ADVENTURE EDUCATION

ADVENTURE EDUCATION

JOHN C. MILES
Western Washington University

SIMON PRIEST
Brock University

Venture Publishing, Inc.
State College, PA 16801

Copyright © 1990
Venture Publishing, Inc.
1999 Cato Avenue
State College, PA 16801
(814) 234-4561

Cover Design by Sandra Sikorski
Editorial Assistance by Michael D. Casper
Production by Bonnie Godbey
Library of Congress Catalog Number 90-71690
ISBN 0-910251-39-8

CONTENTS:

Introduction

To adventure is to venture forth into the unknown, to undertake an activity that has an uncertain outcome for the adventurer and may be risky or dangerous. One goal of a normal daily routine is to minimize adventure, to reduce or eliminate risk so that life may be lived comfortably and successfully. A basic human need is to be safe from harm, and much effort is made to satisfy this need. Yet, while safety is usually a goal, there are times when people purposely place themselves at risk in some enterprise. The risk may be physical, financial, social, spiritual or intellectual. The risk is taken in pursuit of some goal, rarely for the sake of itself. The adventure is usually undertaken to achieve an end that cannot be reached any other way.

The subject of this book is adventure for the goals of growth and human development. Adventure education involves the purposeful planning and implementation of educational processes that involve risk in some way. The risk may be physical, as in a trip in a mountain wilderness where people may be caught in storms, may become lost or may be injured by falling rocks. It may be social, as in asking someone to expose their fear of speaking before groups or otherwise risk social judgement. the risk may be spiritual, as in placing the learner in a situation where he or she must confront the self or perhaps the meaning of life and death. The defining characteristic of adventure *education* is that a conscious and overt goal of the adventure is to expand the self, to learn and grow and progress toward the realization of human potential. While adventure education programs may teach such skills as canoeing, navigation, rock climbing and rappelling, the teaching of such skills is not the primary educational goal of the enterprise. The learnings about the self and the world that come from engagement in such activities are the primary goals.

The use of adventure as a process for learning is a relatively new development in modern education. In one sense it is an ancient approach to learning. Many ancient societies placed their young people in situations where they would be challenged and from which they would learn what life and leadership in that society required of them. They were tested by the elders who were attempting to ascertain which of the members of younger generations should be trained and raised to leadership roles. Modern education, that process usually done by using symbols in media such as books, a process of teaching young people the abstractions they need to function in society, moved away from testing young people in these ancient experimental ways. It did not send them out on vision quests and walkabouts. It tested them in classrooms and judged them suitable for societal roles on the basis of such tests. As this book is compiled late in the twentieth century educators are realizing that both approaches to growth and development may be necessary for a complete education. Thus, adventure education has emerged on the educational scene.

On the surface, adventure education seems a simple process. Yet, as the authors in this volume suggest, there is more to it than is readily obvious. The aim of the process is to learn from risk-taking, not to be damaged or destroyed by it. How can this be managed? How can there be real risk involved, yet danger to mind and body minimized? Can programs involving real adventure also be run safely: Can educators ethically place young people in situations where there is real potential for harm? How are the risks and benefits of such activities to be weighed? The authors tackle these questions from various angles.

As the editors solicited contributors for this volume, they met with various responses. Some potential contributors did not like the term "adventure education." It smacked too much of purely physical challenge activities, of a militaristic orientation and machismo. They would prefer some other title, such as "wilderness education" or "outdoor education" or even "experiential education." The subjects to be addressed involve all of these, yet are broader in scope than some alternative terms, and narrower than others. The term "adventure education" is retained and attempts are made to define it, to show how these other "educations" relate to it. Other definitions and approaches could have been used, but this one is taken with recognition of these other possibilities.

A goal of this project is to bring together the thinking of many practitioners of adventure education programming to reveal the extent of the literature of the field. The essays cover many topics and cite a broad literature. They also reveal the limited nature of the literature of adventure education. Practitioners are only beginning to explore the theoretical underpinnings of their work. They are only beginning to ask why they do things a certain way, what the outcomes of their approaches are, what alternatives to their approaches might be. They have little idea which parts of the processes they use result in which effects. They move ahead with confidence that what they are doing is good and right, as well they should. Questioning and probing and theorizing about adventure education may well confirm practitioners' intuitive beliefs about what they do, while suggesting strengths and weaknesses in their approaches, and pointing in fruitful new directions. The aim of this volume is to make a short step toward development of a solid literature in adventure education and related fields.

This volume is not a description of the field, though it is partly that. It is not a "how to" manual, though it contains practical ideas and discussions of the ways to approach training and safety management and other real problems of using adventure processes. It is an introduction to topics in the field of adventure education. The topics are the section headings. The treatments of these topics is not exhaustive. Many important subjects are not, for one reason or another, treated here. The editors have no hesitation in stating that a volume on each section topic can and should be written or compiled soon. This work is in some cases already done, as with Jasper Hunt's comprehensive treatment of the ethical issues of adventure education, and in others the work is now being undertaken. There is no pretense here that this volume is comprehensive. It is a start and nothing more.

Adventure education has grown rapidly in importance during the past several decades. The likelihood of it achieving central importance in the general enterprise of education is not great, but it will continue to develop and grow as a small but significant part of that enterprise. The prospect is for a gradual infusion of elements of adventure education into public schools and other conventional programs. There is also prospect for continued emergence of adventure programs and schools outside of formal educational settings. Experimentation, innovation and creative development of the field will occur in this independent setting. These new ideas in turn will filter into the mainstream.

As former British prime minister Harold MacMillan has said, "To be alive at all involves some risk." While much of society searches for the illusory risk-free world, adventure educators are teaching that venturing forth onto unknown and unexplored ground can add much to the joy and excitement of life and to human fulfillment and potential. The modern world is faced with great problems, and only by stretching and reaching and extending limits will human ability to solve these problems be realized. Adventure education helps in this great work.

Section One

SOME MODEL PROGRAMS IN ADVENTURE EDUCATION

Five Portraits of Excellence

A good starting place in describing adventure education is with examples. What are "adventure educators" doing? How and why are they doing what they do? What common threads connect the diverse activities of this group of educator? Program examples can pose leading questions and establish direction for this collection of readings.

The examples here are not intended to be typical or representative of the range of adventure education programs. There are hundreds of programs that could serve as well as these. The aim is to exhibit the qualities of programs and diversity of aims that characterize adventure education. Most readers will be familiar with Outward Bound. Greene and Thompson provide a sketch of this large enterprise that has inspired many variations over the years. Few may have heard of C. W. HOG, a university-based program for the disabled. Whittaker explains how his personal misfortune and a background in adventure activities led to his personal inspiration that has helped many people to grow despite their disabilities. Adventure education may be a large corporate or small, individual enterprise, with great results in either case.

Three of the largest and most expensive tasks in modern society are public education, rehabilitation of troubled people, and provision of health care. Adventure education can offer assistance in all three challenges. Gillette shows how a dedicated, creative and hard-working teacher in public education can use adventure to lead high school students toward wonder, self-respect and growth. Kimball's experience at the Santa Fe Mountain Center reveals how wilderness adventure can, along with other experiences, contribute to therapy for clients striving to return to mental health. Weider describes both a specific case of adventure-based therapy and the infrastructure in a health care organization necessary to support such an approach. All of these examples demonstrate the scarcely realized potential of adventure education to address many needs of contemporary society.

Most programs described in this collection have developed in North America. Loynes points out, in his description of development training in the United Kingdom, that the use of outdoors for education, at least in the adventure education sense, began in Britain. The British have repeatedly provided adventure education ideas and examples that have spread to other parts of the world and developed and evolved there. Loynes' contribution is a reminder that adventure is truly a global enterprise.

Outward Bound USA

John H. Greene

&

Donna Thompson
Outward Bound, Inc.

The program known to most Americans as Outward Bound grew out of the need to instill a spiritual tenacity and the will to survive in young British seamen whose ships were torpedoed by German U-Boats during World War II. Once, when a great sailing ship weighed anchor, hoisted sail, and left the safety of the harbor for the open sea, seamen said it was "outward bound"—bound for the unknown, for challenge and adventure.

What began as a wartime school for survival has evolved into an action-oriented program for personal growth, service to others, and physical preparedness. Outward Bound enables participants to leave their safe moorings of home, family, friends, and daily routine to cope with the unfamiliar, the uncomfortable, the difficult, and the adventurous, in search of an opportunity to understand, test, and demonstrate their own resources; to leave self-imposed limitations behind and discover endless possibilities. In short, Outward Bound is learning about oneself and the world through adventure and service activities.

Outward Bound conducts courses of a highly strenuous, physically and mentally challenging nature in remote wilderness areas. In this environment, the challenges, mostly physical, are unique for all participants. The wilderness is a classroom. It allows students to become aware of the interdependency of all life. As a teaching medium, the wilderness provides a metaphor for the individual to develop self-confidence, concern for others, and self-awareness as well as a sensitivity to our fragile environment.

In everyday life, hundreds of variables may have to be dealt with daily. The wilderness offers relatively few options, and the consequences are both real and immediate. The Outward Bound participant's area of attention is sharply contracted, and cause-and-effect relationships are more easily understood. Organizing a four-day expedition at sea, crossing a stream during spring run-off, or taking part in a search for a lost hiker are experiences clearly understood by all, and the outcomes are very real.

Traditional education is concerned almost entirely with intellectual development. It underemphasizes the physical and emotional aspects of students and ignores the critical questions of self-image and relationships between people. Yet a fully functioning human being must address these issues. And Outward Bound does. It has evolved a very specific process that deals directly with these important parts of life. Motivated by the perception of risk or the desire to assist others in need, the students learn that they can succeed far beyond their expectations. And, through the same process of rising to unavoidable challenges, they learn the necessity and rewards of working well with other people.

The survival school image of Outward Bound disappeared after the first few years as it was realized the aim was to conquer personal weaknesses through contact with the wilderness, not to conquer the wilderness. In fact, Outward Bound courses are not easy. They are not meant to be. They are vehicles for personal growth. Outward Bound asks each participant to face unfamiliar and sometimes frightening tasks—climbing a rock face, rappelling, or running white water. But the course is structured so that almost everyone can succeed at their own level. There are no tests or minimum standards, only an expectation that each person is willing to try.

Moving far beyond its roots as a survival school in wartime Great Britain, Outward Bound has created a sophisticated adventure-based education program that uses wilderness experiences to stimulate personal growth. In accomplishing tasks they once thought impossible, people learn to expect more of themselves. They come to realize that the limits to their own potential for personal growth are mostly imagined and self-imposed.

The standard Outward Bound course is three to four weeks long. While each of the Outward Bound schools uses the same basic curriculum in its standard course, some of the specific activities vary according to environment and season. During the early part of the course, each student works on physical conditioning through such daily activities as running, hiking, or swimming.

All participants also undergo extensive instruction in technical skills; safety training appropriate to the environment and season in which the course is taking place; the use of specialized equipment; search-and-rescue, emergency evacuation, and first-aid procedures; field food planning and preparation; map and compass use and route finding; traveling skills and expedition planning and control; care and protection of the environment.

After an initial training phase, participants in groups of 8 to 12, accompanied by instructors, take part in one or more short expeditions (mountain climbing, sailing, backpacking, canoeing, skiing); then, also accompanied by the instructors, they set out on an extended journey for which the participants gradually assume responsibility. Each student embarks on a solo, which is a period of wilderness solitude with a minimum of equipment, lasting up to three days. Most courses will include rock climbing and rappelling; a marathon event; a service project performed by students for the benefit of others; time devoted to reading and discussions; and a final expedition that is student-planned and student-led, with a minimum of instructor supervision.

During all these experiences, students discover new things about themselves. They are sure, where before they were hesitant. They know what it is to meet fear and conquer it. They have learned to share, to lead and follow, to work as a group. Traveling miles across mountains, lakes, or oceans may mean aching muscles, cold, and rain, but these experiences bring the valued understanding of working as a team and pride of achievement.

The standard courses have been developed specifically for young men and women between the ages of 16 and 22. A three-week Outward Bound course gives a young adult the chance to discover innate self-confidence and the ability to work as a team member to achieve specific goals. These lessons are invaluable throughout life.

But Outward Bound has become an experience that knows no age limit. Special courses for 14 and 15 year-olds are designed to give young people a chance to get out of their usual summer routines, try new things, investigate new attitudes, and meet new people in a supportive, challenging environment. These courses are much like standard courses but are geared to the energy and abilities of younger students.

On the opposite end of the spectrum, Outward Bound offers courses for adults over 55. In between lie a number of special courses directed at youngsters in trouble with the law, the physically and mentally disabled, recovering alcoholics and drug addicts, Vietnam veterans, and business managers.

Outward Bound's Directive and Ascent programs for "youth at risk" are carefully structured educational programs for dealing with motivation and behavior problems. By overcoming the challenges of the course, the students find what may be their first opportunity to recognize and use the power they all have to choose the kind of adults they will become.

In dealing with the physically and mentally disabled, Outward Bound works to broaden their perceptions of their own capabilities. As in the standard courses, disabled students are taught to solve tasks that initially seem impossible. Mastering these tasks brings lasting behavior changes, allowing the individual to better adapt and cope with a disability. Improved self-esteem increases functional independence.

In 1978, the Colorado Outward Bound School collaborated with Denver's St. Luke's Hospital to create an Outward Bound experience as part of the treatment of patients in the hospital's Alcoholism Recovery Unit. Since that time, more than 4,000 patients have participated in similar Outward Bound treatment programs throughout the United States.

Courses for both alcohol and drug abuse vary in length from 4 to 30 days. The Outward Bound program is designed to address problems common to patients with alcohol and drug dependencies: low self-esteem, immaturity, learned helplessness, social isolation, and lack of trust. The program provides an opportunity to confront these issues and fears, to discover a renewed sense of competence, and to begin to build trust relationships. Outward Bound alcohol and drug programs are adjunctive to therapy. The minimum age is 12, and there is no maximum age. Courses are run throughout the year, and many are available without professional referral.

Almost 50 years have passed since Kurt Hahn's creation of the first Outward Bound school in Great Britain, sparked by the stresses of World War II. Today, Outward Bound is once again providing a solution to war-related problems through its program for the "forgotten Americans," veterans of the Vietnam War who suffer from reactions to the violence, fear, and pain of battle—problems ranging from flashbacks, alienation, rage, and depression, to loneliness and drug and alcohol dependence. Conducted in cooperation with the Veterans Administration hospitals across the country, Vietnam veterans courses include traditional course elements but are distinguished by the amount of time and effort devoted to talking and listening, counseling, and drawing metaphors from the Outward Bound experience. The course provides participants with renewed self-esteem and allows each to experience again the pride of accomplishment, teamwork, and human interdependence that many of them found in Southeast Asia but lost when they faced a hostile homecoming.

Outward Bound Professional Development courses help maximize managerial potential by simulating problems frequently encountered in normal business situations. For a 4 to 9 day period, managers scale 14-foot walls to learn about problem-solving skills, and climb mountains or negotiate rapids to learn the effectiveness of clear communication, teamwork, and decision-making. They learn the process of sequential problem-solving when an apparently insurmountable task is met by a series of graduated steps. They learn to recognize indications of stress and discover how to improve their physical condition as a result.

Both publicly and privately contracted courses are offered throughout the Outward Bound system in the United States, and many Fortune 500 corporations use Outward Bound training for leadership development.

More than 18,000 people, young and old, attend Outward Bound courses every year. Teenagers, college students, business people, grandparents, homemakers, blue-collar and white-collar workers—all look at Outward Bound as an opportunity to develop new skills, to learn more about themselves, and to grow. Each is challenged both physically and emotionally. Each makes decisions and solves problems. Above all, each discovers unknown talents and abilities that will last long after the course is over.

Most Outward Bound students have little wilderness experience, and, while a few may be athletes, most have never carried a backpack, donned a climbing helmet, or paddled on a river.

Outward Bound operates five strategically located schools in the United States. Each offers a wide variety of courses but tends to specialize in specific activities. For example, the Maine school stresses sailing, winter camping, and mountain backpacking; the Minnesota school concentrates on canoeing, backpacking, and dog sledding; the North Carolina school offers mountain expeditioning, canoeing, and caving; the Colorado school concentrates on mountaineering, skiing, and white-water rafting; and the Oregon school stresses mountaineering, white-water rafting and desert backpacking.

Outward Bound USA has made significant strides in developing model programs that supplement this country's traditional educational curricula. The organization's primary mission is to serve the needs of youth, whether they are underprivileged urban children, students with learning disabilities, youth in trouble with the law, or those suffering from substance abuse. In addition, high school and college leadership training courses are conducted throughout the Outward Bound system.

To a remarkable degree, Outward Bound programs remain consistent with Kurt Hahn's educational principles: "No student should be compelled into opinions, but it is criminal negligence not to impel him into experiences." Hahn's philosophy emphasized developing and maintaining "strong awareness of responsibility for others along with the belief that strength is derived from kindness and a sense of justice." His experiential approach to education—learning by doing—has become a powerful complement to mainstream education. The validity of Hahn's message is clear. "Self-mastering through adventure and experiment which test mind and body; compassion through the opportunity and ability to help others in distress."

While over half of Outward Bound's annual enrollment enter courses structured to enhance positive character development within the high school and college participants, a growing trend to reach out to those incapable or unable to be involved in standard Outward Bound wilderness courses has enabled the Outward Bound educational process to be transferred to many special populations that desperately need innovative programs to solve the problems inherent in our educational system.

Model programs, funded by the states of Florida and Maine, have demonstrated significant positive effects on adjudicated youth seemingly trapped in the juvenile court system. Research on Outward Bound's adjudicated youth programs in Florida proves that the program is highly successful and is the most cost-efficient of all the treatment alternatives available to this population in the state.

In 1986, the Hurricane Island Outward Bound School established an urban component, the Baltimore-Chesapeake Bay Program, as part of the movement to reestablish

Outward Bound's commitment to disadvantaged youth. Similar programs are currently being run in Minneapolis by the Voyageur Outward Bound School and in Los Angeles by the Pacific Crest Outward Bound School.

The North Carolina Outward Bound School has offered extended Outward Bound courses for New York City youth with severe literacy deficiencies and is in its second year of managing an alternative high school in Asheville, North Carolina.

The New York City Outward Bound Center was founded in 1987 to run model urban courses for inner-city youth. Major contract work is being conducted by the center for some of the most troubled high schools in New York City. The Thompson Island Education Center in Boston, Massachusetts, begins operation in 1988 to deal specifically with youth in the greater Boston school system.

The objectives of all these programs are to seek and act upon opportunities to help address educational and social issues affecting the welfare of youth. Efforts include literacy enhancement, dropout prevention, fostering relationships between residents of diverse socioeconomic backgrounds, promoting racial integration, and instilling an ethic of service and compassion to the community.

But Outward Bound, as large and diverse as it has become, cannot answer the many needs of special populations throughout the country. It is for this reason that the Outward Bound process has been replicated by literally thousands of schools, colleges and social service agencies nationwide. Throughout its 26 years of operation in the United States, Outward Bound has encouraged other organizations to adapt its curricula, and at least 20 states have used Outward Bound principles for youth rehabilitation programs. Thus, Outward Bound experience goes far beyond the organization's five schools in the United States. Outward Bound methods and principles have been adapted by over a thousand public and private schools and universities.

Outward Bound USA is a nonprofit, tax-exempt organization formed to foster the development of the Outward Bound philosophy in America and to encourage use of the Outward Bound educational concept in traditional educational programs. Each school operates as a private, nonprofit, tax-exempt educational institution, and, combined, they offer programs in 20 states. Outward Bound is supported by contributions from individuals, corporations, and foundations, and admits students without regard to sex, race, ethnic background, or economic status. A third of its students receive some form of financial aid.

The Santa Fe Mountain Center

Rocky Kimball
Santa Fe Mountain Center

For the past five years I've been involved in a bold social experiment. I am the executive director of the Santa Fe Mountain Center, a therapeutic adventure program adapted to fit the needs of New Mexico's comprehensive mental health care system. While our primary clientele have been juvenile and adult criminal offenders, the Mountain Center has developed programs to fit the needs of many special mental health populations, including chronic schizophrenics in transitional care, autistic or emotionally disturbed youth, rapists, pedophiles, victims of rape and sexual incest, and families-in-crisis.

Over the years, experiences have led me to question old assumptions, to modify rhetoric, and to cautiously reframe the theoretical constructs of what we do. It is the goal of this article to pass on to you, the reader, some of that learning. I will emphasize our work with offenders but will offer comments on other special populations as well.

There is great pressure in our society to find a quick fix for social ills—delinquency being one of them. Unfortunately, wilderness therapy as pill-popping doesn't work. Long-term behavioral change is, for the most part, a long-term process.

Of course, we can all point to exceptions to this statement. Many youths commit one-time, situational delinquent acts. Not suffering from any significant pathological disorder, these individuals are best served by the least restrictive intervention. In these cases, according to the National Council on Crime and Delinquency, a wilderness experience alternative avoids the contaminating effects of institutional care, which often results in antisocial attitudes and an undermining of the individual's sense of self.

While our research efforts at the Santa Fe Mountain Center clearly demonstrate positive therapeutic change on a host of variables and differing psychometric tests, program administrators would be well-advised not to oversell the long-term behavioral effects. Delinquent acts must be seen in the relationship between the individual and the totality of environmental stresses. These pressures include poverty, poor housing, low educational levels, unemployment, cultural conflict, dysfunctional family situations, and child abuse. Most behaviorally disordered youth are depraved because they are deprived; and the power of a 150-foot rappel often fades in light of this.

While recognizing that long-term therapeutic change avoids the quick fix, I have come increasingly to appreciate the value of wilderness adventure experiences as an invaluable tool in psychological evaluation. A major first step in therapeutic change is diagnosis or an evaluation of an individual's strengths and weaknesses. In traditional clinical settings the therapist's protocol includes the client's history, objective testing results, a family history, and a DSM III classification.

While this information is valuable and should not be dismissed, it has serious limitations. First, it is garnered in a clinical setting where past behavior is merely reported but never observed. Second, objective psychological measures are limited to assessing certain a priori defined traits or functions. Third, the client often has a fairly clear idea of what the examiner is "testing." This is particularly true on so-called "self-concept tests."

For all these reasons, the Mountain Center wilderness adventure courses are considered a valuable diagnostic test by the Bureau of Mental Health and the Department of Corrections. The counselor's client report is intended to supplement forensic court evaluations. New Mexico judges often rely upon our written evaluations as a deciding factor in sentencing. Likewise, the Parole Board may require a wilderness evaluation report prior to parole.

Successful completion of the course is an excellent litmus test of an individual's ability to function as a positive member of society. Conversely, in over five years of testing, we have found failure on a wilderness course almost 100 percent correlated with subsequent recommitment.

The wilderness adventure experience can be viewed as a projective psychological test. The basic assumption underlying the use of projective techniques is that clients reveal a composite picture of their global personalities in the way they respond to tasks, demands, and stimuli. Unlike a clinical setting, the testing demands of the wilderness are capricious and require adaptability. Although expectations are made clear during the wilderness expedition, a whole range of responses is possible. Personal characteristics and behaviors emerge in sharp focus.

Like the well-known Rorschach ink blots, wilderness challenges are high in ambiguity. The client must interpret or structure the task demands as well as the response to be made to it. The challenges of the wilderness expedition offer great latitude in response. The greater the latitude and the higher the stress, the more likely the client will "project" unique and individual personality aspects into the "test" situation.

By careful observation of the client's responses to a multitude of "diagnostic" situations—rock climbing, route-finding, water rationing—the skilled mental health counselor identifies life-long behavioral patterns, dysfunctional ways of coping with stress, intellectual processes, conflicts, needs, and emotional responsiveness. When properly observed, recorded and articulated, these data can be the basis for long-term therapeutic goals.

While behavioral change and therapeutic growth usually occur, the Santa Fe Mountain Center can only guarantee that, at the least, critical diagnostic information will be collected. An evaluation outline serves to aid our counselors in reporting psychological processes rather than mere behavioral content.

Unlike an institutional environmental or a clinician's office, there is no way to fake one's way through a wilderness adventure experience. More than once clients have been model citizens before a judge or in a correctional facility, but revealed total sociopathic behavior during the stresses of the wilderness.

On the other hand, obstreperous and contumacious individuals, who may react against the stifling authoritarianism of institutional rules and confinement, have revealed flexibility, compassion, and control under the more open rigors and demands of our courses.

The lesson is that institutional conformity is a poor predictor of autonomy and adaptability—necessary traits for success in the real world.

In terms of our success in a comprehensive mental health care system, it has been essential for our staff to view themselves as counselor/therapists first and outdoor instructors second. This does not mean we tolerate a lower level of technical wilderness skills among the staff, but it reminds us that our means (the wilderness) are secondary to our ends (therapy/evaluation).

Analytical ability, writing skills, and familiarity with basic psychotherapy are just as important as the staff member's rock climbing or mountaineering skills. To successfully bridge the gap between the community mental health system or the corrections system with the outdoor world, staff must be bilingual. This is to say, they should be able to discuss the American Psychological Association's DSM III classifications just as coherently as they could communicate the necessary anchors on a tyrolean traverse.

Too many therapeutic wilderness programs, in my opinion, view themselves as an "alternative to the system," whether it be corrections or mental health. We choose to see the Santa Fe Mountain Center as within the system. Some of our most worthwhile and innovative projects have evolved in conjunction with outside agencies, hospitals or groups.

By viewing our program flexibly, we have been able to develop special wilderness experiences for sex offenders, rape victims, schizophrenics, and families-in-crisis. In each case, the wilderness is simply a component part of a larger therapeutic plan. In many cases, the psychologist or therapist will accompany the special wilderness project, while in others, the evaluation report provides the continuity.

This model has allowed for exciting innovations and keeps therapeutic change in the context of a long-term process. Such coordination of services ensures that we receive client groups at a point of psychological readiness and commitment to change.

We have found no magical formula to replace such motivation. It is the key to change. Like the joke, "How many psychologists does it take to change a light bulb?" Answer: "Only one, but the light bulb has to really want to change."

For a client who has insight and motivation, the wilderness experience is an extremely powerful metaphor for personal growth. After five years of experimentation and adaptation of wilderness adventure experiences for a host of clientele, my enthusiasm for the efficacy of what we offer is undiminished. I believe that psychological change and development begin and end in human behavior.

Our work at the Mountain Center is predicated upon the assumption that experience is more therapeutic than analysis. While many clinical approaches utilize counseling to change attitudes in order to modify behavior, I believe that attitudinal change can best follow experiential exploration of new behaviors. It is the role of the wilderness counselor to help the client draw insight into areas of dysfunction.

Perhaps the most unique contribution we can make to the field of mental health, however, is by dramatically demonstrating areas of power and competency as opposed to merely concentrating on dysfunction and failure. Furthermore, because of the strong bonding that usually takes place between counselor and client, many ancillary areas of mental health can be explored, such as the mind-body connection, the role of fitness, nutritional awareness, and diet.

Wilderness adventure programs have much to contribute to the field of mental health. However, a few caveats come to mind. Do not overstate the impact of what we can offer. Post-course outcomes are idiosyncratic and hence, programs should not simply claim to address one psychological variable like self-concept or social competency.

Don't totally reject the traditional. Understand and be familiar with the medical model. Develop projects in conjunction with ongoing groups that can provide long-term therapy both as preparation and as follow-up. Finally, recognize that by working with special populations we must operate with the tools and understanding of both the wilderness instructor and the mental health professional.

CLIENT EVALUATION

Purpose: While many wilderness adventure counselors are excellent at providing outdoor leadership and conducting safe, therapeutic courses, too many fail to appreciate the importance of the client evaluation. The client evaluation is the link between the Santa Fe Mountain Center, the referral source, and all subsequent agencies who may deal with the client. The gifted counselor will garner critical evaluative data which, if properly recorded and articulated, can be the basis for long-term therapeutic goals.

FORMAT (per example)

1. *Introduction.* The introduction is similar from one course to another and includes:

A. A description of the Santa Fe Mountain Center's Wilderness Experience
B. Breakdown of clients and referral status
C. Course format and location
D. Dates of the course
E. Egregious incidents experienced by the entire group

2. *Course Participation.* This section is usually short and is, relative to other sections, the least important. The section summarizes each individual's ability to accomplish thevarious phases of the experience. It also highlights the peaks and valleys of the physical/mental challenges.

3. *Socialization.* This section comments on interpersonal characteristics.

A. With authority
   1. Does the client seek approval?
   2. Is the client hostile, contumacious, obstreperous, resistant?
   3. How does the client react to counseling?
   4. How does the client react to criticism?

B. With peers
   1. Can the client share material items? (cooperation/sharing)
   2. Does the client contribute to group problem-solving? (assistance/resistance)
   3. What role does the client assume in the group? (group role-leader, follower, active, passive)
   4. Was the client accepted or rejected socially? (in-group/out-group)
   5. Does the client seek intimacy or distance from others? (interpersonal space)
   6. How does the client react to inter personal conflicts? (appropriate/inappropriate)
   7. Can the client show compassion and empathy for others? (sociopathy)
   8. Does the client accept individuals in group across ethnic backgrounds? (prejudice)
   9. Can the client take emotional or physical risks? (trust)

4. *Observations.* This is an open area and the section's content is determined by the major behavioral patterns that emerge as an individual's themes.

A. Exaggerated coping devices displayed on the course, such as:
   1. Dependency on staff or others
   2. Hyperemotionalism—tearfulness, instability
   3. Hypoemotionalism—lack of appropriate affect
   4. Restlessness, insomnia
   5. Excessive worrying, paranoia, bad dreams
   6. Preoccupation
   7. Passive aggression
   8. Somatic complaint, hypochondriacal
   9. Explosive temper
B. Personal traits
   1. Ability to channel or direct energy
   2. Positive/negative attitude
   3. Open and flexible or closed and rigid
   4. Impulsive or deliberate personality
   5. Over-incorporates or under-incorporates information
   6. Immature or mature
   7. Sense of values, spirituality
   8. Internal or external locus of control
   9. Superficial or honest in self-assessment
C. Task performance
   1. Ability to follow directions
   2. Attention span
   3. Initiative
   4. Ability to deal with structured tasks
   5. Ability to deal with unstructured tasks
D. Physical manifestations (related to diagnosis)
   1. Physical appearance
   2. Eye contact
   3. Quality of speech—intensity and level, relevant, coherent
   4. Thought pattern—logical or loose associations
   5. Reality orientation—awareness of time, place, and person
   6. Coordination and balance

5. *Recommendation.* The purpose of this section is to indicate those measures the evaluator feels need to be taken as the next step in the client's therapeutic struggle. Since there are different categories of clients, there are many different needs ranging from family therapy to drug counseling or vocational training. The recommendation section is particularly important for a client who is in transition—about to be paroled, about to leave a group home or residential treatment center, etc. It is also critical for the client who is in limbo, such as a probation violator, a pre-sentence referral, or a client who is serving an evaluation/diagnostic period, etc. In these cases, the evaluator must be candid and honest, or risk jeopardizing the credibility of future evaluation.

O.T.O. - Opportunities to Teach Ourselves: A Classroom Community

Ted Gillette
Andrew Ward High School

It was one of those memorable days in mid-September in the Adirondack Mountains. The valley we were hiking through on our way to Haystack was green with the summer vegetation of a rainy August. As we climbed in altitude, the season began to change right before us. The colorful leaves were brilliant, and as we looked down from the outcroppings along the trail, puffs of color caught our eyes as if they were chrysanthemums flowering in an autumn bed. And then the leaves of fall disappeared and we were in November, and just above the tree line we entered December, snow-capped and clear. Within just a few hours of vertical ascent, we had trespassed through three seasons of the year. The experience was incomprehensible, for we seemed to travel through space in a time warp. And then just ahead, there was the last steep climb to the summit, our lookout destination for the day. We were breathing hard, and despite the chill of the wind, we were sweating. We seemed caught between seasons, not quite sure of which layer to keep on or take off. One last surge of energy, one last thrust upward by the lower thigh, and we would be at the top. I followed closely behind the group of students, for we were tightly bunched, almost anticipating the huddling we would do at the top. My practice teacher was in the lead. She was the first to look around and was the first to speak.

"Oh, this is very pretty," she said. "What a fine perspective. When I was hiking in Switzerland, there were many peaks like this. Actually, the mountains in Switzerland are higher." I listened to what she was saying and watched the faces and eyes of those high school students who had just expended more energy than they had ever done in their lifetimes. I walked to the top and looked around, and it was beautiful, incredibly beautiful. And my true joy and exuberance took hold, and I blurted, "Holy S----!" The students heard this and their weariness exploded into a chorus of "Yeah. Holy S----." And their truthful enthusiasm and appreciation for the view and their own accomplishment roared out from that summit and rolled down the valley, echoing and revealing their spirit and their appreciation. And I looked at my practice teacher and I thought. She knew the trail. She had the wilderness skills. She was trained in rescue. She knew so much, and yet she knew nothing. She did not comprehend experiential education. She did not know the power, the immensity of the potential in the experience. She did not comprehend that all experiential education is a quest for a more mature spirituality. She did not ask the key questions. She asked how far to the mountain so that logistics could be determined. She asked how to balance the pack; how to organize the first aid needs; how to reduce impact on the trail. She did not ask:

- How do we educate for growth?
- How do we nurture maturity?
- How do we reveal blessing?
- How do we offer love?
- How do we stimulate awe and wonder and miracle and jubilation and ecstasy?
- How do we reveal self-respect and honesty?
- How do we share the mystery of the ordinary?

Experiential/adventure education is high-impact teaching and learning. Experiential/adventure education centers on spiritual and psychological truths. The two are interwoven and integrated with every aspect of the curriculum. The greatness of experiential programs lies not so much with the skills learned or the activities accomplished, but with the deep meanings of experiences that the students understand and internalize.

ALICE

I am reminded of Alice. She was seventeen. We were hiking just off the Appalachian Trail in southwestern Massachusetts. It was a wondrously clear day in February. There was a light snowfall the night before and the dry flakes rested tentatively on every pine needle that reached high above the trail. The hike down was precipitous; almost 1000 feet in a mile and a half. The trail was slippery with ice-covered rocks and exposed roots. The sun glistened and intensified as it mirrored off the ice and snow down the valley. I was the last person in the long line of multicolored backpacks that snaked their way towards the bottom.

Alice was the last student and directly in front of me. She seemed reluctant to get started down the trail, but after some gentle nudging, we started the descent. After 10 minutes of a snail's pace, she stopped, breathed heavily, sighed, looked up to the heavens, and proclaimed, "I'm bored." Her words hit me with acute acidity. I had been reveling in the brilliance of the day and the excitement of the difficult hike. Her words were cruel words, I thought, for they seemed to be aimed at me and my sensibilities. I composed myself and regrouped my own emotions. "Well, Alice, we have to go down. Let's catch up with the rest."

We started down and it happened all over again about 10 minutes down the valley. Alice pulled up short and blurted, "D---, this is so G---d--- boring." By now I had been seething inside. How could this little wimp so successfully destroy my glorious day? And how could she be so "bored"? How could anyone be bored on such a day, at such a place? After all, these hikers were on the cutting edge, on the brink, existentially alive, aware of the heightened meaning of living. All this was true, I knew it was.

As I heard Alice whine more and string out the expletives, I wanted to shut her up, but the best part of my professional manner overcame me and I active-listened to Alice. "Uh, Alice, you say that you are bored." Alice responded with vehemence and indignation. "You're G--d--- right I'm bored, and don't give me that active-listening s---." You see, Alice was an experienced talker through many sessions with her therapist. She knew the lingo and the methods better than I did.

We hiked our way down to the bottom of the ravine, finally, stopping all the way down for emotional outbursts. I had withstood abuse; I had sacrificed a great day's hiking enjoyment. At the very bottom, we walked on to ice and then had to ford a narrow stream of black, cold mountain water. I stepped over the stream and looked back to see Alice step, slip, and fall into that icy water. Somehow, not thinking, I bent over to lift her out of the freezing stream. She was a heavy girl, a 30-pound pack on her back, and I was carrying about 40 in mine. How I thought I could lift her up with all that weight and reaching from an awkward position I do not know, but I started to pick her up, and she slipped out of my grasp. She splashed into the stream; I began to laugh wildly and she began to cry. And all this happened just when I thought I had reached the teachable moment, the very point when I believed that the two of us had made it, completed the perilous descent, and now we could share our triumph. The teachable moment was shattered, or was it?

Alice changed into dry clothes and warmed herself next to the fire we had built. It was only after that fiasco—real psychological honesty, real suffering, and real sharing—that we could filter through all the externals and get to the core of the matter. Alice was not "bored." Alice was spiritually terrified and psychologically paralyzed. And I had to break the ice of my own egocentric agenda to really hear Alice.

I learned something on that cold February day. I learned that psychological honesty is of fundamental importance if there is to be spiritual and psychological maturity. Without it nothing can take place. But how does one begin to transcend the egocentricity that thwarts all possibility for a life of fullness and meaning? I believe that there are three ways we overcome our egocentricity:

1. Through suffering;
2. Through the recognition of a power, or design, greater than our own will in our lives;
3. Through our coming to care, to love ourselves enough to love someone else.

The O.T.O. program was an experiential/adventure program that always tried to keep this vision clear, to focus on the essential needs of students and teachers. It constantly examined itself through the perspective of asking the relevant human questions. It always asked how it could thwart the modern social diseases of boredom, belonginglessness, and meaninglessness. It constantly analyzed its meaning as trying to help people overcome their spiritual problems. The times that were spent with students were sacred times because they were so important and so unique and so immediate. This sense of intensity and aliveness pervaded every activity. It was this sense of vitalness of life that was caught by the students. It was the sense of ecstasy over being alive that propelled the students and shook them from the lethargy of the society. I am sure that we did not solve student problems. I agree with Carl Jung, who made a striking observation about how people are and are not healed. He wrote:

> All the greatest and most important problems of life are fundamentally insoluble.... They can never be solved, but only outgrown. This "outgrowing" proved on further investigation to require a new level of consciousness. Some higher or wider interest appeared on the patient's horizon, and through this broadening of his or her outlook the insoluble problem lost its urgency. It was not solved logically in its own terms but faded when confronted with a new and stronger life urge.

I think this insight by Jung is crucial. We all have experienced the freshman who is obnoxious and rancorous, and a few years later, when we encounter the same student, he is delightful, reasonable, gentle, and even compatible. What happened to this youngster other than time and experience nurturing new interests and new insights? The beauty of the O.T.O. program, as with all experiential programs, is that we have the opportunity to seize upon our awareness of how people change, and lead them through experiences that have the potential to get to their psyches. Through activities and through community, we can offer heightened moments of real and immediate life. We are fully aware that the experiences of adventure are fraught with risk, and they are painful and do wound, but all of life is a wounding and a healing process. Our task is to help our students experience the wounds and help them heal with reconstructed scar tissue, for scar tissue is tough and strong and deep. It lasts a lifetime.

All this sounds heavy and threatening. To perceive the O.T.O. program as lacking in fun and excitement would be unfortunate and untrue. If the students didn't really enjoy themselves and have fun over the years, they would not have been involved. And if the teachers were always involved in Jungian therapy, they would have gone mad, wringing their hands continuously. The O.T.O. program achieved success because it was a balanced program, one in which youngsters experienced true joy and exhilaration. They experienced a community of individuals who cared about each other, and they came to know adults better than they knew their own parents.

The entire O.T.O. program began on the premise that we had to understand what students wanted out of their lives, what excited them, what would help them invest time and energy over a long period of time. We came to realize that what students needed was exactly what we as adults needed also. To paraphrase William Glasser, everyone needs four crucial areas to be fulfilled, in order to complete fulfilled and whole. We all need freedom (choices), power (importance), fun (pleasure), and love (belonging). These four categories of human needs are very powerful, natural energy sources. To ignore them, as most of our curricula do in public education, is to invite failure and frustration. These four human needs form a strong current dynamism that attracts all people. Experiential education builds upon these four human needs and best satisfies what people really desire. The experiential/adventure programs help students discover themselves and help them harness their own energies for growth and real personal fulfillment. In more pragmatic terms, what do students want?

Students want to:

- explore
- feel responsibility
- have fun
- have real friends
- experience real success
- master skills
- feel confident
- be independent
- understand reasons for realities in life
- be able to make their own mistakes
- get away from home and school for a while

Students do not want chaos. They need and want structure and security and guidance, but of the right kind. They need reality to play with and adults who offer opportunities, listen to their heartbeats, and give them freedom to grow.

It is paramount to focus upon students' needs, but there is another important ingredient to the experiential mixture, namely, the teacher. What is the adult appeal to the experiential mode? Teachers want to own their curriculum. That is, they want to have ultimate input in the developing and the shaping of their professional involvement. They know what students need and they know how to use experience to the ultimate. Often, in addition, teachers crave the input and sharing of other adults, and experiential approaches to teaching necessitate team structures. When the "chemistry" is right, team-teaching can be an enormous uplift for teachers who are essentially alone in the traditional classroom. Beyond this need for professional sharing, the teacher has very distinct goals for his/her students. Often, the living skills that prepare students for mature adult lives are not taught or nurtured in the traditional high school structure. Experiential education teachers want more for their students.

They want:
- critical-thinking opportunities
- self-discovery
- curiosity heightened
- integration of knowledge bases
- development of a community consciousness and a sense of community responsibility
- challenging experiences that build positive self-esteem
- reading comprehension and writing/research skills
- opportunities for participating in the community process

How significant it is to realize that Glasser's insights are crucial to students as well as to teachers. Historically, what the O.T.O. teachers wanted for their students and what the students wanted had to be integrated.

CURRICULUM COMPROMISE

It happened so long ago that I do not even remember the context, but I do remember that we had a crisis in the classroom. There seemed to be an impasse between what students wanted and what teachers expected. A very active discussion had raged on, and suddenly, Lloyd, a rather thoughtful senior who looked the very part of the Woodstock hero, jumped up and started to draw a diagram on the chalkboard. "This is what you guys want," as he pointed to the teachers. "And this is what we want. There has to be a compromise." Everyone stopped shouting and everyone watched as he carefully proceeded. First, he listed some of the "demands" of the teachers, and then he did the same for students. And then he intertwined the arrows, and the strategy emerged with clarity.

Students "wanted" → ← Teachers "demanded"

And so our I.L.E.C. began—Integrated, Learning, Experiences, Community. The classroom community took its form out of the real give-and-take of students and teachers. The genesis emerged from the struggle to make sense, order, and hope out of the chaos of our lives. Indeed, the need for the integration of out-of-class experiences and in-class activities was forged. And I experienced, then, a flashback to my student days that brought everything into focus and perspective.

I can still remember the beach on Long Island Sound where we used to swim as junior high students. The sandy bottom dropped off dramatically; two steps off the sandbar and we were over our heads. We swam at the mouth of a creek inlet and as the tide turned and started to go out, the current from the emptying creek became a torrential river that separated one side of the creek from the other side, not more than 25 yards across. We would run and dive off the beach and try to swim across the current to the other side. We would get swept up in the undertow and struggle against it, flailing our arms furiously in hopes of overpowering the swiftness of the tide. We learned our lessons well. To swim against the current meant danger. If one tried, he would tire quickly, feel the painful fatigue in his shoulder muscles and the deadness in his kick, and then panic for a split second until he turned his body sideways and swam at an angle with the current. I learned how to survive the raging current. There was only one way. Go with the current and use it to your advantage. It seemed so simple. Why didn't I remember the lesson later on? It took Lloyd to point it out. In essence, he said to us teachers: Go with the flow. Listen to what we want and will do. Look carefully and listen carefully, and harness the energy.

And so we did. We searched for the "turn-on" factors that became the underpinnings of the O.T.O. program. And what was so exciting was that what the students wanted was what we wanted. Developing a curriculum and overall structure became easy. The students wanted the outside world, the real world, and all we had to do was to become the keys that opened up that world for the students. We became the gift givers of reality. We had the time to work with the students and we had the power to integrate experiences. The compromise was not difficult. Lloyd's concept, translated through his diagram, took on added significance. It wasn't very long before we were able to develop our understanding of the learning strategy. We asked the students to develop their "road maps" and we developed ours. The three formative questions posed were:

1. What do I want to know?
2. What do I want to feel?
3. What do I want to do?

After we listened carefully to the students and analyzed our goals for student behavior and skills development and our own needs as professionals, we were able to chart the two sets of aspirations. Figure 1 summarizes our new perspective.

One can readily comprehend that once student needs are clearly understood, program activities and strategies can flow naturally from the hopes and desires of the students. The two articulated and shared sets of needs, of students and teachers, were juxtaposed and integrated to develop a compromised learning strategy. Once the natural flow or momentum of the students was identified, all the teachers had to do was plug into the direction of student movement and integrate the kinds of learning activities desired. In other words, it was as if once we recognized the direction of the current, we had only to ride out on the tide and make that power work for us and the students.

HARD-CORE ACADEMICS

Most experiential teachers talk about students and experiences, and that is natural because they are at the core of the teaching reality. But there needs to be a clear explanation of how traditional learning takes place within the experiential mode. The key is that often the attention and the enthusiasm for learning is generated through "the back door." Once students are moving in a direction, a direction they want to move in, it is relatively easy to integrate the academic skills and knowledge bases that are needed and expected. In short, the difference between experiential programs and traditional ones is not so much in the difference of subject matter but in the means by which we teach the subjects. Perhaps, however, the greatest difference I have seen between traditional and experiential teaching modes is the emphasis we place on process learning. Answers are relatively easy to give if someone else provides the questions. The key to learning sophistication is the students' abilities to generate the questions that need to be answered. By focusing at first on adventure situations, we can help the students learn to ask relevant questions that have to be answered before they embark on an experience that is ultimately relevant to them. The adventure trip touches their very existence and their needs and comforts. For example, because students are directly involved, they want to know:

- Where will we sleep?
- What will we eat?
- What if I have to go to the bathroom?
- How will we get there?
- How much will it cost?
- What if I get hurt?
- Who sleeps in which tent?
- Can we stay up all night?
- What if it rains?
- And on and on . . .

Once they begin to ask the questions, they can begin to categorize the questions into logical groups of questions. These logical groupings become the building blocks for student research groups or committees that will report back to the larger class with answers to the original questions that were brainstormed by the entire class. Often, the particular group's research and suggestions of solutions are not acceptable to the larger class,

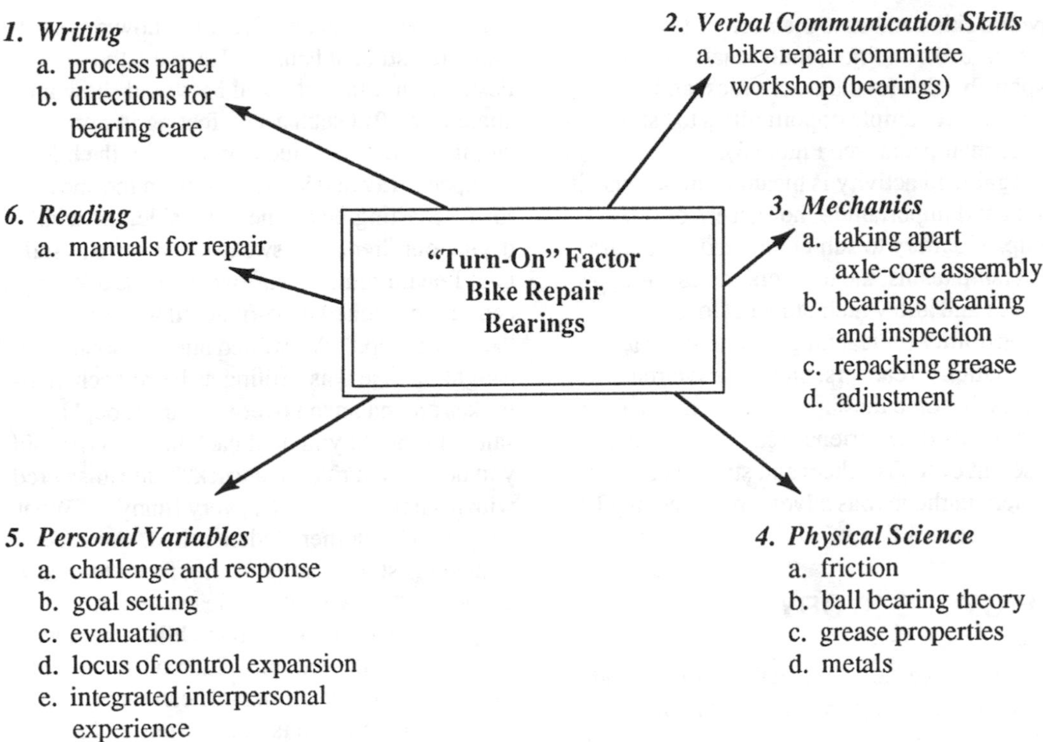

Figure 1
O.T.O. Integrated Learning Experiences Community
Short Term -- 2-Day Lesson Chart

and the class instructs the committee to go back and rework their research and suggestions. There can be no better way to communicate to students the need for accountability than to have students tell other students that they have not done the job adequately. Sometimes this committee report needs to be presented to the group in written form. Here is when students want to learn the correct way to write and communicate because their writing and thinking is on the line before their peers. In the same manner, over the years, we had the students write individual letters to parents (not their own) to explain upcoming trips or to explicate the rationale for what the students were doing. When this happened, the writing always improved dramatically; every student wanted his or her parent to think highly of peers and of the O.T.O. program.

To discuss all the intricate workings of the academic components of the O.T.O. program is not possible in this paper, however, Figure 2 illustrates the complexity and interrelatedness of academic concerns with the other components of the experiential approach. Obviously, if one reads carefully, the integration of factors and ingredients is finely tuned and consciously developed. The unit diagrammed here took place within the context of a week-long bicycle trip to Cape Cod.

The academic flow chart noted in Figure 2 indicates the fusion of academic interests and social/psychological needs. The bicycle trip to Cape Cod serves as a prototype for any long-range target location.

Sequencing or building of activities is crucial, as Figure 1 presents. By developing these kinds of pre-trip activities, the students develop skills and ease themselves toward the adventure. In addition, individuals assume responsibilities for class activities, and students have ample opportunities to "shine" before their peers (see Figure 3).

Again, all activity is meaningful because it is real and important to the success of the group. Contrary to sub-contracted adventure leadership teams, the teachers can assume low profiles and allow their students to take responsibility for teaching crucial skills and information. Teachers, under these circumstances, become the support crew, the enablers for students to experience reality and make sense out of it. Teachers and students become partners in the joyous adventure of seeking life and its possibilities.

A BICYCLE STORY

The hills of western Connecticut are misleading and unforgiving. We found that out on a very hot day in late May. The class had been cycling from the hostel in Massachusetts to Litchfield. Joe was no slouch. He was strong and had the spirit of a bronco, but all of a sudden, he stopped as he looked up at the immense hill in front of us. It was late in the day and we were all tired, but something gave out in Joe. He got off his bicycle, allowed it to fall on the pavement and sat down. "That's it! No more for me. I ain't gonna go. That's it!" Joe had given up. We gathered around him and looked on in amazement. Come on, Joe, the group pleaded, but this senior had had it. It was one of those terrifying moments that teachers have to face sometimes. Do we leave the student behind and keep going, or terminate the activity?

My decision came quickly and we mounted our bikes and started the painful climb. "Joe, if you are going to die, please die on the side of the road." Joe did not appreciate this and responded with the vehement middle finger. Up the hill we pumped. The sweat stung our eyes and the breathing was labored and rapid. But more difficult than the terrain was the beating heart of fear in knowing that I had left a student behind. He knew the destination, I thought, and he would show up sometime. But such a sick feeling in my stomach. We continued, and finally the hill dropped away and we experienced the sheer joy of coasting down the other side, the wind drying our drenched, sweat-laden shirts. And then I heard him. It was one of those adolescent, high-pitched, two-fingered whistles. "Hey, wait up." We waited and Joe soon caught up. He was smiling as he screeched his brakes and balanced over the bar. "Joe," I said, "I thought you died back there. What did you do, hitch a ride on a truck?" Joe answered with a sarcastic, "Ha, Ha, very funny." "What happened?" another student asked. And Joe related his story that I have not forgotten for 20 years. "I saw you guys leave me. It got very quiet and I looked up the hill. There was this old barn, the red one. Did you see it? Well, I said to myself that if I can make it to that barn, then I'll make up my mind. I rode up the hill, got off my bike and walked for awhile, and got to the barn. And then I kept going." And then Joe paused, a long pause. "I guess I figured it out. If I divided the hill into shorter parts, it wasn't so bad. Sometimes you get scared of something, but it ain't so bad if you divide it up."

I could have kissed him right then and there. Everyone listened to what he had to say, and they all seemed to understand what he was saying. That was the teachable moment. That was the time for some real self-understanding. And that was the time that an adult just listened and shook his head in agreement. Joe graduated and over the years he kept in touch. He became a car mechanic, moved out to Colorado, became a trouble shooter for Dodge, moved back to Connecticut, went to school at night, and one day he called me up for some advice. He was 25 and had just completed his first semester at the technical college with a straight A average. I said, "Joe, it's time to climb that hill once again. I think you are ready. This may sound crazy, but I

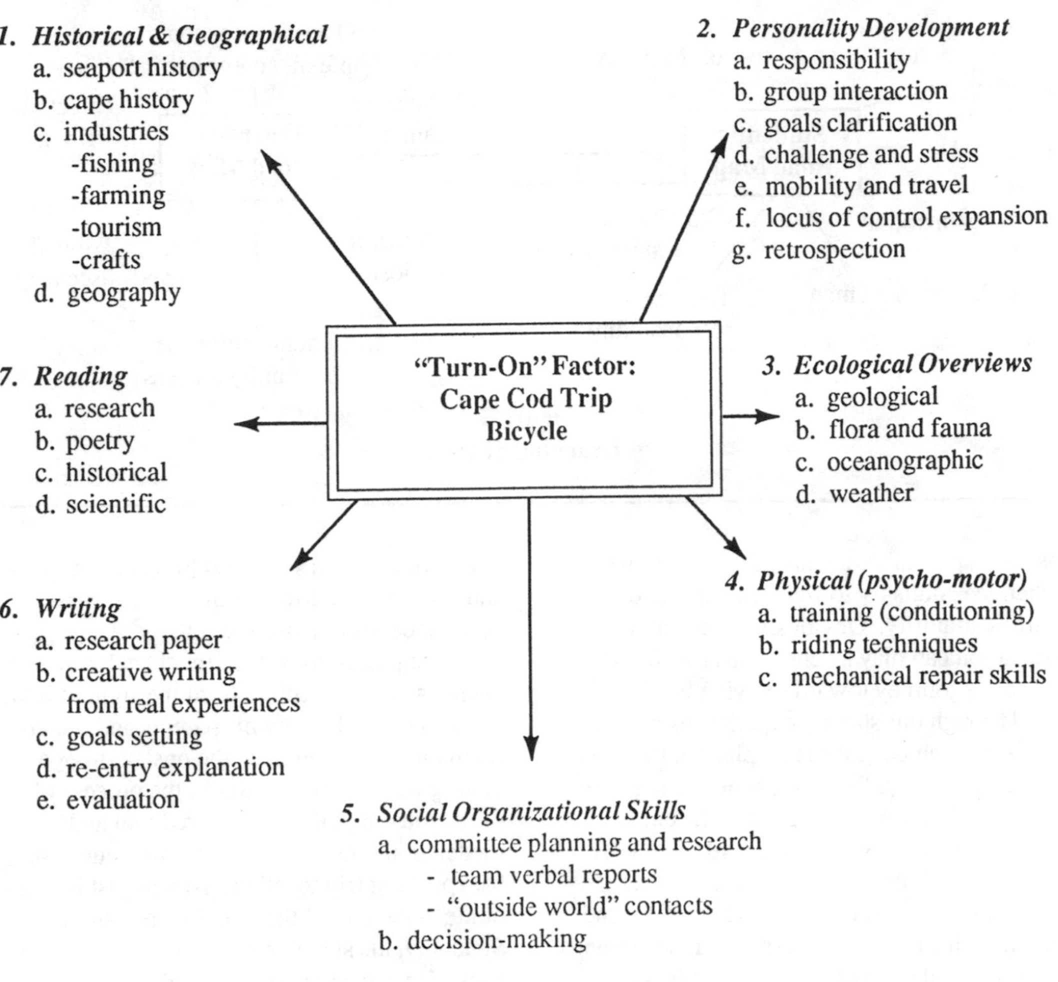

Figure 2
Long Term Flow Chart

want you to apply to M.I.T." He laughed, but he did apply and was accepted with a scholarship, and he graduated, and is now working for Digital. I like to think— no, I know that the opportunity of that bicycle ride in the heat, years before, kept plaguing Joe and nudging him and spurred him on. It was the real experience and the real opportunity to learn from mistakes with confidence that made the difference.

TEACHABLE MOMENTS

Much has been written about the "teachable moment." It is often that the experiential teacher encounters his student within the context of an experience that liberates both the teacher and the student from the restrictions of the traditional classroom setting. I find out more about my students from one country hike than I could ever learn in months of regular classroom teaching. Teachable moments are

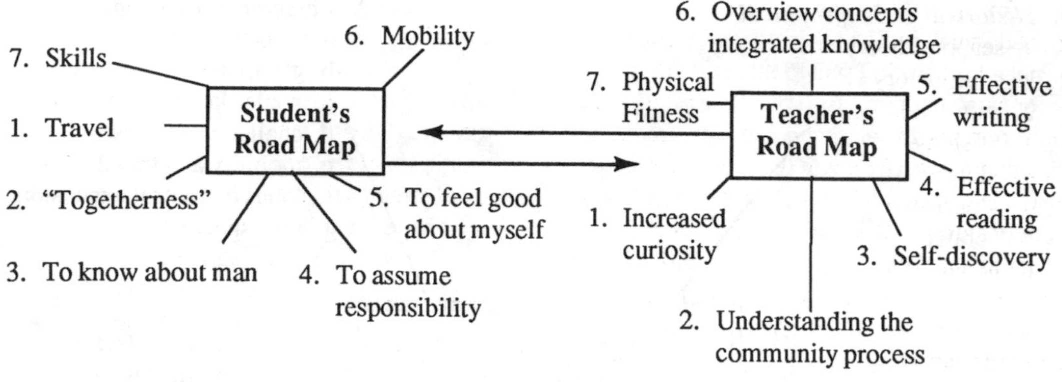

Figure 3
A Learning Strategy

psycho-spiritual moments. They are times when we adults try to wean students and nurture maturity. Obviously experiential education can play an enormous role in the student's journey toward growing up.

Through our sharing experiences with students, we can be at the right place at the right time. It is within this context of dealing with values and spiritual matters that the entire experiential education movement ultimately succeeds or fails. It is within the context of the shared experience that there develops the potential for new awarenesses and the tapping into personal strength and insight. It is this "tapping into" that makes the ultimate difference in a formative experience that lasts a lifetime.

AL

Just the other day I heard the honking of a Town Parks Department truck and I saw Al leaning out the window, shouting a warm hello to me. Al and I go back almost 20 years. He will never cease to amaze me. When I met him, he was a hostile and shy young man. He was born with a severe birth defect. One of his eyes was off-center and blind. If someone got too close to him or caught him off-guard, he would turn his head with the distorted and contorted side of his face and literally give the "evil eye." It was supposed to scare one away and disarm him. Most of the time, Al was very successful in this attempt.

He appeared to be the Hunchback of Notre Dame, as many recoiled from the sight of him. Al had been babied by his parents and understandably protected from the onslaught of a glaring outside world. But in the process of their protecting, they smothered him and rendered him helpless. I remember our first backpacking trip together. Al was just in front of me at the end of the long line of campers. Suddenly, his sleeping bag fell off of his frame pack. He became very distraught. We stopped. "Al, take your time and put your bag back on your pack. I'll wait for you. No problem." But there was a problem. It came out in conversation that Al's father had tied the sleeping bag on the frame the night before. He felt that he could not lash the bag to the frame correctly. He threw the most astonishing and frightening temper tantrum I had ever witnessed. He ranted and raved and drove his fists into the ground. He swore at his father, the pack, and at me for not tying the bag for him. Then I said that I would show him how to tie the bag. He stood over my shoulder as I kneeled down. I could see the slight gleam in his eye. He thought he had conned me into tying the bag for him. I wrapped the bag with the cord and attached it to the aluminum frame and finished off the job with a slip knot. Al bent down to put on his pack, and just as he grabbed the pack, I pulled the cord and the knot came undone. Al flew into a rage again, and soon began sobbing deeply, his frustration and anguish surfacing in the most tormented way. He carried on for half an hour and then finally slumped down on the ground from sheer exhaustion. "Al, I want to help you, but I cannot tie the bag for you. Can I teach you how to do it for yourself?" He listened very carefully, and nodded in resignation. I showed him how to tie the cord and I repeated the technique several times. Then it was his turn, and after several false starts, he tied the bag to the frame. He got up, put on his pack, turned away from me, and then suddenly whirled around with his hand outstretched. "Do you still like me?" he asked. I nodded my approval; I could not speak even if I wanted to. I was exhausted from the emotional interchange.

We set out on the trail and soon caught up to the rest of the students in the class. When the other students saw Al and me approaching, they began to cheer and welcomed Al as if he had just won a race. In truth, he had won a race, perhaps the most difficult one in his life. Once in a lifetime, we are privileged to observe growth and miracle happen right before our eyes. That is what happened that day for Al. He changed that day from a small child of tantrums and self-pity, to an emerging young adult who began to assume responsibility for his own welfare and his own growth. And ultimately, our job as teachers and loving adults is to help young people emerge into self-confident individuals. Al was weaned, the hard way, from dependence to freedom. He was never the same. Today he is married, with two lovely children. He is productive and loving, and smiles easily.

So often, our wilderness treks challenge our students physically and psychologically. Deeply buried in their memories are the stark revelations of doubt and fear, and on the other hand, surety and exhilaration and confidence. But most importantly it is within the community experience, the sharing and pulling together, that we provide the terrain of love and caring. For many students, this limitless energy of love is experienced for the first time with us. The taste of people caring and pulling for each other is a lasting one. It just might be the only relief from the physical and psychological stresses that tend to make the student feel so vulnerable and so much alone.

Through the real experience of group interaction, the student enters the real world of ethical living and moral responsibility. It is upon this new bedrock that the student ventures out into the real world that awaits him. He departs from his high school adventure in living and community with clearer understanding of the poem that we read at the base of the mountain, or by the bank of the river, or at the entrance to the city subway.

Look to this day
for it is life
The very life of life
In its brief course lie all the realities
and truths of existence
The joy of growth
The splendor of action
The glory of power
For yesterday is but a memory
And tomorrow is only a vision
But today well lived
Makes every yesterday a memory of
   happiness
And every tomorrow a vision of hope
Look well, therefore, to this day!

All experiential teachers understand this poem. It is, in truth, our watchword, our faith, and our hope.

C. W. HOG: Pathways to Understanding in the Outdoors

Tom Whittaker
Cooperative Wilderness Handicapped Outdoor Group (C. W. HOG), Idaho State University

&

Conner W. Shepherd
Mesa State College

We travel the vast compass of the oceans, gaze at the splendor of the mountains, wonder at the circular motion of the stars and all the time we pass by ourselves.

(St. Augustine, 300 A.D.)

The Cooperative Wilderness Handicapped Outdoor Group, C. W. HOG, was founded in 1981. The program is a regionally oriented support group and operates from the outdoor program office at Idaho State University. C. W. HOG serves individuals with disabilities from the local Pocatello, Idaho area, the intermountain region, and the nation.

The history and inception of the Cooperative Wilderness Handicapped Outdoor Group can best be understood through an account of the personal history and a revelation of the personal philosophy of its founder and present director, Tom Whittaker:

> In 1979, I was driving back to my home in Sun Valley, Idaho, from a Thanksgiving vacation when an out-of-control car struck me head-on. I suffered multiple fractures and damage to both legs. Surgeons repaired and reconstructed what they could. But they were unable to save my right foot. It had to be amputated.
>
> Before the accident I had been an avid outdoor enthusiast. Among other pursuits, I was a competent kayaker. But after my accident and period of rehabilitation, I was frustrated in my first attempts to run rivers with my friends. On the evening before the first river trip since my accident, my friends held a meeting without me and decided two things. One, I was not the same person I was before my injury. Two, they did not want to have to take responsibility for me out on the river.
>
> The first objection to my coming was obvious and irrefutable. I was different than I had been before my accident. But I felt it was still no reason to exclude me. The second objection was fatuous. I had not asked for, nor expected, anybody to take responsibility for me prior to my injury. As far as I was concerned, nothing had changed. I could still take care of myself. But as far as they were concerned things had changed.
>
> Perhaps as significant as their reaction was the fact that the decision was made in my absence and then relayed to me by a group

> member. I understood that the change in their attitude toward me did not stem from a lack of feeling for me or a desire to deny me a pleasure. Rather, they were concerned for my safety. However, the results was the same. They went. I stayed home.
>
> The rejection I experienced and the lack of involvement in the decision-making process were two of many realities I began to face as a person with a disability. Whether the source was attitudinal, physical, or emotional, the result was always the same. I was excluded from an experience because of my disability.
>
> Life is not a spectator sport. I realized that if I wanted to tango, I'd better get off my duff and make it happen. Sitting on the sidelines waiting for an invitation wasn't going to cut it anymore. At the time of the accident, the Pocatello community helped pay my medical bills. The inception of C. W. HOG was as much the result of the personal experience with my friends as it was inspired by my desire to repay a debt of gratitude for the infinite kindness shown me by the people of Pocatello and Idaho State University.

Whittaker based the organization, structure, and goals of C. W. HOG on four basic interrelated personal convictions.

Building an identity: a rehabilitation concept.

People with disabilities share common attitudes that lead to dysfunctional behavior and alienation from society. They include a lack of identity, a lack of self-confidence and self-esteem, a lack of self-sufficiency and reluctance to accept responsibility, and a lack of motivation and sense of purpose. The complex emotional rehabilitation of people with disabilities is a gradual process that continues in a community setting beyond the hospital or institution. Before people with disabilities can complete their personal rehabilitation, they need to establish positive identities—both collectively, and as individuals. This is best initiated in a supportive, caring environment outside the confines of an institution.

Decision-making is part of identity-building.

An individual with a disability, possessing full cognitive and emotional functioning, can make decisions for him or herself about any activity or trip. The cornerstone of this philosophy recognized a vital difference between taking responsibility for someone and taking responsibility from them.

Recreation and a support group play a role in the rehabilitation process.

A supportive recreation group can be a catalyst which provides the identity that circumstances have taken away. A supportive recreation group also acts as a cushion between the institution and the real world, softening reentry into the community by providing a sense of belonging. Within recreation support groups, individuals practice skills and competencies, build self-esteem, and become physically and emotionally robust. When the community sees people with disabilities successfully meeting challenges in recreation experiences, it responds with feelings of admiration, respect, and acceptance. It is easy, however, for people without disabilities, whose identities intertwine with their careers, social status, recreational interests, family and friends, to take for granted and overlook the benefits recreation can bring to a person who has either lost, or does not have access to, the essentials of a positive self-concept. Once people with disabilities gain a realistic understanding of their gifts and capabilities through recreational experiences, it is imperative that they transfer the application of wilderness problem-solving and identity-building skills to the community and workplace (Wright, 1983).

Work—the essential cornerstone for full integration.

It is the responsibility of society to recognize people with disabilities as contributing members of society and to allow them full integration into the work force. The culmination of the rehabilitation process must be the opportunity for full, productive employment. Selye (1974) believed that our primary aim as human beings was to maintain an identity and earn the respect of others. For Selye, work was a vital element in identity building and maintenance.

THE BIRTH OF A PROGRAM

From the outset, the purpose of C. W. HOG was to help people with disabilities realize their recreational dreams in the wild outdoors. Whittaker was not interested in providing a guide service or package tours for people with disabilities. His idea was to produce a supportive, self-help group that was governed by individual interests within the group. Whittaker was not interested in limiting the scope or diversity of activities. These would be real adventures, not contrived ones. The group would not be involved with token or watered-down experiences. His intention was to close a fun gap that obviously existed in his community for people with disabilities. Having worked in outdoor recreation for many years, Whittaker was committed to its positive value for individuals and society.

According to Whittaker, "What I had done, in my naivete, was produce a situation, through the C. W. HOG program, in which people with disabilities could create a collective and personal identity." The collective identity was the result of being part of a self-help group that did ordinary things in the wild outdoors that might be considered extraordinary for people with disabilities. The gains in self-esteem and personal growth that he witnessed among C.W. HOG members far exceeded his previous experiences observing persons without disabilities engaging in similar activities.

Within the safety of the group, individuals with disabilities learned to risk, experiment, be accountable, accept responsibility, cooperate, seek solutions, and undertake activities that once had seemed inappropriate or out of reach. In short, C. W. HOG members learned to be creative individuals and pursue their visions with love and courage. By portraying themselves as dynamic individuals, they earned the admiration of a community. They also gradually freed themselves from the degrading dependency fostered by reliance upon the directive social service and welfare community.

C. W. HOG: A SELF-HELP GROUP FOR PEOPLE WITH DISABILITIES

To stimulate self-expression, personal growth, and creativity, C. W. HOG activities follow the same informal format adopted by adventurers without disabilities. There are no requirements, rules, or regulations. Behavior is governed by the group. Trips are organized on a "common adventure" principle that ensures maximum involvement at a minimum cost. Anyone can initiate an activity. There are no paid leaders. All expertise is given gratuitously, as from one friend to another. And all participants share equally in the expenses for each adventure.

Legal liability is also governed by the "common adventure" principle or joint venture doctrine. Joint venture recognizes that common adventurers do not owe one another a duty of care (nor does the institution). With more than 90,000 man-hours of active recreation involving more than 1,100 individuals with disabilities and over 2,800 volunteers, C. W. HOG has yet to record its first accident.

Participants have the opportunity to take advantage of the tremendous recreational opportunities available to all Idaho citizens. Participation in vigorous outdoor recreation is encouraged because it requires individuals to risk, to be accountable, and to rely on each other. C. W. HOG activities have included: sea kayaking; camping on uninhabited islands of the Broken Island chain in Berkeley Sound, and Desolation Sound, B. C., Canada; and rafting and kayaking the Middle Fork of the Salmon River, the Main Salmon River in Idaho, the Yampa River in Colorado, and the Green River in Utah. Twice C. W. HOG members embarked on an 18-day, 250-mile journey down the Colorado River through the Grand Canyon.

C. W. HOG members have been horse packing in Yellowstone National Park, dog sledding in the Grand Teton National Park, and skied in premier resorts throughout the western United States. They have ridden in hot-air balloons, scuba-dived, taken martial arts classes, and golfed. They have taken part in wheelchair tennis and amputee soccer tournaments, sailed, rock climbed, rappelled, involved themselves in fitness programs, and enjoyed all manner of social and cultural events.

All of the activities are self-directed and carried out without the assistance of commercial resources or motorized back-up support. These are real adventures, planned and executed by disabled people without a fanfare of publicity or media attention. They are accomplished by ordinary people doing things that are considered no less extraordinary for people without disabilities.

The organizational structure of C. W. HOG is such that it does not define people with disabilities by deciding what is, and what is not, an appropriate activity. An overriding philosophy at C. W. HOG is that an individual with a disability, possessing full cognitive and emotional functioning, can make decisions for him or herself about any activity or trip.

ORGANIZATION AND MANAGEMENT OF C. W. HOG

The day-to-day group activities are directed by members who meet once a week. A quarterly calendar updated by periodic newsletters provides members with news about upcoming events. An organization that to a large extent relies on its members for creativity and programming is extremely cost-effective. C. W. HOG requires only a small staff to administer it. In 1987-88, on an $85,000 budget, the C. W. HOG program provided recreation for more than 400 different disabled individuals assisted by 1,300 volunteers. The program generated 19,000 man-hours of recreational activities for a population that had virtually no such provision six years ago.

The financial control of the program is administered through Idaho State University. Endowment funds established by the C. W. HOG program have been placed in the Idaho State University Foundation. The investment of endowment funds enables C. W. HOG to receive a higher and more stable income, and assures benefactors that funds are professionally managed. The specific use of endowment funds is determined by the C. W. HOG Board of Directors. The Board of Directors includes members of the medical profession, a certified public accountant, a lawyer, university representatives, and individuals with disabilities.

The relationship between C. W. HOG and Idaho State University extends well beyond a financial partnership. Universities need programs similar to C. W. HOG as much as the programs need the universities. The positive regard created within the community by a program such as this is beyond measure. The service opportunities it provides for a university's young people, for professional development, training, and for research, are themselves valuable assets to a university.

On the other side of the coin, the university can give a great deal to such programs. Apart from obvious access to services, expertise, and facilities, the gains in status a person with severely diminished self-esteem derives from association with a university are considerable. Not only is C. W. HOG's success due to the fact that it is attached to Idaho State University, it is also because of its physical location within the Pond Student Union. The accessibility of the resource, housed in the social center of the institution, provides excellent opportunities for C. W. HOG members to integrate and socialize with students without disabilities and to capture the gregarious atmosphere of the building.

A CASE STUDY

Until stories are personalized, we tend to ignore the problems and fail to recognize the triumphs of people challenged with physical disabilities. As a result, we have been slow to embrace individuals with physical disabilities in our society. According to Whittaker, one such personal triumph is Kyle Packer.

> At 21, Kyle Packer was a mouse. Strangled by his umbilical cord, Kyle was revived by doctors. His life was saved—but at a cost. Although the rational part of his brain was spared, the part that governed his gross motor function was in disarray. The resulting spasticity twisted his limbs and affected his speech and ability to eat.
>
> When I met Kyle, he was in his second year at Idaho State University, pushing his 54 pound Everest and Jennings wheelchair backwards with inturned feet. Although a familiar sight on the ground floor of Pond Student Union, he was never seen on its main floor, the social center of the campus. Kyle was racked with anxiety and on the verge of flunking out of school. A recluse, he lived a lack-luster existence, afraid to eat in public or talk on the phone. After pulling a sagging 0.98 grade point average to a 4.00 in his final semester, Kyle was nominated for the 1984 Outstanding Student of the Year Award by the Governor's Committee for Employing the Handicapped. Now a married man with a career, Kyle advocates independent living skills for a group with which he has special empathy—the physically challenged.
>
> So what was it that caused the amazing about-face in Kyle's life? To state the case simply, Kyle discovered how to have fun. It didn't happen overnight. It evolved slowly through a process of discovery and experimentation. With each experience his confidence grew, his self-image improved, his physical and emotional functioning strengthened. Kyle for the first time established an identity and a sense of belonging based on a real understanding of his abilities. Kyle achieved this by joining a self-help outdoor recreation group for people with disabilities, and as a result, he became enthusiastic about his options in life and chances for success.
>
> As a result of Kyle Packer's enthusiasm for sit-skiing, he started working out. On his first attempt, he could not raise 35 pounds in a bench press. His personal best now stands at 200 pounds. By his own admission, Kyle was scared stiff of water. Yet, not only has he learned to swim, he also has oared an 18-foot raft, he learned how to scuba dive, and he has gone on a 10-day sea-kayaking trip.
>
> Upon his return from Illinois, Kyle and his new bride came by my house and I showed him the manuscript for this chapter. I asked him what I should say. He replied, 'You know, Tom, we all have silly fantasies. Mine was to be a football star. Yet trapped in a body like this, I couldn't even try, and that hurt. Really hurt. But with the HOGs, I've done it all. Stuff I can't even believe. In light of all of these, (he waved a stiff arm in a circular motion), 'being a football star's pretty limp.'

CONCLUSION

It has been demonstrated, as is the case with Kyle Packer and many other disabled individuals, that a recreation program, encouraging responsibility and interpersonal relationships, can create dramatic changes in an individual's self-esteem. Before becoming a ski instructor for the C. W. HOG program, Don Carr recalls, "I was watching a mud wrestling contest that took place between all the candidates before Homecoming King and Queen were determined. Kyle Packer was one of the candidates and out there on his knees in all that mud. Not knowing Kyle, at that point, I had to figure nothing bothered him. At first I was kind of embarrassed and then filled with admiration for Kyle. I remember watching Kyle at the crowning ceremony at the Homecoming football game later that week. By the time the runner-up was announced and Kyle's name still had not been mentioned, I felt crushed and disappointed, if not resentful, that he had put himself in a circumstance where he was almost guaranteed to be hurt. I was so wrapped up in my thoughts and projected feelings for Kyle that the announcer's words seemed fuzzy and distant. I found myself on my feet along with a near-capacity crowd cheering and whistling. Kyle's arms were raised in a victory salute. Everywhere orange hats were in the air. Untypically, the majority of the crowd had stayed to witness the outcome of this particular Homecoming gala. And now, their deafening applause was honoring Kyle's guts and tenacity."

This ability to risk oneself and take part, despite one's differences, takes a supreme act of courage which, when witnessed by others, can positively imprint, not only on an individual, but also on a community's values. In three years, Kyle had made the transition from a social recluse to someone a large proportion of the student body knew and cared for. By daring to be different, he learned that he could not only transcend his disability but turn it into an advantage.

REFERENCES

Seyle, H. (1974). *Stress without distress.* Philadelphia, PA: J.B. Lippincott.

Wright, A. N. (1987). Youth development through outdoor adventure programs. J. F. Meier, T. W. Morash, & G. E. Welton (Eds.), *High-adventure outdoor pursuits: Organization and leadership.* Columbus, OH: Publishing Horizons.

Experiential Therapy: An Adventure in Self-Discovery Enters the Psychiatric Hospital

Richard Weider
Healthcare International

AN OVERVIEW: THE ROPES/ CHALLENGE PROGRAM AT HEALTHCARE INTERNATIONAL

The ROPES/Challenge Program is an innovative form of therapy that uses the power of action-oriented experiences to help psychiatric hospital patients make positive changes in their lives. With a variety of group and individual activities on a specially designed obstacle course, ROPES challenges participants to master unusual tasks. At first these tasks seem impossible to accomplish, but in fact become fun and enjoyable to complete.

A primary goal of ROPES is to place individuals in physically, emotionally, and intellectually demanding situations where skills of cooperation, problem-solving, goal-setting, and self-awareness are rapidly developed. Each ROPES event encourages participants to deal with an issue in the "here-and-now," such as a problem communicating with others or a need to feel successful.

A high level of fitness or physical ability is not required to participate in ROPES. What is more important is each individual's willingness to take appropriate risks with other group members.

The ROPES/Challenge course consists of cables, ropes, pulleys, and wood beams set between utility poles or built in trees. Three types of activity areas are included in the ROPES course:

Group Initiative Area

Initiative events are used to challenge a small group of individuals to work together to achieve tasks that initially seem impossible. The process enables each individual to contribute to the group effort. For example, one initiative called "The Wall" challenges group members to help each other over a 12-foot high wall.

Low ROPES Activities

Built close to the ground, these low activity areas provide individuals with situations that require coordinated physical, emotional, and thoughtful effort. From these experiences, participants develop a better sense of personal control and determination resulting in enhanced self-esteem and confidence as well as interdependence and trust in others.

High ROPES Events

These events require the individual's choice and commitment to attempt a series of events approximately 35 feet in the air. The activities are built upon the positive attitudes developed on the low ROPES course, but are primarily designed to encourage initiative and appropriate risk-taking, and to provide participants with feelings of accomplishment. Other group members provide support and encouragement from below.

Preparation. The therapist and ROPES facilitator plans a ROPES session that addresses each individual's needs and goals. The participant's health history is reviewed so that appropriate activities can be planned around any physical limitations or recurring medical problems.

Size of Group. Generally, the ROPES groups are small, consisting of 6 to 12 participants. Often these individuals share common goals.

Sequence of Events. ROPES activities are presented in a sequence of increasingly challenging events that help participants to gradually gain greater self-confidence. A ROPES motto is "start low and slow." Individuals begin with activities on the low-level course. As they learn to trust themselves and their fellow participants, they work up to the more challenging activities.

Discussions and Follow-Up. An important aspect of the ROPES process is group discussion. Before, during, and after each session, the ROPES facilitator and therapist lead participants in discussions of the group's achievements and experiences on the ROPES course. During this time, participants are encouraged to draw conclusions, gain new insights, and make personal discoveries.

ROPES and Safety. The ROPES Program is as safe as it is challenging. An integrated safety management system is always in effect during each ROPES activity. Although the perceived risk of a ROPES event may appear significant, the actual risk is minimal. Safety is ensured by the program's accreditation process, teaching methods and proper use of high-quality equipment. An integrated safety system with back-up support at all critical points ensures the physical safety of each participant. The ROPES methods and equipment are standardized according to proven safety practices. Each participant (and guardian, if participant is under 18 years of age) signs an acknowledgment of risk form prior to involvement. This form states that participation in the ROPES Program requires full attention and cooperation in maintaining safety for self and others.

The ROPES Staff. A blend of therapeutic skills and outdoor knowledge—The ROPES Program is supervised by a trained hospital therapist and operated by full-time ROPES facilitators who represent such disciplines as social work, psychology, education, and wilderness adventure programming. ROPES facilitators are chosen for their therapeutic skills, extensive experience in working with groups, and proven expertise in outdoor education. To reinforce program safety and effectiveness, ROPES facilitators receive ongoing training in ROPES course safety techniques and the group development process.

An Experience of Lasting Value. ROPES is often called a "metaphor for life" because many of the ROPES activities blend physical challenges with imaginative scenarios that can relate to real-life situations.

The following skills and insights gained from ROPES often have a direct, beneficial application to daily life:

- A more positive self-image and enhanced self-esteem
- Effective teamwork and cooperation
- Improved communication and listening skills
- Willingness to take appropriate risks
- An ability to set and achieve goals
- Creative problem-solving skills
- Feelings of accomplishment and success.

In addition, participants experience these benefits in a supportive and rewarding atmosphere with other group members.

AN ANECDOTAL SESSION: FOUR DEPRESSED ADULT WOMEN

Four women, ranging in age from 25 to 45 and hospitalized for diagnoses generally categorized as severe depression, attend their third session of the ROPES program. After greeting the patients at their hospital unit, the facilitator and patients walk out to the ropes course area and begin the session with some mild exercise and stretching. They breath in deeply and comment on the pleasantness of the weather and the air.

The group is next instructed to engage in a game of triangle tag as an aerobic warm-up activity. Three women hold each others' hands in an inwardly facing triangle while a fourth member is left outside the triangle. They are instructed that the outside person is to attempt to tag a member of the triangle opposite her vantage point and that the other two are to protect the targeted individual from the pursuer. The game starts and the dynamics emerge. In light-hearted fashion each person's role is attempted with general success, though the target is eventually tagged. At this point, the roles change and the game continues. The women laugh while focusing on the task. They express pleasure at the activity.

Next they are introduced to the game of Smaug's Jewels. The participants are asked to identify a quality that they are searching for in their lives that they want to pursue. Two younger members each say they want to gain more trust of others. Another member wants more self-confidence, and another wants greater self-esteem. They all acknowledge each others' desires, and the facilitator goes on to explain that a small sack on the ground nearby contains the qualities they are searching for. These qualities, in effect, are the jewels. The game begins with the facilitator assuming the role of protector of the "jewels." The others are instructed to attempt to grab hold of the sack laying on the ground and protected by the enforcer. "If the enforcer tags you before you get the sack you are frozen in place and are out of this session. If you get the sack, you win and you become the enforcer." Before engaging in the sport one of the members observes that, given the outcomes of past experiences at ROPES, they would be advised to take some time to make a plan among themselves to ensure their success. They huddle for two minutes and then come out and set off to grab the sack. Within a minute they are successful. The round continues four more times, and each time there is a winner. The facilitator commends them on their planning and reliance on each other as a team in their pursuit for collective success.

The group next moves on to the main initiative event of the day: the Acid River. The facilitator takes them to the "bank" of the river and explains that the river contains all those toxic characteristics that have dragged them down in the past. He asks them to mention those characteristics. He informs them that they are on the shore of a river and must get across to avoid falling into the arms of people who have been a negative influence on them in the past. He asks them to mention the first name of one or two such individuals. They are then instructed that the "rocks" (cinder blocks) set across the "river" (open field) can only be bridged with the two boards set at their feet. "You can't jump from block to block. You are being pursued by your bad influences and you need to use your strength of character to work together as a team to bridge the blocks above their toxic tendencies to safely get to the other side. If you do fall into the drink or drop a board, you may be handicapped with blindness."

They begin the task of working together to consider solutions to the geometric puzzle. They quickly solve the first bridging problem but then need to execute the solution. One person begins to swing a board on her own without help from the group. The younger members assume a lot of individual effort and manage to get out to the second row of blocks where balance and teamwork are critical to success. Despite their perceived balance problem due to medication, they each retain a high degree of balance in the event. However, teamwork is lacking and both younger women drop a board in the bridging process. They are instructed to return to the starting point, where they are blindfolded and must rely on the two older women for guidance and support. The two older women now muster their strength and begin to retrace the initial plan. They successfully create the bridge, not only relying on themselves, but also involving the two blind participants in roles to help support the maneuvering of the boards. The activity proceeds as they gain the third row of blocks. The task becomes more complicated now as the progression of the four must be planned out. Two women frequently need to stand on one block at a time as they reposition the boards. The boards by now are precariously balanced, and they are instructed to improve on the bridge structure before they can safely cross it. They seem stumped. Then a blindfolded participant realizes that the bottom cross member needs to be pushed more to the edge of one block so the top piece can gain greater support on the other block—insight gained by the feel of her foot. Even the blindfolded women are deeply involved in solving the problem.

At one point during busy activity on the fourth row, an older woman on the third row jumps ahead anticipating the next level solution. In her excitement to put her idea into action she attempts to transfer a board by herself without the others' help and drops the board in the 'river.' She also realizes that her 'solution' would have left a blinded member stranded on a block. To handicap her would likely ensure the group's failure at the task. All note the seriousness of her haste, and encourage her to accept help from the group to retrace her steps and reinvest herself in a team-based solution to the problem. The group continues and soon safely reaches the other side without further mishap. They are ecstatic, jumping up and down with satisfaction and congratulating each other on their collective success. The facilitator reaffirms their success and asks them to retreat to the discussion circle where they can talk about the events of the last 70 minutes.

In the discussion circle they recount what has just transpired. They focus on the acid river activity and talk about how they rebounded from the initial failure and had to work with each other to complete the task. They talk about how befuddling some of the required solutions were, but how they each made input that gradually solved their dilemma. The two younger women remarked on how they had to trust the other two participants to guide them across, while the other two women reveled in how they had to muster confidence to not only assume primary responsibility for the successful solution, but also guide the blinded women across. They note how they had to make a distinction between the solution and the execution of the solution—two distinct steps— and that the problem changed constantly, requiring continual attention to the task.

The facilitator affirms their success, and notes that each of the characteristics that they had sought in Smaug's Jewels were exhibited by them in the course of solving this problem: trust and confidence. And that self-esteem is an outgrowth of successful experience. He asks them about their rebound from the first failure and resultant handicap. They comment on how often they don't give solutions a second chance in their lives, and that they often become overwhelmed with disappointment at their first failure and don't make second attempts. He notes how good it feels to get beyond that initial disappointment and realize that second chances are a normal part of life.

He then asks the group to identify the most gut-wrenching point in the activity. They think for a moment and identify the time that the older participant dropped the board in midstream and left the blind member stranded. He turns to her and asks her to recount her thought process. She shyly notes that she was so excited with her assumed solution that her enthusiasm took over, she flung into action without relying on the rest of the group, and then not only failed by dropping the board, but more unsettling, would have left the blind member stranded. She notes how this is how she often reacts when she's excited—jumping into things without thinking them through or looking for help from others. The facilitator notes that this trait isn't uncommon for all of us at times, and that it is important to note the result and keep this lesson in mind in the future. Examples are offered on how this reaction has been a part of past patterns for each of them. "We need to separate the solution from the execution and seek other people's support to ensure our own success."

Group members also talk about their disappointment that is lingering over an incident that occurred in the previous day's ROPES group, when a member not present today got frustrated in the course of solving a problem and blamed the group for not listening to her. The group became apologetic and attempted to make amends and agreed to include her, but she huffed off, wouldn't accept their apology and removed herself from the group. This incident was a powerfully depressing experience for the women, as it symbolized the rejection from others that often sets them into a tailspin of guilt. The facilitator asks them what they could have done differently about the situation. They note that they did work better with each other that day, and had wanted to demonstrate that same willingness the day before. However, with this person walking off, they were left to feel guilty. The facilitator notes that this is sometimes a ploy that one depressed person uses on others to ensure others feel as badly as she does. At this point, given her departure from the group, these women can't change yesterday's outcome. (The facilitator had noted this incident in the charting for use by the person's primary therapist in a follow-up session.) Then one member notes that they have learned they can't control how other people react to them, and that they can only try their best at amends and not come under the guilt- tripping influence. The facilitator notes how today's positive experience holds much richer lessons for them about the personal strengths they do have. He expresses that the positive feelings they now have experienced can override their depression, and then encourages them to think instead about this time until the next ROPES session, and about how they can apply the lesson of thoughtful teamwork, trust, and confidence to other areas of their lives. The good feelings from this experience can lead them to seek additional positive experiences in their lives, and get beyond the first level of setbacks that have set them into tailspins in the past.

The group ends the session with a simple group hug, and they head back to their units to prepare for lunch. On the way back, one of the older women walks with the facilitator, exuding a sense of satisfaction and confidence. She compliments the two younger women on the progress they are making, and comments on how much progress she feels she has made while at the hospital. She states that this group was empowering, affirming, insightful, and that all took place in an atmosphere of fun and light-heartedness. This was what she felt was helping her accept herself better and discover dormant strengths and qualities, while still being open to learning from setbacks and failures. She thanked him and he affirmed her strengths exhibited that day and wished her success with her recovery. Thus ended another 90-minute ROPES session; one of over 200 such sessions that would take place that week at a Healthcare International Psychiatric Hospital.

Experiences like the one just depicted are becoming more and more common in the daily operation of psychiatric hospitals across the United States. A new therapeutic phenomenon is emerging with the introduction of Experiential Therapy programs in the milieu of acute and long-term residential psychiatric facilities. The greatest impetus for this development has occurred in the new for-profit sector hospitals located in Sun-belt cities across the Southern and Western United States.

My particular involvement emerged as a direct result of the initiative of Healthcare International, one of those for-profit Sunbelt-oriented hospital management corporations, aiming to position experiential programs as a distinctive advancement in psychiatric hospital treatment resources. Besides the commitment to the concept by the corporate officers and facility administrators, the medical directors and the staff of psychiatrists became strong supporters of the concept in the hospitals. The concept has expanded to the point where within two years we have initiated the program at all 17 of our psychiatric hospital facilities. Additional initiatives are underway to establish wilderness-based, experientially oriented residential treatment centers in the Eastern, Southern, and Western United States. A team-building program is also promoted to other large companies throughout the United States.

The main focus of this article, however, is the operation of the experiential therapy program at the psychiatric hospital setting. The structure of the current program serves a variety of needs; it provides an exciting and effective treatment program for hospital patients, as reflected in the consistent feedback in exit surveys that ROPES is one of the two most highly valued resources provided to patients. Given the credentialed qualifications of our ROPES therapists, the program is a billable therapy (revenue generator) for the hospital. In addition, the hospital promotes ropes course activities to community organizations, schools, and a variety of social service organizations as an outreach program. It is a tremendous goodwill generator for the hospital that draws attention to the facility's resources and helps to direct potential referrals to the inpatient hospital program. Everybody wins with ROPES! In effect, we have developed an outdoor adventure program as an urban-based community resource in a growing number of cities throughout the United States, miles from wilderness and requiring only a few hours' commitment to experience its benefits.

OPERATIONAL AND MANAGEMENT ISSUES

Experiential therapy programs are in the early stages of development as a psycho-therapeutic resource within the psychiatric hospital setting. Full-time professional positions have been established at a handful of hospitals across the country and are being filled by individuals with a wide range of ability. High-quality programs require staff that are clinically oriented, technically competent and skilled at group process. The experiential learning process needs to be at the core of credible programs, and staff should be trained to employ all of these skills in a complete program format that is integrated into the treatment plans of patients and the milieu of the hospital.

An Experiential Program Coordinator needs to be trained in three broad areas of responsibility:

- Experiential therapy processing
- Technical skill requirements
- Administrative management.

Standards are now being established that will set basic parameters to ensure that responsible and safe programming is being provided to patients.

Most competent program leaders have gained their training from resources outside of the hospital arena, such as Outward Bound or Project Adventure. In addition, they have clinical training from accredited schools. Understanding the administrative side of program operation tends to be a less-developed ability among some of the best practitioners. Some shun this aspect of the job and prefer to focus on direct service to patients. Whatever the motive or desire of the practitioner, nothing can replace firsthand experience as a participant in the process. Insofar as the programs' roots have emerged from the traditions of Outward Bound and similar adventure-based programs, participation in an extended wilderness program that credibly employs the experiential learning process is a recommended initiation into the field. Many quality organizations that offer these opportunities are networked within the Association for Experiential Education (AEE).

My management approach at Healthcare International is to focus on networking the practitioners and program coordinators from among our hospitals. I do not aim to establish myself as the central expert. Rather, I am a learner among peers. We are developing this field within the hospital setting as we go. After four years of experience we have agreed upon a common set of standards and operating procedures that we feel identify the core of a credible, high-quality operation. The desire is to set a baseline standard and to acknowledge high achievers within the fold. A premium value is placed on the development of new strategies and techniques for working effectively with patients. Effort also focuses on refining approaches for a variety of wellness and outpatient clients.

In general, a good program will have a well-defined process for the referral, assessment, and screening of participants. It will have a tracking mechanism or feedback loop relating to the efficacy of planned activities and their processing related to treatment objectives or other identified strategies. Operating procedures are spelled out relating to the safety practices to be followed for specific activities, basic program formats to be followed given a set time frame, plus staff-to-client ratios. A termination process is required for each participant, and their evaluation of the program is sought. Administrative issues such as utilization norms, staffing efficiencies, maintenance schedules, and financial controls are standardized to the extent possible so that administrivia doesn't overwhelm therapeutic focus.

A training regimen exists for the orientation of new facilitators, and upgrades are planned for higher-level skill development, as well as new technical or therapeutic developments in the field. A professional seminar or workshop series can also be made available for sharing information from among the best practitioners in the network. Our interest is not to control information but to encourage that it be shared and responded to within the network. It is also important that we do not become myopic among ourselves, but actively seek input from other professionals engaged in similar work throughout the country. Beyond this we also conduct peer reviews of each others' programs on an ongoing basis. One year a coordinator will spend three days at another program reviewing all aspects of the operation and critiquing them with the on-site professional. A report is submitted to the hospital administrator with recommendations on how the program might be further refined in the next year. The following year the roles are reversed, though likely with different hospitals for both parties. The sharing that takes place enhances every program significantly on a level that can't be replicated as well any other way.

A strong infrastructure allows program therapists to focus on the issue that is truly important: how to maximize therapeutic efficacy and adapt the process to meet the needs of varying client groups, given their critical issues and potential. Facilitators have developed intervention strategies that enable family dynamics to be honestly and openly explored; that encourage bolemic or anorexic patients to develop greater respect for their physical attributes; that impel conflicting parties to confront interpersonal conflicts while developing greater mutual respect; that generate metaphors of success for patients preparing to return to their homes and communities; that greatly increase the insight that a clinician needs to complete a thorough assessment of a new client; and that provide opportunities for a therapist to develop a stronger trust bond that a chemically dependent/recovering patient requires. Good experiential programs can have immediate payoffs for the participants. The positive impact can be seen and felt among the group of participants who encourage and support each other. Appropriate risk-taking becomes a positive new learning experience.

The highly visual, physical nature of the program, with the image of high ropes and intense group challenges, can overwhelm the fact that the most critical facet of a high-quality experiential program is often the reflection and discussion that accompanies the activity. The facilitator's skill in managing the process for the participants is critical to the efficacy of the program. Learning occurs as a result of thinking and sharing thoughts about powerful interpersonal experience. The integration of thought, feeling, and action is what characterizes experiential programs. The intensity of the discussion is directly related to the impact of the experience. Participants are usually eager to talk about how these presumably unrelated activities have meaning to them metaphorically. These discussions are an exciting aspect of the program, and frankly, without them the activities are incomplete.

Insight, however, cannot be forced. If there is no connection for a participant, suggesting an interpretation could be helpful, but it is less desirable than spontaneous commentary. Facilitators are encouraged not to overlay their interpretation for others, but to allow the activity to stand symbolically for the person, freeing them to further reflect and apply meaning at a later time if they so desire. The facilitator's responsibility is to ensure that, whatever happens, it is not miseducative in any overt context. To the extent that conflict occurs or events deteriorate, the facilitator's responsibility is to attempt to frame the experience so that participants are encouraged to focus on actions or outcomes or sequences that could offer positive insight or affirmation on some level for the group members.

The facilitator as therapist is a demanding role when interacting with high-risk psychiatric patients whose lives are in turmoil and who suffer from the effects of many past miseducative experiences. The facilitator's role is to lead the group without being the focus of the group. The finest facilitation can occur when a patient group succeeds at a difficult task or confronts a serious problem successfully and the facilitator is hardly noticeable in the process. It is likely that the facilitator needed to do significant prodding or deflection. However, a skilled facilitator will do this with a keen awareness of the group process and with strong sensitivity of how not to over-intrude. The skill of being an effective facilitator comes with experience and perhaps best from apprenticing with a seasoned enabler.

The modern psychiatric hospital has evolved from a secure lockup that existed to keep misfits out of the community, to a safe haven for those debilitated from emotional pain. Experiential programs are now used to encourage today's patient to learn new coping skills as a result of taking a reasonable risk to challenge their perception of who they are. Our message is that you can be more than you ever thought you could be if, with the support and encouragement of a caring group, you take a chance, push a new limit, are open to discovery and self-awareness. The activities are structured by a skilled facilitator to plan for success. In the event one fails, which is the real risk every participant takes, the group is available to help put that failure into context, assess the reasons, offer feedback, and ultimately affirm that positive action and initiative are preferable to inwardly focused criticism and despair. As facilitator/therapists, we aim for a true, empowering catharsis that can generalize an exciting positive experience into a lasting metaphor for life. For anyone who participates, experiential programs offer a symbol of hope, promise, and mutual support.

APPLICATION

Typically, over 75 percent of the patients in our hospitals participate in experiential therapy programs—wholly 95 percent of adolescent patients, but something less than 60 percent of adult patients. There are varying reasons for the substantially lower level of involvement among adults, ranging from short lengths of stay, degree of acuity, and the physical condition or age of the patient. All patients must first have a psychiatrist's order before participating, and ultimately all participation is voluntary, though attendance is expected for most adolescents. We are currently developing on-unit programs for less able adults, and are also doing a greater degree of marketing to adults: describing the intent and benefits of the program and allaying fears relating to height and the physical nature of the activities. Once at the program site, no one is coerced into participation. A fundamental program-tenet is that the individual chooses to participate from activity to activity, with a prohibition against peer pressure. Encouragement is solicited but not overdone.

In planning the activity for the day, the facilitator considers the group as a whole and each participant in particular. The staff review the diagnoses and the treatment plans' critical issues in light of the most recent report on each patient's behavior. Then staff identify experiences that could produce the desired teaching moments. We plan for success, but allow patients to discover this themselves. Experiential programs make the assumption that how you act in one situation is generalizable to other situations.

The program is particularly helpful for adolescents, as it enables them to physically interact with each other under controlled stress, and can lead to observations as well as modeling that couldn't be achieved in a traditional all-talk based therapy session. Adults tend to respond well to these programs because of the unusual character of the activity and their ability to abstract the key learnings into metaphorical insights relating to critical life issues.

Among the types of clients that are involved in the programs, most common are the hospital unit groups consisting of individuals with varying diagnoses. Specialized groups are becoming more common, and targeted groups have been conducted that focus on issues relating to:

- Depression among adults
- Character disorders among adolescents
- Chemical dependence (recovery from drug or alcohol abuse)
- Eating disorders
- Victims of abuse
- Schizophrenics
- Multiple or dual diagnosis
- Combined medical/psychiatric patients (including the head-injured)
- Groups for families of patients
- On-unit crisis intervention
- Client-therapist bonding
- Young children
- Sexual perpetrators
- Use as an assessment tool
- Use for family assessments
- Transition groups

In addition, programs are frequently conducted for hospital staff, as a tool to foster teamwork and improved working relationships and communication between departments. When the program activities can demonstrate their efficacy directly to staff, enthusiasm for the program tends to be contagious with patients.

STANDARDS

As with any program in a psychiatric hospital, experiential therapy programs are structured to meet all JCAH (hospital accreditation) and CHAMPUS (federal government) required guidelines as a group therapy where such requirements apply. In other instances the program is considered one of the activity therapies, though most often independent of recreational therapy. Although many good therapists originally were trained as recreation therapists, the program is distinctively separate within our facilities. The standard program coordinator is typically a master's-prepared therapist, experienced in the hospital setting with a prior exposure to experiential concepts and a predisposition to adventure experience in his or her own life. We look for an ability to administer and supervise several support staff, and the coordinator is involved in their ongoing training.

TRAINING

Those interested in becoming experiential therapists should gain an exposure to various psycho-therapeutic orientations and receive some level of clinical training. A personal adventure experience in a recognized experiential education program is highly recommended. Opportunities to intern in a hospital experiential therapy program are available, and are also highly recommended. Hospital organizations that currently have experiential therapy programs at several of their facilities include Healthcare International, Psychiatric Institutes of America, Charter Medical, and Hospital Corporation of America. Over 50 programs are currently operating, and more are starting every month.

In addition, the Hurricane Island and Colorado Outward Bound schools operate Health Services programs for several independent psychiatric or drug rehabilitation programs, as does the Santa Fe Mountain Center and Project Adventure. Any of these organizations or their related hospitals can be contacted regarding job opportunities, as can the Association for Experiential Education in Boulder, Colorado.

Development Training in the United Kingdom

Chris Loynes
National Association for Outdoor Education

The use of the outdoors for education began in Britain because two men felt it was the right thing to do. They were concerned about the moral fiber of young men and saw the outdoor challenge as part of an approach to education that would address the need to develop them physically, socially, morally, and spiritually. The modern equivalent is called Development Training, and it is perhaps appropriate that the current popularity of this approach is so well founded in the roots of the concept. The two men were Baden Powell and Kurt Hahn.

Baden Powell (usually known as B. P.) recognized positive benefits of the outdoor life on young scouts while fighting in the Boer War. The ingredients of adventure, challenge, a common purpose, comradeship, and living together were all recognized at this stage. On his return to England, B. P. set out to find a moral alternative. His first experiments in simple camps operating a troop structure with an adventurous program set precedents in methods, such as the residential setting, working in groups, new and adventurous experiences, and self-reliance. Once published in a form eagerly read by boys, market forces soon established the validity of his insights, with the movement blossoming spontaneously. This was quickly followed by the Guide Movement for girls. Often the initiative for the formation of a troop came from the boys, who then sought a leader.

B. P. also set standards for leadership, being first and foremost interested in the development of young people, understanding their needs, leading by example, delegating responsibility, and using a discovery method of learning. If backwoodsmanship set a bad example in environmental ethics, it was through ignorance rather than by design. The modern Scout and Guide movements are still founded on these essentials and are the largest worldwide voluntary youth movement. The outdoors and the expedition are still major and central parts of their curriculum.

The expedition was also a central part of Hahn's early thinking, being part of the personal development program at Gourdonston School where he was head teacher in the 1930s. The pilots of what was to become the Duke of Edinburgh's Award Scheme, also inspired and initiated by Hahn, took place in Scotland and also incorporated an expedition. The overall scheme and its aims bear a striking resemblance to those developed by the Scout Movement. The two now work closely together.

Both schemes recognize, however, that Adventure is not something one does, but rather a way one feels—that, as an attitude to life, it is perhaps the best way to encapsulate the kind of relationship a healthy person will have with one's environment and one's community. As such, the other ingredients in the two schemes reflect this, and include community service and personal challenges such as the commitment to a hobby and a fitness test.

It was with Outward Bound (OB) that Hahn made his biggest impact, and OB is really the birthplace of Development Training. Starting in 1941 with the first school at Aberdovey on the Welsh coast, OB developed month-long adventurous programs incorporating adventure activities, expeditions, community work and working in groups. Challenge, self-reliance, and leadership were key ingredients. The aim was character-building, and the forum—wild country. Despite popular opinion, the schools were not elitist, recruiting participants from factories and borstals as well as schools. Nor did the approach emphasize athletic achievement but, rather, tenacity of pursuit and the education of the whole person. Courses for girls began in 1951. Six schools were founded in Britain, of which five remain. There are now many more worldwide.

THE BIRTH OF OUTDOOR EDUCATION IN SCHOOLS

In 1950, the Derbyshire Local Education Authority founded Whitehall Open Country Pursuits Center and began a trend that became a rising wave of activity in the outdoors that acquired the name Outdoor Pursuits. The increasing number of schools, youth clubs, and colleges that became involved during the 1960s initially used land-based activities. Participation was mostly outside school time and so, voluntary in nature. Participants, then, were mostly of average intelligence, fit, motivated and obedient, and the expectations leaders could have of such participants were factors in the kind of experience offered. The aim of such programs was proficiency and self-sufficiency, very different from the personal development aims of OB and the Scout Movement. The focus was on the activity rather than the participant. With this emphasis on skill development, teaching styles were heavily directive and inflexible. Early and justifiable concerns about safety tended to reinforce this approach as the best way to ensure the necessary ability for performance in safety.

FIELD STUDIES

In parallel with this movement was the development of centers offering field study programs primarily for geography and biology students aged between 14 and 21. This work was pioneered by the Field Studies Council, which now operates 10 centers throughout the UK. In developing courses for students taking higher school and university subjects related to the environment, the council devised an approach that was quickly adopted by schools. Attendance at a field studies course is currently the commonest means by which students gain residential experience, and participation is frequently required by the examining boards' syllabuses.

DEVELOPMENT AND CHANGE

Over the last 15 years, the three strands of personal development, outdoor pursuits, and field studies have seen many developments and much change. More young people are involved in a wider range of activities, some of which, like board-sailing and mountain biking, are very recent innovations. Many of the activities have developed offshoots that bear little resemblance to the pure forms from which they sprang. For example, abseiling is often provided as an activity in its own right completely divorced from climbing.

Improvements in the range and standard of equipment now available also permit groups to operate at higher levels of achievement without lowering safety margins. A good example is the change from canvas to glass fiber and now plastic and aluminium canoes. The Ambleside Area Adventure Association (the 4As), a voluntary community group in the English Lake District, has a strong canoeing club working with all ages (in the UK, canoeing is a generic term for the sport, the 4As use kayaks). In competition, the club has trained junior national and world champions and has several members competing in the premier UK slalom division. Expeditions include a 100-mile, four-day trip on the Wye, a Welsh river with several rapids, undertaken independent of adults by 12-year-olds, and a sea tour off the Scottish coast with a group whose ages ranged from 13 to 40. Quality coaching and committed members made this possible, but so did modern materials and designs, without which the progress made with young members would have been impossible, the risks faced on the Wye and the sea unacceptable, and the competition achievements unattainable.

The settings in which activities take place have also diversified. For logistical and financial reasons it is often easier to bring the activity to the client than it is to take the client to the activity in its natural surroundings. Increasingly, adventure activities can be found in the wasteland aftermath of urban renewal, and canals and small reservoirs are being used for water-based sports. The ultimate extension of this has been the creation of artificial environments such as dry ski slopes and climbing walls.

Perhaps the leading example is the Ackers Trust, within a mile of the center of Birmingham, on an old waste tip (garbage dump) where a canal and a railway cross. Nearby are the derelict buildings of the old BSA works. The area is characterized by old residential housing, a poor district with a wide variety of ethnic groups represented. The BSA social club was taken over as a community center, the derelict land set aside as a nature reserve and park. The contours of the rubbish heap have been used as the base for a motorbike scramble course and road training facility. A trim trail quickly sprouted, followed by a ski slope on the biggest mound of rubbish and a climbing tower was built in the center of the park. There are plans for an indoor equestrian center in an adjacent empty factory. The canal has been dredged (there are more miles of canals in Birmingham than in Venice) and two narrow boats and a fleet of canoes are available. There is open access to the local community as well as educational and recreational groups. The site managers provide supervision where necessary, but prefer to train group leaders in the skills needed to run their own sessions.

THE GROWTH OF DEVELOPMENT TRAINING

With the raising of the schools leaving age in 1974, the experiential approach of outdoor education increasingly found a home in the school timetable as a more relevant way of learning for low-achieving pupils. Also, the recently introduced programs of personal and social education in many schools often used outdoor education. This further increased the use of the local environment as the arena for outdoor education. Cumbria Local Education Authority was the first to issue a policy statement on Outdoor Education:

> Outdoor Education is widely accepted as the term to describe all learning, social development and the acquisition of skill associated with living and journeying in the outdoors. In addition to physical endeavour, it embraces environmental and ecological understanding. Outdoor Education is not a subject but an integrated approach to learning, to decision-making and the solution of problems. Apart from opportunities for personal fulfillment and

> development of leisure interests, Outdoor Education stimulates the development of self-reliance, self-discipline, judgment, responsibility, relationships and the capacity for sustained practical endeavours.

The Authority owns and staffs three residential centers and has mounted an in-service training programme for teachers to acquire the necessary skills and concepts. They state:

> Outdoor Education embraces 3 interlinked areas of experiential learning, through outdoor pursuits, outdoor studies and the residential element.

A curriculum model incorporates these three strands from age 4 to 19, and advisory teachers have been appointed to promote and resource its implementation.

EXPERIENTIAL LEARNING

Few would disagree that outdoor education and experiences in a residential setting have a unique part to play in extending the opportunities for young people to develop, learn and grow, because of the range of opportunities available for experience-based learning. This approach to education and training relies almost totally upon the participants being completely involved in their learning and taking a genuine responsibility. They are invited to think, share ideas, make decisions, and exercise independence in the carrying out of activities. However, educationalists assumed that learning automatically occurred as a result of experience-based activities; that, having subjected participants to a range of exciting and challenging activities, attitudes are automatically molded or reshaped. There is little evidence to support this assumption, and the realization of this has seen one of the more recent major developments in approach.

If activities are to affect personal and social development and have full impact and more relevance, then there must be opportunities for preparation, evaluation, and reflection. This has led to a change in the approach of many leaders, who have adopted a facilitative approach, a long way from the conventional styles of imparting, instructing, and directing. In particular, it requires sensitivity to draw out the personal learning as a result of an activity or experience, not, as one trainer put it: "I do reviewing. I sit them down at the end of each activity and tell them what they did wrong"! This process has become known as reviewing.

The Brathay Hall Trust, founded in 1946, was the first residential center to develop this approach and is now widely regarded as a center of excellence. It was responsible for coining the phrase "Development Training," and has applied this approach to activities like work experience, as well as to the outdoors—which it regards as only one, albeit potent, of the tools available. Development Training is based on Kolb's learning model, "do, reflect, generalize, apply." After an experience, people in the learning group articulate their reactions, reviewing how they worked together, drawing conclusions, and applying these to real-life situations. The tutor facilitates this process by helping members of the group structure their thinking and confront the issues that arise.

The Brathay Hall Trust has found this approach particularly useful in management and leadership training, therapeutic work, and for personal development at times of transition, such as school to work.

Environmental Education has also seen development that contributes to Development Training. Increasingly, project work and excursions are made in the local environment. The approach has shifted from the use of the field as an outdoor classroom to its use as a laboratory applying a discovery method of learning. Recent work takes an issues-based approach. The learning model involved can be summarized as "head, heart and hands," that is, from knowledge and understanding to empathy and action. One Devon school prepares a center spread on community issues for the local newspaper researched and written by the students. The Primary School curriculum lends itself to work based around outdoor visits. Here are found some of the best examples of curriculum enrichment, with the outdoor experience being integrated into every aspect of the schools' work. Additionally, basic concepts of global and local ecology are being introduced, and environmental awareness is practiced rather than preached.

RESIDENTIALS AND EXPEDITIONS

Residential experience as an aid to learning is not a new idea. In 1963, the Newsom Report confirmed the conviction of many teachers that a wide range of activities developed in a residential context provided an abundance of opportunities to enhance and extend learning. Out of it emerged an almost unique environment to promote social and personal development and to bring teachers and young people into closer contact. In the last 20 years the increasing use of residential centers by schools, youth clubs, and colleges testifies to the rapid demand for such provisions. Significantly, most of the major curriculum initiatives currently being developed stress the potential value of a period of residential experience. Many education authorities have their own centers, often in distant wild country locations. Some schools use other facilities as a base for running their own programs.

A recent trend has been the acquisition of simple accommodation by individual schools often quite close to home for maximum accessibility. The Peers School in Oxford is an example. The simple hut, on its own wind-generated power and water supplies and two fields from any road, is within half an hour of the school. The rural setting, simple lifestyle, and teaching style are deliberately in contrast with the school environment. Groups can use the center on a part-day or residential basis, and it is built into the curriculum in many ways including field studies, personal and social education, outdoor pursuits, and class tutorial work. In such a setting it is easy to have a different kind of relationship with pupils.

It has also become common to recognize that pupils who are involved in the design of their own experience will learn a great deal more from it due to their investment in the outcome. A Bradford school uses a series of day and multi-day journeys designed, organized, and carried out by the pupils as the center of a curriculum for low-achieving pupils. Their literacy, numeracy, practical skills, and life skills are all focused on the task of carrying out the residential program. This is achieved on a minute budget and no more than a day or two's cycle ride from the school. The danger has become that the rest of the school's pupils would like the same approach! In Dudley one school has done just that, and each pupil carries out a residential program in each year of their school career with increasing amounts of responsibility. However, right from the start each student chooses the activities, the location, and the staff member who will help them.

It is apparent that the most effective residential programs are carefully structured to meet predetermined aims and the learning experiences integrated with the curriculum. The use of the residential has also expanded across the age range with many effective examples from the primary sector.

Yet another popular approach incorporating many of the above factors is the expedition. The Young Explorers Trust, the umbrella body of youth expeditions in the UK, annually advises and supports some 40 trips and is aware of some 40 others. This is the tip of an iceberg, as it only includes overseas trips. There will be many more within the UK. Destinations range around the world with recent venues in Nepal, Peru, and China as well as the Arctic, the desert and rain forest. Projects range from adventure and field work to community service. The recent trip to Nepal by St. Xavier's school from Essex, five years in the planning, combined with a Nepalese school to climb in the local mountains. All the equipment was homemade, and that which was used by the Nepalese students was left with them along with the equipment to make more and the training to do it. This was an excellent example of both cultures learning about and from each other, for in return the Essex students received some Gurkha-style survival training from the Nepalese.

DIVERSITY

Traditionally, most user groups have operated within the structures of local education authorities. However, recent developments have encouraged other groups to use the outdoors for their own, equally valid purposes. Social services, recreation programs, the Manpower Services Commission, and community groups are all part of this growth.

The opportunities to gain proficiency in the skills of an activity are no longer confined to remote and inaccessible outdoor centers, but can increasingly be found in the community as part of the recreation department or youth service provision.

Fringe groups only marginally related to mainstream education are becoming increasingly involved in exploiting the potential of the residential. Where a residential experience is recommended as part of a course, as is the case with the Youth Training Scheme for unemployed 16- to18-year-olds, it is often associated with some use of the outdoors as a medium to develop personal effectiveness. IBM runs such a scheme over two years, during which the trainees attend 3 five-day residentials. The first aims to develop the participants' confidence and their ability to work together. The second explores taking responsibility for standards and making things happen. The last is a chance to reflect on their own abilities and aptitudes and put them into practice. The supervisors of the trainees also attend a residential to experience what the trainees have gone through firsthand and acquire facilitating skills to help them transfer the learning to the workplace.

The Trident Trust, a charity dedicated to bringing Development Training to programs aimed at helping the transition from school to work, also uses outdoor and residential events. However, they take the wider view of adventure and incorporate community involvement and work experience into the scheme as well.

The social service and the probation service have been exploring the value of outdoor and residential programs for restoring self-esteem and developing positive attitudes in young offenders and children at risk. This is meeting with increasing success, especially when it is linked with continued opportunity for participation back in the community. The Drake Fellowship, which arose from the successful Operation Drake, forerunner of Operation Raleigh, operates teams of staff in the inner cities of a dozen towns. Their task is to identify disadvantaged young people from all backgrounds and use outdoor programs to give them a new direction and perspective on themselves. After a standard two-week program, there are opportunities for several exciting extension projects and drop-in facilities in the urban center. Some undertake community work and make available a great deal of advice and counseling. Many of the staff are in fact past students of the program. Although the scheme has the advantage of accessibility and street credibility in the towns where these people work, they also face the burden of the seemingly insurmountable circumstances of inner cities and their crushing effect on people. The Fellowship is often the only positive opportunity for many.

There are many new programs with therapeutic goals that encourage the mentally and physically handicapped to extend themselves, work toward independence, and mix with able-bodied people. The Calvert Trust in the Lake District aims to give disabled people as equal an access as possible to adventure activities by adapting equipment and appropriate supervision. There is a strong feeling that disabled people have as much right to the benefits of risk-taking and challenge as anyone. They often display qualities of determination and courage others cannot manage and the delight is always apparent.

Outdoor activities are not just the domain of the young anymore, with a number of schemes aimed at increasing participation among the unemployed and retired. The male-dominated approach to challenge and adventure is beginning to be reassessed, and feminine values are being introduced with a priority on young girls' participation. Outward Bound Eskdale ran the first all women's course to help participants explore themselves, their attitudes, and their capabilities. The Water Activities Center run by Manchester Youth Service has also addressed female participation by various strategies, including all-girls sessions, changes in teaching style and content, and positive discrimination, all of which have doubled girls' participation in the center over five years.

RELEVANCE

The impact of diversity has brought about what are perhaps the most important developments in Development Training to date. There have been fundamental changes in philosophy. The natural environment and its activities have come to be regarded by many no longer as simply a subject to be taught. The outdoors is seen as a medium and the concern is to use it as a vehicle to provide situations for learning with the aim of developing self, social, and environmental awareness. The common strands between outdoor and other experiential approaches to development, such as community involvement, are increasingly being utilized. The emphasis is moving from learning about a subject or an activity to the process of learning itself. And the common ground is the sense of adventure. The early thinking of B. P. and Hahn is undergoing a reappraisal and, with updated values, is being found to be increasingly appropriate as an approach to learning for a modern world.

REFERENCE

Cumbria Local Education Authority. (1974). Statement on Outdoor Education. Unpublished memorandum.

Section Two

ORIGINS OF ADVENTURE EDUCATION

An Historical Overview

How did adventure education evolve into the important education enterprise that it is in the final decade of the twentieth century? What individuals and organizations led the development of this field? These are the central questions of this section. A comprehensive and analytical history of adventure education remains to be written, but the essays here are a step toward such a history.

Kurt Hahn and Outward Bound are treated in the section's two lead essays. Any history of adventure education must start with Hahn. Minor writes as a disciple of Hahn and as a "founder" of Outward Bound, at least in the United States. He shares a "present at the creation" perspective on the birth of this adventure education prototype. Richards complements Minor with his more scholarly and comprehensive treatment of Kurt Hahn.

The history of adventure education is one of leaders such as Hahn, Minor, Paul Petzoldt and others. It is also a history of organizations. Since adventure education is outside the educational mainstream, the strength of numbers, of organized and focused group effort has been necessary for progress and development of the field. As Garvey reveals, the Association for Experiential Education (AEE) has played a key role in linking the diverse elements of the field. Practitioners of adventure education are often rugged individuals, risk-takers and adventurers who are iconclasts and have little tolerance for bureaucrat and organization. The history of AEE is one of attempting to meld this motley crew into a group to promote their common interests and coordinate their diverse activities—to encourage sharing and cooperation to achieve a measure of efficiency in developing programs and meeting challenges.

The Wilderness Education Association (WEA) has been more narrowly focused than AEE. Its aim has been to teach responsible outdoor leadership, and especially use of that basic adventure education resource—wilderness. This association stands in the center of one of the more important issues facing the field—certification of outdoor leaders. The origins of the WEA are important to an understanding of this issue.

Two of the most important programs in the history of the field are unquestionably the National Outdoor Leadership School (NOLS) and Project Adventure. Bachert describes how NOLS appeared and evolved into the leader that it is today. Readers will learn how NOLS came from Outward Bound through the medium of Paul Petzoldt and how WEA, with Petzoldt again the catalyst, emerged from NOLS. All of this is a history of emerging priorities and goals for adventure education.

Project Adventure has grown over twenty years as a very influential form of adventure education. It has, as Prouty's history recalls, been a vehicle to extend adventure education into conventional educational settings. WEA has begun to reach into higher education. Project Adventure has especially influenced common schools and continues to grow and extend its influence in that arena.

What emerges from a reading of the selections in this setting is a picture of programmatic evolution and extension. This extension has been in fits and starts, influenced by strong personalities and marked by disagreement and often outright conflict. Yet the circle of the influence in education generally has grown and the field has exhibited increasing breadth and depth.

The Creation of Outward Bound

Joshua L. Miner
Outward Bound, Inc.

Adventure-based education has its roots in many sources. It has no one "father." But if for some reason we wanted to single out an individual for that honor, Kurt Hahn would most certainly be a likely candidate. This great 20th century educator of German birth and British citizenship, a gentleman of the old school who has been proclaimed "a citizen of global mankind," was an inventor of institutions.

Hahn's Salem Schule in Germany, created in the throes of that nations ordeal of defeat following the first world war, was one of the fine innovative schools of the Western world. Imprisoned by the Nazis, and rescued at the behest of the British government, Hahn recreated the essence and espirit of Salem in a new school in northern Scotland. This unique version of a British public school, where the future Prince Consort of England and the future Prince of Wales would be educated, was Gordonstoun. That school—or more explicitly, the Hahnian principles that identified Gordonstoun—has in turn inspired an international consortium of schools whose headmasters gather annually in what they call their "Round Square Conference" (named after the distinctive building of that name at Gordonstoun. The Conference meets annually to share the member schools' successes and problems and to help keep alive the educational-humanitarian spirit of Gordonstoun's founder).

Out of Gordonstoun, and Hahn's genius for working with people and events, came the first Outward Bound school, and in time the global Outward Bound movement, with its schools in England, Germany, Africa, Australia, New Zealand, Canada, and the United States. Notably, in the American case, there came also the extraordinary array of Outward Bound spinoffs and adaptive programs that have taken root in and deeply influenced American education and other special initiatives. It was through our long association in Outward Bound that I came to know and treasure the friendship of Kurt Hahn.

Out of Gordonstoun, too, along with 18 years of patient, persistent effort, came the British County Badge Scheme. Personally launched by an ultimately convinced Prince Phillip as the Duke of Edinburgh's Award Scheme, this was Hahn's plan for making a comprehensive form of adventure education and service opportunity available to all British youth. Out of that Scheme have come counterpart programs in 29 countries, not least being the Congressional Award plan in the United States.

Even with that remarkable bundle of achievement as a social inventor, Hahn was not through. In 1955, Air Marshal Sir Lawrence Darvall, Commandant of the NATO Defence College, said to him, "The conservative, nationalistic officers attending our school are achieving a remarkable degree of international understanding in a mere six-month course. Think how much more could be accomplished by a nonmilitarist school for young people with an international student body!" Fired by Darvall's concept, Hahn joined forces with him in the seven-year campaign that brought forth Atlantic College (now United World College of the Atlantic) in Llantwit Major, Wales, a two-year pre-college school enrolling students from many nations. Recognizing that international understanding cannot be inculcated in the classroom alone, the skills program included a distinctively Hahnian component, referred to as its "humanitarian curriculum"—rescue and community services to those "in danger and in need." This was the start of the United World College movement.

Rowing bareheaded on a blazing hot day in his 19th year, Kurt Hahn suffered a severe sunstroke. The injury, centering at the cerebellum, where the spine joins the base of the brain, threatened to cripple him. To ease his suffering he spent a year in a darkened room. Periodically thereafter—"despair stalking him like a sinsister shadow," as Henry Brereton has written—the affliction returned in full force, casting him back into the dark. Even after a great London neurosurgeon performed a series of brain-decompressing operations that helped him greatly, light and heat remained his lifelong torment.

In those lonely ordeals of his young manhood he was working out a life principle that years later a remarkable physical educator would articulate and Hahn would make his leitmotif: "Your disability is your opportunity." To make his confinement productive, he devised regimens of physical activity and disciplined thought. He practiced the standing high jump—scarcely to the delight of the Oxford students living beneath him—and the legend is that he broke records in that event. With the study of Plato's *Republic* fresh in his mind, he conceived a new kind of school, where the worlds of thought and action would no longer be divided into hostile camps. Later he wrote out the concept and put it away for future reference.

Hahn was born into a cultured Jewish family in Berlin in 1886. His father was a successful industrialist. His mother was a beautiful woman of artistic temperament and powerful faith in the innate goodness of man. One of her forebears was Jecheskiel Landau, Chief Rabbi of Prague in the eighteenth century, whose writings on the Talmud are still taught at academies of Jewish studies. His grandmother on his mother's side was his adored "Anschulka," whose wise and droll sayings he noted down in a book. ("Anschulka, which of your eight children is the best?" "A mother is like a shopkeeper—she has various kinds of goods.") The home in which he grew up, radiating human warmth, was a gathering place for the city's intelligentsia and artists.

His father, enamored of England, built the family summer residence Wannsee in English country-house style. Kurt, the eldest of three sons, was a born teacher. In the summers at Wannsee he would gather the young people in the pavillion and read them tales of heroic adventure. Often he led them on long hikes over rough terrain. At Gottingen, one of several German universities he attended, his

Greek professor told him, "If you are interested in the old in order to help the new, it is not the German universities that can help you, but Oxford." He studied at Oxford from 1910 to 1914. On August 1, 1914, he took leave of his English friends to return home. Two days later Great Britain declared war on Germany.

In the war Hahn held a succession of minor Foreign Office posts from which he nevertheless emerged as a person of influence. He worked with the moderates—against unrestricted submarine warfare, for a negotiated peace—and became one of their spokesmen. Although his counsel did not prevail, the quality of his work won the attention of persons in high places. He was made advisor to Colonel von Haeften, who was in turn political adviser to General von Ludendorff.

At the war's end Hahn was assistant to Prince Max of Baden, Germany's last imperial chancellor. The prince was a scholarly, humane man who in a speech in 1917 dared to say, "To love your enemy is the sign of those who remain loyal to the Lord even in time of war." The two men shared an enthusiasm for Plato's educational ideas, and in 1920 Prince Max founded a coeducational boarding school with Hahn as headmaster. This was the Salem (shalom, salaam, peace) Schule; it was the school Hahn had conceived seven years before.

The times were, quite literally, fearful. Defeated Germany was on the edge of anarchy. The school thwarted two plots, one by Communists to kidnap Prince Max, another by nationalists to murder Hahn. (Typically, Hahn was more concerned over his would-be assassins' despair for the nation's plight than he was to see them punished.) Guerrilla bands were setting fire to farms. Salem boys joined the night patrols guarding the lonely countryside. It was in that time that William Butler Yeats wrote the lines, so prophetic of the coming European tragedy, that Hahn would come to quote often, a statement of his lifelong concern:

> The best lack all conviction, while the worst
> are full of passionate intensity.

Yeats was defining the very condition that Prince Max and Hahn had set out to deal with. Through Salem, and by spreading the Salem gospel to other educators, they sought to nurture a German youth with convictions rooted in personal responsibility, kindness, and justice. The intent, in Hahn's words, was to equip young people "to effect what they have recognized to be right, despite hardships, despite dangers, despite inner skepticism, despite boredom, despite mockery from the world, despite emotion of the moment." The school's report to parents, developed at Salem and later used at Gordonstoun, evaluated the degree to which the students displayed these traits.

Hahn was at once a champion and hard taskmaster of youth in its conflicts with the elder generation. If young people were to play an influential role in society, he insisted, they must earn the right. Even as he welcomed the German youth movement of that time, he took sharp issue with indulgent adult attitudes. Long after I first knew him, in the time of the youth revolt in the England and United States of the 1960s, it was uncanny to discover that in the Germany of 1928 he had said: "With phrases such as 'Youth Culture' these people besmear the souls of the young with the ointment of flattery—as though the young no longer had to become anything, but were everything already. They rob them of their joy of development and do violence to the natural process of spiritual growth."

Inevitably, the ideals of Salem clashed with the spirit of Nazism. Apprehensive of the growing strength of Hitler's movement, Hahn stepped up his efforts to win the German educational community over to Salem principles. But the Nazi tide continued to rise. In 1932, five storm troopers trampled a young communist to death in front of his mother. They were arrested, tried, and condemned to death. In his notorious "Beuthen telegram," Hitler hailed them as comrades and demanded their release. "Your freedom," he said, "is our honor." For Hahn this was in fact the hour when men of honor must declare themselves.

He sent a letter to all Salem alumni: "Hitler's telegram has brought on a crisis that goes beyond politics. Germany is at stake, her Christian civilization, her good name, her soldiers' honor. Salem cannot remain neutral. I ask the members of the Salem Union who are active in a S.A. or S.S. to break with Salem or with Hitler." It was, said a Briton who was teaching at Salem at the time, "the bravest deed in cold blood that I have witnessed."

Sir Roger Birley (Rohrs, 1970), who was Hahn's contemporary as headmaster of Eton, has given us a record of his courage in the German crisis. Discussing the education provided under Hahn at Salem, Birley wrote:

> But there was a second element quite as important. It was impressively expressed in an address Kurt Hahn gave in Hamburg on 16 February 1933. (The significance of the date, seventeen days after the Nazis gained power, will be obvious.) It began with a study of the Fascist state and educational ideals, and an account of Fascism which seems to make inevitable the uncomfortable statement which is to be found in the address, that, if one looked at the educational principles of the Italian youth organizations, "you find that you might be quoting the whole Salem Certificate of Maturity with its capacity to endure hardships, to face dangers, a talent for organization, prudence, a fighting spirit, presence of mind, success in dealing with unexpected difficulties" — and then come the words, "Only one item is and must be missing: The power of carrying out what is recognized to be just." And a little later, "*Sacro egoismo*, sacred egoism. There is also sacred lying, sacred killing, sacred perjury, sacred breaking of promises." To speak in this way of Fascist principles at that moment was indeed courageous, but Kurt Hahn went on to turn to his own country, and it was with continual references to the state of things in Germany that he gave his reasons why Salem rejected Fascist education. Among these was to be found this one: "We need to be able to feel that as a people we are just and kindly. On this consciousness depends our inner strength."

Hahn became a marked man. In the mass arrests following the Reichstag fire in February 1933, he was jailed. The shock waves swiftly reached Britain, where his friends — some from the Oxford days, others gained as Salem's fame had spread—took up his cause. When Prime Minister Ramsay MacDonald made official representations, Hahn was let go. In July he left for England.

In those first months of exile he was profoundly depressed. At 47, he had lost his homeland, his school, the battle for German youth. A man of means, overnight he had become a nearly penniless refugee. Worse, his spiritual resources were depleted. When he was asked to found a new school along Salem lines, he lacked the will. When he was offered an established school to work with, he said, "I do not have time to overcome the inertia of tradition." Then he returned to Moray, the north of Scotland country where he had spent the convalescent summers of his Oxford years. He met old friends among the fishermen and crofters of the district. On the wharf in Hopeman Harbor, he listened to Captain Danny Main tell tales of men of simple courage against the forces of the sea. With another friend, Lord Malcolm Douglas-Hamilton, he inspected the empty castle at Gordonstoun, badly in need of repair, as a possible site for a school. Its vistas seized his spirit, and he knew again the truth that he would summon so often in guiding others: "Your disability is your opportunity."

Gordonstoun opened as a school for boys in April 1934; by September there were 21 students (among them a Greek prince of Danish blood named Philip, who one day would marry the future queen of England). The board of governors included the Archbishop of York, later of Canterbury, the headmaster of Eton, the master of Trinity College at Cambridge, a distinguished British historian, and the future governor-general of Canada. The school's enrollment grew steadily.

In 1938, Hahn became a naturalized British subject. It was in character that even as he struggled to cope with the acute problems of an expanding, unendowed school, he poured part of his energies into national concerns—alerting the British people to the dimensions of the Hitlerian threat, calling on them to hear the muffled cries from the concentration camps, campaigning at the War Office for a system of training that in months, he declared, could make British infantrymen the equal in stamina, hardihood, and self-confidence of German soldiers whose training had started years before in the Hitler Youth.

War broke out. The British Army commandeered Gordonstoun, and the school had to trek to wartime headquarters in Wales. The move was a major disability. In it Hahn found a new opportunity—and brought forth Outward Bound.

Opportunity's name was Lawrence Holt. Hahn had been trying to launch a "County Badge Scheme," an ambitious national plan for fostering physical fitness, enterprise, tenacity, and compassion among British youth. But in the wartime climate his prestigious County Badge Experimental Committee—scientist Julian Huxley, historian George Trevelyan, and others—had made small headway. At that same time, Holt, a Gordonstoun father and Hahn admirer who was partner in Alfred Holt & Company, a large merchant-shipping enterprise, was gravely concerned about the human toll in the Battle of the Atlantic. He was convinced that due to faulty training, many seamen on torpedoed merchant ships were dying unnecessarily. Unlike sail-trained old-timers, he maintained, the younger men and youths had not acquired a sense of wind and weather, a reliance on their own resources, and a selfless bond with their fellows. "I would rather," he told Hahn, "entrust the lowering of a lifeboat in mid-Atlantic to a sail-trained octogenarian than to a young sea technician who is competently trained in the modern way but has never been sprayed by the salt water."

Hahn proposed they join forces to start a new kind of school offering young people one-month courses that would use Hahn's County Badge Scheme to implement Holt's quest for training to turn attitudes around. Holt agreed, his company providing funds and the maritime staff members. The school, called Outward Bound at Holt's insistence, opened at Aberdovey, Wales, in 1941. It was not, as the mythologized version has it, a school for young merchant seamen. While many of the students were youngsters sponsored by Holt's Blue Funnel Line and other shipping companies and from the government training ship H.M.S. Conway, others were apprentices sent by industry, or police, fire, and other cadets, or boys on leave from their regular schools or about to go into the armed services. It was Holt himself who articulated a Hahnian concept in words Hahn never forgot. "The training at Aberdovey," Holt said, "must be less a training *for* the sea than *through* the sea, and so benefit all walks of life." The month-long course was, in fact, a mix of small-boat training, athletic endeavor to reach standards of competence, cross-country route-finding by map and compass, rescue training, an expedition at sea, a land expedition across three mountain ranges, and service to the local people. The school was fortunate from the outset in two key staff members. Jim Hogan, a resourceful young schoolmaster whom Hahn had recruited from the national educational system to be secretary of his County Badge Experimental Committee, was warden. His assistant in charge of athletic activity was Captain B. Zimmerman, who had been a great innovative physical educator in Germany until he fled his country to avoid Nazi imprisonment. Hahn had brought him from Switzerland to Gordonstoun. It was "Zim" who first exhorted his charges that their liability was their opportunity, who—seizing on Holt's phrase—talked of "training through the body, not of the body," and worked on each student until he could proclaim, "The bug has bit!"

Although beset by a prodigious series of start-up difficulties, Outward Bound worked from the first. The youths who came were the products of Britain's dozen years of depression and dole. Invariably, when they were told what they were expected to achieve in 30 days, murmurs of incredulity and derision ran through the group. But they were soon caught up by "the magic of the puzzle," Hahn's odd phrase for the phenomenon he knew so well—that when a young person "defeats his defeatism" to meet a challenge, it primes him to try for still more difficult achievement. There was a half-concealed pride of accomplishment in the assertion of the Cockney boy, exhausted and footsore after his first cross-country effort: "Cor blimey, if this had been Larndon, they'd shift them bleedin' hills." A moving human story underlay the statement of the half-caste lad from Liverpool, warmed by his watchmates' acclaim for his self-improvement: "This is the first time in my life I have seemed to matter." Wise old Alec Fraser, the former missionary who served as the school chaplain, saw what was happening: "They come for the wrong reasons, and they leave sorry for the right ones that it's over."

Holt's prepositional distinction—training through rather than for—was always to be the essence of the Outward Bound dynamic. Life-enhancing experience is obtained through the sea, the mountains, the wild lake country, the desert. Outward Bound has evolved since those early Aberdovey days. But it has not departed from Hahn and Holt's essential concept of an intense experience surmounting challenges in a natural setting, through which the individual builds his sense of self-worth, the group comes to a heightened awareness of human interdependence, and all grow in concern for those in danger and in need.

In my year and a half as a member of Hahn's staff at Gordonstoun, I came to know his philosophy as an educator in day-to-day practice. The core of his educational purpose was to conserve and strengthen the attributes of childhood into manhood. "What happens in adolescence," he asked, "to your children who in the nursery are so self-confident and happy?" Too often youngsters who were joyous, zestful, and enterprisingly curious, with the gift of wonder and an inborn compassion, grew "dimmed and diluted." Adolescence became "the loutish years," a shallow pre-maturing while strengths remained undiscovered and untrained. Hahn pledged himself "to unseat the dogma that puberty need deform." To this end he sought to create an educational environment where "healthy passions"—craving for adventure, joy of exploration, zest for building, devotion to a skill demanding patience and care, love of music, painting, or writing—would flourish as "guardian angels of adolescence."

One of my early responsibilities was The Break. It was essential, in Hahn's thinking, that a healthy youngster "have his powers of resilience, coordination, acceleration, and endurance purposefully developed." The Break was his unique contribution to physical education. He had invented it in the early Salem days, and from the beginning had made it an imperative part of the Gordonstoun scheme. Four mornings a week, during a 50-minute break in what Hahn called "the sedentary hours," each boy took part in two of a half-dozen events—sprinting or distance running, long or high jumping, discus or javelin throwing. He competed only against himself, trying to better his previous best performance. The frail youngster who broke 10 feet in the long jump for the first time in his life got as big a cheer as the track team star beating his previous mark at close to twenty. Every boy had to do every event. That same star jumper might be a dud at throwing the discus. It was as important to overcome a weakness as to develop a strength.

When I was put in charge of The Break, I became a fascinated witness to its remarkable results. It was not just that the average performance would have put the average American schoolboy to shame. The great satisfaction lay in seeing the physical duffer discover that through trying from day to day; he could do much better than he would have dared to dream. He had learned, in Hahn's phrase, to "defeat his defeatism." You could see him shed—Hahn again—"the misery of his unimportance." His new-found confidence would carry over into his peer relationships, his classroom performance, the quality of work on his project. It was not unusual for a timid or sensitive boy with an undeveloped physique to emerge from the chrysalis of his underconfidence a competent athlete, surprised to find himself confirming what the headmaster had so often told the school: "Your disability is your opportunity."

Hahn was then 65. He was running the school, making frequent trips to London to raise money for it and advance other projects, and shuttling across the Channel in his campaigns to influence the postwar education of German youth. "I am," he told me, "an old man in a hurry." I wondered how many obstacles he had hurdled with that trumpet cry of his determination. The hurry part was literally true. He climbed stairs two at a time, took an entire downflight in a single r-r-r-p-p! His day marched. Frequently it began with three separate breakfast meetings. In theory they were staggered, but usually he wound up circulating from one to the other.

But however tight the day's schedule, he found time to reconnoiter about the school. "A headmaster's job," he said, "is to walk around." His antennae were always out, fine-tuned and waving, probing for each lad's potential strengths that they might be developed, for his innate weaknesses that they might be overcome. Repeatedly he homed in on some shielded aspect of a boy's ego that others had missed and that cast a sudden light on deviant behavior. He was his own psychologist, drawing on a vast bank of observations.

The day's end was signaled at that hour of the evening when Hunter brought the London taxicab around to Gordonstoun House. Hunter would drive him across the moors to the sea cliffs. Then Hahn would get out and jog along the line of the cliffs, his way illuminated by the headlights of the cab following behind.

But the days did not always end so routinely. Periodically, roused from slumber by his call, four or five of us—housemaster, teachers, activity leader—would make our way through the night to his study. The call would have but one meaning—some boy was in trouble. Perhaps a student had been caught stealing. Hahn would have spent a long evening getting the report, talking with the boy and with the student leaders who knew him best. Conscious of the contrast between our disheveled aspects and his neat daytime attire, we would wait for him to stop pacing the floor and tell us why we were there. Finally, when he had given us the facts, came the inevitable dreaded question, the blue eyes boring in: "Josh! When did you first notice this boy was in difficulty, and what did you do about it?" —dreaded because one had sensed and done nothing. When a boy was in danger of expulsion at Gordonstoun, it was not he but the adult community who was on trial. A boy steals because he has some deeper trouble. If one is sensitive enough, if one cares enough, one can detect symptoms of the trouble early, when there may still be time for remedy.

On the morrow Hahn would decide the penalty, posting the facts on the bulletin board to prevent the rumor-mongering he detested: "Put it on my tombstone, 'Here lies Kurt Hahn. He scotched a rumor every day.' "

He ran the school in tensile fashion. It began with his hiring strong people who would stand up to him. Offering Henry Brereton the post of director of studies in 1935, he said, "You must defend your department. If I want to send a boy into the hills for his health just before examinations, you must resist me." He staffed the school's nautical department with a Royal Navy officer and a Merchant Navy officer, in the belief that the inevitable conflict of two traditions would be a creative force—as it proved to be. When I became director of activities, I found that Brereton and I were duty-bound to maintain a rival stance, lest either poach on the other's share of school time. If Hahn thought we were not being wary enough, he took some subtle action, created some threat of encroachment, to put us on guard.

The same tensilizing principle infused his way with the young. His core tenet, stated a thousand times as though it were cut in bronze, was: "It is the sin of the soul to force young people into opinions—indoctrination is of the devil—but it is culpable neglect not to impel them into health-giving experiences." The indoor type was to be chased outdoors, the introvert turned inside out, the extrovert outside in. The tough were to be gentled, the timid emboldened. Above all, the complacent were to be disturbed. "It is my mission in life to molest the contentedly unfit."

He was an intrepid traveler; a journey with him was exhilarating. To see him cope with the usual frustrations of getting from one place to the next was to observe in microcosm ways in which he advanced his grand designs. Policemen, taxi drivers, ticket agents were his instant confidants. No matter how negative an agent's initial response, the ensuing friendship almost surely produced the needed overnight train accommodation or pair of plane tickets. Henry Brereton, who accompanied him on trips to Germany in the difficult travel years right after the war, has provided a lovely reminiscence: "Timetables seem to adjust to his whim, engine-drivers are in league with him and hold up the start of the express whilst he conducts an excited invalid infinitely slowly to her reserved compartment, saying with irritating assurance as guards blow whistles and porters shout and safely seated travelers stare from the windows, 'We have plenty of time, my dear. Don't hurry. There's plenty of time.' "

Brereton's vignette catches Hahn in a moment that, in its small but touching way, reflects the very heart of his personal philosophy. This was his profound commitment to the Samaritan ethic. He had one hero above all: the compassionate traveler on the road to Jericho. Again and again he called for the Parable of the Good Samaritan to be read to the school. In the years to come I was to witness the growing power of his ultimate conviction—that through help to those in danger and in need, youth can strike the deepest chords of the human spirit. It would become a creed: "He who drills and labors, accepts hardship, boredom, and dangers, all for the sake of helping his brother in peril and distress, discovers God's purpose in his inner life."

In the 1960s, Kurt Hahn made periodic trips to this country. His visits to Andover were great occasions—for renewing our friendship, hearing his views about the state of the world, telling him about developments in U.S. Outward Bound, getting his counsel. He took a keen interest in my Outward Bound briefings. In the beginning it pleased him greatly that we had been drafted to set up the final training for the Peace Corps. He was enthusiastic about the American innovation of the solo; in his philosophy, periods of solitude were an essential human need. "You cannot harvest the lessons of your life except in aloneness," he said, "and I go to the length of saying that neither the love of man nor the love of God can take deep root except in aloneness." Sometimes he had concerns. Were the schools giving first aid in place of honor in the timetable? Did this or that school operate so far into the wilderness as to get away from other people and hence from opportunities to give aid or effect rescues? Only once, however, in my time as Outward Bound's president, did he give me a directive: "You will not let the word Christianity creep into Outward Bound. You will simply practice it." He was captivated by the adaptive program phenomena, so different from what had happened in Britain.

Invariably his counsel enriched us. Usually the advice I sought was on some question of strategy or tactic, and he had a way of elevating the discussion to one of principle. I remember once asking him whom at Phillips Academy he thought I should go to for help in weaving Outward Bound philosophy into the fabric of the school. He said, "There are two people—your doctor and your leading historian. If the doctor is worth his salt, he is concerned about the physical well-being of young people, and their future well-being as adults. If the historian is worth his salt, he will have detected the symptoms of a decaying culture, and will be sympathetic to what you're trying to do."

For all of Hahn's intense interest in what we were doing in Outward Bound, I was aware that his main concerns were elsewhere. It is a remarkable fact that in his long, intimate association with the Outward Bound movement, he never held an official position. As an inventor of institutions, it was a part of his genius that he was content to leave their administering to others.

On most of those visits his primary interest was in advancing the Atlantic College project in Wales and its subsequent United World College movement. Atlantic College—later United World College of the Atlantic—with its concept of bringing together students from many nations in a pre-college program, was an immediate success. Today there are also the Lester Pearson United World College of the Pacific in British Columbia, the United World College of Southeast Asia in Singapore, the United World College of the Adriatic in Italy, the Waterford Kamhlaba United World College of Southern Africa in Swaziland, the Simon Bolivar United World College of Agriculture in Venezuela, and the Armand Hammer United World College of the American West in Montezuma, New Mexico.

Rescue and community services to those in danger and in need. The late Earl Mountbatten of Burma, long the movement's international leader, confirmed a heartfelt Hahn thesis: "It's hard to hate someone when you're both helping to save a life."

That is a variation of Hahn's "Whoever saves a life will never take a life." No other human being, perhaps, responded as avidly as Hahn to William James' call to seek "the moral equivalent of war." He recognized that Tennyson's "peace of the broken wing"—peace that softens rather than tests moral fiber—was itself a menace to peace. The answer, Hahn was convinced, lay in "the passion of rescue." His moral equivalent of war was to "enthrall and hold the young through active and willing Samaritan service, demanding care and skill, courage and endurance, discipline and initiative." With each new visit I observed the conviction grow more resolute.

While U.S. Outward Bound evolved in many ways that Hahn had never contemplated, there was no aspect of that evolution that he failed to approve. On the contrary, he was an enthusiastic, though always thoughtful, receptor to each new development. In the beginning much of the change related to a broadening of the student constituency for our schools. The initial constituency was simply that defined for us by the British precedent: boys and young men from age 16 1/2 to 23. From very early on we ensured that that constituency would be as broad as possible by requiring that half of each school's enrollment be scholarship students. This was a deliberate decision to prevent Outward Bound from developing a "preppie" stigma. Knowing that it would be fatal to our purposes if the organization came to be thought of as available just to the affluent, we wanted a broad socioeconomic mix. One important consequence of this policy was that a share of the scholarships went to disadvantaged youngsters in the inner cities, many of them entangled in difficulties with society, some of them already adjudicated. This was one of the factors that led to Outward Bound's pioneering of large-scale projects, successfully employing adventure-based education as a rehabilitation vehicle in working with delinquent youth.

The first major break with our constituency precedent was the introduction and astonishing success of courses for young women, along with the equally "astonishing" discovery that girls could handle—at times even with a superior blitheness—the same courses, of the same degree of difficulty, that had been designed for boys. Then came highly popular adult coed courses. These were followed, inevitably, by courses for adult women, likewise highly successful—to the discomfort of whatever remnants there were of a once rather pure macho esprit. By then all adult age limits were off, and some of the schools also introduced junior courses.

Another way in which the Outward Bound program has evolved is in the increasing importance accorded the service project that is a component of every course. At the same time, often responding to needs not unrelated to those revealed in service activity, schools have introduced into their programs a growing variety of courses for particular student constituencies. These range from courses especially designed for business executives and other enterprise managers, to those for individuals whose special needs entail some form of handicap. Heartening results are being achieved with students who are, for example, physically handicapped or hearing-impaired, or who, again for example, are seeking release from drug or alcohol dependency or are emotionally disturbed. In one such undertaking, a prominent New England treatment hospital and an Outward Bound school have joined forces in an adolescent chemical dependency rehabilitation program. In another that has attracted national attention, Outward Bound is conducting a therapeutic program for Vietnam veterans afflicted with Post Traumatic Stress Disorder, or PTSD, a mental condition marked by combat-induced flashbacks, feelings of isolation and depression, violent outbursts, and low self-esteem.

The city as an Outward Bound environment has long intrigued the schools, and several are embarking on urban-based programs. The current outstanding instance is New York City Outward Bound. Adults—often young business executives—are paired with inner city teenagers in three-day courses that manage to incorporate urban versions of the various wilderness challenges—including rock climbing and a tyrolean traverse—encountered in a regular OB course. The service project may be providing recreation to children crowded with their families into one of the city's hotels for the homeless, or taking a group of black women living in a Brooklyn home for battered women on an ice skating expedition.

Most of the foregoing is illustrative of the fact that in the last decade OB has become increasingly concerned for the well-being of persons who have been visited with misfortunes that the more fortunate among us have escaped. This appears to confirm something that Kurt Hahn seems always to have known: that there is a force inherent in the Outward Bound dynamic that generates compassion.

In 1968 Hahn made what proved to be his final journey to the United States. Deeply concerned about the worldwide violence generated by youthful rebellion and racial conflict, he was looking for guidance from the American experience. Long before, he had given to Sir Robert Birley, headmaster of Eton, counsel that Birley never forgot: "Whenever you have to deal with a boy who is a rebel, remember that you must get him to face the question: Are you going to be a fighter or a quarreler?" Now he was looking for ways to harness productively the fighting spirit of young people.

For two months he crossed the continent and back, from Harvard to West Coast campuses, from Harlem to Watts, seeking new knowledge about student and racial tensions, new leads to healing forces. Fred Glimp, who was Dean of Harvard during the student riots there that year, still marvels at Hahn's keen comprehension of the issues and events on the Cambridge campus. Five years after his 1968 visit to the headquarter of the National Urban League's street workers in Harlem, they had vivid recall of the 82-year-old gentleman from England who came up the stairs two at a time. On Hahn's visit there, a boy who had recently returned from a course at Hurricane Island told him, "It gives you a feeling of great power if you breathe life into a dead person." This was one more affirmation of the message he was carrying on his cross-country safari: "The passion of rescue releases the highest dynamic of the human soul." As he made that safari, his sun-induced affliction was heavy upon him. At such places as New York's Horace Mann School, Wayzata, Minnesota, and the Athenian School in Danville, California, people still remember the dim, imposing figure at the front of a darkened, crowded room, tirelessly answering—and asking—questions, offering his ideas ("I am anxious to carry conviction on this") in response to theirs.

He was intent on inventing a new institution. His dauntless mind worked toward a grand plan under which a "Service by Youth Commission" would coordinate forces, enabling young people to contribute productive energies that otherwise would be spilled in confrontation or drained by frustration. Central to the plan was the removal by aid-and-rescue agencies of age restrictions preventing service by adolescent volunteers, and an international call to young men and women to help in the fight against unnecessary death and suffering. "Lifesaving," Hahn kept telling his American audiences, "is the job of the layman. The less serious things we can leave to the doctors."

In the Watts section of Los Angeles he listened eagerly for two and a half hours as Ted Watkins, chairman of the Watts Labor Community Action Committee, talked about his work with ghetto youth. Ted told him about the Watts young people painting telephone poles to spruce up the streets, starting a chicken and pet farm, converting derelict lots to "vest-pocket parks." Ted said, "Every youngster should be called on to make a sweat investment. He needs something he can protect." Hahn liked that. He made it a theme of his Service by Youth plan.

As his grueling safari ended, his affliction worsened. I drove him to the Boston airport with blankets blacking out the car windows. He wore the homburg hat with the broad, turned-down brim, an arrangement of green felt lined with lead foil shielding the back of his neck, and two pairs of dark glasses. At the plane's door his hand came up in the familiar farewell geture. I was wrenchingly aware of that aircraft carrying off one whose comprehending concern for our sick world was irreplaceable.

Back in London and Scotland he worked on the Service by Youth plan. For all the grandiose scale of his thinking, the ideas he set down were cogent, down-to-earth, feasible. In a very real sense, I believe, he foresaw the coming tragedies of student shootings at Kent State and Jackson State and was working to prevent them. But he was not able, as he always before had been, to exert the force of his personal drive in support of that project. Struck by a car on a country road near Gordonstoun, he never fully recovered from the accident. Yet he turned even that misfortune to opportunity. The mishap gave him a new idea. He wrote Prince Philip, urging his support for a plan to reduce road deaths by including first aid in the driving test. The prince did take up that cause, giving it his earnest backing.

In retirement at last in Hermannsburg, Germany, living in an apartment at one of Salem's satellite schools, Kurt Hahn died on December 15, 1974. He was 88.

There was one "unfinished business" aspect of Outward Bound's evolution that always concerned Hahn, as it has long concerned Outward Bounders everywhere, that I must mention. This is the perennial question of the "follow-up."

U.S. Outward Bounders sometimes do an unconscious disservice by quoting out of context the closing line of Hahn's address at the 1965 Outward Bound Conference at Harrogate, England, where follow-up had been one of the important debated subjects. His concluding words were, "Outward Bound can ignite—that is all—it is for others to keep the flame alive." The line is usually quoted under the impression that Hahn in a sense was negating the follow-up question by relegating the responsibility to a vague, undefined "others." The error of the impression lies, I think, in failure to appreciate (perhaps not even to have seen) what the context was. For in his preceding paragraph Hahn (1968) had quite clearly defined whom he meant by "others," and quite clearly stated the form he believed follow-up should take:

> I believe that the challenge of Samaritan Service, if properly presented, rarely fails to capture young people, body and soul, not only in the Western World. I hear encouraging news about the young behind the Iron Curtain — many of them look westward, with distrust but also with hope. They ask a question which makes us blush: "Are you in earnest about the ideals you profess?" Who shall give an answer? Young men and women who render hard and willing service to their fellow men in danger and in need.

A few months later, visiting in Andover, Hahn gave me a photograph of himself. Part of the inscription, in the form of a charge, was an even more explicit restatement of the thought he had left with the conferees at Harrogate:

> To Josh Miner ... May he remember that the best service he can render to Outward Bound is to recognize its limits: Outward Bound can kindle the flame but it will be extinguished in many cases unless Outward Bounders, returning to their schools and workshops, are confronted by the challenge and the opportunities to go on active service to help their fellow men in danger and in need. Their resolution to do so will be strengthened if we can build up an aristocracy of service throughout the free world, whose example will create a fashion of conduct.

That "aristocracy of service" was the new institution the 82-year-old Hahn was seeking to invent in the aftermath of his 1968 U.S. safari. The lengthy memorandum he wrote upon his return home and sent to his Outward Bound and other American friends is a kind of testament to all of us who care about the well-being of his institutions. In the memorandum's final paragraph, using the designation *helper* for those performing Samaritan service, he stated the salient, consuming idea one more time:

> One would hope that one day the status of helper would be recognized throughout the Western world — thereby a new and challenging avenue of distinction might be opened. Such development would go far to solve the baffling problem of the "followup" for Outward Bound and kindred enterprises.

Henry Brereton said it so well: "Kurt Hahn, who often appears so Victorian in language and manners, belongs in a deep sense to the new age of hope. Like the great artists and scientists, like the astronauts, he is a citizen of global mankind" (Rohrs, 1970).

REFERENCES

Hahn, K. (1968). (Personal Memorandum). Unpublished.

Rohrs, H. (1970). *Kurt Hahn*. London: Routledge and Kegan Paul.

Kurt Hahn

Anthony Richards
Dalhousie University

The phenomenom that has become known as "Hahnism" (Skidelsky, 1976) is the unique aproach to experiential education explicated by Kurt Hahn and embodied in the many institutions he founded, as well as a host of adventure-based experiential education programs, one of which is Outward Bound.

There were four discernable phases in Hahn's life. The first is the period of his childhood, youth, and schooling, which eventually took him to universities in Germany and England. This was a time when he was strongly influenced by both family and teachers. The second phase did not begin until he was 34 years of age, when he opened his first school in Germany. This is a relatively late age to start into the field of education. He would probably have remained with this school, Salem, in Germany, and would not have had an international reputation had it not been for the Nazi movement and Hahn's imprisonment by Hitler. It was the result of this imprisonment and his subsequent release that led him to seek exile in Britain and begin the third phase of his life. This third phase was particularly important because of the number of educational ideas he spawned that led to the establishment of several new schools, programs, and indeed, institutions. Hahn was in his late forties when he opened Gordonstoun School, in Scotland, and Anavryta School in Greece. He also created during his middle age the County Badge Scheme and its outgrowth, Outward Bound. The fourth phase started with Hahn's serious illness at the age of 67, which forced his retirement as headmaster of Gordonstoun. A successful operation in 1955 enabled Hahn to continue to initiate educational projects. The Duke of Edinburgh Award Scheme and Atlantic College were established during this phase, and as an octogenarian he was still active in some of the decision-making at various board meetings.

During some of the most turbulent times in recent history, including two world wars and educational reform, Hahn was still able to make his mark with a brand of education that has continued to be prominent today. However, it was his unity of purpose without a unity of focus that allowed continual adaptation. One of his weaknesses was his inability to let go and hand the reins over to someone else. Whenever another person or group took over his program (e.g., Outward Bound Trust in 1946), he immediately took this adversity and turned it into an opportunity to create something new. He was a living example of one of his favorite sayings, "your disability is your opportunity." However, in his twilight years he was gracious enough to favorably recognise the variety of agencies that had taken over his programs and ideas.

Hahn was a trained propagandist. His apprenticeship with Prince Max von Baden as a political writer in the German Foreign Office helped him to articulate his position in a very convincing manner. Hogan (1968) felt that Hahn was an "artist with words," and that he was always able to gain "maximum emotional consequence." This was particularly evident in his speeches. His style of presentation utilized aphorisms and anecdotes generated from concrete examples. He was often accused of speaking with an economy of truth and inventing statistical evidence when little or none existed. The translation from German to English was not as precise as it might be. This resulted in some of his phrases and expressions being perceived as offensive or radical. For example, in reference to normal adolescent sexual development he used the expressions, "deformities of puberty" and the "poisonous passions." Nevertheless, Hahn made no attempt to moderate these expressions because they had substantial effect and impact during his speeches.

For all the limitations that Hahn had with respect to his language, suspect sources and dogmatic style, he was still able to impress the "right people." The result was substantial support for his ideas, both fiscally and morally. When he was promoting a new idea or program he would leave no stone unturned in order to achieve success. This tenacity of pursuit became one of his trademarks and a notion that pervades all of his programs.

Kurt Hahn was not a prolific writer. Most of his original writings are in the form of transcribed speeches. On several occasions he issued a limited edition of a particular article or would stamp the manuscript "confidential." There appears to be no reason for this other than the fact that he did not want his writing to be made available to the general public for fear that he would be challenged on the grounds that the information was his definitive statement on education. There is no doubt that he had a brand of education that was eclectic in nature but seen as unique and original.

From the very early days of Salem, Kurt Hahn would say of the school's methods that "there is nothing new." They were borrowed from many sources: from Plato, from Dr. Arnold of Rugby, from Eton, from Abbotsholme, from Hermann Lietz, from Fichte, and from Wilhelm Meister. Each of them had proven successful in his own time, and Hahn attempted to take the best from each. He was not concerned that some of the sources were not German. As patriotic as he was, he was still liberal enough to accept ideas from other countries provided that they were useful. He had no time for his colleagues who would reject ideas on the basis of their origin and not consider their merit. He would often say, "....nor do I sympathize with the continental (German) gentleman who refused to be vaccinated because Jenner was an Englishman" (Hahn, 1940, p. 11).

Hahn was extremely clever at borrowing without copying. His adaptations and application of the elements he borrowed were unique. He had the ability to manipulate and create a new and novel way of delivering an educational experience from common practices such as was evidenced in the English Public School system, or from the fundamental educational ideas expressed by Plato.

Hahn's conception of education was simple. Its purpose was to develop a righteous man who is vigilant and an active citizen, who has a sense of duty to his fellow man and to God. Whereas this notion was not particularly earth-shattering, the process by which he achieved his ends made his educational style effective. So much so that his delivery ideas began to take on the ambience of a philosophy rather than a mere novel teaching method.

In Hahn's writing, he seldom refers to academic achievement as being the primary purpose of his schools. In fact, he frequently provides examples of end-of-term reports that are sent home to parents. In these reports he lists, in his order of importance, the categories in which the teacher is to comment. The evaluative items are: public spirit, sense of justice, the faculty of precise evidence, the power to do things right in the face of dangers (e.g., exhaustion, hostile public opinion, scepticism, and boredom), imagination, and the power of organization. At the end of the priority list comes Latin, Greek, mathematics, and other academic subjects (Hahn, 1947, 1956, 1957).

Educating for active citizenship was fundamental to Hahn's philosophy. He believed that every child was born with innate "spiritual powers" as well as an innate faculty that enables him/her to make correct judgments about moral issues. As the child progresses through adolescence, he/she loses the "spiritual powers" and ability to make correct judgments, because of what Hahn referred to as the "diseased society" and the impulses of adolescence. In addition, he criticized the "nerve exhausting" practices employed in other schools (e.g., examinations). There is always, of course, the counter-belief that such powers and conscience are acquired characteristics and not innate, but such beliefs were not Hahn's.

Hahn was obsessed with the social "declines" or social diseases which occurred in his society. These declines have been variously identified by Hahn as:

- Decline of fitness due to modern methods of locomotion;
- Decline of initiative and enterprise due to the widespread disease of spectatoritis;
- Decline of memory and imagination due to the confused restlessness of modern life;
- Decline of skill and care due to the weakened tradition of craftsmanship;
- Decline of self-discipline due to the ever-present availability of stimulants and tranquilizers;
- Decline of compassion due to the unseemly haste with which modern life is conducted.

Hahn (1934) concluded that the civilization of the day is diseased, often sapping the strength of the young before they can grow up. In 1938, he referred to the "phlegmainousa polis" (the inflamed city) in which youth grow up. The only solution to these problems, Hahn believed, was through education. It is interesting to note that the concerns, and sometimes the criticism of youth, in the 1980s, are centered on these same declines even though the turn of phrase and manifestation may be a little different. For example, a simple study conducted in 1943 of the outcomes of an early Outward Bound course in Aberdovey showed that the boys returned home some 10 pounds heavier as a result of the good food and exercise. A claim of a modern North American Outward Bound school may be that the participants would return home following a course 10 pounds lighter. Opposite results, but both programs are addressing the first of Hahn's concerns, the decline of fitness.

Each of the "declines" was addressed by Hahn through prescriptive activities that would bring about a collective cure to each disease. His rationale varied according to the group he was addressing or the kind of project at the time. The solution to the six declines appears in the justification for all of Hahn's educational enterprises: Salem School, Gordonstoun School, the County Badge Scheme, Outward Bound, the Duke of Edinburgh Award Scheme, and the United World Colleges. Hahn's solutions to the six declines are as follows.

THE DECLINE OF FITNESS

There was widespread "physical illiteracy" around the time that Hahn was developing the curriculum for Gordonstoun School. He believed that it was curable. His solution was to introduce a 45-minute daily physical activity program. Each boy participated in running, throwing and jumping activities. These track and field events had a specific set of standards to be achieved by each boy. The reason for having to work toward these standards went beyond the physical benefits. It was as important for each boy to develop and improve on his weak events as it was to nurture his talents. In fact, the phrase used by Hahn (1961) was that each boy should "defeat his own defeatism."

Another phrase that has become more popular with Hahn "disciples" is, "your disability is your opportunity." This occurred frequently in the physical activity program where boys often found hidden talents; witness Hahn's story of a sprinter discovering that he was a better distance runner when a slight injury prevented him from competing in the shorter, faster event. The carry-over into the real world allowed many of the boys not to be discouraged by minor setbacks—but to look at them as an opportunity to move in a new direction.

This daily physical education program differed from those of other English public schools, which had a strong emphasis and even stronger tradition of team-games. Both Salem and Gordonstoun confined their team-games to two afternoons per week. This allowed more time for personal development. It was Hahn's experience that this somewhat extensive physical activity program during the morning break did not disturb, but actually enhanced the subsequent classroom work (Hahn, 1938).

Another reason for including an extensive physical activity program was the concern for decline in vital health, which was more than a mere absence of illness (Hahn, 1962a). On several occasions Hahn made reference to "underexercise" contributing to coronary thrombosis. He believed that middle-aged men and women could not be expected to take part in regular exercise when the joy of movement has already been extinguished in puberty (Hahn, 1962b).

It is quite easy to see the similarity with the lack of fitness in young people in the 1980s. Also, the more recent interest in holistic wellness bears some resemblance to Hahn's notion of vital health. It may be worth re-justifying the physical activity programs in modern schools with the principle that it may contribute to lifelong wellness and healthy lifestyles.

THE DECLINE OF INITIATIVE AND ENTERPRISE

The decline arose from the inactivity and passive pursuits of young people. Hahn felt that it was akin to a disease that he called "spectatoritis" and credited its origin to the "Americans." He claimed that when a boy sat in a movie theater or listened to the radio, he experienced the thrill of a great adventure and the associated stirring events with unconscious movements of his body and without leaving his seat. He felt part of the action, but Hahn claimed that "the sensation was bogus and transitory but was always hotly desired" (Hahn, 1962, p. 4). This conclusion has been corroborated in contemporary research on the effect of television on children and youth (Mander, 1978).

The solution to this decline was the introduction of the "expedition" to the curriculum. The expedition into the mountains or the ocean nourished the spirit of adventure. George Trevelyan (1943), in a speech at the christening of the boat Garibaldi, at Aberdovey Outward Bound School, said, "without the instinct for adventure in the young men, any civilization however enlightened must wilt and whither." Hahn was fond of this quote because it illustrated the importance he placed on expeditions that generated oportunities for adventure. He felt that the rigor of expeditions could stretch young boys beyond the track and field activity program. As the training for track and field would help the boy defeat his own defeatism, so the expedition gave the boy the power to overcome (Hahn, 1960). It also revealed the inner worth of the man, the edge of his temper, the fiber of his stuff, the quality of his resistance, the secret truth of his pretenses, not only to himself but to others (Hahn, 1961b).

The expeditions were not always popular with the students, despite their value. Hahn relates a story of a boy who had just completed a sailing expedition around the Orkneys. After encountering three gales, he was asked how he enjoyed the adventure. The boy replied: "Magnificently, but not at the time!" This story was used in nearly every speech where Hahn was explaining the virtues of expeditions and adventure as an integral part of the school curriculum.

THE DECLINE OF MEMORY AND IMAGINATION

This occurred, according to Hahn, because of an increased pace of life and the rapidly changing political climate of the time. Boys did not have enough opportunity to stop and reflect. There was a need for periods of aloneness. Hahn stated that "neither the love of man nor the love of God can take deep root except in aloneness" (1961a, p. 15). These times alone were the opportunity to look to the future as well as to reflect.

At Gordonstoun, the silent walk to chapel became an important feature for each boy to use to develop his memory and imagination. There were also other activities, such as journal writing, which would encourage reflection. Most of these opportunities were short in duration, unlike the extended solo often used in the North American Outward Bound schools.

In addition to the opportunity to reflect, Hahn believed that these solo experiences helped to develop memory, which was vital. He had a story to illustrate the hazards of a poor memory:

> There was once a famous banker on the Continent who gathered his five sons round his death bed and gave them this piece of advice, "never tell lies, my boys, your memory is not good enough. If our audiences have a bad memory, and particularly the audiences of politicians, there is a great temptation for the speaker, I won't say tell lies, but to operate with an economy of truth." (Hahn, 1962a, p. 4)

THE DECLINE OF SKILL AND CARE

Because of an increase in technology, there was a reduction in the demand for craftsmen. It was the care and pride associated with artists and craftsmen that was disappearing. One of the reasons the Salem students had to spend time with the artisans in the Cistercian Monastry was that craftsmen were far less likely to accept second-rate or unfinished work in the same way as the schoolmaster (Hahn, 1934b).

An indication of the extent of this decline is illustrated in Hahn's story of the boy who produced a very shoddy piece of work. Hahn said to him, "Now this is really awful! Aren't you ashamed of yourself?" The boy grinned and said, "It's the genius of the British race to muddle through." And in his innermost heart he believed that he was contributing to the genius of the race! (Hahn, 1961a)

A job of skill often requires a substantial degree of patience. Hahn (1938) referred to the modern boy as having an impetuous lust for quick results. To encourage this patience and pursuit of quality, each boy was required to select a project. Extended periods of time were devoted to the project and it was expected that each boy would pursue his task through to excellence. The final product was not necessarily evaluated on its finite level of excellence, but rather on the tenacity of the pursuit.

These projects were referred to as "the grande passion" and the idea came about as a result of Hahn's concern about the problems that arise in boys during puberty.

> The discovery of sources of passionate interest can protect the growing young against what have been called the "deforming influences of puberty," resulting in irritability, listlessness, the lack of mental and physical coordination; which some psychologists have regarded as unavoidable symptoms of adolescence. (Hahn, 1965, p. 7)

Hahn believed the psychologists to be wrong. He contended that if a substitute passion could be found, then there was no reason a boy could not pass from childhood to adulthood without being contaminated by an unnatural sex drive (Hahn, 1934).

> If you look around the professions, who would you say has preserved the strength—you might also say the beauty—of childhood? The hunter from the hill, the sailor from the sea. Why? Because their adolescence was guarded by health-giving passions. (Hahn, 1938, p.5)

THE DECLINE OF SELF-DISCIPLINE

In order to overcome this decline, Hahn devised a system of daily exercise and healthy habits known as the "Training Plan." Each student was only permitted to participate in the Training Plan provided that he had proved to the faculty that he could be trusted to complete the daily ritual unsupervised. Each day the students were required to complete all of the following: one warm wash, two cold showers, 30 skips, high jump, running, throwing, no eating between meals, report all illness, account book, and a duty.

Hahn's concern that self-discipline was declining was spirited by his opinion that the availability of stimulants and tranquilizers was so easy that without self-discipline, young people would be "swallowed up" in such things as smoking, drinking, reading undesirable books, indiscriminate hearing of the radio, too frequent visits to the cinema, and staying out late (Hahn, 1934).

The Training Plan was created at Salem. When Hahn introduced it to Gordonstoun, many people warned him that British children would not respond to the regime. However, the Gordonstoun boys accepted the principle with enthusiasm, and many of the subsequent alumni agreed that it was useful to them in later life. To have experienced a sensible precedent of self-denial proved to be of value to those alumni who were influenced by Hahn. It is interesting to note that when Hahn left Gordonstoun, his successors did not understand the rationale for the Training Plan and it soon became used more as a punishment than a privilege.

THE DECLINE OF COMPASSION

This was considered to be the worst decline of all. The haste with which life was conducted did not allow the time for people to be compassionate. An illustration of the decline is reflected in the story about the time Hahn was driven through Lehrter Station in Berlin in 1945. At this time, there were refugees arriving in cattle trucks, many of whom were close to death. The driver of the car was an American sergeant with a kindly, friendly face. While they were driving through the scenes of misery and death he listened to jazz on the radio. He was asked by Hahn's host to turn it off. When Hahn was questioned as to what had happened to the young sergeant, he responded, "He has a dispersed soul which he could not assemble even before the majesty of death" (Hahn, 1947). Hahn therefore looked for deliberate ways of including activities that developed compassion.

The antidote Hahn introduced to counter the decline of compassion was the element of service. He was very fond of using the parable of the Samaritan. This provided a metaphor for the service-oriented activities that became an outstanding feature of Hahn's educational programs. At Gordonstoun it was the coastguard service and the volunteer fire brigade; at the Outward Bound schools it was the mountain rescue teams; and at Atlantic College it was the adoption of the surf rescue service. Kurt Hahn (1962b) believed it to be the supreme task of education to help the young to achieve a balance of power in their inner lives so that the love of man could take charge. The saving of life contributed to this objective.

A cliché that Hahn and many of his supporters used is the concept of an "aristocracy of service." This evolved from an article by William James on the "Moral Equivalent of War." The title seemed to catch their imagination and was still used many years later in the promotion of American Outward Bound schools. Whereas James deplored war, he did admit that war satisfied a primative longing that will never be extinguished: the longing to lose oneself in a common cause that claimed one's whole being. Everyone needed a "Holy Grail," but it was unreasonable to expect that a war be arranged every time society or an individual needed to realize himself (Hahn, 1962b). Therefore, a moral equivalent was needed. Hahn maintained that not only was his Samaritan ethic an eqivalent, but it was capable of releasing the highest dynamics of the human soul. In every article and speech delivered by Hahn after 1949, the rescue service or Samaritan ethic was always considered to be more than the moral equivalent of war.

These six declines formed the core of all of Kurt Hahn's educational ideas and achievements. Over the past 50 years they have undergone many interpretations, but generally are as applicable today as they were in 1933. The fact that most of Hahn's programs and schools are still operating today is testimony to the robustness of his ideas. What was an issue and a need for young people in the 1930s is still current today. In some sense Hahn was ahead of his time in creating a delivery system in education that is pervasive among experiential educators today.

Of all the sayings that Hahn used, the most famous was the following:

> We believe that it is the sin of the soul to force the young into opinions, but we consider it culpable neglect not to impel every youngster into health-giving experiences, regardless of their inclinations. (Hahn, 1935)

The essence of this statement lies in its emphasis on non-indoctrination while at the same time advocating nudging the child into action. The most recent clarification by Hahn was in 1967, when he responded to the original manuscript of a book by Robert Skidelsky. He expands the original statement:

> You and I would agree that indoctrination is of the devil and that it is a crime to force anybody into opinions but I, unlike you, consider it culpable neglect not to guide and even plunge the young into experiences which are likely to present opportunities for self discovery. If you spare the young such experiences, in deference to their wishes, you stunt their natural growth of basic human qualities which they will need for their own happiness and for service to their fellow men. (1967 p. 2)

It seems that most adventure-based experiential education programs, whether they have their roots in Outward Bound or not, all have program goals and objectives that are consistent with Hahn's sentiments expressed in this classic quotation.

In summary, it would be fair to say that Kurt Hahn's philosophy of education was somewhat limited in range as compared with some of the "greats." However, he was a master of capturing some profound ideas and presenting them as simple notions. He had a unique talent of being able to rework many statements to suit the needs of the occasion. When he was embarking on a new project that required funding and support, he could present a rationale that was not only inoffensive, but was immediately compelling.

REFERENCES

Hahn, K. (1934, January 17). A German public school. *The Listener*, 90-92.

Hahn, K. (1935, July 18). Report to annual meeting of Gordonstoun School, London.

Hahn, K. (1938). *Education for Leisure.* Conference of schoolmasters and college tutors at Magdalen College. Oxford: University Press.

Hahn, K. (1940, December 22). *The love of enterprise, the love of aloneness, the love of skill.* Lecture delivered in Liverpool Cathedral.

Hahn, K. (1947). *Active Citizenship.* Address to Elgin Rotary Club.

Hahn, K. (1956). Juvenile Irresponsibility. *Gordonstoun Record, 22*(2), 15-21.

Hahn, K. (1957, November 17). Speech at meeting with Friends of Gordonstoun, Admiralty House, London.

Hahn, K. (1960). Education and changes in our social structure. *B.A.C.I.E. Journal, 14* (1), 1-5.

Hahn, K. (1961a, April 2). A cure for the lawless young, *The Sunday Telegraph.*

Hahn, K. (1961b, April). *Service by youth.* Address to directors of Bournville Co. Ltd.

Hahn, K. (April 26, 1962a). Unnecessary deaths. *The Listener*, 715, 716.

Hahn, K. (1962b, July). State of the young in England. *The Listener*, 52-53.

Hahn, K. (1965, May 9). *Outward Bound.* Address at the Conference at Harrogate.

Hahn, K. (1967, October 30). Letter to Robert Skidelsky.

Hogan, J. (1968). *Impelled into experience; The story of Outward Bound.* Yorkshire: Educational Publications, Ltd.

Mander, J. (1978). *Four arguments for the elimination of television.* New York: William Morrow and Co., Inc.

Skidelsky, R. (1976). A respectful farewell. *The Encounter, 46*, 86-90.

A History of the AEE

Daniel Garvey
Association for Experiential Education

As the flight attendant announced our arrival in St. Louis, I awoke from a not-so-sound sleep, gathered my personal belongings from the overhead compartment and floor space in front of my seat, and shuffled off the plane into the airport. Another annual AEE conference! Could this possibly be number 16 for the association? My thoughts drifted back to previous gatherings of the association, and as I made my way to the baggage claim area, I privately reflected on these yearly get-togethers and the wonderful memories created during a brief four days every fall.

This conference will be different, not only in the ways that all conferences take on their own character, but because my role within the association has changed. This year (1988), instead of arriving with one piece of carry-on luggage, I have arrived with three suitcases (actually, trunks would be a better word), because this year I come as the executive director of the association. In addition to several changes of clothes, these trunks contain most of the important records of the AEE; minutes of previous board meetings, by-laws, ballots for the board election, and an assortment of other documents and office supplies.

Driving from the airport in St. Louis to the conference site at the Touch of Nature Environmental Center in Carbondale, Illinois, I attempted to piece together the history of the AEE and found I couldn't even be sure of which years conferences were held in certain locations: Was the Portsmouth, New Hampshire, conference in 1978 or was it '79? Placing conferences with their dates was less difficult than attempting to put significant activities of the association within a historical context.

This paper is an attempt to write a brief history of the AEE. I have not said "*The* History" because I expect others who have lived through the development of the association will continue to deepen our understanding of the activities of the past 16 years. In researching this paper I have attempted to read whatever I could find about the Association for Experiential Education. Of particular help has been the compilation of board minutes pulled together by my friend and former association officer, Betsy Dalgliesh. In addition to the "written word," I have also had formal and informal interviews with Joe Nold, Dick Kraft, Tony Richards, Keith King, Peggy Walker-Stevens, and Jim Keilsmeier, each of whom has played a significant role in the birth and/or continuation of the association. There are many others, to be sure, who could/should have been contacted to gain insight and factual information. I hope this paper will serve as a beginning, and I encourage all who read it to offer their version of history for future updates.

The Association for Experiential Education (AEE) is a member-supported international organization made up of approximately 1,300 individual and 120 institutional members. The association is committed to the practice and promotion of learning through experience, and to the collection and dissemination of information related to the broad topic of experiential education. One of the major foci of the association has been in the area of "adventure education." Since many of our members are involved in the use of experiential techniques in wilderness and adventure settings, the association has maintained a strong commitment to the development of safe practices for adventure programming. In 1980, the Adventure Alternatives Professional Group was formed within the AEE This group has been a powerful collective of practitioners interested in the application of experiential techniques with populations in corrections, mental health, and groups with special needs.

The AEE publishes the *Journal of Experiential Education* three times per year, eight books specifically focused on the topic of experiential education and its application in a variety of settings (including the Directory of Adventure Alternatives, edited by Michael Gass, which identified 137 organizations and agencies "providing programs that link therapeutic strategies with experiential practices"), periodic newsletters, and the Jobs Clearinghouse, a listing of positions available throughout North America. In addition to publications, the association also convenes regional and national conferences to help practitioners upgrade their skills and provide a meeting time for like-minded people to come together to exchange ideas and renew friendships. Within the association in 1988 there are four professional interest groups: Adventure Alternatives, Programming for the Disabled, Schools and Colleges, and Women in Experiential Education. The AEE office is located within the School of Education at the University of Colorado, Boulder.

THE FORMATION OF AN ASSOCIATION

The story might begin by placing the birth of the AEE within the context of the "progressive" education movement, as has been described by Albert Adams and Sherrod Reynolds (1985). The purpose of my paper is to recognize the rich history of experiential education and to focus more directly upon the Association for Experiential Education as a relatively unique adaptation of this educational philosophy. During the late 1970s, Outward Bound began to focus upon teacher training as one way to help influence the direction of the American education system. The apparent success of Outward Bound programs on previously disinterested students was well-documented, and a small group of colleges and universities began to explore the idea of including these techniques within their formal teacher training programs.

In 1968, the Colorado Outward Bound School, under the direction of Joe Nold, began to affiliate with the University of Northern Colorado in Greeley in offering teachers practice. The goal of these "Teacher's Courses," as noted by Hawlkes and Schulze (1969), was to produce a different type of teacher by addressing the criticism that "... methods classes, certification requirements, and eight-week teacher-training courses, have failed to produce quality educators" (Hawkes

& Shulze, 1969). Another program was located at Appalachian State University in Boone, North Carolina. In 1971, Keener Smathers, an assistant professor of secondary education, began to offer a summer teacher training program that included an Outward Bound course at the North Carolina school.

The success of this program and interest shown by other colleges and universities led Smathers to write to Henry Taft, president of Outward Bound, Inc., seeking his assistance to help organize a conference that would bring together members of the academic community with staff from the various Outward Bound-schools to discuss the value of Outward Bound: type activities at the post-secondary level. Taft responded by sending John Rhodes, program coordinator at Outward Bound, Inc., to work with Smathers at Appalachian State, and the two of them planned a conference for February 1974 (Minor & Boldt, 1981). The First North American Conference on Outdoor Pursuits in Higher Education was convened February 10, 1974, at Appalachian State University. One hundred and thirty-six people preregistered for the conference, and over 200 attended. One of the attendees, Keith King, who was running his own program at Keene State College in New Hampshire, vividly remembers this first gathering: "I always took students with me to conferences, so I guess there were a dozen or so with me. When I heard about the conference, I just knew I had to go. There wasn't much support for what we were doing, most of us weren't sure if anyone else was trying to teach students this way." Dave Hopkinson, a student of Keith's, recounted to me that he was "blown away by the experience of being with this exciting group of people at this first gathering."

Henry Taft delivered the keynote Address, "The Value of Experience." He ended his talk with the following statement, "Finally, I would hope that some sort of national organization on outdoor experiential education at the college level may evolve from this trailblazing meeting. You are in unexplored territory, and about to be impelled into experience. Good luck" (Taft, 1974). A group of conferees, headed by Alan Hale, presented an outline for a possible national association as a follow-up to the conference. One of the recommendations included the formation of a national steering committee to oversee the development of a future conference and the possibility of a larger association. This first steering committee consisted of Bob Godfrey, University of Colorado; Don Kesselheim, University of Massachusetts; John Rhodes, Outward Bound, Inc.; Richard Rogers, Earlham College; and Keener Smathers, Appalachian State University.

The second conference was held 8 months later, in October, at Estes Park, Colorado. The organizer of this gathering was Bob Godfrey. The Estes Park conference was noteworthy because of the wide variety of educators who were in attendance. Unlike the previous conference in North Carolina, where Outward Bound staff had come together with college faculty, the Colorado conference was attended by "regular classroom teachers."

Reflecting upon this stage of what was to become the AEE, Tony Richards suggested that this inclusion of educators from outside the outdoor pursuits area had opened the conferences to a diversity of participants, and had helped ensure that "you didn't have to be vaccinated with an Outward Bound course to be a member of this group."

Perhaps the most vivid memory of those in attendance at the Estes Park conference was the address delivered by William Unsoeld, which he titled, "The Spiritual Value of the Wilderness." In this speech Unsoeld provided a well-articulated rationale for "adventure activities." The effect upon participants was profound. Again quoting Keith King, "We came out of his speech 45 feet in the air, and we didn't come down until we hit New Hampshire."

The 1975 conference was convened by Alan Hale, at Mankato State University. The use of Outward Bound activities on university and college campuses was gaining popularity, and the need for a more formal organization was solidifying. Following the 1976 conference, hosted by Bob Pieh at Queens University in Kingston, Ontario, a group of interested participants met and finally pulled together this rather loose group of affiliated individuals and institutions into the Association for Experiential Education. Rick Medrick authored the Articles of Incorporation, which were filed in the state of Colorado on June 17, 1977. The stated purpose of this new association was to "promote experiential education, support experiential educators, and further develop experiential learning approaches through such services as conferences, publications, consulting, research, workshops, etc." (AEE, 1977). The registered agent for the Association was Maria Snyder, who was working as a secretary with Joe Nold in his "Project Center" at the Colorado Outward Bound School in Denver.

This was the beginning of the AEE. The need for college faculty using experiential methods to affiliate, and the financial and emotional support from Outward Bound combined to form a lasting bond that helped create this new organization. Though most of the early members of the association were "cut from the same cloth," the AEE would soon move from its university focus to a much broader appeal to mainstream education and to people working with special populations of clients, primarily in the fields of corrections and mental health.

THE DEVELOPMENT OF THE AEE AND THE STRUGGLE FOR SURVIVAL

"A movement starts out with dedication and then, if it is to survive, faces success with noble resolution to deal with discomforts of size, with the need for professional recognition, with the issues of recruitment, training, the development of curriculum, the business of doing business and the insurance and management expertise this requires" (Shore, 1978).

Thus Arnold Shore aptly described the development of the AEE from 1977-84. The formation of the association was a concrete example of what a group of committed individuals interested in starting a movement within education could accomplish. Having created the AEE, the next question facing the leaders was, "what should this association do?"

The administration of the AEE was the responsibility of the newly organized "Coordinating Committee," which held its first official meeting on April 15-16, 1977, in Denver, Colorado. In attendance at the meeting were John Rhodes, Dan Campbell, Ron Gager, Rick Medrick, and Maria Snyder. The group discussed the need for increased member services and the production of the *Journal of Experiential Education*, which was scheduled to be published soon. In an attempt to more fully use the talents and energies of other interested members of the association, the Coordinating Committee created four standing committees: (a) membership and promotion; (b) networking, services, and publications; (c) conference and (d) administration and finance. Much of the current organizational structure in the AEE was established during the initial stages of these committees' efforts.

The founders could not rest on their laurels. The 1978 conference was held in St. Louis, Missouri. The choice of this site created substantial difficulties for many of the members, since Missouri had not been one of the states to ratify the Equal Rights Amendment. During the Annual General Meeting at the conference, a resolution, submitted by Linda Chin representing the Women's Issues Special Interest Group, was unanimously adopted by the membership. This resolution notified the Board of Directors that a boycott of the conference was taking place, and called for the following action:

1. That the location of subsequent conference sites be chosen in states that had ratified the E.R.A.

2. That the content of future conferences includes concerns particularly relevant to women more extensively than has been done in this year.
3. That efforts be made to eliminate sexist language in the presentations and publications of this association and its conference (AEE, 1978).

This resolution called attention to the fact that the AEE had an obligation to conduct its activities consistent with the values of its membership. Despite the contributions of several women such as Maryann Hedaa, Sherrod Reynolds, Gruffie Clough, and Maria Snyder in the early development and leadership of the association, the AEE was primarily a male organization. Of the 130 people preregistered for the first conference in North Carolina, 17 were women. If, the AEE was to grow and fulfill the dreams of a broader representation of educators, it would have to address the problems presented in this resolution.

The next serious attempt to change the composition of the association occurred the very next year, at the Portsmouth, New Hampshire conference. In the closing moments of the Annual General Meeting, Arthur Conquest was recognized from the floor and addressed the issue of minority representation within the AEE. He urged the leadership of the association to seek ways in which those who have been participants in Outward Bound programs, often minority students from urban areas, could also be members of the AEE. Conquest's comments resulted in a 27-point plan created by the Board of Directors to help increase the participation of minorities in the AEE. Maryann Hedaa assumed responsibility for this endeavor.

One of the more significant problems to face the AEE was looming on the horizon—financial solvency. As the association headed into the 1981 conference to be held in Toronto, there was a $6,288 deficit projected, with $7,531 remaining in the fund balance. The need for a financially successful conference was not apparent to the leadership.

When most of the expenses from the Toronto conference were calculated, the association was deeply in debt. President Rich Weider reported the following budget summary to the Board of Directors during their 1982 gathering: "In the 1981 budget it was planned to keep $8,000 in a fund balance in case of emergencies. Expenses were cut by $8,000, the Journal publication was deferred, bills weren't paid, and the Colorado Outward Bound School wasn't paid, so that with the $25,000 over budget of conference debt and $8,000 in administrative bills, the organization entered 1982 with a $33,000 debt" (AEE, 1982). In addition to the financial problems facing the association, Stephanie Takis, the executive officer, resigned, stating her belief that the AEE could no longer afford to pay someone in her position.

Faced with a substantial debt, the resignation of the executive officer, and the lack of funds to operate or rent an office space, the association was near collapse. Minutes of board meetings from this era reflect the tension and obstacles facing this group.

While no single person could claim to have saved the AEE, the imaginative and dedicated activities of Jim Keilsmeier, Peggy Walker-Stevens, and Dick Kraft certainly contributed to its rescue. Without the efforts of these individuals, and the other members of the Board of Directors, the association would certainly have floundered and collapsed. Kraft, a faculty member at the University of Colorado, offered space within the Education Department for the AEE. The move of the AEE from Colorado Outward Bound School to the University of Colorado was, in some ways, an appropriate relocation. C.O.B.S. and the University of Colorado had enjoyed a long history of cooperative activities, including the formation of a jointly run Masters in Education Program. In addition, many of the dominant forces within the AEE had either been adjunct faculty in the Education Department (Bob Godfrey and Joe Nold, for instance), or they had studied with Kraft, John Haas, and Stan Ratliff, senior faculty members at C.U. (Jim Kielsmeier, Rocky Kimball, and Tony Richards).

The accounts of the board minutes from this period detail the dedication of a group of determined individuals who were resolved to keep the association alive. Peggy Walker-Stevens arranged her vacation time so that she would be able to journey from New Hampshire to Boulder and work in the office. Keilsmeier and Kraft established the equivalent of martial law regarding the expenditure of money and the operation of the office. The other board members helped subsidize association expenses by covering phone charges and copying costs. The number of yearly board meetings was reduced, and when they met they slept on the floor of a host member's house to help save the costs of hotel rooms.

The efforts of these board members, coupled with a small but well-run conference at Humboldt State University in Arcada, California, convened by Mike Mobley, allowed the leadership and membership of the association to breathe a sigh of relief. At the Annual General Meeting in 1983, Dick Kraft reported "there were 554 people in attendance at this conference and the break-even point was 350." He said he had "come to the conference prepared to declare the organization bankrupt, but the success of the conference made that unnecessary" (AEE, "General Meeting," 1983). The financial scare of the early 1980s led to a conservative budget-planning process for the mid-80s, so that the financial stability of the organization continued to grow. Despite the relatively healthy status of the budget, the last of the debts from the Toronto conference was only finally retired in 1987.

THE CERTIFICATION ISSUE

From the very first meeting in North Carolina, the question of how one determines the relative competence of outdoor instructors has been debated. This question has sometimes been whispered by the membership and at other times shouted from the floor of a general meeting. All discussions concerning the topic of certification were viewed by different factions within the association as biased. To help bring some order to this controversy, the board turned to the expert advice of Jed Williamson, Karl Johanson, and a small group of interested practitioners. This group, termed the Safety Committee, forged a near-consensus regarding the direction that should be taken by the AEE in its efforts to help create and maintain safe wilderness leadership.

In 1984, the Safety Committee published *Common Peer Practices in Adventure Education.* This document was the culmination of endless hours of negotiation and hard work by the people involved. In addition, it brought the association together in a united effort to determine those techniques and practices that could be mutually agreed upon as contributing to the safety of adventure activities. This publication is perhaps the best compilation of standards in adventure programming available.

CURRENT TIMES AND FUTURE DIRECTIONS OF THE AEE

The AEE entered a period of growth and maturity marked by a strong financial base and stable leadership. Questions concerning the board and the membership were ones of direction rather than existence. Discussion at Board meetings focused on concerns about how the association should be managed. The Association began to reach out to like-minded organizations in an attempt to broaden the base of support for mutually agreed- upon agendas for educational change. The 1983 conference at Lake Geneva, Wisconsin, was a joint project of the AEE, The Council for the Advancement of Experiential Education (C.A.E.L.), and The National Society for Internship and Experiential Education (N.S.I.E.E.). In 1985, the AEE became a member of the Forum for Experiential Education, a group of 12 organizations that shared a common commitment to the goal of improving education through the application of a wide variety of experiential education techniques. These outreach efforts, coupled with a more vigorous recruitment program, resulted in a dramatic increase in the individual and institutional membership of the association.

At the January 1985 board meeting, Dick Kraft submitted his Executive Director's Report: "With this report, I believe that you will agree with me that the association is now again on solid grounds, so I hereby tender my resignation as executive director, effective on June 30, 1985 or at such time as a new executive director has been appointed" (AEE, Board of Directors, 1985). The board accepted his resignation and moved to hire Mitch Sakofs as the new executive director. Mitch had worked in the office as associate director with Dick for the past year and was a natural choice to fill the position. During the next two years, Mitch computerized the records of the association, improved the publication of books and resource materials, and generally systematized the activities of the Boulder office. All of these activities were consistent with the major theme of this period: "the professionalization" of the AEE. In 1987, Mitch resigned his position to take a job with Outward Bound, Inc., and was succeeded by Eileen Burke, who assumed the newly created position of association administrator.

The resignation of Mitch Sakofs resulted in a series of prolonged discussions regarding the long-term leadership of the association and the proper role for the board of directors. The result of these discussions was to begin the process of hiring a full-time executive director. Throughout the history of the AEE, there had been several discussions regarding the possible merits of a full-time executive director, but the Association had never been in a financial position such that this could be recommended. Finances had improved to the extent that, in 1987, the association was in a position to hire a full-time director. Rita Yerkes, for the board, began a national search for an executive director in November 1987, and I was hired in August of 1988.

One would have good reason to be optimistic concerning the future of the AEE. Our nation's educational system is suffering from a lack of resources, lack of faith by students and parents, and a lack of clear direction for viable alternatives that can be implemented to help recapture the interest and intellect of our youth. The success demonstrated by member organizations of the AEE has much to offer this ailing system.

In the past, those who comprised the AEE were, in large measure, only marginally connected to the educational establishment. Outward Bound instructors and the highly creative classroom teacher have provided a model for many regarding the education that is possible, but they have not been in positions to effect broad-based educational change. Today we are witnessing a new alliance. Large multinational corporations are sending their top executives on training programs that use experiential education approaches. Ernest Boyer (1987), former commissioner of education, writes in his recent book evaluating the college experience: "A good college affirms that service to others is a central part of education. The questions we pose are these: Are students encouraged to participate in voluntary service? Does the college offer the option of deferring admission to students who devote a year to service before coming to campus? Are the service projects drawn into the larger educational purposes, helping students see that they are not only autonomous individuals but also members of an intentional community? And does the faculty set an example and give leadership to service?" Service learning has long been an integral part of experiential education, and is one of the major tenets of the Outward Bound credo: "To serve, to strive, and not to yield."

The members of the association are not alone in their view that the educational system is in need of significant change. Conservatives and liberals are interested in listening to a voice that has for many years only been heard by a small group of progressive educators. The AEE, and the educational philosophy it represents, will not be a panacea for the ills that have overtaken our educational system, but it may present sound alternatives for some of the problems.

The specific accomplishments of the association are less important than the fact that it exists and supports a different view of educational practice. The AEE has evolved from the basic challenges of surviving to solving problems of effective management, and finally to a position of leadership in educational innovation. I hope the next person to write the history of the AEE will view it as a group that went far beyond an ability to support its members, to an organization deeply involved with supporting change within an educational system that sorely needs it.

REFERENCES

Adams, A., & Reynolds, S. (1985). The long conversation: Tracing the roots of the past. R. Kraft (Ed.), *The theory of experiential education.* Boulder, CO: The Association for Experiential Education.

Association for Experiential Education (1977). Article of incorporation, June 17, 1977, State of Colorado.

Association for Experiential Education (1982). Minutes of Board of Directors meeting, St. Louis, MO.

Association for Experiential Education (1985). Minutes of Board of Directors meeting, September 8, Denver, CO.

Association for Experiential Education (1985). Minutes of Board of Directors meeting, January 31, Boulder, CO.

Boyer, E. (1987). *College: The undergraduate experience in America.* New York: Harper Row.

Hawkes, G., & Schulze, J. (1969). *Evaluation of Outward Bound teachers practica.* Reston, VA: Outward Bound, Inc.

Minor, J., & Boldt, J. (1981). *Outward Bound, USA: Learning through experience in adventure-based education.* New York: Morrow.

Shore, A., & Greenberg, E. (1978). Challenging the past, present, and future: New directions in education. *Journal of Experiential Education, 1*(1), 42-48.

Taft, H. (1974). The value of experience (unpublished address).

Historical Evolution of NOLS: The National Outdoor Leadership School

Delmar W. Bachert
Appalachian State University

The National Outdoor Leadership School (NOLS) is a non-profit school headquartered in Lander, Wyoming, and is recognized as a leader in the field of wilderness education and outdoor leadership. NOLS was founded in 1965 to meet a need for instructors who were masters of outdoor living skills and capable of leading others in the wild outdoors. NOLS currently has branch schools in Africa, Mexico, and the states of Alaska, Washington and Wyoming.

> NOLS teaches outdoor skills and leadership. We believe that effective outdoor leadership is a function of skill, knowledge, and judgment. We develop this potential through continual practice and actual leadership experience. (NOLS, 1986, p. 6)

The *NOLS 1986 Catalog of Courses* lists four major program objectives: leadership development, outdoor skills, minimum impact conservation techniques, and expedition dynamics. The NOLS core curriculum is common to most courses and suggests the comprehensive nature of the NOLS learning experience:

- Minimum-Impact Camping and Resource Protection
- Travel Techniques
- Outdoor Living Skills
- Safety
- Environmental Awareness
- Expedition Dynamics (p. 3)

The "NOLS Experience" is the term that students have come to use when describing their adventures in learning at the National Outdoor Leadership School. The aim here is to document and interpret the historical evolution of NOLS. The intent of this documentation is to trace the development of the school and its curriculum and the impact it has had on wilderness education and wilderness management.

The relationship between wilderness education and wilderness management is largely unexplored. Wilderness education can be viewed as a reasonable alternative to regulation as a wilderness management tool. NOLS serves as a case study.

One paper in this collection delves into the history of Outward Bound. A subsequent one explores the foundation of the Wilderness Education Association. The NOLS story is closely connected to both via the work of Paul K. Petzoldt.

The NOLS Experience emanates in large part from the life of Petzoldt. NOLS was his dream and represents an extension of his life experiences. A glimpse of his accomplishments and lifestyle will prove invaluable in understanding the development of NOLS. It will provide a link to the development of the Colorado Outward Bound School and the eventual development of the Wilderness Education Association as well.

Petzoldt claims that it was on his fateful climb of the Grand Teton, in 1924, that he was ingrained with the need to learn as much as he could about the outdoors and how it could be used. He began a career as a climbing guide in the Tetons soon after this ascent. While guiding, Petzoldt had a tremendous opportunity to gather knowledge and techniques from others. He also began to perfect techniques for training climbing guides for the first mountaineering school in America.

The goal of the Petzoldt-Exum School of American Mountaineering differed from European guiding, where the object was to get the clients to the top, even if they had to be hauled up. In the Tetons they tried to educate the clients, to make them into knowledgeable mountaineers, and get them to the summits. Patricia Petzoldt describes the qualities Petzoldt sought in his Teton guides, criteria that would guide the selection of NOLS instructors decades later:

> They were chosen for other qualities as well as their climbing ability. They had to have great strength and endurance, sound judgment, plenty of horse sense, and a knowledge of people. They must be able to cope with emergencies as they arose. And they had to have plenty of patience. They tried to be good hosts as well as good guides. (Petzoldt, 1953, p. 225)

Petzoldt's reputation and skill as a mountaineer and climber continued to grow and develop. He made a double ascent of the Matterhorn in one day. The climb was internationally acclaimed as a "feat of unusual endurance." He made the first ascent on the North Face of the Grand Teton in 1936. In that same year, long before winter mountaineering was widely practiced, he made the first winter ascent of the Grand Teton (Petzoldt, 1953, p. 209).

In 1938, Petzoldt was asked to join the 1938 expedition to K2, the second-highest mountain in the world. In a discussion of the K2 Expedition members, Houston describes the factors involved in Petzoldt's selection for the team:

> His great experience with mountain camping, winter weather and climbing of exceptional technical difficulty made him a splendid addition to our group. (Bates, Burdsall, House, Houston, Petzoldt, & Streatfield, 1939, p. 31)

In the 1960s, the Outward Bound concept was introduced to America. The involvement in and influence of Petzoldt on the Colorado Outward Bound School (COBS) in its early stages were significant. His experience at COBS in turn helped him clarify the need and goals for NOLS. Petzoldt served in three different capacities during the formative years of COBS. In 1962, he was asked by an old acquaintance from the Ski Troops, Ernest "Tap" Tapley, to examine the school's mountaineering practices. In 1963, he became the mountaineering adviser for the school and in 1964, the Chief Instructor for COBS. Miner and Boldt (1981) describe his impact:

> Paul brought to the school a superb expertise in his mountain expedition specialty. This was not simply because his involvement exposed instructors and students to the experience-garnered wisdom of a veteran

> mountaineer of the first rank. It was more particularly due to Petzoldt's having massaged that experience with an analytical turn of mind, that together with his fervor for communication, his love of the wild outdoors and a gift of communication, made him a fine teacher of wilderness adventuring. (p. 112-115)

The first effort was made in 1964 to have an instructors' course at COBS. According to Petzoldt (1983), this effort consisted of "Tap (Tapley) taking off with the fellas for a hell of a trip!" During the summer of 1964, Petzoldt openly discussed his intent to start a school in Wyoming. In a debriefing session with one four-man group from C-10, the tenth course at COBS, he stated:

> I'm going to have a school in Wyoming, in the Wind Rivers. Maybe we'll have one Outward Bound course like they have here and maybe we'll have two courses in leadership for older fellas. (Petzoldt, 1964b)

During his tenure at COBS, Petzoldt identified three great needs that would influence the creation of NOLS. The first need was to expose the participants to challenges inherent in a wilderness experience. The second was quality instructors that would meet his standards as outdoor leaders. The third was for a program that would meet the interests of those Outward Bound graduates who wanted to progress to greater levels of outdoor skill.

In 1963, Petzoldt actually had begun to promote his idea for a Wyoming Outward Bound school. A headline in the *Wyoming State Journal* of July 30, 1963, reads: "Petzoldt believes beginning could be made next year on Outward Bound camp here (p. 12)." In a letter to Josh Miner, founder of Outward Bound in America, Petzoldt (1964a) comments:

> My personal wishes, of course, would be to have an OUTWARD BOUND Leadership School here, drawing principally on the students who have finished a course in another OUTWARD BOUND school and who, then, are ready to profit by the training that we could give them here to make them real outdoor leaders for their communities or, if you wished, for other OUTWARD BOUND schools in the future.

The Wyoming Outward Bound school was not to be. Miner was involved not only with supporting the fledgling COBS but the development of both the Minnesota and Hurricane Island Outward Bound schools in the mid-1960s. Concern was also expressed about the geographical expediency of another Outward Bound program in the Rocky Mountain region. Petzoldt's commitment to an outdoor leadership school never waivered once the idea was firmly established in his mind:

> Both Mr. Tapley and I realized very early in our experience with the Colorado Outward Bound School that their program could not really come to maturity without instructors with more training and background than we were able to secure in the United States or even from England. Mr. Tapley and I therefore started this school with the idea of supplying good instructors for all outdoor schools and programs. This program should be considered as a crash program in order to raise the standard of outdoor leadership for all groups using the outdoors in America. (1965g)

Wilderness, specifically the Wind Rivers Mountain Range of Wyoming, was chosen as the medium in which NOLS would train outdoor leaders. "OUTDOOR LEADERSHIP SCHOOL FORMED HERE", reads a headline of the March 23, 1965 *Wyoming State Journal* published in Lander. Success came quickly for NOLS. They graduated over 80 students in the summer of 1965. Tapley and Petzoldt shared field leadership and were assisted by six patrol leaders, several with Outward Bound experience. Petzoldt's philosophy is reflected in part by a promotional tape recording he made:

> In order to have outdoor adventure that will compete with the adventure that youth has developed in his own close-knit little teenage society, we have to have something that is

> good. We have to have something that is real adventure: like climbing mountains, like fording wild rivers, like exploring wild country, like facing the storms, like surviving alone in the wilderness. In order to supply this outdoor adventure, at least in order to supply it safely, takes real leaders. (Petzoldt, 1965, Personal Communication)

The *Articles of Incorporation of the National Outdoor Leadership School* (1965) elaborate on the purpose of the school:

> The purposes for which this corporation is formed are as follows: to develop and teach wilderness skills and techniques; to develop and teach wilderness use that encourages minimal environmental impact; to develop and teach outdoor leaders. (NOLS, 1965a)

A key factor in any successful organization is the personnel. Petzoldt recruited tremendous talent for the school, including Tapley and Rob Hellyer. Both were instrumental in the early success of the school in the field. Also instrumental in backing NOLS were Lander, Wyoming residents Judge Jack Nicholas, Dr. William Ericson, MD, and legislator Ed Breece. They formed the nucleus of the early Board of Directors (Nicholas, 1983).

The fee to attend NOLS in its first year of operation was $300 for the 36-day course. The salary of the director was fixed at $650 per month. The school was started with few resources. Petzoldt penned 40 letters a day in early 1965 to gain recruits.

Based on the success of the first summer, plans were laid for 1966. A decision of special significance was made to involve women on the wilderness courses. Petzoldt said: "We expect to expand the course next year. We'll even have a course for girls" (*Wyoming State Journal*, August, 1965, p. 1). The NOLS Experience apparently appealed to women as this comment, made two years later, indicates: "Our women's course was a success and we will have three women's courses in 1967" (Petzoldt, 1967). Soon the men's and women's courses merged into a practical and popular coed wilderness experience.

There were other demands early in NOLS' development. One was for a course for younger students. Another was to offer college credit (Petzoldt, 1967). The nature of the program as well as its initial success led to rapid expansion. NOLS graduated 83 in 1965 and nearly 1,000 in 1970. Branch schools were established in Tennessee, Alaska, Washington, Mexico, Connecticut and Africa. All but Tennessee and Connecticut continue to function today.

NOLS has been successful in part because of the desire of so many young Americans to have a "wilderness experience." It carries with it a certain appeal and represents a rite of passage for many. The wilderness classroom and the wilderness education it promises offer a stark contrast to the educational doldrums they may have been experiencing. The NOLS core curriculum promises adventure and a lifetime of skills to be practiced and honed. It suggests an "Outdoor Life-Field and Stream" lifestyle, if somewhat less consumptive than the outdoor sport norm presented in those magazines.

There were other factors in the early and continued success of NOLS. The creation of NOLS was timely. It coincided with the Wilderness Act of 1964. One impact of designated wilderness was to create an increased demand for backcountry experiences. NOLS offered a challenging and appealing package to a growing number of wilderness seekers. The demand for Outward Bound, adapted Outward Bound, and other backcountry programs created a growing demand for outdoor leaders. NOLS, unlike Outward Bound, philosophically and specifically set out to train a supply of leaders to meet this need.

NOLS met certain intrinsic needs of many young people in the 1960s. Some were seeking alternatives, seeking immersion in a context of reality. The impact of the wilderness; the explain, demonstrate, and do approach to teaching; the energy and enthusiasm of the instructors, all led graduates to spread the word about the NOLS Experience. On campus, at camp, on the trail, this word of mouth became NOLS' best advertisement. Employers began to seek NOLS graduates as applicants.

The curriculum was another reason for the school's success. The content and delivery offer those seeking outdoor-related careers a chance to learn from first-hand experience. It suggests an opportunity to become a leader of outdoor pursuits in addition to being a participant. The "must-knows" was the terminology used by Petzoldt to describe what he considered the minimal knowledge and skills that an outdoor leader must possess. The development of good judgment was a primary goal set for NOLS participants. A five-week mountaineering expedition became the primary "method of education" for delivering the curriculum to the students. Petzoldt (1974) describes both the limitations and the strength of the curriculum:

> While there are many factors of outdoor living that are interesting or enjoyable to know, our primary concern must be immediate protection of the individual, the environment, and the equipment. Thus, time and space limit us to teaching those things which must be known. (p. 23)

The NOLS curriculum was put to the test in the summer of 1965. Petzoldt and Tapley provided primary instruction and leadership with support from Jack Hyland, Jerry Taylor, Bruce Barrus and Burt Redmayne on the first course (*Wyoming State Journal,* August 17, 1965). Ideas, activities, and techniques were incorporated and others were discarded. The NOLS curriculum was tested and revised in the field. In 1974, Petzoldt published a summation of his work and the heart of the NOLS curriculum in the *The Wilderness Handbook.* Wilderness education later received updates in: *The National Outdoor Leadership School's Wilderness Guide* (Simer & Sullivan, 1983), and in Petzoldt's (1984) revision of his book, titled *The New Wilderness Handbook.*

The context and manner in which NOLS delivers the "must-knows" and attempts to develop judgment is critical to understanding the NOLS Experience. The expedition format of NOLS' course is really a special application of the small group process. The process is intense and experiential. The expedition as a mode of education forces both students and instructors to think, and the consequences of their response to challenges in the wilderness are very real. The flow of a lengthy expedition allows for both horizontal and vertical instruction in the practice of skills, technique and judgment.

NOLS is noted for pioneering minimum-impact camping techniques. In the early days this was referred to as "practical conservation" by Petzoldt and the course leaders. Peter Simer (1981), past executive director of NOLS, called for this:

> An agenda for the next 15 years aimed at educating the American wilderness user to state-of-the-art techniques would really only introduce common sense into contemporary American camping. Minimum impact camping is as essential to wilderness as safe driving habits are to the highway. (p. 3)

An explicit and unique claim of Petzoldt and NOLS curriculum is that judgment is a basic element in the foundation of a competent and safe outdoor leader, and NOLS attempts to teach it. If the must-knows are the warp then judgment is the woof of the weave that makes up the NOLS experience. All of the skills, abilities, and techniques an outdoor leader can possess are qualified, modified, and tempered in their application by the exercise of sound judgment. Reporting to the Board of Trustees after the NOLS courses in 1965, Petzoldt wrote:

> Our theory of teaching corresponding judgment along with techniques was successful, and is one of the important and distinguishing factors between our instruction and other instruction in the field of outdoorsmanship and mountaineering. (Petzoldt, 1965e, pp. 3-4)

What has been the impact of NOLS in two decades of offering a wilderness education, a wilderness experience, to over 20,000 participants? Steff Kessler (1983), NOLS instructor and staff director at the time, offers:

> I look for a subtle form of leadership on NOLS' courses—students learning something about themselves as they interact with each other and the wilderness. They are learning to size up situations and intervene in a way that changes reality. Instead of feeling powerless, acted upon by weather, terrain, or group problems, they become actors, problem-solvers, using their skills and experiencing the success of their actions.
>
> A NOLS course affords people with the chance to take charge, a chance often denied in our complex, technological society. Instead of passive recipients of events, NOLS students shape their own society and reality within the mountains. What they learn is, I think, transferable to their lives beyond the mountains. (p. 6)

REFERENCES

Bates, R. H., Burdsall, R. L., House, W. P., Houston, C. S., Petzoldt, P. K., & Streatfield, N. R. (1939). *Five miles high: American Alpine Club American Kharakorum expedition, 1938.* New York: Dodd, Mead & Co.

Kessler, S. (1983). Beyond wilderness skills. *(NOLS) Alumnus,* Fall/Winter: 6.

Miner, J., & Boldt, (1981). Outward Bound USA: *Learning through experience in adventure-based education.* New York: Wm. Morrow.

NOLS (1965). *Articles of incorporation of the National Outdoor Leadership School.* March 4. Lander, WY, NOLS archives.

NOLS (1986). *Catalog of courses.* Lander, WY.

Petzoldt, P. (1953). *On top of the world: My adventures with my mountain-climbing husband.* New York: T. Y. Crowell Co.

Petzoldt, P. K. (1964a) Letter to J. Miner, February 27. NOLS archives.

Petzoldt, P. K. (1964b). Tape recording, Debriefing of C-10 (Tenth course at Colorado Outward Bound). NOLS archives.

Petzoldt, P. K. (1965a). NOLS review and report to the Board of Trustees. NOLS archives.

Petzoldt, P. K. (1965b). Tape recording, NOLS promotional slide/tape, NOLS archives.

Petzoldt, P. K. (1965c). Taper recording, Letter dictated to Mrs. Price, NOLS archives.

Petzoldt, P. K. (1974). *The wilderness handbook.* New York: W. W. Norton & Co., Inc.

Petzoldt, P. K. (1984). *The new wilderness handbook.* (2nd ed.). New York: W. W. Norton.

Simer, P. (1981). NOLS director calls for new wilderness agenda. *NOLS Alumnus,* Winter: 3.

Simer, P., & Sullivan, J. (1983). *The National Outdoor Leadership School's wilderness guide.* New York: Simon & Schuster.

Wyoming State Journal, July 30, 1963, p. 12.

Wyoming State Journal, March 29, 1923, 1965, p. 1

Wyoming State Journal, August 17, 1965, pp. 1 & 8.

Three levels of certification were set. They were:

1. Skills—a user's certification
2. Leadership—a leader's certification
3. Instruction—an instructor's certification

It was expected that most course participants would have camping backgrounds and career interests related to wilderness education or leadership.

Christie, Gregory, Lupton, and Petzoldt agreed on basic course content and organizational details. They agreed to ask the following people to also serve as members of the organizing committee of the newly formed Wilderness Use Education Association: Gene Fear, president of the Survival Education Association, Tacoma, Washington; Patrick LaValla, president of the National Association for Search and Rescue, Tacoma, Washington; Henry Nichol, U.S. Department of Agriculture (retired) Outdoor Recreation consultant, Potomac, Maryland. All of them accepted the invitation to serve. Dr. Christie was selected as chairman, Dr. Lupton became vice chairman, and Charles Gregory became secretary of this new organization. Gregory, who had been a participant in the 1977 summer program under Petzoldt's leadership, sent organizing committee members a draft copy of the *General Course Content Outline,* which included the purpose and the nineteen program components as agreed upon at the October 22 meeting. Those components became the basis for the 18-point curriculum that evolved later. The following is a copy of the draft that Gregory compiled.

GENERAL COURSE CONTENT OUTLINE

Statement of Purpose

To improve the quality of the wilderness and wilderness experience through education of users and the certification of outdoor leaders.

The outline of the wilderness experience is directed at teaching the basic competencies necessary so the wilderness user will have a safe, enjoyable experience with little impact on the environment.

"The best instructor has a good sense of timing." The following basic content will be taught and practiced some time during the course with flexibility given to the instruction to compensate for variable factors such as weather, terrain and seasonal changes. In order to obtain a Wilderness Use Certification, basic competencies must be met.

Expedition Behavior. Good expedition behavior is a practicing awareness of the relationship of individual to individual, individual to group, group to individual, group to other groups, individual and group to the multiple uses of the region, individual and group to administrative agencies, and individual and group to the local populace. It is this awareness, plus motivation and character to be concerned for others in every respect as one is for oneself.

Environmental Ethic. The practice of utilizing the wild outdoors with little impact on the environment. The topic area will be interrelated and introduced within other areas such as basic camping techniques and health and sanitation. During the course, the participants are expected to gain an understanding of the environmental ethic and demonstrate, by practice, those skills and techniques that promote low impact on the environment.

Trip Planning. At the completion of the course, the participant should be able to effectively plan a wilderness experience for his group. The topics in this area will include permits, legal aspects, budgeting, site selection, transportation, selection of participants, use of governmental agencies.

History and Culture. It is encouraged that before the wilderness experience, the participants will examine, through discussion and readings, the site's history and culture. The participants will become aware of the site's history and culture during the wilderness experience. Integration of the area, particularly flora and wildlife as well as special geological processes, will be included in the experience.

Equipment. The selection, design, repair and storage of equipment will be discussed and practiced. Participants will be instructed in specific equipment needed for individuals, sub- group, and groups. Cost, availability, weight and quality of equipment will be discussed. Special equipment and instruction in its care will be determined by participation in special activities that may be included within the basic outline.

Clothing. Clothes should suit the type of activity planned. Instruction in the proper selection and fit of clothing to fit the location and season will be given. Sources of clothing, cost, repair, cleaning, and variety of substitutions will be reviewed.

Rations. By instruction and practice each participant will be able to adequately plan, package, and cook his or her own rations for a two-week experience. Knowledge of food cost, nutritional value, weight, and availability will be detailed within the course. Emphasis will be placed on low-cost, personally selected foods that allow for variety in self-planned menus.

Basic Camping Skills. Emphasis is placed on camping in a way that has a low impact on the environment. Very much integrated with the environmental ethic attitude will be basic skills such as when and where to camp, the camping fire, cooking area, pitching a tent. The basic camping skills will also concern the safety of the individual and protection of equipment.

Health and Sanitation. The techniques to be taught and practiced are essential to the well-being, safety, and comfort of the wilderness user. In the area of sanitation, water quality, and care of human waste, preparation of food will be outlined and practiced. Health practices for being in the out-of-doors as well as bathing and laundry will be included in this section.

Navigation. The art of getting from one place to another, and understanding how it is done efficiently and safely. Map interpretation, use of a compass, limiting factors of weather, physical restrictions, and motivation of the group will be included in the course content.

Trail Techniques. Safety, comfort, and group organization on the trail. Prehiking plans that encompass a time control, energy control, and climate control plan will be practiced. Rhythmic breathing and walking techniques, and trail courtesy are included in this section.

Weather. Identification of sources for weather information and the implications of the effects of weather on the comfort and safety of the group. Instruction given during the course will be reading the signs of changing weather and general characteristics of weather patterns in the specific region where the course is held.

Emergency Procedures. The care and treatment of those injuries that are most likely to occur in the wild outdoors. Specific skills to be covered are treatment for broken bones, fatigue, shock, bruises and blisters, hypothermia, and strains. Evacuation procedures, litter construction, and signaling will be instructed and practiced. Emphasis on avoiding emergency situations will be stressed.

Survival Techniques. A major emphasis will be placed on avoiding survival situations but instruction will be given on emergency survival training. Survival techniques will include food gathering and shelter construction. Search and rescue procedures, legal implications and cost factors involved will also be covered in this topic area.

Aquatic Safety Procedures. Practice of river crossing techniques such as a tyrolean traverse and stream-wading procedures. This area would also include using and preparing water for drinking purposes.

Specialized Knowledge of One Mode of Travel. Depending on the particular emphasis of each course, the participant will be exposed to specialized knowledge in one mode of travel. Examples of specific modes of travel are hiking, canoeing, horsepacking. Specialized knowledge will be outlined to provide the participants with an opportunity to practice skills that will enable them to travel with more enjoyment and safety.

Supervised Leadership Experiences. Each participant will have the opportunity to apply personal knowledge and judgment to instruct peers under supervision. The leadership experience will require the participant to synthesize and apply safety, leadership ability, and environmental impact principles to the experience he is leading.

Judgment in Leaders. To encourage the development of judgment in decision making through experience. This will take place through the opportunity of learning and practicing the basic skills necessary to bring a group to the wild outdoors and applying the skills through leadership experiences during the course. Through supervision, the participant will be instructed to always teach the "why" of any techniques.

Evaluation (Phase I). Before completion of the wilderness experience, the following evaluations will take place: participants' evaluation of participants in skills and techniques, leadership abilities; instructor's evaluation of participants; participants' evaluation of instructor; and participants' evaluation of themselves in relation to other participants. Phase II evaluation will take place three weeks after the experience with a listing of "questions for final discussions" that will be distributed before the course.

Petzoldt added his wisdom to the results of the October meeting in December of 1977 when he wrote a draft of his ideas on the purpose of the Wilderness Use Education Association and sent it to organizing committee members for their reactions. A copy of that draft follows.

WILDERNESS USE EDUCATION ASSOCIATION

Rough Draft of Purpose (December 1977)

The purpose of the association is to encourage enjoyable, safe *use* of our wilderness and the *conservation* of our wilderness through education of the user and group leader.

The above is timely and necessary since laws, regulations, and use restrictions cannot protect the environment against the uneducated user. Most unenjoyable outings, accidents, searches, deaths, and environmental damage can be prevented by education of the user and the group leader. Insurance rates might be lowered for groups having leaders with certified outdoor education. Those selecting leaders for wilderness trips and those individuals depending on the group leader for safety and competence would have a basis for evaluation. Administrators of public lands and others might find such standards useful in planning land use, conservation, and permit issuance.

The association will certify "course leaders" who are capable of planning, outfitting, conducting, and teaching certification courses of at least four weeks' duration in actual wilderness environment. The association has done research with such groups and has developed a course outline of the basics to be taught. These are basic skills, techniques, knowledge, judgment, every outdoorsman should possess. Those passing courses led by course leaders certified by the association will be certified as having the training and education. Graduates of the courses should be able to plan and execute outings for their lifetime recreational needs and act as leaders and advisors to others.

In addition, this training is a necessary foundation for all who wish to pursue specific outdoor specialties such as outdoor teaching, leading wilderness trips, or hunting, fishing, mountaineering, canoeing, backpacking, skiing, and river running activities. Such training would be helpful to persons managing lands for recreational use and conservation.

The association will inspect courses in the field and improve and change programming as judgment indicates. Certification and the follow-up on activities of certified users and certified course leaders will be done by the association. Members of the association are acting as individuals who believe that education of the user and group leader is a necessary aspect of wilderness recreational use and wilderness conservation.

The Wilderness Use Education Association was incorporated in the state of Wyoming as a non-profit corporation (certificate of incorporation in Appendix) on January 2, 1979. The original Board of Trustees included the following persons:

1. Dr. Robert Christie, director of Bradford Woods, Indiana University
2. Eugene Fear, president, Survival Education Association
3. Charles A. Gregory, director of Stone Valley Outdoor Center, Penn State University
4. Patrick LaValla, president, National Association for Search and Rescue
5. Dr. Frank Lupton, Jr., professor and coordinator of ECOEE, Western Illinois University
6. Henry Nichol, U.S. Department of Agriculture (retired)
7. Paul Petzoldt, founder of NOLS (National Outdoor Leadership School)
8. John L. Vidakovich, attorney from Lander, Wyoming

The word "Use" was dropped from the name of the organization in 1980 and it became the Wilderness Education Association. After functioning as the director of the organization from its early beginning, Paul Petzoldt was officially appointed executive director at a salary of $12,000 per year in 1980. Over the years he contributed to WEA thousands of hours of time and many thousands of dollars to help keep the organization going. He traveled thousands of miles to many university campuses to speak with students, faculty, and administrators. He also spoke at a number of conferences and workshops informing people about the new certification/education program. As a result of his efforts, many students were recruited to programs, and a number of universities became affiliates.

An advisory committee comprised of persons from throughout the United States was formed in 1978 and 1979. While it never was utilized as much as anticipated, it provided a group of persons who were supportive of WEA and were willing to give input as requested.

The Wilderness Education Association headquarters was located at Paul Petzoldt's lodge at Alta, Wyoming, near Driggs, Idaho, for several years until 1986 when Sandy Braun, the executive director at that time, resigned to pursue other interests. It was also at this time that WEA became a membership organization. The Board of Trustees took action to move all courses that were being offered through WEA headquarters to various universities that were already offering courses. Headquarters was moved to the campus of Western Illinois University where WEA President Frank Lupton was chairman of the Department of Recreation and Park Administration. He functioned as the acting executive director for nearly two years, until a $28,000 grant was received from the Adirondack North Country Association through the efforts of Jack Drury.

The terms of the grant included moving WEA headquarters to Saranac Lake, New York, to space provided by North Country Community College, home of Jack Drury, writer of the grant proposal, WEA board member, North Country Community College associate professor and head of their Wilderness Recreation Leadership Program. At the June 1988 meeting of WEA, Drury was elected as the new president. Jeff Brown was hired as the new executive director and started his duties in September.

The Wilderness Education Association created the Paul Petzoldt Award for Excellence in Wilderness Education, which was awarded to Ernest "Tap" Tapley at the 1988 WEA Saranc Lake meeting. This meeting also included a reception for Jeff Brown, new executive director, open house for new WEA, offices, recognition of others who have played significant roles in the evolution of WEA and the recognition of Jack Drury as the new WEA president.

Project Adventure: A Brief History

Dick Prouty
Project Adventure

Can any of the insights traditionally gained in a wilderness Outward Bound setting be learned in the course of a twice a week, forty-five minute high school Physical Education program? Can lessons about how to solve problems in a group learned in a Physical Education class be transferred to cooperative work in a Biology class? Can new physical activities be invented to help students to go beyond previously set limits to risk taking? Can public school teachers and counselors learn to use a cooperative style of education which challenges them to be a bit more vulnerable to the students? ...And learn to like it? Can students help solve problems for groups in their communities, serve real needs, and learn valuable curricula and social lessons in the process?

In 1970, these questions were beginning increasingly to show up in the conversations of educators interested in reform. The Outward Bound movement had stirred real interest in using a new set of methods. Jerry Pieh, the young principal of Hamilton-Wenham Jr./Sr. High School in Hamilton, Massachusetts, was one of those asking such questions.

As a young graduate student of education, Jerry had helped his father, Bob Pieh, start the Minnesota Outward Bound School in 1962, and had shared the excitement of those early years. This experience had given Jerry had a strong appreciation for the power of the Outward Bound approach. As principal of Hamilton-Wenham Jr./Sr. High, Jerry was in a position to examine those questions in a practical way. He and a colleague, Gary Baker, wrote a three-year development proposal to the federal Office of Education that would try to answer the question of how to 'mainstream' the Outward Bound process into a secondary public school setting. He called the new program "Project Adventure."

In attempting to bring Outward Bound strategies to a school setting, Jerry Pieh was returning to the basic roots of Outward Bound. The founder of Outward Bound, Dr. Kurt Hahn, was foremost an educator, with roots in the classical private schools of Germany and

Britain. Dr. Hahn felt that the classical school curriculum was not enough for the development of the whole child. His work with the Gordounstoun School in Scotland had led, during World War II, to the establishment of the first Outward Bound School and later to the worldwide Outward Bound school movement. Hahn's original impulse, however, had been to work within the confines of a traditional school. Jerry Pieh sought in his Project Adventure program to bring these ideas back to the setting in which they were first practiced. This had been done before: Lincoln-Sudbury High School in Lincoln, Mass., had an Outward Bound-type course in the late sixties, for example. That particular program, however, was taught by Outward Bound staff, not by public school teachers. Such activities, however, tended to be isolated from the standard curriculum and were almost totally dependent on teacher interest. Pieh wanted more than that. He sought to have the Outward Bound process become a part of the standard high school curriculum.

The funding of the Project Adventure grant in 1971 allowed Jerry to hire key staff with Outward Bound backgrounds and to begin the planning of a new curriculum approach. Many teachers were involved in the planning of this grant, and involved themselves in Outward Bound and other training experiences. Teachers, Project Adventure staff, and administrators then set to work writing and experimenting with curriculum. The largest component was focused on tenth grade physical education, but English, history, science, theater arts, and counseling were also explored in the context of what came to be known as "Adventure Activities."

Bob Lentz was the first director of Project Adventure. Bob had been a teacher, a principal, and had worked at Outward Bound as director of their teacher training programs. Bob also had a deep understanding of the power of the experiential learning process. Here he describes one of his original insights about the effect of an experiential/internship program on students:

> We got back report after report on these kids about what a lively, alert, intelligent, responsible student this is. And you would visit the student on his project and my God, he was alive, and alert and responsible. You'd look through his records and ask teachers about him and the answer you'd get was, "wasn't alive, was lethargic, wasn't alert, wasn't responsible." A kid would come back off his project — for a few days he'd be alive and alert, then his old behavior would come back. That simply said to me, we're missing some vital things here.

Bob found in the Project Adventure curriculum a way to help students become more "alive, alert, and responsible" inside schools, and to institutionalize the process. As Josh Miner and Joe Boldt say in their history of Outward Bound (1981; 336), "No other innovative educational proposal spinning off from Outward Bound has enjoyed a greater success with the educational establishment than Project Adventure." The reason for this success was the willingness and ability of the Project and its staff under Bob Lentz's leadership to work with teachers and schools, empowering them to institutionalize the curriculum changes.

The nature of these curriculum changes were creative and profound, yet not so dramatic that the teachers could not relate them to their existing schedules and class objectives. The original Hamilton-Wenham model was an interdisciplinary concept that focused on the sophomore class. Every sophomore took a year-long Project Adventure physical education class that went through a sequence of innovative warm-ups, trust building exercises, initiative problems, and low and high ropes course elements. Two basic goals were constantly sought and reinforced: that the students would learn how to solve problems in a group more creatively and efficiently; and that preconceived barriers to what was possible often held both the group and the individual from increasing achievement. Concurrently, the curricula in the sophomore's English, social studies and biology classes had units written by their teachers that reinforced the same goals in pursuit of traditional academic course objectives. For example, a student may have learned that the value of planning to use the resources of the group, and keeping a watchful eye on the time alloted for the task, were both necessary to the successful accomplishment of an initiative problem. In biology class, the same student may have put both of those learnings into use again in planning how the student's learning group was to gather data for their investigation of the fresh water swamp behind the high school. The student would finally participate in the adventurous 'Swamp Walk' where the student's data, gathering role in the small cooperative learning group of the class would have been negotiated before the trip. Later, the students would use class time to work in groups to prepare the report.

Other classes would have similar experiential units, using cooperative group strategies. Two-to-three day camping trips that used the environment of the campsite to learn course objectives were valuable as peak experiences where students "put it all together." For example, the annual trip to Arcadia National Park in Maine allowed the biology students to gather specimens for their saltwater tide pool unit. The Hahn service ethic was honored and fused with learning objectives in cross-age tutoring projects, recycling projects, and other activities done for accredited learning classes coordinated by PA staff.

EVALUATION

During the second and third year of the grant, the program was submitted to a rigorous evaluation by one of the full-time staff members, Mary Smith. Finished during the third year of the program, 1974, the evaluation covered the full sophomore class that took the program each year—224 in 1971, and 231 in 1972. Six instruments were administered pre- and post-program application. The instruments were the Tennessee Self-Concept Scale, the School Climate Survey (based on David McClelland's Classroom Climate Survey), two different kinds of student survey, the AAPHERD physical fitness test, and the Rotter Scale of Internal vs. External Control. The specific goals of the evaluation were as follows:

1. To improve self-concept, confidence, and sense of personal competence among participants.
2. To increase psycho-motor skills, especially in the areas of balance and coordination.
3. Go overcome pervasive passivity, apathy, and uninvolvement among students.

The full evaluation report showed strong positive results with statistically significant changes on the Tennessee and Rotter Scales, and consistently strong qualitative data. "Qualitative data" is the evaluation term for those individual reports that come from various types of participants. The following statement is from the qualitative write-up section of the 1974 report: "Not as shy as I used to be but I am still quite shy. Have stayed after school more to get involved in other things. Got up enough courage to stand in front of about 20 sixth grade kids and conduct a lesson." The "change in self-concept" that the evaluation indicates somehow makes more sense through this girl's comments than through the dry numbers. This particular comment from what might be termed a reluctant participant in the P.E. component, demonstrates the type of carryover in "involvement" and "courage," to use the girl's own words, we have found to be typical of an average student's participation.

NATIONAL DEMONSTRATION SITE AWARD

The strong evaluation results, were responsible for the award in 1974 by the federal Office of Education of National Demonstration School Status and subsequent National

Diffusion Network Model program status and funding for dissemination. The National Diffusion Network (NDN) was a new Office of Education program founded on the belief that excellent programs that have had a rigorous evaluation should be shared nationally, with the original teachers of the new program sharing the methods with other teachers directly. From 1974 to 1981, the Hamilton-Wenham School District received a Dissemination grant each year from the NDN to subsidize the 'adoption' of the PA model by other schools nationally. As Director of the PA dissemination effort for the Hamilton-Wenham Schools, Bob Lentz each year set a goal of how many adoptions were likely to occur and how they were to happen.

It is no exaggeration to state that the NDN years literally put Project Adventure on the map nationally. The interest in the PA program was strong anyway, and with a nationally-based program with assistance offices and some funding available in each state, the "disseminating" of the PA model was made much easier. The "adoption process," as the NDN language put it, happened in many different fashions. A typical adoption path would be as follows: a teacher would hear of a great new program (PA) from a friend or at a convention; the teacher would call PA and learn about the NDN and about PA workshops offered; the teacher would convince her administrator to contact the nearest NDN state facilitator's office and apply for a grant; the teacher and perhaps several associates would take a five-day PA workshop in either the P.E. or academic model; if a ropes course was necessary, PA staff would construct it on site, usually partially funded by the NDN; follow-up assistance and training would occur over the next year. By 1980, over 400 schools in most of the states of the country had adopted at least one component (academic or physical education) of the original PA program at Hamilton-Wenham.

Involvement in the NDN process required that the PA staff be more accountable and rigorous in the spreading of the PA model than they otherwise might have been. Follow-up surveys, tracking of the adoptions numbers, tracking of the "key elements" in place at each site, evaluation of workshops, and a review of the strategies in dissemination efforts that had and had not worked, were required on annual reports for funding extensions. The key elements concept was especially helpful. The idea was to identify what elements of the original adoption were responsible for the significant evaluation results, and be able to target the trainings of new teachers and staff at adopter sites so that the evaluation results could in principle be replicated. The key elements checklist was then available to a state facilitator, or anyone who could visit an adopter and see what was occurring or not. The original Hamilton-Wenham program had been a large and complex effort, and most schools would not ever reach that level of adoption. A variety of the key elements checklist, as devised by Bob and his staff, are still used today by the PA staff as a valuable teaching tool and vehicle to think about what we are really talking about when we say "adopt the program."

KEY ELEMENTS OF AN ADVENTURE CURRICULUM

In developing your curriculum, the following components should be an integral part of the final product. It is, however, appropriate to stress some elements more than others, depending on the curriculum you plan. The qualities that make up the Adventure Approach curriculum include:

1. A sense of adventure, unpredictability, drama and suspense. This tone may emerge from the situation (a cliff, slum, or canoe trip) or from the teacher who builds drama, anticipation, suspense, and mystique into the learning experience for students through stories, comments, and even humor.

2. A consistently high (but accomplishable) level of expectation demanded and created by both the intrinsic and external forces. Students need to be convinced that not just anyone could have done this, and that the teacher CARES that the goal is reached.

3. A success orientation in which growth is supported and encouraged and in which the positive is emphasized. Encouragement is one crucial ingredient in resolving the conflict between high expectations and the need for a successful experience.

4. An atmosphere of mutual support in which cooperation, encouragement, and interpersonal concerns are consistently present.

5. A sense of enjoyment, fun, and the opportunity to laugh at a situation, each other, and oneself.

6. An approach to learning which makes use of group problem-solving, which allows for a variety of personal contributions and which presents problems that can't ordinarily be solved individually. The rewards are set up for group effort rather than individual success or competition.

7. The use of a learning laboratory that is more complex, more engaging, less predictable and less familiar than a school classroom.

8. The merging of intellectual, social, physical, and emotional learning and development.

9. A significant amount of cognitive work related directly to abstractions and questions previously developed in the classroom, or subsequently to be developed.

10. The combining of moments of active involvement with moments of personal and group reflection and evaluation. An awareness that teachable and learnable moments are unpredictable but necessary ingredients in curriculum.

11. A definite organization and structure which define the limits of the experience and state expectations, but within which the participants have freedom to make decisions, choices, and even mistakes.

12. An economic and structural reasonableness which allows the curriculum to effectively compete for dollars and other resources within an educational economy which is limited in its resources. Neither too long, nor too exotic nor too expensive.

ADVENTURE-BASED COUNSELING

The potential for the use of the Project Adventure activities with the Special Needs populations of the schools had always been recognized by the PA staff. Self-concept improvement is basic to the needs of most Special Needs students. Work with these students was not a first priority, however, as the PA model was intended to be a comprehensive school model affecting all the students. But there was significant work in early years in two ways: first was the Action Seminar at Hamilton-Wenham Regional High School, an interdisciplinary four-period class which drew on a wide mixture of students (outlined under the same title in the Project Adventure book *Teaching Through Adventure*). This class was taught by PA staff members Jim Schoel and Steve Webster. Those students participated in Adventure activities, group construction and craft projects, and community service. No formal assessment of the students was made prior to entry, but quiet referrals insured that half the students were experiencing trouble in school and required an "alternative" form of instruction. The Action Seminar concept was later carried into the Gloucester Public Schools, where it was incorporated as the Gloucester Museum School, and later as Project Alliance.

The second expression of Adventure Counseling was an outpatient therapy group at the Addison Gilbert Hospital, Gloucester, Mass. Beginning in 1974, Paul Radcliffe, a PA-trained school psychologist, worked under the supervision of Dr. Phil Cutter, and teamed with Mary Smith, a PA staff member, to conduct a weekly two-hour Adventure group. The hospital therapy group concept, with its intake and consultation process, was subsequently incorporated into the Gloucester Public Schools' psychological services, and was called the Learning Activities Group.

The development of the Adventure-Based Counseling (ABC) process into a curriculum equivalent to the earlier interdisciplinary work at Hamilton-Wenham took place with the funding of a Massachusetts State Department of Education grant in 1980-1983. Paul Radcliffe and Bill Cuff worked with personnel from Gloucester, Hamilton-Wenham, and Manchester, Mass., to refine the process of intake, grouping, staffing, activities selection, and staff training. This development grant was significant in that it put the PA work with special needs students in schools on the same footing as the original PA work. The evaluation was extensive and again showed significant gains on the Tennessee in students in three systems over two years. On the basis of the evaluation, the Massachusetts State Department of Education awarded the program validation as a State Model Program.

The development of the ABC model and its formal evaluation actually accelerated a trend that had been there in seed form from the beginning. The NDN had encouraged the dissemination of the PA model beyond schools into all types of "educational service providers," the bureaucratic term for camps, youth centers, clinics and really any place where an educational function was occurring. The first Adventure-Based Counseling Workshop was offered in May of 1979, and the response was strong, with over thirty persons attending the four-day workshop. Persons from residential clinics and hospitals, therapeutic camps and drug treatment centers attended, as well as school counselors, psychologists and alternative school teachers. The adapting of the program's activities to all these sites continued after this workshop, and the movement of the PA outreach into these types of organizations increased.

TRANSITION TO INDEPENDENCE

I had first met Bob Lentz in the fall of 1970 when Jim Schoel, one of the original four PA staff, introduced me to him. Jim had been one of my instructors on an Outward Bound Teacher Practicum course that had been run by the Hurricane Island School out of Bartlett's Island off Maine the preceding summer. As a social studies teacher and director of an Experiential Education program at the neighboring Manchester Schools, I worked closely with both Jim and Bob through the seventies, organizing Adventure-type programs in both the Manchester and Gloucester schools. The Adventure work was involving, frustrating, and exciting; often all at the same time. When we started an early ABC group in Manchester for kids in difficulty in the junior high, I had some of my most meaningful teaching times. In late 1979, Jim, Bob, Paul Radcliffe, and I began meeting to write a grant to develop and refine the ABC model. I enjoyed the challenge of writing the grant, and was intrigued by the possibilities of helping PA grow. I applied for a leave in early 1980, and Bob and I agreed to terms of employment.

In the spring of 1980, Bob Lentz announced that he was resigning as director to assume the principalship of Groves High School in Birmingham, Michigan. After nearly ten years with Project Adventure at Hamilton-Wenham, Bob was ready for a new challenge. The chance to influence change in a public school in the position that research showed had the most direct influence, the principalship, was just such a challenge. He left Project Adventure in good shape, with a new NDN cycle of funding, the good will of the host school system, a strong reputation for quality, a group of experienced key staff, and a system of helping a complex program adoption process happen with minimal problems. Most importantly, he left with a feeling of accomplishment, because the original goal of devising a system to mainstream the goals of Outward Bound into schools had been advanced significantly. Not that there wasn't *plenty* of work left to do, he told us.

Karl Rohnke assumed the director's position after Bob left. Karl had been with PA since its start and in many ways was the most well known staff member. As author of the PA text, *Cowtails and Cobras*, Karl had brought to the many readers of that book a real hands-on understanding of the techniques, methods, and spirit necessary to implement the physical education curriculum that had started at Hamilton-Wenham. Karl's creative abilities had guided the evolution of the ropes course elements and the games, stunts and initiatives that were the core of the curriculum. Karl's ability to play and have obvious fun in a workshop was invaluable modeling for teachers and staff being trained. Karl enjoyed using these strengths and continued as director to construct courses, lead workshops and write up new curriculum ideas. Karl was also decisive in letting us know what he did not like about his new role; thinking about budgets, organizational issues and paperwork hassles. He and I agreed about a year after I started that I would assume the director's role, and he would concentrate on what he did best, which was writing, researching new activities and ropes course elements, and leading workshops.

The early eighties were tough times for education of all sorts. The Reagan revolution was causing increasing cutbacks in funding for schools. The "back-to-basics" movement in public schools was increasing and giving people who wanted to get students to learn in new and creative ways a few more hurdles to jump. Yet, in spite of the mood, the flow of people to training workshops for PA and on to subsequent adoptions continued. The PA budget as part of the Hamilton-Wenham schools in 1981-82 was $345,000, of which only $55,000 was federal money from the National Diffusion Network. The remainder was revenue from workshop fees, ropes course construction and the sale of supplies and books. There were five full-time staff members in the Hamilton offices. In addition, Alan Sentowski, who had been a biology teacher at Hamilton-Wenham and a key early staff member, had started a satellite office in Savannah, Georgia.

In a series of meetings in 1981, we decided with the Hamilton-Wenham administrators that it would be best if PA were to separate from the school. The growth of PA had surpassed the expectations of the school, and while justly proud of the spread of their home-grown product, they felt it best for the increasing growth to go on separately. The decision to separate seemed to fit for everyone, as the PA staff also sensed that PA had the potential to grow in new and important ways and that this could best be done independently. In the next year an amiable agreement was drawn up, a Board of Directors chosen by Karl and I, and the formal incorporation of Project Adventure Inc. as a non-profit 501-(c)(3) organization was made in September 1981. The articles of incorporation affirmed that the main purpose of the new corporation was the " dissemination" of PA programs. We had chosen to continue the basic direction that we had been operating under at the school, but now there was a sense of anticipation that new possibilities awaited.

STEADY GROWTH

The original grant in 1970 had funded a staff of five to work closely with the Hamilton-Wenham staff. The staff of PA in 1981 was six full-time staff, and an additional 10 certified trainers. Certified Trainers were encouraged by the NDN as teachers who could teach training workshops nationally with the same "fidelity" as original staff but with more cost-effectiveness. The staff of PA in early 1989 was 37 full-time persons, with a National Certified Trainer staff of 50 that includes facilitators with expertise and practical experience in all workshop areas. The growth since separation has been continuous with an increase in revenue each year averaging over 30 percent. The sources of revenue are in the same categories as they were in 1981—now they are called "revenue centers"—workshop and training, catalogue sales, Ropes Course construction, and grants and contracts for research purposes. The organization has continued to serve the schools who wanted to expand an existing program or start a new one. The momentum of the word of mouth advertising of the existing "installed base" of PA school programs was strong. As teachers and administrators moved on to new jobs, they often brought their favorite program with them. Both Jerry Pieh, as headmaster of Milton Academy, and Bob Lentz, as principal of Groves High, had PA help them implement a program. Important new work was also done in urban schools in Cambridge, Savannah, Pittsburgh, Columbus, and New York, as the ability of PA activities to motivate for achievement and develop group cooperation proved effective for the multi-ethnic populations of urban schools.

Although work with schools continued to grow, the main reason for the growth of PA was the staff's ability to work with a variety of organizations other than schools and to help them customize a program for their needs. Through the eighties, PA staff, worked with camps, youth agencies such as the Boy Scouts and Girl Scouts, therapeutic agencies, drug and alcohol treatment centers, psychiatric hospitals, colleges, conference centers, corporate training centers, children's homes, job training centers, outdoor education centers, and state agencies. Throughout this expansion of the audiences that the PA staff served, the continuity of the early training models served as a starting point for new work, and the in-house expertise of the organization contracting with PA for assistance was used to draw out a customized program.

While the range of groups served by PA seems wide, the trainings have followed four generic models: Adventure Programming which served physical education and recreation programs; Adventure-Based Counseling which served therapeutic programs; Academic Programming, which served classroom academic programs; and Staff Development Programming, which served educational and corporate adult training needs. Project Adventure has an entry level workshop in each area which uses essentially the same activity base with some modifications. Each workshop, however, is taught by PA staff or certified trainers who have experience and expertise in the program area which the workshop is addressing. By the end of each 4- or 5-day workshop, the participant is ready to design a more expansive program with more specified training, and often is ready to start a modest program in their area.

SOUTHERN OFFICE

One of the key supports of the growth of PA in the eighties was the Southern office. Alan Sentowski had begun the office at an outdoor education center in Savannah in 1980. The office was moved in 1984 to Atlanta to take advantage of the central location of Atlanta. One of the important groups being served by the Southern office in 1984 was the Georgia Department of Youth Services. Cindy Simpson, a school psychologist, had attended a PA workshop in 1981 and gone on to develop a community-based, six-week program for juvenile offenders in the state. Working closely with Juvenile Judge Virgil Costley of Covington, Cindy had developed a program that used a tightly structured Adventure-Based Counseling approach and infused it with academic support, parent counseling,and career counseling. An evaluation of the program from 1983 to 1986 by the Georgia DYS showed that 94 percent of the youths that started the program finished and that the recidivism rate was 15 percent for the three years after the program.

In 1984, Cindy joined Alan Sentowski in the Atlanta office and teamed up with staff associate John Call, who coordinated construction and technical trainings. The Atlanta office relocation proved to be a good decision, as the small staff began to experience a rapid increase in the demand for PA, services soon after the move was made. Alan left PA in June of 1985 to pursue other interests, and Cindy Simpson took over the leadership role. The growth in staff and services rendered has continued and accelerated under Cindy's leadership. The development of innovative community-based direct service models such as Challenge has become a research and development specialty of the southern office. An alternative school model and a jobs training model were started successfully.

By 1989, the southern office had sixteen staff and accounted for about one third of the total PA budget. All of the functions of the Hamilton office were carried on in the southern office with the exception of the catalogue sale of ropes course equipment and PA publications. The growth was made easier by the move of the office in the summer of 1988 to a new site in Covington, Georgia, 30 miles southeast of Atlanta. With the help of Judge Costly and Pierce Cline, another member of an advisory board that PA had formed for the Southern office, Cindy had managed to acquire in 1987 an unoccupied former Elks Club lodge on a five-acre pond. Located on a total of 70 acres, the 12,000 square-ft building was renovated, and housed the Atlanta-based PA staff and programs by the fall of 1988.

THERAPEUTIC PROGRAM GROWTH

The history of PA clearly shows that as the organization works with other client organizations to help them implement a PA program, the resulting customizing process often breaks new ground. The unique issues and needs of the client result in modifications and new designs of existing PA models that often can then be used by other organizations of a similar type that PA helps. This process has clearly been at work in the dissemination of the ABC model. Therapeutic institutions that ranged from public schools to therapeutic camps to counseling centers to residential treatment facilities and psychiatric hospitals implemented a variety of the ABC model in the eighties.

One of the more important early ABC adoptions was as a result of our work with the Institute of Pennsylvania Hospital in Philadelphia. In 1981, four staff of the Therapeutic Recreation department led by Rick Thomas attended an ABC workshop in Hamilton. A grant by a local benefactor to the hospital, one of the oldest and most respected psychiatric institutions in the country, had paid for the training and later for the ropes course that we constructed on the rolling grounds of the hospital. Under the leadership of Rick Thomas, who worked closely with PA staff Paul Radcliffe and Jim Schoel, the Institute began to use the ABC model with a short-term residential adolescent group. The hospital evaluations of the patients' progress in the program were excellent. The therapeutic recreation department has worked with the clinical staff of the hospital to expand the program to other groups including mixed diagnosis adult treatment groups, drug and alcohol groups and eating disorder groups. The schedules and length of the ABC activities in these groups are somewhat different, but they all occur on the grounds of the hospital and often include the ropes course.

Rick Thomas (1981) has some interesting comments on why the ABC model works so well in the hospital setting:

> We want to help patients be more independent, decrease their feelings of helplessness, and get away from the idea that someone else has the secrets about their well-being and who they are. We try to educate patients about their strengths, not looking for pathology. The people we see need experience in doing differently, to experience themselves as different. They're not ready for insight. They need to be brought up to another level before they acquire that. They need to learn by *doing* first. They simply do not have the ability for abstract thinking. Generally, if they do abstract, it is merely a form of intellectualization, with few feelings attached. As Glasser says, "Act differently, even if you don't feel differently."

Rick's comments help explain the power of the ABC model to help the psychiatric patient. The eighties saw PA work with hospitals and other residential care facilities on an increasing basis. By 1989, we had helped over 100 hospitals implement a variety of the ABC program. The use of an integrated adventure-based hospital program was becoming more widely accepted in the psychiatric field by the end of the eighties, and the increased refinement of the program was proceeding rapidly. Cindy Simpson from the Southern office and Paul Radcliffe from the Hamilton office teamed up to lead PA's efforts in this emerging area.

The need for a PA text for the emergence of the ABC field began to be critical as the number of trainings and requests for assistance increased in the early eighties. In 1985, we received notice that the Culpepper Foundation of New York City had funded our proposal to research and write a new text for the ABC field. The book was written in a collaborative effort, with Jim Schoel assuming the lead author position and Paul Radcliffe and I assisting. Jim had one full year funded by the grant to research, interview, and write. It took another unfunded year of work by the three of us to complete the book, but when it was finished, we were pleased with the result. We had a text, *Islands of Healing*, that would guide all those workshop participants at the more than 300 institutions of some sort that had an ABC model and others in the field to share the results of more than a decade of development work. It was a fitting complement to *Cowtails and Cobras* and the other PA texts for the other models, and should, we thought, more firmly establish the credibility of the model for all practitioners.

EXECUTIVE REACH: CORPORATE TRAINING

In the late seventies, Karl Rohnke and Bob Lentz had taught education courses at Boston University in adventure education and had met Tony Langston of the faculty. They discussed and planned how to use the PA activities base with the business school classes that Tony was beginning to work with. Tony went on to start a corporate training program at BU. The new program, Executive Challenge, found a good reception in the high tech clients of the Route 128 area in the late seventies, and quickly became the leader in this new way to work with corporate training: non-wilderness trainings using the range of initiatives, and ropes course elements. Other consultants began to hear of the success of the Executive Challenge model and began to approach PA for assistance in developing a program. As a result of these inquiries, we began to think seriously in 1983 about this emerging area and how it fit into our organization.

In the winter of 1984, we received a call from a human resource group at Digital Equipment Corporation. They had heard about our programs and wanted us to design a team building workshop for their work group. Paul Radcliffe and I worked with the team leader to design a four-day workshop. The result was a great success from the work-team's viewpoint. A three-month follow-up visit on site revealed improved communication, levels of trust, and an ability to take initiatives involving risk with more confidence. A twenty-minute video was produced with Digital's help, and was designed for both Digital and PA use.

We did work with other Digital groups as a result of this initial effort and decided that we should develop the capability to do corporate training. In 1985, Ann Smolowe joined PA to help develop and market a PA corporate model. Ann had a varied background that included a business school education, three years working for the American Stock Exchange, and a complete thru-hike of the Appalachian Trail. Most importantly, she had a strong desire to bring innovative outdoor training to the corporate setting. Our mutual goal was to develop a PA staff development model that would allow us to eventually have the capability to train others in adventure-based corporate training skills. In addition, we hoped to be able to generate revenue from our direct service efforts with companies to help our overall mission in other areas.

By 1989, we had developed a significant track record with a number of larger Fortune 500 companies as well as smaller firms. We had developed customized trainings around the themes of encouraging innovation, culture change initiatives, multiskill retraining, leadership, risk-taking motivation, as well as more standard team building option. The ability to train others easily because of our overall mission had helped define some of our trainings. Frank Iarossi, president of Exxon Shipping in Houston, had heard Elizabeth Ross-Kanter of the Harvard Business School expound on the need for companies to master change, and had become convinced of the need for his company to begin to change its culture. We contracted with Exxon Shipping in 1987 to train teams of company facilitators, who in turn led all 1,000 employees through a one-day team building and skill training that was part of a larger week-long training for all employees, designed by an outside consulting firm. Exxon Shipping was on the way to becoming less hierarchical, less rigid, more able to identify problems earlier and work toward their resolution. In a modern technological environment, the supertanker captain no longer had all the answers or even a knowledge about what many of the problems were. Specialization of knowledge and skills made flexible workteam strategies a must.

THE ACTIVITY BASE

All the program models in the world wouldn't work if we did not have an effective arsenal of activities that could be used to accomplish the program aims. The games, prop and nonprop initiatives, and Challenge Ropes Course elements that the original staff modified and created for the short 50-minute P.E. sessions at Hamilton-Wenham were responsible for the ability of all the subsequent programs to be able to work on-site, indoors if necessary, and to imbue almost any training curriculum with the aims and energy of the PA learning goals. The constant renewing of this activity base and the refinement of the skills training and assessment methods that were necessary as the numbers of adoption sites and participants mushroomed were two key tasks that have helped sustain PA's growth.

One of Karl's strengths is the ability to create new activities and the enjoyment he gets from doing so. An environment of creativity, of pushing for the new modification or of putting together two previously separate things has been important to renewing our base. Karl also works easily with others creating and likes to give them liberal credit, always important in developing new things. PA now has a fifty-element repetoire of ropes course elements, including the following notable PA inventions: Wild Woosey, Mohawk Walk, Proutys Landing, Pamper Pole, Hickory Jump, Seagull Landing, and the Flying Squirrel. The first indoor elements were built in the Newburyport, Mass. gym in 1972, and by 1985 every outdoor element had also been constructed in some sort of indoor environment. The refinement of the technology and equipment for the ropes course has been constant with the following at one point being an innovation: galvanized cable, through-bolting, strand vices, telephone poles and accompanying guy technology, custom-made pulley systems for the belay cable and for the Zip Wire. The invention of new activities was even more pronounced in the initiative and game area, and the publication of *Silver Bullets: A Guide to Initiative Problems and Adventure Games*, was a notable benchmark for the organization. The possibilities continue to expand as PA has become a gathering point for others' ideas in this area.

The direct construction of ropes course elements for others was a service of PA as early as 1972, when Karl built the first PA indoor climbing wall for Newburyport High School. Since then, the direct construction of elements for others has become one of PA's key services. PA will build over 100 courses this year, and will provide repair and safety check services at many more. Located all over the United States, and this year in Australia, Singapore, Hong Kong and Europe, these 100 will join the approximately 1,000 courses PA has constructed since it started. PA runs a catalogue supply service for materials to construct courses and to resupply the existing courses with rope and other equipment. One of the more recent developments in the way we help people construct has been the creation of the package, Challenge By Choice. This is a manual with accompanying two-hour videotape and telephone support which gives a willing person the instructions necessary to construct a low ropes course. *Cowtails and Cobras* had construction information of an informal type in several chapters, but by the mid-eighties, it was out of date. Construction help is now available from PA only through Challenge By Choice or direct service by PA staff. PA is the clear leader in the field of initiative and ropes course design and construction and we remain committed to continuous improvement in both areas.

The safety of the activity base had always been important. But as the number of programs grew, questions on safety and liability issues came more frequently. The second level workshop, Advanced Skills and Standards, first designed and taught by Steve Webster in 1982, was a successful offering that focused on ropes course technical skills, program management and design issues, and possible rescue techniques. In 1981 and later in 1986, we conducted a survey of adopting sites and published what we called the Ten and Fifteen Year Safety Studies. Both showed a level of accidents, defined as a day out of school or work through an injury, at a rate below that of the standard public school P.E. program. In addition, there were no reported accidents of the severely disabling variety that were everyone's concern. These studies proved valuable when the field of outdoor adventure experienced particular adversity with the general liability crisis of 1985-87. We were able, with the help of these studies, to forestall many programs from losing insurance, but the problem of obtaining insurance was difficult for some areas of the country. In 1987, with the help of a new site-specific and voluntary accreditation program, we were able to convince a top-rated insurance company to offer liability insurance for all accredited programs. A new generic *Manual for Ropes Courses and Initiatives* has recently been written by Steve Webster. The accreditation program uses the manual as a guideline for acceptable technical skills and safety issues.

PLANNING FOR THE FUTURE

In 1985, at the urging of a key PA Board member, we worked with an outside consultant to implement a long-range planning process for PA. We assessed strengths and weaknesses, looked at mission, set objectives, and designed strategies and action plans to make the objectives happen. After some discussion, we arrived at this statement of our mission: *The mission of Project Adventure Inc. is to be the leading organization helping others use adventure education as a catalyst for personal/professional growth and change.*

The key phrase is "helping others use." By this we mean that we consult, train, and empower others to start, maintain and improve PA program models that use our innovative program base of games, initiatives, and ropes course elements. Direct service such as our existing programs with youth at risk, schools, and corporate groups will continue to grow and be a source of important research and development opportunities, and revenue stability; but the primary focus of the organization is to help other organizations use PA models to promote growth and change in their students, clients, and organizations.

There is a definite trend worldwide toward incorporating adventure activities into educational and training programs. The main reason for this trend is the recognition that team synergy is a major driving force in both economic productivity and social change possibilities. To help both educational and training institutions address these realities with creative new models is our principal long-range goal. PA's unique access to many types and levels of organizations allows us to accent the catalyst role of our mission, and to help communities of interest develop among those we serve. Our focus on a clear mission has helped us grow strongly since 1985, and it will be even more important to maintain as we head into the next decade. To help this focus, we have begun to use the phrase "Bring the Adventure Home" to describe both our mission goal and our process of encouraging an adventurous "challenge-by-choice" attitude as a goal of all programs. There are definitely many possibilities ahead, and our commitment at PA is to continue choosing our challenges with the same spirit of fun and Adventure that has been our trademark from the beginning.

REFERENCES

Miner, J. L. and Boldt, J. (1981) *Outward Bound U. S. A.: Learning through experience in adventure-based education.* New York: William Morrow and Company.

Smith, H. (1974) *Summary evaluation statement. Project Adventure:* Mamilton, MA.

Thomas, R. (1981) Unpublished Personal Correspondence.

Section Three

FOUNDATIONS OF ADVENTURE EDUCATION

A Philosophical Overview

What beliefs underlie the approaches to teaching and learning referred to as adventure education? A coherent philosophy establishes a foundation upon which to build theory and action. Does adventure education have such a foundation? Jasper Hunt, the philosopher thinking most thoroughly today on these questions, thinks there is such a foundation for adventure education.

Hunt finds in Plato the earliest blocks in this foundation. Plato obviously was not thinking about adventure education as practiced today, but his thoughts on virtue and experience can be applied by modern practitioners in this arena. So too with Aristotle, William James, Alfred North Whitehead, John Dewey, Hahn and the late Willi Unsoeld. The philosophy of living and theory of knowledge that emerge from the works of these philosophers, Hunt argues, provide adventure education with a sound philosophical heritage.

In his second paper in this section, Hunt builds on the points made in the first about the importance of virtue to adventure education. What is a good or bad adventure educator? What should be the "standard of excellence" in this field and who should decide? To what moral virtues is it necessary for practitioners to adhere? Hunt writes of honesty, compassion, justice and courage. His thinking should help adventure educators formulate the critical questions they must ask in order to create and adhere to a solid ethic for their profession.

This section begins with Priest's attempt to define the key terms used throughout this book. There is a confusing array of terminology that must be clarified and assumed as discussion in the field of adventure education progresses. The schema presented here is only one attempt to sort out the semantic difficulties. It is certainly not the only possible schema. The editors, in fact, are not in complete agreement on definitions. Still, some assumptions about the meaning of terms must be made. Priest offers useful guidance in this regard.

The Semantics of Adventure Education

Simon Priest
Brock University

In the previous chapter, the portraits of five model programs used a variety of words to explain the thing they do, called ADVENTURE EDUCATION. This brief article is an attempt to define the terms used throughout this book and to bring some differentiation of agreement to the various words we use to describe our profession and the experience.

OUTDOOR EDUCATION

The broad field known as outdoor education encompasses everything from scaling a major Himalayan peak without oxygen, to taking school children outside the classroom for their learning, to bird watching from the bedroom window. Outdoor education has been described as a place (natural environment), a subject (ecological processes), and a reason (resource stewardship) for learning. It has been called a method (experiential), a process (sensory), and a topic (relationships) of learning. However, these explanations have failed to address the facts that outdoor education may take place indoors (trip preparation) and may be concerned with more than ecology (human interactions).

One definition includes all these valid points: outdoor education is an experiential method of learning with the use of all senses. It takes place primarily, but not exclusively, through exposure to the natural environment. In outdoor education, the emphasis for the subject of learning is placed on relationships concerning people and natural resources.

This definition implies that outdoor education is more than just learning about nature. Historically, two branches of outdoor education have been identified: environmental education and adventure education. Truly functional outdoor education incorporates aspects of both approaches. Here are explanations of the two approaches in relation to the key point of relationships.

ENVIRONMENTAL EDUCATION

Environmental education is concerned with two relationships: ecosystemic and ekistic. Ecosystemic relationships refer to the interdependence of living organisms in an ecological microclimate. In other words, basic biological concepts like the web of life, the food chain, the energy pyramid, etc. Ekistic relationships refer to the key interactions between human society and the natural resources of an environment. In other words, how people influence the quality of the environment (water pollution or strip mining) and how, in turn, the environment influences the quality of their lives (clean drinking water or the spiritual beauty of nature).

ADVENTURE EDUCATION

Adventure education is also concerned with two relationships, but different ones: interpersonal and intrapersonal. Interpersonal relationships refer to how people get along in a group (two or more people). These include communication, cooperation, trust, conflict resolution, problem-solving, leadership influence, etc. Intrapersonal relationships refer to how an individual gets along with self. These include self-concept, spirituality, confidence, self-efficacy, etc.

The premise of adventure education is that CHANGE may take place in groups and individuals from direct and purposeful exposure to: *C*hallenge, *H*igh *A*dventure, and *N*ew *G*rowth *E*xperiences. This is not to say that adventure education causes change; just that it highlights a need to change and supports any personal decisions to make changes.

The purpose of adventure education is to bring about an awareness for these positive changes. A sub-purpose is to enhance the self-concept and improve social interaction. For these reasons, adventure education has become a powerful tool for modifying the behaviors of many client groups—from functionally disabled persons, to individuals who feel socially and personally inadequate, to incarcerated people who are disruptive or destructive to society.

The process of adventure education involves the use of adventurous activities such as recreational pursuits in the outdoors or the so-called artificial adventure environs (ropes courses and group initiatives). These activities are used to provide a group or individual with tasks to accomplish. These tasks often involve problem-solving and challenge. The problem-solving requires decision-making, judgment, cooperation, communication, and trust. The challenge may take the form of testing one's competence against mental, social, or physical risks. To maximize safety, the risk is structured such that it is perceived as being enormously high, while in reality it is controlled at acceptable low levels.

The product of adventure education is personal growth and development. By responding to seemingly insurmountable tasks, groups and individuals learn to overcome almost any self-imposed perceptions of their capability to succeed. They are able to turn limitations into abilities; and, as a result, they learn a great deal about themselves and how they relate to others.

OUTDOOR RECREATION

Very simply put, outdoor recreation is any activity done outdoors. This broad definition spans the spectrum from gardening, to camping out, to racing cars.

OUTDOOR PURSUITS

Outdoor pursuits are a subset of outdoor recreation. They represent the self-propelled activities performed in an outdoor setting. Some common examples include walking, backpacking, rock climbing, mountaineering, skiing, snowshoeing, orienteering, bicycling, spelunking, sailing, kayaking, rafting, and canoeing. They do not include other outdoor recreational activities that are motorized (such as snowmobiling, motorcycling, car racing, and power boating) nor animal powered (such as horse riding and dog sledding). While the latter are definitely outdoor recreation, they lack the low-impact environmental philosophy that is expected to go hand-in-hand with outdoor pursuits.

LEISURE

Recreational activities take place during an experience known as leisure. In leisure, the process of the experience is the most important part; as opposed to work, where the product is all-important. For example, playing music to earn money is work; playing for the sheer enjoyment is leisure. For an experience to qualify as leisure, it must meet two criteria. First, it must be entered into voluntarily and of free choice; and second, it must be intrinsically motivating in and of its own merit.

ADVENTURE

Adventure is a subset of the leisure experience. For something to qualify as an adventure experience it must meet the two criteria mentioned above, and also meet a third criterion: The outcome must be uncertain. Consider two individuals who go for a walk in the woods. The first is walking because she enjoys getting exercise and likes the outdoors (she is at leisure: free choice and instrinsic motivation). The second is walking because he is placating her, doesn't want to be there, and hopes to get back to the TV as quickly as possible (he is not at leisure: obligatory attendance and extrinsic motivation). If some uncertainty arises, only she is capable of experiencing an adventure. He may become excited and may even enjoy the event, but by definition, the experience cannot qualify as adventurous since he is not at leisure.

UNCERTAINTY

The outcome of an adventure is uncertain when information (critical to the completion of a task or the solution of a problem) is missing, vague, or unknown. For example, on an outdoor journey the outcome is uncertain when the necessary skill or confidence may be lacking; when the leadership influence, task definition, or group morale may appear unclear; and when the weather might be somewhat unpredictable. These conditions all lead to uncertainty through risk.

RISK

Risk is the potential to lose something of value. The loss may lead to physical (broken bones), mental (psychological fear), social (peer embarrassment), or financial harm (lost or damaged equipment). From moment to moment, no one can be fully sure that a loss will actually occur, hence the uncertainty creating adventure in a leisure experience. Risk is created from the presence of dangers.

DANGER

Danger gives rise to risk. The two are not the same. Dangers are present in both people and their surroundings. Dangers may be classified as either perils or hazards.

PERIL

Perils are the sources of the loss. A lightning bolt is one example. It is the source that leads to the risk of electrocution.

HAZARD

Hazards are the conditions that influence the probability or likelihood of a loss actually occurring. An intense thunderstorm is one example. It is the hazard that accentuates the number of lightning bolts.

HUMAN DANGERS

Dangers (perils and hazards) may originate from the people in a group. Peer pressure, lack of attention, horseplay, and incompetence are all examples of human dangers. These are said to be subjective or under the control of the group and their leader.

ENVIRONMENTAL DANGERS

Dangers (perils and hazards) may also come from the natural surroundings. Avalanches, white-water rapids, poisonous plants or animals, and temperature extremes are all examples of environmental dangers. These are said to be objective or not controllable by the group and their leader.

ACCIDENTS

The accident is an unexpected occurrence that results in a loss (illness, injury, or fatality). An accident only becomes an emergency if the group and their leader are not prepared to respond correctly. The potential for an accident occurs if the human and environmental dangers are permitted to occur simultaneously. Kept separate, white-water rapids and horseplay are just fine; but allowed to combine at the same time, they lead to the possibility of an accident. This does not mean an accident will always be probable. They can be prevented by effective leadership. However, the concern is not a matter of *will* there be an accident, but *when* it will happen. Be prepared!

INCIDENTS

Incidents or close calls are the unforeseen happenings that do not develop into emergencies. Through effective leadership, the accident is prevented or the consequences are reduced. Incidents can be thought of as minor accidents where the losses are acceptable (cuts, scrapes, bruises, etc.). Acceptability is a personal matter. Acceptable losses to one person may not be acceptable to another. Death is acceptable to some Himalayan climbers, while a bump on the head may not be to a child's mother.

RISK

Once again, risk is the potential to lose something of value. The risks may be physical, mental, social, or financial. Risk may be subdivided into two types: real and perceived.

REAL RISK

Real risk is the true potential for loss: that which actually occurs in an adventure. If no loss occurs, then the real risk was zero. If a person dies, then the real risk was extreme. No one can tell with absolute certainty where the real risk lies at any time. However, it can be estimated. Effective leaders with sound judgment and plenty of experience can usually perceive the risk accurately, but not always.

PERCEIVED RISK

The best estimation of real risk in known as perceived risk. For a first-time participant, the perception of risk may be flawed. Fearful people tend to overperceive the risk, while fearless people tend to underperceive it. Only through intensive and extensive experience can a person gain an astute perception of risk.

COMPETENCE

An adventurer uses competence (a combination of skill, attitude, knowledge, behavior, confidence, and experience) in an attempt to solve the problem or accomplish the task. Like risk, it may have two possible manifestations: real and perceived.

REAL COMPETENCE

Real competence is the true ability of the individual: that which is actually mustered in an adventure. If no loss occurs, then the real competence was sufficient. If a person dies, then the real competence was insufficient. No one, not even the adventurers, can tell with absolute certainty where their real competence lies at any time. However, like real risk, real competence can be estimated. Effective leaders with sound judgment and plenty of experience can usually perceive an individual's competence accurately, but not always.

PERCEIVED COMPETENCE

The best estimation of real competence is known as perceived competence. For a first-time participant, the perception of competence may be grossly inaccurate. Timid people tend to underperceive their competencies, while arrogant people tend to overperceive theirs. Only through intensive and extensive experience can a person gain an astute perception of competence. Perceived competence is closely allied with self-efficacy: a measure of effectiveness and efficiency to perform a competency. In other words, the personal belief that a task can be accomplished or a problem solved.

FACILITATED ADVENTURE

The facilitated adventure is used to create astute adventurers. By manipulating perceived values of risk and competence, while keeping real values at acceptable levels, a reasonably well-controlled adventure experience is possible. Depending on the objectives and precise structuring of such an experience, misperceiving individuals will slowly come to better recognize real risk and real competence.

Philosophy of Adventure Education

Jasper S. Hunt, Jr.
Mankato State University

"But," says one, "you do not mean that the students should go to work with their hands instead of their heads?" I do not mean that exactly, but I mean something which he might think a good deal like that; I mean that they should not play life, or study it merely, while the community supports them at this expensive game, but earnestly live it from beginning to end. How could youths better learn to live than by at once trying the experiment of living?

(Henry David Thoreau, *Walden,* p. 51)

The idea of impelling people into adventurous situations in order to gain certain educational goals is not new. There is often a tendency to view adventure education as a fairly recent development in Western culture. Many people in the field of adventure education, when asked to trace the philosophical development of adventure education, will begin discussing the history of Outward Bound or the Boy Scouts and Girl Scouts, or other 20th-century manifestations. The first thing I want to accomplish here is to argue that adventure education is not a recent educational invention, and that an understanding of the philosophy of adventure education must go much further back in history than the 20th century. This is not the place to do a detailed historical analysis, but some basic issues and sources need to be examined.

Plato, the ancient Greek philosopher, was born about 427 B.C. and died in 347 B.C. During his life of about 81 years, Plato composed many philosophical works. The most famous work was the *Republic*, written in the latter part of his life. On its face, the *Republic* is a treatise about the ideal city-state. However, the *Republic* can also be read as a detailed theory of education. In Book 5 of the *Republic*, there is a fascinating discussion about the best way to raise children to assume the obligations and responsibilities of adulthood. Specifically, the issue is raised about teaching young boys and girls the virtues needed to assume leadership roles in the city-state. The word virtue, in the sense in which the Greeks used it, should not be confused with the modern use of the word to denote sexual purity exclusively. To be virtuous for an ancient Greek was to exhibit an excellence demanded by some practice. For instance, a virtuous potter would be one who had mastered the art of pottery as evidenced by his or her excellent pottery. Therefore, in order to participate as leaders in the city-state, certain virtues had to be taught to young people, just as certain virtues of pottery-making had to be taught to young potters-to-be. The four cardinal virtues needed by the future leaders of the city-state were wisdom, bravery, temperance, and justice.

How best to teach these virtues to young people takes up a major portion of the *Republic*. The issue of participating in war and the defense of the city comes up, and Plato offers an interesting proposal for teaching young people the virtues demanded of warriors. Plato writes,

> For as for their wars, I said, the manner in which they will conduct them is too obvious for discussion.
>
> How so? said he.
>
> It is obvious that they will march out together, and, what is more, will conduct their children to war when they are sturdy, in order that, like the children of other craftsmen, they may observe the processes of which they must be masters in their maturity, and in addition to looking on they must assist and minister in all the business of war and serve their fathers and mothers. Or have you never noticed the practice in the arts, how for example the sons of potters look on as helpers a long time before they put their hands to the clay?

- and later -

> What you say is true, I replied, but, in the first place, is it your idea that the one thing which we must provide is the avoidance of all danger?
>
> By no means.
>
> And, if they must incur danger, should it not be for something in which success will make them better?
>
> Clearly.

- and later -

> Still, we may object, it is the unexpected that happens to many in many cases.
> Yes, indeed.
>
> To provide against such chances, then, we must wing the children from the start so that if need arises they may fly away and escape. (Hamilton & Cairns, 1961)

This selection from Plato contains within it several features that I will argue serve as a philosophical foundation for all adventure education in the late 20th century. It seems obvious to Plato that the best way to learn about what one needs to know for one's maturity, is to experience it directly as a young person. Just as the young potter-to-be needs direct experience with pottery, so does the warrior-to-be need direct experience with war. It is interesting to note what Plato does not say here about learning the virtues of a practice. He does not say that one ought to sit the young people in rows and lecture them about either war or pottery. He does not say that the best way to learn these things is to develop a standardized test to examine the retention of facts memorized about the virtues. Indeed, there is a hint of irritation on Plato's part that this subject even needs discussion at all. It is "too obvious for discussion" says Plato. Plato's interlocutor does not bother to question the point Plato is making about how to teach these things. Rather, the questions asked are about such things as whether complete safety must be guaranteed, what constitutes success, and what must be done if too much danger presents itself to the young people. (I will return to these three questions later.) What is accepted is the notion that the virtues are best learned through direct experience of them by young people.

I do not cite this ancient example because of a desire to root a philosophy of adventure education in preparations for war. I suspect that some of my readers will object to this example because of its connection with waging war. War is not the point. The point is that as far back as Plato the notion was put forth that young people could learn lessons about virtue best when impelled into adventurous situations that demanded that virtues be exercised.

Another key ancient source is Artistotle (384 B.C. - 322 B.C.). Aristotle was a student of Plato and developed the notion that education should be concerned with the development of virtue in young people. What is interesting to note about Aristotle and the development of moral virtues is his essential agreement with Plato that in order to learn the virtues, one must live the virtues. In Aristotelian language, the way one learns a virtue is by the development of right habits.

> Neither by nature, then, nor contrary to nature do the virtues arise in us; rather we are adapted by nature to receive them, and are made perfect by habit.
>
> Again, of all the things that come to us by nature we first acquire the potentiality and later exhibit the activity... but the virtues we get by first exercising them, as also happens in the case of the arts as well. For the things we have to learn before we can do them, we learn by doing them, e.g., men become builders by building and lyre-players by playing the lyre; so too we become just by doing just acts, temperate by doing temperate acts, brave by doing brave acts.

- and later -

> It makes no small difference, then, whether we form habits of one kind or another from our very youth; it makes a very great difference, or rather all the difference. (McKeon, ed., 1941)

If Aristotle is right about virtues being best learned by the development of right habits and if developing right habits involves education, then it follows that education is connected with the development of virtue. My view is that both Plato and Aristotle are right about education being directly concerned with learning virtue, and that this concern with learning virtue is foundational to any philosophy of adventure education.

A similar theme is articulated by a modern writer. William James, the 19th-century philosopher and psychologist, wrote an essay titled, "The Moral Equivalent of War." In this essay James argues that war, repugnant as it is, nevertheless brings out many virtues in people in ways that are unique. His point in the essay is to wage a war against war, not to argue for the benefits of war. As James (1949) writes,

> The war against war is going to be no holiday excursion or camping party. The military feelings are too deeply grounded to abdicate their place among our ideals until better substitutes are offered than the glory and shame that come to nations as well as to individuals from the ups and downs of politics and the vicissitudes of trade.

James' point is that military feelings represent certain cultural ideals that cannot be met by simple politics or commerce. As he says, "better substitutes" must be found to learn the ideals taught through war. In the essay, James draws from the military theorist S. R. Steinmetz and lists the following as virtues that are uniquely habituated by war: "Fidelity, cohesiveness, tenacity, heroism, conscience, education, inventiveness, economy, wealth, physical health and vigor."

James applauds the military virtues. He says,

> Militarism is the great preserver of our ideals of hardihood, and human life with no use for hardihood would be contemptible. Without risks or prizes for the darer, history would be insipid indeed; and there is a type of military character which everyone feels that the race should never cease to breed, for everyone is sensitive to its superiority.

While James applauds the military virtues, he abhors the use of war to teach these virtues. Risk-taking is admired by James, but the use of war to encourage risk- taking is not admired. What is needed, says James, is a substitute for war that will bring out the desired virtues. The substitute James proposes is impelling young people into adventurous situations, utilizing nature as the medium.

> If now—and this is my idea—there were, instead of military conscription a conscription of the whole youthful population to form for a certain number of years a part of the army enlisted against Nature, the injustice would tend to be evened out, and numerous goods to the commonwealth would follow. The military ideals of hardihood and discipline

> would be wrought into the growing fibre of the people; no one would remain blind as the luxurious classes now are blind, to man's relations to the globe he lives on, and to the permanently sour and hard foundations of his higher life.

- and later -

> Such a conscription, with the state of public opinion that would have required it, and the many moral fruits it would bear, would preserve in the midst of a pacific civilization the manly virtues which the military party is so afraid of seeing disappear in peace.

- and later -

> I spoke of the "moral equivalent" of war. So far, war has been the only force that can discipline a whole community, and until an equivalent discipline is organized, I believe that war must have its way.

One need not agree with James about the conscription issue to see his broader point about using nature-based adventure as a means to moral education and the teaching of virtue in young people. In addition, readers who may be offended with James' assumption that the virtues are male ones should remember the cultural context in which these words were written. Conscription and sexism are not the key issues. The use of nature as a means to teach human virtues is the key point. Indeed, war is the enemy for James, and he wants to provide an antidote to its allure and acceptability in modern civilization.

As William James was growing old (he died in 1910), across the Atlantic Ocean in Germany, a young man emerged who took the philosophical tradition of Plato, Aristotle, and James, and put it into practice. Kurt Hahn, the founder of Outward Bound, should not be omitted from a philosophy of adventure education. This is not the place to discuss the life of Kurt Hahn or the history of his educational endeavors. It is the place to outline the key philosophical notions behind his activities in adventure education.

Hahn's thinking about education drew heavily from the Greek tradition outlined above. It was Hahn's view that educators should be concerned with the development of the virtues as well as the traditional academic goals. However, a shift occurs with the advent of Hahn that includes virtues which are omitted in discussions centered around the military and war-based virtues. In an essay about Kurt Hahn, Joshua Miner and Joe Boldt refer to a talk Hahn gave where he was discussing Italian Fascism and the educational virtues embraced by fascism. Miner and Boldt (1981) quote Sir Roger Birley's report of a talk Hahn gave in Hamburg, Germany in 1933 where he referred to Italian, fascistic virtues in education.

> ...you find that you might be quoting the whole Salem Certificate of Maturity (Hahn's program) with its capacity to endure hardships, to face dangers, a talent for organization, prudence, a fighting spirit, presence of mind, success in dealing with unexpected difficulties... Only one item is and must be missing: *The power of carrying out what is recognized to be just* (emphasis added).

- and later -

> We need to be able to feel that as a people we are just and kindly. On this consciousness depends our inner strength.

For Kurt Hahn, the fascistic philosophy of using adventure to teach virtue lacked one of the fundamentals articulated long ago by both Plato and Aristotle: justice. Hahn was revolted by the fascistic movements in Italy and Germany with their disregard for justice. Just as William James sought to use nature in the war against war, so, too, did Kurt Hahn want to use adventure education as a tool to arm young people against the allure of fascism and war.

Hahn's educational thought rapidly evolved into the Outward Bound program. I am assuming that readers of this book already know about Outward Bound and I will not, therefore, discuss Outward Bound per se. I do need, however, to mention something, drawing from the philosophy of Kurt Hahn, that is pivotal to a philosophy of adventure education far beyond Outward Bound.

A fundamental philosophical concept that is common to Plato, Aristotle, James, and Hahn in the teaching of virtue, is that whatever methods are used to instill the virtues are mere *means* to the *end* of virtue. The ultimate goals are not to be confused with the means used to get there. Specifically, as Hahn's ideas about adventure education matured, the realization that adventure was at the service of much different goals became clear. Kurt Hahn's confederate in the origination of Outward Bound, Lawrence Holt, is credited by Boldt and Miner (1981) not only with originating the use of the term Outward Bound, but also, more importantly, with formulating the following philosophical notion:

> The training at Aberdovey, Holt said, must be less a training *for* the sea than *through* the sea and so benefit all walks of life (emphasis added).

The wilderness adventure experience does not stand alone in a philosophy of adventure education. Adventure is a mere means to a much loftier end—human virtue. Holt's idea that adventure is a means and not an end is reflected in Plato, Aristotle, and James. In Plato, the young people are taken out to the battle fields in order to learn virtues needed for leadership in the city-state; in Aristotle, habits are developed in order that virtue be learned; and in James, the use of nature as a teacher to avoid war. The common thread that runs through all of these sources is the importance of adventure as a means and not as an end in itself.

In the initial quotation of this chapter from Plato's *Republic*, three issues were raised that need to be addressed as foundational to a philosophy of adventure education. The three issues were (a) whether all danger should be avoided, (b) what justifies the use of danger in the education of young people, and (c) what to do if too much danger manifests itself. Plato's position on these issues is clear from the quote. From Plato the argument is put forth that no, all danger should not be avoided; the use of danger is justified by making better people; and care must be taken to rescue the young people if too much danger presents itself. It will be helpful in developing a philosophy of adventure education to expand on Plato's ancient advice on these matters by examining these ideas from a modern perspective.

William F. Unsoeld (1926-1979) was a modern adventure educator and philosopher who spent much reflective time responding to the questions raised above by Plato. A great deal of philosophical mileage can be gained by outlining some of Unsoeld's thoughts on these issues. In May 1974, Unsoeld gave a talk on adventure education in Kaiserslautern, Germany (Unsoeld, 1974). During that talk he broached the subject of using risk as an educational tool.

> I've got to put in a pitch for risk. Because, somehow, I see our youth of today being conditioned in the other side of the tracks too much, being warped over here to the conviction that, if its *risky*, its *bad.*

- and later -

> I think that you pay too great a price when you excise risk from your total economy.

- and later -

> We used to tell them in Outward Bound, when a parent would come and ask us, "Can you *guarantee* the safety of our son, Johnny?" And we finally decided to meet it head-on. We would say, "No. We certainly can't Ma'am. We guarantee you the genuine chance of his death. And if we could guarantee his safety, the program would not be worth running. We do make one guarantee, as one parent to another. If you succeed in protecting your boy, as you are doing now, and as its your motherly duty to do, you know, we applaud your watch dog tenacity. You should be protecting him. But, if you succeed, *we guarantee you the death of his soul!*"

Of all of the quotations that I could have selected to begin the discussion about Unsoeld's response to Plato's issues, this is probably the most controversial. But space is limited and I want to get to the heart of the matter. Unsoeld agrees with Plato that risk is a legitimate educational tool. Adventure educators in general also agree.

To guarantee that risk has been completely eliminated from an adventure education program would be to contradict oneself. Adventure logically implies risk. But why go forth, adventure, at all? Because that is the nature of reality. When a person lives, that person goes forth into reality every moment of every day. For a living organism, what will be is never full predictable. To be is to become. To become means to venture forth into an emergent world. The world of living creatures provides complete safety only in looking backwards. What has faded into the past is safe and predictable because it is the past, and is, therefore, no longer emergent. Unsoeld's comments about risk in education are rooted in the metaphysical notion stated above that to be is to become. Alfred North Whitehead (1978) had this to say about the process of becoming.

> The world is thus faced by the paradox that, at least in its higher actualities, it craves for novelty and yet is haunted by terror at the loss of the past, with its familiarities and its loved ones. It seeks escape from time in its character of "perpetually perishing." Part of the joy of the new years is the hope of the old round of seasons, with their stable facts—of friendship, and love, and old association. Yet conjointly with this terror, the present as mere unrelieved preservation of the past assumes the character of a horror of the past, rejection of it, revolt:
>
> *To die be given, or attain,*
> *Fierce work it were to do again.*
>
> Each new epoch enters upon its career by waging unrelenting war upon the aesthetic gods of its immediate predecessor.

Whitehead articulates one of the deepest metaphysical problems of human existence. On the one hand we long for safety and security, to hold on to what we are. Yet, we must live and grow. Literally, not to grow and live means to die. What stands behind Unsoeld's response to the hypothetical mother who wants a guarantee of safety for her son, Johnny, is Unsoeld's understanding that the universe is so constructed that complete safety is a metaphysical impossibility. To succeed in securing complete safety is to deny reality. As Whitehead (1978) puts it,

> The universe is thus a creative advance into novelty. The alternative to this doctrine is a static morphological universe.

It was Unsoeld's view that the denial of reality in the education of young people could only result in the destruction of their souls. It was for this reason that he refused even to attempt to guarantee complete safety to students and parents.

Not guaranteeing complete safety is a far cry from not providing any safety at all in adventure education. Plato recognized this long ago. This issue of impelling students into adventurous situations, while at the same time protecting them from too much danger, presents a point of paradox that must be addressed in a philosophy of adventure education. Too much safety results in killing students' souls. Too little safety results in dead bodies.

Plato's advice (Hamilton & Cairns, 1961) on this matter is to "wing the children from the start so that if need arises they may fly away and escape." The wings that Plato refers to are horses that can be ridden away from danger and toward safety. The importance of providing a means of escape, of protecting a student's safety, is critical for adventure education. The deeper philosophical problem of determining how much risk is to be desired and how much safety is to be desired remains to be addressed.

Since I have based the discussion of a philosophy of adventure education in the teaching of virtue, it is useful to seek guidance in resolving the paradox of risk and safety by examining the notion of virtue in more detail. One virtue that most adventure educators hold dear is the virtue of courage. I have never met anyone who denied the desirability of the virtue of courage and I suspect that all adventure educators would agree that courageous people are better than cowardly people. But what does it mean to be courageous?

According to Aristotle, developing the virtue of courage rests upon avoiding two excesses. Too much courage results in recklessness. Too little courage results in cowardice. Aristotle writes,

> Now it is a mean between two vices, that which depends on excess and that which depends on defect; and again it is a mean because the vices respectively fall short of or exceed what is right in both passions and actions, while virtue both finds and chooses that which is intermediate.

- and later -

> With regard to feelings of fear and confidence courage is the mean; of the people who exceed, he who exceeds in fearlessness has no name..., while the man who exceeds in confidence is rash, and he who exceeds in fear and falls short in confidence is a coward. (McKeon, 1941)

It would be a gross misreading of the virtue of courage, at least from Aristotle's perspective, to equate courage with recklessness. For Aristotle, recklessness is as great a vice as is cowardice. Were adventure educators to forget this, then they would fail in teaching virtue. Indeed, they would succeed only in teaching vice.

What prevents the virtue of courage from degenerating into rashness or recklessness? Safety. It is my view that one cannot possibly argue for the acceptability of adventure education as a means to courage, and ignore a concomitant commitment to safety, without degenerating into conceptual incoherency. The upshot is that adventure educators are saddled with a very difficult task indeed. On the one hand they embrace risk, and on the other hand they embrace safety. What results is a conceptual tension that is, in my opinion, quite healthy. Once again, William F. Unsoeld (1976) has an interesting comment on this tension.

> You emphasize safety in a high risk operation. You emphasize safety, but *you don't kill the risk*. You emphasize safety as a rational man's effort at survival, but we're going to go right ahead and stick our head in the noose... that's the game. But we're going to be so careful in doing it, at the same time and that delicate balance, you know, I think it just has to be transmitted all the time. We don't do anything stupid. There's enough out there to get you anyhow.

The "delicate balance" that Unsoeld talks about demands that adventure educators acknowledge the paradox of adventure and safety as endemic to the profession. Any time one is forced to keep a balance between two conflicting ideals, there is always the possibility of losing the balance and giving one too much attention at the expense of the other. Proponents of safety at all costs will be met with resistance by adventure advocates, and proponents of adventure at all costs will be challenged by those concerned with safety. A sort of philosophical checks and balance results that can provide a source of intellectual honesty for all adventure educators. What would be intellectually dishonest would be to ignore the paradox or to dissolve it by embracing one side at the exclusion of the other.

In the final pages of this essay, I want to argue that a philosophy of adventure education has implications far beyond the confines of wilderness-based programming. One commonality between Plato, Aristotle, James, Whitehead, Hahn, and Unsoeld is the importance that the virtues be lived in order that they be *learned*. Adventure education provides a vehicle that enables students to live the virtues. Fundamentally, this idea of living in order to learn presupposes a theory of knowledge that has applicability far beyond the teaching of the moral virtues.

There is a marvelous quotation from Thoreau (1973) that leads in nicely to the broader applications of adventure education.

> Which would have advanced the most at the end of a month,—the boy who had made his own jack-knife from the ore which he had dug and smelted, reading as much as would be necessary for this,—or the boy who had attended the lectures on metallurgy at the Institute in the mean while, and had received a Rodgers' penknife from his father? Which would be most likely to cut his fingers?—To my astonishment I was informed on leaving college that I had studied navigation!—why, if I had taken one turn down the harbor I should have known more about it.

The contrast Thoreau presents between learning about knives from listening to lectures, then being presented with a knife as a gift, and building his own knife from scratch is striking. So is Thoreau's reaction to being informed that he had studied navigation while in college. Thoreau saw a difference between learning about knives and learning about navigation and knowing knives and knowing navigation. This difference illustrates precisely what I mean by a broader application of adventure education far beyond the confines of wilderness adventures.

To equate learning with sitting passively in a lecture hall or classroom and regurgitating facts back to a teacher who talks 95 percent of the time is the antithesis of adventure education. To measure scholastic aptitude by scores obtained from students filling in the proper computer bubble responses to questions posed in a booklet is the antithesis of adventure education. In either case, what is rewarded is a student's ability to make safe, predictable answers. For a student to attempt any sort of creativity is to risk, not genuine adventure, but censorship and punishment. I will label the sort of education that Thoreau refers to, above, as the conservative theory of education in contradistinction to adventure.

The conservative theory of education assumes that knowing is a simple matter of listening plus mental cogitation. Adventure educators argue that knowing is much more complex than the conservatives assume.

A philosophical source that I have not yet mentioned is John Dewey. Dewey spent a great deal of time and effort on the issue of knowledge and the implications of a theory of knowledge for education. In opposition to the dominant conservative trend, Dewey argued that the quest for knowledge is itself an adventure. For a person to think at all implies adventure, according to Dewey (1916),

> It also follows that all thinking involves a risk. Certainty cannot be guaranteed in advance. The invasion of the unknown is of the nature of an adventure; we cannot be sure in advance. The conclusions of thinking, till confirmed by the event, are, accordingly, more or less tentative or hypothetical.

Thinking for John Dewey is primarily forward-looking and is not restricted to the confines of the past. Although the past sets the stage for the future, the past does not provide the starting point for thought. Thought begins and is rooted in the process of inquiry. Inquiry is a disciplined response to a situation that is indeterminate and which demands intellectual resolution (Dewey, 1938).

> Inquiry is the controlled or directed transformation of an indeterminate situation into one that is so determinate in its constituent distinctions and relations as to convert the elements of the original situation into a unified whole.

- and later -

> Inquiry and questioning, up to a certain point, are synonymous terms. We inquire when we question; and we inquire when we seek for whatever will provide an answer to a question asked.

A key idea in this quotation from Dewey is his analysis of what constitutes an indeterminate situation. In Dewey's theory of knowledge, an indeterminate situation is not just a mental state of confusion. Rather, an indeterminate situation is one that is rooted in the actual world of a person. Dewey (1938) writes,

> A variety of names serves to characterize indeterminate situations. They are disturbed, troubled, ambiguous, confused, full of conflicting tendencies, obscure, etc. It is the *situation* that has these traits. *We* are doubtful because the situation is inherently doubtful. Personal states of doubt that are not evoked by and are not relative to some existential situation are pathological.

If a necessary condition for thought to occur at all is the existence of situations of the type that Dewey describes, then it follows that adventure is intimately bound up in thought as such. Whenever educators impel students into indeterminate situations in order to facilitate thought, they are using adventure as a means to thought. To ask a student to question any aspect of his or her world is to risk many things. The complete security of the settled past is abandoned in favor of an uncertain future opened by inquiry. The exercise of the human imagination is fundamentally an exercise of adventure when it reaches out to an uncertain future. If to think is to inquire, then, to think is to risk being wrong.

If adventure is an effective means for learning virtue, then I want to argue that it is a good means for learning other things as well. As adventure education shows its effectiveness in the moral education realm, it gains additional justification for branching out into other educational areas. Thoreau thought that there was more to knowing navigation than his professors at Harvard imagined. Most adventure educators would agree with him.

There is no way to impel students into indeterminate situations without impelling them into adventure. Whenever a student encounters situations that are incomplete and which demand inquiry, he or she is faced with uncertainty and with possible outcomes that are not pre-set. Outcomes that are not pre-set are often intolerable for those whose highest educational aspirations are toward safety and predictability.

As I write this chapter, the American educational establishment has been in the grip of conservative educational reformers for nearly eight years. Most of the reforms have involved increased emphasis on student passivity, rote memorization, standardized testing, and other reforms that seek to eliminate adventure from education. The very things that Thoreau criticized about his own education have become the centerpieces of much of recent educational reform. Where Thoreau and Dewey encourage questioning and risk-taking by students, many current reforms encourage unquestioned acceptance of authority and the elimination of risk from education. Instead of the existentially real, indeterminate situations that Dewey writes about, students are too often being given material that is dead, wooden, and far removed from their own experiences.

My goal here is not to offer a critique of recent educational reforms. It is to make the point that a philosophy of adventure education includes a theory of knowledge that has applicability in many other areas of education. Kurt Hahn was not primarily an outdoorsman. His main concern was with education in general and with the use of adventure as a broad educational tool. Earlier in this chapter I discussed adventure as basically a philosophy of living. The philosophical implications of adventure education reach into the very core of civilization and what direction the modern world will take. Alfred North Whitehead discusses adventure as foundational to the positive directions the modern world might take.

> But, given the vigor of adventure, sooner or later the leap of imagination reaches beyond the safe limits of the epoch, and beyond the safe limits of learned rules of taste. It then produces the dislocations and confusions marking the advent of new ideals for civilized effort. A race preserves its vigor so long as it harbours a real contrast between what has been and what may be; and so long as it is nerved by the vigor to adventure beyond the safeties of the past. Without adventure civilization is in full decay.

Whitehead suggests that a philosophy of adventure is vital to the prevention of the decay of civilization. A philosophy of adventure education, therefore, has much to offer the broader social context in which it occurs. In this sense, then, adventure educators can lay claim to a philosophical heritage that is arguably one of the sources of the preservation and endurance of a vital and alive civilization.

REFERENCES

Dewey, J. (1916). *Democracy and education.* New York: The Free Press.

Dewey, J. (1938). *The theory of inquiry.* New York: Irvington.

Hamilton, E., & Cairns, H. (Eds.). (1961). *Plato: Collected dialogues.* Princeton, NJ: Princeton University Press.

James, W. (1949). *Essays on faith and morals.* New York: Longmans, Green & Co.

McKeon, R. (Ed.). (1941). *The basic works of Aristotle.* New York: Random House.

Miner, S. L. & Boldt, J. (1981). *Outward Bound U.S.A.* New York: William Morrow Co.

Thoreau, H. D. (1973). *Walden.* Princeton, NJ: Princeton University Press.

Unsoeld, W. F. (1974). Outdoor education: Lecture at Kaiserlauterm. Unpublished lecture.

Unsoeld, W. F. (1976). Outdoor education: Lecture at Wright Academy. Unpublished lecture.

Whitehead, A. N. (1978). *Process and reality.* New York: The Free Press (corrected edition edited by D. R. Griffin & D. W. Sherburne).

Whitehead, A. N. (1933). *Adventures of ideas.* New York: The Free Press.

Ethics

Jasper S. Hunt, Jr.
Mankato State University

The goal of this chapter is to convince readers that ethical issues are intimately bound up with every aspect of adventure education and that ethics must be dealt with by adventure education practitioners. It is not my intent to deal with specific issues or to suggest ways of resolving ethical conflicts when they arise. Rather it will be enough to present a case for the inclusion of ethics within the broader scope of adventure education in general. Once this crucial first step has been taken, the details of ethics will follow naturally for practitioners in the course of their professional lives (Hunt, 1986).

In my other chapter in this book, "Philosophy of Adventure Education," I spent some time on the Greek origins with particular attention paid to the concept of virtue as a key educational goal of adventure educators. The idea of virtue will be used in this chapter to outline my case for the inseparability of ethics from the study and practice of adventure education.

Adventure education is not an abstraction with no concrete manifestations in actuality. To talk about adventure education is to talk about programs that do things with human beings. Students are taught. Budgets are formulated. Staff members are hired and trained. Programs are implemented. In short, adventure education manifests itself in the actual world of human affairs. Therefore, it is useful in articulating the argument for the inclusion of ethics in adventure education to root ethics within the context of actual programs. My assumption is that all adventure programs share certain generic features and that ethics can be grounded within these generic features.

Any adventure education program that is developed will have certain activities, procedures, and policies that will be used to achieve the goals of the program. The goals of the program constitute the end or ends toward which the program aims. The ends will vary from program to program, but the very fact that a program exists implies some end towards which the program aims. So the first generic trait of all adventure programs is that they all have ends toward which they aim.

Ends are not achieved from nowhere. Ends are achieved by putting together activities that lead toward ends. These activities constitute the means by which the program operates. It is impossible to arrive at an end without doing something to get there. The second generic trait that all programs share is the use of means to get to ends.

For instance, a program may have as its end the development of sound judgment by its students. Developing sound judgment as a surgeon is very different from developing sound judgment as a mountaineering leader. Good judgment is not a generic skill that is applicable to any situation. Rather, good judgment resides within the scope of a range of activities with discernible boundaries. One does not teach judgment skills in mountaineering by putting students in hospital operating suites. The point is that the activities used to achieve desired ends will define a program as much as the existence of the ends themselves.

Therefore, all adventure programs are partially defined by the practices that they employ as means to their desired ends. The term *practice* as I use it here is a technical one and is crucial for grounding ethics within adventure education. Philosopher Alasdair MacIntyre (1984) describes a practice in the sense in which I am using it here.

> By "practice" I am going to mean any coherent and complex form of socially established cooperative human activity through which goods internal to that form of activity are realized in the course of trying to achieve those standards of excellence which are appropriate to, and partially definitive of, that form of activity, with the result that human powers to achieve excellence, and human conceptions of the ends and goods involved are systematically extended. Tic-tac-toe is not an example of a practice in this sense, nor is throwing a football with skill; but the game of football is and so is chess.

Coiling a climbing rope is not a practice in MacIntyre's sense, but teaching rock climbing is. Just as I can be an excellent surgeon or a poor surgeon, so too can I be an excellent adventure educator or a poor one. The goods or "standards of excellence" achievable by a surgeon, a football player or an adventure educator, are goods attainable only by those who participate in the practice of medicine, football, or adventure education. Participating in a practice presents the practitioner with the potential of achieving various goods, excellences, which inhere in the specific practices.

The use of the term "goods" is open to a confusion that should be mentioned. MacIntyre makes a distinction between goods that are internal to a practice and goods that are external to a practice. Suppose, for illustration, that an adventure education program was to hire an instructor who was primarily seeking employment in order to finance a personal mountaineering expedition. The instructor does an adequate job, is appropriately compensated, and goes on the expedition as a result of the pay. The good which this hypothetical instructor receives is the money. There is no reason for this instructor to do more than the minimum required in order to be paid for the job done. Indeed, if the instructor can do less than is called for, and not get caught, then the instructor still receives the pay and can be called successful. This sort of good achieved by the instructor is what MacIntyre calls a good external to a practice.

Internal goods, on the other hand, are goods attained purely because of the excellence achieved by participating fully in a practice. An adventure educator pursuing internal goods will receive personal satisfaction by being recognized as achieving a level of excellence only attainable by participating in the practice. This does not mean that internal and external goods are mutually exclusive. An adventure educator who is well-paid financially may at the same time receive internal goods from a job well done.

Thus, it makes sense to talk about a good or bad adventure educator. Presumably what is desired is good adventure educators rather than bad ones. This is where ethics begins to emerge as inherent to the very core of what it means to participate in the practice of adventure education. Practices logically imply standards of excellence for practitioners to measure themselves against. As MacIntyre (1984) argues,

> A practice involves standards of excellence and obedience to rules as well as the achievement of goods. To enter into a practice is to accept the authority of those standards and the inadequacy of my own performance as judged by them. It is to subject my own attitudes, choices, preferences and tastes to the standards which currently and partially define the practices.

I may aspire to achieve excellence as a baseball player. However, I am only able to hit the ball if I am allowed five strikes at the ball, instead of three. The point of MacIntyre's quote immediately above is that inherent to achieving the label of "a good baseball player" is the idea that I am only allowed three strikes at bat. Any more than three strikes and I am no longer playing baseball. The three-strike rule provides a standard of excellence by which my performance is judged. If I am to achieve excellence as a baseball player, it will only be possible insofar as I conform to the standards as the goods internal to the practice of baseball.

It is at this point that the transition can be made to the discussion of virtue. If the teaching of virtue is foundational to a philosophy of adventure education, as I argued in my earlier chapter, then how does talk of virtue apply to the practitioners themselves? In other words, if adventure educators are to teach virtue to others, does it not make sense that they are themselves virtuous? Therefore, the next step in discussing ethics in adventure education is to describe what it means to be a virtuous adventure educator.

If someone achieves levels of excellence set by a practice, that individual may be called a virtuous person. In formulating the definition of virtue, MacIntyre (1984) writes,

> But what does all or any of this have to do with the concept of the virtues? It turns out that we are now in a position to formulate a first, even if partial and tentative definition of a virtue. A virtue is an acquired human quality the possession and exercise of which tends to enable us to achieve those goods which are internal to practices and the lack of which effectively prevents us from achieving any such goods.

The first step, then, in formulating a conception of a virtuous adventure educator is to look at the practices that make adventure education what it is. For it is only as a person functions within the practice of adventure education that he or she can attain the status of a virtuous adventure educator. The achievement of goods internal to the practice of adventure education is the key to achieving virtue in this context.

There is often a tendency to restrict discussion of practices to purely technical practices. In other words, a practice could be limited to articulating the standards of excellence purely in terms of such things as hard skills, soft skills, and other technical skills needed to function as an adventure educator. If this was the case, then virtue in adventure education would reduce to the mastery of purely technical skills and the issue of ethics would, therefore, convert to a discussion of technical skills. I have mastered these technical practices; therefore I am a virtuous adventure educator, one could argue. This argument would be valid as far as it goes. Certainly, mastering the internal technical goods of the practice of adventure education is a vital part of the virtues of adventure education. But there is more to virtue than just technical practices.

Aristotle discusses two kinds of virtue that are very helpful.

> Virtue too is distinguished into kinds in accordance with this difference; for we say that some of the virtues are intellectual and others moral, philosophic wisdom and understanding and practical wisdom being intellectual, liberality and temperance moral.

- and later -

> Virtue, then, being of two kinds, intellectual and moral, intellectual virtue in the main owes both its birth and its growth to teaching (for which reason it requires experience and time), while moral virtue comes about as a result of habit whence also its name ethike is one that is formed by a slight variation from the word ethos (habit). (McKeon, 1941)

Aristotle makes the distinction between intellectual virtue and moral virtue. Knowing how to perform the technical practices of adventure education falls under the umbrella of intellectual virtue. The intellectual virtues, however, cover only part of the territory of virtue. A moral virtue is one which must be developed in order that the intellectual virtues be guided and controlled toward their proper ends. For example, I may achieve the excellence of making good safety judgments about appropriate technical rock-climbing routes to do with students. Suppose, however, that I am lazy and therefore evade doing these routes because they make my job more difficult. My laziness becomes a character flaw within me that gets in the way of my exercising the intellectual (technical) virtue of being a good rock-climbing educator. Unless I develop the moral virtue of industriousness as well as the intellectual virtue of good technical rock skills, then I will never achieve the internal good of being an adventure educator who utilizes rock climbing as an educational practice. Without the moral virtue I could become a rock-climbing instructor but I could not become a good rock-climbing instructor.

According to Aristotle, therefore, ethics become the formation of the right habits needed to guide the intellectual virtues.

> This, then, is the case with the virtues also; by doing the acts that we do in our transactions with other men we become just or unjust, and by doing the acts that we do in the presence of danger, and being habituated to feel fear or confidence, we become brave or cowardly.

- and later -

> Thus, in one work, states of character arise out of like activities. This is why the activities we exhibit must be of a certain kind; it is because the states of character correspond to the differences between these. It makes no small difference, then, whether we form habits of one kind or another from our very youth; it makes a very great difference, or rather all the difference. (McKeon, 1941)

If MacIntyre is right about virtue being a necessary ingredient for achieving goods internal to practices, then the virtues become essential for practitioners to achieve their ends. If Aristotle is right that ethics is the development of right habits needed to guide the intellectual virtues, then it seems reasonable to conclude that in order to have a practice of adventure education, ethics and virtue are needed as inherent to the practice.

Readers may wonder at this lengthy justification for the place of ethics within the practice of adventure education. Many may assume that ethics obviously have a place within adventure education. My experience is that even to justify the place of ethics within the practice of adventure education is difficult with many practitioners.

I recently met with a young adventure educator who described the following scenario to me. He had been employed by an adventure education program this past summer. That program has a first-rate high ropes course used in most of the school's programs. The belay method used utilizes the "Y Tail" (also called the "Lobster Claw") technique to protect students from falling to the ground. As with all such belay methods, it is necessary for instructors to be prepared to effect the rescue of a student who might fall from the course and is unable to get back on the course unaided. In order to be able to effect a fast rescue, the course has a "rescue box" that contains all of the necessary gear for a rescue high up on the course.

During staff training, the young man raised the question of how instructors should respond to students who might ask, "What is the box for?" The instructor was worried that students, if told what the box was for, might become overly fearful, since the presence of the box might be a constant reminder of the possibility of falling off the course and of a rescue. The senior staff member present during the staff training replied that of course the instructor should tell students that the box contained "maintenance gear" in order to avoid scaring students unnecessarily. The instructor then asked the senior staff member if giving such a deceptive reply was an ethical thing to do. The senior staff person became irritated and retorted that ethics did not have anything to do with it. He said that it was a policy issue and that he did not have time during staff training to deal with ethics.

Presumably the senior staff member wanted his instructors to be good instructors. Yet when confronted by the problem of determining what constitutes a good instructor, the senior staff member precluded the attainment of a good internal to the practice of adventure education. Without time allowed to discuss the problem of deceptive replies to students' questions, the moral virtue needed to guide the intellectual virtue of being competent to run a ropes course with students was left out of the picture. Therefore, the practice of adventure education taught to the young instructor was an incomplete practice.

The moral virtues that are a part of the practice of adventure education are not an option to practitioners. To leave out the moral virtues and attempt to practice adventure education as a purely technical enterprise is impossible. If such an attempt is made, the moral virtues will be present in programs but they will be unconscious and assumed to be true without being acknowledged. Unconscious assumptions in ethics are problematic at best. At worst they can produce bad practices and bad practitioners. To return to the example of the rescue box, I make no judgments at this point whether or not lying to students about such things is good or bad. Maybe the policy promulgated by the senior staff member was the right one. The judgment I do make, however, is that the senior instructor's refusal to deal with the ethical issues was intellectually incoherent and irrational.

As a practical matter one might ask at this point, where does one go to find the virtues needed to resolve problems like the rescue box issue? It is one thing to recognize the problem for what it is. It is another thing to try to rationally resolve the problem. In the end, students either are told the truth about rescue boxes or they are not.

Practices and the virtues needed to realize the goods internal to the practices do not come out of nowhere. Every practice emerges out of a history that gave rise to the practice. The modern physician is the heir to the practice of medicine with a long history. Modern physicians do not practice medicine the way the ancient Greeks did, but they do turn to Hippocrates, an ancient Greek physician, for guidance in pursuit of what it means to be a virtuous physician. The Hippocratic Oath is not simply an oath. It is a moral connection with the history of the practice of medicine. It is a reminder to the modern physician that there are virtues attendant to the practice of medicine to which he or she had better pay attention. Failure to do so can result in the physician only attaining external goods and never achieving the internal goods open to medical practitioners.

Alasdair MacIntyre (1984) has this to say about the importance of history to practices.

> What I am, therefore, is in key part what I inherit, a specific past that is present to some degree in my present. I find myself part of a history and that is generally to say, whether I like it or not, whether I recognize it or not, one of the bearers of a tradition. It was important when I characterized the concept of a

> practice to notice that practices always have histories and that at any given moment what a practice is depends on a mode of understanding which has been transmitted often though many generations. And thus, insofar as the virtues sustain the relationships required for practices, they have to sustain relationships to the past—and to the future—as well as in the present.

One thing that might be a great aid to the people involved in the issue of the rescue box would be look back and think about what has defined and sustained the student-teacher relationship in adventure education in the past. The question could be faced about the role of truth-telling as a virtue for the practice of adventure education. Has lying to students enabled practitioners of adventure education to achieve the internal goods of the practice in the past? Has truthfulness been an aid or an impediment to the practice of adventure education throughout its history? In short, has honesty been considered a virtue in the history of adventure education? If it has, then modern practitioners need at the very least to take account of this. If honesty has not been a virtue and lying has been a virtue, then this ought to be taken account of.

In addition to historical sources, practitioners can turn to the current practices of their fellow practitioners for guidance in recognizing the virtues. To enter into a practice is to enter into membership in a community of other practitioners. When I am deciding to install a belay system in a high ropes course that I use in my professional life, I consult other practitioners about the latest developments in ropes course belay techniques. Checking on such things as safe belay techniques would fall under the heading of an intellectual virtue for Aristotle. There is no reason why one could not check with one's fellow practitioners for guidance in the moral virtues as well.

This need not imply that other practitioners are always right about their views on moral matters. The same holds true for technical issues. There is a good deal of disagreement about what the safety standards should be for belays on high ropes courses. Check with a variety of practitioners and there will not be a concensus on many technical issues. The same holds true for moral virtues.

However, certain virtues will be common for all practitioners both in the technical and moral areas. For instance, there may be disagreement about the best belay techniques, but there will be no disagreement that students should have a belay when on a high ropes course. Agreeing that a belay is needed in the first place at least sets the stage for the ensuing argument about the best technique to use.

The same holds true for moral virtues. Without the sharing of certain fundamental moral virtues by all practitioners, the practice of adventure education would be impossible in the first place. For instance, the practice of adventure education would cease to exist if practitioners were not honest, were cowardly, or unjust. How could I possibly value a colleague's opinion about safe belay techniques if I was unsure about whether or not I was being told the truth about my colleague's opinions about safety? A precondition for entering into a practice is that practitioners be honest with each other. It is for this reason that the medical profession, for instance, is so harsh on practitioners who publish phony research results in medical journals. Physicians who treat patients based on false research data risk endangering the health of their patients. To harm a patient is to violate the very nature of the practice of medicine. Therefore, honesty becomes a cardinal virtue in the practice of medicine. Without honesty there would be no practice of medicine. The same holds true for the practice of adventure education.

An adventure educator who is a coward would be unable to practice adventure education. I argued in my chapter on philosophy of adventure education that adventure logically implies risk. Eliminate the risk and the adventure is eliminated. Therefore, a practitioner who is a coward and as a result denies risk, is unable to achieve the internal goods of being an adventure educator. How much risk is morally acceptable within the practice of adventure education is debatable, but the acceptability of cowardly practitioners is not debatable.

Justice is another virtue essential for the practice of adventure education. Without concern for what one is due, for what is fair, practitioners would be unable to function. Suppose a student was to pay for an adventure education program and was told upon arrival that it was all a joke, there really was no course and that, in addition there would be no refund of money to the student. Although this is a bit outlandish to consider, the point is that without some conception of justice and fairness guiding the practice of adventure education, there would be no reason not to do such things.

The same can be said of the virtue of compassion. Kurt Hahn is on record as believing that compassion was one virtue that must be common to all adventure education programs. To impel students into adventurous situations in order to learn the virtue of compassion in a compassionless manner or under the tutelage of a practitioner who lacked compassion, would render adventure education absurd. If compassion is a fundamental virtue students should be learning from adventure educations, then it is essential that virtue permeate the entire practice of adventure education.

The presence of the virtues within the practice of adventure education does not eliminate moral conflict or controversy from the scene. Some practitioners might be tempted to conclude that the acceptance of the moral virtues would render ethical decision-making easy. This is not the case. It might be a very difficult matter indeed to determine within a given context what the virtuous course of action might be. Decisions must be made on a case-by-case basis as to what the various virtues demand. Problems like when does courage become recklessness, when does honesty become brutality (must I really tell Aunt Alice that the new dress she has just purchased and which she is so proud of is hideous in my opinion?), when does compassion become mere sentimentality, etc., must be faced. These are not easy problems to solve. The important point to gain is that the virtues at least provide a standard from which to operate when facing specific difficulties. I may decide not to be totally honest with Aunt Alice about my opinion of her new dress, but I at least confront that problem with the virtue of honesty as the standard to which I turn or from which I depart.

Aristotle in his discussion of the virtues warns that the virtues are not rigid edifices that take away the burden of thoughtful decision-making from people. The very nature of ethics as the science of right action precludes neat, tidy, thoughtless answers to complex and difficult problems. To thoughtlessly apply the virtue of honesty in my interaction with Aunt Alice and ignore the virtue of compassion would be an improper use of the virtues.

Another warning that adventure education practitioners ought to take note of is the too-easy identification of the virtues only with the virtues of the past. There is no reason to think that the virtues of adventure education are contained in a neat "Sears and Roebuck Catalogue of Ethics" someplace. As the relatively young practice of adventure education grows and develops, new and different virtues will need to be recognized and practiced.

There is always the potential for the virtues that are accepted by practitioners to equate directly to the interests and needs of those in power and with what I will call the "ethical establishment." In the practice of slavery, for instance, a virtuous slave is one who submits well to his or her master. It could be the case that, on the contrary, a virtuous slave is one who works with all his or her might to end the practice of slavery or in some way change it. Of course most slave owners would hardly recognize this possibility of the virtuous slave as the most rebellious one! Practitioners need to be very careful that the ethical standards which develop not be allowed to result in a static, self-satisfied tool to maintain the status quo as an end in itself. The classic example that comes to mind are the Old Testament prophets who attacked the dominant interests and demanded a reexamination of what it meant to be a virtuous Hebrew. Every practice needs its "prophets" to shake things up.

My final recommendation for practitioners of adventure education is that they take the time to discuss what they are doing within the contexts of their various programs. While there are some generic features common to all adventure education programs, there will also be differences between programs that might demand different virtues from practitioners. However, unless time is taken to think about these issues, thoughtful recognition and resolution of specific issues cannot happen.

I have made no attempt to list what I think the virtues are for the practice of adventure education. Readers should not conclude that since I mentioned justice, honesty, courage, and compassion in this chapter that I am implying that these are a complete set of the virtues. Far from it. I do think these four virtues are common to all adventure education programs, but they hardly represent a complete picture. It is only within the context of a much wider discussion that an adequate account could be given of the virtues essential to the practice of adventure education. I will be content here if I have convinced readers that there is at least something worthy of consideration in the issue of ethics in adventure education.

REFERENCES

Hunt, J. (1986). *Ethical issues in experimental education.* Boulder, CO: Association for Experiential Education.

McIntyre, A. (1984). *After virtue* (2nd ed.). Notre Dame, IN: University of Notre Dame Press.

McKeon, R. (Ed.). (1941). *The basic works of Aristotle.* New York: Random House.

Every Trail Has a Story: The Heritage Context as Adventure

Robert Henderson
McMaster University

There is something exciting in the first start even upon an ordinary journey. The bustle of preparation—the act of departing, which seems like a decided step taken—the prospect of change, and consequent stretching out of the imagination—have at all times the effect of stirring the blood and giving a quicker motion to the spirits. It may be conceived then with what sensation I set forth on my journey into the arctic wilderness ... Before me were novelty and enterprise; hope, curiosity, and the love of adventure were my companions; and even the prospect of difficulties and danger to be encountered, with the responsibility inseparable from command, instead of damping rather heightened the enjoyment of the moment.

(Back, 1970)

These words would pull the heartstrings of any adventurer today, but the date and place suggest this was no "ordinary" adventure. This was no ordinary "stretching out of the imagination."

George Back's 1833 exploration into the central barren grounds of the Canadian Arctic was unquestionably an adventure then and remains an unquestionably adventurous route for today's traveler. The river run remains an opportunity to put one's competence to task with the risk inherent in the travel. Such adventure travel experiences rarely, hopefully can never, fall into that problematic category of adventure without risk that is possible with overly structured safety criteria and a watered-down adventure curriculum. Most adventure travel programs maintain the qualities of novelty and enterprise and deliver the goods in line with George Back's explorations, for adventure is a state of mind. The risk is real and is a modern-day goal in itself. We share this adventure attraction motivator with our historical precursors, though rarely was this a goal in itself in former times. But there are other goals available for the modern explorer—the cultural explorer.

Then, in 1833, the stretching out of the imagination was a wide-eyed stare into the unknown—the never-recorded. This quest upstaged any concern for common sense and safety, though at all times common sense and safety would have governed Back's conduct. As compared to some cohorts such as Sir John Franklin's string of misadventures, his safety record proves this. The modern adventure can recapture this drive for the unknown, granted maintaining a more easily found sensibility for common sense and safety. But another quality can be carried along today that brings an added dimension of "prospects of change and consequent stretching out of the imagination."

This quality embodies an affinity with what has passed before, tapping a rich heritage of adventure on the trails and waterways of those lands whose natural integrity has remained relatively intact. This abstract sense of relatedness—being part of history—being tradition, is something extra, something more, complementing and perhaps creating the adventure. The feeling of "fit" with the experience of a George Back and the fit into the "mindscape" of another time serves to enrich the present reality and warm the spirits of the land. As Sigurd Olson (1969) said, "...and when they did (seek these spirits), the land glowed with warmth and light." Such spirits—whether native, voyageur, pioneer, cowboy, mountain man, or early recreationalists—can become celebrated partners on the trail, a companionship of past and present. This in itself can be that quality of adventure sought on the trail—another kind of unknown, perhaps part of an evolution of what is the adventure of the trail.

Such stretching of one's aspirations bespeaks the potential that awaits the cultural explorer, who, added to or growing out of the adventure at hand, brings a poetic imagination for the sharing of time and place, a sublime expression of imprinting with a time, person, or travel style. Such connection is not accessible everywhere and at all times, but it is accessible as a compliment to modern adventure far more than we avail ourselves to it. We make things beautiful, adventurous with our imagination. It is with imagination that adventure finds its starting point and its further depth: its added qualitative dimensions. George Back's bustle of preparation describes his imagination at work. Today the adventurer and/or adventure educator can pull the same heartstrings. As Canadian novelist Peter Such (1978) has said, "We all need a sense of our past, and how our present and indeed our future grow out of it, to see ourselves as part of that continuing tradition as it keeps evolving and not separate from it."

A JOURNAL EXCERPT

Huddled around an evening fire before a difficult height of land watershed crossing, we sat staring and wondering into the fire. Would years of historical use have maintained a worn portage trail, or is this today only an obscure, poorly marked waterway connection? Would we even find such a trail? Would our loads be too heavy for our stamina? For some, this might have been the last straw, a turning back point due to the frustration of an adventure gone wrong. Leonidas Hubbard, a 1903 adventurer's misadventure in Labrador, springs to mind. This adventure turned to pure adversity. Many other such stories from the past creep into our present. P. G. Downes' 1940s description of a challenging portage and searching for trails, and Grey Owl's narrative of getting lost (misdirected) are tales for the telling by the fire this night. These stories we keep alive by the fire, creating a tangled web of heritage context; preserving oral tradition with the drama of a canoe travel legacy composing our present adventure.

> How we were "part of the verb to explore. ...The search being not for a material thing as much as it is for an attitude or a quality of imagination" (Perkins, 1983)

We were part of a scene that has been repeated for all first-timers through this canoe route and countless other routes. Our maps did not place us out of context; they helped define the context. How many have huddled by a fire at this campsite with the same sense of adventure and apprehension for the long height of land portages ahead? For fleeting moments, the shared humanity was comforting, revealing an added depth to our adventure. In the morning the portage trail we would seek was "their" trail. They were real and we were living their story. For every trail has a story! Whether specific in nature or only general to the broad sweep of history and the land, the bush is alive with the stories that await our imagination as told in travelers' journals, from old-timers or simply from an old trailblaze marking a now forgotten height of land portage.

THE SPECIFIC HERITAGE CONTEXT

Retracing George Back's trip down the river that now bears his name with his journal in hand is an example of a specific in-context challenge that is less demanding for the imagination compared to general themes. To share an adventure with an 1833 group through a largely unchanged landscape, aware of the similarities of circumstance and yet not naive to the differences dictated by water levels, modern equipment, and modern knowledge and temperaments, is to be at all times thinking/fusing past and present. Here is a twofold adventure; one physical and one visionary or mythical.

One need not be in the arctic for such adventure. The Voyageur canoe routes and horseback treks into mountain passes can offer the same insights with "real people" in context with specific mysteries and unknowns to explore. Lewis and Clark on the Missouri, William Butler on the Voyageur Waterways, LaSalle on the Mississippi, and Mary Schaffer and John Colter in the Rocky Mountains are among the many possible personalities with whom one may share a common quest for adventure; yet for today's explorer, the trail is also graced with the genius of this past. Questions arise, such as from what vantage point would this sketch have been drawn? What inspired a particular journal entry? Where is the old gravestone so meticulously recorded by another? Such retracing of experiences bring history to direct interpretation. Thinking in terms of education, the experiential experience takes one from studying history to realizing "that history is me" (Brown, 1971). In short, the particular fascination with experiencing the similarities and differences with the likes of explorers George Back, William Butler, and John Colter, is itself an adventure.

The affinity can also be discovered with a specific out-of-context nature. The Bennett Outdoor Education Centre in Edmonton, Alberta, has a program where school groups study the specific circumstance of David Thompson's 1812 winter discovery of the Athabasca Pass. Thompson's hired canoe men mutinied and with great difficulty finally ascended this northern gateway to the Pacific.

School groups capture this moment on the steep ravine slope behind the center with a mock Thompson dressed the part shouting orders to browbeaten mock voyageurs. The exercise can be an initiative task of hauling weighted sleds up a pitch or the challenge of freighting gear over the Athabasca Pass, the major obstacle in the Atlantic/Pacific fur trade, while putting up with the belittling, arrogant Thompson. In both cases the imagination is stirred. In the latter, additional questions arise that create context and a mythical quality to the immediate task. Such questions may be, why was Thompson belligerent to his men? Why attempt the pass in the winter months? Why this pass anyway? The answers for these questions and more are solvable puzzles that again bring history and adventure alive. The asking brings the experience alive in a specific context of Thompson on the Athabasca without the specific setting.

What we experience is not the initiative alone, but the experience exposed to our methods of questioning that may include the specific context of a David Thompson, the Voyageur, the Piegan Indians, and the life on the land of that time. All the various players must become involved as the questioning becomes more complex and demanding. Imagination here exposes a broader perceptual and conceptual method of questioning. One's sense of the unknown is given a broader base or grounding. Carefully chosen interpretive questioning strategies of educators keep the past within reach for all ages.

THE GENERAL HERITAGE CONTEXT

This bridging of past and present is also accessible in a most general sense, without specific places, people, and times. Picture a beautiful winter's day! Somewhere in the Canadian Shield, you ascend a steep, forested ridge on snowshoes, through 3 feet of snow to arrive at a level ridgetop. Intentions had been to get a distant view, but the forest blocked all possibilities. The large pine of this area have been cut, so climbing a tree would not help. You walk the ridge awhile, then slowly descend. No adventure, no real success, little physical challenge to your endeavors and yet you feel wonderful, outside yourself with contentment. Your climb was merely recreational. You were not a timber cruiser of the past identifying woodlots, not a surveyor overcoming land obstacles, not a native hunter using the ridge to hunt moose where less snow prevails, offering choice winter moose habitat; not an explorer trying to use a vantage point to discern any future course. You were none of these, yet they are all stored fuel for the imagination. With each step of your snowshoe you connect with the spirit of this technology so brilliantly adapted to such winter terrain—so necessary for all of the above. Each step with your snowshoes puts you deep into the romantic prints of its past and its utility. As Sigurd Olson (1956) has said of the snowshoe's close cousin, the canoe, it "makes you a part of all it knows." Here the travel mode captures a general flavor of the experiences of the nameless people, places, stories, and mostly with a time when snowshoe was king and of course, at times, it still is. Some of the wisdom of this technology comes with such steps, confusing your present with an adventure of possible relatedness where no adventure seems apparent. Your adventure now is one of sensitivity and homeness, comfort and sense of place in the bush (not wilderness) with knowledge of those who passed before. This is not the wilderness, but a homeland; it demands less aggression and more sensitivity.

For the educator, the challenge can be to impart the touch of this imagination in others so that snowshoes (canoe, horseback) are not just snowshoes, but doorways to this notion of being history. Whether general or specific in context, adventure on the land may offer this potential of relatedness to a larger reality. Contemporary Canadian painter Ivan Eyre has said of art,

> "When I look at a painting it isn't only the painting that I see, but the thing that I am. If there is more in the painting than I am, then I wouldn't get it" (Woodcock, 1981)

This is also true of adventure education and travel in a heritage context. With travel in settings (where natural integrity remains relatively intact) such as the north shore of Lake Superior specifically, much of the Canadian Shield, Rocky Mountains, and Arctic Barren Grounds generally—where the travel mode has a rich heritage such as horseback riding, snowshoeing, and canoeing—with travel that can tap the insights/adventures of others through their journals and stories; with all of these, it is not only the adventure that is available but an added thing that is in each of us. Part of each of us desires to be grounded in a heritage, to see ourselves as reflections of a past, yet evolving! We all desire a sense of place in a geography that offers hope and faith. This helps define who we are.

It is because there are so many cultural explorers adding this "grounding" to their travel experiences through study and exploration that it seems possible to say, "We do see it," for there is not more in the adventure than we are. Because if there were more in adventure than we are, then we wouldn't get/see it; and we *can "get"* these sleeping stories of the past, ready to be awakened with our imaginative qualities.

Gregory Bateson has said,

> "In choosing our beliefs we are therefore also choosing the images that will guide, create, and pull us along with our culture,

into the future. The world partly becomes—comes to be—how it is imagined" (Bateson, 1972)

We can hope that adventure education helps us choose images that add a feeling of relatedness to our heritage on the land so that we evolve from a sole adventure frontier perceptive of many of those we study to a grounding, a homeness that comes with a sense of past and roots. "The continuity and context of this sort of physical and mythical reality is even more essential to humanity than adventure in the realm of the unknown" (Franks, 1981). We take the pioneer, explorer, frontier spirit and evolve through it to a modern rootedness, a more *connected* culture to our landscape. Hopefully, we can merge our immigrant status with an indigenous one. Being history, this abstract magical affinity, taken in fleeting moments captured whole or savouring a general ambience, helps us see who we are and all we are. It helps us see that history is in me and I am in history. It can be either a plus to an adventure, a feeling beyond the adventure; or perhaps even a mindscape that grows to negate the adventurous sense. From these perspectives, one of heritage, the self gains images of caring, respect, awareness of culture and diversity and how we all must evolve *with* and *within* our landscape.

The stretching out of the imagination we share with George Back can tap two unknowns: the physical adventure of risk testing competence, and the mythical adventure of the self extending its boundaries of time and place. In both there is great promise.

The Australian aborigines relate to their homeland through a labyrinth of invisible pathways known as songlines or dreaming-tracks. Perhaps the North American native pictographs and petroglyphs served much the same end. More literally, these pathways are the "Footprints of the Ancestors" who sang the world into existence (Chatwin, 1987). The songlines provide direction for the young man's walkabout or vision quest: a cultural rite of passage where ecological maturity or grounding in nature is imparted and fostered. Often judged as primitive, this notion is perhaps also essential. The cultural explorer/adventurer/educator can channel a mythical association of self and landscape toward a beautiful, caring adventurous imagination. Canoeist/artist/filmmaker Bill Mason called such connections "The Song of Paddle" (Mason, 1988). Though we remain of largely immigrant status with the modern concept of "wilderness," if we approach our travel and adventures within a historical context, then songlines can exist for us in the North American landscape. Every trail and waterway has a story. These are the bush travelers' dreaming-tracks that, when listened to, can help sing a new "first start upon an ordinary journey."

REFERENCES

Back, G. (1970). *Narrative of the arctic land expedition to the mouth of the Great Fish River, 1836.* Rutland, VT: Charles E. Tuttle Co.

Bates, G. (1972). *Steps to an ecology of mind.* New York: Ballantine.

Brown, G. I. (1971). *Human teaching for human learning.* New York: Penquin.

Chatwin, B. (1987). *The songlines.* New York: Penquin.

Franks, C. E. S. (1988). Canoeing: Toward a landscape of the imagination. J. Raffan & B. Horwood (Eds.), *Canexus: The canoe in Canadian culture.* Toronto: Betelgeuse Books.

Mason, W. (1988). *Song of the paddle: An illustrated guide to wilderness camping.* Toronto: Key Porter Books.

Olson, S. (1956). *The singing wilderness.* New York: A. A. Knopf.

Olson, S. (1969). *Open horizons.* New York: A. A. Knopf.

Perkins, R. (1983). *Against straight lines: Alone in Labrador.* Boston: Little, Brown & Co.

Such, P. (1978). *Vanished peoples: The archaic Dorset and Beothuk people of Newfoundland.* Toronto: NC Press.

Woodcock, G. (1981). *Ivan Eyre, Fitzhenry and Whiteside.* (Unpublished).

RESOURCES

This list serves to entice, to draw the adventurer into the rich treasure chest of historical writings as an actual "doing." The sources provided pertain to themes presented within the text.

Baheless, J. (1950). *The eyes of discovery: The pageant of North America as seen by the first explorers.* Philadelphia, PA: J. B. Lippincott Co.

The adventures of North America's first explorers, including LaSalle and Lewis and Clark.

Belvin, W. (1973). *Give your heart to the hawks: A tribute to the mountain man.* Los Angeles, CA: Nash Publishing.

The mountain men told through story form. Great campfire reading, including John Colter's travels.

Butler, W. (1891). *The great lone land: A narrative travel and adventure in the Northwest of America.* (14th ed.). London: Sampson, Low, Marston & Co.

An early adventurer travels across the Canadian western interior. Also, see William Butler, The Wild North Land, for a winter travel account.

Merrick, E. (1942). *True north.* New York: Charles Scribner's and Sons.

A classic account of snowshoe travel in Labrador from a man who "got out" and got into the bush.

Oleson, D. (Ed.). (1981). *A wonderful country: The Quetico-Superior stories of Bill Magie.* Ashland, WI: Sigurd Olson Environmental Institute.

A collection of old-timer recollections and connections to place.

Schaffer, M. (1980). *Old Indian trails of the Canadian Rockies.* Banff, Alberta: The Whyte Foundation (Reprinted as A hunter of peace).

Exploration in the Canadian Rockies by a sensitive Quaker woman.

Thompson, D. (1971). *Travels in western North America 1784-1812.* (V. G. Hopwood, Ed.). Toronto: MacMillan.

The opening of the western interior of North America as told by the one man who could make that claim.

Wallace, D. (1905). *The lure of Labrador.* New York: F. Revell. (Reprinted in 1977 by Breakwater Books, Portugal Cove, Newfoundland).

A firsthand account of an epic misadventure.

Section Four

THE SOCIAL PSYCHOLOGY OF ADVENTURE EDUCATION

The Nature of the Experience

Priest earlier addressed the problem of defining key terms, one of which was "adventure." This section takes up, with reference to psychology, the key question, "What is adventure?" Why do people engage in adventure? What rewards does it provide? All of the answers come to this: People seek adventure because it enriches their lives. How so?

Henderson argues that adventure grounds one in his or her natural and cultural heritage. People need to know and understand the context of their lives, he suggests, and adventure is one path toward this understanding. An adventure is a mixing of physical and mythical experience. It stirs the imagination, especially if the adventurer contemplates the adventurers that have preceded him or her. Adventure can be exploration of a geography of hope and faith, a connecting to landscape. Barry Lopez has written recently of the "internal landscape" that responds, morally and spiritually, to the external landscape. Henderson suggests that adventure is a vehicle to connection of these landscapes.

Quinn approaches the question, "Why adventure?" more analytically than Henderson. He dissects the adventure experience and finds there subjectivity, discovery, desire, striving, uncertainty, excitement, fun, exhilaration and growth. The world can be a small and narrow place, he argues, unless one seeks to explore. Adventure is exploration, which requires extension of self. This extension leads to growth, which feels good, leads to further exploration, and thus do people move toward fulfillment.

The Csikszentmihalyis carry the analysis further. Their concept of "flow" is well known, and they present it again here in the context of adventure and adventure education. Flow is a useful way of describing and understanding the elements of the adventure experience—of what happens to a person in such an experience. The Csikszentmihalyis research yields insight into why people seek adventure and what they gain from it.

All of this essential analysis can be complex and confusing. Priest attempts to diagrammatically present a simple model of the adventure experience, a conceptual model based partly on the work of the Csikszentmihalyis. He explains how risk relates to competence in the adventurer, and what the various outcomes of the adventure experience may be. He reveals the positive and negative feedback loops that may be set off by adventure experiences. His approach yields useful visualizations of this experience.

Klint closes the section with a review of what developmental psychology has revealed about the value of adventure education. What effect does it have on self-concept, self-efficacy and perception of competence? She concludes that research has given insight into the outcome of the adventure experience, but has shed little light on the process. What specific elements of the adventure experience produce which results? There is, says Klint, much work to be done, but at least past inquiry gives clear direction to future research. Practitioners and researchers have only begun to think about and understand the psychology of adventure education.

The Essence of Adventure

Bill Quinn
Northern Illinois University

Goethe said: "Whatever you can do or dream you can do, begin it. Boldness has genius, power and magic in it."

Adventure. Adventure speaks of beginning, boldness, and power. Adventure connotes participation and active involvement in life. An adventure, a quest, begins because of a human desire, a drive to experience that which is hidden and unknown. "We are attracted by a deep forest or lake because it gives the impression that there is some truth to discover, some secret to abduct from the heart of the object. It is the eternal seduction of the hidden" (Dufrenne, 1973, p. 398). The discovery, the unveiling, is the recompense of the adventurous seeker. A desire for adventure may have directly contributed to the emergence of the human species from equatorial Africa untold eons ago. Ardrey (1976), in *The Hunting Hypothesis*, contends that a primordial sense of adventure stimulated early humans to discover and inhabit the world. He stated,

> The magnet of our nature commanded that we investigate certain blue Ethiopian hills, and what lay beyond. And so in the vast concourse of time we moved on past the veto of desert, into the chill of winters that our equatorial existence had never anticipated. But we did not go back. And that is what is so interesting. (p. 135)

Ardrey believes that the ancient drives of simian curiosity and propensities of predation combined together to create the desire for adventure in the human species. He continued:

> There had to be ancient winds within us, old primate curiosities, newer predator demand for exploration. These were not so much the biological consequences of cultural advance, but very old biological demands—that inhabit us still, to become a dominant quality in the life of our species. Adventure. (p. 136)

Adventure does not lie only within the objective natural world. It lies deep within oneself, within the spiritual, emotional, and intellectual spheres of personhood. An adventurous undertaking need not always be outwardly evident. High, dangerous, or spirited adventure may exist privately and be outwardly unobservable. Consider the appearance of two chess players engaged in an important match. Outwardly, they are as stoic as possible, but inwardly they are functioning intensely.

The question remains as to what the essence of adventure is. It is a desire for a something, a condition, which is absent. It is a process that begins with the acceptance of a situation where one knows one will need to call upon one's own *supposed* talents and spontaneously, irrevocably, act upon them. During the process of accepting the idea of placing oneself in a tenuous situation, one *must* harbor doubt as to the adequacy of one's ability. Without question, when complete confidence and competence reign, adventure cannot exist. Yet the essential feeling of adventure varies in degree. The stranger the new ground trodden upon, the further one goes beyond one's imagined talents, the more intense and profound the adventure becomes. Duration is a functioning part of the feeling of adventure. The longer the final outcome remains obscure, the closer one comes to the edge, the deadline, before culminating action resolves conflict, the more concentrated and reverberating the adventure becomes. Yet there are no final outcomes, only episodes.

The price of failure is always the same—there is loss. However small or great depends upon what has been originally risked. Loss, the result of error, may be physical—the skinning of the knee or the forfeiture of life; emotional—hurt feelings or the shattering of self-confidence; intellectual—a missed exam question or a situation where one's ideas are compelled to crumble; social—a lonely afternoon or ostracism by peers; or spiritual—a momentary lapse into indifference or the devastation of cherished beliefs. Inevitably, there is casualty.

But, what is a life that is dominated by the fear of pain? If pain appears as an archenemy, an intruder to be avoided at all costs, a person would be restricted to asking "Would this action I am contemplating hurt?" rather than "Would it be good to take a chance in this way?" To the person who assumes a risk, pain, if it does occur, will not feel less, but will matter less. There is so much more in the striving that matters (Kohak, 1984). The essential feeling of the striving is what Mitchell (1983), and Csikszentmihalyi (1975) before him, described as "flow." The flow state refers to a "a kind of personal transcendence" (Mitchell, 1983, p. 153), brought on by engaging in activity solely to inculcate the inherent rewards of that activity. But this explanation is not enough. Mitchell further elucidates the idea by describing the flow state as one where "a level of involvement such that consciousness at hand and the doing of it blend, that action and awareness become indistinguishable" (p. 154). The flow state, or personal transcendance experienced when risk is courted and met, describes a reason for inviting adventure into one's life.

The price of success may be even more harrowing. Triumph carries the requirement to continue for anyone honest to himself. As Eugene O'Neill (in Ferguson, 1980) put it,

> Those who succeed and do not push on to greater failure are the spiritual middle classers. Their stopping at success is the proof of their compromising insignificance... ...Only through the unattainable does man achieve a hope worth living and dying for—and so attain himself. (p. 673)

If a climber hasn't fallen, he hasn't climbed; and if a canoeist is dry, she hasn't paddled. Real fear comes from knowing that there is no honest place to hide.

But O'Neill has missed something—the knowledge that through adventure, peace is obtainable. Maybe its duration is ephemeral, and feelings of peace certainly vary from person to person, but peace is an outcome of adventure. D. H. Lawrence (1936) stated, "Peace is the state of fulfilling the deepest desire of the soul. It is the condition of flying within the greatest impulse that enters us from the unknown" (pp. 117-118). To fly, wrapped in an impulse from the unknown toward the unknown, lies close to the heart of the experience of adventure. Peace comes from confidence gained and the fulfillment of success. "When a man yields himself implicitly to the suggestion which transcends him, when he accepts gently and honorably his own creative fate, he is beautiful and beyond aspersion" (Lawrence, 1936, p. 671). He is also enmeshed in adventure and will soon be at peace. The reward of peace is the difference between adventure and thrill-seeking. The thrill-seekers find no peace.

In our contemporary society accolades are heaped upon those who, through their personal adventuring, achieve the stupendous and visibly great deeds. Grand adventurousness is recognized in those who confront death while seeking excitement. The price of a mistake is so great. Scaling Everest, diving to the ocean depth, mushing to the North Pole, or leaping from airplanes, is perceived as adventure to most onlookers and may well be perceived as adventure by the participant. William James (in McDermott, 1968) expressed an essential quality of adventure that is apparent through obvious risk:

> The element of precipitousness, of strength and strenuousness, intensity and danger. What excites and interests the looker on at life, what the romances and the statues celebrate ... is the everlasting battle of the powers of light with those of darkness; with heroism reduced to its bare chance. (p. 648)

He continues with the ideas that describe adventure and remind us again of O'Neill:

> Sweat and effort, human nature strained to its uttermost and on the rack, yet getting through alive, and then turning its back on success to pursue another more rare and arduous skill—this is the sort of thing the presence of which inspires us. (p. 648)

Visible actions of a stupendous nature catch the public eye because of the immediacy of confrontation and the extremity of the price of failure. A real sense of urgency is felt. However, there are magnificent adventures in human lives that are not applauded because of their commonality, even though these undertakings are no less compelling. Raising children honestly, choosing a career faithfully, maintaining a marriage continually, now these are adventures! I have seen adventure in the deep darkness of my daughter's eyes, in the recesses of my mate's feelings, and in the expressions of those whom I served.

To engage in adventurous activity and to fail will necessitate some sort of loss. But what is the price of choosing not to seek or purposely avoiding tenuous situations? The price is torpidity, and the result is stagnation. One must actively seek an adventurous way of life; otherwise there is only a small and narrow world to explore. A diminutive existence then ensues. D. H. Lawrence (1936) conceptualizes,

> We all must die. But we need not all live ... We may refuse to live, we may refuse to pass into the unknown of life; we may deny ourselves to life altogether ... Unless we submit our will to the flooding of life, there is no life in us. (p. 673)

So the answers to the questions, why risk, why engage the possibility of penalty and discomfort, and why approach one's personal limit, become obvious. Without actively seeking, without attempting to, and going beyond what one already knows one can accomplish, there is no growth. Strenuousness of mind, heart, and body engenders growth. Where there is no growth, where stagnation is the rule, a human being offers nothing, either to one's self or to society.

Even without regard to any of these thoughts, without conceptualizing the need for adventure in one's life, individuals would still seek it. Adventure is courted because it is rewarding, it is exciting, fun, and exhilarating.

Taking part in some discovery about oneself and one's environment is pleasurable. Self-knowledge is always an outcome of adventure, be it happy or sad, uplifting or degrading.

But the emotions that precede and lead to exhilaration and excitement are often fear, hesitation, and apprehension. Again, one is mired between an enlivened state and a static, stagnant existence. The catalyst is the need for committed action. So, the frightening question comes back again. Granted that I am the master of my own destiny, how shall I fulfill that destiny? (Novak, 1970) Why scale that rock wall to the east? Why make that national presentation? Why complete a doctoral dissertation? One is inevitably drawn back to the desire for the hidden, the inexplicable human urge to experience that which is just out of range of prior background, to supplement insight with experience previously unknown.

René Daumal (1967), in *Mount Analogue*, expresses the feeling thus:

> You cannot stay on the summit forever; you have to come down again—so why bother in the first place? Just this; what is above knows what is below, but what is below does not know what is above. One climbs, one sees, one descends; one sees no longer, *but one has seen* [emphasis added]. (p. 103)

As a result of an experience like this, one also has a broader base from which to attempt to see again, and again. An attitude that permits a person to seek adventure in life feeds upon itself and renews itself. Any life worth living is worth living with the advent of a venture.

REFERENCES

Ardrey, R. (1976). *The hunting hypothesis.* New York: Atheneum.

Csikszentmihalyi, M. (1975). *Beyond boredom and anxiety.* San Francisco, CA: Jossey- Bass

Daumal, R. (1967). *Mount analogue.* San Francisco: City of Lights Books.

Dufrene, M. (1973). *The phenomonology of aesthetic experience.* Evanston, IL: Northwestern University Press.

Ferguson, M. (1980). *The aquarian conspiracy.* Los Angeles, CA: J. P. Tarcher Inc.

Kohak, E. (1984). *The embers and the stars.* Chicago: University of Chicago Press.

Lawrence, D. H. (1936). *Phoenix, the posthumous papers.* New York: Viking Press.

McDermott, J. (Ed.). (1968). *The writing of William James.* New York: Random House.

Mitchell, R. G. (1983). *Mountain experience: the psychology and sociology of adventure.* Chicago: University of Chicago Press.

Novak, M. (1970). *The experience of nothingness.* New York: Harper and Row.

Adventure and the Flow Experience

Mihaly Csikszentmihalyi

&

Isabella Selega Csikszentmihalyi
University of Chicago

It has not been easy for the human race to survive. Through millions of years our ancestors have been challenged by all kinds of trials and tribulations: ice ages, saber-toothed tigers, droughts, and diseases. If we are still here, it is because they were able to develop a superb array of survival tools. Some of these are well known: our complex brain, our nimble fingers, our ability to cooperate, and of course the various technologies these made possible, ranging from the taming of fire to the splicing of genes. But there is one advantage we know less about, even though it must have been indispensible to our ancestors in their long struggle to survive in a mysterious and dangerous environment. This advantage is the enjoyment we derive from exploring the unknown and confronting the unexpected.

During the course of evolution, we have learned to enjoy those activities that are necessary for individual survival and the reproduction of the species. Human life would have disappeared from earth long ago if we did not derive pleasure from food and sex. Physiological rewards have been built over time into our bodies so that we may feel good when we do what needs to be done. But man does not live by bread alone. To survive in an unpredictable and dangerous environment, human beings must also enjoy a certain amount of novelty and danger.

And this is indeed the case. Someday we shall be able to document exactly the physiological benefit that "adrenaline rushes" provide rock climbers or sky divers, or the release of endorphins that a "runner's high" brings to the nervous system of athletes. In the meantime, even though we lack an understanding of the biological mechanisms, it is quite clear that facing the challenge of the unknown is generally pleasurable to most people. The "spirit of adventure" is not dead, and it must have been strong and healthy through the endless stretches of nameless centuries in which our ancestors struggled to gain a foothold on the earth.

In our studies, we have found that people involved in adventurous pursuits such as rock climbing (Csikszentmihalyi 1975; Mitchell

1983), solo long-distance sailing (Macbeth 1988), polar explorations (Logan 1985), spelunking (Massimini & Carli 1986), and a variety of similar endeavors, report a state of optimal experience we have called flow. To understand why adventure is so attractive, it is important to understand what happens to people when they experience flow.

CHARACTERISTICS OF THE FLOW EXPERIENCE

Flow describes a state of experience that is engrossing, intrinsically rewarding, and "outside the parameters of worry and boredom" (Csikszentmihalyi, 1975). Since its introduction some 14 years ago, the flow concept has been applied theoretically in a variety of disciplines, including psychology, cultural anthropology, and sociology. Its impact has probably been strongest in the study of free time: play, sports, leisure, and recreation (Csikszentmihalyi, 1969, 1975). On a wider level, the cumulating research from these years has resulted in its application in educational, clinical, and commercial settings (Csikszentmihalyi & Csikszentmihalyi, 1988).

The flow concept emerged from observing and interviewing people who expended much time and energy on activities that provided few extrinsic rewards such as money or recognition: artists, rock climbers, dancers, music composers, amateur athletes, high school basketball players (Csikszentmihalyi, 1975). Their answers suggested a common set of characteristics that constituted a feeling of enjoyment, well-being, and competence that distinguished their particular involvement from the less satisfying events common to most of everyday life. Since what motivated the activity usually seemed not to be external rewards but the activity itself, the conclusion was that it was *the quality of the subjective experience itself* that made the behavior intrinsically rewarding.

What are the elements of the flow experience that make it a desirable and motivating state? Certainly a crucial one is the person's level of absorption with the activity. In a flow state there is characteristically a total involvement with the chosen activity, one that typically offers constant challenges that have to be met with appropriate skills, and the ability to match these provides immediate and gratifying feedback. An underlying assumption of flow-producing activities is that there "are ways for people to test the limits of their being, to transcend their former conception of self by extending skills and undergoing new experience" (Csikszentmihalyi, 1975, p. 26). Although ideally flow would be the result of pure involvement, some people need other inducements, such as competition, extrinsic rewards (money, recognition, or the prestige and glamour associated with certain activities), and the risk involved in physical danger, to get involved in flow activities. But when the activity itself becomes the goal, when it becomes a flow-producing experience, the following characteristics are what make it worthy of repetition to the participant:

1. A person in flow knows clearly what must be done, and gets quick feedback about how well he or she is doing. Goals and means are logically ordered, so that it is possible to foresee the results of alternative actions. A tennis player always knows she must return the ball to the opponent's court, and the goal of a chess player is to mate the opponent's king before his own is mated. The many ambiguities of everyday life are banished. However, in flow there is no pause to evaluate the feedback, the person is too involved with the experience to reflect on it. Action and reaction have become so well-synchronized that the resulting behavior is automatic. This is true even in endeavors that are not as clear-cut as those of a tennis or chess player. A composer of music or an explorer set for themselves tasks that are much more open-ended; however, they must have within themselves certain internalized goals that allow them to recognize positive feedback. For instance, the composer's goal is to write down certain chords and harmonies imagined in the mind; if the notes sound right when

played back, the feedback is positive. The explorer may not have a specific goal in mind, but each day some objective must be set and achieved. Without knowing whether they are doing well, neither could feel the enjoyment that makes their efforts a flow experience.

2. Because goals and feedback are so clear, the flow experience involves a merging of action and awareness. A person in flow has no dualistic perspective: There is awareness of the actions but not of the awareness itself. All the attention is concentrated on the relevant stimuli, and one stops being aware of oneself as separate from what is being engaged in. This feeling was aptly described by an expert rock climber in our sample: "You are so involved in what you are doing [that] you aren't thinking of yourself as separate from the immediate activity ... You don't see yourself as separate from what you are doing." A dancer described her feelings when a performance is going well in very similar terms: "Your concentration is very complete. Your mind isn't wandering, you are not thinking of something else; you are totally involved in what you are doing ... Your body is awake all over ... Your energy is flowing very smoothly. You feel relaxed, comfortable, and energetic." Although the flow experience may appear effortless, it often requires strenuous physical exertion or highly disciplined mental activity. For this reason it is difficult to maintain for any length of time without at least momentary interruptions.

3. This merging of action and awareness is made possible by a third characteristic of flow experiences: a centering of attention on a limited stimulus field. To ensure that people will concentrate on their actions, potentially intruding stimuli must be kept out of attention; that is to say, one's consciousness is "narrowed" so that irrelevant stimuli are excluded. In play and leisure activities, the rules of the game tend to perform this function. In less-structured activities, certain routines and settings facilitate the limiting of the stimulus field and the keeping of attention on what is going on. The important thing is that irrelevant information is weeded out. A mountaineer describes the results of this complete focusing of attention on what is going on: "When you're [climbing] you're not aware of other problematic life situations. It becomes a world unto its own, significant only to itself. It's a concentration thing. Once you're into the situation, it's incredibly real, and you're very much in charge of it. It becomes your total world." A basketball player expresses the same idea: "The court—that's all that matters... Sometimes on court I think of a problem, like fighting with my steady girl, and I think that's nothing compared to the game. You can think about a problem all day but as soon as you get in the game, the hell with it!" And a dancer sums up the benefits emerging from this centering of attention on a limited stimulus field: "I get a feeling that I don't get anywhere else ... I have more confidence in myself than any other time.... Dance is like therapy. If I am troubled about something, I leave it out of the door as I go in [the dance studio]."

4. A consequence of this intense concentration is a fourth characteristic of the flow experience, often described as "loss of ego" and "self-forgetfulness." When an activity completely involves a person with its demands for action, the self that serves to negotiate between a person's actions and those of others is no longer necessary. Although in some situations a person may lose touch with personal physical reality, in others there may be a heightened awareness of internal processes. What is usually lost in flow is not the awareness of one's body or of one's functions, but only the self *construct*, the "I" as the actor or intermediary that a person learns to interpose between stimulus and response. A person making a difficult ascent has to concentrate on the role of the mountain-climber in order to survive and cannot afford to bring into question any other aspect of the personal self. Even the possible threat from the mountain

itself does not intrude because a good climber feels well-equipped to face the challenges presented to him, and does not need to bring the self into play. The loss of the sense of self is sometimes accompanied by a feeling of union with the environment, whether it is the mountain one is climbing, or one's team, or even the universe. The sense of time may also change: Hours may seem to pass by in minutes, or the intensity of the concentration and the heightened awareness may give seconds a feeling of incredible depth and infinity. This lack of preoccupation with the self, this loss of self-consciousness paradoxically allows people to expand their self-concept: What emerges is a feeling of self-transcendence, of the boundaries of the self being expanded. Thus a good violinist, surrounded by the stream of sound she helps to create, may feel she is part of the "harmony of the spheres." A climber may begin to feel a sense of kinship developing between fingers and rock, between the vulnerable body and the surrounding stone, sky, and wind. An ocean sailor during a long night watch will begin to feel that the boat is an extension of himself, moving to the same rhythms and to a common goal. In each case the person becomes part of a concrete system of action greater than the individual self. This expansion of one's being, accompanied by a successful matching of skills to challenges, is deeply enjoyable, and at the same time it produces a person enriched by new achievements and a stronger confidence.

5. People in flow feel potentially in control of their actions and of the environment. Rather than an active awareness of control, however, one ceases to worry about losing control, as one often does in real life. This feeling is true even in situations where the objective dangers are quite real—hang-gliding, deep-sea diving, spelunking, race car driving, rock climbing—yet they are seen as predictable and manageable. Risk-takers often claim that their enjoyment comes not from the danger itself, but from their ability to minimize it, from their feeling that they are able to control potentially dangerous forces. Rock climbers must always be aware of two types of problematic situations: "objective dangers" such as falling rock, drastic drops in temperature, sudden storms, even avalanches; and "subjective dangers" related to the climber's lack of skill, such as being unable to correctly estimate the difficulty of a rock face in relation to one's ability. Yet the whole point of climbing is to avoid objective dangers as much as possible, and to eliminate subjective dangers entirely by rigorous discipline and sound preparation. As a result many good climbers maintain that their mountaineering exploits are far less dangerous than crossing a busy street in a large city: They feel that the objective dangers presented by the crowds, buses, and taxi drivers are less predictable than those on a mountain, which can be overcome by skills. Sailors who have circumnavigated the earth's vast oceans alone on a small boat have expressed the same types of feelings. It is this confidence of being able to exercise control through one's skills that not only makes flow experiences enjoyable but also ensures a desire for their repetition.

6. The final characteristic of the flow experience is its autotelic nature. The components of the flow state are usually so enjoyable and psychically rewarding, and so unlike the drudgery of most of life, that there is a desire to repeat activities that produce the flow experience. Even if initially done for extrinsic reasons, the activity becomes intrinsically rewarding. Some surgeons get so involved in their work that they volunteer their services to local hospitals while on vacation because they find using their skills more enjoyable than sitting on a beach. Children forced to take music lessons may in time get to enjoy playing music for its own sake if they begin to hear the results of using their skills. The same happens to high school mathematics students who are able to match their skills to the increasingly complex problems being presented in the classrooms.

THE IMPORTANCE OF THE FLOW EXPERIENCE

Why is the flow experience important? Probably because it provides a key to understanding the strivings of the self and illustrates the human search for an improved quality of individual well-being. The fact that many flow activities are rarely extrinsically rewarded, or at least not rewarded to the extent of the effort involved, illustrates the fact that man needs more than the fulfillment of genetically programmed needs. Both Csikszentmihalyi (1975) and Mitchell (1983) have shown that persons with jobs and statuses viewed as highly desirable by others look for flow experiences outside their everyday work and social settings. Moreover, as modern life becomes more and more complex, feelings of apathy on the one hand and alienation on the other may become even more widespread, and increasing numbers of persons will strive to find situations in which they feel that what they do is of their own choice and under their own control.

An extreme example of this search for improved experience are the full-time ocean cruisers studied by Macbeth (1988), many of whom feel that everyday life contains meaningless goals, alienates the person from the rhythms of nature, and is antagonistic to the autonomy of the individual. In ocean cruising they find the sense of fulfillment and enjoyment of life that was missing in their previous endeavors. As a result they go so far as to drop out of society to pursue an autotelic but solitary *lifestyle* that they feel gives them autonomy and choice, and enhances their identity and sense of competence. These, of course, are the same goals that are central to *activities* such as rock climbing, chess playing, or adventure-seeking; the difference is that such flow experiences are rarely pursued full-time. Most people will continue to find their flow experience in free-time activities, although some are lucky enough to find it on their jobs. Other people, who may possess what we call an "autotelic personality," are actually able to structure flow into compulsory activities such as school or work—situations to which many others respond with boredom or frustration. Ideally, of course, school and work, which take up so many years of a person's life, would be structured to provide flow experiences to a maximum number of people (Delle Fave & Massimini, 1988; Rathunde, 1988).

FLOW AND ADVENTURE EDUCATION

Where does adventure education fit into the picture? Certainly it responds to the human desire for novelty, discovery, uncertainty, and problem-solving. The pursuit of these attributes assumes that people are motivated by intrinsic rewards, in addition to extrinsic rewards based on physiological drives, stimulus-response, and social conditioning. Hebb (1955), Berlyne (1960), and others have introduced into modern psychology the idea that organisms need to do more than satisfy pre-programmed needs, that an optimal level of stimulation is also needed. One may extrapolate from this position that a person will enjoy an activity if it offers a pattern of stimulation not ordinarily available in the environment; it must also have been freely chosen (deCharms, 1968; Deci & Ryan, 1985) and allow the person to use his physical, sensory, or intellectual potential in a new or challenging way. However, this does not explain why certain activities are considered enjoyable and others are not. By interviewing participants in "autotelic" activities in our pilot studies, we were able to separate eight items that were regularly cited as reasons for enjoying such activities. These items were then introduced to the later sample groups studied, who were asked to rank their particular activity according to a questionnaire containing both intrinsic and extrinsic reasons for enjoying the activity (Csikszentmihalyi, 1975). The "autotelic factor" of each activity was determined by the ranking given to each reason. The eight factors were:

1. The enjoyment of the experience and the use of skills
2. The activity itself: the pattern, the action, the world it provides
3. Friendship, companionship
4. Development of personal skills
5. Measurement of self against own ideals
6. Emotional release
7. Competition, measurement of self against others
8. Prestige, regard, glamour

Adventure participants would probably rank the reasons for the activities they undertake in an order very similar to that given by rock climbers (Csikszentmihalyi, 1975) and full-time ocean cruisers (Macbeth, 1988), who rated "the enjoyment of the experience and the use of skills," and "the activity itself: the pattern, the action, the world it provides," as the two top items. Adventure activities, having few extrinsic rewards, are a way of challenging oneself to participate in experiences that are removed from everyday opportunities, that may use skills not called for in daily routines, or conversely, as a way of developing skills that one admires and would like to acquire. The milieu in which these skills are practiced—the environment as well as the individuals sharing the same interests and goals—is probably also an important factor. The importance of the other items is likely to vary with the person and the particular activity engaged in.

Like participants in other autotelic activities, adventure participants are searching for a peculiar state of experience, an experience that is rarely accessible in everyday life. As Mitchell (1983) has pointed out in connection with the choice of mountaineering as an avocation, "The key concept, the desirable condition, the sought-after goal of climbing is the social-psychological condition of flow." What is being sought is the experience corresponding to an unusual match between person and environment. The challenges and skills in question are based on real elements of the situation—such as the waves confronting the sailor—but what effectively determines the quality of the experience is the person's subjective estimation of what the level of challenges and skills are at any given time.

The flow model suggests that to derive enjoyment from life reliably requires the ability to get into flow, stay in it, and make the process evolve. This in turn depends on a capacity to structure interaction with the environment in a way that facilitates flow. Specifically, the characteristics of the autotelic experience correspond to capacities to (1) focus attention on the present moment and the activity at hand, (2) define one's goals in an activity and identify the means for reaching them, and (3) seek feedback and focus on its informational aspects. In addition to these abilities, the dependence of enjoyment on a balancing of challenges and skills suggests the importance of a capacity to continuously adjust this balance by using anxiety and boredom as information, and identifying new challenges as skills grow. Being able to tolerate the anxiety-provoking interactions that test one's skills also appears to be important. Finally, other attributes are likely to have an effect outside of the particular interaction; among these would be the ability to delay gratification, which is necessary for the eventual enjoyment of activities that require a significant investment of energy before they start providing intrinsic rewards. Clearly all of these are important in adventure activities. As Priest and Baillie (1987) have pointed out, good adventure education consists of an accurate evaluation of both the environmental dangers being pursued (risk) and the individual ability of each participant to confront them (competence). It is the careful matching of risk and competence in situations of progressing complexity that produces the experiences characteristic of the flow state. Eventually those who are able to find enjoyment in adventure activities made on purpose to provide autotelic experiences, are more likely to begin finding flow in other areas of life as well. Indeed, a new range of activities may be opened to them as avenues for enjoyment. And when people derive enjoyment from their daily lives, they will spend less time feeling apathetic, anxious, or bored.

This ability to match ever-complexifying skills and challenges produces feelings of enjoyment and achievement that lead to a stronger and more confident sense of self. Over the millions of years of evolution humans have been challenged by many trials. Rather than giving up, they have met these head-on, and have even managed to derive pleasure from facing the unknown and the unexpected. By being able to turn adversity into flow experiences, they have managed to control nature and free themselves from many of the constraints imposed by the need to survive. However, at each stage of development, after having found a comfortable adaptation to the environment, humans have not been content to rest on their achievements but have pushed on to new frontiers, led by the enjoyment of the unknown. At present, when we are faced with a daunting array of possibilities for action, the ability to find flow may be as big a challenge as mankind has ever encountered before.

REFERENCES

Berlyne, D. E. (1960). *Conflict, arousal and curiosity*. New York: McGraw Hill.

Csikszentmihalyi, M. (1969). The Americanization of rock climbing. *University of Chicago Magazine, 61*(6), 20-27.

Csikszentmihalyi, M. (1975). *Beyond boredom and anxiety*. San Francisco, CA: Jersey-Boss

Csikszentmihalyi, M. & Csikszentmihalyi, I. S. (1988). *Optimal experience: Psychological studies of flow in conscious.* New York: Cambridge University Press.

deCharms, R. (1976). *Personal causation: The internal affective determinants of behavior*. New York: Academic Press.

Deci, E. L., & Ryan, R. M. (1985). *Intrinsic motivation and self-determination of human behavior*. New York: Plenum Press.

Delle Fave, A., & Massimini, F. (1988). Modernization and the changing contexts of flow in work and leisure. M. Csikszentmihalyi & I. S. Csikszentmihalyi (Eds.), *Optimal experience: Psychological studies of flow in conscious* (pp. 193-213). New York: Cambridge University Press.

Getzels, J. W., & Csikszentmihalyi, M. (1976). *The creative vision: A longitudinal study of problem finding art*. New York: Wiley Interscience.

Hebb, D. O. (1955). Drives and the CNS. *Psychological Review, 62*, 243-254.

Logan, R. D. (1985). The flow experience in solitary ordeals. *Journal of Humanistic Psychology, 25*(4), 70-89.

Macbeth, J. (1988). Ocean cruising. M. Csikszentmihalyi & I. S. Csikszentmihalyi (Eds.), *Optimal experience: Psychological studies of flow in conscious* (pp. 214-231). New York: Cambridge University Press.

Massimini, F. & Carli, M. (1986). La selezione psicologica umana tra biologia e cultura. F. Massimini & P. Inghilleri (Eds.), *L'esperienza quotidiana* (pp. 65-84). Milan: Franco Angeli.

Mitchell, R. G. (1983). *Mountain experience: The psychology and sociology of adventure*. Chicago: University of Chicago Press.

Priest, S., & Baillie, R. (1987). Justifying risk to others: The real razor's edge. *Journal of Experiental Education, 10*(1), 16-22.

Rathunde, K. (1988). Optimal experience and the family context. M. Csikszentmihalyi & I. S. Csikszentmihalyi (Eds.), *Optimal experience: Psychological studies of flow in conscious* (pp. 342-63). New York: Cambridge University Press.

The Adventure Experience Paradigm

Simon Priest
Brock University

Paradigms are merely conceptual models and theories designed to view and explain phenomena in life. One such recent perspective, the Adventure Experience Paradigm (Martin & Priest, 1986), was designed to interpret adventure experiences. Based on the works of Ellis (1973), Csikszentmihalyi(1975), and Mortlock (1984), the paradigm is diagrammed in Figure 1 on the following page. Before reading on, a review of the definitions given in the chapter on semantics is now warranted.

Note the model has two axes: those of risk (the potential to lose something of value) and competence (a synergy of skill, knowledge, attitude, behavior, confidence, and experience). Recall from the last section on philosophy that challenge is the interplay of risk and competence. In this model, five such conditions of interplay are shown. The condition, or results, depends on the balance of risk and competence.

When risks are low and competence is high, a condition termed "exploration and experimentation" exists. Using the common activity of canoeing, this is likened to practicing paddle strokes on a calm lake. As risks increase, and/or competence decreases, the conditions of "adventure, peak adventure, and misadventure" occur. Returning to canoeing, these would be respectively analogous to paddling on gently moving water, successfully running a fierce rapid, and dumping overboard in white water. These four conditions are acceptable learning opportunities for any adventurer. Learning basic skills, applying them to a challenging task, testing one's limits on the razor's edge, and having to deal with the consequences of error are the mainstay of education from and through adventure.

However, the fifth condition of "devastation and disaster" is a place where few adventurers choose to tread. Occurring when risks are high and competence is low, this frightening condition should have no role in educational experiences. People may learn from misadventures, from which they may recover, but deaths result in negative adventure experiences and only reverse the educational merit of adventure.

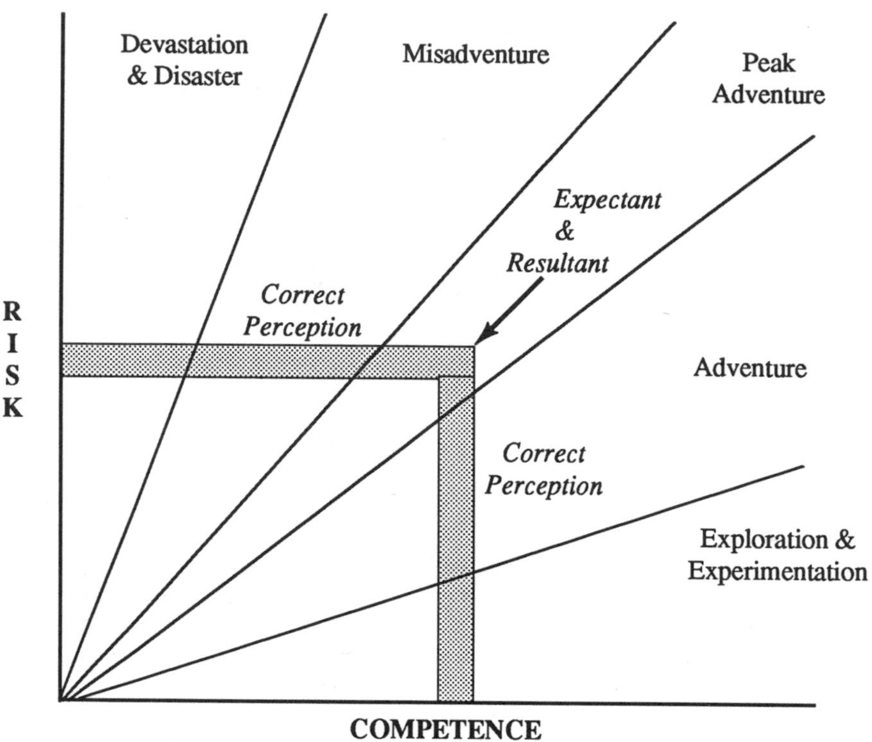

Figure 1
The Adventure Experience Paradigm © 1985 by Simon Priest & Peter Martin

The key to an experience being adventurous, then, is uncertainty of outcome (Priest & Baillie, 1987). In fact, adventure is simply leisure with uncertainty (Carpenter and Priest, 1989). The uncertainty comes from the risks inherent in the activity and becomes challenging when a person applies personal competence against the risks in an attempt to resolve that uncertainty. Furthermore, people tend to select risks that balance their competence in order to achieve optimal arousal (Ellis, 1973), a state of flow (Csikszentmihalyi, 1975), and/or peak adventure experiences (Priest, 1987).

For these reasons, adventures are personally specific (based on personal competence) and situationally specific (based on situational risks). In other words, an adventure for one person, in a particular place, at a given time, may not be adventure for another, or for the same person in a different place or time. Like leisure, adventure is purely "a state of mind" (Mitchell, 1983).

The state-of-mind concept dictates human behavior and, in turn, is driven by human perceptions of reality. Hence, both risk and competence (the two axes of the model) may be thought of as having two possible values: real and perceived. Unfortunately for most people engaged in adventures, these are often not the same value. Novices tend to misperceive the risks and competence of an adventure experience. Two types of such novices are common.

First, timid and fearful people overperceive the risk (this is going to be dangerous) and underperceive their competence (I can't do this). If we consider that the perceptions of these people tend to dictate their expectations, then they are likely expecting a condition of misadventure (see Figure 2). Also, if the real values of risk and competence dictate the actual outcome, then a condition like exploration and experimentation may result. This adventure experience is undesireable because,

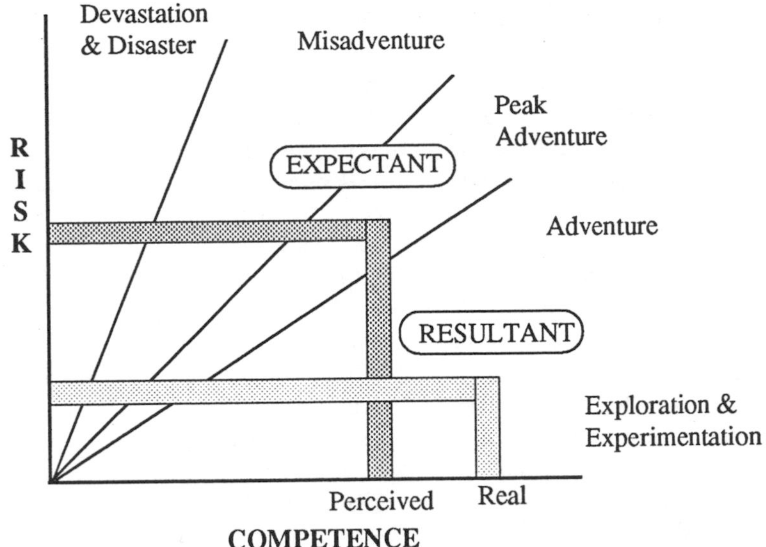

Figure 2
Profile of the Timid and Fearful Individual

when left to their own accord, the timid and fearful will miss their opportunity to experience a self-actualizing adventure, and this is a shame (see Figure 2).

Second, arrogant and fearless people underperceive the risk (this is going to be a breeze) and overperceive their competence (I can do this the best). Again, if the perceptions of these people tend to dictate their expectations, then they are likely expecting a condition of adventure (see Figure 3). Also, if the real values of risk and competence dictate the actual outcome, then a condition like devastation and disaster may result. This adventure experience is equally if not more undesirable than the one above, since the arrogant and fearless will injure themselves and may likely take some other adventurers with them, and this is unacceptable (see Figure 3).

These kinds of shortcomings are often avoided by experienced adventurers. Through repreated exposure to the risks and by repeated application of their competence, these people have become astute: accurate in their perceptions. Hence, one goal of adventure education should be to create astute individuals: people who correctly perceive the situational risks and their personal competence, plus seek adventure experiences where the two variables are matched for a peak adventure.

The solution to the problems elucidated above is known as the faciliated adventure experience. Through structured and controlled experiences under the supervision of a facilitator or leader, people can make advances toward astuteness. These experiences are said to be structured, since the facilitator sets up the level of challenge as a custom fit for the individual; and are said to be controlled, because the risks that are manipulated are strictly the perceived values (the real values are maintained at acceptable and/or low levels). The key to the operation is the facilitator, who must be sufficiently experienced and astute enough to perceive the risks and the people's competence more accurately than they can. Two examples are shown in Figures 4 through 7 on the following pages.

By way of illustration, consider a timid and fearful man on a high ropes traverse. The facilitator has structured an experience where this person is asked to walk across a tight rope fifty feet above the ground with only a rope strung from the far tree for balance and support. Based on perceived values, he is expecting a misadventure or, even worse, devastation and disaster! In actuality, the real values are quite different, since he is belayed (protected by a safety line). After considerable coaxing and assistance from the facilitator, he completes the traverse with the accompanying feeling of elation. The facilitator assists him in reflecting on his adventure and after some thought and discussion he now realizes that the task was not so dangerous and that he really was capable enough to complete it. This learning may later transfer to daily living concerns, where perhaps the man expresses timid and fearful behaviors when meeting new people.

As a second case, take an arrogant and fearless woman on a rock climb. The facilitator has structured an experience where she is asked to climb a particularly difficult route that has previously been the topic of some bragging on her part. Based on perceived values, she is expecting exploration and experimentation or, at best, mere adventure! In actuality, the real values are quite different, since she is belayed (protected by a safety line), but the facilitator has chosen a very difficult route and expects her to fail. After considerable effort, she has fallen off the crux of the climb repeatedly and is exhausted. The facilitator now assists her in reflecting back on her misadventure and after some thought and discussion she realizes that the task was indeed more difficult than she expected and that she really was not as good as she was saying. This learning may later transfer to daily living concerns, where perhaps the woman expresses arrogant and fearless behaviors when working on projects as part of a small group.

These types of facilitated adventure experiences are repeated in different contexts, but with similar structuring and control. The upshot is that people slowly shift their perceptions toward becoming "in tune" with reality: they slowly become astute! With astuteness often comes improvements in self-concept and in socialization. Interpersonal and intrapersonal relationships benefit from such adventure experiences. The paradigm described helps visualize how this takes place.

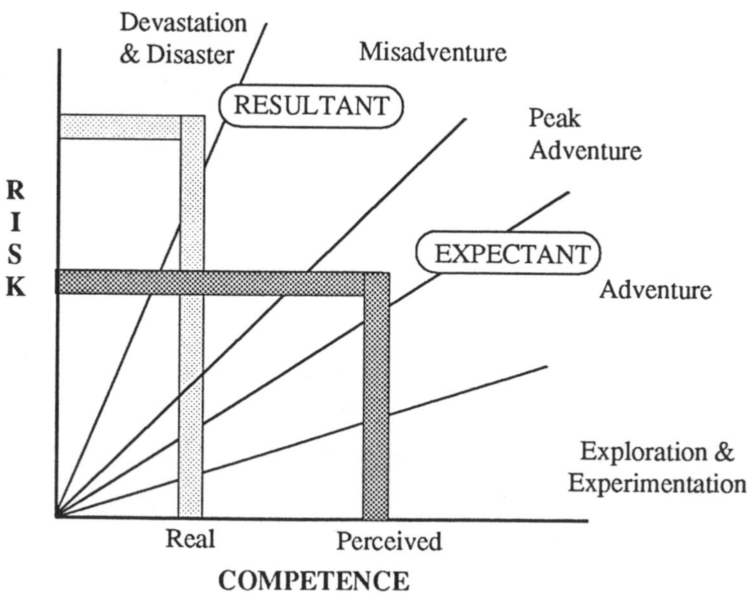

Figure 3
Profile of the Arrogant and Fearless Individual

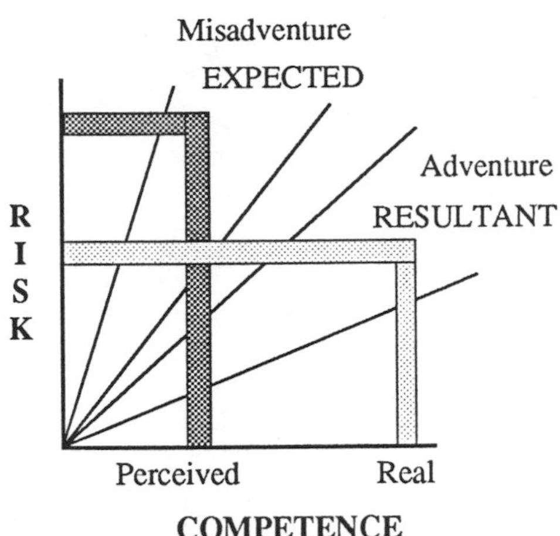

Figure 4
Before the facilitated adventure experience for the timid and fearful participant

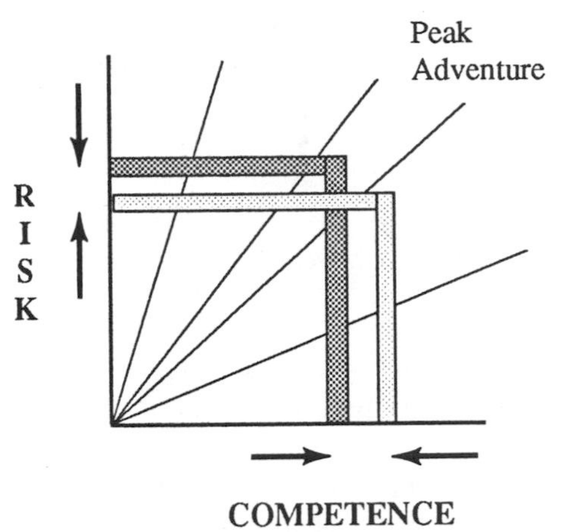

Figure 5
After the facilitated adventure experience for the timid and fearful participant

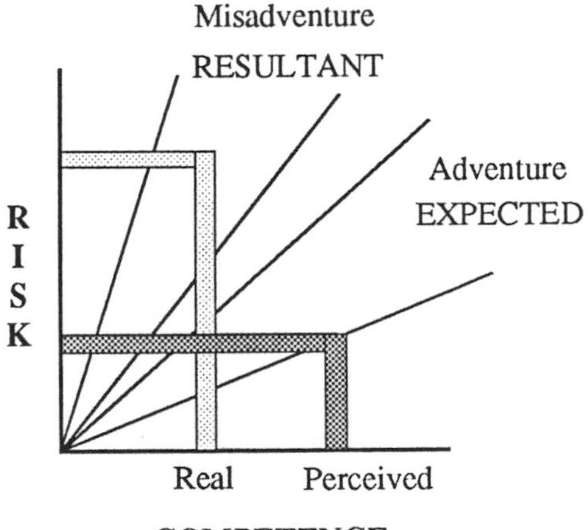

Figure 6
Before the facilitated adventure experience for the arrogant and fearless participant

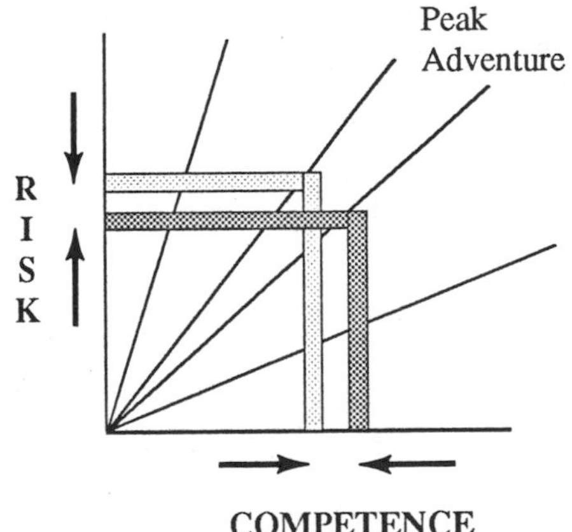

Figure 7
After the facilitated adventure experience for the arrogant and fearless participant

REFERENCES

Carpenter, G, & Priest, S. (1989). The adventure experience paradigm and non-outdoor leisure pursuits. *Leisure Studies, 8*(1), 65-75.

Csikszentmihalyi, M. (1975). *Beyond boredom and anxiety.* San Francisco, CA: Jossey-Bass.

Ellis, M. J. (1973). *Why people play.* Englewood Cliffs: Prentice-Hall.

Martin, P., & Priest, S. (1986). Understanding the adventure experience. *Journal of Adventure Education, 3*(1), 18-21.

Mitchell, R. G. (1983). *Mountain experience: The psychology and sociology of adventure.* Chicago: University of Chicago Press.

Mortlock, C. (1984). *The Adventure Alternative.* Cumbria, United Kingdom: Cicerone.

Priest, S. (1987). Modeling the adventure experience. R. Yerkes (Ed.). *Outdoor education across America: Weaving the web,* (pp. 7-12). Las Cruces, NM: ERIC CRESS.

Priest, S., & Baillie, R. (1987). Justifying the risk to others: The real razor's edge. *Journal of Experiential Education, 10*(1), 6-22.

New Directions for Inquiry into Self-Concept and Adventure Experiences

Kimberley Ann Klint
University of Oregon

The adventure experience has been attributed with the potential for enhancing human development in the physical, cognitive, and affective domains (Ford & Blanchard, 1985). Benefits associated with the adventure experience in the physical domain include increased levels of strength, cardiovascular and muscular endurance, and feelings of well-being. Cognitive development centers around the development of an enriched body of knowledge associated with a variety of topics, including the environment, safety skills, and activity skills. Finally, self-concept, senses of achievement and motivation, and stress control represent some of the affective components that may be influenced by an adventure experience. This latter area is of particular interest to many adventure programmers. If adventure experiences can indeed enhance affective development, then planned adventure experiences could be considered attractive alternatives to therapeutic programming and human development.

The notion that adventure experiences offer opportunities for affective development is not new. The Outward Bound Movement has been the guiding ship for adventure education around the world since its conception in 1941 (Wichmann, 1976). The original aim of the movement was to build character and develop survival skills in young seamen. These goals directly address all three areas of human development: affective, cognitive, and physical. The initial Outward Bound experiences were deemed a success, and soon Outward Bound programs were established around the world. Other adventure programs also were initiated, many modeling themselves after the Outward Bound program. The Outward Bound Movement came to North America in 1963.

Since its conception, the Outward Bound experience has been subject to the researcher's microscope. In particular, researchers have tested Outward Bound's claim that it is an experience through which personal growth and self-perception are enhanced (Ewert, 1983). Support for this hypothesis has been forwarded on repeated occasions. An Outward Bound experience has been found to enhance self-confidence and other self-perceptions (Fletcher, 1970; Lee & Schoder, 1969; Nye, 1976; Hendy, 1976; Stremba, 1977; Wetmore, 1972); reduce recidivism (Kelly & Baer, 1969); enhance motivation levels (Kolb, 1965); and enhance self-actualization (Vander Wilt & Klocke, 1971). The benefits of adventure have not been limited to the Outward Bound experience, since similar results have been associated with many other adventure programs (c.f Ewert, 1983).

These studies are to be commended because they have attempted the difficult task of gaining quantitative understanding of affective development while maintaining the integrity of the adventure experience. Unfortunately, as with many compromising situations, these results paint a far from complete picture. Study findings support the hypothesis that the adventure experience can influence affective development. However, they fail to provide clues as to how this influence is developed, and more importantly, what aspects of the adventure experience are salient to the development of affect. In other words, there is understanding about what adventure experiences can potentially accomplish, and yet there are few insights as to how these potentials are fulfilled. Future research needs to move away from identifying products associated with adventure experiences and toward understanding the process. The testing of theoretical frameworks could provide a starting point for such studies. The purpose of this paper is to review theories of self-concept that may be applied toward understanding the adventure experience.

SELF-CONCEPT

Self-concept is a generalized term referring to the mental image one creates about oneself. Other terms such as self-esteem, self-efficacy, self-confidence, and self-image refer to specific aspects of the self, and sometimes their meanings overlap. For example, self-esteem refers to satisfaction and confidence in oneself, while self-confidence connotes confidence in one's abilities and powers to accomplish a goal or task.

Interest in "the self" as an influential factor of behavior dates back to the first century B.C. (Ewert, 1983). However, notions about how "the self" was involved were not crystallized until William James (1890) posed a theory of self-concept. He hypothesized that self-concept was related to achievement. He proposed that one's feelings of worthiness were a function of the ratio of one's actual achievements to one's aspirations. According to James, affect was viewed as central to the development of self-concept.

Cooley (1902/1956) challenged James' hypothesis that achievement and affects were the underlying aspects of self-concept. Cooley argued that social interactions were fundamental to the development of "the self." He felt that a sense of worth was developed through one's perceptions of how significant others felt about behaviors and appearances. In other words, self was a "looking-glass self," created from the information received from others.

Mead (1934) expanded Cooley's theory to include a cognitive perspective. Mead stated that sense of self was developed through a cognitive process, involving interpretation of self in the social context. Rosenberg (1979) further elaborated on the notion that self-concept was associated with cognitive processes. However, Rosenberg suggested that the cognitive processes involved with self-concept development changed with the maturation process. Specifically, younger children rely on different information and processes in their self-concept development compared to older children and adults.

Many other theories of self-concept development have been forwarded; however, they are too numerous to be described here. Many of these theories have expanded on one small aspect of the fore-described theories. However, acknowledgment of these theories is important since they encompass the fundamental principles of self-concept, as we currently understand it (Weiss, 1987). These principles include:

1. Self-concept is a function of social interactions;
2. Self-concept is multidimensional;
3. Affect is associated with the development of self-concept;
4. The degree to which successes and failures influence self-concept is a function of the importance one attributes to the activity;
5. Self-concept levels influence motivation levels.

It was suggested at the beginning of this chapter that further probings into how self-concept is affected through the adventure experience should start with theoretical frameworks. However, quantitative research relies on theories that are testable and can be broken down into variables with identified constructs and relationships. Very few theories of self-concept meet these requirements. Fortunately, there are a few testable theories that include a self-concept component in their explanation of another human phenomenon such as motivation. These theories may be useful as a starting point for understanding the process of self-concept development in the adventure experience. These theories include Bandura's (1977) theory of self-efficacy and White's (1959) model of effectance motivation and its expansion into Harter's (1978, 1981) theory of competence motivation.

SELF-EFFICACY

Bandura's (1977) theory of self-efficacy is a cognitively based explanation of the motivational process. The theory revolves around one's feelings of self-efficacy under mastery conditions. Self-efficacy is defined as the strength of an individual's belief that he or she can successfully accomplish a task that tests ability levels. According to Bandura, self-efficacy is based on information derived from internal or external sources. Levels of self-efficacy, in turn, influence future mastery attempts through choice, effort, and persistence. Thus, perceptions of self-efficacy levels play the central role in the motivational process.

Self-efficacy has three dimensions: magnitude, generality, and strength. These dimensions hold important implications for mastery performances. Magnitude of self-efficacy levels is influenced by perceptions of task difficulty. If a number of related tasks were ordered according to difficulty levels, one's efficacy expectations might only include the simple tasks, or they could be extended to include the more difficult tasks. In other words, one individual may hold expectations for success with only the simple tasks, while another person may believe that success will be achieved for all the tasks, including the most difficult. Generality refers to the degree to which one limits or extends self-efficacy levels to different situations. For example, one may limit efficacy expectations to identical tasks, while another may generalize expectations for success to a range of situations. Finally, the strength dimension refers to how long one will hold on to high expectations for success despite contradictory information. For example, one with a weak strength dimension may lower self-efficacy levels after one failure, while one with a strong strength dimension may maintain high self-efficacy levels in the face of many past failures.

In summary, high efficacy expectations may be defined by strong degrees of magnitude, generality, and strength. One may have low self-efficacy levels if magnitude, generality, and strength dimensions are weak, and the task is novel. Intermediate levels of self-efficacy are determined by an interaction among the three dimensions.

Bandura's theory also states that self-efficacy levels are determined by the cognitive interpretation of information derived from four possible sources. These sources include performance accomplishments, vicarious experiences, verbal persuasion, and physiological arousal. Performance accomplishments refer to an individual's past experiences of success and failure in mastery experiences. Success increases mastery expectations, while repeated failures decrease expectations. The effects of single failures on expectations depend on timing and circumstances. Failures early in learning tend to be more influential than failures in later stages. Also, failures that are later overcome by increased effort levels can strengthen self-efficacy levels to a greater degree than failures overcome by chance. Information gained through performance accomplishments is thought to be the most influential and stable source of information because it is based on actual experiences.

However, actual experiences are not the only means by which information about self-efficacy is gained. Vicarious experiences can also provide meaningful information. Thus, seeing another pursue similar mastery attempts without negative repercussions can enhance the observer's efficacy expectations. The modeling effects of vicarious experiences are relatively weak and unstable influences on self-efficacy. However, the more similar the actor is to the observer, the stronger the modeling effect is.

Efficacy expectations can also be affected by verbal persuasion. Again, this source of information is relatively weak compared to actual experience. However, in combination with vicarious or aided experiences, verbal persuasion can be a mobilizing factor. On the other hand, verbal persuasion followed by failure can have detrimental effects on self-efficacy levels.

Finally, physiological arousal levels can provide valuable information about self-efficacy. Since high arousal levels usually undermine performance, persons experiencing high anxiety levels might expect failure. Additionally, expectations for failure can further elevate arousal levels since the anticipation of failure may confirm thoughts about personal inabilities. Thus, arousal levels can influence self-efficacy levels, particularly for individuals who use arousal states to assess perceptions of vulnerability and stress.

In summary, expectations for success are enhanced if an individual has a history of success with similar tasks. The observation of similar others experiencing success, verbal persuasion from social sources, and low arousal levels may increase self-efficacy levels to a lesser degree. Finally, these four sources can influence self-efficacy levels independently or interactively.

According to Bandura, efficacy expectations determine performance through choice or avoidance of activities, the amount of effort associated with mastery attempts, and how long effort will be sustained in failure or stressful situations. Self-efficacy levels can influence one, two, or all three of these motivated behaviors to different degrees. Bandura also suggested that the relationship between self-efficacy and performance is reciprocal: elevated efficacy expectations influence performance, and performance outcomes, in turn, influence self-efficacy levels.

In conclusion, Bandura's theory hypothesizes some possible antecedents and consequences of self-efficacy levels. Researchers in many different fields have applied Bandura's theory in attempts to understand how specific experiences influence self-efficacy levels. To date, only one published study has applied Bandura's theory to the adventure experience.

Brody, Hatfield, and Spalding (1988) investigated the generality dimension of the self-efficacy construct. Specifically, they were interested in how the levels of perceived self-efficacy developed through rappelling (a perceived high-risk adventure pursuit) were generalized to other perceived high-risk adventure pursuits such as rock climbing and scuba diving, as well as everyday, potentially stressful situations like speaking to a group of strangers or coping with test anxiety. The study involved 34 male undergraduates with no experience in high-risk outdoor activities. The experimental group was exposed to two 2-hour sessions of rappel instruction. The other group received no treatment. The results revealed that self-efficacy levels associated with rappelling were enhanced after the treatment. More importantly, the perceived increases in self-efficacy were generalized to the other high-risk adventure activities, but not to the everyday, potentially stressful activities. The authors concluded that the generalization of self-efficacy levels can be extended to similar activities.

This study marks one direction that future inquiries testing Bandura's theory of self-efficacy in the adventure context can take. It has moved beyond describing consequences of adventure experiences and provides insight into how these consequences, namely increased self-concept levels, are developed.

PERCEIVED COMPETENCE

White's (1959) model of effectancy motivation offers another perspective on the motivational process. It is a simple model that states that behavior is the result of an "urge to competence." More specifically, individuals are motivated toward mastery attempts because they wish to have an effect on their environment. If a mastery attempt is achieved by a competent performance, then the urge is satisfied by feelings of efficacy or pleasure. These feelings of efficacy, in turn, increase or maintain effectance motivation. If motivation levels are increased, then future mastery attempts are initiated. Figure 1, on the following page, displays White's model of effectancy motivation.

White's model was revolutionary because it challenged earlier notions that behaviors were instinctive. However, the theory was not operationalized, and thus, it could not be tested. Almost 20 years later, Harter (1978, 1981) built White's framework into a theory of competence motivation. It should be noted that Harter's theory is a developmental theory. It was specifically developed to understand the motivational process in maturing children. However, the directions in which Harter moved away from White's basic theory should have implications for understanding adult behavior. Harter expanded White's model to include the effects of social and interpersonal factors, as well as the effects of positive and negative experiences. She also hypothesized that the motivational process is domain-specific. Figure 2 on the following pages shows a model of Harter's theory of competence motivation.

The construct of perceived competence is one of the central components of Harter's theory. It is also the construct related to self-concept. According to Harter, perceived competence is a domain-specific measure of self-esteem. Thus, one develops a perceived competence level for each domain with which one is involved. This is in contrast to earlier theories, which discuss a general sense of self. Harter also suggested that perceived competence levels were influenced by many factors: success or failure after mastery attempts; perceptions of control; motivational orientation; positive or negative reinforcement and approval from significant others; and characteristics of the task. In turn, perceived competence levels, in conjunction with perceptions of control, influence affective responses and effectance motivation. Effectance motivation levels are then associated with future mastery attempts.

The complexities of Harter's theory may best be explained through an example. Suppose an individual decides to attempt a new rock-climbing route. If the level of route difficulty matches the skill level of the climber, then the task is described as optimally challenging. The achievement of optimally challenging tasks has a proportionately greater impact on self-perceptions. If the climber is successful in the attempt, then positive affects such as enjoyment or intrinsic pleasure are experienced. Additionally, success can increase levels of perceived rock climbing competence and enhance the likelihood that internal perceptions of control are developed. In other words, the climber attributes the success to

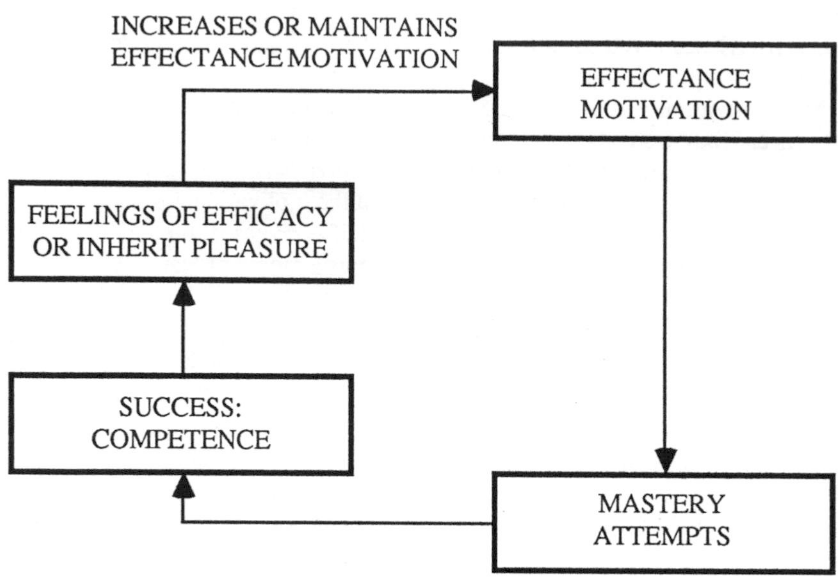

Figure 1
White's Model of Effectance Motivation

internal sources like effort and ability. The climb attempt can also receive positive reinforcement and approval from significant others like climbing friends. If this is the case, then the information provided in the reinforcement is internalized to develop self-reward systems. Specifically, the climber develops an intrinsic motivational orientation, meaning that the climber chooses activities that provide self-satisfaction and meet self-determined standards of performance. An intrinsic motivational orientation further enhances perceived competence levels and internal perceptions of control. These self-perceptions augment affective reactions such as pleasure. The combination of positive self-perceptions and affects, in turn, increases motivational levels. The climber is likely to attempt the task again.

On the contrary, failure in the climbing attempt can diminish motivational levels as negative affects and self-perceptions are experienced. Repeated failure eventually reduces perceived climbing competence levels, and might lead to external perceptions of control. In other words, the climber may attribute the failure to external reasons such as difficulty of the route or that bad luck was involved. Additionally, the lack of reinforcement and approval from significant others may result in the development of extrinsic motivational orientation. The climber may begin to choose routes that meet other people's approval and strive to meet external standards of performance. An extrinsic motivational orientation tends to decrease perceived competence levels and enhance external perceptions of control. Decreasing self-perceptions and negative affects such as anxiety, in turn, decrease effectance motivation. The climber may not attempt that particular route again.

This generalized explanation of Harter's theory does not suggest that a single success or failure experience has an immediate effect on future motivation levels. Past experiences play an important role in the process. However, self-perceptions are probably modified to a slight degree by single experiences.

To date, Harter's theory has not been tested in the adventure domain. This can be partially attributed to the fact that the theory

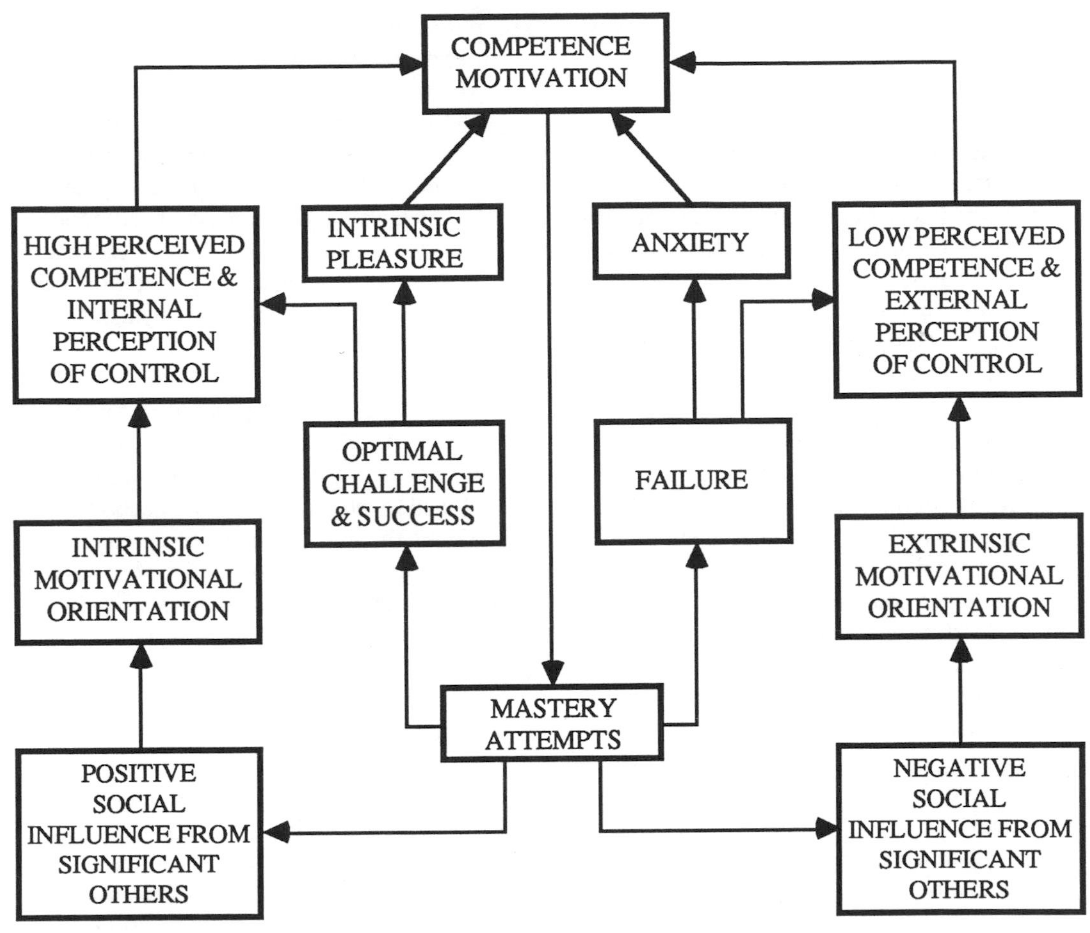

Figure 2
Schematic of Harter's Theory of Competence Motivation (Weiss, 1987)

and the instruments created by measuring various variables are directed toward children between the ages of 7 and 16 years. However, this theory could form the basis for adventure experience research, since it is testable and many of the constructs have been operationalized. Further, many of the instruments have been modified to domain-specific versions. For example, the perceived physical competence scale developed by Harter has been modified to sport-specific scales in basketball, baseball, soccer, and gymnastics.

FUTURE RESEARCH

Inquiry into the adventure experience needs to move into the next stage, from describing the product to understanding the process. It was suggested that theoretically based research could serve as a starting point for these future inquiries. However, the call for theoretically based research on the adventure experience does not mean that experimental research designs are the only direction to follow. The theories presented in this paper were offered because they identify some of the elements apparently involved in the development of self-concept.

Future inquiry based on Bandura's theory can focus on determining which information sources are associated with the adventure experience, and more importantly, which of these information sources are involved in the self-concept changes that result from adventure experiences. Further, inquiry can investigate which of the three dimensions of self-efficacy is most susceptible to change in the adventure experience. Additionally, the meaning or implications of changes in these self-efficacy dimensions are worthy of future study.

White's and Harter's theories of competence motivation can also provide a valuable framework for theoretical research. Again, Harter's theory designates antecedents of perceived competence. These include success/failure, degree and type of reinforcement from others, motivational orientation, and perceptions of control. Inquiry into the adventure experience can examine which of these factors are associated with the experience and which are related to changes in perceived competence levels. Additionally, further studies can explore which of these factors influence perceived competence levels to the greatest degree, and how the influences of these factors can be maximized in the adventure experience.

In summary, quantitative and theoretical researchers can test these theories in the adventure context by creating situations that isolate the selected factors. Thus, they can begin to identify which aspects of the adventure experience influence self-concept levels, and how this phenomenon occurs. This, in turn, would allow adventure programmers to enhance the adventure experience by focusing on these salient factors.

However, future inquiry into self-concept development in the adventure experience is not limited to quantitative research. The self-concept theories of Bandura, White, and Harter can also serve as starting points for qualitative researchers. The hypotheses of these theories can function as the first working hypothesis in an emergent design (see Lincoln & Guba, 1985). The inquirer can then purposefully seek knowledge that supports or refutes the working hypothesis. The additional information will gradually allow the inquirer to modify the working hypothesis so that it conveys the essence of self-concept in the adventure context. Eventually, the inquirer should create an understanding of self-concept as relates to the adventure experience. This context-specific understanding of self-concept can then be quantitatively tested by a quantitative researcher.

The theories of self-concept can also assist the qualitative inquirer by identifying respondents from qualitative study. For example, the inquirer can use the quantitative instruments developed to measure specific aspects (variables) of a theory. The inquirer can then purposefully select respondents whose answers support the theoretical hypothesis, as well as those whose answers are unpredictable. This type of respondent selection will facilitate the development of a context-specific understanding of self-concept development in the adventure experience.

In conclusion, inquiry needs to move forward toward an understanding of *how* the adventure experience influences human perceptions and behavior. However, this inquiry process does not need to start in square one. The body of knowledge created by social psychology can serve as a departure point. The theories of Bandura, White, and Harter, among others, probably have application to inquiry into the adventure experience. Both quantitative and qualitative inquirers can benefit from the works of our social psychology peers. Both types of inquiry can be combined to create a holistic understanding of the essence of the adventure experience, an essence that can be communicated to those not yet enlightened.

REFERENCES

Bandura, A. (1977). Self-efficacy: Toward a unifying theory for behavioral change. *Psychological Review, 84*:191-215.

Brody, E., Hatfield, B., & Spalding, T. (1988). Generalization of self-efficacy to a continuum of stressers upon mastery of a high-risk sport skill. *Journal of Sport Psychology, 10*:32-44.

Cooley, C.H. (1902/1956). *Human nature and the social order.* Glencoe, IL: Free Press.

Ewert, A. (1983). *Outdoor adventure and self-concept: A research analysis.* Eugene, OR: Center of Leisure Studies, University of Oregon.

Fletcher, B. (1970). *Students of Outward Bound schools in Great Britain: A follow-up study.* (ERIC Document Reproduction Service No. ED 050 325).

Ford, P., & Blanchard, J. (1985). *Leadership and administration of outdoor pursuits.* State College, PA: Venture Publishing.

Harter, S. (1978). Effectance motivation reconsidered. *Human Development, 21*:34-64.

Hendy, C. (1976). *Outward Bound and personality: 16PF profiles of instructors and ipsative changes in male and female students 16-19 years of age.* Unpublished doctoral dissertation, University of Oregon.

James, W. (1890). *The principles of psychology.* New York: Henry Holt.

Kelly, F., & Baer, D. (1969). *Outward Bound: An alternative to institutionalization for adolescent delinquent boys.* Boston, MA: Fandel Press.

Kolb, D. (1965). Achievement motivation training for underachieving high school boys. *Journal of Personality and Social Psychology, 2*(6).

Lincoln, Y. & Guba, E. (1985). *Naturalistic inquiry.* Beverly Hills, CA: Sage.

Lee, R., & Schoder, H. (1969). Effects of Outward Bound training on urban youth. *Journal of Special Education, 3*(2).

Mead, G. H. (1934). *Mind, self and society.* Chicago, IL: University of Chicago Press.

Nye, R. Jr. (1976). *The influence of an Outward Bound program on the self-concept of the participants.* Unpublished doctoral dissertation, Temple University.

Rosenberg, M. (1979). *Conceiving the self.* New York: Basic Books.

Stremba, R. (1977). *A study of the relationship between participation in an Outward Bound program and changes in self-esteem and locus of control.* Unpublished doctoral dissertation, Indiana University.

Vander Wilt, R., & Klocke, R. (1971). *Self-actualization of females in an experimental orientation program.* National Association of Women's Deans and Counselors Journal, 34(3).

Weiss, M. (1987). *Self-esteem and achievement in children's sport and physical activity.* M. Weiss & D. Gould (Eds.), Advances in pediatric sport science, vol. 2. Champaign, IL: Human Kinetics.

Wetmore, R. (1972). *The influence of Outward Bound school experience on the self-concept for adolescent boys.* Unpublished doctoral dissertation, Boston University.

Wichmann, T. (1976). *Affective role expectations for deliquent youth in environmental stress-challenge programs.* (ERIC Document Reproduction Service No. ED 156-394).

White, R. (1959). Motivation reconsidered: The concept of competence. *Psychological Review, 66*:297-333.

Section Five

THE LEARNING OF ADVENTURE EDUCATION

The Experience Cornerstone

The essence of adventure education—of any approach to education—is learning. How might educators wishing to use the process of adventure for learning best achieve their students' learning objectives? What does the literature of education contain that might be useful to adventure educators? This section begins to shift from theory to practice. The authors offer suggestions on how learning through adventure might be facilitated.

Kraft, in the introductory essay, lingers in the realm of theory. What does learning theory offer to adventure educators? He briefly reviews behaviorist, social, cognitive and developmental theories of learning. What have Gardner, Dewey, Piaget, Coleman and Resnick offered that might help adventure educators? Kraft notes that adventure educators often think the work of educational theorists in the laboratory is of no relevance to them. Not so, he argues. If the aim is to conduct the best learning experience, then insight must be gleaned from all available sources. Kraft does a brief, but comprehensive job of suggesting where the best gleaning may be done.

Hammerman and Knapp move to more practical issues and methods. The former explains the inquiry approach to teaching and learning, and provides examples of how it can be applied in adventure education settings. Knapp suggests how leaders can help participants in a program process their experience. He offers guidelines for helping people internalize meaning from experience. This is not a task, he notes, to be taken lightly. The facilitator is "playing with fire," and there is much to know in order to do the job correctly. He offers many suggestions on how to do this critically important work.

In the section's final essay, Gass addresses the critical issue of transference of learning. How can learning experiences during adventure serve the learner back home? What can adventure educators do to increase the long-term effect of the experiences they facilitate for their students? Gass reviews relevant theory, then offers a model for transfer. His discussion comes down to specific techniques useful for enhancing transfer.

As with all sections of this book, the authors here can only suggest the vast array of ideas and methods that might be useful for understanding the challenges of learning through the experience of adventure. The purpose here is to suggest general directions in which adventure educators might travel in their search for insight and resources for their task. These few essays can only be a beginning.

Experiential Learning

Richard J. Kraft
University of Colorado

Everybody experiences far more than he understands. Yet it is experience, rather than understanding that influences behavior.

(McLuhan)

Despite the repeated calls over the Reagan/ Bush era for a "return to the basics," generally interpreted to mean the formal classroom with its traditional reading, writing, arithmetic, classics, Shakespeare, American history, and Western Civilization, experiential learning is alive and well as we head toward the 21st century. McLuhan in the above quote gives us a clue as to why experiential learning has always been and will continue to be a major, if not *the* major, way in which most of us attempt to make sense of our universe. Vicarious and symbolic forms of learning dominate our schools and classrooms, but it would be foolhardy to claim that these are the only, or even the dominant, ways in which we as human beings learn. In this brief chapter, we shall attempt to explore a few of the philosophical and psychological relationships between experience and learning.

Educational psychologists usually define learning as "a change in the individual caused by experience" (Slavin, 1986, p. 104). Change can and does obviously occur in the formal classroom as the result of such educational interventions as the lecture, laboratory, discussion, recitation, and testing. On the other hand, it is equally obvious that change in the individual or in behavior can and does occur in the non-school environment, and thus learning is not something confined to the school, nor only that which occurs under certified teachers and in interaction with state-approved curricula and textbooks.

It is only in this century that learning in the formal school setting has become the dominant mode for the majority of persons in the "developed" world, and it is only in the past quarter-century that a majority of children throughout the Third World have had their learning formalized and curricularized in the classroom. The purpose of this essay is not to deny that important learning does occur in the traditional school setting, but to look at what learning theory, educational philosophy, the psychology of learning, theories of intelligence, and research on learning can tell us about how learning occurs in the non-school environment.

Learning theories are generally divided into two principal types: behavioral and cognitive. Observable behavior in or outside the classroom is the major focus of the behavioral theories, while the mental processes individuals use to learn and remember information or skills are the focus of the cognitive theories. Adventure educators and others who use "real life" experiences as their major teaching/learning tool, often ignore or denigrate what laboratory learning theorists have discovered, not recognizing that our carefully programmed outdoor experiences or work-study, apprenticeship programs make use of the same principles of learning, only in a different setting. We also hope, as evidence is slim, that these nontraditional learning environments will result in greater, more beneficial behavioral change, greater learning, longer retention, and all the other points made so cogently in the learning laboratory.

BEHAVIORAL LEARNING THEORIES

Numerous principles of behavioral learning theories can be found in the practice of adventure and other forms of experience-based learning. The principle that behavior changes according to its immediate consequences is perhaps the most important in both classroom and non-classroom learning environments. In the adventure setting, countless examples of the immediacy of consequences can be given through such things as ill-fitting boots leading to blisters, improperly tied knots leading to injury or death in a fall, a tent being washed away if set up in a streambed, dehydration from lack of prepared water, and literally hundreds of other examples.

The use of positive and negative reinforcers, rewards and punishments, has been well-documented with laboratory animals, with students in the classroom, and in the wilderness. While researchers in the laboratory reward rats with pellets of food, and teachers use such positive reinforcers as stars and grades, or aversive stimuli such as tests or various punishments, outdoor adventure educators can and do use rewards such as praise for an activity well-done, or a wide range of positive or negative reinforcers when working in therapeutic settings with alcoholics, drug abusers, and delinquents. The ropes course setting may differ from a psychiatrist's office, a detoxification center, or a locked youth facility, but the basic behavioral principles remain the same. While adventure educators may not be as overt, as specific, or as well-planned in the behavioral conditioning process as B.F. Skinner (1968) or Ivan Pavlov, the basic principles remain the same.

SOCIAL LEARNING THEORY

Albert Bandura (1969), in his Social Learning Theory, uses the basic principles of the behaviorists, but suggests that we also learn vicariously through modeling or imitating others' behavior. In social learning theory, not all learning is shaped by consequences, but rather can be directly learned from a model. Bandura suggest that there are four phases to this form of learning: attentional, retention, reproduction, and motivational.

In the attentional phase, the learner is presented with appropriate cues, and novelty is used to motivate the student to pay attention. In adventure education, activities early in a course such as crossing a Burma Bridge, participating in cooperative games or initiatives, or the group leader setting the metaphor (Bacon, 1983) are examples of the attentional phase.

In the retention phase, the instructor models the behavior and encourages the student to imitate and practice the behavior. Knot tying in preparation for a belay and paddling technique in preparation for the rapids are among the many examples in which adventure educators model the behavior and then have students practice it, before getting into the more dangerous setting.

The reproduction phase is the time in which students match the instructor's behavior and their ability is assessed. Adventure educators pride themselves in their instruction of behaviors that have obvious meaning for the learner, and which must be properly performed if individual or group disaster is to be avoided. Assessment is immediate, as the raft might turn over or the tent blow away if the appropriate behavior has not been learned.

In the final motivational phase, the learners model the appropriate behavior because they believe that in doing so they will increase their chances of being reinforced. Whether reinforcement comes in the form of praise from the instructor, in the successful climbing of a rock face, or in more traditional classroom reinforcements, the learning process is the same.

COGNITIVE LEARNING THEORIES

As with the Behavioral Learning Theories, only a cursory overview will be provided, and only those aspects of the theories that appear to relate to adventure education will be discussed.

Information processing theories attempt to analyze by what process information is absorbed and how students can be helped to retain the information. Short-term and long-term memory are an important part of the research. Information from the senses (sight, hearing, touch, smell, taste) meets the sensory register, and if nothing happens in the first few seconds, it is rapidly lost. Adventure educators pride themselves in using "all the senses" in their work, and while the research evidence is limited, it would appear that the memories of many of the experiences that are part of our adventure programs are retained much longer than the less profoundly moving experiences in the classroom. What is learned or remembered, however, has never been carefully researched, and it would behoove experiential educators to limit their claims.

Space does not permit any discussion of critical cognitive learning research on perception, attention, automatization, levels of processing, or verbal learning. Schema Theory, however, attempts to deal with questions of meaningful learning as opposed to rote learning, and holds that long-term memory is enhanced when information fits into an existing schemata. Outdoor, adventure, and other experiential educators constantly raise the importance of schemata in helping their students to learn new skills or function in new environments. Without well-developed schemata, the learner in any environment is involved in rote, or "meaningless" learning. The memorization of the names of trees, without the ability to place them in a broader schema based on leaves, needles, size, color, bark or a variety of other criteria, is rote memorization and in most cases will not lead to longer-term memory.

Experiential educators also pride themselves in the teaching of concepts, not unrelated facts, and in addition often claim greater transfer of learning and problem-solving skills than is found in the typical classroom setting. There is once again little research on the transferability of skills learned in the wilderness to one's home, school, or community, although some of the recidivism studies on delinquents would appear to point toward such a transfer. Problem-solving and critical thinking are major areas of research by cognitive psychologists, and the educational reform movements of the 1980s were unanimous in their advocacy of these important areas. It is in these areas that experiential educators make their greatest claims, and would appear to lead in pedagogy. Rather than deal with abstract mathematical problems in a textbook, the experiential educator seeks to place the student in a setting that forces appropriate problem-solving behavior. Rather than develop critical thinking skills unrelated to the real life of the student, the experiential educator places the learner in an environment in which those skills can be used to solve problems around them.

THE THEORY OF MULTIPLE INTELLIGENCES

Howard Gardner in his influential book, *Frames of Mind* (1983), defines intelligence as the "ability to solve problems or to create products that are valued within one or more cultural settings." He goes on to propose eight distinct criteria for intelligence and seven human competencies. Among other critiques of traditional I.Q. measurements, Piaget's developmental stages, and information processing research, he suggests that all of these emphasize linguistic or logical-mathematical intelligences to the near total exclusion of forms of intelligence.

Reviewing the basic biological research, Gardner concludes that there are seven distinct intelligences: (a) Mathematical-Logical—the ability to organize thoughts sequentially and logically; (b) Verbal-Linguistic—the ability to understand and express ideas through language; (c) Bodily-Kinesthetic—the gaining of knowledge through feedback from physical activity; (d) Musical—sensitivity to tone, pitch and rhythm and the ability to reproduce them; (e) Visual-Spatial—the ability to learn directly through images and to think intuitively without the use of language; (f) Interpersonal Intelligence—the ability to notice and make discriminations regarding the moods, temperaments, motivations and intentions of others; and (g) Intrapersonal—having access to one's own feeling life. Space does not permit a detailed discussion of Gardner's research criteria, but he makes a strong case that all seven intelligences meet certain biological and psychological specifications, and that all can and have been isolated in various parts of the brain.

Gardner and other educators are only just beginning to discuss the pedagogical implications of his theory, but some of them for experiential, adventure educators are quite clear. Gardner outlines the forms of education and intelligences used in nonliterary societies and discusses the use of linguistic and musical skills in oral verse, spatial intelligence in sailing, numerous examples of bodily-kinesthetic intelligence in the work in the village or tribal settings, and many interpersonal intelligences passed on throughout the tight-knit group. He points to the transitional "schools" of the rites of passage or initiation rites, bush schools and the apprenticeship systems, and their emphasis on a range of intelligences. The modern scientific secular school, however, concentrates its efforts on the logical-mathematical intelligence, with some lesser emphasis on the interpersonal and linguistic.

If Gardner's theory continues to gain acceptance among educators, it is likely to affect the way public schools look at learning and intelligence. Experiential educators have always felt uncomfortable with the near total emphasis in traditional education on the logical-mathematical and linguistic skills, and have sought to provide a more holistic learning environment. Gardner's theory provides a solid research rationale for the wide variety of bodily-kinesthetic activities used in adventure programs, and for the wide range of intrapersonal and interpersonal activities that form such a critical part of the pedagogy for both the therapeutic and nontherapeutic outdoor education programs. Rites of passage and apprenticeships, found in traditional societies, have been resurrected by experiential educators as having relevance in the late 20th century, and with the current emphasis in education on critical thinking and problem-solving, adventure educators and others dealing with the role of experience in learning can justifiably take the lead in providing a range of learning activities that use all the intelligences.

DEWEY AND PROGRESSIVE EDUCATION

John Dewey and the Progressive Educational Movement in the 1930s took seriously the role of experience in and outside the schools. The educational reform movements of the 1960s and early 1970s also attempted to bring the world into the classroom and reconnect the school with the broader society. Following a decade of "back to the basics" and a return to traditional education, it appears that the 1990s may be a time in which experiential learning both inside and outside the classroom will again be looked upon with greater favor and with the same consideration as the more traditional information assimilation and symbolic and vicarious learning approaches that still dominate our schools. With the massive failure of the schools to reach the "forgotton half" of the students, particularly among the poor and minorities, researchers, psychologists, educators, and a few public policy-makers are returning again to some of the basic ideas of experiential learning. It appears that American education is still going through periodic swings of its educational pendulum, and that many of the ideas that focus the argument go back almost a century to the original writings of Dewey, or even two centuries to Rousseau and other European writers. Perhaps the pendulum will stop when educators admit the need for both symbolic and vicarious learning that is predominantly classroom-based and for experiential learning, which involves all the senses, all the intelligences, and a range of learning environments.

While Dewey warned against unjustified dichotomies, he differentiated between progressive and traditional education in his classic 1938 work, *Experience and Education.* (Dewey, pp. 19-20).

> To imposition from above is opposed expression and cultivation of individuality; to external discipline is opposed free activity; to learning from texts and teachers, learning through experience; to acquisition of isolated skills and techniques by drill, is opposed acquisition of them as means to attaining ends which make direct vital appeal; to preparation for a more or less remote future is opposed making the most of the opportunities of present life; to static aims and materials is opposed acquaintance with a changing world.

Dewey also warned that experiences could be miseducative if they prevented further growth, or lead to callousness or lack of sensitivity. Growth must be physical and moral, not just intellectual. Dewey constantly emphasized the social aspects of learning and the importance of learning contributing to the good of the society, not just narcissistic pleasure. He emphasized the need for rigor and discipline in learning, whether in the classroom or on a mountaintop. Adventure educators and other advocates of experience-based learning would do well to heed Dewey's warnings, or we shall surely be condemned to further swings of the pendulum.

PIAGET AND DEVELOPMENTAL THEORY

Part of the impetus for the revival of experience-based learning in the 1960s came from the work of Jean Piaget (1952), the Swiss psychologist, whose work on the developmental stages of cognitive growth emphasized the importance of active learning and concrete experiences. Piaget's theory of development holds that there are four interrelated factors that influence mental development: (a) physical maturation; (b) experiences that involve handling, moving, and thinking about concrete objects; (c) social interaction, particularly with other children; and (d) equilibration that results from bringing the other three factors together to build and rebuild mental structures. Piaget went on to delineate the stages of growth as from 0-2 years of age, sensorimotor control; 2-4, extracting concepts from experience; 4-7, intuitive thought; 7-11, concrete operational thought; and 11-15, formal or abstract operational thought.

The implications of Piaget's theory are critical for experiential educators of children and adults, as it posits the active nature of all learning, that children learn best from concrete experiences, and that even adolescents and adults who are capable of formal abstract thought need concrete experiences in order to develop new physical knowledge. Some research on Piaget's stages would appear to indicate that many adults remain at the concrete operational stage for much or most of their learning. Elementary educators in the

United States, Britain and other countries have been profoundly influenced by Piaget's work, but his warnings about overemphasis on symbolic learning and rote memorization and the need for active physical and social interactions with one's environment have generally been ignored by secondary, higher, and adult educators. Adventure educators, who spend a large majority of their time providing experiences that involve active, concrete learning in interaction with the physical environment and in social interaction with members of the group, could take a leadership role in the 1990s in putting Piaget's ideas into practice in adult learning environments.

COLEMAN: INFORMATION ASSIMILATION vs. EXPERIENTIAL LEARNING

James Coleman (1977) differentiates between the information assimilation process of the regular classroom and the experiential learning process. In the traditional classroom information assimilation model, the student generally receives the information through a symbolic medium such as a lecture or book, and then assimilates and organizes the information so that the general principle is understood. Inferences are then drawn to a particular application of the general principle and the learner finally moves from the cognitive and symbol-processing sphere to the sphere of action where the knowledge gained is actually applied. Critics of contemporary education, such as Brazilian philosopher Paulo Friere, suggest that modern schools seldom get past the third step of Coleman's model, or what Friere calls the reflective stage, and into the world of action, where genuine change occurs.

Coleman suggests that the experiential learning process occurs in almost a reverse sequence and at least initially does not use a symbolic medium for transmitting information, as the information is generated through the sequence of steps itself. The steps in the experiential learning process then are to carry out an action in a particular instance and see the effects of that action. Understanding the effects in a particular instance and the consequences of the action, the learner then moves towards an understanding of the general principles involved, and finally applies, through action, what has been learned in a new circumstance.

Coleman suggests that schools use the information assimilation model, to a far greater extent than the experiential model, as it can reduce the time and effort needed to learn something new. On the other hand, for children, adolescents, or adults who have not mastered the complex systems of symbols used in reading, mathematics, and other disciplines, the information assimilation model leads to almost guaranteed failure, as they are unable to translate the learnings into concrete sequences of action. The traditional learning model also is dependent on artificial and extrinsic motivation, as action (the intrinsic motivation) comes at the end of the learning sequence.

The experiential learning mode, on the other hand, is a time-consuming process because it involves actions sufficiently repeated that the learner is able to generalize from the experience. Ideally it uses no symbolic medium, and consequences follow actions immediately. Motivation is intrinsic, as actions with real consequences occur as the first step in the learning process. Finally, experiential learning appears to be more deeply etched into the brain of the learner, as all learning can be associated with concrete actions and events, not just abstract symbols or general principles.

It is difficult to generate research evidence backing Coleman's theory, as most evidence of learning is shown through pencil and paper tests, which are dependent upon mastery of symbolic media. When a mechanic cannot explain in writing what needs to be done to repair an automobile, but can carry out the necessary work, or when a rock climber cannot explain the physical motions needed or the physics of his activity, but can climb a 5.12 rock face, one is faced with the issue of behavioral evidence versus "book learning."

RESNICK: LEARNING IN SCHOOL AND OUT

Adventure educators face the challenge of "proving" the efficacy of the learning that occurs on their courses using traditional symbolic research models, or in creating new models that document what has been learned.

One indication of the pendulum swing once again toward experiential learning in the final decade of the 20th century is the growing interest on the part of the educational research establishment on what is learned "in school and out." Lauren Resnick, in her 1987 Presidential Address to the prestigious American Educational Research Association, explicated some of the differences between "practical and formal intelligence." Using research by anthropologists and psychologists in such disparate settings as navigation practice on U.S. Navy ships, black market lottery bookmaking in Brazil, mathematics knowledge among dairy workers, and arithmetic performance by people in a Weight Watcher's program, Resnick concludes that school learning differs from other learning in four basic ways: (a) individual cognition in school versus shared cognition outside; (b) pure experimentation in schools versus tool manipulation outside; (c) symbol manipulation in school versus contextualized reasoning outside school; and (d) generalized learning in school versus situation-specific competencies outside.

Resnick suggests that school learning often becomes a matter of manipulating symbols rather than connecting with the real world. It often becomes the learning of rules disconnected from real life, and concludes that "there is growing evidence, then, that not only may schooling not contribute in a direct and obvious way to performance outside school, but also that knowledge acquired outside school is not always used to support in-school learning. Schooling is coming to look increasingly isolated from the rest of what we do." She also suggests that there is limited evidence of direct transfer from school to out-of-school use. Before experiential educators get too excited with these statements, however, she also suggests that much of the situation-specific learning that occurs in our experiential programs can be very limiting, with little transferability to other settings.

With the shift away from apprenticeship models in both the trades and the professions toward formal school settings, Resnick suggests that technical, management, and professional education are adhering to too great an extent to forms of teaching found in the traditional classroom; that there is too little engagement with the "tools and materials of work," and more time given to theory than to developing truly expert performance skills. She concludes that we need to help students gain skills for learning even when optimum conditions do not exist. We need learners who can transfer skills from one setting to another and who are adaptive learners. The discontinuity between the worlds of school and work suggests that we should not focus so much on "symbols correctly manipulated but divorced from experience." Successful schooling must involve socially shared mental work and more direct engagement with the referents of symbols. Schooling should begin to look more like out-of-school functioning and include greater use of reflection and reasoning.

Resnick has clearly laid out the challenge for adventure and other experiential educators in coming years. With claims of an educational process that is dependent on shared cognition, skills directly related to real life settings, learning in environments that demand a wide range of reasoning skills, and a range of specific competencies that provide immediate feedback and are transferable to other life settings, experiential education would appear to be uniquely poised to help overcome the current deficiencies of both traditional schooling and much of vocational-technical training as it occurs today. The rapid growth in adventure programming for the criminal justice system, many public schools, businesses, therapeutic centers, teacher training universities and in youth leadership, to name but a few of the institutions now using the methodology, would appear to indicate a growing acceptance of this form of experiential learning. The challenge now is to carefully document what is being done and its therapeutic and learning effects.

CONCLUSIONS

In this brief overview of experiential learning, we have attempted to provide insights from only a few of the many philosophers, psychologists, educators, and researchers who have spoken to the issues of the role of experience in learning. Had space permitted, we would have gone into the work of learning style theorists such as Kolb (1976), McCarthy (1980), and Gregorc (1977), who provide valuable insight into how learners differ in both style and emphasis. Friere (1973), with his naming, reflecting, and acting, has developed a pedagogy for liberation that is sweeping the Third World, while Kurt Hahn (1970) developed the theory and practice underlying the Outward Bound schools, and Maria Montessori (1972) gave her name to a whole pedagogy based on concrete experiences. Many experiential educators have looked to humanistic psychologists such as Maslow (1968) and Rogers (1969) for insight into personal growth, group processes, and openness to new experiences.

In conclusion, perhaps the educational systems in the United States have finally come of age in their recognition that not all children, young people, or adults learn in the same manner or at the same speed. They have begun to learn that the insights gained from adventure programs and other experiential learning environments have great potential for use in the mainstream of our educational settings, whether in schools and colleges, in therapeutic programs, or in the worlds of business and industry.

REFERENCES

Bacon, S. (1983). *The conscious use of metaphor in Outward Bound.* Denver: Colorado Outward Bound School.

Bandura, A. (1969). *Principles of behavior modification.* New York: Rinehart and Winston.

Coleman, J.A. (1977). Differences between experiential and classroom learning. In M.T. Keeton (Ed.), *Experiential learning: Rationale characteristics, and assessment,* pp. 49-61. San Francisco, CA: Jossey-Bass Publishers.

Dewey, J. (1938). *Experience and education.* New York: Collier Books.

Freire, P. (1973). *Pedagogy of the oppressed.* New York: The Seabury Press.

Gardner, H. (1983). *Frames of Mind: The theory of multiple intelligences.* New York: Basic Books, Inc., Publishers.

Gregorc, A.F., & Ward, H.B. (1977). *A new definition for individual.* NAASP Bulletin.

Hahn, K. (1970.) *The educational thought of Kurt Hahn.* London: Routledge and Kegan Paul Ltd.

Kolb, D.A. (1976). Management and the learning process. *California Management Review,* Spring.

Maslow, A.H. (1968). Some educational implications of humanistic psychologies. *Harvard Educational Review, 38,* No. 4.

McCarthy, B. (1980). *The 4 MAT system.* Arlington Heights, IL: Excel, Inc.

Montessori, M. (1972). *Spontaneous activity.* New York: Schocken Books.

Piaget, J. (1952). *The origins of intelligence in children.* New York: Basic Books.

Resnick, L.B. (1988). Learning in school and out. *Educational Researcher, 16*, No. 9.

Rogers, C. (1969). *Freedom to learn.* Columbus: Charles E. Merrill.

Skinner, B.F. (1968). *The technology of teaching.* New York: Appleton-Century-Crofts.

Slavin, R.E. (1986). *Educational psychology: theory into practice.* Englewood Cliffs, NJ: Prentice-Hall.

Teaching by Inquiry

Donald R. Hammerman
Northern Illinois University

Inquiry is by no means a new approach to learning. Socrates, Plato, and Aristotle are said to have employed inquiry as a means to provoke comprehension on the part of their followers. Inquiry is time-consuming. It involves a high degree of interaction between teacher and learners. The teacher/leader is the asker of questions, not the one who gives answers. Students rely on their own observations and analysis of data. The teacher stimulates the learning process by posing questions to students, causing them to think about (a) what they have observed, (b) what is likely to occur next, and (c) a course of action or steps to pursue in order to bring about a certain action or solve a particular problem.

The term "inquiry" is often used synonymously with exploratory learning, discovery learning, problem-solving, and Socratic questioning. While they are closely related and contain elements that reinforce and complement one another, inquiry, discovery, and problem solving are not one and the same. The process of inquiry can lead to discovery, to making inferences, to arriving at generalizations and drawing conclusions. These elements, in turn, can be a part of the problem-solving process.

INQUIRY TRAINING

Inquiring or inquiry is a very natural way to learn. It is the way most of us go about learning on our own outside of formal learning situations. We pose questions like: I wonder why? How did this happen? How does this work? What do you suppose would happen if?

In a more formal sense, inquiry training refers to a model for teaching students some of the techniques and applications of scientific or scholarly inquiry pioneered by J. Richard Suchman. In Suchman's model, students are usually presented with a puzzling or discrepant event and then invited to direct their questions to the teacher. This reverses the traditional role of teacher asking and students parroting back information gleaned from the textbook.

The students must test their hypotheses by framing questions that can only be answered with a "yes" or a "no."

Picture the following scenario:

A group of wilderness campers are out for a day's trek in the Colorado Rockies. They have paused for a brief lunch break just below the timber line, seeking shelter from the biting wind before continuing on to the summit. One of the group poses the question: "Why do the trees not grow above this elevation?" Rather than launch into a long-winded verbal explanation, the leader turns the question back to the group: "Why do you think there are few trees beyond this point?" The following dialogue ensues:

Hiker: "As we've climbed there has been a definite drop in temperature. Does climate have something to do with it?"
Leader: "Yes."
Another hiker: "The air also feels much drier up here than down below, am I right?"
Leader: "Yes."
Hiker: "Other than for a few patches of old snow here and there, there is no running water; that would seem to support the lack of moisture theory, right?"
Leader: "Correct."
Hiker: "The few trees remaining as we approach timberline are definitely smaller and more thinly spaced. Does this mean a much shorter growing season at this altitude?"
Leader: "Yes."
Hiker: "Why are most of the trees just above us gnarled and deformed?"
Leader: "Rephrase your question please so that I can answer it with a yes or a no."
Hiker: "I've noticed that the wind is blowing harder up here. Could that deform a tree over a period of time?"
Leader: "Yes."

Thus the questioning-answering process continues until basic concepts are grasped or a puzzling situation is solved.

INSTRUCTION THROUGH INQUIRY

The traditional approach to imparting "skill knowledge" is through lecture/demonstration, that is to say, "I'll teach you what you need to know about this specific skill by showing you what to do and explaining how to do it." In situations in which the safety of the participant is of paramount importance, this is usually the most efficient procedure. Inquiry techniques can be employed in combination with lecture-demonstration without diminishing the effectiveness of the instruction. In fact, in most cases, by varying instructional strategies and introducing techniques such as inquiry and problem-solving, learner involvement is increased and student interest heightened.

As our first example, let us consider the teaching of specific canoeing skills, namely, some of the basic canoe strokes. All of the essential safety instruction concerning launching the canoe, proper seating or kneeling position, what to do if swamped, will already have been covered. Now we are ready to handle the canoe on water. Beginners usually experience difficulty keeping the craft moving in a straight line. Thus it is essential to begin with basic strokes that will enable paddlers to move the canoe forward in a straight line, and then proceed to strokes for changing direction and reversing direction. The traditional mode of teaching would have the instructor demonstrating and giving appropriate verbal explanation.

Consider the following scenario employing inquiry process along with lecture/demonstration as an alternative. In this example, two students are in each canoe; one in the bow, the other in the stern—canoes gathered in front of the instructor on a quiet lake.

Instructor: "To move the canoe forward, it works best if the sternperson and bowperson paddle on opposite sides of the canoe. Place your hands on the paddle like this and take long, smooth, strokes." (demonstrates) "Now try it." (Students try this for a few minutes.)

Instructor: "Now both of you paddle on the same side of the canoe and see what happens." (Students try this for a few minutes.)

Instructor: "This is the sweep stroke, and this is the reverse sweep." (Demonstrates both strokes.) "With bowperson and stern-person paddling on opposite sides once again, see what happens when one of you sweeps and the other reverse sweeps. Make the canoe move in different directions." (Canoers experiment for a while.) "Now let's review. Bowperson paddle on the right, sternperson on the left. To change direction to the right what stroke should the bowperson use and what should the sternperson do?" (Answer: Bow-person reverse sweeps, while sternperson sweeps.) "To move the canoe to the left which stroke would each paddler use?" (Answer: Bowperson sweeps; sternperson reverse sweeps.)

The students practice these maneuvers, changing from one side of the canoe to the other, until they get used to the feel of both strokes from a left-handed and right-handed paddle position.

Instructor: "In running a river it is sometimes necessary to veer the canoe quickly in one direction or the other in order to avoid a rock, a submerged log, or some other hazard. To do this the bowperson does a bow rudder (demonstrates) or a cross-bow rudder (demonstrates) while the stern-person executes a broad sweep stroke on the opposite side." (demonstrates) "Bow-person, assume you are paddling on the left side of the canoe, and you wish to veer left, which stroke will you use?" (Answer: bowrudder.) "What should the sternperson do?" (Answer: Sweep on the right.) "Bowperson, you are still paddling on the left, but you need to veer quickly to the right. What do you do?" (Answer: cross-bow rudder.) "And the sternperson?" (Answer: Either a reverse sweep on the side on which he/she has been paddling [the right], or a broad sweep on the opposite side.)

These maneuvers are practiced by both paddlers on each side of the canoe and in both the bow and stern position. Additional examples of inquiry-type questions are: "What will happen if you use this stroke in the bow and this one in the stern?" "If you want to turn your canoe around to reverse direction, what combination of strokes would you use?"

Other basic strokes such as the draw stroke and the J-stroke can be presented in similar fashion. These examples should suffice, however, to demonstrate that it is possible to present some basic skill information by incorporating questions and inquiry into the lecture/demonstration process.

For our next example to illustrate how teaching by inquiry can be applied to adventure education, let us assume that a small group of backpackers has set off on a week to 10-day trekking expedition in the western Rockies. This involves moving from site to site every day or so. Once beyond the trail-head, the trip leader must map out daily hiking routes. The leader who wishes to use inquiry teaching methods and involve participation in the decision-making process might conduct a discussion along the following lines:

Leader/Guide/Instructor: "Tomorrow we intend to break camp and move to a new site on the other side of the mountain." (At this point the leader brings out a topographic map and compass.) "Let's map out a route that will be scenic and not too vigorous since we're just at the start of our trip and still adapting to the altitude."

Hiker: "The shortest route appears to be straight over this pass."

Leader: "Yes, you're right; that is the shortest line in distance, but what kind of climb is it?" (The group examines the map and determines that they are at an elevation of 7,000 feet, and the pass is situated at about 9,800 feet.)

Leader: "That may be a little more than we want to tackle on only our second day out. Are there some alternative routes?"

Hiker: "What if we followed this stream through the valley between the two mountains?"

Leader: "That's a possibility. Let's figure out the distance." (They check the scale on the map.)

Hiker: "It looks to be about 9 miles with little change in elevation. We should be able to handle that easily."

Leader: "I agree. And an added advantage is that we'll always be close to a water supply. Why is that a good idea?"

Hiker: "Because we need to take in plenty of fluids at these elevations to keep us from dehydrating."

Later that day the group approaches its destination and must begin searching for a suitable campsite. The trip leader continues the teaching by inquiry process.

Leader: "What factors do we need to keep in mind in selecting our campsite for to-night?"

Group: "We want to be sheltered from the wind. We want to locate the tents so they catch the early morning sunlight. We want to be fairly close to our water supply."

Once the campsite is selected, other questions follow:

Leader: "Which direction should our tents face? Where should the cooking area be set up? Where should we locate the latrine?"

Thus the instruction continues with the leader/instructor subtly providing certain bits of information and guiding learning to acquire additional information and grasp other concepts as the participants confront real-life situations and come up with appropriate solutions.

ADDITIONAL CONSIDERATIONS

In adventure education, there are some skills that are so technical—where procedures are so exact, and where safety is at such a high premium—that there is little room for teaching by inquiry. An example of this would be in the realm of rock climbing, where certain basic skills must be acquired; safety measures must be adhered to exactly, and in the interest of efficiency there is usually a best way to do it. In situations like this there is no question as to the most efficient method—straight demonstration-explanation.

Once the basic skills are learned and a certain amount of proficency is attained, however, some inquiry may be applied to help a group investigate and/or solve a particular problem. For example, "Now that we know what we know, which specific climbing techniques will work best in getting around this ledge, or in ascending this crack?" Or, returning to our previous section on canoeing: "Which design works best in various conditions, such as large bodies of water as opposed to rivers, or fast water as opposed to smooth water?" "What are the advantages of a longer canoe versus a shorter canoe, or the reverse under different conditions?" "What are the advantages of a broader-beamed canoe versus a narrow-beamed craft?" "Round-bottomed versus flat-bottomed?"

A FINAL WORD

Adventure to some is a state of mind, not so much a place or a physical risk as a mental challenge. One can find adventure in the most unlikely places—in the midst of a teeming metropolis or in a secluded ocean cove as well as on a wild river or on a mountain peak. Whatever the setting, the wise instructor/leader recognizes the value of allowing learners to experience the joy and thrill of learning by oneself.

Processing the Adventure Experience

Clifford E. Knapp
Northern Illinois University

"What is of greatest consequence in a person's life is not just the nature and extent of his or her experiences but what has been learned from them."

(Cousins, 1981)

"You do not learn by doing ... you learn by thinking - acting - thinking - acting, etc. In and of itself, doing, like experiencing, can be a mindless affair."

(Sarason, 1984)

Every moment of life is an experience. Some moments bring pain, pleasure, boredom, or a variety of other emotional responses. Some experiences are planned and others seem to just happen to people. In order for experiences to be more than mindless affairs, they must have meaning that enables us to behave in useful ways in the future. Put briefly, we need to learn from them.

Whitehead (1929) in his essay, *The Aims of Education*, stated that "the problem of education is to make the pupil see the wood by means of the trees." (p. 18) Adventure educators can assist their participants in acquiring better lives through helping them identify "trees" of knowledge in the woods of experience. These trees consist, in part, of the intrapersonal and interpersonal skills needed to function alone and with others.

Leadership involves more than merely selecting outdoor tasks such as canoeing, backpacking, soloing, or climbing a 14-foot wall. Leadership also entails conducting these tasks safely and skillfully, as well as facilitating the process of making sense from what is learned. This act of processing or helping others internalize meaning from experience has also been described as debriefing, reflecting, analyzing, and generalizing, or simply sharing outcomes from the activity. Traditionally, this event occurs in a group gathered together to verbalize about personal feelings, thoughts, and human interactions under the guidance of an adventure educator.

Walter and Marks (1981) define processing as "... primarily a discussion of the completed activity [which]...provides detail, order, and meaning to the participants' experiences" (p. 166). The principal facilitation tools are observing, listening, providing feedback, questioning, and structuring activities to help participants reach the program objectives.

WAYS OF LEARNING

Koziey (1987) contrasts two ways of learning. He describes the traditional, deductive model used in most schools as the "Learn-Look- Do" approach (p. 20), in which students *learn* about something (usually through hearing or reading), then *look* at someone else applying it, and sometime later *do* what has been learned. An alternative inductive model, more appropriate to adventure education, is the "Do-Look-Learn" approach, which provides for the discovery of truths that have been personally assimilated through experience. During the *look* or reflection phase of this model, participants "... examine the subjective experience of doing the activities, and then determine what happened, how it happened, and what forces were present that influenced the way things happened" (p. 21). In the *learn* phase of this model, participants internalize "... through extrapolating data to other real-life situations ... through the use of theoretical inputs for understanding processes and activity;" and "through making decisions about how insights gained can be utilized for personal growth or for being effective in the world" (p. 22). Particularly during the *look* and *learn* phases of Koziey's model, facilitators can assist learners by helping them process the experience.

UNDERLYING ASSUMPTIONS ABOUT PROCESSING

In describing the theory and practice of processing experiences, several assumptions have been made:

1. Skilled facilitators can assist participants in gaining understanding from human experience through the application of effective processing techniques.
2. Human relations process skills can be practiced and learned best through interactions with others in a controlled group setting.
3. Much of the group learning that takes place can be applied to situations outside the group if the participants are assisted by skilled leaders.
4. Stress-producing outdoor challenges and the accompanying processing sessions can provide the necessary stimuli for making lasting life changes.

These assumptions indicate the underlying premise of this section: Adventure educators must possess group processing skills in order to expand the personal meanings of outdoor experiences for participants and attain the program objectives.

HARD AND SOFT SKILLS

Adventure educators generally accept the need to develop both hard and soft skills. The hard skills are defined as the technical competencies needed to conduct physical activities skillfully and safely. A few examples are setting up a system for belaying a climber, cooking a meal, or paddling a canoe. The soft skills are defined as the human relations competencies needed to guide personal growth and achieve group unity. A few examples are empathizing accurately with others, resolving a conflict, or drawing out individual feelings. Perhaps the term "soft skills" originated because of the stereotypical image of females as being physically "soft" and also skilled in listening, expressing feelings, cooperating, maintaining relationships, and nurturing others. Whatever the semantic roots of the term, adventure educators agree that men and women need hard and soft skills to be complete and effective leaders. The overall skill of conducting a processing session consists of a variety of soft-skill components.

Because human group interaction is a complex phenomenon, creating a comprehensive list of soft skills is difficult. Gardner (1984) divided human relations skills (which he termed personal intelligence) into two categories—intrapersonal and interpersonal. Intrapersonal skills permit "... access to one's own feeling life ..." (p. 239) to guide personal behavior. Some examples are becoming aware of feelings, affirming personal worth, recognizing personal power, and taking risks. Interpersonal skills include those that allow individuals "... to notice and make distinctions among other individuals ...," especially their moods, temperaments, motivations, and intentions (p. 239). Some examples are: communicating thoughts and feelings, empathizing, interpreting nonverbal language, cooperating, and listening to others. Adventure educators can help the "participants develop and practice these skills in outdoor settings and provide guidance in applying them to other life situations."

SUGGESTED GROUP NORMS FOR COMMUNITY-BUILDING

Norms, or standards of behavior, can only be suggested, not mandated. However, the designated leader is usually given a considerable amount of power in determining the norms under which the group will operate. The following norms have been shown to increase the probability that a caring and trusting community will form:

1. Confidentiality should be preserved within the group.
2. Participation in the group activities should be encouraged as much as possible.
3. Participants should ask for what they need and want although they should not expect to get all they ask for.
4. Participants should speak for themselves rather than assume that they can speak for others in the group.
5. Discussions should focus on the "here and now" as much as possible rather than including frequent references to other people and situations outside the group.
6. The dignity of everyone should be respected by avoiding putdowns and encouraging validations.
7. Participants should be encouraged to take appropriate risks to promote positive changes.
8. Participants should be in charge of designing their own plans for personal growth.
9. Participants should demonstrate openness and honesty with their thoughts and feelings whenever possible.
10. The privacy of the group members should be respected at all times.

BARRIERS TO COMMUNITY-BUILDING OBJECTIVES

Building a supportive community involves learning and applying intrapersonal and interpersonal skills. In order to function effectively, a group needs to adopt a set of enabling norms that promote unity. Many adventure leaders agree that certain behaviors inhibit the attainment of a sense of community. These behaviors could be described as "restricting" norms. For example, the following norms generally impede the formation of caring communities: dishonesty, competition, rigidity, mistrust, avoidance of conflict, defensiveness, pessimism, and criticism. One goal of the facilitator is to influence the norms operating within the group so that they become enabling rather than restricting.

THE ROLE OF THE FACILITATOR IN PROCESSING

The facilitator's role is to create situations in which participants encounter opportunities to learn about themselves and others through direct experience. Facilitators should make it easier for the group to form a supportive community. Facilitators cannot do this for the group, but their knowledge and interventions can help the process along. Groups usually pass through various predictable stages before they reach a state of unity in which the members work well together. Facilitators first outline the tasks (e.g., climbing a mountain, pitching a tent, using a map and compass to find a destination) to be accomplished. Sometimes participants already have the necessary hard skills, but often these skills need to be taught or perfected. These tasks are designed to help participants reach the program objectives established by the sponsoring institution.

The difference between the tasks and the objectives must be clear to both the leaders and the participants. In ideal situations the group members usually prefer to complete the task (e.g., fording a river) and to achieve certain program objectives (e.g., cooperating, building trust, gaining self-confidence). However, if the group fails to successfully cross the river (assuming that no one is hurt or drowned), the objectives can still be met. If completion of the task is viewed as the sole end in view and the objectives are ignored or minimized, the benefits to the participants will be limited.

The role of the facilitator during the processing phase of the experience is to help the participants reach as many objectives as possible, whether the tasks are completed or not. According to Jordan (1987), "An overly aggressive or autocratic leader or an overly lackadaisical or laissez-faire leader may inhibit both the number and quality of participant contributions... The leader should take care not to inadvertently tell participants how they are functioning and feeling, but rather probe and verbally guide the participants into discovering their own emotions and attitudes" (p. 74). "Throughout the discussion it is important that the leader maintain an open and caring attitude toward all group members. By being attentive to his or her own nonverbal language, tone of voice, and choice of words, the leader will develop a better understanding of the group" (p. 76).

Facilitators must also be aware of and capitalize on both the content (what is discussed) and the process (what is communicated nonverbally) to maximize the participants' learning. By being attentive to the content and process involved in the experience, the facilitator will be better able to guide the development of the group from a collection of individuals into a cohesive community.

PRE-PLANNING THE PROCESSING PHASE

Some pre-planning can be accomplished if leaders have access to some information about the participants beforehand. This preliminary data can be obtained through personal contact or written documentation. Knowing certain facts about the population, such as age, gender, special needs, physical disabilities, purposes for attending, or behavioral characteristics can be helpful, although even this is insufficient to fully plan the processing session. Facilitators may want to prepare a list of questions related to some predictable issues that may arise. For instance, many individuals in newly formed groups have difficulties communicating effectively, deferring judgments about others, listening, cooperating, respecting human differences, trusting others, and leading or following others. Pre-planned lists of questions have limitations; however, they can prove useful as checklists for what to look for. (Note: For examples of pre-planned questions organized under various objectives, see Knapp [1984], "Designing Processing Questions to Meet Specific Objectives.")

ADDITIONAL GROUP ISSUES TO PROCESS

One of the most difficult dilemmas for leaders is deciding what issues to process. If guiding a community is the main focus, then any barriers to achieving this goal become crucial group issues worthy of time and attention. Some additional group issues to watch for and process are:

1. Participation/involvement in group activities
2. Level and style of influence exerted by individuals
3. Group decision-making methods (i.e., voting, consensus seeking, or domination by a verbal minority

4. Expressions of belonging or feeling rejected (group membership)
5. The extent to which feelings are openly expressed
6. The amount of putdowns and critical comments
7. Obvious attempts to control others against their wills
8. Evidence of low self-esteem and lack of confidence
9. Unresolved conflicts
10. Aggressive or hostile behavior
11. Unwarranted gender stereotyping

Facilitators should design a plan of action to achieve pre-selected objectives, but must always be flexible enough to alter the plan if necessary. The best preparation for processing the group experience is a thorough understanding of psychological and sociological principles as they occur in structured adventure situations.

SUGGESTED STEPS IN PROCESSING

Step 1: Establishing rapport, norms and ground rules. After the group members have been prepared for participation in the outdoor task, they should be oriented to the purpose of the processing sessions. Facilitators need to establish a rapport with the participants and should outline some minimal behavioral expectations. Individual leadership style and philosophy dictate the extent to which the group is instructed about the objectives, expected norms, and ground rules prior to the activity. Participants need to feel safe both physically and psychologically and therefore some ground rules are helpful in the beginning of the session. Insisting on the importance of respecting confidentiality and individual privacy, giving permission to not participate verbally, and prohibiting verbal putdowns helps the group members to develop feelings of safety. The facilitator must create and maintain a humane climate in the group, or honest expressions of thoughts, feelings, and actions will be inhibited.

Step 2: Observing, reporting, and questioning. When group members interact as they move toward completing assigned tasks, there are literally hundreds of human content and process observations that can be made. Facilitators need to identify the relevant issues to process. The program objectives are important guides in making these decisions. In these matters there is no substitute for experience and sound professional judgment. Group issues can range from those that are relatively nonthreatening to those that are potentially volatile and value-sensitive. For example, issues that can be emotionally powerful include those related to gender stereotyping, flagrant disregard for safety rules, personal competence and self-esteem, or deeply held prejudices. Facilitators should always be alert to incidents that evoke strong feelings in the participants. The leader has the responsibility to make key observations and to report them to the group or raise questions so that key issues will become more apparent to the participants. Usually, these observations are directed first toward concrete behavior and not to the inferences drawn from these actions. For example, when a participant stays physically apart from the rest of the group, this act is merely described or probed through questioning. It is risky to interpret the reasons for a person's separation from the group. Identifying and discussing factual observations are less problematical than trying to uncover the underlying motivations for these behaviors. Later in the session, when more trust and mutual support have developed, the facilitator can ask for feedback about the feeling associated with the behavior. Hammel (1986) suggests that *Bloom's Taxonomy of Education Objectives Handbook I: Cognitive Domain* (1959) can guide the sequence of the processing session. This method involves becoming aware of the concrete aspects of the experience first (eliciting information about knowledge, comprehension, and application) through directed questions such as "What happened when ...?" or "How did you feel when ...?" (p. 22) Next, the group could examine the more abstract ways of thinking about the experience such as analysis, synthesis, and evaluation by answering questions such as "Do you see any patterns?" "Have you learned anything about yourself?" or "What was the highlight for you?" (p. 22)

Step 3: Other types of facilitator intervention. This step is somewhat more controversial and not always included in a typical processing sequence. Some types of facilitator interventions are especially applicable to the more contrived situations involving group initiatives or ropes challenge courses. Some facilitators may choose to stop the group before the task is completed to process certain interactions while they are still vivid. If a participant contributes a significant element to the solving of a group problem, the action could be stopped to process it. In another instance, if the group demonstrates a restricting norm, the action could be stopped to discuss the situation and to suggest a more appropriate enabling norm. Another type of facilitator intervention is to respond to specific behaviors by changing the rules for completing the task. For example, if one of the physically strong participants always contributes to the group in that way, the facilitator could create a hypothetical situation in which that person "breaks" both arms. This would force the group into a different problem-solving strategy and would provide that physically strong person with opportunities to contribute in other ways. Alternative ways to "disable" the participants are to render them temporarily blind (using blindfolds), mute, or deaf (using earplugs) in order to change the dynamics of the group.

Step 4: Summarizing, evaluating, and reaching closure. The final step in the processing sequence is to help the group summarize, evaluate, and transfer the adventure program to future situations. This phase can be done at the close of a two-hour session, or at the end of a 26-day course. Reaching closure is important for participants, especially if they have achieved a sense of community and developed strong feelings for each other. When people feel cared for, trusted, and supported by others, they often want to bid others farewell through a structured celebration or ritual. Even if the group remains intact upon returning home, closure activities can relate to leaving the place and completing a valuable program. Part of the closure ceremony involves helping the participants transfer and apply what is learned to other settings. Closure activities can be as simple as allowing every one an opportunity to verbalize the highpoints of their time together, or planning how they will apply what they learned at home; or as complex as writing and performing a poem, song, or skit that captures the positive experience, or developing and signing a self-contract related to proposed personal attitudinal and behavioral changes. Sometimes participants may plan their own activities for accomplishing closure. However the closure phase is achieved, it is important to include this step before the group disbands. Adequate time should be devoted to discussing the transition from the group experience to the situation back home. Usually the norms established in the group are different from those operating outside of the group. Participants should be cautioned about assuming that everyone in other settings have fully accepted norms such as expressing feelings openly, listening by reflecting back what is heard, taking behavioral risks in order to grow, or validating each other in verbal or nonverbal ways. The participants gains from the adventure experience can be erased if they encounter problems of rejection or hostility in back-home situations. Potential reentry problems need to be addressed with care in order to ease the transition from one group culture to another.

ALTERNATIVE MODES FOR PROCESSING

Although the traditional image of a processing session is a leader-led group of people sitting in a circle discussing the impact of the experience, other methods for acquiring personal meaning should be considered. Smith (1987, pp. 34-37), outlines several other ways that allow participants to process their experiences:

1. *Relaxation/Centering/Introspection.* Provide time, either in silence or with back-ground music or natural sounds, to reflect on the experience. Sometimes con trolled breathing and relaxation exercises can help to create the conditions necessary for quiet ntrospection and learning.
2. *Special Places.* Assign special places outdoors for participants to "become one" with the environment, and to process their experience. They can be asked to find special objects such as a tree or rock to use as sounding boards for a "conversation" with nature.
3. *Solos.* Direct participants to spend time alone outdoors. This period can be as short as several minutes or as long as a few days. They can also use this reflection time alone to eat or to watch a natural event like a sunrise or a bee pollinating flowers.
4. *Guided Fantasy.* Provide verbal input in order to influence the thoughts and feelings of the participants. The mono logue could take the form of a story that has relevance for the group and evokes mental images related to the impact of the experiences on the individuals.
5. *Journal Writing.* Direct the participants to write about their experiences in a struc tured or unstructured way. Use sentence stems, diagrams, and other written thought stimuli to trigger appropriate responses or to suggest stream-of-consciousness writing to record insights and questions.
6. *Small Groups.* Suggest that participants share in several small groups, which usually permits more verbal interaction and feelings of belonging. These sessions can be open-ended or structured to varying degrees. If a group issue such as how decisions are being made arises, the participants can divide into trios or pairs to talk about good and poor decision-making examples observed in their group.

SOME CAUTIONS TO CONSIDER

Interacting with people who express thoughts and feelings in stressful group situations can be as dangerous as playing with fire. Leaders must have a clear picture of what they wish to accomplish, their own skill levels, and as much information about the participants as possible. Processing, as conducted in most adventure settings, is not designed as a therapy session. Participants are not there to be healed of mental disabilities in most situations. The leader is not there to be treated either and should not take "group time" to raise and pursue personal emotional issues. If leaders feel intense emotions or bring in burdensome problems from outside the group, they should not conduct the processing session until these distracting feelings or problems can be put aside. A co-facilitator is usually helpful to take over in these extreme cases. Knowing one's limitations is just as important as knowing one's strengths. Facilitators can only suggest more gentle slopes in reaching life's mountain peaks; they cannot do the climbing for the participants.

SUMMARY

Processing the experience is part science and part art. This section has attempted to deline-ate some of the science of processing so that facilitators can develop clearer objectives and use more precise methods. Because process-ing the experience involves making on-the-spot judgments based on new factual informa-tion and intuitive predictions, all the steps can not be outlined in cookbook fashion. If adventure educators focus carefully upon who is in the group, how they interact as they complete their tasks, and the objectives they would like to achieve, the art and science of processing experience will be practiced more effectively.

Developing a Code of Ethics for Processing Adventure Experiences: A Self-Inventory

Directions: The following statements are possible components of a personal code of ethics for processing adventure experience. A code of ethics is a set of ideas that establishes a standard for what is right and good. Read the statements through once and then rate them on a scale using the numerals 0, 1, 2, 3, 4, or 5. (0 = no value as a component of a code of ethics and 5 = an essential part of a code of ethics)

1. Select educational objectives that you are qualified to process.
2. Share the educational objectives with the group.
3. Find out as much as possible about the group prior to working with them.
4. Allow adequate time for doing and processing each activity.
5. Share the expected ground rules and norms of behavior for the group.
6. Stress the importance of maintaining confidentiality among the participants.
7. Respect a participant's right to remain silent or to "pass" during the processing session.
8. Respond to participants in ways that enhance their self-esteem and build their confidence.
9. When possible, avoid opening up traumatic issues in the lives of the partici pantsunless you have the time and expertise to adequately follow-up.
10. Limit the giving of advice about how people should live their lives.
11. Provide opportunities for all participants to meet their needs in the group.
12. Continually learn more about psychology, communications, and group dynamics through personal involvement in groups, reading, lectures, and other means.
13. Provide time to discuss the transition from the group to back-home situations to help participants apply newly-acquired knowledge and skills.
14. Be cautious about "pushing" participants beyond the limits they choose for themselves.
15. Intervene when an important group issue surfaces in order to help the participants understand the dynamics of the situation.
16. Begin the processing session with a clear plan for reaching specific objectives, but remain flexible and open to change.
17. Create a rapport with the participants and build a climate of safety and support.
18. Devote time and attention to group issues and avoid spending time on your own personal issues.

What other essential components of a personal code of ethics would you add to this list?

REFERENCES

Bloom, B. S. (Ed.) (1956). *Taxonomy of educational objectives handbook, I: Cognitive domain.* New York: David McKay Company, Inc.

Cousins, N. (1981). *Human options: An autobiographical notebook.* New York: W.W. Norton and Company.

Gardner, H. (1983). *Frames of mind: The theory of multiple intelligences.* New York: Basic Books, Inc.

Hammel, H. (1986). How to design a debriefing session. *The Journal of Experiential Education, 9*(3), 20-25.

Jordan, D. (1987). Processing the initiative course experience. *The Bradford Papers Annual, II*, 73-78.

Knapp, C. E. (1984). Idea notebook: Designing processing questions to meet specific objectives. *The Journal of Experiential Education.* 7(2), 47-49.

Koziey, P.W. (1987). Experiencing mutality. *Journal of Experiential Education. 10*(3), 20-22.

Sarason, S. B. Quoted in Smith, V. (1984) Book review: Schooling in America, scapegoat and salvation. *Phi Delta Kappan. 66*(3), 224-225.

Smith, T. E. (1986). Alternative methodologies for processing the adventure experience. *The Bradford Papers Annual, 1*, 29-38.

Walter, G. A., & Marks, S.E. (1981). *Experiential learning and change: theory design and practice.* New York: John Wiley and Sons.

Whitehead, A. N. (1929). *The aims of education and other essays.* New York: The Macmillan Company.

Transfer of Learning in Adventure Education

Michael Gass
University of New Hampshire

As seen throughout this text, the growth of adventure experiences has produced a wide variety of applications. Some of these applications have been used to provide and/or enhance leisure or recreational experiences. The focus of these types of experiences is on the activity itself, and while there may be applications to future recreational experiences, the major intent of these activities is on the leisure experience.

However, when the focus of adventure experiences is on educational or therapeutic goals, the intent of the process pertains not only to the immediate activity, but also to the relation of the experience to future issues for the participant. The true value or effectiveness of the program lies in how learning experienced during adventure activity will serve the learner in the future. Dewey (1938) goes as far as to say that this quality of application to future learning "discriminates between experiences that are worthwhile educationally and those that are not" (p. 33). This aphorism is especially true for adventure education/therapy programs. Whether it has been a juvenile offender developing more appropriate social behaviors, a freshman student obtaining a more beneficial educational experience at a university, or another program where adventure is used as a valid educational or therapeutic medium, the credibility of programs using a challenging environment is based upon the positive effects they have on their students' or clients' futures.

This effect that a particular experience has on future learning experiences is called the transfer of learning, or simply "transfer." Not only is transfer important for adventure education programs, it also has been identified as critical for the support, continuation, and/or livelihood of such programs. For example, when describing the value of adventure programming as a milieu used to prevent delinquency, the U.S. Department of Justice (1981) states that:

> Despite having some plausible theoretical or correlational basis, wilderness programs without follow-up (transfer) into clients' home communities should be rejected on the basis of their repeated failure to demonstrate effectiveness in reducing delinquency after having been tried and evaluated. (p. 2-77)

While transfer is critical to the field of adventure education, probably no other concept is so often misunderstood. Much of the confusion plaguing the transfer of learning has resulted from two main factors. First is the concern that the initial learning usually takes place in an environment (e.g., mountains) quite different from the environment where the student's future learning will occur. Second is the lack of knowledge concerning the variety of methods available to promote transfer. Neither of these problems is limited to adventure education, but there are certain theories, models, and techniques that pertain directly to the field and can assist in eliminating much of the confusion surrounding the topic, and enable individuals to strengthen the transfer of their program's goals.

THEORIES CONCERNING TRANSFER

Concerning the application to adventure education, three central learning theories pertaining to transfer exist that explain how the linking of elements from one learning environment to another occur (see Figure 1). Bruner (1960) describes the first two, specific and nonspecific transfer, in attempting to show how current learning serves the learner in the future.

> There are two ways in which learning serves the future. One is through its specific applicability to tasks that are highly similar to those we originally learned to perform. Psychologists refer to this specific phenomenon as specific transfer of training; perhaps it should be called the extension of habits or associations. Its utility appears to be limited in the main to what we speak of as skills. A second way in which earlier learning renders later performance more efficient is through what is conveniently called non-specific transfer, or, more accurately, the transfer of principles and attitudes. In essence, it consists of learning, initially, not a skill but a general idea which can then be used as a basis of recognizing subsequent problems as special cases of the idea originally mastered. (p. 17)

The following example from a student's notebook illustrates the use of specific transfer in adventure education:

> Today during the class we learned how to rappel. Initially I was quite frightened, but I ended up catching on to the proper techniques and enjoying it quite a bit! One thing that helped me in learning how to rappel was the belaying we did yesterday. With belaying, our left hand is the 'feel' hand while the right hand is the 'brake' hand. With rappelling, it is the same; our left hand is the 'feel' hand and our right hand is used to 'brake' our rappel and control our descent.

In this example, the student's previous experiences of specific hand skills learned while belaying positively affected her ability to learn the necessary and correct hand skills of rappelling. Figure 1 illustrates these events occurring—the initial stage of learning how to belay, the development of the proper and safe habits while belaying, and finally, the use of these skills while rappelling.

The next example from another student's notebook highlights what Bruner describes as nonspecific transfer, or the use of common underlying principles in one learning situation to assist the student in a future learning experience:

> ...'as a result of the wilderness course', I've seen myself developing more trust in my friends at school. The no-discount policy helps me quite a bit, but I think what helped the most was learning how I receive as well as give support to others. I felt that this was the most important thing I learned 'while on the wilderness course'.

In this second example, the student has taken the common underlying principles that she learned about developing trust (i.e., receiving and giving support from/to others) from the wilderness course and generalized those principles and attitudes to a new learning situation (i.e., school). This ability of the learner to generalize is crucial for nonspecific transfer to occur. Figure 1 on the following page shows the connection of two learning situations by common underlying principles or non-specific transfer. In this example, the student, through an initiative such as the willow wand exercise supplemented with a no-discount policy, learns valuable principles and attitudes about developing trust in peer relationships. She takes these principles, generalizes them, and transfers them to a new learning situation, such as developing meaningful relationships at school based on trust.

The third transfer theory associated with adventure learning also requires the student to generalize certain principles from one learning situation to another. But the principles being transferred in this theory are not common or the same in structure, but are similar, analogous, or metaphorical. The following passage illustrates a student making the connection between the similar underlying principles of canoeing and his group working together:

> There has been a certain jerkiness in the group. It's like the progress of a canoe. When the people on each side paddle in unison, with each person pulling his weight, the canoe goes forward smoothly. If certain people slack, or if there is a lack of coordination, progress becomes jerky. The canoe veers 'from' side to side. Time and energy are wasted. (Godfrey, 1980, p. 229)

In this particular situation, the student is not using the principles of efficient canoeing for future aquatic learning experiences. He is instead transferring the concepts or principles of canoeing as metaphors for another learning experience that is similar, yet not the same.

This third type of transfer, metaphoric transfer, is also illustrated in Figure 1. Here the student takes the similar underlying principles mentioned in the example above, generalizes them and applies them to a future learning experience with similar elements. The future learning experience represented in Figure 1 for metaphoric transfer is a group situation where the necessity of everyone working together efficiently is vital (in this case, working for a business corporation).

One individual who has done a great deal of investigation into the use of metaphoric transfer with adventure learning is Stephen Bacon. In the following passage, he further explains how the use of experiences that are metaphoric provides a vehicle for the transfer of learning:

> The key factor in determining whether experiences are metaphoric is the degree of isomorphism between the metaphoric situation and the real-life situation. Isomorphism means having the same structure. When all the major elements in one experience are represented by corresponding elements in another experience, and when the overall structure of the two experiences are highly similar, then the two experiences are metaphors for each other. This does not imply that the corresponding elements are literally identical; rather, they must be symbolically identical. (Bacon, 1983, p. 4)

A PROGRAM MODEL FOR TRANSFER

When reviewing the three transfer of learning theories previously discussed, it can be seen that the key to increasing transfer often lies in the selection or design of appropriate learning activities and the teaching methodology. One of the major faults of adventure education has been the lack of planning for the transfer in either of these areas. Transfer must be planned, much in the same manner as an educational objective or a properly planned learning skill.

Figure 2 portrays the learning process of an adventure program interested in procuring positive transfer for a student. As seen in the model, once the needs of the student and the goals of the program are properly identified and matched, learning skills, activities, teaching strategies, and transfer models and

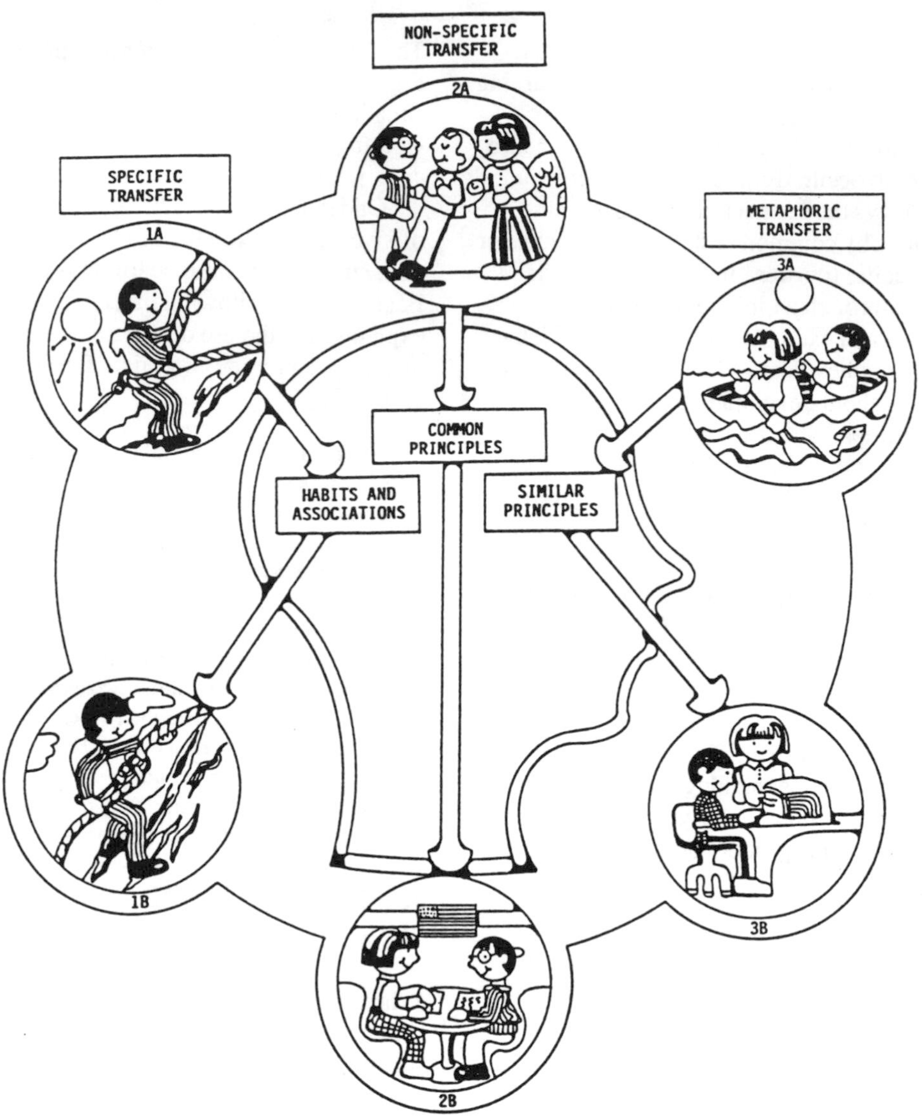

Figure 1
Three Theories of Transfer in Adventure Education

The above diagram illustrates how learning in adventure education is linked to future learning experiences. In the first theory, specific transfer, the learner takes the habits and associations acquired during a previous experience (Diagram 1A—the hand skills of belaying) and applies them to a new experience to assist him in developing a new skill (Diagram 1B—the hand skills of rappelling). In the second theory, nonspecific transfer, the learner generalizes the common underlying principles received from a previous experience (Diagram 2A— developing trust from an initiative game) and employs them in a new learning situation (Diagram 2B—developing trust with peers at school). The third theory, metaphoric transfer, shows the earner transferring the similar underlying principles from canoeing (Diagram 3A) to working with other individuals in a business corporation (Diagram 3B).

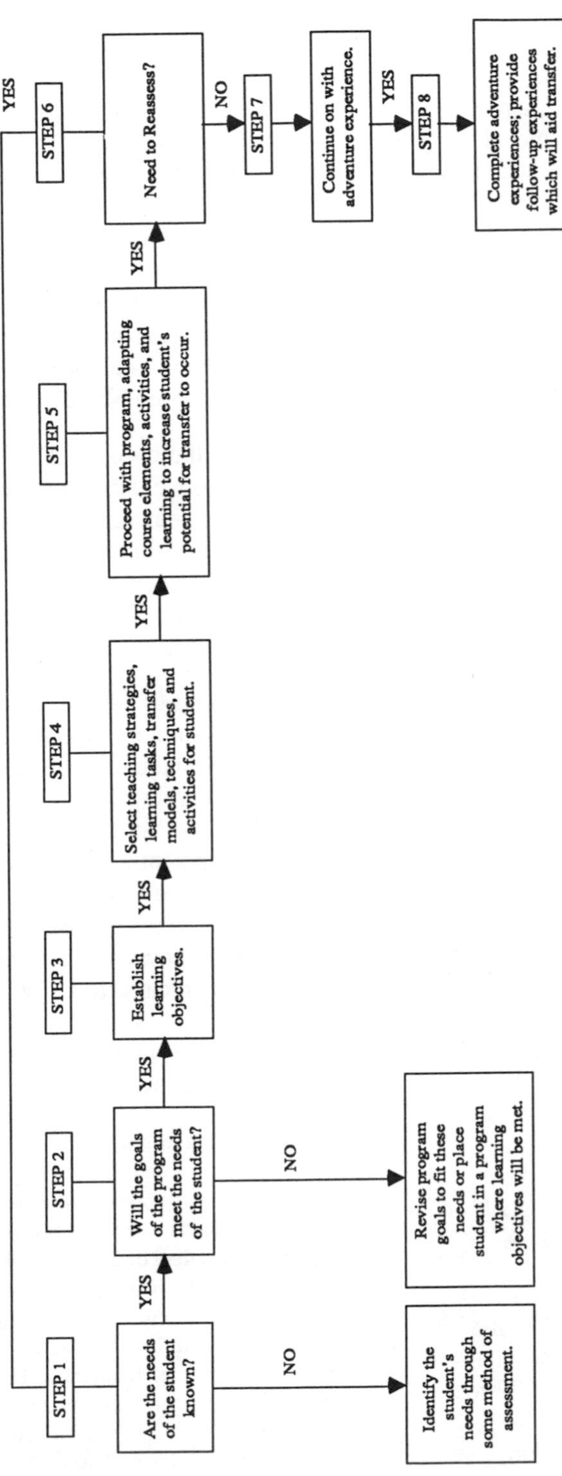

Figure 2
Learning Process Model with an Emphasis on the Transfer of Learning

techniques are planned. A strong emphasis is placed on providing the connection between the present and future learning environments to increase the amount of transfer that will occur. Note that throughout the program, if the needs of the student change, the model directs the instructor to assess these changes and adapt new learning activities and transfer elements to the student's new behavior. At the completion of the adventure experience, follow-up activities are also used to enhance positive transfer.

FACTORS/TECHNIQUES THAT ENHANCE TRANSFER OF LEARNING

Given the information in Figure 2 for programming transfer, what are some of the factors or techniques adventure educators can use to assist them in increasing the transfer of their students' learning? (Shown by Step 4 in Figure 2.) Many researchers have presented exhaustive lists of elements that can lead to positive transfer, but some of these are unalterable (e.g., genetic factors concerning intelligence), while others have little application to the "non-traditional" atmosphere where most adventure learning takes place.

As stated in the program model, it is necessary for adventure educators to select not only the proper transfer of learning theories, but also the techniques and activities involved with the increase of transfer applicable to their program. Ten techniques adaptable to the transfer of learning occurring with adventure activities are presented here as examples. Many other techniques exist and should be selected for their ability to transfer the goals of the specific program and according to the theory of transfer one is using.

1. Design conditions for transfer before the course/program/learning activities actually begin. Several steps can be done prior to a learning experience that can aid in the transfer of learning from an adventure activity. Examples of these steps include:

   a) Identify, develop, or establish a commitment to change in the student.
   b) Have a student set goals for the experience.
   c) Write and set tight learning objectives for the student in the program.
   d) Place the plans and goals made by the student in writing to create a stronger commitment for transferring the learning.
   e) Plan adventure experiences based on their ability to enable students/clients to transfer learning from the adventure experience into future experiences.

   Each of these steps illustrates the need for instructors of adventure education/therapy programs to think and plan proactively. Using such conditions enhances the strengths of using adventure experiences for educational or therapeutic goals.

2. Create elements in the student's learning environment similar to those elements likely to be found in future learning environments. Learning environments with strong applicability to future experiences have greater potential for a more positive transfer of learning. The following example of a "youth at risk" in a wilderness program shows how elements of the program were created to assist him in transferring a behavior, in this case, a greater self-concept, into a subsequent learning environment.

   Throughout the course, Kurt was presented with a variety of challenging tasks. He overcame strong personal fears and doubts and succeeded at many of the tasks that required a great deal of initiative. The staff noticed that after he had developed a stronger belief in himself, he was especially zealous on tasks that required a great deal of trust and responsibility (e.g., belaying). Throughout the course, the staff continued to place Kurt in progressively more difficult situations that demanded a strong, realistic belief in himself as well as other members in the group. Many

> of the discussions at night were about the relationships between the elements they faced as individuals and as a group in the wilderness and how these elements mirrored the situations they would encounter when they returned to their communities.

Other learning behaviors are often presented in a similar manner to increase their relevance and application to future learning environments for students. Certain programs have found that by approaching problem- solving and decision-making skills in a general manner, their students succeed in creating elements valuable for future use (Gass, 1985a, p. 5).

3. Provide students with the opportunities to practice the transfer of learning while still in the program. There was probably no better time for Kurt to practice the behavior to be transferred (i.e., an increased self-concept) than during the adventure experience. The variety of contexts in which to practice transfer, the number of times Kurt could practice transferring the behavior, and the strong support within the group that developed during this outdoor adventure program all helped Kurt focus on necessary generalizing and conceptualizing skills. These skills proved valuable in strengthening his ability to transfer the enhanced self-concept for future learning situations.

4. Have the consequences of learning be natural—not artificial. One can think of the consequences of learning as either being natural or artificial. "Natural consequences are those that follow or would follow a given act unless some human system intervenes. Artificial consequences follow or would follow a given act, if, and only if, some human system anticipates or responds to the initial act and causes the artificial consequence or modifies a natural consequence" (Darnell, 1983, p. 4).

Superficially viewing the field of outdoor education, one would think all learning that takes place in the outdoors would have natural consequences. Unfortunately, far too often this is not the case. Whether it has been from an "overly" caring instructor or an overpowering one, too often the student becomes dependent on, is shielded by, or anticipates the instructor as a reinforcer of learning. Once the course is over and the reinforcer (i.e., the instructor) is removed from the student, learning behavior is severely hampered or terminated. In this way, with artificial consequences the result of learning transfer is extremely limited.

However, if outdoor programs could make their students' learning more experiential, natural consequences would be more likely to occur. This would result in the stronger formation of learning behaviors likely to be available in future learning situations, hence increasing the amount of transfer. Some experiential learning techniques that could foster the development of natural consequences include relying upon the students' intrinsic rather than some external source of motivation; placing more responsibility for learning on the student (see #8); and not shielding the learner from the consequences of what is learned, whether they be positive or negative.

5. Provide the means for students to internalize their own learning. The ability for a student to internalize learning creates the concepts and generalizations central to the transfer process. Adventure educators have differed to a great extent on how this is best accomplished. Many believe that by getting their students to verbalize or place their own learning into words, the internalization of the concepts to be transferred is increased through self-awareness and reflective thinking (Kalisch, 1979, p. 62). Others feel that conscious

efforts such as verbalizing are secondary to other methods of internalization, such as the subconscious development of metaphors for transfer (Bacon, 1983, p. 2).

Methods that enable students to internalize learning behaviors from adventure programs often use reflective processes to aid internalization. An example of one method often used by adventure education programs that increases transfer through reflection is the "solo" experience. Certain programs feel that such an experience, when appropriately implemented, reinforces the learning that occurs in the adventure program and helps students/clients to identify how they are going to use the experience in the future (Gass, 1985a, p. 6).

6. Include past successful alumni in the adventure program. Sometimes the incorporation of successful alumni in courses or programs assists in the transfer of learning for students/clients. The following example demonstrates how one program uses this technique:

> By listening to how these alumni used the skills they had learned from the program in their lives, students began to envision how they might use elements of the program in future situations. While not always advisable or possible for some programs, many individuals felt this "vicarious" method of planning future transfer strategies aided in the transfer of learning for students (Gass, 1985a, p. 5)

7. Include significant others in the learning process. The inclusion of other individuals closely associated with the student's/client's learning process has often been found to heighten the transfer of learning (Gass, 1985a, p. 2). Some of the persons used to fill this vital role have been peers, parents, counselors, social workers and/or teachers. The following example illustrates how one program includes significant others in the learning process to provide positive transfer for a student:

> Before Cristina participated on theadventure portion of the family therapy program, several objectives were established for her family, counselor and school teacher—as well as herself. Cristina and her family met with the staff, other participants and their families prior to the adventure experience in order to familiarize both the students and the parents of the reasons for their participation on the course. Another reason for this meeting was to inform them of possible changes in the student that could occur. The program continued to stay in close contact with Cristina's family in order for them to adjust to and support possible changes in Cristina's personality and behavior.
>
> Cristina also created several "goal contracts" in a pre-trip meeting with the assistance of a staff member in the areas of personal, family, school and peer development. The contracts were discussed on the course and monitored monthly, with proper adaptations, for the next six months. These contracts were agreed to and supported by Cristina's family. Cristina's teacher also participated on several portions of the wilderness course, enabling her to support, reinforce, and try and use the observable changes during the adventure program with Cristina in the classroom.

8. When possible, place more responsibility for learning in the program with the student/client. Many programs, especially those invested in teaching adventure education experientially, believe that placing more responsibility with the student in the program not only increases the student's motivation to learn but also the incentive to apply what is learned in future experiences. Examples of this range from programs involving students in the planning of food menus to programs that have students organize and conduct an entire adventure experience on their own. Certain programs have implemented strong service components that have a definite focus on future experiences outside of the adventure experience (MacArthur, 1982, pp. 37-38) and enhance the self-responsibility within the student, which can lead to a greater transfer of learning.

No matter what techniques programs use to involve their students/clients in the planning and operations of an adventure learning experience, their involvement should depend on their ability to accept responsibility for learning and their willingness and desire to do so. A person that willingly accepts responsibility for learning will transfer information much more readily than an individual who approaches such a task with a sense of indifference or resentment.

9. Develop focused processing techniques that facilitate the transfer of learning. In many adventure education programs, processing/debriefing/facilitating is often used to enrich a student's learning experience. The length and intensity of these debriefings can differ from a quick and informal sharing of the day's occurrences to a lengthy and formalized discussion of a particular incident with a specific set of rules and guidelines. Despite this vast difference in the application of techniques, there are certain general characteristics that, if included in the processing of an experience, will assist in the transfer of learning. Some of these characteristics are:

    - Present processing sessions based on the student/client's ability to contribute personally meaningful responses. Use feedback that is well-intended, descriptive, specific, and directed toward positive change.

    - Focus on linking the experiences from the present and future learning environments together during the processing session. This can often be accomplished by actually contracting with the students for this to occur.

    - When possible, debrief prior to and throughout the learning experience and not just at the end of it. This allows students to continually focus on the future applicability of the adventure experience.

10. Provide follow-up experiences that aid in the application of transfer. Once a student begins transferring learning, the presence of follow-up activities (e.g., continued communications, feedback on learning decisions, processes, and choices) serve to heighten transfer abilities. Again, one reason for this might be the positive effects of reflection between learning situations. Reflection gives the student the opportunity to see and evaluate the results of past learning behaviors, garner learner motivation, and plan future learning strategies and directions.

CONCLUSION

As educators who use the outdoors and challenging situations to help students learn more efficiently, we all aspire to teach our students something usable; and therein lies the value of our program. But unless we assist our students in providing their own linkages, bridges, and connections to their learning, the utility of much of the education we work so hard to bring about is put away in the equipment room along with the ropes and backpacks. As we strive to become better educators and proponents of the value of adventure education, let us look upon transfer as a device to excite students by showing them the future value of their current learning experiences. This motivation, provided by the opportunity to use their learning again, can furnish one of the strongest incentives for our students' continued learning and the field's success.

REFERENCES

Bacon, S. (1983). *The conscious use of metaphor in Outward Bound.* Denver, CO: Colorado Outward Bound School.

Bruner, J. (1960). *The process of education.* New York: Vintage Books.

Darnell, D. K. (1983). *On consequences, learning, survival, and "the good life."* An unpublished report. Department of Communications, University of Colorado.

Dewey, J. (1938). *Experience and education.* New York: MacMillan Publishing Company.

Gass, M. A. (1985a). *Strengthening adventure education by increasing the transfer of learning.* Durham, NH, University of New Hampshire. (ERIC Document Reproduction Service No. 255-335).

Gass, M.A. (1985b). Programming the transfer of learning in adventure education. *Journal of Experiential Education. 8,* (3), 18-24. This article can also be found in Meier, J. F.; Morash, T. W., & Welton, G. E. (Eds.) (1987). *High adventure outdoor pursuits: Organization and leadership* (2nd ed.). Columbus, OH: Publishing Horizons, Inc. 246-258.

Johnson, G.; Bird, T.; Warren-Little, J.; & Beville, S. L. (1981). *Delinquency prevention: Theories and strategies.* U.S. Department of Justice: Office of Juvenile and Delinquency Prevention, Center for Action Research, Inc.

Kalisch, K. (1979). *The role of the instructor in the Outward Bound process.* Three Lakes, WI: Honey Lakes Camp.

MacArthur, R. S. (1982). The changing role of service in Outward Bound. *Journal of Experiential Education. 5* (2), 34-39.

Mitzel, H. (Ed.) (1982). *Encyclopedia of educational research.* 5th Ed. New York: Free Press, Volume IV, 1947-1955.

Rhoades, J. S. (1972). *The problem of individual change in Outward Bound: An application and transfer theory.* Dissertation Abstracts International. Amherst, MA: University of Massachusetts.

Richardson, B. L. (1978). *The transfer of learning from high-risk activities in adventure-based outdoor education programs.* An unpublished report, Northern Illinois University.

Section Six

THE LEADERSHIP OF ADVENTURE EDUCATION

A Most Critical Ingredient

Leadership is a critical element in any field of activity, but especially so in one like adventure education where the safety of participants is of central concern. Adventure, by its nature, involves elements of risk and uncertainty. It occurs in environments containing both objective dangers like falling rocks and lightning, and subjective ones like fear and irresponsibility of participants. Outdoor leadership demands many skills, and especially judgment. This last is an intangible quality that is very difficult to teach and to assess. One may not know whether he or she has it until a situation demands it. If judgment is lacking, disaster may be the result.

The authors in this section tackle, from various angles, the problems of defining good outdoor leadership and of educating and training good leaders. Priest starts off with another useful definition of terms. Green, noting that leadership cannot be taught in any single workshop, course or even degree program, suggests that outdoor leadership training must be a lifelong, or at least career-long, process. He offers his opinion on what should be the basic ingredients of a training program.

Phipps and Swiderski turn their scholarly minds to the "soft skill" dimension of outdoor leadership. They explain how soft skills—those of group development, conflict resolution, and decision-making, among others—are critical to effective leadership. Safely navigating the physical environment is much simpler than finding one's way through the personalities, aspirations and eccentricities of a group under the pressure of an adventure. Phipps and Swiderski argue for a systematic approach to soft-skill leadership training, and suggest a model to be used.

Raiola examines the state of leadership training in colleges and universities. He briefly describes four training programs and offers an outline for an outdoor leadership curriculum. The nine elements of this curriculum are derived from survey research and from a review of literature. Institutions can, Raiola contends, make a critical contribution to leadership development, though they might not be able to do the complete job.

Cain and McAvoy tackle the issue of judgment in outdoor leadership. What is it and how can it be acquired? They present a theoretical foundation for development, evaluation and documentation of an experience-based judgment process. Cain has done a Delphi study to assess the views of professionals in outdoor leadership on experience-based judgement. He presents the interesting results of that study and the authors conclude that a model process of judgment can be identified and should by developed, evaluated, taught and applied.

Where, by whom, and how should judgment in outdoor leadership be taught? Who should assess its presence? How should competency in this field be defined and recognized? These are some of the issues Cockrell addresses in the concluding essay in this section. He reviews the certification issue, the arguments for and against certification, and the history of this argument. He notes that certification programs are already in place in certain special subfields of outdoor leadership. The problem is with comprehensive outdoor leadership certification. Cockrell concludes that comprehensive certification may be undesirable and impossible. He supports a "modular" approach to training and certification.

This section examines broad questions about outdoor leadership. It focuses especially on the problem of training outdoor leaders. There is no attempt to treat the "hard" skills of outdoor leadership. Excellent treatments of these skills are available for the many activity areas that comprise adventure education.

Outdoor Leadership Components

Simon Priest
Brock University

As this section considers the topic of leadership, a brief introduction to terms is warranted.

LEADERSHIP

Leadership is a process of influence. The group member doing the most influencing at a given moment in time is the leader of that group. Leadership can be broken into three areas: concern for the group, or relationship orientation; concern for the problem, or task orientation; and concern for the favorability of influential conditions, such as environmental danger, individual competence, group unity, leader proficiency, and decision consequences. Based on the various combinations of these three areas of concern, a leader will influence through one of three styles: autocratic (keeping all decision-making power to self), democratic (sharing the decision-making power with the group), or abdicratic (giving decision-making power to the group).

OUTDOOR LEADER

An outdoor leader is someone who is designated, by the agency sponsoring the adventure, to be in charge of the adventure. Being in charge means holding legal and moral responsibility for the organization, instruction, and supervision of the group, and for the safety, protection, and enjoyment of the individuals and the environment.

OUTDOOR LEADERSHIP PREPARATION

The preparation of outdoor leaders is necessary in response to increasing use of the outdoors. People are being injured and the natural resources are sustaining damage. To counter these trends, experts have recommended education of the users by effective outdoor leaders. These candidates may be prepared (selected, trained, and assessed) by any one of several curriculum schemes that currently operate in North America and around the world.

OUTDOOR LEADERSHIP CERTIFICATION

If desired, certification follows preparation. As evaluated by a certifying body, certification is a means to guarantee that minimum standards of competency have been met or exceeded by the candidates. Although no nationally accepted bodies exist in North America, certification is the source of much controversy. Some experts believe it should be abolished. The main reason is a difficulty in assessing judgment based on experience: the most important attribute of an outdoor leader.

LEADERSHIP SKILLS AND ATTRIBUTES

Seven skills and seven attributes combine in a recipe for the effective leader:

Technical Activity Skills

Those competencies concerned with the outdoor pursuits being led. Some examples include being able to rock climb at a certain standard or level of difficulty, and being able to paddle a certain section or grade of a whitewater river. So as to maintain group control during the adventure, outdoor adventure leaders need to be able to perform at a proficiency equal to or greater than that of the group members.

Safety Skills

Those competencies (specific to the technical activity skills) necessary to enjoy the activity in a safe and sensible manner. Examples of such safety skills are navigation, survival, weather interpretation, body temperature regulation, wilderness first aid, accident response, search and rescue, and water safety.

Organizational Skills

Those competencies needed to plan, prepare, execute and evaluate an expedition or field trip with attention given to the special needs of participants. For example, outdoor adventure leaders need to arrange transportation, food, and lodging for a group, schedule activities, plan routes, and secure the necessary permits, equipment and clothing to make the trip a success.

Environmental Skills

Those competencies necessary to prevent negative damage to the natural surroundings. For example, outdoor adventure leaders must practice and encourage minimum impact travel and no-trace camping by modeling behaviors such as carrying out the garbage and not cross-cutting switchback trails.

Instructional Skills

Those competencies required to teach the group other skills related to the activity, environment, and safety. For example, teaching skiing technique in a series of progressions, teaching safety by the inquiry approach, and effectively using instructional aids to teach environmental concepts are all important instructional skills.

Group Management skills

Those competencies keep the group dynamic intact and which keep the members working toward their task. For example, outdoor adventure leaders need to resolve conflicts, communicate effectively, and foster personal trust and group cooperation.

Problem Solving and Decision-Making Skills

Those competencies that enable outdoor adventure leaders to accomplish tasks and deal with incidents, accidents or emergencies. More will be said about these skills (and judgment) later in this article.

Motivational Philosophy and Interest

The underlying reasons that cause (or motivate) outdoor adventure leaders to have interest in leading other people in the outdoor setting. These might include a desire to introduce others to nature, to work in the outdoors, or to share skills with others. Rarely, if ever, are outdoor adventure leaders in the job for the money!

Physical Fitness

The agility, coordination, endurance, and strength necessary to perform the tasks associated with being an outdoor adventure leader. Outdoor adventure leaders need to be physically and mentally fit enough to work long hours, sometimes under considerable stress.

Healthy Self-Concept and Ego

This refers to outdoor adventure leaders who are *not* entirely devoted to themselves and who know their true abilities. Potentially disastrous consequences are possible from a leader who is leading in order to be the center of attention, rather than to honestly help others. Outdoor adventure leaders who know their own strengths and weaknesses, who reserve pushing their own limits to times when they are engaged in personal trips, and who are aware of their own egos, can devote time and effort to developing healthy self-concepts in others. Outdoor adventure leaders who take groups outdoors so that they, themselves, may benefit from climbing a new peak or running a new river with the students along for the ride, are obviously not responding to the needs of the group and therefore cannot be expected to provide enjoyable growth experiences for others.

Awareness and Empathy for Others

This relates to more than mere sympathy for people. Outdoor adventure leaders must be aware of how group members might feel under certain circumstances. This awareness comes from the outdoor adventure leader having previously been in a similar situation. A leader who has never been through an activity similar to that of a group member may lack the experience necessary to truly appreciate the predicament the member may be experiencing. If a leader is unaware of the emotional status of a group member, then that leader cannot possibly help the member reach toward personal goals!

Personable Traits and Behavior

This refers to the set of model actions and one's personality that combine to create a rapport between outdoor adventure leader and the group. For example, a leader needs to embody such traits as unselfishness, confidence, honesty, punctuality, humor, and eagerness. Leaders are also held up as role models by those they lead, and as such, they must exhibit model behavior when in the presence of their charges. They must demonstrate a C.A.R.E.S. ethic (concern, admiration, respect, empathy, and safety) toward both environment and people. For example, they should wear lifejackets and protective helmets when such equipment is called for, they should avoid leaving any trace of their presence in the wilderness, and they should behave in a manner that is socially acceptable to others.

Flexible Leadership Style

This means knowing how, why, and when to apply differing approaches for sharing the role of decision-maker. Under most conditions, the decision-making of a group will be democratic or shared. In an emergency, leaders must be autocratic: giving orders and expecting them to be carried out. When the experience is progressing well, the leader may choose to be abdicratic: entirely delegating responsibility for decision-making to the group. In the latter case, the leader remains on hand ready to assume more decision-making power if called for.

Judgment Based on Experience

This is only needed when critical problem-solving information is unknown, missing, or vague. By calling on past experiences and using sound judgment, outdoor adventure leaders substitute values for unknown, missing, or vague information, and permit the problem-solving process to continue. Sound judgment is the glue that binds all the other components together to create the truly effective outdoor adventure leader.

ANALYTICAL PROBLEM-SOLVING

The problem-solving process is composed of two important phases: analytical and creative. The analytical phase follows several steps represented by questions. If the answer to each question is known and immediately obvious, then the problem-solver progresses to the next question. The seven questions are:

1. *Recognition*: Does a problem really exist?
2. *Definition*: What is the precise crux of the problem?
3. *Anticipation*: What is the desired outcome after resolution?
4. *Identification*: What are some possible solutions?
5. *Selection*: Which solution appears most probable?
6. *Execution*: Solution put into action? (after *decision* has been made)
7. *Evaluation*: Does the solution bring about the desired outcome?

DECISION-MAKING

Decision making is one part of the analytical phase. Selection and execution (the steps of discriminating a probable solution from the list of possibles) are the steps where the decision is made.

CREATIVE PROBLEM-SOLVING

If the answer to any question in the problem-solving process is not immediately obvious, because information is unknown, missing or vague, then the creative phase becomes necessary to arrive at an answer. This phase includes such techniques as:

1. *Brainstorming*: openly expressing all ideas without fear of criticism.
2. *Extended Effort*: generating the last ideas when all others have ceased.
3. *Attribute Listing*: inventorying the characteristics indicative of ideas.
4. *Forced Relationships*: comparing ideas in order to create new ones.
5. *Deferred Prejudice*: keeping an open mind, not choosing the first idea.
6. *Experience-Based Judgment*: estimating results based on past experience.

Judgment becomes extremely important when the act of delaying a decision (in hopes that new information will arise) might result in a further compounding of the problem. By drawing upon past experience, estimated values may be substituted for the missing, unknown, or vague information. By estimating these values, based on what happened last time, the process of solving the problem may continue.

Sound judgment comes from surviving past judgment calls (good or bad); from analyzing those successes and failures, and from retaining that analysis for future situations. In turn, this requires that problem-solvers gain plenty of intensive and extensive practical field experience over the years. However, possession of a great base of experiences in no way assures sound judgment on the part of anyone, but on the other hand, lack of experience cannot possibly provide the critical foundation required for the interpolation or extrapolation of values for missing, unknown, and vague information.

Outdoor Leadership Preparation

Paul Green
Eastern Washington University

The education of an outdoor leader is an ongoing effort to renew skills and acquire knowledge necessary to successfully and safely lead outdoor pursuits. (Traditionally, a strong emphasis has been placed on the professional education of outdoor leaders by the leaders themselves.) The education of a leader falls on a continuum that places the novice leaders on the beginning of the spectrum and professional, skilled leaders toward the other end of the continuum. It is important to realize, however, that all leaders must strive to continually update their skills throughout their careers, in order to stay current in the knowledge, techniques, and procedures related to the outdoor pursuits they choose to lead.

novice ———————————————— skilled professional

The Outdoor Leader Education Continuum

Several facts and assumptions of outdoor leadership preparation that are an integrated part of the education continuum. These are important to the discussion of outdoor leadership preparation and should be mentioned at the beginning of this discussion.

1. The education of a leader of outdoor pursuit activities is continuous and ongoing throughout the leader's career. New skills must be acquired and learned skills and knowledge must be renewed, as they will deteriorate over time.

2. No standard outdoor leadership preparation curriculum has yet been established in the United States (Swiderski, 1981).

3. The development of a leader's hard skills and soft skills is a tremendous individual commitment. Additionally, learning skills and knowledge about outdoor leadership techniques and procedures requires a long period of education.

4. No single course, workshop, or degree program can adequately prepare an outdoor leader for the demanding task of educating and guiding the individuals under the leader's charge.

Since no standard curriculum exists for the preparation of outdoor leaders, the following guidelines are recommended. The guidelines have been established through a review of the literature available in the field of outdoor leadership preparation (see references) and are designed to give direction to the leaders who are on the continuum of education toward a professional, full-time career in outdoor pursuit activities, organization, and leadership.

FIRST AID

The minimum credentials in first aid for outdoor leaders who direct participants in outdoor recreation activities is advanced first aid with CPR and a wilderness or backcountry-oriented first aid course. Van der Smissen, in "The Legal Aspects of Outdoor Pursuits," states that "the outdoor leader must not only be knowledgeable in first-aid, but must be knowledgeable in the first-aid related to the type of adventure activity that they are leading" (1980). An outdoor leader who directs wilderness activity should be familiar with the first aid and rescue techniques related to wilderness or backcountry accidents.

The wilderness first aid standards can be met by enrolling in a wilderness first responder's course, a wilderness second aid, mountaineering first aid, mountain medicine or wilderness Emergency Medical Technician (EMT) course. It is important to realize that EMT training is not always desirable for an outdoor leader. In some counties the EMT program is extremely hard to recertify and, having met the EMT standards, a certified technician must be able to adequately train to meet the minimum recertification requirements. Unless outdoor leaders have the opportunity to put in the considerable time necessary to maintain the EMT certification, they should not pursue the training, because the legal standard-of-care level required of an EMT is higher than that level required of individuals with advanced first aid and a wilderness-oriented first aid course. If gross mistakes are made in the management or treatment of injuries, higher liability standards may be applied to the caregivers' actions.

HARD SKILLS: TECHNIQUES AND PROCEDURES

The outdoor leader who accepts the responsibility for a group of people participating in an outdoor pursuit activity has an obligation to have basic mastery of essential hard skills. The hard skills are those involved a variety of outdoor pursuit activities, including cross-country skiing techniques, basic rock-climbing techniques, rapelling, land navigation, route-finding, crevasse rescue training, white-water rafting, and so on. The skills are regional in nature and require the leader to establish basic mastery of the essential skills in their area. Networking with a variety of established leaders in a geographic location will help the novice determine the essential skills to be mastered and the level of proficiency expected of a leader in that given region.

SOFT SKILLS: PROCESSING, COMMUNICATION, AND GROUP DYNAMICS

The soft skill education of an outdoor leader is greater than an ongoing commitment to gain communication and listening skills, since each outdoor pursuit activity has a set of objectives for the participants to reach on the outing. Processing skills, communication skills, and an understanding of group management are three essential soft skills that require mastery by the outdoor pursuit leader. Other soft skills are identifiable by geographic leaders within a region. Most skills can be enhanced by reading journals, attending professional conferences, and by establishing specific soft skills to be reached for the individual leader. Establishing a written list of skills to be polished on every outing will enhance the leaders' ability to communicate, teach, process, understand, and manage the groups they lead.

JUDGMENT, PROBLEM-SOLVING AND DECISION-MAKING

Beyond the knowledge of technical hard skills and soft skills are the core skills of judgment and decision-making. Judgment and decision-making are critical core skills of outdoor leaders who are charged with the responsibility of safely educating the participants in an outdoor activity. In a given day a leader might have to make 10 to 100 good decisions, and many of those decisions will involve problem-solving and good judgment. Learning safe decision making is the leader's main goal, and this can only happen through experience, practice, networking, and an ongoing commitment to personal inservice education. It is recommended that leaders attend conferences and workshops sponsored by the professional organizations in their field. It is also recommended that they closely network with other outdoor leaders and communicate not only on program development, funding, staffing, and so on, but, on decision-making in order to gain a deeper understanding of the variables that are used in decision-making and problem-solving. The higher the level of skill expected of the participant and the more demanding the environment, the greater are the decision-making and problem-solving techniques demanded of a leader. Several case study texts are being planned at this time to be utilized as decision-making aid for leaders to review decisions of other leaders in outdoor activities.

MINIMUM-IMPACT CAMPING—PHILOSOPHY AND PRACTICES

The minimum-impact or low-impact camping practices utilized by outdoor leaders to lessen the group's impact on a specific environment are essential to any group leader's education. Low-impact camping techniques are also regional in nature and are dictated by the type of terrain and vegetation the participants are traveling. Outdoor leaders must be cautious that they teach and practice the current accepted procedures for camping, care of waste water, care of human waste, and so on, for the area in which they are operating. Each government land management agency, such as the U.S. Forest Service, the National Park Service, the Bureau of Land Management, or the State Department of Natural Resources will have specific recommendations for group leaders as to the methods of low-impact camping. Publications available on low-impact camping and philosophy include *The National Outdoor Leadership Wilderness Handbook* and *Walking Softly in the Wilderness* by the Sierra Club. Networking with other leaders on how they deal with waste, especially in winter treks, is imperative to the leader in order to be current in this critical area of education.

MAP INTERPRETATION

Map interpretation is defined by the author as the ability of an outdoor leader to analyze a map and propose a route matched to the abilities of the group being led. Topographical maps are available for all areas of the United States, Canada, and Europe. Whether leadership involves backcountry experience for backpackers, skiers, river rafters, kayakers, or climbers, the ability to read the map and analyze the terrain is an essential leadership tool to put the best trip together for a group. Regional guidebooks are available to support topographical maps and give excellent information on campsites, water sources, and travel distances, as well as historical and scenic areas. The U.S. Forest Service's regional offices also have planimetric maps that detail logging roads, trailheads, and various boundaries of importance to the leader. Practice and more practice is the key to map interpretation skills.

LEADERSHIP ETHICS

All outdoor leaders must be solidly grounded in positive leadership ethics to have a well-rounded education for leading groups in the outdoors. An outdoor leader is bound with strong moral obligations to lead an ethical trip. Ethical issues such as creating simulated first aid or rescue situations without prior briefing of the group, favoring female clients over male clients, imposing personal views on participants, or taking advantage of the leadership position, must be handled. Leadership ethics can be learned through reading, by attending seminars, and by networking with other professional leaders.

CONCLUSION

The professional education of an outdoor leader is a continual commitment to learn and review hard and soft skills as well as a variety of core skills. Leaders' responsibilities to the participants they lead dictates that a life-long learning process must be followed in order to ensure knowledge and skills. The guidelines presented in this article only address the concerns of the outdoor leader's additional education in all areas of organization and management of outdoor pursuits.

The "Soft" Skills of Outdoor Leadership

Maurice Phipps

&

Michael Swiderski
California Polytechnic State University

The introductory article in *Trends* entitled "Risk Recreation: Trends and Issues" (Ewert, 1985), begins in the following manner (see Figure 1).

Immediately after the appearance of this announcement in the *London Times,* over 5,000 people applied for the 56 positions in the Shackleton Expedition (Ewert, 1985). This quest for adventure and excitement has carried over into our current recreational system. Outdoor pursuits such as backpacking, mountaineering, rock climbing, spelunking, white-water rafting, canoeing and kayaking, horseback riding, cross-country skiing, scuba diving, and sailing have become popular activities.

There are many adventure organizations planning and executing expeditions, such as the American Alpine Institute based in Washington state, and Nantahala Outdoor Center, based in North Carolina. The National Outdoor Leadership School (NOLS), based in Wyoming, organizes expeditions in the United States and throughout the world, including North and South America, Africa, and Nepal. The Wilderness Education Association (WEA) also organizes expeditions throughout the United States. Besides "organized" expeditions, there are many informal groups, clubs, schools, colleges and universities, scouts, and churches planning and executing their own ventures. Over the last decade, countless educational programs for users of outdoor areas have arisen throughout the United States, Canada, Europe, Australia, New Zealand, and Japan. There are over 400 such educational programs in the United States alone (Ford and Blanchard, 1985).

Many of these outdoor pursuits schools and programs are led by technically skilled leaders. Technical skills are often deemed essential because of the potential danger of outdoor pursuits, but a weakness with the leadership of many of these groups are skills in the affective domain, or the soft skills. The affective side of leadership, the 'soft' skills or 'people' skills, are often neglected.

LONDON TIMES

December 29, 1913
THE SOUTH POLE

A New Imperial
Expedition

Sir E. Shackleton's Plans

ACROSS THE ANTARCTIC
CONTINENT

We are able to announce to-day, with a satisfaction which will be universally shared, that Sir Ernest Shackleton will lead a new expedition to the South Pole next year.

Figure 1
Shackleton's announcement in the *London Times*

An historical look at the evolution of the skills illustrates this development. As part of leader/follower training, Paul Petzoldt, founder of NOLS, introduced a new concept into his courses that he termed "Expedition Behavior" (Petzoldt, 1974). Expedition Behavior deals with interpersonal relationships and behavior. This aspect of outdoor leadership relates to 'soft' skills or 'people' skills. To teach these skills, Petzoldt used insights gained through experiences on personal expeditions and knowledge of other expeditions. In *The Wilderness Handbook* (1974), Petzoldt stated:

> Himalayan expeditions have been full of examples in which poor Expedition Behavior has promoted failure and disaster. The early Germans on Nanga Parbat, the French in the Karakoram, the English on Everest, the Americans and Italians on K2, the French on Annapurna, all had disappointments and tragedies that might have been prevented by previous training in Expedition Behavior. (p. 128)

Such conflicts and poor behavior are not only exemplified in major expeditions as cited above, but during outings of informal groups, clubs, centers, schools, colleges, and camps. These smaller, informal groups also need to understand appropriate responses to expedition problems. An understanding of Expedition Behavior (group norms) alone could be insufficient when enmeshed in the complexities of leadership, group process, and individual personalities. A more comprehensive understanding of the soft skills, including leadership styles, group process, and Expedition Behavior, is essential in order to cope with expedition groups.

Some leaders seem to have natural talents with soft skills, gaining and maintaining respect from their groups. These leaders are often referred to as the "psychological" leaders of a group. They create an atmosphere conducive to team, building and maintain the leadership without undue use of coercive power effected by externally conferred status (Huntford, 1985). Historical references to Shackleton's leadership seem to show that he had these qualities. Shackleton is famous for his expeditions, pulling through tremendous adversity while still taking care of all the members of his group. In strong contrast to Shackleton's leadership styles, another polar explorer who was a colleague (and adversary!) was Scott, who relied on autocratic command and who experienced failure. Huntford (1985) in *The Last Place on Earth* recounted difficulties between the two men on board the *Discovery.* Huntford suggested that Scott needed the rigid naval hierarchy to assert his authority and seemed incapable of sensing the psychological undercurrents that rule human behavior.

What developments have been made in regard to outdoor leadership soft skills in expedition settings in order to cope with these psychological undercurrents? One of the earliest recognized attempts at teaching soft skills was done by Petzoldt and the Wilderness Education Association. The Wilderness Education Association's National Standard Program in Outdoor Leadership curriculum included Expedition Behavior, leadership styles, group process, communication, and other soft skills. Because of their complexity and amorphous nature, instructors sometimes found soft skills difficult to teach, and therefore dealt with these components unsystematically. Outward Bound has also progressed in developing soft skill competencies. Through Outward Bound staff training, manuals, and publications, the importance of group process has been recognized and addressed (Kalisch, 1979). There have also been recent developments in other countries, including the island state of Tasmania in Australia, where an outdoor leadership program is attempting to adapt present leadership theories from the education, military, and business professions (Priest, 1985).

The importance of soft skills in outdoor pursuits has been stressed (Hollenhorst and Ewert, 1985; Priest, 1985). Attempts have been made at teaching soft skills. As indicated, the complexity and nature of the soft-skill components of outdoor leadership make them difficult to teach. Yet, as the number of participants in outdoor pursuits increases, more leaders are needed to ensure both the safety and the effectiveness of the experience, be it recreation or education. It is no longer acceptable to be solely technically competent in hard skills such as navigation, use of equipment, trip logistics, etc. Soft-skill competencies are also needed because many expeditions fail in meeting their goals and objectives simply because of group dynamic and leadership-related problems that are either not addressed, or are inappropriately handled by the usual methods and curriculums in outdoor leadership training.

SOFT SKILLS DEFINED

Soft skills, the interpersonal, people skills of outdoor leadership, can be divided into social, psychological, and communication components. Social soft skills incorporate group welfare and participant interaction, whereas psychological soft skills relate to the participant's behavior and presence of mind. On the other hand, communicative soft skills combine verbal, written, and other nonverbal transmission and exchange of information. Soft skills are complex in nature, yet critical in maintaining harmonious relations in expedition settings. Maintaining harmony, in turn, affects the goals and safety of the group. Some specific examples of these skills are illustrated in the following list (Swiderski, 1987, p. 36).

EXAMPLES OF HARD SKILLS

Physiological

- understanding of the human body (Buell, 1981, p. 105)
- administration of first and second aid
- hypothermia recognition and treatment
- mainteinance of physical fitness, etc. (Priest, 1987, p. 4)
- promotion of health
- Treatment of backcountry ailments

Environmental

- practice of personal and group sanitation (Buell, 1981, p. 103)
- practice of solid waste disposal (Swiderski, 1981, p. 108)
- interpretation of weather systems (Rogers, 1979, p. 15)
- promotion of environmental ethics (Swiderski, 1981, p. 107)
- understanding of ecological principles
- knowledge of the local natural history
- prevention of negative impact on the natural surroundings (Priest, 1987, p. 5)

Safety

- prevention of accidents through awareness of hazards
- practice of group security (Rogers, 1979, p. 16)
- search and rescue competencies (Buell, 1981, p. 106)
- treatment of water for drinking (Swiderski, 1981, p. 108)
- implementation of risk management techniques (Green, 1981, p. 56)
- development of a critical eye for safety
- checking the safety of all equipment (Buell, 1981, p. 103)
- demonstration of safe driving procedures (Swiderski, 1981, p. 109)

Technical

- active participation in the outdoor pursuits being led (Priest, 1987, p. 5)
- maintenance of equipment and facilities (Buell, 1981, p. 106)
- teaching of activities using the recommended progression
- rock/caving/ice competencies such as knots, belaying, etc.
- water-based competencies such as life saving, canoeing, etc.
- snow-based competencies such as skiing, snowshoeing, etc.
- land-based competencies such as backpacking, route finding, etc.

Administration

- establishment of program goals and objectives
- execution of appropriate pre-planning (Green, 1981, p. 57)
- implementation of risk management policy (Buell, 1981, p. 106)
- understanding of legal liability (Rogers, 1979, p. 19)
- development of outing logistics (Buell, 1981, p. 102)
- organization and conducting of functional meetings
- supervision and evaluation skills
- collection and reporting of accident information (Buell, 1981, p. 102)
- compliance with resource regulations (Swiderski, 1981, p. 108)
- development and implemention of sound safety procedures (Buell, 1981, p. 104)
- proficiency in organizational skills (Swiderski, 1981, p. 108)

EXAMPLES OF SOFT SKILLS

Social

- maintenance of intact group dynamics (Priest, 1987, p. 5)
- resolution of conflict (Priest, 1987, p. 5)
- development and provision of a supportive group climate
- sensitivity to the needs of others; empathy (Priest, 1987, p. 4)
- establishment of effective group relations
- recall of names
- provision of opportunity for personal growth (Priest, 1987, p. 23)

Psychological

- creation of a climate of trust (Priest, 1987, p. 5)
- understanding and stimulation of motivation
- management of psychological stress (Buell, 1981, p. 105)
- promotion of values and understanding of attitudes
- attunement of healthy self-concept and secure ego (Priest, 1987, p. 4)
- team building
- assessment of mental and emotional strengths (Swiderski, 1981, p. 108)
- development of environmental ethics
- respect for the counseling/therapy difference (Buell, 1981, p. 4)

Communication

- ability to think on one's feet
- ability to speak in front of groups
- interpretion of nonverbal body language
- ability to listen and respond while conducting debriefing sessions
- persuasiveness
- ability to transfer information by teaching

EXAMPLES OF CONCEPTUAL SKILLS

Judgment

- recognition of potential problems (Swiderski, 1981, p. 107)
- perception of potential dangers (Priest, 1987, p. 4)
- analysis of alternatives
- anticipation of the unexpected
- analytical/creative problem solving (Priest, 1981, p. 5)

Creativity

- generation of new ideas (LeBoeuf, 1980, p. 9)
- perception of trends
- improvisation of equipment and repairs in emergencies (Swiderski, 1981, p. 108)

THE EMERGENCE OF SOFT SKILLS IN OUTDOOR LEADERSHIP

Leaders from around the world were simultaneously recognizing key elements in outdoor leadership: judgment, decision-making, and interpersonal interaction. Jackson, past director of Plas y Brenin, one of the National Mountain Centers in Britain, identified the following six "forces" that influenced leadership, judgment, and decision-making: environmental, physiological, psychological, safety, sociological, and technical forces (Jackson in Rogers, 1979). The elements of judgment, decision-making, and interpersonal interaction fall within Jackson's psychological and sociological forces. Concurrently, Rogers (supported by the Council of Outdoor Education of Ontario and its Task Force on Adventure Activities) purported that: "Training in leadership and training in motor skills are two separate attributes required of a leader. The case is made for the leader obtaining both technical skill certification and leadership development" (1979, p. 1). Rogers suggested that these skills be obtained separately, yet noted a symbiotic relationship existed between the two. He also made a strong case for the understanding of human behavior and small group dynamics:

> The outdoor adventure activity is the epitome of the dynamic small group. Knowledge of how and why groups function and dysfunction is basic to environmental behavior, personal growth, safety and in many instances the acquisition and proper performance of technical motor skills. Group problem-solving is essential in outdoor adventure activities. (p.15)

At the same time, Jenson (1979) actually dealt with the application of small group theory in adventure programs. She emphasized the effects of the environment on an expedition that was "different than being in a safe, familiar environment, where it is possible to interact on a habitual and superficial basis" (p. 39). Group members need to be receptive to new ways of thinking and this can only be maintained in a positive group atmosphere. Jensen explained the importance of emotional support, and in doing so, dealt with conflict using group development theory. The leader's role was explained in terms of types of approach (authoritative or emotional), and it was maintained that judgment was needed to deal with the group, with individuals and their conflicts. Although Jenson presented an accurate picture of what to expect and provided some ways to cope, she did not deal with the problems systematically. March, on the other hand, summarizes his views on learning good judgment by saying, "Good judgment is the result of experience. Experience is the result of good judgment" (1984, p. 37). A bad experience, however, could be the result of bad judgment and such an experience can happen on expeditions if psychological and sociological considerations are not recognized and dealt with. Instructors, particularly the less experienced, could find themselves in a "Catch 22" situation, as described by March above, in being able to apply good judgment.

As has been mentioned, Petzoldt's recognition of participant behavior as a very important aspect of expeditions helped pave the way in the United States for the identification of such soft skills or psychological components of leadership. In his more recent publication, *The New Wilderness Handbook* (1984), Petzoldt includes a comprehensive chapter on outdoor leadership in which he refers to the safety aspects of leadership, cooperation, conflict, and delegation, which are valuable components of a soft skills curriculum.

RESEARCH IN OUTDOOR LEADERSHIP

Several skill competency studies have been completed on outdoor leadership that have confirmed the importance of soft skills (Swiderski, 1981; Green, 1981; Cosgrove, 1984; Priest, 1984). A survey of 648 graduates of Wilderness Education Association (WEA) courses by Cockrell and Detzel (1985) investigated the effect of outdoor leadership certification on safety, environmental concerns, program standardization, and expedition behavior. The study results indicated that safety and environment were perceived to be of prime importance in outdoor leadership considerations. In addition, expedition behavior appeared to be influenced by WEA courses. The results also indicated that group processes and communication skills (soft skills) were not influenced by WEA as much as outside influential sources.

Very little applied research in the form of quasi-experimental design has been completed in outdoor leadership. Two action research studies relevant to soft skills are a master's thesis by McPeters (1976), which investigated group-centered/leader-centered leadership and another Master's Thesis by Baker (1975), who studied changes in leader behavior attitudes affected in basic courses at the National Outdoor Leadership School.

McPeters tested the hypothesis that group-centered leadership leads to less problem behavior among 20 male and female emotionally disturbed adolescents. The results indicated that participation in the camping program with group-centered and leader-centered groups did not improve emotionally disturbed adolescents' levels of interpersonal affect for other group members. Group-centered leadership did lead to increases in liking for the group as a whole more than did leader-centered leadership. It was suggested that more development of group skills was necessary prior to a trip using group-centered leadership or to introduce this style on a more gradual basis. Hersey-Blanchards' life cycle theory of leadership (1982) also suggests that the group-centered leadership be introduced gradually as the followers acquire the group skills and readiness to take on responsibility. The life cycle theory was supported by Jones' theory of group development, (1973), which divided group development into four stages: dependency, conflict, cohesion, and interdependence.

Baker (1975), in his study, explained the teaching method on selected 1974 NOLS courses in this way:

> Instruction in leadership takes the form of discussions and lectures on "optimum expedition behavior patterns" that emphasize consideration and sensitivity towards other members of the expedition, as well as actual experience in leading and having responsibility for a group of one's fellow students in small hiking parties. (p. 21)

He researched 80 subjects on basic five-week courses to investigate if there would be a positive change in students' attitudes concerning leader behavior. Results indicated that there were no positive changes in the students' attitudes toward leadership behavior. In fact, there was a decrease in consideration scores among those who had graduated from college and had previous camping experience. This study lends additional support to the hypothesis that a more effective method of teaching the soft skills is needed on expedition style courses.

Research by Phipps (1986) compared two outdoor groups using a systematic approach with four other outdoor groups using the more traditional "opportunity teaching" approach. The six expedition groups were studied on WEA courses. Results showed the following:

1. Leader behavior was affected positively using a systematic approach.
2. The unsystematic approach used by comparison groups affected leader behavior attitudes negatively compared to positive behavior attitudes in the groups using a systematic approach.
3. The group dynamics were perceived more positively in the task, relationship, positive use of power, and leadership using a systematic approach. There was a relationship between leader effective ness and the participants' positive per ceptions in regard to the group dynamics in all the groups.
4. The research then has shown the importance of the soft skills and that the haphazard approach to teaching them has not been very successful. A systematic approach is suggested to increase understanding of soft skill instruction. The experience of others can be drawn on by using theories and planned experiences in a systematic teaching model. This teaching model enables students and instructors to work through various group dynamic components at appropriate times, prior to, and as they unfold. This in turn can enable better judgment in the process of teaching soft skills.

The systematic approach used by Phipps (1986a) in *An Assessment of a Systematic Approach to Teaching Outdoor Leadership in Expedition Settings* consisted of the integration of three models, Situational Leadership™ (Hersey and Blanchard 1982), Jones' model of group development (1973), and a group dynamics teaching model by Phipps (1987). A combined teaching method called Experiential

Leadership Education evolved from the Phipps study (1986a) using these three models in conjunction with measurement techniques devised for the research. A description of these three models follows.

Situational Leadership, developed by Hersey and Blanchard (1982), is based on the amount of direction (task behavior) and socio-emotional support (relationship behavior) a leader must provide, given the situation and "readiness" of his or her followers. Follower readiness is the ability and willingness of people to take responsibility for directing their own behavior and is the key to the judgment, made by the leader, in choosing one of the four Situational Leadership Styles (see Figure 2).

When looking at group development theory, for example, Jones' model (1973) corresponds to Hersey and Blanchard's Situational Leadership model (see Figure 3).

Using the two models in conjunction may create an understanding, allowing better judgment in selecting an appropriate style of leadership and decision-making in relation to the group (both models are compared in Figure 4).

Both models suggest that as the followers develop, the personal relationships and task functions change. Over time then, as the group/followers become more able to do the task, and assuming that they are willing, the leadership should become more group-centered. In the Situational Leadership model, this would mean that more participating and delegating styles would be used to empower followers.

The group might not progress further than the conflict stage (stage 2—Figure 3). They may reach interdependence (stage 4), then regress, even to dependency (stage 1). if, for example, the task changed. A group may change tasks from mountaineering to kayaking, in which case, followers may need to be oriented again. Consequently, the leader must judge at what stage of development the group is in or at what level of maturity (readiness) in the Hersey-Blanchard model. Hersey and Blanchard (1982) defined maturity as the ability and willingness of people to take responsibility for directing their own behavior. Having gauged the maturity level, the leader then decides which leadership style to use: telling, selling, participating or delegating (see Figure 2). Each style is a combination of task and relationship behavior, the combination that is best needed to influence the group or individual.

Until the group matures to a cohesive unit, the leadership style needs to be more leader-centered. Initially, a telling style is needed to orient the group, as they need basic information only. For example, when arriving at the roadhead they want to know how far they will be going, when will there be rest breaks, and so on. They need only basic task information at first. Later, when using the selling style (in the conflict stage), a high amount of relationship behavior is needed to create an open or supportive communication climate. This entails being descriptive, problem control-oriented, spontaneous, empathic, equally directed, and egalitarian. Selling means that high relationship behavior is needed although the leader remains very directive.

Moving along the curve to the participating style, the leader behavior continues to be high relationship in order to motivate and be supportive rather than directive. Some decision-making can be shared. The leader then is facilitating or assisting the group in decision-making, as the group is cohesive and concentrating on data flow in the task function.

If the group reaches the interdependence stage of development (high maturity or readiness), the leader should delegate most decision-making and keep a low profile. Followers should be *willing* and *able* to do the task. The group may, however, regress in task maturity, so the leader must be prepared to step in if necessary, using one of the other styles.

The group and individual may fluctuate in the job maturity (ability) and psychological maturity (willingness), so the leadership style must adjust by moving back and forth along the curve to the appropriate quadrant in

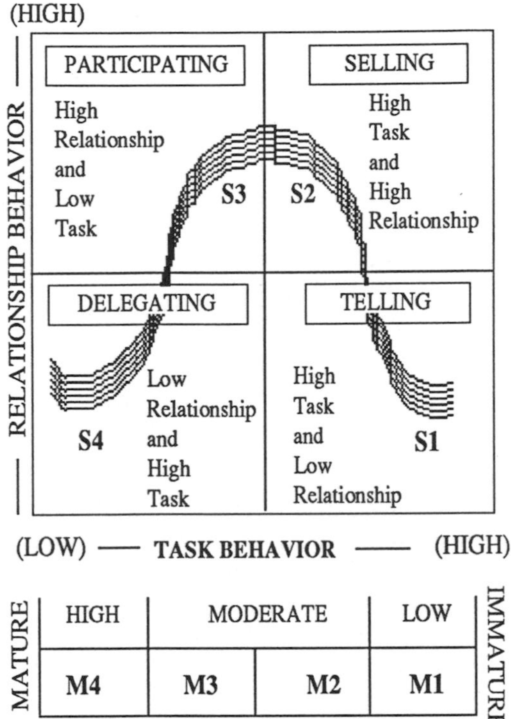

Figure 2
The Situational Leadership Theory

Figure 2. Sometimes in the outdoors and particularly on expedition-style courses, there will be several fluctuations within a single day. For example, after mastering campcraft, the group may need a delegating style of leadership to eat, pack, and move; a participating style of leadership to plan a route; and, in the afternoon, a telling style of leadership to effect a rappel.

The judgment to select the appropriate leadership style is the key to effective leading, but this judgment is best learned experientially. Use of group developmental theory and the Situational Leadership model along with an understanding of group dynamics, will aid in the process of developing soft skill competencies. Acceptance of feedback and reflection on experiences make it possible to learn these leadership skills. An open and supportive communication climate is necessary to accomplish this.

The group dynamics teaching model (Phipps, 1987) was developed experientially on six expedition courses between 1982 and 1984. An understanding of group dynamics permits a better choice of leadership style. A combination of the maturity of the group and individuals, the dynamics within the group, and the situation determines how leadership decisions are made.

The "maturity" or "readiness" of the group, reflected by their behaviors, is often influenced by the internal dynamics of the group. This influence can be positive and negative. The purpose of the group dynamics teaching model is to reinforce positive behaviors by intervention (or specific nonintervention) in appropriate situations. Examples of interventions are:

1. Developing group norms by establishing commonly set expedition behavior patterns.
2. Setting specific times for mutual feedback for followers and leaders with regard to thoughts and feelings in the group.
3. Establishing an open instead of defensive communication climate.
4. Using team-building exercises such as new games, team T-shirts, team initiatives, group fantasies, cookouts, and introductions.
5. Teaching conflict styles and conflict resolution methods.

Sometimes nonintervention is appropriate when a mature and interdependent group has a problem to resolve that is within their capabilities. The leader at this time should delegate the decision-making. Taking the decision-making away from them in this situation could be demotivating and may also defeat the object of the educational purposes of the leadership course. Another example of nonintervention would be a situation where the group has made a decision-concerning a group norm, such as a specific meeting time. If some people wish to change the meeting time, a group decision by

Stage	Personal Relations	Task Functions
1	Dependency	Orientation
2	Conflict	Organization
3	Cohesion	Data Flow
4	Interdependence	Problem Solving

Figure 3
The Group Development Model

3 PARTICIPATING	2 SELLING
DELEGATING 4	TELLING 1

SITUATIONAL LEADERSHIP

3 COHESION (Data-Flow)	2 CONFLICT (Organization)
INTER- DEPENDENCE (Problem-Solving) 4	DEPENDENCE (Orientation) 1

GROUP DEVELOPMENT

Figure 4
A Comparison of Hersey and Blanchard's Model with Jones' Model

consensus entails ownership and increases the effectiveness of the decision.

Being aware of the possible negative behaviors in groups, and making the group aware of these behaviors can allow energy to be spent building a positive atmosphere. A positive atmosphere also creates effectiveness in the task, eventually pulling the group together as a team. Working through the teaching model should help develop soft skill competencies and bring an awareness of the complex interactions that exist in group dynamics.

The group dynamic teaching model includes the following nine elements:

1. Group development
2. Expedition behavior
3. Giving and receiving feedback
4. Conflict strategies
5. Conflict resolution
6. Group dynamics
7. Role functions in groups
8. Defense mechanisms in groups
9. Group dynamics questionnaire (Phipps, 1986b)

It is intended as a flexible guide. The teaching style can involve lecture, discussion, and experiential work applied directly to situations that occur from time to time. Exercises and role plays can also be used, but it is important that the model be used to anticipate and avoid *unnecessary* problems. For a complete documentation of the Group Dynamics Teaching Model, refer to *High Adventure Outdoor Pursuits: Organization and Leadership* (Meier, Morash, and Welton, 1987)

The above theories can be used in the teaching of outdoor leadership, but the objective is to enable students to use the theories and practice the different leadership styles. This involves conscious decision-making. Conscious decision-making can be maximized by using a journal technique as used by Phipps (1988) in *Experiential Leadership Education,* which allows tracking of the use of different styles over time. This allows analysis and measurement of appropriate styles and further develops the soft skill competencies.

The systematic approach is suggested to teach and learn some of the soft skills of outdoor leadership. This will prepare potential leaders more fully to deal with the psychosocial aspect of groups. A fuller understanding of groups will hopefully produce leaders with Shackleton's insights of the "psychological undercurrents that rule human behavior."

REFERENCES

Baker, E. (1975). *Changes in leadership behavior attitudes effected by participation in basic courses at the National Outdoor Leadership School.* Unpublished master's thesis, The Pennsylvania State University.

Buell, L. (1981). *The identification of outdoor adventure leadership competencies for entry-level and experienced personnel.* Ann Arbor, MI, University Microfilms International, Dissertation Information Service.

Cockrell, D., & Detzel, D. (1985). Effects of outdoor leadership certification on safety, impacts and program standardization. *Trends, 22:* 4.

Cosgrove, M. (1984). *Minimum skill competencies required for employment as an outdoor leader in a wilderness adventure program.* Unpublished master's thesis, University of Southern Illinois.

Ewert, A. (1985). Risk recreation: Trends and issues. *Trends, 22:* 4.

Ford, P., & Blanchard, J. (1985). *Leadership and administration of outdoor pursuits.* State College, PA: Venture Publishing Inc.

Green, P. (1981). *The content of a college level outdoor leadership course for land-based outdoor pursuits in the Pacific Northwest: A Delphi consensus.* Unpublished doctoral dissertation, University of Oregon.

Hersey, P., & Blanchard, K. (1982). *Management of organizational behavior: Utilizing human resources.* 4th Ed. Englewood Cliffs, NJ: Prentice-Hall Inc.

Hollenhorst, S., & Ewert, A. (1985). Dissecting the adventure camp experience: Determining successful program components. *Camping Magazine.* Feb: 32.

Huntford, R. (1985). *The last place on earth.* New York: Atheneum.

Jenson, M. J. (1979). Application of small group theory to adventure programs. *The Journal of Experiential Education.* Fall.

Jones, J. (1973). A model of group development. In J. Jones and W. Pfeiffer (Eds.). *The annual handbook for group facilitators.* La Jolla, CA: University Associates.

Kalisch, K. R. (1979). *The role of the instructor in the Outward Bound educational process.* Wisconsin: Three Lakes.

Meier, J., Morash, T., Welton, G. (Eds.). (1987). *High-adventure outdoor pursuits: Organization and leadership.* Columbus, OH: Publishing Horizons Inc.

McPeters, J. (1976). *The effects of different leadership styles on selected behavioral and interpersonal variables of emotionally disturbed adolescents in a camping program.* Unpublished master's thesis, The Pennsylvania State University.

Petzoldt, P. (1984). *The new wilderness handbook.* New York: W.W. Norton and Company.

Petzoldt, P. (1974). *The wilderness handbook.* New York: W.W. Norton and Company.

Phipps, M. (1988). Experiential Leadership Education. *The Journal of Experiential Education , 11:*1.

Phipps, M. (1987). Group dynamics in the outdoors: A model for teaching outdoor leaders. *High Adventure Outdoor Pursuits: Organization and Leadership.* Meier, J. Morash, T. Welton, G., (Eds.) Columbus, OH: Publishing Horizons, Inc.

Phipps, M. (1986a). *An assessment of a systematic approach to teaching outdoor leadership in expedition settings.* Unpublished doctoral dissertation, University of Minnesota.

Phipps, M. (1986b). Group dynamics questionnaire. *An assessment of a systematic approach to teaching outdoor leadership in expedition settings.* Unpublished doctoral dissertation, University of Minnesota.

Priest, S. (1987). *Preparing effective outdoor pursuits leaders.* Eugene, OR. Institute of Recreation, Research and Service, Department of Leisure Studies and Services, University of Oregon.

Priest, S. (1985). Effective outdoor leader ship: A survey. *The Journal of Experiential Education, 7*(3), 34-36.

Priest, S. (1984). Outdoor leadership Down Under. *The Journal of Experiential Education*, *8*(1), 13-15.

Rogers, R. J. (1979). *Leading to share—sharing to lead.* Ontario: Council of Outdoor Educators.

Swiderski, M. (1987). Soft and conceptual skills: The often overlooked components of outdoor leadership. G. Robb (Ed.). *The Bradford Papers Annual, 2.* Martinsville, Indiana, Bradford Woods Center for Outdoor Education.

Swiderski, M. (1981). *Outdoor leadership competencies identified by outdoor leaders of five western regions.* Unpublished doctoral dissertation, University of Oregon.

Outdoor Leadership Curricula

Edward Raiola
Unity College

One of the exciting and, at times, frustrating elements of participating in the field of outdoor wilderness education and recreation involves the issue of ensuring that practicing professionals function with competence, safety and prudence. There is no doubt that camp directors, program supervisors, and administrators need competent and qualified people in charge of their outdoor adventure programs: they all want skilled, safe, knowledgeable staff. Whether one is a parent sending a child to a camp that offers adventure-based programming, a student enrolled in a stress-challenge course, or the director of a therapeutic wilderness-based program for troubled youth, there is a concern about the quality of the staff who lead such programs. Are the leaders knowledgeable and competent enough to provide a safe and enjoyable experience? Do they meet the minimum qualifications to handle such positions as adventure educator, canoe guide, ropes course instructor, or rock climbing specialist?

The past decade has seen extraordinary growth in the use of the outdoors for educational, recreational, and human service programs. Increasing numbers of people have found the outdoors a wonderful place to arouse sensitivity, learn practical living skills, shape values, expand cognitive understanding, develop commitments, and strengthen personalities. As the demand for outdoor activities increases, there is a need for highly skilled outdoor leaders and administrators—professionals who must have knowledge and skills gained from many disciplines and a variety of life experiences.

The field of outdoor wilderness/recreational education is interdisciplinary in that it provides educational, recreational, and therapeutic experiences for people in dispersed recreation areas. It deals with people and the natural environment, and requires knowledge, ability, and skills sufficient to operate in that environment in a safe manner with minimum impact. This field also requires understanding of and competence in: group process, learning theories, leadership, program planning, administration, and a wide variety of outdoor skills.

Individual leaders and administrators of outdoor programs must understand specific characteristics of the people they work with, such as age group traits, socio-economic characteristics, and developmental levels. This awareness will help in understanding behavior and developing appropriate activities and experiences. Leaders are responsible not only for designing and administering outdoor recreational programs, but also for teaching specialized outdoor recreational skills and observing the participants' interpersonal relationships.

RESEARCH IN OUTDOOR LEADERSHIP

During the last 20 years, there have been a number of studies pertinent to outdoor leadership education. Cousineau (1977), Swiderski (1981), and Buell (1983) all identified specific competencies deemed necessary for outdoor leaders. Each of these studies stressed that the education and preparation of competent outdoor leaders is comprised of a variety of components (e.g., experience in the field, leadership ability, skill development, and training experiences).

While several studies identify specific leadership competencies and course topics, the majority have been built from conceptual theory and have not been tested or evaluated. Shiner (1970), Mendence (1979), Simmons (1981), and Priest (1988) developed and recommended theoretical programs for the education and training of outdoor leaders in a higher-education setting. Each of the studies strongly recommended that the programs be interdisciplinary in nature and that there be classroom as well as field experiences.

Building on the work of Green (1981), this author used an interdisciplinary approach to establish, test, and evaluate a curriculum for outdoor leadership education. Respondents in the study included not only experts with both higher-education and field experience in outdoor recreation, but also students who were leaders-in-training. Based on the responses of panel members and students, a review of the literature, and the limitations set forth in the study, nine elements emerged as preferred curriculum content for outdoor leadership education (see pages 237, 238).

CURRENT PRACTICE

After having reviewed the research, it is appropriate to look at what is actually happening in terms of current practice. More and more colleges and universities are offering wilderness-related courses. In a recent study by Hendee and Roggenbuck (1983), 417 colleges and universities were identified as offering wilderness-related courses. The NRPA-SPRE curriculum catalog (1988) lists 17 colleges and university programs that indicated that they had outdoor leadership curricula. This is by no means a complete list of schools that have such programs.

From a review of the curricula of these programs, certain characteristics emerged: large and small schools offer programs, and the names of the degree programs vary from "outdoor education" to "outdoor pursuits" to "outdoor recreation." Some programs are highly skill-oriented, while others stress coursework in the natural sciences and education. The programs are housed in various departments such as physical education, recreation, forestry, and the social sciences. The following is a description of four selected programs that are representative of the variety and focus of current curricula.

At Eastern Washington University, the Outdoor Recreation degree program is shaped to train leaders in a variety of outdoor pursuits they will supervise and/or teach. The program is designed to have three tracks. One track involves land-based outdoor activities, such as rock climbing, backpacking, winter camping, and mountaineering, and focuses on skill acquisition and leadership for those activities. The second track is similar to the first, but deals with water-based activities. The third track is different from the first and second, but supports them. It involves courses such as adventure programming, search and rescue management, and adventure-based counseling.

Ferrum College in Virginia offers an interdisciplinary major in outdoor recreation. Its goal is to enable students to successfully plan, develop, lead and administer outdoor recreation programs. The curriculum is divided into several categories: outdoor recreation activities (skills), outdoor recreation leadership, program planning and administration, safety and legal aspects of outdoor recreation programming, and an in-house certification program for qualified outdoor recreation leaders.

The University of New Hampshire offers an outdoor education degree that is one of five options in the department of physical education. This program focuses on the use of physical movement in the outdoors to achieve educational and therapeutic goals. The curriculum is divided into five sections: activity courses conducted in the field; emergency care; theoretical courses that include philosophy, experiential education, adventure education, and so on; experiential classes where students gain first- hand experience leading or working with specific programs; and supporting coursework from psychology, English, and 20 credits of electives. Besides coursework, students are expected to work on furthering their professional development with outdoor endeavors. An "experiential transcript" is kept on each student to monitor his or her progress in the field.

Unity College in Maine offers a Bachelor of Science Degree in wilderness-based outdoor recreation. The program offers two areas of concentration: field instructor and administrator. Each option in the program is designed to prepare students for a leadership position in the professional field of wilderness-based outdoor recreation or related education programs.

This outdoor recreation curriculum is founded on a solid liberal arts base that seeks to develop qualities of adaptability, creativity, and decision-making necessary to success in a complex society. Special emphasis is placed on writing, speaking, mathematics, and helping students appreciate and learn from their cultural heritage. The curriculum provides a combination of both classroom and field experiences and is divided into four components: outdoor skills, which includes canoeing, climbing, and backpacking; outdoor recreation theory and practice, with courses such as an introduction of outdoor recreation and outdoor recreation for special populations; leadership and administration, which includes coursework in program planning, administration, and leadership; and finally, interpersonal skills, with courses in counseling, group process, and other soft skills. Each student is also required to complete an internship.

Education and training outside the formal curricula is complemented by organizations such as Outward Bound, National Outdoor Leadership School, Wilderness Education Association, and SOLO-Wilderness Emergency Medicine. Each of these organizations offers part-time employment for students, as well as formal courses for credit in affiliation with sponsoring colleges and universities. These courses can offer prospective leaders the possibilities for extended field experiences and immersion in the programs' philosophies and practices, as well as opportunities for advanced skill training.

STRIKING A BALANCE

When considering the components of outdoor leadership development, it is helpful to distinguish between "training" and "education." Such a distinction illuminates the necessary interplay of skill mastery, in the technical sense, and the evolution of a larger context of knowledge with which to practice skills. If one thinks of training as the learning of techniques, whether of fire-making, rope handling, or map and compass navigation, one can view education as the process through which the student comes to understand the appropriate use of technique, as well as the implications of such use.

Through this framework, the need for a balance of training and education in the preparation of outdoor leaders becomes self-evident. One also may become aware that the development of a good leader, as of a good writer, psychologist, or teacher, is an ongoing process.

In the pilot test of the curriculum for outdoor leadership (Raiola, 1986), some of the stages of this ongoing process become evident (see Figure 1). At the beginning of the course, the students were at a level of "unconscious incompetence" relative to their skills and understanding. That is, they were largely unaware of the aspects of capable leadership and were unable to demonstrate these aspects. As they were introduced to the curriculum objectives, they progressed into a level of "conscious incompetence," where the components of effective leadership became known to them, as did their lack of skill and experience.

Over time, the students moved into a state of "conscious competence." With deliberate attention, they were now able to perform competently the tasks of outdoor leadership, yet the degree of self-scrutiny required to do so led to awkwardness. Often, each step of a procedure had to be thought through in order to achieve the desired result.

By the end of the course of instruction, most of the students had arrived at a level of "unconscious competence" relative to most of the curriculum objectives. They had integrated the educational and training experiences to the extent that they could perform their duties competently without constant thought. Their automatic responses had become reliable, and the groundwork for future refinements of their expertise was in place.

Each of these leaders that moves out into new situations and is required to encompass new learning, will pass through the four stages illustrated in Figure 1. This developmental movement, though broadly defined, is subjective in nature and individual to each person; some students move through this process much faster than others.

This process, in terms of leadership development, is generally the same for each person and is a continuing, lifelong evolution as one grows and absorbs new knowledge. Optimally, an outdoor recreation curriculum will provide students with both the fundamental skills and knowledge for beginning their maturation in this field of endeavor, and a sense of themselves as representatives and teachers of the values and ethics of the outdoors.

The education and training of competent and sensitive outdoor leaders/educators have some important social and political implications for the use of and general attitudes toward the natural environment, and thus, the minimization of environmental degradation through use. Highly skilled and aware outdoor leaders are a major resource for the re-education of the increasing numbers of people who are discovering the outdoors. By creating outdoor experiences that embody values of preservation/conservation of nature and promoting, through role-modeling, a non-abusive relationship with one's environment, an outdoor leader has a unique opportunity to shape the practices and attitudes of the public.

In terms of choosing which curriculum objectives should be included in a model outdoor leadership curriculum, the studies cited earlier offer specific recommendations for content as well as sequencing. It is the opinion of this investigator that the application of specific curriculum content should be chosen by individual outdoor recreation educators. For example, the following nine elements that emerged as preferred content of the outdoor leadership education curriculum should be considered as guidelines for a college-level outdoor leadership course. The objectives are not listed in a sequence that reflects a recommended preference for presentation. Rather, they are listed as a guide for the outdoor recreation educator. It is important to note that organizing curriculum objectives around the common threads of *concepts, values,* and *skills and abilities* related to outdoor leadership will help to provide continuity, sequence, and integration in order to reinforce each aspect and produce a cumulative learning effect. The interplay of these organizing principles is considered by this investigator to be critical to the success of any curriculum.

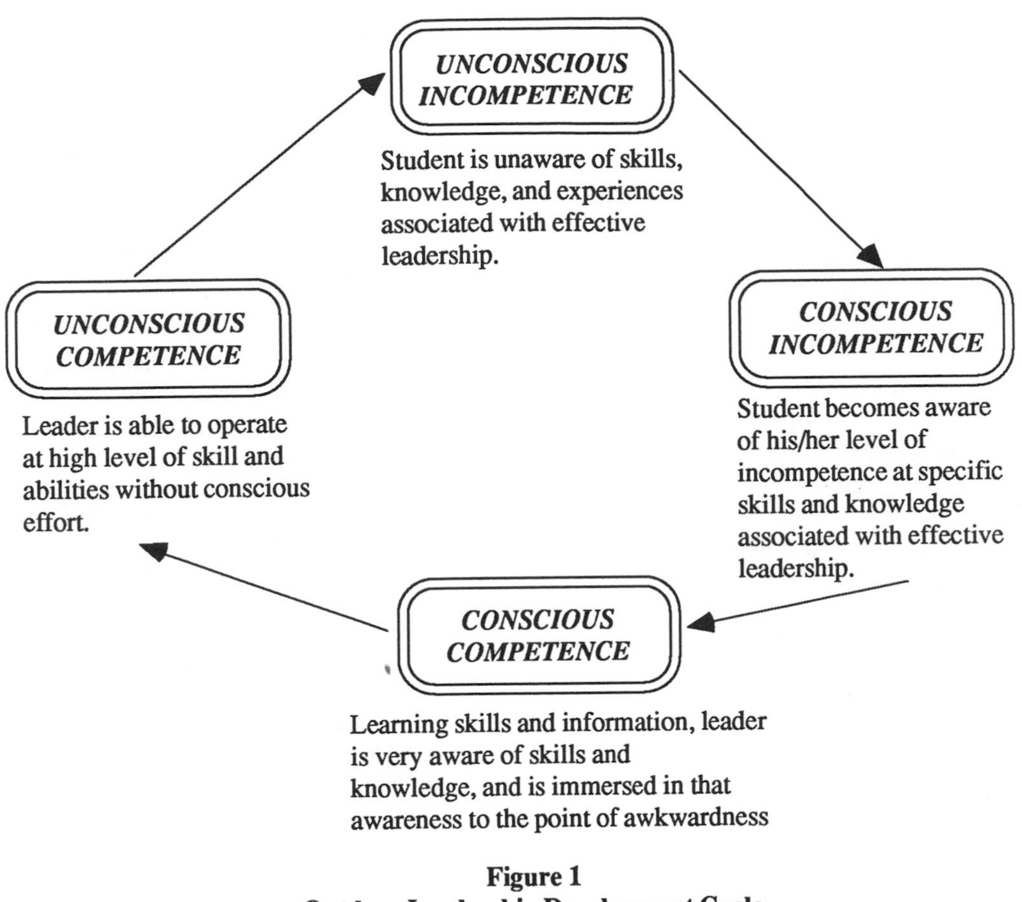

UNCONSCIOUS INCOMPETENCE
Student is unaware of skills, knowledge, and experiences associated with effective leadership.
CONSCIOUS INCOMPETENCE
Student becomes aware of his/her level of incompetence at specific skills and knowledge associated with effective leadership.
CONSCIOUS COMPETENCE
Learning skills and information, leader is very aware of skills and knowledge, and is immersed in that awareness to the point of awkwardness
UNCONSCIOUS COMPETENCE
Leader is able to operate at high level of skill and abilities without conscious effort.

Figure 1
Outdoor Leadership Development Cycle

CONTENT OF OUTDOOR LEADERSHIP CURRICULUM (RAIOLA, 1986)

Based on the consensus of objectives, the review of literature and the limitations set forth, the following nine elements emerged as preferred content of the outdoor leadership curriculum.

1. *Leadership Style.* This element of the curriculum identifies topics, information, and practices that will enhance the knowledge, skills, and abilities of the students to develop their own leadership styles.
   - General knowledge related to leadership styles
   - Characteristics of the leader
   - Responsibilities of the wilderness leader

2. *Judgment/Objective-Subjective.* This element of the curriculum identifies topics, information, and practices that will help students develop their own judgment and decision-making ability for outdoor leadership,
   - Characteristics of sound judgment
   - Potential problems of poor judgment
   - Process of learning sound judgment

3. *Trip Planning and Organization.* This element identifies topics, information, and practices that will help students enhance their knowledge, skills and

abilities in program planning, organization, and evaluation of outdoor leadership.

- Common elements of program planning
- Considerations of activity and site selection
- Evaluation tools for outdoor programs
- Common elements for successful wilderness programs

4. *Environmental Issues.* This element identifies topics, information, and practices that will enhance the students' skills and abilities in minimum-impact practice and environmental considerations that affect wilderness programs.

   - Philosophy of minimum-impact practice
   - Common problems of overuse
   - Minimum-impact practice and procedures
   - Common hazards in wilderness trips
   - Procedures and practices to minimize hazards

5. *Risk Management.* This element of the curriculum identifies topics, information, and practices that will enable students to become aware of the safety and legal issues associated with outdoor leadership and to develop emergency plans and procedures.

   - Common risks in outdoor programming
   - Steps in risk management or outdoor programming
   - Legal liability and standard of care
   - Release forms and acknowledgment of participation
   - Emergency policies and procedures

6. *Instructional Principles.* This element identifies information and practices that will enhance the knowledge and abilities of students to teach and present material in an outdoor setting.

   - Introduction to learning styles
   - Elements of experiential education
   - Opportunities and limitations of instruction in an outdoor setting
   - Teaching techniques for wilderness programming

7. *Navigation.* This element identifies in formation and practices that will help students enhance their knowledge and abilities in map and compass use for outdoor leadership.

   - Topographic map symbols and uses
   - Compass use
   - Use of map and compass
   - Planning routes

8. *Group Dynamics.* This element of the curriculum identifies topics, information, and practices that will help students enhance their knowledge, skills, and abilities to work with small groups in outdoor settings.

   - Techniques for communication and problem-solving
   - Common interpersonal issues associated with wilderness programs
   - Opportunities and limitations of problem- solving with small groups in an outdoor setting.

9. *Nutrition.* This element identifies information and practices that will help students enhance their knowledge, skills, and abilities related to menu planning and preparation for outdoor planning.

   - Components of a balanced diet
   - Practical nutrition for wilderness leaders
   - Organizing, planning and preparation of food for outdoor programming
   - Techniques for food preparation in the field

REFERENCES

Bachert, R. (1977). *Directory of outdoor education degree programs.* Austin. TX: National Education Laboratory.

Buell, L. (1983). *Outdoor leadership competency: A manual for self-assessment and staff evaluation.* Greenfield, MA: Environmental Awareness Publishers.

Cousineau, C. (1977). *A Delphi consensus on a set of principles for the development of a certification system for educators in outdoor adventure programs.* Unpublished doctoral dissertation, University of Northern Colorado.

Elsner, G. H. (1985). *Recreation use trends: A forest service perspective.* Paper presented at the Outdoor Recreation Trends II National Symposium, Myrtle Beach, SC.

Fuller, S. K. (1985). A camp director's view. *Camping Magazine, 57*(6), 25-26.

Green, P. J. (1981). *The content of a college-level outdoor leadership course for land-based outdoor pursuits in the Pacific Northwest: A Delphi consensus.* Unpublished doctoral dissertation, University of Oregon.

Hendee, J. C., & Roggenbuck, J. W. (1984). *Wilderness-related education as a factor increasing demand for wilderness.* Paper presented at the International Forest Congress Convention, Quebec City, Canada.

Jones, P. C. (1980). *Views held by outdoor recreational professionals relative to professional preparation of outdoor recreation.* Unpublished doctoral dissertation, University of Georgia.

Mendence, D. J. (1979). *An integrated-interdisciplinary model in outdoor education for higher education.* Unpublished doctoral dissertation, University of Northern Colorado.

NRPA/SPRE (1987). *Recreation and parks education curriculum catalog.* Alexandria, VA; National Parks and Recreation Association.

Priest, S. (1988). Outdoor leadership training in higher education. *Journal of Experiential Education, 11*(1), 42-47.

Raiola, E. O. (1986). *Outdoor wilderness education: A leadership curriculum.* Unpublished doctoral dissertation, The Union for Experimenting Colleges and Universities.

Rogers, R. J. (1979). *Leading to share—sharing to lead.* Sudbury, ON, Canada: Council of Outdoor Educators of Ontario.

Shiner, J. W. (1970). *Developing professional leadership in outdoor recreation.* Unpublished doctoral dissertation, State University of New York, Syracuse, NY.

Simmons, G. (1982). *An outdoor adventure education baccalaureate degree curriculum and activities model.* Unpublished doctoral dissertation, University of Northern Colorado.

Swiderski, M. J. (1981). *Outdoor leadership competencies identified by outdoor leaders in five western regions.* Unpublished doctoral dissertation, University of Oregon.

Tyler, R. W. (1949). *Basic principles of curriculum and instruction.* Chicago, IL; University of Chicago Press.

Experience-Based Judgment

Kelly D. Cain
University of Wisconsin

&

Leo H. McAvoy
University of Minnesota

One aspect of outdoor leadership is absolute and unquestionable: a leader must be able to make quality decisions, that are based on good judgment, that work, are safe, protect the environment, and accomplish the purpose of the outing (Petzoldt, 1984). Throughout the emergence of the outdoor leadership field, judgment and decision-making ability have been identified as two of the competencies most essential to quality leadership of outdoor adventure education experiences (Cain, 1985; Green, 1981; Hunt, 1984; McAvoy, 1980; Petzoldt, 1984; Swiderski, 1981). But these two competencies have not been emphasized in outdoor leadership curriculums as much as they might be due to their seemingly subjective nature. Thus, there has been a lack of general understanding as to how to develop, evaluate, and document them in relation to outdoor leadership as a professional field. Likewise, the process of developing and understanding experience-based judgment has received rather superficial treatment in the past. This is not due to lack of experience provided in organized adventure education programs and outdoor leadership curriculums, but due to the underutilization of the widely available theoretical foundation of judgment and decision-making before, during, and after the experience.

This paper presents the position that the development of experience-based judgment in outdoor leadership is generally the conscious (both cognitive and physical) application of a generic judgment and decision-making process to "real situations" in the field. This conscious application is essential regardless of whether it occurs in an organized group or personal experience setting. In this paper, the authors present a theoretical foundation for the development, evaluation, and documentation of an experience-based judgment process; give the results of a research project that summarized the opinions of a number of experts in the field; and offer recommendations for future directions.

For the context of this paper, the terms "judgment and decision-making" and "experience-based judgment" will be combined and abbreviated as (J/D-M) unless otherwise noted. The reasons for this are: (1) their often interrelated, substituted, and implied usage in previous literature; (2) by definition, they are mutually dependent; and (3) experience-based judgment is considered the *applied* sense of the common theoretical base.

THEORETICAL FOUNDATIONS

The theoretical foundation for general leadership-based judgment and decision-making has been well documented in the literature and research of a number of fields (leadership, decision sciences, and organizational behavior and administration). In contrast, the development of theory in outdoor leadership is relatively new.

The theoretical foundation for general leadership basically began in the early 1940s with the study of personality traits conducive to leadership (Cattell, 1946; Stodgill, 1948). These researchers were followed by leadership theorists who produced massive amounts of literature on leadership traits, styles, behavior patterns, training, motivational characteristics, decision-making, and attributes of leadership judgment (Gibbs, 1947; Fiedler, 1967; Simon, 1976; Reitz, 1977; Macgregor-Burns, 1979; Rich, 1980).

The primary theoretical foundation of this paper lies in the synonymity of leadership and the judgment and decision-making process. Reitz (1977) explains that when judgments or decisions must be made, there are generally two major factors that should be considered. The first is to determine who the decision-maker will be, and the second involves the choice of which process should be used by the decision-maker to arrive at an appropriate decision.

The decision-makers or leaders are individuals who have learned the behaviors of influencing others. These behaviors typically include leadership styles, goal-setting, decision-making, motivation, communication patterns, and change strategies (Rich, 1980). Leadership style refers to methods selected by the leader to attempt influence over followers. While there is no "one" best style of leadership for all situations, success is measured by the leader diagnosing and selecting the most appropriate style for a particular situation (Hersey & Blanchard, 1982). The leadership style selected theoretically regulates the degree to which the leader shares the judgment and decision-making process with those being led.

The theory behind leadership, and the resulting judgment and decision-making process, can be divided into two contemporary explanations—the classical and the humanistic. The classical theory expects all decisions to be made by the leader, director, or administrator. The humanistic theory reflects the participative and/or laissez-faire approach to the decision-making process and the overriding importance of the group (Rich, 1980). Each of these has found its place in the field of outdoor leadership and is reflected in not only the decisions and actions of individual leaders, but also in the very philosophy by which the leadership of entire adventure education programs is conducted.

For the context of this paper, outdoor leadership is defined as the continual series of judgments, decisions, actions, and evaluations executed by a leader in the interest of maximizing a group's goals in relation to an adventure education pursuit. These goals would generally include, but not be limited to: safety; enjoyment; personal growth/education; and maintenance, if not improvement of, the condition of the environmental resources being used (Buell, 1983; Petzoldt, 1984; Rogers, 1979). This definition implies both the classical and humanistic contexts, since it is common practice for contemporary outdoor leaders in adventure education to delegate the judgment and decision-making process to the group in appropriate situations.

The theory of the judgment and decision-making process itself, as applied to every experiential application in outdoor leadership and adventure education, becomes the central core of this paper. As is the case with leadership, voluminous amounts of literature are available on the theory of judgment and decision-making (Hersey & Blanchard, 1982; Macgregor-Burns, 1979; Reitz, 1977; Rich, 1980; Simon, 1976). Decision-making implies a choice to be made among alternative courses of action. The process of making choices requires judgment, which is only one aspect of the decision-making process. Simon (1976), considered one of the founders of decision-making theory, has stated:

> In so judgments; so far as they involve the implementation of such goals, they will be called factual judgments. (p. 4)

The outdoor leadership field has recently labored in an attempt to define "quality" or "sound" judgment and decision-making ability. Definition of these qualities outside a very specific and quantifiable context has led to criticism. It is necessary, within the outdoor leadership and adventure education fields, to define them in the context of humane idealisms and the "spirit of excellence." We consider "quality" judgment and decision-making ability as two distinctly different, but mutually dependent, entities.

"Quality" judgment is the measure of a leader's ability to use a process for anticipation and recognition of needs or opportunities for action on the group's collective goals. The perception of these needs or opportunities is influenced by situational interactions and what leaders observe and know about themselves, the group, and the circumstances of any specific situation (Petzoldt, 1984; Rogers, 1979). "Quality" decision-making ability is the measure of a leader's power and capacity to consistently make decisions based upon judgments that maximize attainment of the group's collective goals (Petzoldt, 1984; Rogers, 1979).

DEVELOPMENT, EVALUATION, AND DOCUMENTATION

Although Petzoldt (1974 & 1984) is regarded as the first outdoor leader in this country to emphasize its importance, the concept of judgment as the "glue" by which all other competencies are cemented in outdoor leadership has been identified by a large number of writers in the field (Buell, 1983; Cain, 1984; Ford & Blanchard, 1985; Hunt, 1984; Rogers, 1979). Prior to this emphasis on judgment in outdoor leadership in the United States, a solid foundation for it had already been established in Britain and Canada. John Jackson, former director of the Plas y Brenin, the National Mountain Leadership Training Centre for Britain is often credited with the earliest associations of judgment and decision-making to outdoor leadership:

> There is plenty of room for an individual approach and each good leader will solve problems in his or her own way, but *the decisions made and solutions to problems will obey certain basic rules and will be determined by the individual's ability to make sound judgements based on knowledge and experience.* (Jackson, no date)

As an outgrowth of Jackson's influence, as well as of the certification issue in Canada, Rogers (1979), in *Leading to Share—Sharing to Lead,* developed the theme of objective judgment. He based sound leadership on the development of six broad areas with objective judgment as their controlling factor. The six areas are the environmental, physiological, psychological, safety, sociological, and technical forces inherent in any situation. He holds that outdoor leadership development should be accomplished through a "symbiotic relationship" between two separate schemes. Technical outdoor skill training (e.g., rock climbing, canoeing) might be obtained from certifying groups. Leadership development, (e.g., communication skills, group process) should be provided through separate and specific leadership education curriculums. He points out that only through a long individual growth process can objective judgment emerge as a mature leadership skill and be based on more than knowledge and facts (Rogers, 1979).

In the United States an argument has raged since the advertisement of judgment as a major curriculum goal by the National Outdoor Leadership School in the sixties, over whether judgment can be "taught." If it can be taught through various pedagogies and curriculums, what are the specific generic techniques that can be used to maximize its development?

The controversy appears to be centered around the word "taught" because of the implication that there exists a "recipe" on how to teach judgment. When the word "developed" is substituted, the argument subsides because it connotes more broad-based techniques and flexible methodology. This methodology can range from minimally goal-oriented personal experiences in childhood to the most stringent certification program that can be imagined. As in all other aspects of experiential education, each person will learn differently and a wide variety of techniques should be available.

Whatever the combination that has been or will be the most effective for an individual to acquire judgment, there is still the theoretical argument about how it happens. How can judgment be developed? March and Petzoldt provide a strong contrast in opinion on this question. March (1985) states that a safe level of leader judgment can be acquired only after long periods of personal experience. In contrast, Petzoldt (1984) points out that these periods of personal experience must include a structured and/or systematic investigation into how facts about specific situations are gathered and analyzed. This would include explaining why, how, and by whom various leadership decisions are made in regard to the choice of behavior and technique used in various situations.

Although judgment and decision-making are typically explained in the context of the individual leader, it is common within most organized programs to also consider them as a group process. This concept of shared judgment and decision-making has long been a component in Outward Bound programs (Kalisch, 1979), the National Outdoor Leadership School, Wilderness Education Association, Project Adventure, and many other university-based programs (McAvoy, 1987). The intricate dynamics of group decision-making and its effect on leadership has been researched in other outdoor programs by Phipps (1987).

The most contemporary treatment and measure of maturity of J/D-M ability in outdoor leadership and adventure education is reflected in the recent writings of Ewert (1987), Miles (1987), and Priest (1987). These three pieces, along with those soon to be released in a special theme issue of the *Journal of Experiential Education,* will move J/D-M ability into the spotlight of discussion.

A DELPHI STUDY OF EXPERIENCE-BASED JUDGMENT

Within the last three years, a research study (Cain, 1988) was conducted to summarize the opinions of recognized experts about experience-based judgment in general. The specific purpose of this study was to assess consensus of professionals in the fields of outdoor leadership and adventure education on the development, evaluation, and documentation of judgment and decision-making ability in students and practitioners of those fields.

A three-round Delphi process was used to elicit from a panel of 26 experts their professional opinions as to whether judgment and decision-making ability in outdoor leaders can be: (a) developed, and if so, in what specific ways; (b) evaluated, and if so, in what specific ways; and (c) documented, and if so, in what specific ways as well as why it would be professionally beneficial to do so for the field and its individual members. As part of the solicited information on documentation, current sentiment on the various forms of certification were also sought. The experts on the panel represented the major outdoor adventure education programs in the United States (Outward Bound, National Outdoor Leadership School, Wilderness Education Association, and Project Adventure); other adventure programs; and academic institutions in both the United States and Canada.

Among the 26-member panel, there was 100 percent agreement that J/D-M ability *can be developed* in students and practitioners of outdoor leadership through various methods. The panel did note, however, that the phrase "J/D-M ability *can be developed*" cannot presuppose that these skills be developed in *all* students and practitioners, but that a talent, predisposition, or demonstrated capability for these skills must first exist. This also implies that J/D-M skills can be developed in individuals with varying degrees of success, just as can any other ability. From this foundation, the panel cited 49 development methods, of which 33 were considered to be "important" in the development of J/D-M ability. Of those 33, the top six generalized development methods were:

1. Experience in a variety of environments and seasons, with varying conditions of intensity;
2. Realistic opportunities for students to lead peers in stress and non-stress situations;
3. Experience with participants with varying abilities and disabilities;
4. Instructor explanation and discussion with students and/or practitioners about their own J/D-M process in actual field experiences;
5. Experience under a variety of instructors who serve as role models and/or mentors;
6. Opportunities for processing student-led experiences with emphasis on the discussion of the student leader their own J/D-M process with peers and instructors.

The general sentiment of the panel appears to be that an outdoor leader with good J/D-M ability benefits from adapting judgments and decisions across a wide variety of external circumstances other than just a variety of group members and co-leaders. This does not mean that a leader with experience in only one type of ecosystem, climate, season, and type of clientele cannot develop excellent J/D-M ability. Rather, it means that ideally, J/D-M ability is developed more through personal experience of experientially adapting judgments and decisions across a variety of environments and clientele than by academically or conceptually doing so.

As for evaluation and assessment, there was also 100 percent agreement by the panel that J/D-M ability *can be evaluated* in students and practitioners of outdoor leadership through various methods.

Of the 24 total methods cited by the panel for evaluating J/D-M ability, eight of those were categorized as "important." The top five generalized methods were:

1. Opportunities for a supervisor/mentor to evaluate the student or practitioner in unfamiliar or risk/stress situations in which J/D-M is required;
2. Instructor's written appraisal of the student or practitioner's field experience, including self and peer evaluations;
3. Ongoing, structured, and cumulative evaluation of a student/practitioner by a variety of instructors/supervisors/ mentors over a long period of time and in a variety of field leadership situations;
4. Past outdoor related job experience/ performance rated by self and supervisors/employers;
5. Self-evaluation of J/D-M ability.

Diverging from the previous measures, there was only an 88 percent level of agreement by the panel that J/D-M ability *could be documented* in students and practitioners of outdoor leadership through various methods. Of the disagreement registered by a minority of the panel, the ability to document J/D-M ability in such a way as to make it a trustworthy indicator for future performance was a major concern.

In all, 22 total methods for documenting J/D-M ability were evaluated by the panel. Of those, only three were considered "important." These methods were:

1. A combination of: logged experience; personal, professional, and student references; education; [various "hard" and "soft" skill] certifications; personal interviews; field or specialized evaluations; and chronologically listed job experience;
2. Records of regularly structured performance evaluations from organizations or other actual leadership positions where the student or practitioner has done fieldwork;
3. A list of professional references from whom qualitative/quantitative evaluations can be obtained regarding a student's or practitioner's J/D-M ability in fieldwork experience.

Interestingly, certification of outdoor leaders as a documentation method received a very mixed level of support. It is noted, though, that *if* certification were to be used, the panel most favored certification by "special schools" and by "professional organizations," respectively, as opposed to "registration" or "licensing" by state agencies.

It is important to note that in the study collectively, there was a very large number of methods cited for developing, evaluating, and documenting J/D-M ability and that relatively few are discussed here. As such, the authors encourage the reader to consider that those not discussed could contribute a great deal to in-depth investigation of this subject.

RECOMMENDATIONS

The right person
Having the right people
In the right place
At the right time
With the right knowledge
And the right equipment
(Jackson, 1973)

Various kinds of decision-making processes have been developed over the years (Rich, 1980) that incorporate and/or can be applied to the value judgments and factual judgments described by Simon (1976). The one favored by the authors, due to its simplicity yet comprehensiveness and adaptability to the outdoor leadership field, is the "Normative Model" as outlined by Reitz (1977).

The Normative Model is divided into seven steps:

1. Setting objectives
2. Recognizing a problem
3. Evaluating the problem
4. Searching for alternatives
5. Evaluating alternatives
6. Choosing among alternatives
7. Carrying out and following up the decision

As a result of the literature reviewed here and the results of the Delphi study, the authors propose the following model process for experience-based judgment and decision-making in outdoor leadership:

1. The observation and recognition of a need or opportunity to act on behalf of maximizing the group's collective goals and objectives;
2. The collection of all available information that describes the conditions of the need or opportunity;
3. The identification and analysis of potential options of action that can be executed to satisfy the need or opportunity based upon the observations and collection of information;
4. The identification of potential consequences that may be incurred by execution of each individual option or combination thereof;
5. The selection of one or any combination of the most appropriate options;

6. The execution of that decision; and
7. The evaluation of the outcome and consideration of subsequent decision-making and action if necessary (Petzoldt, 1984; Reitz, 1977; Rogers, 1979).

As the reader can see by comparison of the two models, the authors have adapted and redefined Reitz's Normative Model of the decision-making process. The basic model has been left intact except for the setting of objectives, which was incorporated with step 1 of the refined model. As Rich (1980) points out, the process of making decisions becomes most important *after* specific goals have been established. Therefore, the setting of goals and objectives becomes a decision-making process in itself. Goals and objectives are necessary to measure the direction and success of the decision-making process, but a new set of objectives may or may not be established each time the process is carried out.

The authors are convinced that the development, evaluation, and documentation of J/D-M ability must be accomplished through an interwoven web of the experiential and the theoretical base. While the consensus for a single generic process need not be adopted across the entire field, the authors find it difficult to believe that the experiential development of J/D-M ability can be solely left to the often haphazard processing of random experiences, regardless of whether they be in verbal or in journal form. The theoretical thread of J/D-M must guide that process as it applies to J/D-M as a "life skill" in any context of an individual's life.

Closely related to this point is whether J/D-M must be developed, evaluated, and documented in terms of a particular adventure education activity or setting. The expert panel in the research study was strongly split on this point, with those against arguing that J/D-M is a generic leadership skill that can theoretically be developed separately and then transferred across all activities and settings. Others argued that a basic level of skill training in a particular activity or setting is a prerequisite to sound judgment, and that the two are mutually dependent. It appears to the authors that much of the divisiveness of the arguments is in the willingness or unwillingness to trust an individual's predisposition for transfer of learning into unfamiliar settings. The argument rests heavily on whether leaders know their strengths and weaknesses and accept responsibility accordingly.

Thus surfaces a basic philosophical dilemma between outdoor leaders and adventure education administrators. On one hand, administrators philosophically want to trust leader judgment for the safety of participants, the success of programs, and experiential education in general. But they feel pressed to defend themselves with the legalistic, liability reducing, rule-based policy approach for handling complex field situations. As Hunt (1984) points out, this is "very strange and incongruent" in light of "an educational movement that espouses responsibility, initiative, and freedom." The authors would suggest that individual outdoor leaders must be given the flexibility by administrators and program policy for allowing a tolerable level of negative learning. That is, outdoor leaders (students and practitioners) should be allowed to make tolerable mistakes for the sake of educating themselves and others—for the sake of developing J/D-M ability. The authors would agree that good judgment is often the result of surviving "tolerable" bad judgment (Ewert, 1987).

With flexibility for developing J/D-M ability comes the determination of how much stress is appropriate in any particular situation. The Delphi panel of experts was quite outspoken, but again divided on this point. To the authors, it appears that the growth of J/D-M ability is based upon the corresponding proportion of "stressful" experience with relatively tolerable outcomes. In other words, the potential rate of development of J/D-M ability will rise proportionate with the degree of exposure to "stressful" experiences in general; whether they be related to environment, season, leading of peers, variability of participant characteristics, the realization of responsibility, or any other stress-inducing element. This also means that J/D-M ability can be developed in non-stressful situations, but at a rate lower than in stressful situations. It should be acknowledged though, that all of this discussion is grounded in the fact that stress is relative to the one experiencing it and that a stomach-wrenching experience to one may be a cake-walk to another.

The appropriate level of stress induced by a leader is in itself a "quality" judgment. For while they are trying to maximize the development of J/D-M ability in participants, they are also juggling the delicate levels of perceived and real risk, participant enjoyment, group cohesiveness, and environmental and behavioral ethics. As one panelist put it, "Qualities of good J/D-M are demanded most critically when the heat is on" for both leaders and participants.

As was pointed out earlier in the literature, leadership is skill in the influence of behavior of others. The ultimate level of developing leaders in adventure education is mentoring. The importance of mentoring was brought out by the panel in all areas of the study. There was a 92 percent level of agreement that it is a highly valued method for developing, evaluating, and documenting J/D-M ability. The only noted shortfalls were the potential for negative role modeling, the fact that some mentors might be profit-driven, and the possibility that a mentor may or may not be able to actually "teach" J/D-M. There are few competent outdoor leaders who could solely cite themselves for their own developed wisdom. The authors would contend that mentoring has and will continue to play an extremely important role in outdoor leadership and adventure education, and that it will demand that mentors be able to specifically communicate in terms of judgment and decision-making ability.

The discussion of experience-based judgment and of leadership development will undoubtedly continue as the adventure education field continues to grapple with the problem of providing qualified program leadership. There are growing pains involved in any journey toward maturity. One panelist in the study succinctly describes the J/D-M dilemma in outdoor leadership and adventure education:

> What makes for good judgment is having a series of challenge/risk experiences and surviving. It is doubtful that within the *time context* and *legal/moral restrictions* of institutionally sponsored "leadership training" that such experiences could be provided. Judgment may be enhanced somewhat by "leadership training," but the critical/dominant element of judgment comes from "real life" experiences.

REFERENCES

Buell, L. (1983). *Outdoor leadership competency*. Greenfield, MA: Environmental Awareness Publications.

Cain, K. D. (1985). Wilderness education association certification. J. Miles & R. Watters (Eds.), *Proceedings of the 1984 Conference on Outdoor Recreation* (pp. 53-61). Pocatello: Idaho State University Press.

Cain, K. D. (1988). *A Delphi study of the development, evaluation, and documentation of judgment and decision-making ability in outdoor leaders of adventure education programs*. Unpublished doctoral dissertation, University of Minnesota.

Cattell, R. (1946). *Description and measurement of personality*. New York: Yonkers on Hudson.

Ewert, A. (1987). *Decision-making in the outdoor pursuits setting*. Paper presented at the 1987 National Conference of the Association for Experiential Education. Port Townsend, WA.

Fiedler, F. E. (1967). *A theory of leadership effectiveness*. New York: McGraw-Hill.

Ford, P., & Blanchard, J. (1985). *Leadership and administration of outdoor pursuits*. State College, PA: Venture Publishing Inc.

Gibbs, C. A. (1947). The principles and traits of leadership. *Journal of Abnormal Psychology, 42*, 267-289.

Green P. (1981). *The content of a college-level outdoor leadership course for land-based outdoor pursuits in the Pacific Northwest: A Delphi consensus*. Unpublished doctoral dissertation, University of Oregon (University Microfilms No. DEO 82-01832).

Hersey, P., & Blanchard, K. H. (1982). *Management of organizational behavior: Utilizing human resources*, (4th Ed.). Englewood Cliffs, NJ: Prentice-Hall, Inc.

Hunt, Jr., J. S. (1984). Opinion: The dangers of substituting rules for instructor judgment in adventure programs. *Journal of Experiential Education, 7*, 20-21.

Jackson, J. A. (no date). *Notes on party leadership*. Unpublished manuscript.

Jackson, J. A. (1973). *A few thoughts on party leadership*. Plas y Brenin N.M.C. Unpublished manuscript.

Kalisch, K. R. (1979). *The role of the instructor in the Outward Bound educational process*. Three Lakes, WI: Unpublished.

Macgregor-Burns, J. (1979). *Leadership*. New York: Harper & Row.

March, W. (1985). Wilderness leadership certification—Catch 22—Assessing the outdoor leader: An insoluble problem? In J. Miles & R. Watters (Eds.), *Proceedings of the 1984 Conference on Outdoor Recreation* (pp. 37-41). Pocatello: Idaho State University Press.

McAvoy, L. H. (1980). Outdoor leadership training. In J. Meier, T. Morash, & G. Welton (Eds.), *High adventure outdoor pursuits: Organization and leadership* (pp. 116-123). Salt Lake City: Brighton Publishing Company.

McAvoy, L. H. (1987). Education for outdoor leadership. In J. Meier, T. Morash, & G. Welton (Eds.), *High adventure outdoor pursuits: Organization and leadership* (pp. 459-467). Columbus, OH: Publishing Horizons, Inc.

Miles, J. C. (1987). The problem of judgment in outdoor leadership. In J. Meier, T. Morash, & G. Welton (Eds.), *High adventure outdoor pursuits: Organization and leadership* (pp. 502-509). Columbus, OH: Publishing Horizons, Inc.

Petzoldt, P. K. (1974). *The wilderness handbook.* New York: W. W. Norton and Co.

Petzoldt, P. K. (1984). *The wilderness handbook.* New York: W. W. Norton and Co.

Phipps, M. L. (1986). *An assessment of a systematic approach to teaching outdoor leadership in expedition settings.* Unpublished doctoral dissertation, University of Minnesota.

Priest, S. (1987). *Preparing effective outdoor pursuit leaders.* University of Oregon Press.

Reitz, H. J. (1977). *Behavior in organizations.* Homewood, IL: Richard D. Irwin, Inc.

Rich, D. W. (1980). *Leadership training handbook.* Published Doctor of Education project in lieu of dissertation, University of Northern Colorado, Greeley, CO.

Rogers, R. J. (1979). *Leading to share—sharing to lead* (Monograph). Ontario, Canada: Council of Outdoor Educators of Ontario. (ERIC Document Reproduction Service No. ED 178 234.)

Simon, H. A. (1976). *Administrative behavior.* London: The Free Press.

Stodgill, R. M. (1948). Personality factors associated with leadership: A survey of the literature. *Journal of Psychology, 25,* 35-71.

Swiderski, M. J. (1981). Outdoor leadership competencies identified by outdoor leaders in five western regions. *Dissertation Abstracts International, 42,* 3753A.

Outdoor Leadership Certification

David Cockrell
University of North Carolina

The emergence of Outward Bound in America in 1962 clearly transfigured basic North American notions of outdoor education in many ways. Outward Bound has given identity here to the term adventure education and provided us with a renewed vision of outdoor programming as a legitimate professional activity. With that vision, however, have arisen a number of rather thorny professional issues, not the least of which is who should be considered qualified to be described as an outdoor leader. Certification of outdoor leaders has been a topic of widespread controversy in the United States and Canada since about the mid-1970. As of this writing (early 1989), the heat of the debate appears to have died down somewhat, but the truly central issues of the controversy have yet to be squarely addressed by any quorum within "the industry."

The purpose of this paper is to provide an overview (a broad perspective, as from above) of the certification controversy. I first lay out the arguments for and against certification as they have been voiced by leaders in the field of adventure education. I then summarize research that has been conducted on various aspects of the problem. A variety of existing certification programs are also summarized, and I close with some personal speculation about where the near future may find us.

ARGUMENTS FOR AND AGAINST CERTIFICATION

Much of the impetus behind the American certification concept owes to the works of Paul Petzoldt. As the first chief mountaineering instructor for the Colorado Outward Bound School in 1963, Petzoldt began to see a need to train instructors (Bachert, 1987). The need for a standardized instructor training course eventually led Petzoldt to establish the National Outdoor Leadership School in 1965. While NOLS has traditionally certified graduates of certain of its outdoor leadership training courses, the school has not taken a decisive stance on the issue. Petzoldt's next venture, the Wilderness Education Association (WEA) did take an unequivocal stance on certification. The WEA philosophy is outlined in detail in Petzoldt's (1984) book, *The Wilderness Handbook.*

Petzoldt presents two arguments in favor of outdoor leadership certification. First, outdoor recreation in general is experiencing a trend toward greater challenge and risk (Ewert, 1985). This trend is associated with escalating numbers of backcountry accidents for which the taxpaying public has traditionally taken responsibility (Petzoldt, 1984). In an effort to partially reduce mounting public expense, McAvoy and Dustin (1981) proposed the controversial alternative of no-rescue wilderness, requiring recreationists to arrange their own rescues. For many reasons, this idea has not yet found wide appeal. Education and certification of wilderness leaders with demonstrated good judgment and knowledge of emergency procedures would seem to provide a more moderate tactic that emphasizes preventing accidents.

Second, there is a growing sensitivity to the ecological impacts of wildland recreation. Cole (1979, 1982) has shown that extremely light use levels often account for much of the impact. Studies by Miller and Miller (1979) and others have shown the painstaking efforts necessary to rehabilitate impacted wilderness soils, vegetation, and wildlife populations. On the other hand, studies of wilderness education (e.g., Fazio, 1979; Bradley, 1979) have shown considerable success in changing the practices of wilderness users. It now seems clear that prevention of impacts through light-handed educational contacts is preferable to more heavy-handed use restrictions or to rehabilitation (Hammitt and Cole, 1987).

Questions of safety and impacts are exacerbated by the growing numbers of educational, therapeutic, and organized recreational user groups (Hendee and Roggenbuck, 1984). Uninformed organizational trip leaders can precipitate more than their share of rescues and impacts. Secondarily, participants in organized programs constitute an important audience of future independent users who may need training in safe and ethical use practices. Such opportunities should not be lost. If organizational trip leaders were carefully trained and certified as knowledgeable about safety and minimum impact use practices, the trickle-down effect of standardized practices would be greatly enhanced.

Arguments against the certification idea also fall into two general groups. The essence of the first argument is that it would really be impossible to certify a leader to be safe. This argument has been articulated by Bill March (1987), former deputy director of the National Outdoor Training Center in Scotland, and currently coordinator of the Outdoor Pursuits program at the University of Calgary. Because wilderness environments vary so dramatically in the pattern of objective dangers and safety factors presented to a trip leader, March feels that only sound judgment developed through years of encounters with wilderness can prepare a person for leadership responsibilities. March questions the assumption that demonstration of good judgment during a certification assessment is a valid indicator of comparable performance in different situations later.

Further, March believes the assessment process itself may significantly alter the performance of a certification candidate in the British system. Candidates may falsely believe that a test problem has been contrived by the instructor and therefore contains no objective risk. Assessors' attitudes may artificially intimidate certification candidates or artificially encourage compliance. Candidates may conduct prior reconnaissance trips to assessment sites or otherwise "cheat" on assessment tasks. Subjective evaluation schemes will almost certainly be subject to differences in values among instructors.

Of course, other professions (airline pilots, surgeons, teachers) do attempt to assure the public of the adequacy of a professional's judgment. There are many techniques for improving the success rate of the certification assessment: documented experience logs, standardized training apprenticeship sequences, certification boards, and nationally standardized examinations, among others. March suggested five "standards" that he felt could encourage a valid certification process in outdoor leadership:

1. All assessors or certifiers should be professionally trained in assessment techniques;
2. All assessors should be re-assessed on an annual basis;
3. All assessors should be legally liable for their certification;
4. All assessment candidates must have access to an independent appeal process if dissatisfied;
5. All assessors should be evaluated by assessment candidates.

Without such safeguards, March (1987) describes outdoor leadership certification as "a meaningless charade, a license to kill, and a scapegoat for the bureaucrats." Perhaps the reason these challenges have become arguments against certification in outdoor leadership is the heterogeneity of the field. I have suggested that Outward Bound may be viewed as a "central tendency" or prototype for adventure education, but the variance from this central tendency is quite large. There are wide variations in program goals, populations served, environments utilized, and activities employed. It is not at all immediately obvious what an outdoor leader in North America should be certified to *do*. In a discussion of certified public accountants, Gregory, Mueller, and Tabor (1976) identified five essential elements for an occupation's admission to the status of "profession":

1. A specialized body of knowledge with a high degree of intellectual content;
2. A recognized educational process and standards for admission to the profession;
3. A self-imposed code of professional conduct;
4. A motive for service oriented to the precedence of public interest over personal gain and self-interest; and
5. A recognition of status by persons outside the profession.

Certainly an outdoor leadership certification system provides a standard for admission to the profession and some recognition of status by various publics. Such a system seems presumptuous, however, unless it is developed in conjunction with the other elements of the profession.

A specialized body of knowledge is emerging in outdoor leadership with a grounding in social science theory (Ewert, 1987). Continuing research on the processes and outcomes of outdoor adventure programming is needed to advance this element of professionalism. Educational curricula for preparing new professionals are emerging in the field, and the present volume is an important example. Efforts at curriculum coordination and evaluation should be undertaken. The role of the universities in the educational process is an important and as yet undecided issue. Employers must ultimately invest in the standardized professional preparation process by hiring trained professional staff.

A self-imposed code of professional ethics is perhaps a step or two further away, but many of the elements of a professional code of outdoor leadership already exist (Hunt, 1986). The placement of a human service motive above profit may be an easy criterion of professionalism for some outdoor leaders, but the priority should be made an explicit element of the profession. Certainly the legitimacy of outdoor leadership certification is dependent on the success of the field in each of these basic professional endeavors.

There is a final argument against certification that is more philosophical in nature and perhaps more fundamental. America's wildland recreation tradition is based on freedom of choice, self-reliance, individual responsibility, exploration, and challenge (Leopold, 1966). It is these very qualities, of course, which have attracted educational and therapeutic adventure programs to the wilderness setting. However, Ewert (1985) identified trends in outdoor adventure toward greater regulation, shorter experiences, diminished knowledge of outdoor skills, and greater reliance on technology. There are also more highly structured programs than ever before. Such trends have probably been influenced by the efforts of outdoor leaders over the last few years to demonstrate a "correct" form of outdoor adventure. By standardizing use practices and certifying leaders, we may be contributing to the erosion of the very values the profession hopes to foster. Ironically, the heterogeneity discussed above as an impediment to professionalism in adventure education may also be one of our greatest strengths.

RESEARCH ON THE CERTIFICATION ISSUE

There have been several descriptive survey research studies conducted to assess support for certification. These have been described in more detail elsewhere (Cockrell & Detzel, 1985; Cockrell, Detzel & Braun, 1986) and will only be briefly summarized here. Senosk (1977) surveyed 148 outdoor pursuits organizations in the United States in 1976. Thirty percent had a certification system in effect and 52 percent expressed a need for such a system. In a second national survey, Ewert and Johnson (1983) found a lack of consensus about who should administer a national certification system or how, but 71 percent of the professionals surveyed supported the concept. Two regional surveys of outdoor professionals have echoed these findings, with 76 percent supporting a certification scheme in Ontario (Cousineau, 1977) and 71 percent expressing support in Virginia (Cockrell, 1985).

Some minor interest in certification has been generated in the resource management community where "merit" is seen as an alternative for rationing wilderness or wild river use, controlling impacts and improving safety. Merit is similar to certification in that permits would be allocated on the basis of some demonstrable skill, knowledge, or past behavior (Shelby, et al., 1982). Shelby and his colleagues examined the preferences of backpackers and river runners for five allocation techniques: pricing, reservations, lotteries, queuing, and merit. Sixty-six percent of the backpackers and river runners felt that a merit system would have no detrimental impact on them. Fewer than 40 percent saw a merit system as fair. Stankey and Baden (1977) were somewhat more supportive of merit systems. They felt merit would be accepted by users if it were seen as an alternative to more authoritarian rationing measures. In general, however, reactions of private wilderness users might be described as guarded, and attitudes of managers as hesitant.

Cockrell, Detzel, and Braun (1986) examined the reactions of certified WEA graduates to their certification courses and attempted to assess the effectiveness of courses in changing knowledge levels and use practices. WEA graduates were found to be well-educated men and women, typically in their late 20s. About half were professionally involved in outdoor leadership. Graduates were generally very satisfied with their courses. They reported being evaluated fairly for the most part, and they rated their instructors favorably. They felt most of the course objectives were achieved.

Interestingly, the knowledge levels of WEA graduates about outdoor safety and conservation practices were not particularly high, as measured by brief scales of multiple choice items reflecting the WEA curriculum. Moreover, the mean number of WEA curriculum areas reported to be implemented into graduates' subsequent programming was 4 out of 16, and one-third of the graduates who were employed in outdoor leadership were not implementing any of the curriculum areas due to the WEA experience. While methodological shortcomings were acknowledged in this study, there were indications that the WEA certification curriculum was not well-standardized across courses, and that the competencies taught may not have had broad application in graduates' professional activities.

In an interesting recent examination of Outward Bound (OB), National Outdoor Leadership School (NOLS), and WEA instructors (n = 184), Sakofs (1987) found 60 percent to favor certification, and 60 percent to support a nationally accredited outdoor leadership curriculum. While there were no differences in support levels for certification across the three schools, there were pronounced differences in support for a standardized curriculum. One hundred percent of the WEA instructors supported a standardized curriculum, while only 46 percent and 50 percent of the OB and NOLS instructors respectively supported standardization. Interestingly, Sakofs found no differences in the importance assigned by the three organizations' instructors to various areas of curriculum content. This finding diverges from Cockrell, Detzel, and Braun's (1986) standardization data for WEA graduates and may indicate a trend toward greater standardization of outdoor leadership competencies in the future.

Finally, Priest's (1987) international survey on outdoor leadership preparation has brought additional perspective on the lessons from the longer British involvement with outdoor leadership certification, as well as important comparisons with Australia, New Zealand, and Canada. There are perhaps three conclusions from this comprehensive assessment that are most directly relevant to the present discussion. First, Americans and Canadians are more concerned about litigation and insurance than the other three countries, and our philosophies of outdoor leadership training are colored by these concerns. Second, support for the certification of technical activity skills and safety is comparable internationally and is at about the same levels reported in prior research (about 70 percent). Finally, beyond technical and safety skills, there is not much consensus concerning the competencies to be certified. The British and Australians predictably support certification of a broader range of competencies, and the Canadians and New Zealanders reject the approach more thoroughly. Priest's U.S. sample had the highest percentage of undecided respondents.

PROFILES OF CURRENTLY EXISTING CERTIFICATION SCHEMES

This discussion has deliberately emphasized the rationales and research surrounding the certification issue. Because adventure education is a young, rapidly evolving field, descriptions of existing certification programs serve only as mileposts on the path to maturity. Nonetheless, a summary of some certification schemes on this continent that have survived a few changes may indicate robust trends for the near future.

An array of specific outdoor sports in America have adopted certification as a means of enhancing quality in performance and instruction. The Hang Glider's Association of America, the Professional Ski Instructors of America, and the Professional Association of Diving Instructors, among others, offer skills-oriented certificates of competency that may be of relevance to outdoor leaders. The word "hard" in this section title is in quotes because these certificates clearly involve more than the performance of psychomotor skills. Judgment and leadership, client assessment, group facilitation, and instructional skills are normally involved. The granting of an advanced certificate in many outdoor adventure sports is a genuine indicator of outdoor leadership competencies, even if limited in scope to a particular activity.

An example is the certification sequence for paddling instructors administered by the American Canoe Association (ACA). ACA's National Instruction Committee promotes a series of basic paddling courses for canoes, decked canoes, kayaks, and sea kayaks. These courses are taught by ACA-certified instructors. The current instructor certification process is divided into three consecutive levels: flatwater, moving water, and white water (Foster, 1987). Instructor candidates are evaluated on their mastery of technical knowledge, teaching skills, and paddling skills. Technical knowledge includes general knowledge of canoesport, safety, equipment, conditioning, paddling theory, river reading, river running strategies, and rescue. Teaching skills include "logistics, lesson organization, class control, teaching of specific technical topics, technique analysis, and demonstration of leadership skills and judgment" (Foster, 1987).

After an ACA instructor has taught for two years, he or she may be selected by a committee to become an instructor trainer candidate. A candidate who successfully co-leads an instructor workshop and is recommended by an instructor trainer then achieves this highest level of certification.

Foster (1986) argues the value of ACA certification in familiar language. Certification provides a forum for the development of skilled instructors. It enhances professionalism in instruction; ensures that minimum standards will be met; provides a vehicle for sharing information; and minimizes liability risks. Foster (1986) insists that the intent of this system is not to downgrade the professionalism of noncertified instructors, but the ACA (and American Red Cross) canoe/kayak instructor certificates have become established standards in the field.

Interestingly, other specific adventure activities have evolved with less investment in the certification process. Climbing and Ropes and Initiatives Course Instruction are noteworthy examples. The training and sanctioning of climbing instructors has proceeded in a highly decentralized way, reflecting the individualism that is the hallmark of the sport. Several regional organizations have attempted Ropes and Initiatives Instructor certificates, but none has yet achieved widespread recognition. Project Adventure (PA), the best-known ropes and initiatives advocate, has recently become a membership association. In their 1989 literature they claim: "The range of program implementation options is so great that we feel a blanket certification is not appropriate." They do, however, maintain a network of Project Adventure Certified Trainers who have worked at length with PA staff; they accredit programs that meet their standards; and they provide PA association group liability insurance for interested accredited programs.

Certifications for risk management and emergency handling skills might also be mentioned as "hard skills" certificates. The American Red Cross Advanced First Aid and C.P.R. certifications serve as widely standardized basic building blocks. The "wilderness" adaptations of the Department of Transportation's First Responder and Emergency Medical Associates, and Stonehearth Open Learning Opportunities are quickly becoming standards in the industry. Another relevant specialized certification is available in backcountry avalanche forecasting from the American Avalanche Institute.

As interest in wilderness education has become more widespread in the U.S. Forest Service, several national forests have piloted systems of wilderness user certification. Perhaps first of these was the Eagle Cap Wilderness on the Wallowa-Whitman National Forest in Oregon. Their user education program focused on "no-trace" camping. It included contacts with visitors at trailheads and campsites as well as follow-up letters. In the off-season, Forest Service personnel delivered programs for public schools and civic organizations (Bradley, 1979). As an informal incentive to encourage retention, a quiz and certificate of completion were included as a part of their materials.

Similar systems, including certifications, have been implemented by the Superior National Forest in the Boundary Waters Canoe Area Wilderness and by the Jefferson National Forest in Virginia. In the Boundary Waters, completion of a brief educational program and a test have been required to obtain a backcountry permit (G. Coyle, personal communication, April 1986). The programs address wilderness ethics, wilderness philosophy and regulations, and trip planning and leadership. Programs are taught by outfitters, scout leaders and other user group leaders who have successfully completed a four-hour instructor training program. These volunteer instructors are then authorized to conduct user programs and issue certificates and wilderness permits.

The program developed by the Jefferson National Forest in Virginia was based on the Boundary Waters model but expanded both the instructor training and user education components (Kascenska, 1987). Volunteer instructors were recruited from resource management agencies, scouts, Sierra Club groups, community outdoor recreation supervisors and other organized group leaders. A 10-hour instructor training workshop was cooperatively sponsored by the Forest Service and the Wilderness Education Association. Curriculum content included wilderness history and philosophy, ethics, and trip planning and leadership. Successful completion of the workshop and written final examination led to the granting of WEA's "Wilderness Steward" certification. Authorized instructors were then provided with teaching materials and support services to teach a four-hour user education workshop with a variety of organized user groups.

These agency-sponsored user certification schemes appear to have been moderately successful mechanisms for teaching minimum impact skills and enhancing safety (Kascenska, 1987). The breadth of their application is not yet clear, however. As noted above, "merit" systems of permit allocation are still regarded as undesirable infringements on freedom by many recreationists and managers. As voluntary experiences, wilderness education programs are essentially extended interpretive efforts, and the significance of certification is considerably lessened.

COMPREHENSIVE OUTDOOR LEADERSHIP CERTIFICATION

Outward Bound, the National Outdoor Leadership School, the Boy Scouts of America, and many other outdoor programs all administer advanced-level outdoor leadership training opportunities for aspiring staff, sometimes with an associated certification. As these are primarily "in-house" certifications, however, they will not be addressed in detail.

In keeping with its long-standing commitment to professional quality through certification and accreditation, the American Camping Association has promoted a comprehensive outdoor living skills certification program. The lower levels of certification, Campcrafter, Advanced Campcrafter, and Tripcrafter, are programs designed for campers in organized camps. These courses are taught by certified Outdoor Living Skills (OLS) instructors who have completed a brief course assessing their skills and teaching competencies. OLS instructors with a Tripcrafter authorization are eligible to participate in an eight-day Trip Leader Institute that results in certification as a trip leader.

The American Camping Association (1986) clearly indicates that the focal point of this certification sequence is "to help foster safe, intelligent use of the wilderness by organized camps" (p. 3). They do, however, permit completion of Outward Bound, NOLS, WEA, or Appalachian Mountain Club courses as "equivalent skills" to OLS instructors with Tripcrafter authorization. The American Camping Association stance is that the 8-day Trip Leader Institute may be less extensive than other outdoor leadership training opportunities, but that it fills a gap for organized camp staff who already possess some outdoor leadership skills.

At the time of this writing, the Wilderness Education Association is still the primary U.S. organization to espouse a nationally standardized, comprehensive outdoor leadership training curriculum leading to certification.

Descriptions of the organization and curriculum are provided in this volume by Frank Lupton, and elsewhere by Cain (1984), Phipps & Cain (1984), Cockrell & LaFollette (1984), and Petzoldt (1984).

Briefly, the anchor point in the WEA approach is the National Standard Program for Outdoor Leadership Certification: a five-week, 18-point, college-level curriculum. In an effort to separate the certification function from the training agencies, WEA withdrew its own course offerings in 1986 and now only accredits universities to teach the national standard curriculum. Recently, WEA authorized several of its accredited universities to vary the sequencing and organization of curriculum elements and field experiences to best fit the instructional model for that particular institution. Thus, there are now several different approaches to teaching the standard certification curriculum.

The fundamental premise of the WEA philosophy is that cultivation of sound judgment and decision-making ability is central to quality outdoor leadership. Ironically, this is quite consistent with March's (1987) arguments against certification. A corollary to the WEA philosophy, however, is that good outdoor judgment can be taught and learned. Thus, while the certification curriculum addresses wilderness living and travel skills as well as adventure activity skills, these are not the primary focus. Primarily, the certification course teaches the students to evaluate specific situations and decisions from within a context of generalized principles. Thus, evaluation is itself an important curriculum element, and students undergo a rigorous process of self, peer, and instructor evaluation throughout the course. Several accredited universities now interweave periods of field time in the wilderness with more didactic classroom instruction and assessment. WEA's position is that good judgment, evaluation and leadership are skills that are transferable to a wide variety of outdoor environments and activities.

In addition to the National Standard Program, WEA sponsors professionals' courses and occasional instructors' courses through accredited universities. WEA instructors must complete a Standard, Professionals', or Instructors' course, apprentice on a second course, and be recommended for instructor status by the head instructor of the apprentice course. A variety of affiliate institutions now offer WEA Wilderness Steward Programs, shorter courses teaching one or more of the 18 National Standard Program curriculum elements. In addition to its certification program, WEA is also a professional membership organization with a full range of membership services.

CONCLUSIONS

During and shortly after World War II, the philosophies of Geoffrey Young and Kurt Hahn gained prominence in British school systems, and teachers began to take students to the mountains to learn directly from experience and adventure. Through the efforts of Sir Jack Longland and others, the Mountain Leadership Training Board was established, and the Mountain Leadership and Mountain Instructor's Certificates gained widespread recognition. For many, these changes represented the culmination of long-sought aspirations (Mortlock, 1973). Indeed, Americans such as Paul Petzoldt and "Tap" Tapley went to the U.K. to study the system for its applications in this country (Bachert, 1987). Only now are the American Outward Bound schools seeking broad acceptance here by the public schools as has been the case in Britain since the early 1960s (Bacon, 1987).

There were, however, concerns raised about the new field of "mountain education." Traditional mountaineers questioned the proficiency of "teaching mountaineers," the validity of the certification system, and the motives of teachers and students alike taking educational trips to the crags (Price, 1973). The Cairngorm tragedy of 1971, in which a teacher with a Mountain Instructor's Certificate led six teenagers to their death on a winter mountaineering trip, brought the debate to its peak.

There were loud cries for more defined and specific standards, more rigorous certification assessments, and the total elimination of risks on educational trips. There were also, perhaps, even louder calls for recognition that outdoor education and mountaineering should be quite distinct endeavors. These voices argued that when outdoor education depended on adventure for its success, it must not preclude it through standardization and proscription. This latter opinion was formalized in the British Mountaineering Committee's Hunt Report on Mountain Training (1975):

> Those who are being introduced to mountaineering must be safeguarded against accidents arising from exposure to risks that are beyond their experience to cope with. At the same time, they should not be taught attitudes or practices which, by overplaying safety, may stultify enjoyment and restrict their ability to progress in climbing with all its attendant challenges and opportunities.

Certification systems sponsored by the Mountain Leadership Training Board, the British Canoe Union, and others continue to be influential today. The result of the debates in the 1970s, however, has been a narrowing of focus to hard skills certification, a restriction of educational programs to short-term, controlled environments, and an emphasis on skills training for later "true" adventures. A clearer distinction has arisen in British society between outdoor education and wilderness adventure, and the certification systems address strictly the former.

In this paper, I have summarized the arguments for and against certification, research on the topic, existing North American systems, and the longer British history with the idea. I believe some direction for the near future may be induced from these inquiries that might guide our path toward professional maturity.

First, many of the conditions that precipitated an outdoor leadership certification system in Britain in the early 1960s are present in North America today. There is a growing recognition of the efficacy of organized adventure as a growth medium in many different settings. There is a concurrent preoccupation with safety, litigation, and insurance. And there is no standardized training sequence for leaders of adventure experiences. These conditions have also argued for some form of credentialing in numerous other professions.

Second, research has quite consistently shown a majority of outdoor educators to support certification here. As in Britain, this support does not extend to the certification of private wilderness users or adventurers. It seems unlikely that American resource management agencies or private user groups (e.g., the Appalachian Trail Conference) will move toward user certification unless they are pushed to do so by demand from untoward organized groups.

Third, again as in Britain, the certification programs that are least controversial here and most definable are those that focus on circumscribed skills and concrete knowledge. Trends in outdoor adventure are leading to shorter, more specialized, and professionally led experiences. Outdoor leadership training is similarly trending away from the long comprehensive course, and toward more convenient modular training segments in activity skills, safety skills, knowledge of the environment, and administrative skills.

This is not to say that multiple certifications of specific skills and concrete knowledge can supplant good judgment as the basis of quality outdoor leadership. It is simply to say that the demonstration of competent skills in appropriate circumstances is a more concrete vehicle for assessment. The recent acceptance by the WEA of modular training segments leading to the National Standard Certificate is an important step in recognizing this approach.

It is my hope that the profession will turn more and more to the universities to provide this modular training and certification. The university course structure can provide curriculum modules in "Risk Management in Wilderness Settings," "Vertical Techniques," "Conflict Resolution," etc. Degree programs in outdoor leadership provide thorough exposure to the various curriculum areas over an extended time frame, and students can take specific courses that accommodate all the usual constraints of scheduling, finances, and prerequisites that face students of other professions. There is time to gain the documented field experience that most agree is critical to the development of good judgment. If the profession of adventure education would invest seriously in universities as training vehicles for entering professionals, perhaps a college degree would be the only certification we would really need.

REFERENCES

Bachert, D. W. (1987). *The NOLS experience: Experiential education in the wilderness*. Unpublished doctoral dissertation, North Carolina State University, 1987.

Bacon, S. (1987, September). *The use of wilderness for human resource development*. Paper presented at the World Wilderness Congress, Estes Park, CO.

Bradley, J. (1979). A human approach to reducing wildland impacts. In Ittner, R., Potter, D. R., Agee, J. K., & Anschell, S. (Eds.), *Proceedings of the Recreational Impacts on Wildlands Conference* (pp. 222-226). Seattle, WA: U.S.D.A. Forest Service Pacific Northwest Forest and Range Experiment Station, Publication R-6-001-1979.

Cain, K. (1984). *Wilderness education association certification*. Paper presented at the National Outdoor Recreation Conference, Bozeman, MT.

Cockrell, D. (1985). Opinions of Virginia's outdoor educators concerning standards, certification and training. *Virginia Journal of Health, Physical Education and Recreation, 7* (2), 17-18, 21.

Cockrell, D., & Detzel, D. (1985). Effects of outdoor leadership certification on safety, impacts and program standardization. *Park Practice Program Trends, 22* (3), 15-21.

Cockrell, D., Detzel, D. and Braun, S. (1986). Certified wilderness trip leaders: Their knowledge levels, safety records and opinions of certification courses. Lucas, R. (Ed.), *Proceedings—National Wilderness Research Conference: Current Research.* Ogden, UT: U.S.F.S. Intermountain Research Station Gen. Tech. Rep. INT-212.

Cockrell, D., & LaFollette, J. (1985). A national standard for outdoor leadership certification. *Parks and Recreation, 20* (6), 40-43.

Cole, D. N. (1979). Reducing the impact of hikers on vegetation: An application of analytical research methods. Ittner, R., et al. (Eds.), *Proceedings of the Recreational Impacts on Wildlands Conference* (pp. 71-78). Seattle, WA: U.S.F.S. Pacific Northwest Experiment Station, Publication R-6-001-1979.

Colen, D. N. (1982). Wilderness campsite impacts: Effect of amount of use. Ogden, UT: U.S.F.S. Intermountain Forest and Range Experiment Station Research Report INT-284.

Cousineau, C. (1977). A Delphi consensus on a set of principles for the development of a certification system for educators in outdoor adventure programs. Unpublished doctoral dissertation, University of Northern Colorado, 1977.

Ewert, A. (1985). Emerging trends in outdoor adventure recreation. In McLellan, G. (Ed.), *Proceedings - 1985 National Outdoor Recreation Trends Symposium II* (pp. 155-165). Atlanta, GA: U.S.D.I. National Park Service.

Ewert, A. (1987). Research in experiential education: An overview. *Journal of Experiential Education, 10* (2), 4-7.

Ewert, A., & Johnson, W. (1983). Outdoor adventure leadership: A study of current issues facing the profession. *Proceedings: Inter-mountain Leisure Symposium.* Provo, UT: Brigham Young University.

Fazio, J. R. (1979). Information and education techniques to improve minimum impact use knowledge in wilderness areas. In Ittner, R., et al. (Eds.), *Proceedings: Recreational Impact on Wildlands Conference* (pp. 227-234). Seattle, WA: U.S.F.S. Pacific Northwest Experiment Station, Publication R-6-001-1979.

Foster, T. (1986). The value of certification. *American Canoeist, 8*(2), 5.

Foster, T. (1987). A new approach to the certification process. *American Canoeist, 9*(2), 5.

Gregory, W. R., Mueller, G. G., & Tabor, R. N. (1976). *Periodic recertification of CPA's: New labels on old packages.* Seattle, WA: University of Washington Press.

Hammitt, W. E., & Cole, D. N. (1987). *Wildland Recreation: Ecology and Management.* New York: Wiley.

Hendee, J. C., & Roggenbuck, J. W. (1984). *Wilderness-related education as a factor increasing demand for wilderness.* Paper presented at the International Forest Congress Convention, Quebec City.

The Hunt Committee (1978). Hunt report—Annex, A., and Wilson, K. (Eds.), *The games limbers play* (p. 661). San Francisco, CA: Sierra Club Books.

Hunt, J. (1986). *Ethical Issues in experiential education.* Boulder, CO: Association for Experiential Education.

Kascenska, J. R. (1987). *A program for wilderness education in Virginia.* Unpublished master's thesis, Virginia Polytechnic Institute and State University, Blacksburg, VA.

Leopold, A. (1966). *A Sand County Almanac.* New York: Ballantine Books.

March, B. (1987). Wilderness leadership certification—Catch 22. In Meier, J., Morash, T. W., & Welton, G. E. (1987). *High adventure outdoor pursuits.* Columus, OH: Publishing Horizons.

McAvoy, D., & Dustin, D. L. (1983). The right to risk in wilderness. *Journal of Forestry, 79*, 150-152.

Miller, J. W. and Miller, M. M. (1979). Propagation of plant material for subalpine revegetation. Ittner, R., et al. (Eds.), *Proceedings—Recreational Impacts on Wildlands Conference* (pp. 304-210). Seattle, WA: U.S.F.S. Pacific Northwest Experiment Station, Publication R-6-001-1979.

Mortlock, C. (1978). The philosophy of adventure education. Wilson, K. (Ed.), *The games climbers play* (pp. 656-658). San Francisco, CA: Sierra Club Books.

Petzoldt, P. (1984). *The new wilderness handbook.* New York: Norton.

Phipps, M. , & Cain, K. (1984). Wilderness Education Association, one plan for U.S. certification and comparison to British outdoor qualifications. *Adventure Education, 1* (6), 24-26.

Priest, S. (1987). An international survey of outdoor leadership preparation. *Journal of Experiential Education, 10* (2), 34-39.

Sakoffs, M. (1987). The field instructor's orientation toward certification. *Journal of Experiential Education, 10* (2), 40-42.

Senosk, E. M. (1976). *An examination of outdoor pursuit leadership certification and licensing within the U.S. in 1976.* Unpublished master's thesis, University of Oregon.

Shelby, B., Danley, M. S., Gibbs, K. C., & Petterson, M. E. (1982). Preferences of backpackers and river runners for allocation techniques. *Journal of Forestry, 80,* 416-419.

Stankey, G., & Baden, J. (1977). *Rationing wilderness use: Methods, problems and guidelines.* Ogden, UT: U.S.F.S. Intermountain Forest and Range Experiment Station, Publication INT-192.

Section Seven

THE MANAGEMENT OF ADVENTURE EDUCATION

Administering the Resources

Discussions of leadership in adventure education and outdoor pursuits in general usually examine the challenges of field leaders. Behind each field leader, of course, lies leadership of another sort—that which creates and maintains the organization. Such leadership offers different challenges and satisfactions than those facing the field people, but is no less critical to the success of adventure education. The essays in this section examine general topics central to organizational leadership.

All programs start with an idea, and many end there. Costello offers a few hints on how to get off the starting line. Do a realistic assessment of your possibilities, prepare an action plan, determine the finances, and start. When the start is made there will be a tremendous work-load, as Watters notes. A successful program requires long hours, thorough planning and emotional commitment. Tight budgets, politics and protocol will produce a lot of stress on staff, and burnout will be a real risk. Burnout must and can be avoided. Watters correctly points to personnel management as perhaps the most critical ingredient of successful program administration.

Part of personnel management is staff growth and development, and Teschner and Wolter take this as their subject. What is the ideal field staff person, and how do you develop him or her? They identify the qualities of this ideal staffer, then suggest an approach to staff development that yields the greatest likelihood of achieving the higher level competencies they seek in staff. Their aim is the synergistic interaction of experiential, supervisory and formal approaches to training, and they explain how this synergism (an outcome greater than might be achieved by any one approach to staff development) can be reached.

Sometimes the organization cannot or will not do all the work required and so decides to contract out part of that work. Strong describes why this can be a good approach, and explains the process one should use to achieve a good contract. This can be a complex legal matter that requires great care. Strong's aim is to alert the manager to the potential and the problems of this approach.

Whether or not parts of the work are contracted to others, two aspects of adventure education program administration can never be avoided—safety and evaluation. Wade writes about general principles of safety management in adventure education. He uses examples from Outward Bound to illustrate his points, and describes how each part of that large and complex organization is involved in safety management. Warner takes a comprehensible look at the state of program evaluation and finds it lacking. Evaluation is essential, he argues. Program administrators have not used evaluation as a program development tool as they should. Individual programs and the field of adventure education as a whole would be better if evaluation was thoroughly done. The gut feeling that good work is being done will no longer suffice. Professionals in adventure education must know what principles, theories and circumstances combine for the best results for specific types of participants. Warner offers helpful advice on how this critically important evaluative work can be done.

The essays here focus on only a few important dimensions of program administration. Obviously, there are many more that should be treated, enough in fact to comprise an entire book on program administration alone. (The same, of course, might be said for other sections of this book.) Management of outdoor pursuit programs involves all of the matters of managing any enterprise, along with some unique to this field of activity. While much can be learned from the conventional management literature, the editors recognize a great need for research and writing about the special challenges of effective administration of adventure education programs.

Starting Your New Outdoor Program

Phil Costello
Project U.S.E.

Many individuals involved in instructing and managing adventure programs reach a point in their career when they consider the possibility of starting their own program. In some cases, usually after being involved with a number of different adventure education programs, and developing different skills along the way, an individual will consider taking on the challenge of starting and managing their own program. In all cases, the start of a program begins with an idea.

THE IDEA STAGE

Many individuals reach a point where they have an idea for a program they would like to develop. Some of these ideas will prove to be solid and should be developed, others will need a lot of adjustment, and still others should be dropped.

How do you know if your idea has a good chance of making it?

1. Develop and write your first program description. Include a clear and specific purpose of your idea, as well as goals and objectives.
2. Put together a list of six to eight people you would like to have review your idea. Send them your written description in advance, then meet with them and discuss your idea in detail. Ask each of these individuals to suggest others who should review your idea.
3. Find out if any groups, organizations, or individuals in your area are already involved in activities similar to your idea.
4. Do some basic research to find out if the services you want to offer are needed.
5. Begin to think about whether or not you want to have one or more partners to help develop your ideas.
6. Review your work thus far and rewrite your program description.

THE ACTION PLAN

If you consider all of the information discussed thus far and you feel ready to further develop your idea, you will need to begin to consider some of the organizational options. There are a wide range of possible ways to structure a program. Following are points to consider regarding four options:

1. Incorporate as a profit-making corporation.

   good points
   - maximum amount of control
   - you could develop a marketable business and eventually sell it at a profit
   - better chance of getting back any personal investment

   bad points
   - very difficult to obtain funding from private foundations
   - some school systems and organizations prefer working with nonprofits
   - will not qualify for surplus food and equipment
   - tax payments

2. Incorporate as a nonprofit corporation.

   good points
   - tax-exempt status
   - donations are tax deductible
   - bulk mailing permit
   - eligible for surplus government food and equipment
   - eligible for private foundation funding
   - high degree of control

   bad points
   - limited lobbying ability
   - Board of Trustees control overall program
   - regulation of earnings and fees
   - if corporation dissolves, all assets must be given to another nonprofit corporation

3. Develop your program under the "umbrella" of a larger organization.

A number of successful organizations were initiated as smaller programs operating under the umbrella of larger existing corporations with the "goal" of eventually "spinning-off" to become their own program. In each state there are a number of private educational corporations that are involved with contracting with the federal and state governments for their services. Once your written program is refined, locate a private educational corporation in your area and present your idea to them. You may want to seek out a corporation with a strong network of contacts that would be helpful to you for developing your program, that may not be heavily involved in experiential education, but is receptive to the concept. This arrangement may be beneficial to the larger corporation by giving them new services to market.

good points
- fairly easy to initiate
- least difficult way to obtain proper insurance coverage
- very efficient way to develop a client market
- highly probable that you will survive first two years
- good intermediate step to being on your own

bad points
- you will not have complete control of your operation
- could be difficult to disengage and "spin-off" on your own, especially if your program is successful

This option has a great deal of potential, but problems can occur if there is not a clear agreement regarding expectations, ownership of assets, long-range planning, and accumulated deficits or surpluses.

4. Develop your idea in a tri-school arrangement.

Sell your idea to three or four schools or a mixture of several schools and a college or university. Base your program in one of the schools and provide services to each school. Develop a "menu" of all the possible program ideas, including services to special needs groups: potential dropouts, disruptive and disabled students.

good points
- client base in central area
- potential for impact
- community-based

bad points
- you would have to sell three schools in same general area
- if one of the schools wouldn't adopt your program, you might have to in corporate
- change in school administration that could change status.

5. Getting off the ground.

Once you determine the direction you want to go with your idea, such as incorporating as a private nonprofit corporation, you will be anxious to get started and will want to jump in with both feet immediately. However, it is recommended that you work one full year prior to going operational. A preferred arrangement would be to have a full-time position and a stable financial base for the year before going on your own.

"Pre-Flight" Checklist

1. If you decide to incorporate, check with state officials to identify all legal requirements for proper compliance. Requirements for profit and nonprofit corporations vary from state to state.

2. Begin to develop an advisory board of key individuals that are interested in your program. Eventually you will want representatives from law, banking, medicine, education, fund-raising, and so on.

3. Develop diverse funding possibilities rather than relying on one or two sources. Explore federal and state sources, private foundations, donations, and client sources for developing an income base.

4. Most private foundations will not support a new organization for several years, but if they think you are a potential candidate for funding, they will watch the progress of your program.

5. Select primary and secondary clients on which you would like to focus.

   - public elementary, middle, and secondary schools
   - independent schools
   - colleges/universities
   - alternate education programs
   - special populations: emotionally disturbed, developmentally disabled, physically handicapped, etc.
   - teacher training
   - juvenile justice system: corrections, probation, residential centers, youth agencies
   - adult and continuing education programs
   - youth groups, clubs, church groups, local recreation programs
   - families, parent/child
   - open enrollment courses for youth/adults
   - corporations: management training, employee courses
   - military organization/units

6. Develop and run a series of 1-day invitational programs that will enable key people, including potential funding sources, to meet and spend time with people to whom you plan to offer services.

7. Do not rely on letters, phone calls, or mailings to establish yourself with clients. Make it a priority to personally meet and spend time with people to whom you plan to offer services.

8. Seek advice from others in the field before preparing your first public relations materials.

9. If you conduct any programs during your pre-flight stage, be sure they are of the highest quality possible. Begin to develop a reputation as a strong, reliable, professional program regardless of the status of your program.

10. Research possible locations where you will be able to conduct your programs—federal land, state parks and forests and private outdoor centers are possible locations. Some private landowners are more than willing to have programs conducted on their property.

11. Approximately a dozen states have a Camp Safety Act Program usually admini stered by the State Department of Health. Check to see if your state has a Camp Safety Act Program, as this will have a major effect on your program.

CONSIDERATIONS

Many outdoor programs that managed to get off the ground did not last long for two primary reasons: (a) lack of capital to invest in starting up the program; (b) poor overall management of the program.

Capital Investment

Obviously, the more money you have to get started, the easier it will be. If your capital is limited and you do not want to take out a bank loan, you can still make it work, but you will need to operate on a strict budget and stick to it. If your capital is limited for start-up, you will need to develop skills for scrounging, bartering, checking out surplus property, and requesting donations from equipment companies.

Management

As your program starts to grow, get to know every aspect inside and out. Find out how much it costs to operate every aspect of your programs so you will be able to make decisions to help you survive. As you discover aspects of program management that you don't enjoy and tend to put off, check yourself to be sure these areas get covered.

Insurance

The insurance market changes every year. During most of the 1980s, it would have been nearly impossible for a new small program to obtain insurance. In 1988, it is currently less difficult, but still not a simple task. A good place to start is by contacting other experiential education programs and talking with their insurance agents. Do some shopping. Check out different-sized programs from various parts of the country. Some states have regulations regarding the minimum amount of liability insurance required to operate an adventure program.

Scrounging

A great deal can be accomplished through scrounging and bartering. Equipment companies, lumber yards, and corporations are generally willing to help but they should be approached personally. While scrounging can prove beneficial, the down side is that it is time-consuming and sometimes needs to be a low priority for the use of your time.

A FINAL WORD

Be willing to take risks! Keep your sense of humor!

Management and Administration of Outdoor Programs

Ron Watters
Idaho State University

Since the heady, hectic days of outdoor programming in the 1960s and 1970s, a slow, maturing process has settled upon the field. The field is still young, of course, and full of promise for meaningful experiences for participants and stimulating job opportunities for professionals. But the field is at a point where most program directors find themselves wearing the hat of an administrator more than that of an outdoor educator.

It's not because those of us in the position dreamed of shuffling papers. Rather, it is a necessity brought on by the changing nature of outdoor education and society. Outdoor employees are seeking reasonable salaries and benefit packages. Participants want quality instruction and services. Upper level administrators ask for travel requisitions, risk management plans, and written justifications of programs. And the law profession continues to cast its menacing shadow over programs.

All of these and more require our attention in an administrative and managerial capacity. And, like any form of management, the style utilized is dictated by the service or product provided. In our case, the service is outdoor recreation, and there are some management procedures and techniques particular to the field that are helpful in running outdoor operations. I won't attempt to cover the entire topic in the limited space of this paper, but I will touch on a few key areas that I've found helpful in my 18 years in the field. One of those areas is the most vexing, yet rewarding parts of outdoor management: personnel.

PERSONNEL MANAGEMENT

The nice thing about outdoor education is that it attracts good people, willing to devote inordinate amounts of their time and energy. Certainly, there are a few misguided souls who would be better off in more sedentary positions. But on the whole, it has been my experience that finding the right people is not the problem. Rather, the challenge of personnel management in outdoor programs is dealing with the over-enthusiastic and eventually over-worked employee.

Outdoor program jobs are far different than the typical working situation of 8 to 5. A staff member might work a full weekend on a backpack trip, then be back in the office on Monday morning . . . and then work several evenings teaching kayaking during the week . . . and then work the next weekend. It's not unusual during the height of ski or summer seasons for an employee to work 4 or 5 weeks without a break.

Upon hearing about such work hours, the standard layman's impression is, "Well, it's easy work. He's just out playing." Certainly it's play, but it's other people's play. And that is the catch. There's a big difference between personal recreation and recreation that is done for the benefit of others. Even in the least structured of all styles of outdoor trips, the common adventure trip, outdoor program staff are burdened with the responsibility of helping guide the democratic process within groups. Democracy even within small groups is never easy, and dealing with personality conflicts within the unsettling environment of the outdoors can be and is wearing. When you're doing it every weekend, it's work.

What is at the heart of the matter is an emotional commitment to the job and the participants. Some trips go smoothly, of course. But others are different. Like a raft with a slow leak, an outdoor staff person staggers home at the end of emotionally demanding trips, flaccid and deflated. Often the next morning they'll be back at the office, cleaning up the van, putting away gear and tying up the loose ends. Throw several of these trips together, and with time, burn out enters the picture and quietly does its damage.

The cure, of course, is time off. Outdoor program directors need to keep an eye on how much their staff is working and watch for signs of burnout. A little time off to enjoy one's own personal recreation or do something different can greatly improve an employee's outlook and productivity.

The method in which time off is given will depend upon the appropriate protocol of the sponsoring institution. In my situation, for years we were able to provide time off on an informal basis. The idea was that if you worked a weekend, you took two days off. Stricter state requirements now require us to record compensation (comp) hours. It is difficult to calculate the number of hours outdoor program employees work when they're on trips, but generally giving eight hours of compensation for each extra day beyond a regular five-day week is accepted as fair. For instance, a person working a weekend trip receives 16 hours of comp time (8 for Saturday and 8 for Sunday). This method requires greater paperwork, but from a procedural standpoint most personnel departments will be more comfortable with it than with informal methods.

It is very important that your superiors, the people who are above your program, understand the amount of time and emotional commitments being put in by your staff. I'll talk about communication with superiors later in the paper, but you need to make a concerted effort to remind those in authority of the good work and dedication put forth by your staff. With this understanding, your superiors can set the record straight to higher administrators.

PROGRAM PLANNING

I don't want to state the obvious, since everyone's fully aware of it. But it won't hurt. Plan carefully. Assiduous planning is the key to a smoothly functioning program. While there are various stratagems that can be employed, I found that two elements greatly assist the process. One is regular staff meetings, and the other is a large calendar with lots of space to write down ideas. The regular staff meeting (once a week) is used to touch base with everyone, to find out how trips went, and to generate ideas for upcoming events.

I would suggest scheduling the planning meeting early in the week, since the staff can make last-minute preparations of activities occurring later that week. For specific days, Monday is okay, but Tuesday is better. Mondays are often poor days since staff members who have just worked the weekend come in to the meeting tired. Tuesday seems to be a much more energetic day, and staff members are more enthusiastic and better inclined toward rolling up their sleeves.

The large planning calendar comes to meetings as well. As ideas are discussed, they are penciled in on the calendar. The calendar serves to remind staff members of events coming up. By using pencil, the calendar is easily altered and updated. When it comes time to print out schedules, the calendar serves as a convenient rough draft.

VOLUNTEER MANAGEMENT

Few in the outdoor program business have the luxury of working with liberal budgets. Often funding is tight and there's little to spare. Thus, methods must be found to stretch hard-earned funding dollars. The use of volunteers is one such method.

Volunteers can serve many functions in an outdoor program. They can help organize and take out trips, run workshops, conduct evening programs, help with programs for people with disabilities, or even assist with office duties. Those with programs at universities have an advantage here. The student population on a college campus serves as a great pool from which young, enthusiastic volunteers can be drawn.

But volunteers don't necessarily always need to be young or come from the campus. Volunteer resources are available in any community. Take evening programs for instance. A good many emergency room doctors are more than happy to do sessions on emergency first aid procedures in the backcountry. A geologist might be interested in doing a program on the geology of a popular climbing area. A member of a nearby ski patrol could likely be talked into doing a program on avalanche safety. Even the local insurance agent might turn out to be a good prospect for a program, particularly one who has just returned from a trek to Annapurna. It is a pleasant marriage. Volunteers are happy to do their program and share their knowledge and skills, and you are happy to have the free offering.

Some volunteers require extra time, particularly those that will be assuming coordinating or leadership positions in the program. Many programs have found the extra time spent training to be well worth the effort. The University of California-San Francisco is an example of a program that provides training for volunteer coordinators in its successful common adventure trip program. Programs for people with disabilities throughout the country provide training courses and utilize volunteers extensively in such programs as skiing, rafting, sailing, horse riding, and so on.

Before unleashing volunteers, let me issue a warning. Volunteers are not a cure-all. Many prospective volunteers are initially enthusiastic, but when the routine work begins, they suddenly disappear. Others are simply unreliable. It takes work to interest the right people, and once the right people are found, it takes more work to cultivate and keep them motivated. Show personal interest in volunteers. Follow up good helpers with phone calls. Invite volunteers to social events, like a pizza evening after a day of ski touring, or the annual Christmas party at the end of the year.

People who volunteer do so not only for the personal satisfaction of helping others. There are other reasons, and often it is the other reasons that are most important. They may have a need to be part of a group. They may get an ego boost from being in a leadership position. Or they may enjoy the extra recognition and prestige that comes from leading. It is an understanding of these other motivations that can help you keep volunteers on-track and enthusiastic. One point to remember is to always give recognition. Don't be afraid to be profuse. Making the extra effort to compliment and say thanks over and over will pay many dividends. If you keep that in mind, you'll have a windfall of volunteer help in your program.

RECORDKEEPING

There's little joy in it, this recordkeeping business. Nobody looks forward to it, but directors of outdoor programs more than anyone need to keep good records. There are reasons. Good recordkeeping shows a level of sophistication. By having data on participation, results of participation satisfaction surveys, or an analysis of costs and benefits, you are in a much better position to justify the expenditure of funds for your program. Programs with no records or poorly tabulated participation figures appear—even though they might not be—loosely organized and poorly run.

Recordkeeping need not be taxing as long as it is done on a regular basis. I utilize the weekly staff meeting as a time to keep records up-to-date. While the staff meeting is underway, a master data sheet can be passed around and members of the staff can update their entries for the past week. A variety of records can be kept, but at the very least, good participation records should be maintained. Even if your sponsoring agency or institution doesn't require one, prepare an annual report with total numbers of participants and information on the year's highlights.

The journal method is one way of collecting records and information as the year progresses. The journal, which is basically a scrapbook, can include participation figures, copies of news releases, photographs from trips and complimentary letters from participants. At the end of the year, the annual report can be easily prepared by paging through the journal and picking out significant events. The journal, if left in a prominent place in the outdoor office, also serves as a good promotional tool. People stopping in at the office invariably pick it up and page through it.

THE POLITICS OF OUTDOOR PROGRAMMING

The smoky, sultry world of politics is probably the last arena in which an outdoor program director wants to get involved. But the political arena described here is not that sultry kind, nor is it the kind that involves the surreptitious jockeying and power positioning that sometimes takes place within the bureaucracy of institutions. Rather, this is about its more subtle form: the wise, tactful, and artful way of getting things done.

When you are in charge of an outdoor program, the tactfulness of your approach often means the difference between good administrative support and poor administrative support. Or, put more practically, it's the difference between a good budget and a poor budget.

Artful politics involves the understanding of power structures within institutions. One way of categorizing institutional power is to look at it from the perspective of two dimensions (Banning & Sherman, 1988). One dimension is authoritarian power. Authoritarian power is that which is assigned by the institution. The power that your superior possesses to hire, to supervise you, or to approve your budgets has been given to that person by the institution. Most institutions have flow charts showing the network and chain of command of authoritarian power.

The other dimension of power, influential power, is not assigned by the institution. This is the kind of power that comes through personality, tact, and persistence. It also comes through friendly contacts, respect for work, and logical and compelling proposals. And if it is carefully nurtured and used, influential power can effect positive change.

Outdoor programs are always low on the authoritarian power scale. This is never more obvious than by looking at the institutional flow chart, where the rectangular box housing the outdoor program often appears at the bottom of the page—if it appears at all. It is, then, influential power that must be utilized by outdoor program directors. The development and use of influence doesn't happen overnight. It takes time.

What is important is that you understand your institution's protocols, the chain of command in which you fit, and which individuals in that chain are the key people. Keep supervisors, especially your immediate supervisor, informed of your program's activities. When supervisors hear from you on a regular basis, they become comfortable and stay comfortable with your program. That's the way you want supervisors to be. If they are not familiar with the program, you'll have little support when the chips are down.

Administrators higher in the chain of command are more difficult to reach. But nevertheless, you should take advantage of occasional opportunities to make contact when they present themselves. If the community newspaper runs a complimentary article on your program, you may wish to send a higher administrator a copy of the article. Supervisors and presidents like good press—and good mail. When you have enthusiastic participants who just had a wonderful time on a trip, have them drop a line to the president.

Sometimes help comes from unexpected corners. Our program occasionally runs climbing demonstrations for high schools around the area. At one of the out-of-town demonstrations, we learned that a teacher who helped organize the event was a state senator on a key legislative committee. When we found this out, we asked if he wouldn't mind dropping a line to our immediate supervisor and the president of the university. He didn't mind, and wound up writing a complimentary missive on legislative letterhead.

As a postscript to the story, I recently submitted a proposal for extra funding that will be considered by the president of our university. The extra funds are sorely needed in our program for people with disabilities. Will the letter from the legislator help us? You bet it will.

Become familiar with how decisions are made in your institution. When developing funding proposals, start with your immediate supervisor and work up through those above. You'll find that there are appropriate times and routes to take. Much of how you tailor your approach will be guided by your experience and by the experiences of those who have been in the system for a long time. Persistence is the key. You'll be unsuccessful more times than you are successful, but keep coming up with ideas and trying them out. Eventually, something will click, and you'll have a success. With time and a little luck. you will be able to increase the budget, provide better pay for your staff, and improve services to your participants. That's when playing politics becomes worth all the trouble.

REFERENCE

Banning, J. H., & Sherman, R. (1988). The politics of change: A different view of working together. *ACU-I Bulletin,* November, 4.

Beyond Minimum Competencies: Toward an Integrated Model of Staff Growth and Development

Douglass P. Teschner

&

John J. Wolter
The Wilderness School

If the laborer gets no more than his employer pays him, he is cheated, he cheats himself.

(Henry David Thoreau, 1971, p. 357)

The hiring, training, and supervision of staff are among the functions of experiential education program administrators. It is our belief that these functionally separate tasks are philosophically integrated. This paper is a discussion of their interconnectedness and relationship to program quality.

THE ISSUE OF COMPETENCIES: MINIMUM VS. IDEAL

Before one can effectively hire, train, or supervise staff, it is essential to designate appropriate qualifications, be they certifications, theoretical knowledge, skills, experience, and/or personal characteristics (including attitudes and behaviors). The model most often used in experiential education is delineation of "minimum competencies" that are desired and/or necessary for employment. While the minimum competency model has proven useful for administrators and staff alike, it has several associated problems.

First, the use of minimum competencies necessitates that there be some means of agreement upon whether or not a given minimum has been achieved. Unfortunately, those competencies that are easiest to demonstrate and/or measure—and, therefore, the most likely to be selected—tend also to be the most trivial. For example, it is relatively simple to become certified in first aid, but quite another matter to be able to effectively manage an emergency medical situation in a remote wilderness area. Certification is a widely used minimum competency, while the latter (and far more important) skill is difficult to measure and, thus, rarely used as an employment prerequisite.

Second, the rigid adherence to designated minimum competencies may foster a "black box" perspective on the hiring process. Every individual is unique and may possess strengths that could prove valuable to the program—even though they do not appear on the minimums list and may, therefore, be ignored by the person doing the hiring. Further, the use of a minimum competency "checklist" fails to consider the synergistic interaction of competencies: An individual may fail to possess a required qualification, but his or her combined strengths in other areas will often more than compensate. For example, a mature individual with extensive life experiences may prove very effective in working with troubled youth despite having no prior experience with this population.

Third, the designation of minimums may foster an attitude that, once the minimums are achieved, no further development is necessary. As a result, program mediocrity may be inadvertently promoted.

Lastly, the minimum competency model is useful for hiring and pre-service training, but of limited value for inservice training and supervision. Although the addition of "advanced" competencies could eliminate or reduce both this and the previous concern, we sought instead a model that would be more comprehensive and would also eliminate the first two problem areas.

It is our experience with hiring and training staff that it is far more useful to focus on "ideal" rather than "minimum" competencies. We begin our thinking by defining as comprehensively as possible the characteristics and qualifications of the theoretical "perfect staff member."

Ultimately, each organization must define its own ideals for each of the various types of positions for which it hires. In the case of our programs, which primarily serve youth with special needs, we hire staff for a variety of positions including classroom teachers, vocational instructors, dormitory parents, and wilderness trip leaders. Wilderness staff lead canoe and backpacking expeditions of 2 to 8 weeks in duration to the Florida Everglades, Southern Appalachians, New Mexico's Gila Wilderness, New Hampshire's White Mountains, and other areas. Trips incorporate experiential learning of academic subjects and outdoor skills, teamwork and group dynamics, and individual and group counseling. As a specific example of designated ideals, we offer a generic description of the perfect qualifications of the trip leader.

THE IDEAL WILDERNESS TRIP LEADER

We have found it useful to classify the ideal characteristics and qualifications in five broad categories: personal characteristics, experience, skills, theoretical knowledge, and certificates.

Personal Characteristics

- Sound judgment (the ability to proactively evaluate situations, promote student well-being, and prevent accidents; wisdom)
- Integrity (high standards; consistency)
- Desire to learn (open-mindedness; curiosity; openness to experience and constructive criticism; willingness to follow directions)
- Sense of adventure (willingness to be vulnerable)
- High self-image (self-knowledge and confidence)
- Charisma (ability to inspire others)
- Flexibility (adaptability, patience, tolerance for ambiguity)
- Commitment and energy (desire and ability to work hard and long hours)
- Initiative and self-reliance
- Persistence (can accept defeat as well as victory; unflappable; steady; motivated)
- Compassion (caring; wanting to help; nonjudgmental attitude; respect for the individual)
- Cooperative outlook (desire and ability to work with others)
- Ability to communicate effectively
- Willingness to accept responsibility (and concurrent accountability)
- Awareness (perceptive; able to anticipate)
- Creativity (able to be innovative)
- Sense of humor (able to laugh at self)
- Maturity
- Healthiness and physical fitness
- Positive role model
- Personal philosophy congruent with the program's

Experience

- Wilderness (broad-based, including expeditions of two weeks or longer in varied seasons and terrain; solo experiences)
- Leadership (especially wilderness expeditions with special needs youth)
- Rescue and emergency first aid (applied in real-life situations)
- Teaching (especially that which is experiential in nature)
- Counseling (group and individual)
- Child care (residential experience with troubled youth)
- Prior employment experience in our programs
- Prior experience at trip locale (for example, Florida Everglades)

Skills

- Wilderness (campcraft, hiking, canoeing, etc.—in excess of level necessary for execution of trip)
- Leadership (ability to direct and motivate others)
- Health and safety (first aid, cardiopulmonary resuscitation, and wilderness medicine; lifesaving and water safety)
- Teaching (curriculum and lesson plan development and implementation)
- Counseling (attending skills; processing behavior; generalization of gains; internalization of behavior; problem-solving and resolution techniques; enhancement of self-esteem)
- Child care (crisis de-escalation; physical restraint)
- Organizational (logistics)
- Interpersonal communications (including conflict resolution)
- Writing (reports)
- Driving

Theoretical Knowledge

- Wilderness (navigation, meteorology, etc.)
- Leadership (philosophy; psychology; alternative models)
- Health and safety (including nutrition, personal hygiene, use of medications, etc.)
- Teaching (experiential education theory; theoretical knowledge of subjects being taught on trips)
- Counseling (philosophy; alternative models)
- Child care (philosophy; rationale for crisis de-escalation and restraint)
- Adolescent development (including psychopathology and the nature of behavioral change)
- Trip site locale (potential safety hazards; prevailing local standards; administrative agencies)
- Philosophy, policies and procedures of Becket Academy

Certificates

- College degree (science background preferred)
- First aid: Emergency Medical Technician (preferred) or American Red Cross Advanced or Standard First Aid
- CPR: current certificate
- Water safety: American Red Cross Water Safety Instructor (preferred) or Advanced Lifesaving
- Canoeing: American Red Cross Basic Canoeing
- Safe driving record

It may appear that there are redundancies in this listing. For example, the term "wilderness" appears under the categories experience, skills, and theoretical knowledge. We believe that such distinctions become very important when this model is applied to reality. As an example, we might interview a number of individuals who can talk extensively about rock climbing (and thus possess much theoretical knowledge), are able to tie knots (thus possess at least one relevant skill), but have never done a multi-pitch climb (thus lack significant experience). As a general rule, experience is a far more valuable indication of competency than skill alone, which is in turn more valuable than theoretical knowledge. Further, those who have experience usually (but not always) also possess the associated skills and theory.

As for certificates, we believe that such "paper" qualifications are useful for credibility, but of limited relevance to program effectiveness. Usually certificates are very narrow in scope. A further issue is described by Tom Lyman:

> The very obvious problem with certification ...is that there is really no way for the school or certifying agency to honestly evaluate, or guarantee, the instructor's capability, effectiveness, or sound judgment *in truly difficult situations*. (1981, p. 33)

We further believe that, as experience is usually more significant than skill, knowledge, or certification, personal characteristics are more important than experience. In our view, personal characteristics are, in fact, derived from experience (and associated reflection). While such characteristics may have some genetic basis, we nevertheless believe they can be acquired given the appropriate commitment and circumstances. Further, our use of the concept "personal characteristics" refers only to those traits that are highly internalized and thus emerge intuitively. We do not consider behavior or attitudes that are superficial or expressed in a highly conscious manner to be true personal characteristics.

BEYOND THE IDEAL: ACKNOWLEDGING PROGRAM REALITIES

Unfortunately, an inevitable initial reaction to defined ideals is dismay. While there are individuals who possess some (or many) of the individual qualifications, the person who has them all is, of course, nonexistent. This being the case, how can one run quality programs without such perfect leaders? The answers are several.

First, it is important to accept that we live in a *real* world; no human endeavor is ideal, so it is unrealistic to expect anything different from outdoor programming. At the same time, however, it is essential to make every effort to approach the ideal as closely as possible. The ideal must be viewed as the ultimate goal. Effective leadership necessitates this dualistic perspective: accepting the real, striving toward the ideal.

Second, we hire the very best staff available, placing special emphasis upon personal characteristics and experience. We also look for staff who seem especially keen to learn and grow, and thus have long-term potential.

Third, we try to be flexible as regards the specifics of a given wilderness trip and its associated activities. It is our belief that programs can be most effectively built upon the qualifications of available staff rather than trying to rigidly fit staff to existing job descriptions and programs. We try to design trips that allow staff to fully utilize their strengths.

Fourth, we attempt to match staff with those having complementary strengths so that each trip's staff *as a whole* more closely approaches the ideal. As noted by Bert Horwood (1983, p. 26), this technique is applied in other programs as well.

Fifth, we believe it is essential to recognize that staff competency is only one of a myriad of factors that contribute to program success. Other variables that can be administratively manipulated include the quality and quantity of supervision, the availability of support services (such as boat captains or seaplanes), organizational policies and procedures (especially quality and comprehensiveness), advanced trip planning, equipment (for example, availability of a two-way radio), local knowledge of the trip area, the nature of the trip (i.e., land-based vs. water-based), the nature of the individual students (sex, age, emotionally disturbed versus mentally retarded, etc.), the number of students and staff-student ratio, the length of the trip, the location of the trip, the nature of the itinerary (i.e., 15 versus 8 mile days), and the trip goals and activities (i.e., academic versus recreational vs. therapeutic emphasis; long-term wilderness expeditions versus short-term wilderness experiences coupled with historical or ecological field trips).

Sixth, we train staff to become more effective and thus come closer to approaching the ideal. It is this final area of augmenting program effectiveness upon which we will focus in the remainder of this paper.

STAFF DEVELOPMENT: A CRITICAL COMPONENT OF SUCCESS

Our broad perspective on staff development extends into the domain of organizational development (which "has organizational change as its explicit, central focus and sees the change of individuals through training as a means of organizational change" [Lynton & Pareek, 1967, p. 46]). For our purposes, we have defined staff development as an organization's efforts to promote employee growth: more specifically, helping staff move beyond present competencies toward perceived ideals.

The use of the word "perceived" requires some discussion. A central question is who does the perceiving: the supervisor or the individual staff member? In our case, we most often design pre-service training efforts to meet specific organizational goals, but—as a staff member continues with the organization—increasingly shift the goal-setting burden to the staff member.

In either case, clarity about goals is important (see, for example, Aaker, 1981, p. 28) and staff need to feel that training is tied to their needs (Weick, 1979, p. 7). Involving staff in the planning process (including informal needs assessment) invariably creates a climate of trust: In this sense, the process is as important as the product. But we also feel that it is essential to move beyond organizational goal clarity and the process of staff involvement to helping staff clarify their individual goals and needs. Who do they want to be? What do they want to become?

Initially, most staff are threatened by this empowering perspective. Despite our national preoccupation with the abstract concept of freedom, people generally seem most comfortable when they are told—directly or indirectly—what to do, how to act, and what their goals and values should be. But as we develop ongoing relationships with staff members we are usually successful in catalyzing them to confront these existential questions.

As an organization we benefit from a staff member's self-knowledge since he or she is better able to decide if personal goals are congruent with the organization's (and thus whether this line of work is personally appropriate). As Hersey and Blanchard observe, "the closer...the individual's goals and objectives to the organization's goals, the greater will be the organizational performance" (1969, p. 117).

The wide-ranging and comprehensive nature of our previously stated description of the ideal leader is advantageous since its diversity allows each individual staff member latitude to select specific areas where he or she wants to develop. For example, an individual may decide that he or she really wants to become effective in counseling—a competency congruent with the needs of our wilderness program. It is, of course, essential that communications between staff and supervisor are open with the goals of each clear to the other. There is also a need for collaboration and negotiation that involves some degree of give-and-take, since rarely will individual and organizational goals be perfectly synonymous.

Once the goals are clarified, the staff development process is designed to achieve them. But, before proceeding to the specifics of our staff development model, it will be worthwhile to enumerate several of the assumptions upon which it is based.

First, people intrinsically want to learn and grow and do their very best. This positive and optimistic view of human nature, which has gained increasing acceptance in the latter part of this century, is rooted in the work of Carl Rogers and other humanistic psychologists.

Second, ongoing staff growth is regarded as essential to program success. As Roland Barth observes, "when teachers stop growing so do their students" (1980, p. 147).

Third, ongoing realization of personal growth is intrinsically more important to staff than pay and other benefits. This assumption is rooted in the work of Abraham Maslow and Frederick Herzberg. It is somewhat surprising that our highly developed society continues to rely on "low level" physical and security needs as primary motivators (Aaker, 1981, p. 32).

A parenthetical issue related to these first three assumptions is the much-discussed "staff burnout." We wonder if this phenomenon is less a result of long working hours and high demands than of an absence of ongoing personal growth. Our suspicion is that staff only burn out when they stop feeling that they are growing.

A fourth assumption is that learning occurs in a myriad of ways, both anticipated and spontaneous.

Fifth, program administrators can significantly enhance staff growth (as well as other organizational change efforts) by "a proactive planning model based on a clear statement of what we want to cause to happen rather than a reactive problem identification/solution model" (Aaker, 1981, p. 5). More specifically, administrators can develop situations in which spontaneous learning is likely to occur, create opportunities for staff to reflect upon and assimilate learning, and plan and implement staff development programs. To achieve these aims, we offer the following model.

AN INTEGRATED STAFF DEVELOPMENT MODEL

We envision staff development in a broader context than that in which it is generally perceived. This comprehensive model incorporates three major subcomponents: experience, supervision, and formal training.

Experience

While experiential learning methodologies can—and should—be utilized in formal training programs, our use of the term "experience" refers specifically to on-the-job learning (including pre-trip planning). Our approach is consistent with what Lynton and Pareek (1967) describe as the "activity strategy," except that we have broadened it to incorporate every aspect of an employee's involvement with the organization (with the exception of supervision and formal training).

It is not without irony that educational programs extolling the virtue of experience for their clients often fail to recognize its significance for training staff. This is not to say that the value of experiential learning is unappreciated. After visiting a number of experiential education programs, Horwood observed that, "learning is definitely not confined to the clients" (1983, p. 26). Further, the practice of pairing new staff with veterans (who act as mentors and role models) is very common.

It is our belief, however, that the role of experience in staff development is often understated and thus its potential effectiveness not fully realized. Further, even high-quality experiences do not result in learning unless complemented by equally high-quality reflection.

We believe that experiential learning is enhanced if supervisors set high standards and clear expectations, develop a climate of trust, and are both caring and accepting of the individuals with whom they work. The most effective supervisors have a "sixth sense" that enables them to accurately predict the degree of responsibility that each of their staff is capable of assuming. Through such programmed success, a supervisor both achieves the organization's goals and enhances employee learning and self-esteem.

On their part, staff can maximize their own experiential growth by being accepting of responsibility, motivated to learn, willing to take risks and be vulnerable, and able to internally reflect upon and process their experiences. The essential trait of being open to experience requires a lack of defensiveness (see, for example, Carl Rogers' description of the "fully functioning person," 1969, pp. 278-297).

But as our colleague Earle Fox observes, "the very ability to have experience at all and make rational sense of it is becoming increasingly marginal for many people" (1983, p. 3). While we recognize this statement as characteristic of many youth, it is also true—to a significant degree—of most adults as well. In this regard, experience as the sole form of staff development often fails: Staff are not always able to fully extrapolate lessons from even the most potentially useful learning experiences. It is in this respect that supervision—the second component of our staff development model—takes on increased importance.

Supervision

Unfortunately, supervision has a bad reputation, in part—we believe—because of the common failure to make clear distinctions among its various subcomponents. We have found it helpful to distinguish between two major types of supervision.

We call the first type "directive" supervision. This model is hierarchical, involving a traditional superior-subordinate relationship between the supervisor and staff member. The supervisor makes the decisions and gives clear and explicit instructions to staff. If they are not successfully carried out, appropriate actions by the supervisor include reprimand, punishment, or—in a severe case—firing.

The second type we call "collegial" supervision, borrowing the term used by Dr. A. Peter Mattaliano. (Alternatively, Morris Cogan (1973) uses the adjective "clinical.") The supervisor and staff member are engaged in a mutually supportive, dialogical relationship in which they work jointly to develop and achieve the staff member's goals as consistent with organizational needs (see earlier discussion). Collegial supervision necessitates a climate of mutual trust in which neither partner feels threatened and both are thus able to move beyond the all-too-common "primitive quality of human relationships" (Barth, 1980, p.170). As Cogan observes, the collegial supervisor must "learn to recognize the springs of his own behavior" (1973, p. 43), and acknowledge "the imperative for openness, flexibility, and examined judgments" (p. 41). The effective collegial supervisor is able to catalyze the internal reflection process in staff members, helping each one develop an ability to process experience *without* such assistance. Collegial supervision is a time-consuming process and an exacting skill that demands a high level of "disciplined intuition" (Cogan, 1973, p. 146).

But which type of supervision—directive or collegial—is most appropriate? The most effective supervisor is able to employ both modes—and know which one is more appropriate in a given situation. As a general rule, the collegial model serves the needs of both the organization and staff, while the directive approach only serves the former. Ultimately, of course, it is the organization to which the supervisor owes primary allegiance. Thus there are situations when the supervisor must act appropriately to protect the program and clients—even if this is counterproductive to the needs of the staff. The directive model is appropriate when the program is in crisis or otherwise seriously compromised (in the case of wilderness programs, most notably as regards issues of health and safety).

We do not mean to suggest that staff do not grow by being reprimanded or even fired. Instead we are arguing that a model of collegial supervision is generally a more harmonious and efficient way to achieve ongoing staff development. It is our suspicion that many supervisors have a limited "bag of tricks" and thus employ directive methods in instances where the collegial model would be far more effective in achieving their ends. For example, the regular use of reprimands tends to create a defensive posture: Unless the staff member has a high degree of openness to experience, personal growth is not an immediate byproduct.

The distinction between directive and collegial supervision is blurred in the model described by Ken Blanchard in the best-seller, *The One Minute Manager*. Although the one minute manager is philosophically allied with the collegial supervisor, the use of "one minute reprimands" is a creative integration of both the directive and collegial philosophies. Such a reprimand incorporates specific criticism followed by a humanistic affirmation of the individual's strengths and capabilities.

Formal (written) evaluation is yet another supervision technique. While this may serve the need to maintain records on employee performance, we agree with Barth that, "it has only a limited influence upon staff development" (1980, p. 167).

Formal Training

Formal training programs are the third staff development strategy. In addition to providing concrete learning, training sessions foster team-building by creating an opportunity for staff to informally interact. Effective training programs are well-conceived and planned (see, for example, Wood, Thompson, and Russell, 1981), and tied to program realities.

Consideration must be made to what Joyce and Showers call "level of impact" (1980, p. 380): Is the desired outcome issue awareness? Understanding of theoretical concepts? Skill acquisition? Trainers commonly fail to make these distinctions. For example, it is possible to "cover" vast amounts of material (what Lynton and Pareek [1967] describe as an "academic strategy"), but it should never be assumed that, "participants can translate the abstract generalizations into improving their actual performance in concrete real-life situation" (p. 41). Lectures or discussions can make staff aware of issues related to, for example, coastal navigation, and may even promote theoretical understanding. But it is improbable that a lecture will result in *skill* acquisition or the ability to apply the knowledge to program contexts.

In planning training programs, it is essential to clarify and narrow staff development objectives to those that can be realistically achieved in the time available. Specific activities must be designed to meet the objectives. Weick (1979) describes a number of possibilities, including lectures, open forum discussions, performance tryouts, brainstorming, agenda-setting buzz groups, fishbowls, demonstrations, structured discussions, and roleplays. Critical incidents are another technique we have used with much success.

It is also important to distinguish between pre-service and inservice training programs. The former are useful for team-building, developing an awareness of organizational policies and procedures (especially in conjunction with prior reading of the program's staff manual), introducing theoretical knowledge, and teaching low-level skills (for example, CPR, if not previously acquired). But, unless staff have prior experience in a similar program (or other relevant life experience), it is unlikely that pre-service training can achieve significant assimilation of information or higher-level learning. In terms of realization of staff growth, pre-service training is usually very limited in impact.

Programs for veteran staff (inservice) are likely to be more effective—as regards acquisition of more sophisticated knowledge and higher-level competencies—since they build upon an experiential base. It is our belief that presentation of theory is most relevant when it follows experience—even though our nationwide educational structure is based upon the opposite sequence.

Effective inservice programs incorporate the analysis of experience either explicitly (for example, through group discussions) or implicitly. As an example of the latter, a lecture on a particularly relevant topic may stimulate internalized reflection.

STAFF DEVELOPMENT SYNERGY

But which of these three components—experience, supervision, and formal training—is most important? To answer this question, we must return to our earlier discussion of the ideal staff member. You will recall that as a general rule, we recognized personal characteristics, experience, skills, theoretical knowledge, and certifications in descending order of significance as regards the effectiveness of a staff member. Unfortunately, we believe that the relative ease of an organization to empower qualifications and competencies is in inverse relationship to their importance (see Figure 1).

This suggests that formal training efforts—being limited in time duration—may be effective in achieving certifications, theoretical knowledge, and (possibly) skills—but cannot realistically achieve higher-level competencies. As we stated previously, the development of personal characteristics evolves from experience—thus it comes as no surprise that this strategy (which requires the most time and energy) is most likely to achieve higher ends. Experience is so important, in fact, that it is not only a means, but also an end in itself!

We are not suggesting that formal training programs be eliminated—they are, indeed, valuable. But the real answer to the question of which strategy works best subsumes all three possibilities. While each strategy alone is useful, the synergy of employing all three will achieve the highest level of staff growth. Experience is the most important of the three, but necessitates quality reflection—which can be enhanced through supervision. A preservice training program is an excellent opportunity to explain the supervisory process, thus enhancing its effectiveness. Specific on-the-job experiences may suggest a need for particular skills, which can in turn be introduced in an inservice program. In this manner, the three strategies enhance and support each other, sustaining a whole that is more than the sum of its parts.

CONCLUSION

Implementation of an integrated model of staff development requires significant energy and commitment. As Wood, Thompson, and Russell observe:

> Professional growth is a complex, human task. It requires a climate conducive to learning and change. It is based upon clear goals and objectives derived from careful needs assessment. It is promoted by the effective use of diverse resources. It includes opportunities for field-testing, feedback, and adjustment. All these things take time to achieve. (1981, p. 88)

Anything less, however, prevents programs from achieving their full potential.

Our argument extends beyond the domain of staff development: At a higher level we are suggesting a philosophical basis for supervisor-staff relationships. If we want our programs to achieve the highest level possible, we must constantly act to enssure that our staff achieve their highest levels. Staff development must be integral to the functioning of the supervisor, permeating all thinking about hiring, training, and supervising staff—as well as other program decisions that will impact on them. As for the supervisor's development, we see it as essentially the synergy of the staff's growth and achievement.

REFERENCES

Aaker, J. B. (1981). *School teams using planned change as an educational strategy.* Coral Gables, FL: United States Office of Education Region IV Resource Center, University of Miami.

Barth, R. S. (1980). *Run school run.* Cambridge, MA: Harvard University.

Blanchard, K. H. (1983). *The one-minute manager.* New York: Berkley Books.

Cogan, M. L. (1973). *Clinical supervision.* Boston, MA: Houghton-Mifflin.

Fox, F. E. (1983). The spiritual core of experiential education. *Journal of Experiential Education, 6*, 3-6.

Hersey, P., & Blanchard, K. H. (1969). *Management of organizational behavior: Utilizing human resources.* Englewood Cliffs, NJ: Prentice-Hall.

Horwood, B. (1983). Southwestern sojourn. *Journal of Experiential Education, 6*, 23-26.

Joyce, B., & Showers, B. (1980). Improving inservice training: The messages of research. *Educational Leadership, 37*, 379-385.

Lyman, T. G. (1981). Safety the paramount concern: Evaluating outdoor personnel. *National Association of Secondary School Principals Bulletin*, February, 31-36.

Lynton, R. P., & Pareek, U. (1967). *Training for development.* Homewood, IL: R. D. Irwin.

Mattaliano, A. P. *Self-help for teachers: collegial supervision in urban schools.* Unpublished manuscript, University of Massachusetts.

Rogers, C. R. (1969). *Freedom to learn.* Columbus, OH: Charles E. Merrill.

Thoreau, H. D. (1971). *Walden and other writings.* J. W. Krutch (ed). New York: Bantam.

Wieck, C. (1979). Training and development of staff: Lessons from Business and Industry. *Education Unlimited,* September, 6-13.

Wood, F. H., Thompson, S. R.; & Russell, F. (1981). Designing effective staff development programs. *Staff development/ organizational development.* Alexandria, VA: Association for Supervision and Curriculum Development.

The Contractual Process

Michael C. Strong
University of Oregon

In 1976, the International City Managers Association found that only 11 percent of California cities had contracted recreation services to the private sector. In 1979, a study by California State University at Hayward revealed that 81 percent of the 216 cities, counties, and special districts responding to the survey were involved in the contracting process. What happened? The passage of Proposition 13 resulted in sharply decreased financial resources, forcing program administrators to seek creative solutions. "Contracting out" has emerged as a good vehicle for enhancing program scope and quality, for transferring liability costs and risks, and for maintaining a stable level of service during these times of financial constraint.

A contract is a formal agreement between two parties and involves the performance of specific promises in return for consideration, usually expressed in dollar values (Kaiser, 1986).

Contracts may be "limited" or short-term, or "extended." This article focuses upon the preparation, implementation, and evaluation of short-term contracts, with emphasis upon their applicability to adventure education specialists seeking to employ this alternative method for diversifying program offerings. The following lists explain the advantages and disadvantages of contracting out:

ADVANTAGES OF CONTRACTING OUT

1. Possible to transfer the liability costs and risks to another party, making contracting out well-suited to high-risk activities.

2. Safe, high-quality experiences or activities can be provided by qualified professionals, when the necessary expertise is not available "in house."

3. It is possible to increase program scope, especially into areas requiring specialized equipment (such as sailboats, scuba gear, etc.).

4. The contractor assumes a percentage of the administrative responsibilities and problems, permitting an agency's employees to more efficiently direct their energies toward the performance of other tasks.

5. Competition between contractors for the provision of services and/or equipment may keep the cost of activities or experiences down.

6. The investment of capital funds for facility improvements (e.g., the construction of a climbing wall or ropes course) or for the purchase of high-cost equipment is not required.

7. The storage, inventory, repair and replacement of supplies and equipment is not required.

8. Efficient use may be made of community resources. In addition, public relations between the public agency and the private sector may be enhanced.

DISADVANTAGES OF CONTRACTING OUT

1. Insofar as the control of an experience or activity is assumed by a contractor, some control is lost by the contracting agency. Program quality may be compromised unless effective evaluation processes are employed.

2. Fluctuations in insurance rates (and other as yet unforeseen economic circumstances) may reduce or eliminate a contractor's ability to acquire and maintain the insurance coverage demanded in the bid specifications, or to remain competitive.

3. Individuals capable of effectively implementing the contractual process may not be employed by an agency interested in contracting out.

4. The cost of an experience or activity may rise to an undesirable or impractical level if there is a lack of competition in the marketplace.

5. The potential exists for the monopolization of a market by one contractor. Healthy public relations may be sacrificed if it appears that there may be bias in the selection process.

6. If the contractor fails to fulfill the agreed-upon promise(s), an experience or course may have to be terminated at an inconvenient time. Furthermore, the solving of problems that may arise throughout the term of the contract may require more employee time and energy than the time-saving benefits anticipated by entering into the contract.

7. State statutes and charters or local regulations and agency policies may limit (or prohibit) an agency's ability to contract out.

The Outdoor Pursuits Program at the University of Oregon has weighed the advantages and disadvantages of contracting out and has been able to utilize short-term contracts to expand a respected, diverse program in the face of externally imposed budgetary constraints. Currently, 48 percent of all outdoor pursuits courses depend upon contractual services and/or goods. Contracting out enables the Outdoor Pursuits Program to offer activities that would not otherwise be a part of the program, without compromising either program philosophy, or the safety and quality of outdoor experiences.

All water-based outdoor activities including white-water rafting, kayaking, canoeing, windsurfing, sailing, and river rescue techniques involve a contract of some kind. In most cases, limited contracts are established for the rental of water-based goods and/or equipment. The Outdoor Pursuits Program maintains control over the instructional processes by providing its own instructors.

Where an outside agency is capable of providing more qualified instructors, the contract for professional services may specify course content, teaching methods, educational goals and objectives, and evaluation processes.

THE LEGAL AUTHORITY TO CONTRACT OUT

The authority for public agencies to enter into contracts is derived from the sovereignty of the state. "Local governments are customarily given a general power to contract which is ordinarily interpreted to authorize all contracts necessary to accomplish the purposes and objectives of the local government unit as expressed in the state constitution, state laws, or corporate charter" (Kozlowski, 1982, p. 28). State statutes will determine if a contract is even necessary for the provision of services and/or goods. The state of Maryland, for example, requires that a written contract be made once expenditures for supplies, materials, equipment, construction of public improvements, or contractual services exceeds $1,000. Most statutes or charters also require that a general appropriation, sufficient to cover the cost of the provision of the requested services and/or goods, precede the contract.

Statutes or charters will also determine the requirements for competitive bidding, the purpose of which is to "benefit the taxpayer by securing competition and guarding against favoritism, improvidence, extravagance or corruption" (cited in Kozlowski, 1982, p. 32). Most statutes declare that public advertising for bids and competitive bidding are required for every contract that exceeds a specified aggregate dollar value. Where competitive bidding is compulsory, most statutes or charters also demand that bidding agencies be given adequate notice as to the kind and nature of the contract so that they may more capably prepare bid proposals.

In many states the process of "competitive negotiation" supersedes that of competitive bidding for contracts involving the provision of professional services. As opposed to an objective evaluation of sealed bids, the process of competitive negotiation involves the public agency bargaining separately with the three most qualified bidding agencies, commencing with the most qualified and proceeding to the others. Statutes may also declare that the award of a contract shall be to the agency submitting the lowest bid, unless it is found that the bidder is "not responsible" (i.e., does not have the experience, skill, ability, or capacity, etc., to satisfactorily perform the tasks stated in the bid specifications). In cases where the agency submitting the lowest bid is denied the contract, this bidder must be informed as to why the bid was rejected.

Since state statutes and charters prescribe the mode of contracting, it is essential for the adventure education specialist to have a working knowledge of the specific legal framework within which the contractual process is administered. Without an understanding of the basic principles of public contract law, a public agency may be exceeding its authority to enter into contracts, or may be planting the seeds for the development of future legal problems. Remember that a valid contract exhibits the following characteristics: "1) mutual consent of the parties to be bound by their agreement, offer and acceptance; 2) an exchange of promises or performance having legal significance, the basis of the bargain referred to as consideration; 3) no defenses which preclude contract formation such as fraud or duress" (Kozlowski, 1982, p. 30).

PREPARATION, ADMINISTRATION, AND EVALUATION

With the legal framework (within which contracts are administered) understood, the adventure education specialist is ready to prepare the preliminary documents of the contractual process. These documents may vary depending on the policies for contract administration in place within an organization. It is essential, however, that as a whole they:

(a) clearly convey the bid specifications, (b) outline the expectations of the contract parties with respect to each other's performance, (c) establish the basis for conflict resolution should problems arise during the term of the contract, (d) provide concise and clear information and directions (for bid proposal submission) to bidding agencies, (e) assist in the objective evaluation of bid submissions, and (f) eliminate the potential for problems (and/or legal confrontations) through the implementation of a legal and binding contract. These documents should be prepared with simplicity and economy of effort in mind. The slogan, "prior planning prevents poor performance" should be kept in mind throughout the process. The documents of the Alpine Ski Program contract at the University of Oregon are offered as examples of one approach that fulfills the above criteria.

The purpose of the Bid Specifications Document is to convey, in clear and concise statements, the services and/or goods requested by the agency. The necessity for paying attention to detail during the preparation of this document cannot be overemphasized. The bidding agency must have a clear understanding of the bid specifications in order to determine if it is capable of providing the requested services and/or goods and in order to submit informed bid proposals. Potential problems in the delivery of services and/or goods are likely to be averted if this document has been well-conceived and is well-written (see the appendices).

The Bid Conditions Document serves the functions of: outlining the conditions that the bidding agency must accept in order to be considered as a contender for the contract; establishing the expectations for the conduct of both parties (from the institution's perspective); of providing the basis for conflict resolution should problems be encountered during the term of the contract (see the appendices).

The adventure education specialist must know the type and extent of insurance coverage required for the implementation of a particular contract. For example, at the University of Oregon, in order to be awarded a Personal Professional Services Contract, the Alpine Ski Program contractor must secure and keep in effect auto and general liability insurance, including contractual liability, with minimum limits of $1,000,000 per occurrence. For contracts in which the Outdoor Pursuits Program rents only equipment or other goods, the Outdoor Pursuits Program Coordinator determines the nature and extent of the insurance coverage.

Bidding agencies are required to submit a certificate of insurance with the bid proposal. The certificate of insurance must state that: the University of Oregon must be informed if the certificate of insurance is canceled or materially changed, and that the university shall be included as additional insureds. This document also includes: a "sanction" clause that allows the university to withhold partial payment in the event that the contract is violated, a "termination" clause which specifies the conditions by which the contract might be terminated, and an "indemnification and hold harmless" clause. It also specifies the manner in which the contractor will bill the university for the services and/or goods provided. The adventure education specialist may also wish to include a "right to inspect equipment clause" as a device for monitoring the quality of the equipment that may be used in the contract. The bidding agency may also submit conditions establishing its expectations for the conduct of both parties. These conditions must be examined carefully. Negotiation may be required to determine mutually agreeable conditions.

The Bid Proposal (see the appendices) ties the "Bid Specifications" and "Bid Conditions" documents together. It requests that the bidding agency submit its price for the provision of the requested services and/or goods. It also requires that the contractor accept the terms of the "Bidding Conditions" document. Finally, the bid proposal states that all of the requested supporting documentation (e.g., the insurance policy, instructional progressions, the statement of philosophy, etc.) must be submitted with this document. Two copies of the bid proposal are sent, so that one copy may be retained by the bidding agency. The cover letter provides clear instructions and directions for the submission of timely bid proposals. It specifies the date on which bid proposals are due, the approximate date for contractor selection, and the individual to whom bid proposals are to be submitted.

THE SELECTION PROCESS

The selection process involves more than just selecting a provider. Contract law requires that qualified bidding agencies be identified, informed of the presence of the contract, and invited to submit bids based upon the contract specifications and the bidding instructions. In most cases, public institutions are required to make an effort to notify all potential bidders within a reasonable distance. Where only a limited number of easily identifiable bidding agencies are capable of fulfilling the contract specifications, public advertisement may not be necessary. For example, when there is only one facility in the immediate area that has an indoor climbing room, and the adventure education specialist is interested in utilizing this facility, it makes little sense to advertise for bid proposals.

The next step is the evaluation of submitted bid proposals. The adventure education specialist should leave unopened any bid proposals returned in advance of the deadline for submission in order to avoid the potential for bias. The initial task for the individual or panel charged with the responsibility for selecting a contractor is to determine if each bidding agency has submitted a valid bid proposal. If the bid proposal does not conform to the bid specifications, it may give a bidding agency an advantage during the evaluation process. In addition, all supporting documentation must be submitted as requested. Documents such as the certificate of insurance should be carefully examined. If the bid proposal is invalid or supporting documentation is missing or inadequate, there are sufficient grounds to reject a bid proposal.

The evaluation process should employ an objective format for assessing each bidding agency's ability to satisfactorily meet the bid specifications. In order to accomplish this task, specific criteria should be identified and weighted to allow for objective comparisons of the competing bids (see the worksheet in the appendices). In the worksheet example, the evaluative criteria are categorized under the headings of Participant Safety, Quality of the Experience, Cost, and Special Considerations. Each criterion is then given a weighting of 1, 2, 3, 4, or 5 signifying the highest level of importance. Criteria under the headings of Participant Safety and Quality of the Experience both receive weightings of 5 on this worksheet. While criteria under the headings of Cost and Special Considerations are important, they are deemed less important than the other two criteria, and hence, receive a weighting of 3. A rating of 1 through 5 is then given for the expected performance of the bidding agency on each criterion, 5 being the highest rating, hence a higher expected ability to perform. The weightings and rankings for each criterion are then multiplied, summed, and a total score is obtained that reflects the bidding agency's perceived ability to provide the requested goods and/or services, the highest total score indicating the most qualified agency.

Bidding agencies responding to the request for the submission of bid proposals should be informed, as soon as possible after the contract has been awarded, of the status of their submissions. In the case of the Alpine Ski Program, the University of Oregon is sensitive to the fact that the staff directors of each ski area must confirm instructor appointments and schedules well in advance of the beginning of the ski contract. Immediately after the contract has been awarded, each area is contacted via telephone and in writing and informed of the ski area to which the contract has been awarded.

The letter invites the director of each ski area not receiving the contract to contact the university ski coordinator for a more detailed explanation as to why his/her bid was not accepted. Agencies responding to this invitation gain valuable information that will assist them in the preparation of future bid proposals and receive a measure of assurance that their bid proposals have been examined in detail and with objectivity. If an agency's bid proposals have been rejected repeatedly without valid explanations of the shortcomings of these proposals, the agency may quit responding to future requests for bid proposal submission, and competition in the marketplace may be reduced.

The adventure education specialist must initiate the contractual process well in advance of the starting date of the contract. The time required for contract implementation will depend on the nature and complexity of the services and/or goods required. Unforeseen circumstances may prevent timely contract selection unless a sufficient cushion of time is allotted between the forwarding of documents to the bidding agencies and the formal announcement of the contractor. Furthermore, each bidding agency should be extended the professional courtesy of advanced notification. By allowing plenty of lead time the contractor will be able to prepare for the delivery of the requested services and/or goods, and unsuccessful applicants will be given sufficient lead time in which to make other plans. The contractual process for the Alpine Ski Program begins as soon as the ski areas begin gearing up for the coming ski season. Requests for proposals are sent as early as possible (by mid-October) and the bidding agencies are allotted sufficient time to prepare informed bid proposals (approximately three weeks). The contractor has been selected and all agencies have been informed as to the status of their bid proposals by the first week in November. If the contractual process proceeds unhindered, there is sufficient time to advertise and promote the ski program, which begins during the first week of the following January.

Once the contract is in place, the work is not yet finished. As Heydt states, "a contract is a dynamic document which must be used to ensure that there has been satisfactory performance by both parties, and is not to be placed on the shelf to collect dust during the life of the contract" (1986, p. 48). The methods and procedures of contract administration originate with the intentions of both parties for entering into the contract and the expectations of the parties with respect to each other's performance. The contract must be interpreted as a whole and should the contract document contradict the true intentions for entering into the contract, this in itself should not obstruct the abilities of either party to perform as originally intended. In other words, neither party should be able to avoid responsibilities that become apparent when the contract is construed as a whole.

The most important and effective element of contract administration is open communication between the parties involved. Effective communication can: establish a harmonious working relationship between parties; head off potential disputes or performance failures; and help to ensure that the contract is successfully completed. It is important to, whenever possible, treat the contractor as a partner rather than an adversary. After all, both parties have entered into the contract in order to work toward the fulfillment of a common goal.

The contract administrator is advised to document the history of events, happenings, conversations, and so on during the contract. Documentation provides information and ideas from which future improvements in the contractual process can be made, and may provide a valuable record should the unfortunate situation arise whereby the contract is terminated and civil litigation proceedings become necessary. Should it become necessary to terminate the contract, the contract should specify the termination procedures and any appeal procedures.

It is advantageous to complete an evaluation of the contractor's performance and to share the results with the contractor. This procedure is particularly important for a limited services contract that may be renewed in the future. Areas of contractor strengths and weaknesses can be identified by the contract administrator. This feedback can be used by the contractor to improve the level of performance should the same contractor be selected to fulfill a future contract. The administrator can utilize the information to refine the renewal process. The utilization of an objective worksheet will allow the contract administrator to focus on the important areas of contractor performance. The worksheet should be prepared in advance along with the other contractual documents so that the contractor can be evaluated at appropriate times throughout the term of the contract.

REFERENCES

Heydt, M. J. (1986). Ten principles for contract administration. *Parks and Recreation, 21*, 48-51.

Kaiser, R. A. (1986). *Liability and law in recreation, parks, and sports.* Englewood Cliffs, NJ: Prentice-Hall.

Kozlowski, J. D. (1982). Statutes dictate public contracting requirements. *Parks and Recreation, 17*, 28-35.

Watkins, Mike. (1985). *Issues associated with the use of contracted services in the University of Oregon SPE Program: A technical report with recommendations.* Unpublished manuscript.

Appendices

UNIVERSITY OF OREGON
Department of Physical Education and Human Movement Studies
Outdoor Pursuits Program

BID PROPOSAL - ALPINE SKI PROGRAM - 1988

COST/STUDENT

A. Eight days of ski lessons and lift tickets and provision of goods and/or services as outlined in the Bid Specifications.

B. Equipment Rental:

1. Cost of boots per day ____________
2. Cost of poles per day ____________
3. Cost of skis per day ____________
4. Cost of skis/boots/poles per day ____________
5. Cost of skis/boots/poles for eight days ____________

AUTHORIZED AGENCY SIGNATURE: ________________________

NAME (please print or type): ___________________________

DATE: ______________________

I understand and accept the terms and conditions outlined in the Bid Conditions.

AUTHORIZED AGENCY SIGNATURE: ________________________

ALL REQUESTED DOCUMENTS MUST ACCOMPANY THE BID STATEMENT

UNIVERSITY OF OREGON
Department of Physical Education and Human Movement Studies
Outdoor Pursuits Program

CONTRACTOR EVALUATION FORM - Alpine Ski Program

	Excellent	Satisfactory	Needs to Improve	Not Applicable
Equipment				
1. Quality of equipment	[ ]	[ ]	[ ]	[ ]
2. Safety of equipment	[ ]	[ ]	[ ]	[ ]
3. Quantity of equipment	[ ]	[ ]	[ ]	[ ]
4. Provision of equipment	[ ]	[ ]	[ ]	[ ]
Contractor Performance				
1. Punctuality	[ ]	[ ]	[ ]	[ ]
2. Ability to communicate	[ ]	[ ]	[ ]	[ ]
3. Working relationship	[ ]	[ ]	[ ]	[ ]
4. Helpfulness/friendliness	[ ]	[ ]	[ ]	[ ]
5. Openness & honesty	[ ]	[ ]	[ ]	[ ]
6. Professionalism	[ ]	[ ]	[ ]	[ ]
7. Impartiality	[ ]	[ ]	[ ]	[ ]
Delivery of Services & Goods				
1. Skill level of instructor	[ ]	[ ]	[ ]	[ ]
2. Quality of instruction	[ ]	[ ]	[ ]	[ ]
3. Concern for safety	[ ]	[ ]	[ ]	[ ]
4. Class content	[ ]	[ ]	[ ]	[ ]
5. Instructional progression	[ ]	[ ]	[ ]	[ ]
6. Interpersonal relations	[ ]	[ ]	[ ]	[ ]
7. Evaluation of students	[ ]	[ ]	[ ]	[ ]
General				
1. Cost of service	[ ]	[ ]	[ ]	[ ]
2. Quality of service	[ ]	[ ]	[ ]	[ ]

Comments (please use the reverse side)

Recommendations (please use the reverse side)

Signature ______________________

UNIVERSITY OF OREGON
Department of Physical Education and Human Movement Studies
Outdoor Pursuits Program

BID CONDITIONS - ALPINE SKI PROGRAM - 1988

Consideration of the Bid Proposal is contingent upon the agency's acceptance of the following conditions:

1. The University reserves the right to cancel the program without prior notice should program enrollment fall below 30 students.

2. Full charges will be assessed for students who remain registered in the program regardless of attendance record.

3. Charges will be assessed by the agency on a prorated basis for students who withdraw from the program at the rate of 1/8 of the eight-week fee per session.

4. The refund schedule of the University of Oregon be acceptable for student withdrawal from the course for sickness, injury or extenuating circumstances.

5. Should the agency fail, for any reason, to provide all eight 1.5-hour instructional sessions, the agency shall make a prorated refund of 1/8 of the eight-session fee for each session canceled per student, and the Agreement shall be considered terminated.

6. If the University buses are unable for any reason to reach the ski area, the contract will be extended for one additional Thursday of instruction in order to provide students with the contracted eight sessions.

7. The agency must compensate ski instructors working in the University program on the basis of number of 1.5-hour sessions taught and not on the basis of number of students in attendance at each session.

8. The agency will bill the University of Oregon for the provision of goods and/or services rendered following the final ski session.

9. The agency shall secure, at its own expense and keep in effect during the term of the contract comprehensive auto and general liability insurance, including contractual liability and products and completed operations, with minimum limits of $1,000,000 per occurrence. This insurance policy is to be issued by an insurance company authorized to do business in the State of Oregon. The State of Oregon, acting by and through the State Board of Higher Education on behalf of the University of Oregon and their officers, employees, and agents shall be included as additional insureds in said insurance policy. Failure to obtain or maintain such a policy shall constitute a breach of this contract. A copy of the agency's insurance policy must be submitted with the Bid Proposal. The certificate of insurance should provide that the insurance company will give a 30-day notice to the University of Oregon if the insurance is canceled or materially changed. The policy should also specifically state that contractual liability is provided for this contract.

10. It should be understood that the agency will be expected to take due care for each person's safety from the moment of arrival at the ski area to time of bus departure. Damage to any and all ski equipment provided by the agency caused by any class participant or instructor shall not be the responsibility of the University of Oregon.

11. In carrying out the provisions hereof, or in exercising any power or authority granted by an Agreement, the agency hereby promises and agrees to save, defend, indemnify and hold harmless the State of Oregon acting by and through the State Board of Higher Education on behalf of the University of Oregon and its officers, agents, employees, and members from all claims, suits, actions and other proceedings resulting from or arising out of the activities of the contractor or its subcontractors, agents, or employees under the agreement.

12. The bidding agency must agree to follow the Equal Opportunity Employer Act.

UNIVERSITY OF OREGON
Department of Physical Education and Human Movement Studies
Outdoor Pursuits Program

BID SPECIFICATIONS - ALPINE SKI PROGRAM - 1988

Bid Proposals are to be submitted based upon the provision of the following requested goods and/or services to the 1988 Alpine Ski Program:

A. Instructional Goods and/or Services

1. A ski program providing lift service plus instruction in beginning, intermediate, and advanced alpine skiing and ski racing, snowboarding, and cross country downhill, including eight sessions of instruction at each level, with a minimum of 1.5 hours of instruction in each session for up to 150 students per day. All sessions will occur on consecutive Thursdays, beginning January 14, 1988 and ending March 3, 1988, provided that the University of Oregon buses can reach the ski area each day. If not, the ending date would be March 10.

2. Lesson plans for each level of instruction, submitted with the Bid Proposal (to include a statement of educational philosophy, course content, teaching methods and progressions, evaluative criteria and methods of evaluation for each level of instruction).

3. Instruction by fully qualified PNSIA Ski Instructors. A list of potential instructors' names, certification levels, and years of experience must be submitted with the bid.

4. A maximum student/instructor ratio of 12/1.

5. A system for recording and reporting attendance which:
   (a.) is accurate and up-to-date.
   (b.) provides the Alpine Ski Program Coordinator with this data on a weekly basis. (Attendance records will be given to the coordinator at the beginning of each ski session for the prior ski session.)

6. Submission, within four calendar days of the last ski session, of complete class records and suggested final grades for each student to the Alpine Ski Program Coordinator.

7. A statement of the total cost of lifts and lessons per student for the complete program as requested in the Bid Proposal.

B. Non-Instructional Goods and/or Services

1. Numbered photo I.D. cards for each student. The numbers must be consecutive. The agency must provide the personnel and equipment to produce and distribute the I.D. cards on campus on Thursday, January 7, 1988, and the personnel and equipment to produce I.D. cards at the ski area on the first ski day, January 14, 1988. The numbers on these I.D. cards should be con secutive with the I.D. cards issued on campus.

2. A rental program providing skis, boots and poles. A description of the rental stock (types and quantities) and rental prices (including any applicable package, group, or multiple rental discounts) must be submitted with the Bid Proposal.

3. A ski pass for the Alpine Ski Program Coordinator, plus one lift ticket for each bus chaperone (limited to one chaperone per bus), plus up to four lift tickets (season total) to be used by the Head of the SHAPE Service Physical Education Program, and/or an Outdoor Pursuits Program representative.

4. A ski patrol system and other safety measures in compliance with United States Forest Service permit regulations.

Safety Management

Ian R. Wade
Outward Bound USA

This chapter deals with the general principles of the safety management of adventure education programs. The principles will be illustrated with examples drawn from Outward Bound. As the largest American adventure education program, with upwards of 19,000 participants each year, and over 1,000 instructors, safety management has necessarily become fairly sophisticated over the 27 years since Outward Bound began.

Any human activity carries with it the chance for accidental death. The National Safety Council publishes data each year which shows that over the last 25 years, an average of 60.4 people (age range 15-24) out of every 100,000 die accidentally each year. By the end of 1987, the accidental death rate for Outward Bound had fallen to 58.4, from a figure nearly seven times higher in the previous decade.

The key to this improvement has been a preemptive safety program that anticipates and analyzes hazards and requires the formulation of appropriate methods for controlling the hazards.

SAFETY OBJECTIVES

In the early years of adventure education programs, fatal accidents were sufficiently frequent events that some field staff and managers came to assume were an inevitable, though regrettable, part of operations. A change in attitude toward safety has taken place, and the first step in effecting this change was to clarify that fatal accidents were considered unacceptable. One example is Outward Bound's formulation of two safety objectives: (a) to eliminate fatalities, disabling injuries and serious illnesses; and (b) to put in place programs that reduce other accidents, injuries, and illnesses.

These two relatively simple statements were widely disseminated and are now shared by all staff who work for Outward Bound. No longer does anyone feel that a certain number of fatalities are inevitable or acceptable within Outward Bound. Every adventure education program should have some unambiguous statement of safety objectives, that is understood and shared by all staff.

RESPONSIBILITIES FOR THE SAFETY PROGRAM

With clearly stated and widely understood goals for safety management, responsibilities must be assigned for performance. All the texts on industrial safety management stress that the commitment of top management is vital, and this is no less true for adventure education programs. While the field instructor often seems to be primarily in control of safety, the process that allows that instructor to be placed in the field is, in the long term, of greater importance. For this reason, each program must examine what the responsibilities of its various levels of management are, or ought to be.

To illustrate how this assignment of responsibility has worked in Outward Bound, the responsibilities of various levels of managers are listed below:

1. Trustees
   - statements of policy
   - monitoring results
2. National organizations
   - biannual safety review by national Outward Bound office
3. Managers at each school
   - program design
   - approving safety procedures
   - establishing organizational structure and job descriptions
   - staff selection, training, placement and evaluation
   - equipment, food, and vehicle selection
   - emergency planning
   - ongoing safety monitoring
4. Field supervisors
   - anticipating hazards due to area, activities, participants
   - curriculum approval
   - assessment of participants
   - participant safety briefings
   - staff orientation and training
   - staff supervision and evaluation
   - evaluating safety for management
5. Instructional staff
   - assessment of participants
   - implementation of safety procedures
   - participant training
   - ensuring potential hazards are backed up
   - incident reporting
6. Participants
   - medical screening
   - assumption of risk
   - evaluation of safety of activities and staff

THE KEY TO SAFETY MANAGEMENT

When we hear or read of an accident, our analytical instincts come to the fore and we are usually able to spot several things that could have been done to prevent or forestall the serious consequences of the unplanned event that resulted in injury. The key to an effective safety program is to think through the probable and reasonably possible things that might go wrong ahead of time, and design operating procedures such that serious harm does not ensue. Records of past incidents in other programs can be an excellent source of the types of potential problems that may need to be anticipated.

The safety responsibilities outlined in the previous section are designed to ensure that this analysis is done in advance. The general methodology used by safety engineers applies to each group mentioned above. They must perform four general functions in the safety program: (a) identification of hazardous conditions and practices; (b) development of hazard control methods; (c) communication of hazard control information to those directly affected, and (d) evaluation of effectiveness of hazard control system.

The safety management process is not a separate part of Outward Bound operations, but is woven into the daily operating decisions of each staff member. It is often the first factor to be considered in evaluating any given action, along with cost and potential benefits. The following sections describe in more detail how the above four-step process is used by each group of people responsible for safety in Outward Bound.

Trustees' Roles in Safety Management

Not-for-profit corporations, schools and colleges are typically governed by a Board of Trustees with final responsibility for all operations. While these people are not necessarily experts in the potential hazards of adventure education programs, they have a duty to:

1. Be informed about potential hazards in the program.
2. Ensure that qualified people develop safe operating procedures.
3. Ensure that systems exist for communicating these procedures to staff and participants.
4. Evaluate the results of operations regularly and institute corrective actions.

In Outward Bound schools, the trustees have established a National Safety Policy, which constitutes their standing orders to management and staff on how to anticipate and address safety matters. Hazards might arise either from the participants, the staff, or the type of activities undertaken. Accordingly, the policy requires that:

1. Screening will be done to assess whether participants have medical or psychological problems that may be harmful to themselves or others during a program.

2. Minimum standards for staff be established and a regular staff evaluation process be adopted.

3. New program must formulate safety procedures. These safety procedures are reviewed and approved by trustees and management and by the national organization before new program operation may commence. The procedures are customized to each geographic area, staff skill level, participant ability level, and the activities being undertaken. A new program may take place in a totally new geographic area or include a new activity in the same area (multi-pitch climbing where only top-rope climbing had previously been done). Alternatively, it might involve a new type of participant in a familiar area (delinquents instead of adults).

4. Participants be warned in advance of probable hazards and trained to understand and protect themselves from hazard during the course.

5. Safety operating procedures be communicated to staff in training sessions and in writing, usually in the form of a staff handbook.

6. A standardized accident reporting system be used and periodic summary reports prepared.

7. A trustee committee at each school be charged with conducting on-site inspection of programs each year.

8. A safety review process be used whereby every two years a school's safety program is independently audited.

9. Emergency procedures be established for major accidents, including the requirement for external review of major accidents.

Trustees, then, are the people who hold ultimate responsibility for safety. Their primary role is to establish policy and provide oversight. Along with experts within and outside the Outward Bound schools they hold in trust, they establish policy, approve procedures, and most importantly monitor results closely. Each trustee safety committee will meet with managers to review results about three times a year. Additionally, trustees make their own fact-finding visits to the field.

Finally, chairmen of trustee safety committees *of all the U.S. Outward Bound schools* meet annually for a full day to discuss the year's safety record in the entire Outward Bound system.

National Organization Role in Safety Management

Larger organizations or ones that belong to a national association may receive some useful safety management assistance from their national organization. The American Camping Association, the American Mountain Guides Association, and the Association for Experiential Education provide various kinds of safety management oversight.

Because each Outward Bound school is licensed by a national organization, systems have been developed for monitoring each of the schools. The most important vehicle is a biannual safety audit, coordinated by the national office of Outward Bound. A review team comprised of experts from other Outward Bound schools and outside specialists in the program activities to be reviewed, visits a school to assure themselves that the safety program is functioning at a high professional standard. The report of the review team may contain recommendations for change in operating procedures and requires a written reply from the school within 30 days, indicating how they plan to comply.

These safety audits provide a valuable way of getting an outside perspective on the safety program and use a process much like that used to accredit schools and colleges. Additional monitoring takes place through periodic review of all significant accident/incident reports, and thorough investigations of any major accidents.

Managers' Roles in Safety Management

Program managers effect safety in a multiplicity of ways. As with other groups, their functions in safety management are to:

1. Anticipate potential hazards in program design and operation;
2. Establish practical ways of coping with the hazards;
3. Ensure staff and participants understand these methods;
4. Set up management information systems to evaluate program operations.

At the Outward Bound schools, the managers' responsibilities typically include:

1. Selection of appropriate program activities in areas that are potentially safe. Before beginning operation in any new area, managers look at the potential hazards and ask the "what if" questions. These questions identify the hazards that could arise with operations in the area and identify ways to control the hazards. Each area will usually have a specific guidebook developed for Outward Bound staff use, showing where activity sites are available and ways to safeguard them.

2. Selection of qualified supervisory and instructional staff is a key responsibility. Staff are selected for a technical skill level considerably beyond what will normally be needed during course operations. While training can be readily provided for upgrading some technical skills (e.g., first aid or rescue techniques), in other areas, qualities such as good judgment, communication, and maturity must be sought. These qualities are further evaluated during an apprenticeship period.

3. Formulation of safety procedures that properly cover the various hazards in their program areas and are adapted to the abilities of each special participant group they may work with. A typical instructor handbook may be 200 pages in length and cover safety procedures very specifically.

4. Equipment, food, and vehicle selection are also the concern of managers. Selection of appropriate and durable equipment is continuously monitored. Lists of equipment to be supplied to each participant, each group, and for emergencies are maintained for every season and operating area by logistics staff. Feedback from instructional staff and participants is systematically incorporated. Menus are planned for each course type, are periodically checked with nutritional advisors, and are also updated in response to participant and staff feedback. Vehicles are carefully selected for carrying loads and driving on rough terrain. Staff undergo an Outward Bound-designed driving screening test before being allowed to drive with participants. Maintenance schedules meet or exceed manufacturers' recommendations.

5. Training of staff is a critical area, given the seasonal nature of Outward Bound and many other adventure programs. Detailed manuals setting out the responsibilities of instructors and field supervisors are given to each staff member and are required reading before employment, and are then carried in the field. Generally, two weeks of pre-employment training is given, with two or more days of orientation prior to each course. Training in specific skill areas is offered outside of the employment period. These offerings are coordinated through Outward Bound's National Training Institute and are available to others working in the adventure education field, too.

6. Managers establish an organizational structure with reasonable spans of control so that performance information can be gathered and acted on effectively. The field supervisor's role is particularly critical in gathering information about staff performance and enabling decisions on promotion, training needs, and program design to be accurately made.

7. Regular field visits to maintain contact with field supervisors and instructional staff enable managers to provide a cross-check on information they receive from the field.

8. Reviewing reports written by participants and instructors that evaluate the safety and impact of every course is a routine part of the manager's responsibilities.

9. Field incident reports are prepared each time first aid is performed or a near-miss occurs. These are used in the preparation of an Annual Safety Report to the trustees. This allows managers to review the year's programs, chart progress against the safety objective of reducing injuries and illnesses, and to determine training needs for the follow ing year. Many schools are now producing quarterly safety reports, to be able to respond more quickly to trends.

10. Ensuring that each program is equipped to cope with likely emergencies in a prompt and professional manner is part of the manager's role. The school's staff can combine their efforts with local emergency medical services to evacuate a participant. Most evacuations can be accomplished in less than eight hours, with 24 hours being a general upper limit. An evacuation plan is prepared for every area so that staff are aware of local resources, such as radio, telephone locations, and helicopter procedures.

Field Supervisors' Roles in Safety Management

Field supervisor are senior instructional staff persons who spend the majority of their time observing groups in the field, and are thus in a position to anticipate and observe developing problems. In some instances, field supervisors may also instruct a group while supervising another, but usually not when three or more groups are operating at the same time. Field supervisor have the same basic four responses:

1. Anticipate hazards peculiar to that course.
2. Ensure that plans exist to control the hazards.
3. Observe whether staff and participants understand how to operate safely.
4. Evaluate the safety of the program for management.

In Outward Bound, field supervisors will typically have three or more years of instructional experience and will have worked in several areas and with different types of participant groups. A close-working relationship with staff gives the field supervisor a critical role in the following activities:

1. Approving the instructor's course designs and modifying them when needed. Each instructor prepares a written itinerary/curriculum prior to the course. The field supervisor's knowledge of the seasonal hazards of an area, the local hazard spots, or the limitations of certain types of participants in coping with hazards, is an important check and balance on the instructor's judgment.

2. Much training of instructional staff is performed by the field supervisor, who spends sufficient time observing individual staff members to be aware of their development needs. Training may also be accomplished in the pre-course orientation, through on the job coaching, or by recommendations for training outside of the employment period.

3. Giving safety briefings to staff prior to courses and at other critical times. Participants also get general safety briefings and specific briefings for certain hazards either from the field supervisor or their delegate.

4. Evaluation of instructional staff is a particularly critical function, especially because of the seasonality of employment and turnover. Each instructional staff member receives a written evaluation at the end of each course. Usually, this will include feedback from a co-worker as well as the supervisor's assessment. Verbal feedback is provided throughout the course, as appropriate. Recommendations for advancement may be instituted by the field supervisor but will be reviewed by managers who have access to all the evaluations of an instructor and who will have insights of their own from training sessions and field visits.

5. Each school has a Certification Program that establishes criteria for the instructors to meet. The field supervisor determines when an individual has met these criteria and is ready to become a fully certified instructor.

6. Reporting on significant safety incidents is the responsibility of the field supervisor. These reports are used to plan future training sessions as well as to upgrade safety procedures. The field supervisor ensures that all significant incidents are accurately reported and assesses recommendations from instructional staff for improved course design, participant screening, or logistical support.

Instructional Staff's Role in Safety Management

The instructor is most directly able to influence safety because of an almost constant interaction with participants. In general, two or more staff members are assigned to each group of 8 to 12 participants, to provide a check and balance on the judgment of a single person and also to provide an apprenticeship period to an incoming staff member.

One person should always be given authority for the group, even if the two are similarly qualified. Instructional staff interprets the same basic four safety management tasks in the following way:

1. Observe and anticipate hazards their group may encounter.
2. Use appropriate methods for allowing each individual to successfully deal with hazards.
3. Provide appropriate training for each participant.
4. Evaluate the program and other staff performance.

In Outward Bound schools, the instructional staff effects safety management in the following ways:

1. Instructional staff observes participants and designs their activities to be within safe and beneficial limits. They can anticipate hazardous conditions and actions of participants and modify activities appropriately.

2. Whenever a potential hazard exists where the consequences of an error would result in serious injury, the instructor must be able to intervene. In general, systems must be in place to make all such situations fail-safe. An example of this is when the rockclimber holding the belay rope is backed up by a second person, in case the first person fails to hold the rope properly. On a snow slope, with a bad run out in the event of a slip, the first line of defense might be the participant using training with an ice axe to self-arrest, yet a fixed rope or belay would be used too, as a backup. In some cases activities where this backup cannot be provided must be avoided, e.g., a dangerous river crossing or running a rapid, where an error may result in entrapment.

3. Each instructor is trained in the technical skills needed for the program environment, at a level considerably above what would benormally required to operate the program. Gaining the needed experience usually takes several years of regular personal involvement in the adventure activities. Thus, instructors have a considerable reserve of experience and are able to appreciate the adventures participants are experiencing without being close to their limits. Screening is strict, and at some schools only half the apprentice staff will advance to an instructing position.

4. Each Outward Bound instructor is trained to respond to medical emergencies:

- Nearly 50 percent hold *EMT certification* (licensing requirement for ambulance attendant).
- *All* have advanced Red Cross or higher certification.
- *All* have CPR Life Support certification.
- *All* have specialized first aid knowledge of wilderness medical problems.

5. Outward Bound offers EMT and First Responder certification courses, which are taught from the perspective of providing care in a remote wilderness location. These courses are available for other adventure education program staff too.

6. Training of participants to acquire skills needed for wilderness living and travel and to make their own informed

assessment of hazards is a critical part of the instructor's role. As participants begin to use their newly acquired skills, instructors must monitor that skills are properly applied.

7. Each instructional staff member writes a report on each course, evaluating safety and documenting any injuries, illnesses, or incidents. Specific hazards encountered in the area are recorded in the course area guidebook, and suggestions for upgrading safety procedures, logistical needs, course design, or participant selection are made.

Participant's Role in Safety Management

The persons most often directly able to influence safety are the participants, who are the potential accident victims. The safeguards discussed should not cause participants to no longer feel responsible for their own safety. Prior to acceptance into an adventure education program, participants should be screened to determine that their skill levels are appropriate for the program, and that they have no medical or psychological problems that may endanger themselves or others. The four general safety management tasks apply to participants in this manner:

1. Being alert to situations they are uncomfortable in undertaking;
2. Following staff instructions and using good judgment;
3. Letting staff or others know when they feel endangered or see others in danger;
4. Reporting problems they observe with the safety of the program to staff and managers.

At Outward Bound, the safety management tasks involving participants are the following: each participant undergoes medical and psychological screening before acceptance on a course. Trained admissions staff review each medical form and consult with school physicians and psychologists when follow-up questions arise. Every effort is made to accept people, but a small percentage are referred to other programs, screen themselves out or are turned down.

Prior to acceptance, a statement from the school director informs the participant of the risks involved in the program. The participant, and a parent or guardian if the participant is under legal age, signs a statement acknowledging these risks. More importantly, participants agree to assume responsibility for protecting themselves from these risks. Participants who are unwilling or unable to assume this responsibility are removed from the programs. Participants evaluate the safety and quality of their course and the effectiveness of their instructor at the end of the course.

CONCLUSION

The powerful effects of outdoor adventure education can only be obtained by operating in an environment that has potential dangers, and in which a certain degree of real risk is present. The safety objective should be to reduce these risks to levels comparable to other human activities, all of which carry some degree of risk.

Safety management of an adventure education program is the responsibility of several groups of stakeholders in the program. Trustees, managers, field supervisors, instructors, and participants all have vital and different roles to play. The general tasks of each group are common, however:

1. Identification of hazardous conditions and practices;
2. Development of hazard control methods;
3. Communication of hazard control information to those directly affected;
4. Evaluation of the effectiveness of the hazard control system.

The safety management system described outlines the preemptive measures Outward Bound has developed. As well as successfully eliminating fatalities, the safety management system described has reduced the non-disabling injury rate. In 1987 Outward Bound had only 0.67 incidents of injury severe enough to cause a participant to miss a day of activity per 1,000 participant days. This means if 150 people went on a 10-day program only one person would experience an injury severe enough to miss a day of the program.

Over the past three decades, safety management systems have evolved in the adventure education field. The great benefits participants report from participation in adventure education programs and their proven educational and therapeutic effectiveness can now be delivered with safety results comparable to the risks of everyday life.

Program Evaluation: Past, Present and Future

Alan Warner
Association for Experiential Education

Adventure-based experiential education traces its roots across a century of critical philosophers and educators from William James, to John Dewey, to Kurt Hahn, not to mention the broader contributions from aboriginal cultures. However, as an educational domain with a sense of definition and self-awareness, it is a very young movement that was only organized in the early 1970s. Research and evaluation questions only started to surface once proponents began to give some definition to their approaches and expected outcomes.

In contrast, domains of psychology such as the learning theory have empirical traditions dating back to the beginning of the 20th century. The youthful nature of research and evaluation in experiential education provides the context for examining past lessons, present prescriptions, and future challenges.

PAST LESSONS

Don't Just Talk About It

Calls for more attention to evaluation and research have been a constant refrain throughout the 1970s and 1980s. However, it is generally accepted that the evaluation and research literature is insubstantial (Conrad, 1979; Conrad & Hedin, 1981; Ewert, 1987; Shore, 1978; Warner, 1982). Why? Relatively little solid work has been completed because evaluation has not traditionally been a priority relative to service, program development, and fund-raising. Evaluation work requires an institutional resource base that is still in its early phases of development. Underlying these practical issues has been an important psychological dimension: experiential educators have a strong sense of mission and belief in their work. The zeal and energy that it takes to chart new educational directions does not necessarily breed critical reflection and self-analysis.

Quality Work Takes Quality Effort

To the extent that evaluation projects were undertaken in the 1960s and 1970s, most frequently they involved giving program participants pre-treatment and post-treatment questionnaires in order to document positive changes across the program on key personality traits and attitudes, particularly self-concept (Ewert, 1983; Shore, 1978). Much of the evaluation work was devoted to one-time outcome studies conducted by researchers from other disciplines, frequently graduate students in education or psychology who were completing thesis requirements. From a quantitative, scientific point of view, the evaluation designs were weak, although the multitude of positive results tended to bewilder reviewers into concluding that there is a documented improvement in self-concept as a result of intensive outdoor adventure programs (Ewert, 1983; Shore, 1978). From a discipline perspective, too much time and effort has been devoted to conducting poorly controlled outcome studies on psychological variables. A few strong studies could have accomplished the same task, leaving more time and resources to be devoted to other issues. Hit-and-run outcome studies do not develop a strong research and evaluation framework for experiential education.

The rationale for all of this work is only understandable at an individual program level, where administrators commissioned projects in order to document positive outcomes so as to justify further funding. But the assumption that quantitative evaluation studies sell programs is simplistic, given the complex, personal, political, and organizational relationships that are the context for funding decisions. A program is rarely funded on its scientific merits. Bureaucrats and politicians who have a positive perspective on a program will be very accepting of data documenting the program's benefits. However, they probably would have supported the program regardless of the data. Decision-makers who have other ideas and agendas will likely refuse to accept the data and can always point to flaws in the research methodology, particularly when it is a "quick and easy" outcome study. Given the time and resources that still must go into these studies, it would seem more productive to put the work into developing sophisticated promotional materials and positive relationships with decision-makers.

Take Responsibility for Your Own Learning

The past low priority and narrow focus of evaluation research has resulted in programs contracting out work to researchers from other disciplines. But by relinquishing responsibility for defining evaluation approaches and borrowing evaluation expertise and methodology from other disciplines, experiential education research has been dominated by evaluation criteria that are philosophically out of tune with experiential theory and practice. As an experiential educator, one must question whether assessment techniques that measure abstract traits and concepts and depend on verbal and cognitive skills should be the primary means of evaluating experiential education programs committed to learning through concrete action and experience (Warner, 1984a). Yet the field has been left with the biases of applied researchers in education and psychology who tend to rely on quick and easy measures of personality traits and attitudes, both as a result of their training and the academic pressures to publish. These types of evaluation studies have also had pragmatic advantages for administrators in that they do not interfere with programming, yet they produce "clean" numerical results. Ironically, even when these research designs are well-controlled, many social scientists question the value of relying only on psychological tests because of their empirical deficiencies in reliability, validity, and ability to predict behavior (Mischel, 1969; Abelson, 1972). It is time that experiential educators take responsibility for their learning through defining their own evaluation strategies.

These past lessons have been well-recognized in experiential education literature (Ewert, 1987; Hamilton, 1979; Warner, 1984a). Given the theory and principles of experiential education, the lessons are common sense: don't just talk about it, quality work takes quality effort, and take responsibility for your own learning. Slowly, a relatively small number of experiential educators have been developing interests and expertise in research and evaluation. Most of them are employed in academic positions where there is time, incentive, and pressure to write and do research. For example, of the 15 identified authors of articles in the 1987 edition of the *Journal of Experiential Education* that were devoted to research and evaluation, five were full-time university faculty, four were graduate or undergraduate students, and five worked or taught in university settings. Only one author did not have any university affiliation. The development of some research expertise within the field can produce more meaningful efforts. It can allow for the development of longitudinal evaluation and research projects and generate more on-going interaction between researchers and practitioners. Experiential educators are now in a position to prescribe new and hopefully more productive directions for research and evaluation (Conrad & Hedin, 1981; Ewert, 1987, Warner, 1984a).

PRESENT PRESCRIPTIONS

Integrate Action and Reflection

Program evaluation is fundamentally a tool for critical reflection but has not been used in this way, given the past focus on one-time evaluation studies. To be meaningful, evaluation needs to be built into the program from the outset, setting up an action-reflection learning cycle for program staff and administrators. For example, experiential education practice typically involves leaders processing activities with participants either immediately or at the end of a day. Programs are processed by staff at their conclusion, if not before. An important but simple evaluation process could involve asking participants after each program activity or day to assess the value of their experience on a three point scale. The rating process would contribute to the program experience by communicating to participants that they have a role in program evaluation. If the ratings were collected across instructors and programs, staff would have a valuable tool to look at what seems to be working and where there are difficulties. New hypotheses may be generated, which in turn require follow-up and/or encourage program innovations. Taking the extra step of writing down ratings allows one to capture patterns beyond the critical incidents that are embedded in the memories of the more articulate participants and staff. For example, ratings may be used to identify specific adventure activities that have special attributes that meet the needs of one set of participants, but not others (Teaff, & Kablach, 1987). Several versions of an activity could be tried simultaneously and the results compared in order to broaden the range of participants who receive significant benefit from it. A simple, daily rating system is not a startling idea and it will not "sell" the program. It is one example of a means to collect useful information that stimulates an action-reflection cycle.

A developmental approach to evaluation involves asking different types of questions at different stages in program development. Initially, the focus is on "formative" or "process" evaluation questions as one works to build the program. Who are the participants? What are their needs? Do the activities really address the program goals? How and why do specific activities work? etc. At later stages in program development, there may be more interest in "summative" or "outcome" evaluation strategies, although process data is typically still needed to interpret the results. But there is little point in drawing firm conclusions or generalizing from outcome data before a program has a consistent and coherent structure. Unfortunately, experiential education as a discipline inverted this pattern by relying on outcome strategies in its early phase of development.

In order to move toward using evaluation as a program development tool, integrating action and reflection, practitioners must take a greater responsibility for program evaluation efforts, both independently and in conjunction with researchers. Practitioners are more in touch with the practical realities of the work and have more vested interest in maximizing the impact of the evaluation efforts. Researchers, even those working within the discipline, tend to be less concerned with direct program impact and more focused on theory, long-term program development, and the accumulation of knowledge. For example, the article that had the most direct connection to programming in the recent *Journal of Experiential Education* issue on research and evaluation, was the only article written by a full-time practitioner (Heinrichsdorff, 1987). Heinrichsdorff (1987) proposes a methodology whereby participants and staff develop their own evaluation criteria at the start of each program. She suggests that this approach immediately clarifies staff and participant expectations, ensures relevant outcome criteria are assessed, and starts the process of participants and staff taking joint responsibility to realize their goals. At the end of the course, the participants and staff already have an investment in providing meaningful data, and there is a greater likelihood that the results will be cycled back into the program. A rigorous, quantitative expert in research methodology would quickly shoot holes in this approach: Where is the control group? how can one trust biased self-reports? etc. But these concerns may not be the priority in program efforts to improve specific practices where there is no intent to generalize to other settings. The goal is to promote program development rather than pronouncing on outcome.

The integrated approach can develop a positive spiral in terms of practitioner involvement in evaluation work. If practitioners begin to see that evaluation efforts provide valuable information to them, they in turn will put more commitment and energy into evaluation, which in turn will create more successful projects.

Focus on the Process

A second related prescription is to focus on the conditions and circumstances under which experiential education practices work rather than simply on whether they work. The discipline is moving beyond the simplistic belief that experiential education is inherently good for everyone under all circumstances. What are the principles, theories, and circumstances that combine to build the most effective programs for specific types of participants? For example, Drebing, Willis, & Genet (1987) looked at how a participant's level of anxiety impacts program satisfaction, self-reported learning, and the person's relationship with the leader. The results indicate that anxiety has a unique relationship with each of these variables. With further work, one might begin to identify appropriate levels of anxiety for specific types of program goals, participants, and activities. Bacon (1983) has developed an intriguing model for understanding the impact of the Outward Bound approach on individuals. He suggests that wilderness activities will have maximum impact to the extent that they provide a metaphor for the individual's life experiences and limitations back in their home communities. This theory could be applied to the evaluation of practical activities in ongoing programs as a step toward looking at the nuts and bolts of program effectiveness. Practitioners and researchers have complementary strengths and need to work together to make their efforts effective. Practitioners often have implicit, experience-based theories of how and why specific practices may work. In turn, researchers can help practitioners articulate and test theories while integrating them with previous work.

Emphasize the Quality of the Experience

Valuable knowledge can be gained by carefully analyzing the components of experiential programs, but since the emphasis in experiential education is on the whole person, there would seem to be some inherent limitations in subdividing people into traits or programs into units. Most experiential educators would not accept the premise that the whole person is equal to the sum of his or her parts (traits), much less that the whole program is equal to the sum of its individual activities. There is ongoing controversy in the field of personality theory and research as to whether it is even helpful to conceptualize people as having identical personality structures with the variance in individuals due to differences in the amount or quality of each trait (Bem & Allen, 1974). By focusing only on the quantifiable effects, the holistic, qualitative experience may be missed. For example, documenting changes in participants across a program on scales of moral reasoning and self-esteem does not provide great insight into the process and implications of the changes for participants in terms of their experience. The scale results also do not provide insight into the nature of the program experience.

There is a need to shift at least some of the evaluation effort to documenting the nature of both the individual's experience and the total program experience. Qualitative and ethnographic evaluation and research methods are probably best equipped to contribute to this task and need greater emphasis (Rowley, 1987). Qualitative work typically involves the researcher implementing program evaluation with a less structured approach based on program participation, observation, and/or interviews. The evaluator attempts to integrate information from various sources into a personal description and analysis of the program. The experience of a program is conceptualized as a subjective, complex, and interactive phenomenon that needs to be assessed in a holistic fashion. One of the advantages of this approach is that the subjective nature of the work is immediately evident, whereas subjective values are often hidden in the "objective" quantitative model. Of course, the very subjective aspect of the qualitative model may be viewed as a limitation.

In recent years, there has been much philosophical debate in the program evaluation field over the relative merits of the qualitative and quantitative models (Filstead, 1979; Smith & Glass, 1987). At a practical level, it seems reasonable to conclude that both approaches have their place in a new field that needs to address a wide range of questions. To date, qualitative work has been minimal. For example, an experienced participant observer, intent on critically documenting and assessing the experience of a program and the individuals within it, can provide a wealth of new ideas, hypotheses, and information, which can be cycled back into the program and the experiential education literature. The observer is in a position to ask questions and raise issues beyond the limits of the program ideology that staff typically adopt, even when they are critiquing and reflecting on their efforts. The prescription is the need to focus on the quality of the experience in a holistic fashion.

Problem-Solve with Multiple Strategies

The development of participants' problem-solving skills is a key element of many experiential education programs. Effective problem-solving involves having a wide range of strategies at one's disposal and then tailoring them in a flexible fashion to the specific issue or situation. Effective program evaluation requires a similar approach, and past work has brought home the limitations of relying on only a few strategies for all situations. A wide range of resources is available. There is a body of literature in education, sociology, and anthropology on ethnographic procedures aimed at qualitative analysis (Goetz & LeCompt, 1984; Guba & Lincoln,

1985). In addition, there are several decades of work in the field of applied behavioral analysis that take a very scientific approach to defining treatments, and assessing change (Haynes, 1978; Simon & Boyer, 1974). For example, sophisticated behavior observation procedures can be used to evaluate changes in participants' problem-solving skills across a program on initiative tasks (Warner, 1984b). Peer evaluation is another approach that has been used to assess a range of educational programs and seems particularly compatible with experiential education philosophy (Beker, 1960; Kaufman & Johnson, 1974; Wiggins, 1973). One might document changes in participants' perspectives of their peers as a tool to analyze group dynamics and leadership styles. Finally, journals are a key element in many experiential programs, and there is extensive literature on extracting themes and insights from open-ended writing through standardized content analysis procedures (Carney, 1972; Holsti, 1969). For example, a careful analysis of self-oriented statements in participants' journals may shed light on changes in self-perception across an experience. In brief, the field should ask a broad range of questions with a diversity of approaches.

Learn from the Consequences

Experiential practice attempts to set up learning situations where feedback and consequences are direct, natural, and concrete. If a group of adolescents cannot work together to cook a meal on a wilderness trip, they do not eat. What if the same learning model was applied to program decisions? If the participants do not demonstrate an increase in cooperative behavior by the end of the program, the program must be changed. Both examples are simplistic, but the notion is that at some point one does need to be concerned with practical outcomes. Ultimately, for many programs, particularly those working with troubled and disabled participants, program goals aim at changing behavior. There is a need to shift the focus in outcome research from looking at changes in attitudes to documenting accomplishments and changes in behavior that can be related back to process-oriented evaluation data. For example, some adventure programs claim that troubled adolescents become more cooperative and socially responsible as a result of their program experiences. There are numerous possibilities for testing this notion by assessing practical behaviors. Do the young people's drinking patterns change as the result of their experiences? Do they become more active in work and recreation activities? Defenders of these programs faced with negative results on these measures could argue that one is being unrealistic to expect changes in participants' behavior back in their home environments with intensive, short-term programs. They would probably be correct, but then the challenge posed by the negative results would be whether the program could do more to reintegrate young people into their home communities and create quality follow-up experiences (McCabe & Harris, 1979).

Attitude measures do have their place in assessing outcome in that they provide a perspective of the impact of the program on the psychological/emotional domain, which is one part of the person. However, one should not ignore the other domains nor restrict outcome assessments to personal changes in participants. For example, the number of hours of service and the actual contributions to the community by participants of a service learning program are important accomplishments that can be documented. The focus should be on what the program is trying to achieve, whether it is a change in participants, a school, or a community.

It may seem contradictory to argue both for increased evaluation emphasis on program process and experience, and also for a shift to practical behaviors and accomplishments to assess outcome. In fact, the two approaches complement each other. Behavioral outcome evaluation will only provide meaningful information if it can be connected to information about program processes and experiences in a longitudinal way. For example, Ross & McKay (1976) developed a sophisticated behavior modification program in a juvenile corrections facility for difficult female offenders. Their initial results were dramatic in terms of a greatly reduced recidivism rate for participants relative to a comparison group. They repeated their program twice with a few "minor" changes, and in these instances the recidivism rates of the participants jumped to a level that was even higher than the standard treatments. After a careful review of the program process and experience, the investigators hypothesized that it was the peer therapist aspect of the original treatment that was the key factor in the initial success, not the more prominent behavior modification procedures. They then dropped the behavior modification program entirely and developed the peer therapist model. As a result, they were able to repeat the very significant decrease in the recidivism rate that had been documented initially. Outcome data becomes more valuable to the extent that it is connected to information about the program process.

FUTURE CHALLENGES

The above prescriptions for evaluation and research are common sense from the perspective of an experiential educator. What could be more logical than to integrate action and reflection, focus on the process, emphasize the quality of the experience, problem-solve with multiple strategies, and learn from the consequences? Unfortunately, it is a relatively easy task to define the needs, and many of the above ideas have been expressed elsewhere (Conrad & Hedin, 1981; Ewert, 1987). The challenge is to overcome the psychological and structural issues that are the roadblocks to moving in these directions. It is not a coincidence that these directions are still relatively uncharted despite the fact that they seem like common sense.

Psychological Roadblocks

One quality of strong leadership is the ability to believe in what one is doing, otherwise participants will not identify with the program's values and goals. The very powerful role of the self-fulfilling prophecy has been well-documented in education literature (Rosenthal & Jacobson, 1968). Outcome research in mental health has indicated that the type of theoretical treatment approach adopted by a therapist can be far less important in predicting outcome than the extent to which the therapist believes in the specific approach (Yalom, 1985). Practitioners need to believe in themselves, both to survive psychologically in intensive programs requiring high energy, and to ensure the success of their programs.

Unfortunately, this needs to believe has a dangerous flip side. Implicitly, often unconsciously, it can be translated into "I am a helpful person, therefore, I would not do anything to hurt anyone, therefore, what I am doing is helpful." Most leaders are keen to make adjustments in programs when they identify trouble spots, but are they willing to step beyond their own biases, paradigms, and ideologies? The role of evaluation in providing a new perspective is often proclaimed, but when push comes to shove, the energy and priority is not there to make the evaluation happen. In part, it is leaders' need to believe in what they are doing that results in evaluation receiving a lower priority relative to other tasks. On the other hand, if one waited until a program approach was proven to be absolutely effective before implementing it, very little, if anything, would get accomplished. There is a middle road, but experiential educators more often tend to err towards too much implicit faith in themselves and their work.

A second psychological issue that blocks practitioners from getting more involved in evaluation and research efforts is the tendency of researchers to use jargon and sophisticated technical procedures that obscure the nature of the evaluation process. Practitioners are implicitly convinced that they do not have the expertise to define program evaluation efforts. Recently, in the early stages of a research design course for practicing teachers, the professor introduced the notion of frequency polygons and histograms. After five minutes, one teacher pointed out to the others that the professor was simply talking about line graphs and bar graphs, which are elementary school mathematics concepts. By the end of the course, the same teachers had gained a very different perspective of the research enterprise and their ability to undertake evaluation and research work in their own settings. They had learned the jargon such that they could review and identify fatal weaknesses and shoddy work in articles published in some of the most "respectable" education journals. Prior to the course, they would not have dreamed of drawing such conclusions, much less reading these "difficult" articles. The sophisticated academic jargon is particularly intimidating when researchers are quick to criticize what they perceive to be the biased evaluation efforts of others in scientific terminology. However, they often fail to acknowledge the inadequacies and weaknesses in their own approaches. Often, the simplest designs produce the most meaningful results.

The key ingredients to defining an evaluation are knowing the phenomena, identifying the key issues, and defining potential evaluation strategies in a creative, logical, and thoughtful fashion. One does not have to conduct major research projects to produce meaningful evaluation data for a particular setting. The priority is to build evaluation and reflection into the program, regardless of the scale of the project. Researchers do have technical expertise, which can be necessary and/or valuable, but typically the expertise is more relevant to the question of how to implement a specific strategy rather than deciding what issue should be addressed and what strategy developed.

Structural roadblocks

Structural issues within the experiential education field combine with practitioners' beliefs in both their practical effectiveness and research ineptitude to further restrict evaluation efforts. A very legitimate complaint among practitioners is that there is simply no time available for evaluation, given other responsibilities. Experiential education organizations are often run on a shoestring and/or programs are spearheaded by committed individuals within larger organizations that do not even recognize the person's experiential activities as their primary job responsibility. Evaluation requires the allocation of staff time at an organizational level, which can only come at some sacrifice to other priorities and services.

There are also typically few incentives and payoffs to the practitioner for evaluation from an organizational perspective. Significant recognition does not often result from the write-up of an evaluation report or a research article. Instead, evaluation may be seen as taking time and resources away from service, while neither generating funds nor having a dramatic short-term impact. Moreover, given the negligible impact of past evaluation work on program development, organizations may have some experience to justify relegating evaluation to a low-priority endeavor. Complimenting the pressures on practitioners are the academic pressures on university-based researchers. Although they have incentives for doing research and writing in terms of career advancement, the pressure can become extreme to the point that the priority becomes the amount of work one has published rather than the quality. Numbers of quick and easy studies can score points with tenure committees. Yet, more carefully developed longitudinal efforts that have meaningful returns to local programs and take more time and effort, do not gain an equivalent level of academic recognition. Practitioners and academic researchers are under different types of pressures that can detract from quality evaluation efforts, and in turn, quality programs.

Confronting the Roadblocks

Developing a meaningful and constructive program evaluation and research base involves overcoming psychological and structural roadblocks. As a young field, experiential education has an opportunity to avoid the alienating research versus practice dichotomy that is entrenched in other disciplines. For example, classroom teachers typically ignore their technical research literature because it seems irrelevant to day-to-day activities. On the other hand, some teachers do not view evaluation or research as essential or even helpful to good practice. One key element to addressing the psychological roadblocks involves integrating research and practice in the training process. If future experiential educators are given a firm grounding in program evaluation and research as a part of their training to be practitioners, it may help them to constructively question their practice while building confidence in their ability to define and develop evaluation strategies. Moreover, evaluation and research teaching responsibilities must not be farmed out to someone from another field. These topics must be taught by an experiential educator in an experiential fashion, addressing relevant examples, methodologies, and issues. Only then will students integrate their evaluation and research experience with their practical work. The ideal standard for undergraduate and master's research should be meaningful, small-scale efforts that can impact specific practices, rather than independent studies that can be published. A diversity of approaches, qualitative as well as quantitative, needs to be addressed.

The leadership in training innovations will have to come from the stronger, cohesive programs that have control over an integrated degree program. Unfortunately, in many places, experiential education is taught across a few courses by faculty who are working within a broader department or division. These faculty often do not have program control over courses taken by students with experiential education interests. However, leadership from the integrated programs can have a substantial impact on the field, while individual faculty can include evaluation and research topics as sections of practical courses.

The structural roadblocks must be confronted by practitioners through their programs and institutions. Inevitably, some time and resources committed to other priorities must be shifted to evaluation work. Over the long run these initial shifts can bring better programs and save resources. Many organizations are beginning to recognize that the traditional outdoor program staffing strategy of utilizing high-energy, committed, young instructors to run very intensive courses, has serious shortcomings in terms of instructor burnout and turnover. By the time instructors have gained experience and are more able and willing to recognize the limits of their missionary zeal, they turn over. Organizations lose the staff who are probably in a better position to identify and put priority on meaningful evaluation projects. Experienced staff are more likely to see the long-term benefits of putting short-term energy into evaluation. Finally, at the initial hiring level, more priority might be placed on hiring staff with a strong commitment to reflection and evaluation.

Another means for organizations to increase their emphasis on evaluation is to carefully integrate meaningful procedures into new program proposals and build the cost in as a budget line. Given the increased push for accountability in education and social programs in recent years, evaluation is one item that granting agencies are more amenable to supporting. Programs may also pool resources, cooperate with universities, and/or build and utilize larger networks as a means to increase priority on program evaluation without making unacceptable sacrifices in other areas. At an administrative level, these strategies demand creativity, commitment, and communication. The return can be substantial for program development.

PUTTING THE IDEAS INTO PRACTICE

The psychological and structural roadblocks will only be overcome through long-term efforts to change organizational and university structures at the local level, though broader networks and publications can facilitate the process. But what are the key questions for those committed and able to develop evaluation projects now? The fundamental question is, "why evaluate?" The priority should be program improvement, rather than to meet external grant criteria, or to justify and sell the program.

The second issue is to consider the developmental stage of the program and its present level of sophistication. What types of evaluation projects will feed back information and contribute to action? For example, assume one is developing a pilot program to build multicultural awareness and sensitivity among high school youth. It includes a short-term, intensive summer experience at a camp setting followed by participants working together in small, independent teams to put on multicultural events in their home communities during the subsequent fall season. How could one build evaluation into the program? A key program issue would involve participants developing the planning skills and the teamwork to put on the community events. One could expect participants to keep journals throughout the process of planning and running the community events in order to document their teamwork and accomplishments. By working with the participants to develop a meaningful planning process during the summer camp, one could ask that specific information be included in the journals: number of meetings, number of community participants, quality of the team process, etc. One could even assist participants to develop their own evaluation strategy for their event, which in turn would contribute to an overall program evaluation. Valuable information can be generated if priority is placed on getting participants to follow through with their journal recordings and if there is a careful analysis of the collected information. One would have a record of program accomplishments, some numerical indicators of impact on the community, and insights into the team process. The requirements of the evaluation also promote meaningful practice: use of a journal, development of planning strategies, and participant reflection and evaluation of their work. This approach is more time-consuming than only administering a couple of pre-treatment and post-treatment attitude questionnaires, but the return in the long run is much higher. Questionnaires might be used in conjunction with this approach, but their value would come in relating their results to the journal data. The above scenario provides one example for a program at one stage of development. A well-entrenched program may benefit from a broader, more rigorous evaluation process with comparison groups or repeated measurements over time. The key is to tailor the approach to the needs of the program.

A third issue and trap that frequently appears in program evaluation work is an attempt to make the program and the resulting evaluation be all things to all people. A proposal for an adventure program for a delinquent population promises improvements in self-esteem, socially responsible behavior, cooperative attitudes, problem-solving skills, empathy for others, etc. The evaluation then ends up involving innumerable questions and sections on a great range of topics.

The result is a little bit of information about everything and not much of substance and value about anything. The root of the problem is often with the program's lack of clarity and specificity in defining goals. The evaluation process, rather than condoning this approach, can be used to raise questions. What are the key goals? How exactly will the program provide experiences that will help participants achieve their goals? There must be a clear vision of the program before one can identify the options for evaluation.

A final issue is the recognition that good work takes time. One needs to assess the extent of what a program can achieve in terms of the time, energy, and resources available. A small, well-implemented project, in which information is carefully analyzed and cycled back into programming, can start a positive spiral by involving staff in the process and creating opportunities for further work. However, intensive evaluation strategies, which may seem exciting in their initial stages, can reinforce negative attitudes if the initial enthusiasm falls off and there is not the time and resources to carry the project through to completion. In short, one needs to be realistic about what can be accomplished, and creative about tapping additional resources. The critical issue when pulling in external resources is to ensure that the people who will be using the information maintain involvement and control over what will be done and how the evaluation will be conducted.

The prescriptions will not be realized in the short term. It is a major challenge to integrate action and reflection, focus on the process, emphasize the quality of the experience, problem-solve with multiple strategies, and learn from the consequences. The psychological and structural roadblocks are substantial, and there are no quick and easy answers. Practitioners' strong faith in their practices, and sense of helplessness with respect to research are attitudes embedded in who they are as people. The organizational pressures and reward structures that inhibit quality work are rooted in institutions and are often beyond the control of experiential educators. However, as more practitioners and researchers work to put the ideas into practice at the local level, the discipline will strengthen its evaluation and research base, and the process of change will gain momentum. It is a major challenge, but that is a key ingredient at the start of the experiential learning cycle.

REFERENCES

Abelson, R. (1972). Are attitudes necessary? B. T. King and E. McGinnes (Eds.), *Attitudes, conflict, and social change.* New York: Academic Press.

Bacon, S. (1983). *The conscious use of metaphor in Outward Bound.* Denver, CO: The Colorado Outward Bound School.

Beker, J. (1960). The influence of school camping on the self-concepts and social relationships of sixth grade children. *Journal of Educational Psychology, 51* (6), 352-356.

Bem, D., & Allen, A. (1974). On predicting some of the people some of the time: The search for cross-situational consistencies in behavior. *Psychological Review, 81*, 506-520.

Carney, T. F. (1972). *Content analysis: A technique for systematic inference from communications.* Winnipeg: University of Manitoba Press.

Conrad, D. (1979). *Experiential education: A summary of the theoretical foundations and a critical review of recent research.* St. Paul, MN: Center for Youth Research and Development, University of Minnesota.

Conrad, D., & Hedin, D. (1981). National assessment of experiential education: Summary and implications. *Journal of Experiential Education, 4* (2), 6-20.

Drebing, C. E., Willis, S. C., & Genet, B. (1987). Anxiety and the Outward Bound process. *Journal of Experiential Education, 10* (2), 17-21.

Ewert, A. (1987). Research in experiential education: An overview. *Journal of Experiential Education, 10* (2), 4-7.

Ewert, A. (1983). *Outdoor adventure and self-concept: A research analysis.* Eugene, OR: Center of Leisure Studies, University of Oregon.

Filstead, W. J. (1979). Qualitative methods: A needed perspective in evaluation research. T. R. Cook and C. S. Reichardt (Eds.), *Qualitative and quantitative methods in evaluation research.* Beverly Hills, CA: Sage Publications.

Goetz, J. P., & LeCompt, M. D. (1984). *Ethnography and qualitative design in educational research.* Orlando, FL: Academic Press.

Guba, E. G., & Lincoln, Y. S. (1985). *Naturalistic inquiry.* Beverly Hills, CA: Sage.

Hamilton, S. (1979). *Evaluating experiential learning programs.* Paper presented at the Annual Meeting of the American Educational Research Association.

Haynes, S. N. (1978). *Principles of behavioral assessment.* New York: Gardner Press.

Heinrichsdorff, A. M. (1987). Course evaluations: Creating a self-fulfilling prophecy. *Journal of Experiential Education, 10* (2), 47-49.

Holsti, O. R. (1969). *Content analysis for the social sciences and humanities.* Don Mills, ON: Addison Wesley.

Kaufman, G. G., & Johnson, J. C. (1974). Scaling peer ratings: An examination of the differential validity of positive and negative nominations. *Journal of Applied Psychology, 59,* 302-306.

McCabe, B. A., & Harris, B. (1979). *Keeping the flame alive: The role of follow-up in therapeutic adventure programming.* Paper presented at the Annual Conference of the Association for Experiential Education, Portsmouth, NH.

Mischel, W. (1969). *Introduction to personality.* New York: Rhinehart and Winston.

Rosenthal, R., & Jacobson, L. (1968). *Pygmalion in the classroom.* New York: Rinehart & Winston.

Ross, R., & McKay, H. B. (1976). Adolescent therapists. *Canada's Mental Health, 24,* 15-17.

Rowley, J. (1987). Adventure education and qualitative research. *Journal of Experiential Education, 10* (2), 8-12.

Shore, A. (1978). *Outward Bound: A reference volume.* Greenwich, CT: Outward Bound Inc.

Simon, A., & Boyer, E. G. (1974). *Mirrors for behavior, III: An anthology of observation instruments.* Wyncote, PA: Communications Materials Center.

Smith, M. L., & Glass, G. V. (1987). *Research and Evaluation in Education and the Social Sciences.* Englewood Cliffs, NJ: Prentice-Hall, Inc.

Teaff, J., & Kablach, J. (1987). Psychological benefits of outdoor adventure activities. *Journal of Experiential Education, 10* (2), 43-46.

Warner, A. (1982). *A social and academic assessment of experiential education trips with elementary school children.* Unpublished doctoral dissertation, Dalhousie University, Halifax, NS.

Warner, A. (1984a). How to creatively evaluate programs. *Journal of Experiential Education, 7* (2), 38-43.

Warner, A. (1984b). Using initiative games to assess group cooperation. *Journal of Experiential Education, 7* (1), 42-43.

Wiggins, J. S. (1973). *Personality and prediction: Principles of personality assessment.* Don Mills, ON: Addison Wesley.

Yalom, I. (1985). *The theory and practice of group psychotherapy, (3rd ed).* New York: Basic Books.

Section Eight

THE SETTING FOR ADVENTURE EDUCATION

Places for Risk-Taking

Nature provided most of the settings for early attempts at adventure education. Kurt Hahn took his boys to sea. Outward Bound in America went to the mountains, lakes, deserts and the sea. Adventure educators sought environments that contrasted to the normal settings of their clients. They sought places that would provide a break with the familiar; places that would add an ingredient of challenge and risk to the adventure. Adventure program participants come from a society dominated by a compelling passion for control of self, of others and of nature. Control would bring comfort, safety and security. What places might offer less of these, might force the student to test and stretch their abilities and yield discoveries about self, society and nature?

One such place, as Miles points out, is wilderness. When wild places are accessible, adventure educators use them. After millennia of efforts to conquer nature and eliminate wilderness, people today seek its risks and uncertainties for the lessons to be learned there. Wild places are rare and fragile today. Miles suggests that educators must nurture, conserve and even restore this resource of central value to them.

Contemporary society has such technological capability that many of the risks posed by nature in wilderness can be reduced or eliminated. Radios, helicopters, even satellites make rescue possible from the most remote locations. Wilderness areas are "managed" by bureaucrats who perceive one of their tasks to be the protection of visitors from themselves. How much protection, asks McAvoy, is too much? He offers a proposal for rescue-free wilderness areas. The very idea is an anathema to land managers and fraught with moral issues for adventure educators. The threat of over-regulated, monitored and policed wildlands, where achievement of challenge and self-reliance are difficult, is a real one worthy of contemplation.

All adventure educators cannot, of course, transport their clients to natural wilderness. Most wilderness is in the rural West, while most adventure education clients are in the urban East. Proudman argues that urban settings are good settings for developing programs for inner-city youth. Curricula and learning models must and can be adapted to this setting. Proudman contrasts the wilderness and urban settings and reviews the issues posed by efforts to use the latter. He argues convincingly that the approaches used by adventure educators offers much to urban communities.

Adventure educators have sometimes also found it useful and necessary to create their own resources, including the settings for adventure activities. Attarian and Rohnke describe the principal directions this creation has taken. Climbing walls have been designed in various ways, pools and gyms have been used, and the ropes course has evolved into one of the most widely used "environments" for adventure education. As adventure education spreads and evolves, the ingenuity of practitioners will yield new ideas for facilitating challenge that will allow widespread access to adventure activities and reduce pressures on natural environments. This promises to be a very interesting and evolutionary process.

Wilderness

John C. Miles
Western Washington University

Wilderness is a place where the processes of nature occur as they always have, where grizzly and wolf, golden eagle and great white shark stalk their prey, where such organisms live and die as they have since their creation. Trees grow there for a thousand years, fall over and rot, giving nutrients to the next generation. The sun rises and sets over land that changes, sometimes quickly but usually slowly, constantly, and according to the inexorable rhythms of nature. Rocks and boulders rattle and tumble off wilderness peaks. Winds pound and snows smother the uplands, while heat shatters the rock of deserts and flood undermines and fells the eagle tree. Individuals and species come and go and life triumphs in wild places. The river of time flows steadily, regularly, predictably.

Such is wilderness, a description of which is difficult without reference to human experience. In human terms, wilderness is "an area where the earth and its community of life are untrammeled by man, where man himself is a visitor who does not remain" (1964, The Wilderness Act). Wilderness is an environment in which people can exercise less control than usual. When a storm descends on wilderness travelers, there is no climate-controlled retreat available. They must cope with the resources at hand. Predictability of experience is reduced by this lack of control —the wilderness traveler faces more unknowns than usual. Can these be handled? This element of uncertainty is always present in wilderness, and this ingredient prompted adventure educators to take their students there.

What qualifies a place to be considered a wilderness suitable for adventure? The pioneering ecologist and wilderness advocate Aldo Leopold once defined wilderness as a place where a person could take a two-week pack trip and not encounter the works of humans. That was the early 1920s. By the late 1960s, with roads in many places that were wild in Leopold's day, the U.S. government thought 5,000 acres a reasonable minimum size for an area to be included in the

National Wilderness Preservation System. The size of the natural area is important only in terms of its effect on wilderness values like solitude, beauty, and naturalness. An uninhabited island of 500 acres surrounded by hundreds of square miles of ocean could be as wild as a two-million-acre tract in a remote part of Alaska.

Another set of qualifications for wilderness involve human experience of a place. Can the traveler find the physical and emotional challenge of the unknown there? In New Hampshire, two small boys pack their rucksacks and venture forth into woodlands in a place settled for 300 years. They are small, the woods are big. They perceive their adventure as risky—wild animals out there in the dark, no parents to help them cope with fear, no McDonald's to tap for food supplies. They camp, in their minds, in a wilderness.

The point is that the wilderness used by adventure educators is both a physical and conceptual place. Wilderness is an idea, a state of mind. It is relative rather than an absolute conception and condition. People are arguing about whether grizzly bears should be reintroduced into the North Cascades of Washington state. "Do it," say some people. "The Pasayten will be really wild with them there." Others argue against the idea. "Grizzlies are too dangerous. The increased risk will reduce the recreational value of the place for me and for others. People will be frightened to go there." All the debaters like to travel to "wilderness." Some like more "wild" in their wilderness than others. Some, like adventure educators, desire an element of risk, of mystery and challenge in the places they go with their students. Other wilderness travelers seek a relatively safe environment where they can retreat from the cares of the world. This illustrates how people have come to variously define "wilderness."

Adventure educators take their students into the full range of wilderness places. They go where they can find environments that challenge the students—onto rivers, into caves, over mountains, across deserts, through swamps, and to lakes and the sea. They look for places that are physically difficult and demanding for travel, that present exacting but soluble problems, that give instantaneous reward for effort, that grant the opportunity for solitude, that allow immersion in the unfamiliar and the unknown with the anxiety that these produce. They seek places where the illusion of total human control of nature is banished, places that engage the whole person—mind, body and spirit—places that are pervaded by a sense of power, mystery, and awe. They go where there is danger but where the danger can be assessed and managed. They help students convert danger, fear, and anxiety into achievement and mastery through skill, cooperation and hard work. Many educators have found these qualities and learning opportunities in wilderness.

Students go into wilderness and most come away changed. Their self-confidence is increased. Some who consider themselves failures come away with a taste of personal success. New skills are learned and perspectives gained. Boundaries defining what is possible for them in various areas of their lives are moved, extending their visions of their personal potential. Most students in wilderness adventure education programs come away more physically challenged and fit than they have ever been before. Some have, for the first time, reflected on some of life's deeper issues. Has wilderness brought about these results? Not by itself. A combination of program and place have produced the results. The educator has designed the experience to take advantage of the qualities of the place that suit his or her purposes. No research has been done to determine how much the place contributes to the achievement of adventure education program objectives. There is no doubt, though, that some learning is made much more possible by the setting of wilderness.

Wilderness is an increasingly scarce resource for adventure education. It is more scarce in some regions than others, and development is inexorably reducing the overall availability of this resource. In 1985, the National Wilderness Preservation System in the United States totaled 89 million acres, 3.78 percent of the approximately 2.3 billion acres of the country.

Many millions of wild acres in national forests, parks, wildlife refuges, and rangelands are not officially part of the system. Struggles to ensure preservation of more wilderness are underway, but every fight is difficult—the forces for development, roadbuilding, mining, logging, snowmobiling, off-road vehicle driving, and tourism development are strong. The wilderness system in the United States may grow to 120 million acres. As this occurs, the total resource will shrink as development advances in unprotected areas.

On the surface, the wilderness resource supply might look good—120 million acres is a lot of land. Unfortunately wilderness is not evenly distributed. There is relatively little wilderness in the eastern United States. Many states have no designated wilderness (yet have most of the human population). Alaska has 56 million acres of official wilderness and California, nearly six million. The majority of the National Wilderness Preservation system is too far from most people to be accessible to them. Thus, while four percent of the American land may become official wilderness with long-term protection from development, access and supply will become an increasing problem as population, recreational use, and adventure education programming grow.

The situation of wilderness worldwide is more difficult to adequately describe. Park and wilderness preservation began in the United States and progressed farthest here. Many nations around the world, even developing countries, have followed the United States' example by establishing national parks and preserves. Still, there is precious little wilderness, and what there is suffers the pressures of development and growing population. Biologist George Schaller traveled the Himalaya mountain range and found wildlife populations decimated everywhere by people desperate for food and cash. Even Antarctica, relatively inviolate until now, faces the juggernaut of oil and mineral exploration and development. There is, in short, little wilderness left on a planet inhabited by a rapidly growing population of more than five billion humans. The future promises continued shrinkage of the wilderness.

Adventure education is a recent phenomenon in the widespread business of teaching and learning. Its emergence has, ironically, coincided with decline of the wilderness resource upon which it depends. This is not surprising since the reason people now program "adventure" is because it is no longer a normal part of life. Humans sought for millennia to subdue wilderness. That process was dangerous, uncomfortable, and often fatal. Now that wilderness seems to be conquered, humans miss the challenges the struggle provided. They recognize the values provided by that struggle, values not appreciated then and not now available in the normal course of life. So, in compensation, they venture forth in growing numbers in adventure sports and even program risk for their youth.

Will adventure education be a flash in the educational pan? Possibly, because there can be no adventure education if there is no physical place for adventure. Thus, it is incumbent upon educators who use wilderness to do all that they can to maintain and sustain this resource. Adventure educators must be advocates of wilderness. They must work for the preservation of the tiny fraction of the world's surface that remains wild. Others are working to do this in political arenas. Enlightened self-interest requires adventure educators to join in that effort.

Secondly, adventure educators should program a proper wilderness-use ethic into the experience of their students. Some programs currently do a better job of this than others. All programs must do this job well. Official wilderness has caretakers, but users cannot leave the wilderness maintenance job to official caretakers. There are too few of them to do the large job. Educational programs using wilderness must train all of their leaders in minimum-impact technique and teach them to effectively teach this technique. All programs must embrace an ethic of service of working to mitigate the inevitable impact they have when they use wildlands, no matter how hard they work to minimize their impact. Damage to wilderness, as to all environments, is incremental—a little here and there, which over time adds up to destruction of the beauty and solitude, naturalness and mystery that make such places useful to educators.

Valuable lessons that are useful in life's larger context are learned in adventure education. Some of these lessons can and should be about the human species' relationship to and its dependence upon, nature. Students, most of whom will come from urban backgrounds, can learn to see nature in new ways, to appreciate how complex, beautiful, and organized it is. Awareness that they, as humans, are nature-bound by ecological constraints, can grow. Humility in the face of grand space and time can give perspective on human enterprise. Human control of nature can perhaps be seen for what it is—an illusion. All of these lessons can help the students understand themselves as humans, as members of the biotic community. Perhaps they can even begin to grasp their special responsibilities as human beings, which derive from their understanding of how nature works. Humans are, as far as we know, the only organisms who are conscious of the process of evolution and can make decisions accordingly. We may come to see this gift of knowledge as a burden and an opportunity, but we will not be able to escape it. Thus, wilderness education can be an introduction to planetary citizenship.

Some may respond that this is expecting a lot of a usually short educational experience confined by specific goals and learning processes, and it is. Yet a visit to wilderness is a rare gift and the most must be made of the opportunity the visit provides. Wilderness travel is to outdoor experience what a symphony is to music—the ultimate opportunity to encounter the depth and scope of the medium. Aldo Leopold, as a pioneering thinker on wilderness and ecology, thought integrity, stability, and beauty were the ultimate values of the natural world. These qualities can be experienced and understood in wilderness settings.

When a person experiences the wilderness often, as most adventure educators do, there is a temptation to become complacent and blasé about the place, to take it for granted and think it commonplace. Wilderness is rare and valuable in the modern world. The educator who uses wilderness should treat it like he or she would an ancient and rare book—with awe, great care, and affection. Much can be learned from the book, but only by those who study it carefully and patiently. Just as educators should treat a rare book gently and cautiously, with careful attention to its fragility and for its longevity, so must they treat wilderness. Only then will they ensure that future generations of wilderness educators and students will be able to take lessons from the wilderness.

REFERENCES

Berry, W. (1987). *Home economics.* San Francisco: North Point Press.

The Wilderness Act of 1964, (16 U.S.C. 1131 et seq.: 78 Stat. 890).

Rescue-Free Wilderness Areas

Leo McAvoy
University of Minnesota

A challenging environment is often stated as one of the necessary experiential components in adventure education programs (McAvoy, 1987). Although challenging environments can be found in school and urban settings, many adventure programs have traditionally utilized the more remote, undeveloped outdoor recreation resources found in National Parks, National Forests, and in designated Wilderness Areas. These adventure programs use Wilderness Areas because of the opportunities to have participants experience the beauty and grandeur of nature, and also because of the risk, challenge, and opportunity for self-sufficiency that the wilderness provides. But some fear that opportunities to experience risk are diminishing in these times of heavy wilderness use and the tendency of wilderness managing agencies (e.g., National Park Service) to assume responsibility for user safety. Will there be opportunities in the future for adventure education programs to utilize wilderness for risk and challenge if current trends in wilderness-management continue?

A 1981 issue of *Journal of Forestry* introduced the idea of a rescue-free wilderness area in which recreationists would have an opportunity for complete self-sufficiency (McAvoy & Dustin, 1981). It was proposed that rescue-free zones be established in some existing remote wilderness areas. In these zones, the wilderness users would be completely responsible for their own safety. The government agencies managing these rescue-free zones would be absolved, indeed prohibited from conducting or sponsoring any search and rescue operations for wilderness users in the area. The managing agency would be responsible for informing the users of the principle risks in the area and that no governmental rescue services would be available for a recreationist there. Otherwise, the rescue-free zone would be managed like other wilderness areas; there would be a user quota system to keep the number of visitors low to protect the resource and the wilderness experience, no motorized vehicles, and no signs, trails, or bridges. The visitors to these rescue-free areas could experience the self-growth that comes from the challenge of testing themselves and taking full responsibility for their actions (McAvoy & Dustin, 1983). The following is a rationale for rescue-free wilderness and how such areas relate to the goals and practices of adventure education.

PHILOSOPHICAL BASIS FOR RESCUE-FREE AREAS

Wilderness is usually regarded as a block of land. The Wilderness Act of 1964 legally defines certain blocks of land as being wilderness. There are now over 88 million acres in the National Wilderness Preservation System (NWPS) in this country, with more being proposed.

Wilderness is also an experience, and it is the opportunity for that experience that attracts visitors to wilderness. If the experience opportunities were gone, there would likely be no wilderness areas today. Our cultural perception of wilderness has many dimensions (Nash, 1982). It is a place to experience beauty, serenity, primeval forces of nature, undeveloped places, primitive and unconfined recreation, historical significance, and a place of scientific wonder. It is also a place to experience freedom, solitude, challenge, risk, and self-reliance. It is these last few experiences (challenge, risk, self-reliance) that some believe we are in danger of losing.

Our cultural value of, and need for, wilderness was articulated in the mid-1800s by the transcendentalist philosopher and author Henry David Thoreau. In 1851, he ended a lecture by stating that in wildness is the preservation of the world (Nash, 1982). Those were radical words for a country that was trying to create a civilization out of a vast wilderness. Over the years since 1851, our society has held that there is more to the preservation of the world than wildness. Yet, we as a society have also decided that wildness is one of the aspects of this world we want to preserve, and so we have, in our wilderness areas. The question is, are we allowing that wildness to slip away?

Early visionaries of a national wilderness system argued that risk and self-reliance were vital parts of the wilderness experience and should be preserved. Bob Marshall, the founder of the Wilderness Society, wrote in the 1930s that wilderness should provide opportunities for complete self-sufficiency (Marshall, 1930). More recently, others interpreting the 1964 Wilderness Act have argued that wilderness is a place where users are responsible for their own safety, where a physical and mental challenge to survive exists, and self-reliance reigns (Nash, 1982, 1985). Part of the definition of "wilderness" in the Wilderness Act states that it is a place that is *untrammeled*, which means uncontrolled and unrestrained. Wilderness is the uncontrolled, and the uncontrolled is unpredictable and therefore potentially dangerous. The uncontrolled and unrestrained are important aspects of what wilderness is, or at least what it was intended to be by the shapers of the Wilderness Act of 1964.

NEED FOR RESCUE-FREE AREAS

The need for rescue-free wilderness zones centers around the three issues of wilderness management agencies taking responsibility for visitor safety, the development of "high-tech" equipment for rescue, and the growth of an insurance mentality. Over the past 20 years, there has been an increase in wilderness management by federal agencies. This has been mainly to protect the integrity of the natural resources from the damage of overuse. In some wilderness areas, regulations have had to be imposed limiting use numbers and use types. This wilderness management has also resulted in governmental agencies such as the Park Service and Forest Service assuming a growing amount of responsibility for the safety of the wilderness user. This is appropriate in most developed outdoor recreation resources, but some question the need to extend this safety-net mentality to all wilderness areas.

Wilderness management is somewhat of an oxymoron. "Wilderness" implies freedom, the uncontrolled, risk and self-reliance, while "management" implies control, restraint, and security. There are still some remote wilderness areas where people can go to experience a feeling of complete self-reliance either because of the remoteness of the area or the current lack of agency-use monitoring. But will these opportunities continue in the light of federal agencies moving further in wilderness management?

The continuing development of high technology equipment is making the wilderness less than wild. Wilderness visitors enjoy the benefits of development in fabrics like nylon for lightweight tents and clothing, and synthetic insulation for sleeping bags. These developments make wilderness accessible to almost anyone. The somewhat negative developments (for self-reliance purists) are the high-altitude/all-weather helicopter, pack radios, locater beacons, etc. Most wilderness users know all too well that should they be declared overdue, ill, or injured, most wilderness is accessible in a few moments time for a helicopter rescue to fly them to the wonders of the modern hospital emergency room. The availability of high-technology rescue techniques causes some individuals and groups to enter wilderness areas ill-prepared to be self-sufficient because they know the governmental managing agencies will coordinate a rescue operation if needed.

A third phenomenon creating a need for rescue-free areas is a general insurance mentality in American society. Many people want to be protected from all risk. They want the benefits of high-adventure activities (personal growth, stimulation, enhanced awareness, self-fulfillment) but they want the potential costs to be borne by others, usually the government (Aharoni, 1981). Persons with this insurance mentality want illusions of challenge, risk, and self-reliance, but they want a government-sponsored safety net (Sax, 1980). And, they tend to believe that everyone else should share this insurance mentality by placing visitor protection as an overriding top priority. An illustration of this trend is the million dollars spent each year by governmental agencies in rescue operations in backcountry areas (McAvoy & Dustin, 1983). Well-meaning governmental managers have often extended the visitor safety policies that are necessary in developed parks to the wilderness, where such policies run counter to the purpose of wilderness.

EXPERIENTIAL BENEFITS OF RESCUE-FREE AREAS

Rescue-free areas would preserve that rare opportunity for self-growth that wilderness can provide. They would provide opportunities for challenge and the personal testing of oneself at the edge of life (Schreyer et al., 1978). But one cannot truly test at the edge of life if not allowed to approach it. One cannot really approach the edge if one knows that it is fenced with a rescue policy. Risk, challenge, self-reliance, and complete self-sufficiency are legitimate experiences to be preserved in the American wilderness.

Freedom and choice are highly valued in American culture. Rescue-free areas would not be forced on anyone. They would be available for those visitors who desire that type of experience. They would expand the range of choices available for wilderness users. They would be a few remote sections of existing wilderness areas where the visitor could experience complete self-sufficiency without the ultimate protection of a governmental agency standby to rescue.

There will certainly be some injuries in rescue-free wilderness zones and there may even be deaths. But they will be rare. Visitors entering such an area would be better prepared and more careful than the average wilderness users because they would know they were responsible for their own safety and for the safety of those in their group. Nearly all visitors to rescue-free areas would return home from their wilderness outing intact and infused with a new sense of confidence in their ability to take charge of their lives. They would have tested themselves at the edge of life successfully, much the way that sky divers and blue water ocean sailors do.

A WORST CASE SCENARIO

The following is a worst case scenario for a rescue-free area if such an area was established as part of the wilderness system. Let's assume that four friends want to visit a rescue-free zone and experience complete self-sufficiency. They receive all necessary information from the wilderness-managing agency. They are advised that no governmental rescue will be available to them. They decide they want to assume responsibility for themselves, and so they go into the area. After a long trek into a climbing area, they set up a base camp in a valley and survey the climbing opportunities. Early the next morning they start up a challenging face in two rope teams. Two members fall and are seriously injured. Neither are able to get off the mountain without assistance.

The rescue-free policy would work as follows. First, the managing agency would not come looking for the party if it was declared overdue. If the uninjured members of the party came out seeking a rescue, there would be no governmental agency rescue personnel, equipment, or service available for that zone. This includes Park Service, Forest Service, military, or local government-sponsored rescue. The party is entirely responsible for the welfare of its members.

Let's say in this case the uninjured party members decide to go out of the area and get friends to help in the rescue. But they would have to abide by use rationing or quota restrictions on use currently in effect for the area. They would have to assume responsibility for themselves, because if they become injured the rescue-free concept would apply to them as well. They would also have to comply with other wilderness use policies, such as no motorized vehicles. In the case of this scenario, the party alone would be responsible for themselves. They must rely on their own resources. Once they decide for complete self-sufficiency and enter the area, they are on their own completely.

RESPONSE TO COMMON CRITICISMS

Criticisms of the rescue-free proposal have been characterized by an undercurrent of negativism (Allen, 1981; Williamson, 1984; Peterson, 1987). The emphasis of these criticisms has been on what could go wrong in a rescue-free area rather than the positive aspects of what could go right. The negative visions of broken bodies lying unattended at the foot of the cliff and desperate pleas for help going unheeded serve to swing attention away from the positive personal and group benefits and growth that would accrue to the overwhelming majority of visitors to rescue-free wilderness. But practicality dictates that a response must be made to such criticisms, even though the potential benefits far outweigh the potential personal and societal costs (in the opinion of this author).

Wilderness-managing agency staff argue that rescue-free wilderness areas are impossible because agency policy dictates that search and rescue services will be available to all visitors. A rescue-free advocate answers this by simply saying the policy can be changed so those services are not available for certain zones. It may take legislative action or executive direction, but agency policies can be changed if enough citizens exert appropriate political pressures.

Another common criticism heard from managing agencies and others is the fear of legal liability. If a managing agency did not provide rescue service wouldn't they be successfully sued by either the injured party or their families? Legal scholars have researched this rescue-free concept and have decided that a managing agency that chose to not provide rescue would not be sued by either an injured party or their family. In undeveloped wilderness areas, the duty of the managing agency is only to inform the prospective visitor of principle dangers and to inform the visitor that no rescue services will be available while in that area (Frakt and Rankin, 1982). The managing agency does not have the responsibility to guarantee absolute protection of a person in a remote wilderness area (Rankin, 1984). There are virtually no cases of successful litigation in undeveloped wilderness areas. Adventure education agencies that sponsor trips to such areas would not have to fear liability problems if they have qualified staff, adequate supervision, inform participants of risks, and have appropriate group responses to handle emergency situations (McAvoy et al., 1985).

The legal question aside, many would argue that it would be ethically inexcusable for a managing agency like the Park Service or Forest Service to refuse a request for search and rescue. The rescue-free advocate would counter by pointing out that it is ethically inexcusable for governmental officials to deny people the opportunity for self-determination. If we are going to give people an opportunity to grow through challenge and by experiencing self-reliance, then we must provide that type of wilderness experience. We should respect the choice of those who would want to visit such a rescue-free area. We are a democracy that prides itself on respecting the rights and desires of the minority. Informal research indicates a significant minority that wants to see rescue-free areas become a reality in the wilderness system.

CONCLUSION

A proposal for rescue-free wilderness is not a macho, extremist, "man against the wilderness" attempt to make the wilderness more dangerous than it already is. It is not a proposal championed by insensitive people. Rather, it is an attempt to preserve a few places to experience what wilderness was intended to be, the untrammeled experience full of opportunities for self-reliance, risk, challenge, and self-growth. It would preserve in the American wilderness system legitimate opportunities for testing and expanding one's capabilities.

It is still possible to get a *de facto* rescue-free experience in little-used wilderness areas. But if wilderness use and wilderness management continue on current trends, all wilderness areas in the future may be as heavily regulated, policed, and monitored as some National Parks are now. Risk, challenge, and self-reliance may not be available in the wilderness of the future unless steps are taken now to preserve these experiences.

The goals of adventure education programs and activities include personal testing, challenge, and risk (Ewert, 1986). Adventure programs assist participants in developing physical, intellectual, and emotional skills that allow them to test themselves at increasingly higher levels of difficulty. To complement this progression of challenge, skills, and personal development, participants should be given increasing amounts of freedom and responsibility to exercise their competence and self-sufficiency (Dustin et al., 1986). Rescue-free wilderness areas appear to be a logical extension of this competency/self-sufficiency component of adventure education. Rescue-free areas may not be the best answer, but adventure educators must consider the role of self-reliance and risk in wilderness and how they can be preserved. If not through rescue-free areas, how?

REFERENCES

Aharoni, Y. 1981. *The no-risk society.* Chatham, NJ. Chatham House.

Allen, S. 1981. Comment: No-rescue wilderness — a risky proposition. *Journal of Forestry, 79*(3), 153-154.

Dustin, D., McAvoy, L. & Beck, L. 1986. Promoting recreationist self-sufficiency. *Journal of Park and Recreation Administration, 4*(4): 43-52.

Ewert, A. 1986. The therapeutic modification of fear through outdoor recreation activities. *The Bradford Papers Annual, 1*: 1-10.

Frakt, A., & Rankin, J. 1982. The law of parks, recreation resources and leisure services. *Brighton Publishing*, Salt Lake City, UT. 315 pp.

Marshall, R. 1930. The problem of wilderness. *Science Monthly, 30*: 141-148.

McAvoy, L., & Dustin, D. 1981. The right to risk in wilderness. *Journal of Forestry, 79*(3), 150-152.

McAvoy, L., & Dustin, D. 1983. In search of balance: A no-rescue wilderness proposal. *Western Wildlands, 9*(2): 2-5.

McAvoy, L., & Dustin, D., Rankin, J., & Frakt, A. 1985. Wilderness and legal-liability: Guidelines for resource managers and program leaders. *Journal of Park and Recreation Administration, 3*(1): 41-49.

McAvoy, L. 1987. The experiential components of a high-adventure program. Meier, J.F., T.W. Morash, & G.E. Welton, (Eds.), *High-Adventure Outdoor Pursuits.* Publishing Horizons Inc., Columbus, OH, 521 pp.

Miles, J. 1978. The value of high-adventure activities. *Journal of Physical Education and Recreation, 49*(4): 27-28.

Nash, R. 1982. *Wilderness and the American mind.* Yale University Press, New Haven, CT. 425 pp.

Nash, R. 1985. Proceed at your own risk. *National Parks, 59*(1-2): 18-19.

Peterson, D. 1987. Look ma, no hands: Here's what's wrong with no-rescue wilderness. *Parks and Recreation, 22*(6), 39-43, 54.

Rankin, J. 1984. Land features, locality and liability in park injury cases. *Trends, 21*(3): 9-12.

Sax, J. 1980. *Mountains without handrails.* University of Michigan Press, Ann Arbor, MI, 152 pp.

Schreyer, R., White R., McCool, S. 1978. Common attributes uncommonly exercised. *Journal of Physical Education and Recreation, 49*(4): 36-38.

Williamson, J. 1984. You can always say no to a rescuer. *Backpacker, 12*(5): 60-63, 68-69, 88, 92.

Urban Adventure

Steve Proudman
Outward Bound Chicago

The aim of this discussion is to challenge thinking and basic assumptions about what constitutes adventure education. Analysis begins with an examination of the problems and realities facing urban youth in American society and the potentials for adventure education of an urban environment. It is assumed that society's future economic, political, and social functions depend on successful transition into adulthood of today's youth. The focus is on urban youth, though many observations also apply to adults in urban settings.

The first section of this discussion explains the rationales for urban adventure programming. The city of Chicago provides an example of the condition of urban youth. The second section explores the potential for developing programs for inner-city youth. Current curricula, experiential learning models, and network utilization are explored. Finally, the third section will examine some emergent issues, such as professional (adventure education) lifestyle conflicts, safety concerns, and the cultural barriers inherent when operating in urban settings.

Passow (1982), writing on urban education's trends and issues for the 1980s, states that:

> "cities constitute rich environments for educating individuals of all ages. The urban environment contains cultural, educational, social, economic, physical, and natural resources that influence the development of its inhabitants. Urban education, when it consists only of that which takes place at that site called 'school', is clearly too limited and limiting."

Adventure education offers the potential to expand learning beyond conventional approaches in urban settings.

WHY URBAN ADVENTURE PROGRAMMING?

Risk-taking is a principal component of any adventure education curriculum. These risks are perceptual and highly controlled in the design and delivery processes. In urban environments, risks are part of a youth's daily existence.

The 1980 Census reports that 503,086 youth, aged 10 to 19, live in the city of Chicago. Sixty-seven percent of these are black and Latino (U.S. Census, 1980). In July 1986, the late Mayor Harold Washington established the Mayor's Youth Development Coordinating Committee (YDCC). The function of the committee was to examine both the successful passage to adulthood and the problems unique to adolescents. In YDCC reports, it was estimated that in 1987:

1. 75,000 youth would be seeking work but would remain unemployed.
2. 50,000 youth would leave school before graduating.
3. 45,000 youth will be arrested by Chicago police.
4. 60,000 youth would have substance abuse problems.
5. 15,000 female adolescents would become pregnant (YDCC, 1987).

Additional statistics revealed the gravity of the problems facing Chicago youth:

1. It is estimated that 1 in 3 children in Chicago live in families with incomes below the national poverty levels ($10,609 for a family of four). More than half of these children in poverty grow up in single-parent, female-headed households (Testa, 1985).

2. The Gang Crime Unit of the Chicago Police Department estimates that there are 120 street gangs in Chicago, with over 15,000 members. There are, on average, one to four gangs present in each Chicago public school. There were 14,000 active gang members arrested in 1986. Gangs are constantly recruiting members, providing safety and a sense of belonging to troubled youth (YDCC, 1987).

3. In 1985, 18.5 percent of all live births in Chicago were to teenagers. That translates to 10,222 babies (YDCC, 1987).

4. An estimated 10,000 youth are living on the streets of Chicago, nearly 4,000 of them pregnant and/or parenting teens. Many of these youth are victims of family violence, abuse, and neglect (Chicago Coalition of the Homeless, 1985).

5. Chicago was the most residentially segregated city in the nation in 1980. The Chicago public schools have the greatest level of black/white student segregation of any city school system in the United States (Chicago Urban League, 1987).

The YDCC reported that the number of "at risk" Chicago youth is growing. A generation of young people is lacking opportunities for positive experiences that will contribute to their transition to productive and contributing citizens of Chicago.

This state of affairs facing many urban youth should be seen as an impelling motivator and challenge to the adventure education profession. How can we better serve the needs of urban adolescents who might otherwise never benefit from our processes of learning? The answer may be to bring the program closer to their world by implementing adventure education in and around the city.

Today's youth are the caretakers of tomorrow's society. The future economic, political, and social success of American society depends on youth to develop the capacities they need for a successful transition into adulthood. Greenberger and Steinberg (1986) state that "rapid changes and multiple choices that currently characterize American society require adolescents to develop capacities that give them the flexibility and competence to meet demands that may change several times during their adult lives."

The Center for Youth Development at the University of Minnesota has done extensive research on youth needs in the developmental process. They state:

> "Development of a sense of self is the critical foundation for the transition into adulthood. Youth need to feel significant, important and unique; experience others being affected by their actions and decisions; interact positively with others; have a sense of belonging; love and be loved, trust and be trusted, respect and be respected. They need to experience a range of emotions, including success and failure, in a supporting context.
>
> Moreover, youth need to develop a sense of engagement: experiment without irrevocable commitment; have opportunities to make contributions to their world; experience a range of cultures, classes, languages; engage in adventurous activities; experiment with ideas and behaviors; and engage themselves physically.
>
> Finally, youth need to develop critical choice: reflect on and discuss needs and feelings; deal with uncertainties and be challenged and excited by change; have the opportunity to discuss conflicting values while formulating their own; gain experience in decision-making; know who can help in developing effective management of their affairs; develop the capacity for sustained, intense involvement in activities."
> (YDCC, 1987)

Present "school" experiences aim to prepare adolescents to become productive members of our materialistic society. They do not need a materialistic experience, but rather a humanistic or spiritual one. Through adventure education, commonly held societal values are taught: persistence, perseverance, compassion for others, critical thinking skills, and a sense of individual strengths and community interdependence. Urban adventure programming can provide a necessary balance of humanistic needs required for the holistic development of adolescents, complementing the functional skill orientation of conventional schooling.

The National Commission on Youth (1981) concludes that young people respond positively when given opportunities for meaningful participation in society. The capacities youth develop are dependent on the opportunities available to them. Opportunities that come as direct experience contribute to the formation of concepts of self, to responsibility, to modes of thinking about moral-social problems, to interpersonal relationships, and to the capacity for feeling joy and empathy (Gilligan, 1982). Adventure education can help build these capacities.

Costello (1980) also identifies four capacities that adolescents acquire, and adults need —and will continue to need—to function in society. These capacities are physical vitality, resourcefulness, social connectedness, and the ability to sustain caring relationships. In a report by the Chapin Hall Center for Children at the University of Chicago (Wynn, et al., 1987) these capacities are now fully described as follows:

1. Physical vitality: optimal health, energy, stamina, resistance, and resilience.

2. Resourcefulness: ability to act effectively to achieve objectives for oneself and others. Components include the possession of practical knowledge and skills (beyond streetwise), the ability to seek and sift information (critical thinking), to learn new things, and to apply knowledge and skills in effective action.

3. Social connectedness: sense an individual has of affiliation with a social community that validates their identity, provides support and services, and requires contribution in return.

4. Ability to sustain caring relationships: capacity to give and accept care in return. Capacity for self-worth.

Outward Bound, as a leading organization in the adventure education field, has shown ways to nurture such capacities in people of all ages, but especially among youth. The philosophical foundations upon which Dr. Kurt Hahn created the first Outward Bound learning model in Gourdonstoun, Scotland, are physical fitness, self-reliance, craftsmanship, and compassion. In comparing these four tenets with those identified by current youth experts, some interesting parallels emerge. Outward Bound's organized group experiences offer the following opportunities:

1. To participate in adventure activities, which are at times designed to be physically demanding. Through these experiences, physical vitality is enhanced as physical fitness is discovered.

2. To learn new skills, cognitive, kinesthetic, and social. By solving problems, working on technical competency, and working with others in cooperative relationships, a sense of craftmanship and self-reliance are developed and resourcefulness is increased.

3. To participate in a group context with peers, toward the pursuit of common interests. A community of bonding results as group members learn to resolve conflicts, express feelings, care for and listen to others. This develops a sense of compassion in relating to others and enhances caring relationships and a sense of social connectedness.

4. To learn knowledge and skills that are directly transferable to their more accustomed "familiar" environments. With help from a community of supports, a student's experience with adventure education programs can be validated and can have a significant meaning in their lives.

As professionals, adventure educators have an obligation to continue to explore the ways their methods and tools can have greater impact on the growing problems in American society, particularly those confronting urban youth. The following section will explore some examples and possibilities.

SHIFTING PARADIGMS—CREATING URBAN PROBLEMS

To broaden the population of youth served by adventure education, programs need to be adapted to the realities of inner-city youth. To be maximally effective and preventative in impact, programs need to be offered to youth aged 10 to 15. Youth are most vulnerable at this age. The pressures for choice are real, yet often the choices and support systems are limited. The challenge to the adventure education profession is to design programs that address the needs of this age group and that are accessible and attractive to them.

Urban adventure programs' views of the city resemble other adventure programs' view of their more traditional outdoor environments. Each environment becomes a dynamic classroom. The city and its multiple physical, natural, and human resources are the classrooms through which curricula are developed. Urban waterways can serve as corridors for adventures for learning natural history, architectural history, and principles of ecology, or as a means to access and explore new neighborhood environments. Through a well-designed urban experience, students can explore new parts of their "hometown" and themselves in a highly interactive process.

Urban exploration in the form of a Group Road Rally curriculum (Woodward, 1988) can be designed to focus on personal growth and group process objectives. The personal growth objectives can include increasing self-esteem, self-awareness, and self-assertion through using map and compass skills, using knowledge of the city, and by interviewing strangers. The group process objectives can include intimacy, mutuality, cooperation, cohesiveness, problem-solving, and conflict resolution. The activities involved can be traveling in small groups to new and unknown places, using consensus decision-making, experiencing limited cash resources for a day, or doing a several-day service project.

Service learning is a worthy endeavor in and of itself and provides another approach to adventure education in the city. In an adventure-based curriculum, its inclusion can serve as the cornerstone of a powerful and relevant experience for students. Lyn Baird, a past director of the National Center for Service Learning believes that:

> "Only reality can prepare students to cope sensitively and compassionately with the real world. The process of service learning involves mutual risk and involvement. Through this process the realization that we need each other hits home. Seemingly opposite concepts—giving and getting, acting and reflecting, serving and learning—begin to emerge." (Baird, 1985)

From community service experiences, students are confronted with values different than their own. Through this exposure comes a deeper understanding of themselves and their roles in society. As they discover their own sense of worth, they learn about self-confidence, courage to risk, and self-reliance. The opportunities for growth can assist a young person's transition from dependent adolescence to responsible adulthood. In urban settings, service learning opportunities abound. They are an essential experience to be included in a program design.

More traditional adventure activities, such as rock climbing and a ropes course, can provide a high-impact experience in a curriculum. Ropes courses and team challenge courses may already exist in an urban area. Through contractual arrangements these resources may be accessible. Natural climbing sites may be scarce to nonexistent near an urban area. "Buildering," the use of building structures for climbing activities, may be an option. Other possibilities might include indoor climbing walls and artificial climbing towers. A solid network of adventure educators in an urban locale may prompt greater utilization of existing resources and expand program outreach. However the components of a program's curriculum are decided, they need to be consistent with the objectives of a selected learning model, not haphazardly or unconsciously conducted for recreational purposes.

Adventure education is an applied method of experiential learning. Pfeiffer and Jones (1973) describe an experiential education model that includes five steps:

1. Experiencing—involvement in the activity.
2. Publishing—sharing the reactions and information.
3. Processing—emergent dynamics are explored and discussed with other participants.
4. Generalizing—extracting generalizations from the experience.
5. Applying—planning applications of principles derived from the experience in other settings. When this new learning is used and tested it becomes a new experience, closing the loop.

Beyond these components of a workable program, Meier (1980) adds several ingredients that add to the desirable effectiveness:

1. A moderate amount of stress;
2. Group living;
3. Success for the individual and the group;
4. A new environment;
5. An individual experience separate from the group, as time for reflection and assimilation.

Urban programs that currently exist in the United States typically use these elements in fashioning a model suited to their situation. Course lengths can vary from one day to single or consecutive weekends, to one week (see Appendix pp. 292-297 for program address). A new environment for inner-city youths may simply be going to a different neighborhood from their own, or it may be exploring a city, county or state park system. Finding a "solo" site may prove to be more difficult (churches have been used). The experiences that become the final adventure program should never be underestimated for their potential educational impact.

The practitioners of adventure education are continually adapting their talents to impact mainstream education. Adventure education alternatives exist in public and private schools' physical education programs, special education courses, and faculty in-service days as part of adult development. Change comes slowly and with difficulty. Yet, by adopting the risk-taking mindset of a social entrepreneur and working within the mainstream educational system, a dedicated educator can address the personal and social needs of urban youth.

Futurist Robert Theobald describes our current era of human development as one of interrelationships of the "compassionate era" (Theobald, 1986). Theobald's vision of this era's characteristics includes the support of diversity and differences, the challenges of cooperation between these differences, the inevitability of uncertainty and change, and the values of honesty, responsibility, humility, faith, and love. Many of these compassionate virtues can be taught through adventure education.

Expanding networks and linkages between the public and private educational sectors, the business and social service sectors, and the multiple institutions and organizations in an urban center, is necessary for implementing new programs. The complexities of these networks will lead to conflicts, but they can and must be resolved. Issues will arise as people attempt to work together in the urban setting.

EMERGENT ISSUES FOR DISCUSSION

Three issues have been selected for discussion here. These are professional lifestyle conflicts between urban-based and wilderness-based adventure programs, safety considerations in planning and implementing programs, and the fundamental issue of cultural barriers in staff compositions and student-to-staff relations.

At the 15th Annual Association for Experiential Education conference in Port Townsend, Washington, November 1987, a workshop on exploring metrophobic biases within the outdoor/wilderness-based adventure professional community was conducted (Moriah and Proudman, 1987). A question was posed to 30 participants, asking them to identify the positive attributes of working in an outdoor (wilderness-based) setting and in an urban setting. The attributes they listed were:

Wilderness-Based

- Multi-dimensional
- Stimulating
- Physically oriented
- Aesthetically pleasing
- Observing participants
- More freedom to participate
- Being a "guru"
- Direct consequences
- Spirituality through contact with nature
- Small group intimacy
- Earth connection
- Rediscovering heritage
- No clocks/watches

Urban-Based

- Modern comforts
- Human cultural diversity
- News and information
- Anonymity and privacy
- Cultural events (Arts, etc.)
- Immediacy of human problems
- Availability of resources
- Continuing support systems

- Raising families (Social systems)
- Recreational opportunities (spectator sports)
- Access to human solutions
- Transforming urban "jungle" into "jungle-gym"
- New challenge

According to the group, outdoor professional settings offered more benefits to an individual's spiritual and ecosophical attunements. Urban areas were places of greater access to human problems and solutions. Is the adventure education profession, by nature of its history and roots, biased in favor of outdoor/wilderness environments for teaching and learning?

Attracting excellent staff away from wilderness settings to work in large urban areas is not easily done. Conflicts in values, and fears and prejudices concerning the urban environment may affect an individual's decision to bring their talents of working adventure education programs into urban areas. It could be argued that a tremendous amount of personal and professional growth can be achieved by existing in both worlds—urban and wilderness. Tom James (1987), writing on the development of an Outward Bound Center in New York City, argues that it is in the urban centers where the best and most talented instructors are needed. By testing their skills in urban program areas, wilderness instructors would, in many ways, be entering directly into the same educational process that students experience coming from urban areas into wilderness programs sites. The benefits to the individual and the subsequent program could be enormously positive.

Ultimately, the decision to choose one's place of work and lifestyle is a personal one. As the level of professionalism increases, perhaps more practitioners will examine their values and will take some risks in expanding their talents and scope of their work.

Safety considerations need to be thoroughly evaluated in the program planning process. Once a curriculum is constructed, a reconnaissance trip is essential for gathering information. A network of supportive volunteers can provide assistance with this. The goals of a reconnaissance effort are to identify potential people to be interviewed, explore the side canyons; that is, the sites of interest along an itinerary path, to assess the important logistical elements of time and timing of sequential events, and to recognize safety hazards, problems, and safe zones.

Urban safety maps can be useful for identifying where a route is planned and what areas are to be avoided. Criteria used for these purposes can be based on crime rates, known gang concentration centers, level of lighting at night, proximity to other people and the level of activity on the streets, to name a few. The evidence can come from police units, local residents, local merchants, neighborhood organizations, and pre-course reconnaissance trips.

Communicating with all of the necessary players in an urban experience is important. Parental or guardian approval and support, administrative clearance, and permission from authorities is important. Retaining a well-informed and briefed field staff helps prevent problems from developing. Good relations with all program contacts is necessary for a positive public image and to ensure program acceptance.

There is a saying in the urban adventure profession that "it is much easier to ask for forgiveness than it is to ask for permission." If the program plan calls for an activity that may need special permits or approval; don't expect an immediate "yes" answer. Rappelling off a public building may at first be prohibited. But with persistence, diplomacy, and education, permission may be granted. All of the contact that occurs in the field, be it personal or professional, has potential public relations impact. Running urban programs can attract a lot of attention and curiosity. Safety needs should never be sacrificed or compromised.

The process of thinking preventively is the same in both wilderness and urban settings. Each place has its unique hazards. Neither should be considered more or less safe than the other. A sharper eye for safety develops over time through experience with running urban programs. Early in the design process before students become involved, always ask the question, "What is unsafe about this activity?"

The final issue deals with cultural barriers. Adventure education staff and participants have largely been members of an upper-middle class Anglican culture in America. This will continue until more effort is made to transcend cultural barriers for recruiting students and staff.

The composition of staff in the field is in need of diversification for several reasons. At present, there are few available role models in the adventure education field for younger black, Hispanic, Asian, and Native American participants. What does this reflect about the values minorities have for the utility and relevance of adventure education? Or is the problem a lack of access to training opportunities? How might the profession begin to remedy this imbalance?

Another reason for lack of minority participation is the difference in cultural values. Are adventure programs willing to examine their premises and assumptions to broaden their inclusion of differing beliefs and values? Many current adventure programs conflict with the basic cultural values of inner-city adolescents. The idea of "pushing one's limits" contradicts having been taught to accept one's own limitations.

The need to communicate across cultural divisions begins with sincere, honest, and compassionate efforts and expressing an openness to learn from each other. Finding commonalities among the differences could lead to greater levels of trust and collaboration. Recognizing, acknowledging, and reinforcing differences is equally important.

Tomorrow's urban world will be more complex than today's and will demand higher levels of mutual cooperation and interdependence. The challenge for the adventure education community is to adapt its strengths to meet the greater needs of society. As the profession matures, this will be a natural and necessary evolutionary step as it merges with the more traditional and mainstream learning approaches from which we are all byproducts. The question remains whether or not we are willing to meet the challenge.

REFERENCES

Baird, L. (1985). *Fanning the flame in experiential education and the schools,* Eds. D. Kraft and J. Kielsmeier. Boulder, CO: The Association for Experiential Education.

Chicago Coalition for the Homeless (1985). *Youth homelessness in Chicago.* Annual Report.

Chicago Urban League (1987). *Basic Facts: National statistic on blacks*—Research Edition. Annual report.

Costello, J. (1980). *Criteria for evaluating and planning public policies for children.* Unpublished manuscript. Chapin Hall Center for Children at the University of Chicago.

Greenberger, E., & Steinberg, L. (1986). *When teenagers work: The psychological and social cost of adolescent employment.* New York: Basic Books.

James, T. (1987). *An urban strategy: Outward Bound in New York City.* A preliminary draft, unpublished. Providence, RI: Brown University, Education Department.

Leroy, E. (1985). *Adventure and education in the theory of experiential education.* Eds.: R. Kraft and M. Sakofs. Boulder, CO: The Association for Experiential Education.

Meier, J., Morash, T., & Welton, G. (1980). *High-adventure outdoor pursuits.* Salt Lake City, UT: Brighton Publishing Company.

Moriah, D., & Proudman, S. (1987). *Overcoming metrophobia: New perspectives on urban adventuring and outdoor lifestyles.* Workshop presented at the 16th Annual conference of the Association for Experiential Education. Port Townsend, WA: November 15-18.

National Commission on Youth (1981). *A bridge too long.*

Passow, A. H. (1982). Urban education for the 1980s: Trends and issues, *Phi Delta Kappan.* April issue. pp. 519-522.

Pfeiffer, J. W., & Jones, J. (1973). *A handbook of structured experiences.* La Jolla, CA: University Associates.

Testa, M., & Lawler, E. (1985). *1985 state of the child in Illinois.* The Chapin Hall Center for Children at the University of Chicago.

Theobald, R. (1986). *The rapids of change.* Wickenburg, AZ: Action Linkage. Section 2.90, p. 2.

U.S. Census Report (1980). Washington, DC: Government Printing Office.

Woodward, T. (1988). Personal correspondence. Minnetonka, MN: Voyageur Outward Bound School—Voyageur in the Parks program.

Wynn, J., Richmond, H., Rubenstein, R. A., & Littell, J. (1987). *Communities and adolescents: An exploration of reciprocal supports.* Chapin Hall Center for Children at the University of Chicago.

Youth Development Coordinating Committee (YDCC) (1987). *A Chicago youth agenda: Meeting the needs of a generation at risk.* Chicago, IL: Mayor's Office.

Artificial Adventure Environments

Aram Attarian
North Carolina State University

Participation and interest in adventure programs and activities is growing. Much of this growth can be attributed to improved technology, which provides safer and lighter equipment; new literature, including guidebooks, instructional texts and periodicals; increased exposure on television and in motion pictures; lifestyle changes with people seeking more exciting and adventurous recreational experiences; and the increase of instructional programs provided by recreation departments, schools, colleges, universities and professional guide services (Dunn & Gulbis, 1977; Skow, 1983; Bishoff, 1986). Often though, suitable facilities or environments for engaging in adventure activities are lacking. However, this does not mean that participation in these activities cannot occur. A number of adventure activities are being conducted successfully in artificial environments created or adapted specifically for the activity. Artificial adventure environments can be defined as any man-made structure, device, or environment that simulates a natural setting, which can be used specifically for teaching or participating in outdoor skills or activities. Teaching takes place in a controlled, safe atmosphere, usually void of the objective hazards commonly associated with the activity. Building walls, swimming pools and gymnasiums have been successfully adapted for use as adventure environments.

The use of artificial environments as adventure settings has the potential to become an accepted alternative for the "real thing." In a recent study, Ewert (1987) found that practitioners in the field of outdoor adventure recreation expect the use of rope courses, climbing walls, and challenge games to increase in the future. Several factors may contribute to this impending trend. As overall participation in outdoor recreation activities continues to grow, greater demands will be placed on our natural resources to support these activities (President's Commission on Americans Outdoors, 1986). Increasing interest in outdoor recreation opportunities close to home, where existing resources and facilities are perceived as crowded, can be minimized by the use of artificial environments. Artificial environments can also provide adventure activities and opportunities to those living in urban areas, or where specific natural settings are nonexistent and long-distance travel is required to get to a usable site. Artificial environments may also be utilized as prerequisite or additional training requirements for beginners prior to trip participation. Most individuals who participate in adventure activities want to receive instruction on how to participate safely in a particular skill or activity before progressing fully into it (Wohlers, 1987).

Rock climbing and water-based activities (canoeing, kayaking) are two of the most popular adventure pursuits that can be conducted effectively in an artificial environment. Other environments include gymnasium activities, first aid and rescue simulations, and artificial snow.

ROCK-CLIMBING WALLS

Although not a new idea, artificial rock-climbing walls are becoming popular as a means of instructing individuals in the sport of rock climbing. One source predicts that artificial climbing walls may become a true member of the mountaineering family tree (Steiger, 1988). The first organization to build and utilize an artificial climbing wall was the William G. Long Camp, located outside of Seattle, Washington, in 1941. This structure was built of natural stone and was known as the "Schurmann Rock." During the latter part of the 1950s, the French developed adjustable wooden climbing walls (Kudlas, 1979). The French Minister of Sport, Maurice Herzog, a respected mountaineer, encouraged the development of wooden climbing walls. Gaston Rebuffat, another well-known mountain guide, was instrumental in the development and implementation of these French climbing walls. These walls were adjustable and could be manipulated to increase or decrease the difficulty of the climbing problem (March & Toft, 1979). During the 1960s, the British made significant contributions to climbing wall technology. The first successful indoor climbing wall in Britain was constructed at the Ullswater School in 1960. The success of this indoor facility caused other schools and programs in Great Britain to design and construct similar climbing walls. By 1970, over 50 artificial climbing walls existed in Britain. Today, over 2,000 climbing walls are scattered over Britain (March & Toft, 1979). A similar interest in climbing wall design and use is currently underway in the United States. Several commercial companies are currently manufacturing artificial climbing walls and paraphernalia for private and institutional use.

Artificial climbing walls have many advantages: (a) if built indoors, the climbing wall provides year-round programming options, regardless of weather conditions; (b) offers rock-climbing opportunities when nearby rock-climbing areas are nonexistent; (c) teaching takes place in a controlled, safe environment; (d) greater student participation occurs through regularly scheduled classes and workshops; (e) the need to transport students, staff, and equipment to a climbing site that may be hours away from campus is eliminated; (f) the environmental impact associated with large groups constantly gathering at one particular climbing area is lessened. On the negative side, a climbing wall may be too expensive to build and maintain, functional wall space or an appropriate facility may be nonexistent, and the lack of administrative support and liability concerns may prohibit construction.

An artificial rock-climbing wall is a structure or adapted structure that may utilize one or a variety of construction techniques and materials to erect a climbable wall, vertical or horizontal in nature. The artificial climbing wall allows the climber the freedom to experience the same faceholds, cracks, overhangs, and other features one might expect to find at a natural climbing area (Attarian, 1987).

Before beginning construction, several considerations must be given. Some climbing walls are designed with too many purposes in mind and are complex, expensive projects, designed to teach every aspect of rock climbing. The upper portion of the climbing wall is used very little, while the lower 10 to 15 feet receive the most use (March & Toft, 1979). The most functional and effective climbing walls are those that have been designed through consultation with experienced climbers. Experienced climbers can provide valuable assistance in the development and placement of handholds, ledges, and other rock features, which will greatly enhance the finished product and experience (Dunn, 1983). The primary function of a rock-climbing wall should be to provide practice in the basic techniques and skills of rock climbing. This includes the use of handholds, balance, and movement on rock. Other amenities, such as equipment, knot and safety displays, descriptions of local rock-climbing areas, and a climbers directory can be included to enhance the learning experience and provide more information on the sport (Attarian, 1987).

Location of the climbing wall is an important factor in its safe operation and management. If the wall is to be constructed indoors, several guidelines need to be considered (Kudlas, 1979; Attarian, 1987):

1. Become familiar with the wall space considered for use. Will it support such a structure? Will other activities or spaces be affected?

2. Be sure the chosen area is large enough to accommodate climbers, equipment storage, and, in some cases, spectators.

3. Be sure the room is large enough dimensionally (height, width).

4. It may be a good idea to locate the climbing wall in an area where similar activities take place; for instance, a weight training room or gymnastics area. These areas can be secured after use or when the facility is unsupervised.

5. Select an area where access and control is limited. This can prevent the area from becoming an attractive nuisance.

If plans are to locate the climbing wall outdoors, consider:

1. A sheltered area away from the rain and wind;
2. Exposure to sun for teaching purposes and maximum daylight use;
3. Whether the area can be secured when not in use.

The type of wall to be constructed depends on the kind of use the wall will receive, location of the completed structure (indoors, outdoors), budget, existing usable wall space, and the capabilities of the designer and/or contractor. There are a number of different methods, techniques, and styles currently employed to design and build effective climbing walls:

1. Traditional or wooden block walls;
2. Faux rock panel or tile walls;
3. Conversion of building walls (March & Toft, 1979);
4. Use of conventional building techniques.

By far the simplest and most creative approach to climbing wall construction consists of a series of wooden, stone, or molded fiber glass blocks attached to a flat or slightly irregular surface. Brick, cinderblock, or concrete are the best surfaces for this type of application. Plywood (3/4 inch to 1 inch) can also be used, since it is economically priced and can be attached either permanently or temporarily to another surface. Holds are attached to the climbing surface by screws, bolts, or epoxy. The best type of epoxy for this purpose is highway marker adhesive. This material is used to glue down highway lane markers. Shear strength is nearly 6,000 psi. When epoxied, the holds become permanent. Plywood or hardwood block holds can be attached by bolts or screws. It's good practice to temporarily attach the holds and try them out before permanent mounting. A climbing wall that is designed with limited or difficult holds may only be appropriate for experienced climbers. Too many holds may make the climbing easy. One advantage with bolted or screw-attached holds is that they can be moved periodically to change the direction and difficulty of the climb.

Several companies, including Project Adventure, Edelrid, Metolius, and Sport Climbing Systems (SCS), are currently manufacturing pre-fabricated holds made of hardwood, fiber glass or a resin-based compound. Individually molded holds are designed to be attached to wooden walls with screws, or to concrete walls with bolts or epoxy. Holds are designed to resemble knobs, edges, pockets, and other natural features.

Commercially made tiles and panels with molded and sculpted features are new to the artificial climbing wall market. A wall built entirely of tiles is aesthetically pleasing, clean and functional. Paneled climbing walls are becoming increasingly popular in Europe, especially for competition purposes.

The Macrotile™, by Metolius, is a molded 18-inch hexagonal plate with a variety of holds molded into its surface. Each tile can be turned six different ways, thus providing six different sets of holds. If attached permanently, a minimum number of holds can be used. Attachment via screws is recommended.

Sculptured Rok™ Tiles have been introduced by SCS located in Berkeley California. These four-sided tiles can be adjusted in a variety of ways to accommodate specific needs and applications. Large Textured Rok™ Panels are also being manufactured by SCS. These panels are ideal for applications where diverse climbing problems are required. Each panel, which covers an 8-square-foot area, contains a grid pattern of threaded bolt sleeves. This allows for the attachment of a bolt on handholds (Roks™) to be mounted to the panel surface. The Portland Rock Gym, Portland, Oregon; has one of the largest tile walls in the United States.

Interior or exterior stone or brick walls can be modified for use as climbing walls. Modification can be accomplished by altering the stone or brick to provide handholds and footholds. Rough-dressed stone walls are the best structures for modification, since the material is natural rock. This type of climbing wall presents the climber with opportunities for face climbing and allows practice in the basics of rock climbing. Absent are large cracks and overhangs. However, the inside corners of the wall may provide opportunities for stemming and laybacking.

Modification can be kept to a minimum if the stone used in construction is rough and irregular, since this provides naturally occurring holds. Sufficient holds will also exist if the mortar joining the rock is recessed. Walls void of holds can be modified by chiseling out mortar at selected joints to provide finger holds. Further modification can be accomplished by cutting blocks of stone or brick from the wall and resetting them either with a one-foot protrusion or recessed to provide larger holds. It is recommended that a brick or stone mason be employed for any modification work. Cost can be kept to a minimum, since an existing structure can be used and major modification work may not be necessary. The most difficult step may be obtaining permission to use and modify such a structure, especially if it is part of a building.

Several different techniques using concrete have been used in the successful construction of climbing walls. The use of concrete can be an expensive and time-consuming undertaking. However, the realism, functionality, longevity, and aesthetic quality of the finished product can make up for the cost.

Don Robinson, a well-known British climbing-wall builder, designs artificial walls consisting of brick and natural stone (Newman, 1984). A brick wall is constructed that is interspersed natural stone. The natural stone provides handholds and footholds. Overhangs and other features are also added. Another technique uses poured concrete slabs with a series of natural stones placed in the slabs. Cracks and belay points are also added. The slabs are then raised and tilted at different angles to represent different climbing problems and situations. The Ackers Trust Climbing Wall in Birmingham, England and the Practice Rock at the University of Washington, Seattle, are good examples of these designs.

Another British builder, Gordon Bendall, manufactures sheets of rock known as Bendcrete. The slabs are built on a wire reinforcing-type mesh with natural stone or other features that is covered by the mesh. Concrete is added, which in turn leaves the natural rock protrusions and features exposed and permanent. The Kelsey Kerridge Wall at Cambridge uses the Bendall technique.

Another technique, guniting, places 3 to 5 inches of blown concrete on a steel and wire-mesh frame. The steel/wire frame gives the structure support, form, and definition. As the concrete begins to harden, experienced sculptors carve and mold realistic cracks, ledges, overhangs, and other natural rock features. To enhance realism, the entire climbing wall is painted with natural colors. North Carolina State University at Raleigh, North Carolina, successfully utilizes a climbing wall of this design.

The artificial climbing wall has many diverse uses and applications. Schools, colleges and universities, the military, private and commercial fitness centers, and climbing schools are all realizing the potential for climbing wall use. Artificial walls are currently being used for instructional purposes, recreation, training, and fitness and competition.

Instructional Use

A number of secondary schools, colleges and universities as well as the military are using climbing walls to supplement existing climbing programs or create new ones. The instruction of safety and basic climbing skills are the main goals of these programs.

Recreation

A climbing wall can add an extra dimension to a school or municipal recreation program by providing opportunities for adventure-based activities where none may have existed before. Programs for specific populations (women, substance abusers, older adults, children) can also be developed with the climbing wall as the central focus.

Training/Fitness

Fitness centers, especially in areas with traditionally large climbing populations (e.g., the Pacific Northwest) are adding climbing walls and related fitness equipment to their facilities (Steiger, 1988). These centers allow climbers to train year-round and perfect technique, strength, flexibility, and balance. Focus on basic rock-climbing instruction is also possible through a well equipped center (Hessburg, 1988).

Competition

A growing worldwide trend toward climbing competition has brought the artificial climbing wall into the limelight. Almost all of the major climbing competitions to date have taken place on artificial walls, constructed from molded panels and/or tiles (Kennedy, 1988; Osius, 1988).

While artificial climbing walls present a controlled and safe environment, it is important to maintain and adhere to strict safety and management guidelines. For some institutions the climbing wall may become a center of attention, mainly due to its uniqueness and location. Several standard safety practices should be maintained by programs incorporating climbing walls. Obviously, other safety guidelines should be generated specific to a particular program or climbing structure.

General Safety Guidelines:

1. All climbers should be belayed or spotted during all climbing activities.
2. All climbers should wear helmets.
3. Climbing areas should be secured after each session.
4. If the climbing wall is located in an area that cannot be secured after use, do not start the climb at floor level.
5. All belays should be anchored.
6. When bouldering:
   - All climbers should be spotted.
   - Climber's feet should not exceed the height of the spotter's shoulders.
   - Helmets should be worn by both climber and spotter.
7. Landing surface:
   - Indoors: mats or a spotter should be used.
   - Outdoors: pea gravel or wood chips are adequate. Maintenance is a must.
8. Develop a maintenance schedule:
   - Test handholds for soundness.
   - If concrete, look for cracks and deterioration.
9. Adequate belay anchors should be in place (5/8-inch steel eyebolts are best).
10. Maintain at the maximum a 12:l instructor-student ratio.

POOL ACTIVITIES

The swimming pool can be used for the instruction of basic canoe and kayaking skills and other adventure activities. In some cases, artificial environments other than pools have been used for instruction and competition purposes. One example of this type of environment is the artificial slalom course (artificial boulders included) constructed for the 1972 Olympic kayak event in Augsburg, West Germany (Warner, 1972). Artificial wave-making equipment and facilities are also gaining in popularity (Aquatic Amusement Associates, Ltd., 1988). The nation's first inland surfing facility, Big Surf, was constructed in Tempe, Arizona, in 1970. The facility is located on a 20-acre site that includes a 2.5-acre, 300-foot-wide lagoon, complete with sand beach and Polynesian landscape. A hydraulic system produces the waves (Odenkirk, 1970). SCUBA, another popular water sport, has been effectively introduced in a pool environment (Wohlers, 1988).

Canoeing and kayaking are among the fastest growing sports nationwide (Lime, 1986). Many river recreationists are novices, with little or no experience (Leatherberry, Lime, & Thompson, 1980). According to Meyer (1979) the most hazardous adventure activities are those associated with moving water. Drowning deaths (8,000 per year) are the third most common cause of accidental death in the United States, and the second leading cause of accidental death for persons between the ages of one and 44 (Dworkin, 1987). With these facts in mind, education of the participant becomes a key issue. If educated in the basic skills and safety practices of boating and water survival, users can become safer and better boaters. For this purpose, the swimming pool can play an important role.

As an artificial adventure environment, the swimming pool can be used for pre-outing instruction to teach participants basic boating skills and safety practices. This in turn provides more actual boating time, since pertinent skills and safety practices have been taught prior to the outing. For competitors, opportunities for off-season training exist. The utilization of the swimming pool for boating activities can also increase the use of aquatic facilities during evening hours or weekends, thus providing a more balanced aquatics program.

Basic Skills Instruction

The swimming pool can be used as a medium to teach and assess basic boating skills and equipment use. Teaching can progress at a rate conducive to the skill and interest levels of the participants. Participants can also be introduced and encouraged to paddle different types of watercraft in a familiar and less threatening environment.

Practice of Safety Techniques

Opportunities to practice a variety of safety skills and techniques can be successfully accomplished in regularly scheduled pool sessions. Safety skills, such as a prerequisite clothed swim, drownproofing, partner and self-rescue, boat rescue, hand paddling, re-entering a swamped canoe, and emptying a swamped canoe should be practiced until they are mastered so that these situations cease to be anything more than incidents, rather than emergencies (American National Red Cross, 1977).

Training

The pool can become a useful environment for off-season training by implementing basic training techniques that require little water space but at the same time simulate outdoor conditions. Some training exercises are listed below (Evans & Anderson, 1975).

The English Gate. Developed in England, this is a complex, back-and-forth, in-and-out maneuver. This exercise is effective training for slalom and assists in the development of quick and precise movement, required for wildwater racing. The object of the English Gate is to go around and through a single gate without touching a pole.

Sequence 1. Pass through the gate in a forward direction three times.

Sequence 2. Back the kayak down the outside of a pole, Eskimo roll, then go forward through the gate and repeat the process on the other side.

Sequence 3. Move down the outside of a pole, pivot, and then go backward through the gate. Once through, pivot again and go backward through the gate.

Sequence 4. Move forward past the outside of a pole, roll, then go backward through the gate and repeat this on the other side.
Each sequence should be done as quickly as possible for best results.

The Chase. This pool game is a three-person chase that lasts for five minutes. At maximum speed, the first boat leads the other boats on an unknown route (rolls included) for five minutes, through and around four to five gates that have been set up across the pool. The objective is for the lead boat to gain distance on the followers to catch and touch the third boat from the rear. All gates must be successfully negotiated.

Sprints. Three to four boats are lined up at one end of the pool. A signal starts them off. The object is to sprint as fast as possible to the other end of the pool. Several strokes (backward, sculling, draw) besides the forward stroke can be used to make the contest interesting.

Sequences. A slalom course is designed through several gates. The first boat through the gates develops a sequence. The sequence is memorized by the other boaters and duplicated. By starting a couple of boats only 10 seconds apart, it is possible to maintain two boaters on the course at a time. Sequences can be designed in which all gates are negotiated in reverse. Rolls can be included to make this task varied and interesting.

Kayak Polo. A game of polo played in an indoor pool with two to three boats per side (depending on pool size) is an excellent activity for the development of paddling skills, stamina, and maneuverability. Paddles are used as mallets to strike a volleyball into the opponent's goal (water polo net). Safety requirements should include helmets for all players and padded bows for all boats. Players cannot use arms or hands to contact the ball, opponent, or boat.

GYMNASIA ACTIVITIES

The gymnasium has several characteristics that can make it an inviting facility for adventure activities. The large floor and wall spaces, along with common gymnasium equipment, can be combined to produce functional artificial environments and activities. Walls are ideal for the construction of climbing structures and rappelling platforms. Floor space can be used for rock climbing instruction, and ceiling rafters and beams can be used for the construction of indoor ropes courses (described elsewhere in this text).

Rappelling

No aspect of rock climbing has excited the beginning climber more than rappelling. Beginners often seem quite eager to learn how to rappel, more so than climb (Loughman, 1981). However, rappelling is a skill that should be taught in a basic rock-climbing course. Sport rappelling should be discouraged since it is an activity that requires supervision and experience to master correctly and safely. Both rappelling techniques and safety/rescue should be taught. This can be done in a number of ways. If a climbing wall is used, a rappelling station or platform should be included. If a climbing wall does not exist and a rappelling platform is constructed, then access can be gained with a ladder. All rappels should be belayed. Some schools use buildings, the back end of stadiums, and bleachers to teach this activtiy. Facility use of this type almost always requires permission from the athletic department or school administration (Rohnke, 1981).

Prusiking

Prusiking is a technique that allows the climber to ascend a fixed rope by using a prusik knot. This climbing procedure is used primarily by climbers in rescue situations. Prusiking can be done effectively by using the traditional 2-inch diameter, 20-foot long manila climbing ropes found in almost every school gymnasium. Standard rock-climbing ropes (dynamic construction) can also be used for this purpose. Caving/rescue rope (static construction) is the best, since it doesn't stretch as much as conventional climbing rope and is easier to "handle" for this application. The use of the prusik technique provides an opportunity for the gymnasium climbing rope to be used in a creative way and allows students to reach the top of the rope. (Note: those unfamiliar with rappelling and prusiking should consult experienced help before attempting these activities.)

Ground School

The best way to describe this activity is to compare it to a pilot learning how to fly. Before actually flying the airplane, a pilot must first attend ground school. Here he or she learns about the instruments, controls, and other essential skills needed to fly the airplane. In an adventure setting, ground school basically means the same thing. The participant is exposed to the equipment, practices, terminology, and in some cases the technique associated with the activity before progressing to the real thing.

Rock climbing is a good example of the ground school approach. All that is needed for this activity is an indoor or outdoor space that can accomodate a group of 12 participants and the appropriate equipment. Several stations are set up to teach a variety of rock climbing skills. Station #1—Belaying, using the sitting hip belay and other mechanical methods. At this station, students actually climb, practice falling and holding a fall (on a horizontal plane), and belay one another while using the correct communication terminology. Station #2—Knot tying. Here, 10-foot pieces of practice rope are supplied along with diagrams showing the climbing knots being used and their applications. Students should be able to tie all knots correctly, with their eyes closed and behind the back. Station #3—Harness construction. If commercially made harnesses are not available, 1-inch to 2-inch webbing is supplied and the student constructs his or her own climbing harness. All participants are instructed to tie the harness in a similar fashion for conformity and safety reasons. Station #4—Rappelling. This station may be optional. Participants actually practice rappelling on a horizontal plane. This allows the student to become familiar with the technique involved and the friction device being used, and allows practice in self-rescue. After the participants have rotated through each station (usually several times), or have had ample opportunity to practice, and are comfortable with their skills, it's time to begin actual climbing on the artificial wall or natural climbing area.

FIRST AID, SEARCH, AND RESCUE SIMULATIONS

Effective and realistic first aid, search, and rescue simulations can be done using artificial environments. All it takes is creativity and imagination on the initiator's part. Simulations are feigned accidents or rescue situations presented to a group as a problem to solve. Every attempt should be made for the simulation to be convincing and realistic, depending on its purpose. Simulations can be powerful learning situations if executed properly. Several guidelines should be kept in mind when implementing a simulation (Morrissey, 1983). Initially, the activity should be done for a specific purpose. Is it being done just because it sounds good, or is first aid being taught? Be specific. This will make planning and execution easier. Second, the activity should be properly planned and executed. Are the appropriate materials on hand? Have other staff been notified of the impending "accident"? Third, a thorough debriefing should follow the simulation. Was the activity worthwhile? Was anyone offended? What did the participants learn as a group, as individuals?

Simulations can:

1. Motivate students to learn first aid and emergency procedures;
2. Provide skill training in emergency procedures;
3. Achieve group cohesion through a common challenge;
4. Provide a high-energy, meaningful adventure;
5. Demonstrate the complexity and difficulty of rescue operations.

Litter Lowers

Stairwells, bleachers, abandoned railroad trestles, and buildings can be used as effective "litter lowering sites." Litter lowers teach the techniques and complexities of rigging a litter and rescue skills, and provide opportunities for teamwork, leadership, and communication. This activity can also be used to reinforce previously learned rock-climbing skills.

Search and Rescue Practice

Search and rescue practice allows the individual to learn and put to use map and compass skills, and provides for group interaction and teamwork. If combined with a rescue situation, first aid skills may be called upon.

Caving

Caving techniques and cave rescue can be practiced in an artificial environment set up in a dark room or in a underground system of drain pipes or similar systems. A maze, constructed from tables, chairs and desks, can simulate a cave environment. Crawls, tight squeezes, and narrow passages can all be created to provide a cave-like atmosphere. To duplicate the darkness, participants may be blindfolded. Improvised cave rescue can also be conducted by introducing a stokes or SKED litter into the maze. In this situation, participants get a feel for the difficulties and frustrations of carrying, dragging and passing a litter through narrow passages.

SNOW AND ICE

"Plastic snow" has successfully been manufactured and can be used by ski areas for extending the ski season or developing skiing in areas that receive little or no snow. Areas for indoor or outdoor training and equipment demonstrations can also be designed using this product. The snow is made of EVA (ethylene-vinyl acetate), which is a soft, rubberlike material that produces a ski trail that is both soft and flexible. This material exhibits the same characteristics of real snow. The snow structure resembles a lattice-work design and consists of criss-crossed plastic strips dotted with stubby toothbrush-like blades. Ski trails are made by press-fitting together 1.2 by 1.2-foot sections of the strips.

REFERENCES

Attarian, A. (1987). Rock climbing in the great indoors. *Parks and Recreation, 22*(12), 43-45.

Aquatic Amusement Associates, Ltd. (1988). Aquawave Product Brochure. Albany, New York.

Bishoff, G. (1985). National outdoor outfitters market report. *National Outfitters News, 10* (8), pp. 10-13.

Dunn, D. R., & Gulbis, J. M. (1976). The risk revolution. *Parks and Recreation, 11* (8), pp. 12-18.

Dunn, I. (October, 1983). Mountain scene: Climbing walls. *Mountain,* p. 23.

Dworkin, G. M. (1987). Pool management: Eight steps to a safer facility. *Parks and Recreation, 22* (2), pp. 38-40.

Evans, J., & Anderson, R. R. (1978). *Kayaking: The new whitewater sport for everybody.* Brattleboro, VT: Stephen Green.

Ewert, A. (1987). Outdoor adventure recreation: A trend analysis. *Journal of Park and Recreation Administration, 5* (2), 57-67.

Hessburg, J. (1988). The vertical club: Seattle's cure for the midwinter climbing doldrums. *Summit, 34* (3), pp. 26-27

Ice and snow—who needs it?. (1972). *Parks and Recreation, 7* (5), 41.

Kennedy, M. (1988). Competitions: Showdown in Grenoble. *Climbing, 106*, pp. 44-46.

Kudlas, J. (1979). *The Rock Climbing Teaching Guide.* Reston, VA: American Alliance for Health, Physical Education, Recreation and Dance.

Leatherberry, E. C., Lime, D. W., & Thompson, J. L. (1980). Trends in river recreation. *Proceedings, 1980 National Outdoor Recreation Trends Symposium, Vol. 1.* General Technical Report NE-57. April 20-23, 1980, Durham, NH, pp. 147-164. USFS Northeast Forest Experiment Station.

Lime, D. W. (1986). River running and natural resource management: A focus on river running and boating. *President's Commission on Americans Outdoors: A Literature Review,* Appendix to the Report of the President's Commission on Americans Outdoors, (management), 127-150.

Loughman, M. (1981). *Learning to rock climb.* San Francisco, CA: Sierra Club.

March, W., & Toft, M. (1979). The conversion of exterior wall facings for climbing activities. *Journal of Health, Physical Education, Recreation and Dance*. *50* (1), 30-32.

Meyer, D. (1979). The management of risk. *Journal of Experiential Education, 2* (2), 9-14.

Morrissey, D. M. (1983). Chicken gizzards and screams in the night. *Journal of Experiential Education, 7* (3), 40-42.

Newman, B. (1984, November - December). Gear spotlight: Want to buy a climbing wall? *Mountain, 106*, p. 44.

Odenkirk, J. E. (1970). Inland surfing. *Journal of Health, Physical Education and Recreation, 41* (11), 26-27.

Osius, A. (1988). Round 2: Hill and Destivelle bout. *Climbing, 107*, pp. 38-41.

President's Commission on Americans Outdoors. (1986). *The Report of the President's Commission: Americans Outdoors—The Legacy, the Challenge*. Washington, DC: Island Press.

Rohnke, K. (1981). *High profile*. Hamilton, MA: Wilkscraft.

Skow, J. (1983, August 29). Risking it all. *Time*, pp. 52-59.

Steiger, J. (1988). Tools of the trade: Building a better rock climber. *Climbing, 107*, pp. 106-113.

The American National Red Cross. (1977). *Canoeing*. New York: Doubleday.

Warner, R. C. (1972, November- December). New events at the 1972 Olympic games. *Physical Education, 70* (2), pp. 6-7.

Wohlers, R. (1987). Designing and developing a safe, successful scuba diving program. *Parks and Recreation, 50* (2), 50-55.

Ropes Courses: A Constructed Adventure Environment

Carl E. Rohnke
Project Adventure

Ropes course? What's that? I'm often tempted to facetiously answer, "a ropes course is a ropes course is a ropes course," because of the generic proliferation of uses and challenge applications that have been made of combining logs, ropes, trees, poles, and cables, but quoting a cliché is tedious, and simply repeating the topic, no matter how generic, is obviously the easy way out. So here's the way I see it—and have seen it over the last 20-plus years.

Because I've been involved with ropes course design and construction since 1968, interested people are certain that I have the history of challenge courses well-defined and recorded. I don't. I've always been more interested in design and implementation, and even writing this less-than-definitive essay on ropes courses doesn't tempt me to "go for the roots." Nonetheless, here's what I've experienced, read, heard, and been told.

George Hébert, an officer in the French Navy during the late 1800s, as part of his military commission, became responsible for the physical training of all French Navy recruits. Hébert, somewhat of an original thinker and quite the physical person himself (performing as a professional acrobat at one point in his career) favored "natural exercises:" walking, crawling, climbing for conditioning purposes, rather than the traditional and often tedious exercises that were favored by exercise professionals during the latter part of that century.

Hébert must have been as persuasive as he was personally fit, because he developed a following of supporters who enthusiastically promoted his off-beat ideas about exercise with missionary-like zeal. There was no mention made at this time about growth of self-concept, increased communication, or developed cooperation; just exercise. Hébert and his disciples developed and adapted "natural" exercises into something that could be compared to the modern ropes course approach. Because of my occupational affiliation with Project Adventure, Inc., I am, of course, referring to PA's developed curriculum that utilizes ropes courses as a tool for increased self-awareness in addition to physical growth, group cohesiveness, and so on.

An interesting account of that development is presented in the book, *Hébertisme*, by Claude Cousineau, a professor at the University of Ottawa in Canada. Cousineau writes, "Hébert was opposed to analytical exercises and controlled movements which he considered artificial and purposeless. ...The exercises had to be functional, useful and in the open air. Everything was based on the fundamental movements of human beings: walking, running, crawling, climbing, jumping, balancing, throwing, lifting and carrying. Therefore, every indigenous physical obstacle became the essence of Hébertisme." There seem to be quite a few of these Hébertisme courses extant in Canada and used primarily by summer camps to allow exactly what Hébert had in mind: affective and psychomotor growth through natural exercises.

Other organizations have used challenge courses as part of their goal to increase physical fitness, the military being a prime example. But a change was taking place; the "ropes" venue was being more frequently used as a site for building character and practicing group problem-solving tasks than strictly for physical training and conditioning. Used by the military, however, the choice of participating or not participating was "do it fast, or do it slow—but *do it*." In a disciplined military situation where people's lives depend upon immediate reaction to orders, there is not much room for rugged individuality.

I have visited two well-known military obstacle courses (an obstacle course is a ropes course that you *have* to do). Each had elements that displayed design ingenuity and were well put together. Each one also had events (40 feet plus) that had no belay system: so much for civilian participation. I asked one of the attending sergeants, "Do you ever have any accidents on the high events that have no protection ropes?" His terse answer told me more than I wanted to know. It was simply, "Yes sir."

Considering the quasi-military set-up of the initial Outward Bound schools in Europe and Kurt Hahn's rationale for initiating a "survival" type of training for British merchant seamen during World War II, it's not surprising that most of the current OB schools in the world currently use a ropes course as part of their self-confidence/awareness programs. But the discipline emphasis and pressure to perform have changed significantly over the years. Now a student is introduced into a realistic situation (rock climbing, rappelling, rafting, etc.) and asked to perform or participate as part of a cohesive team toward overcoming a tangible problem that may or may not be fabricated (on-site initiative problem versus a river crossing, for example). The implicit challenge at Outward Bound is, as the result of training and confidence-building exercises, to go beyond perceived capabilities. However, the civilian participant in this case has a choice that is not determined by someone else's ego or sense of discipline.

Project Adventure started in 1971 at the Hamilton-Wenham Regional High School in Hamilton, Massachusetts, and is of particular interest to me because I began building ropes courses for the Project then and I'm still employed by the Project now.

It was during these early years of innovation at Project Adventure that the Challenge By Choice concept began to emerge. The original staff was heavily imbued with this continent's interpretation of Kurt Hahn's Outward Bound philosophy. As new employees of a fledgling adventure organization, we were ready to "serve, strive, and not yield," but weren't quite sure how that was going to fit into the flow of the public school organizational format. Could we get permission to take students from class for a three-day solo, and where were we going to fit in the final expedition? That's a bit facetious, but the first few weeks of the program did have us scrambling for "civilized" ideas, and wondering if our wilderness orientation was going to do us any good in the "'burbs." Specifically, how were we going to transfer the most usable and effective techniques available in a 26-day residential wilderness program, into three 50-minute class sessions per week— a formidable task. It happened, however, and the Project prospered as the result of being the right program presented at the right time in the right place, and also because the "people" situation was also in tune. The administration (Principal Jerry Pieh) had initiated the idea. The curriculum coordinator (Gary Baker) was enthusiastic about writing the grant proposal. And the physical education teachers (Sherm Kinney, Cliff Mello, Sally Woodsum, and Jennifer Swisher) were so enthused that each of them volunteered to attend a 26-day Outward Bound session. And finally, the original Project Adventure staff (Bob Lentz, Mary Ladd Smith, Jim Schoel, Karl Rohnke) were attuned to what was situationally needed in this newest of challenge venues: the public schools. When you have that many people at various organizational levels all enthusiastically zeroed in on the same educational goal, that goal becomes a reality.

The one thing that we knew was transferable (other than the proven OB concepts) was the challenge ropes course, and it became a priority to get one built on the school property. When I began work on the course at HWRHS, I had two ropes courses "under my belt" and remember feeling confident in my knowledge and expertise level. Even considering all that we know now about improved construction techniques and safety systems, I'm still pleased in retrospect at how well the challenge elements went together in and among that beautiful stand of mature beech trees behind the high school. The ropes course at Hamilton-Wenham was state-of-the-art for many years, and is still being used as part of the ongoing full-year physical education adventure program. Since that time, Project Adventure, Inc. has been directly responsible for the construction of well over 1,000 indoor and outdoor challenge ropes facilities.

The first few courses that I built as an employee for Project Adventure were patterned after what I had learned and observed at the Outward Bound schools. As we continued to fit adventure into the public school 50-minute time slot, it became more obvious that the characteristic OB ropes course consisting of contiguous events was functionally giving way to individual challenge events spaced throughout a wooded area. Having only a comparatively short time to work with the students, it made more sense to build the events separate from one another so that at the end of a class period the instructors didn't have half a dozen students stranded at height on a series of connected events. Sequenced events make a lot of sense in a residential program where time is not a factor: We were adapting again to the needs of a daily school schedule.

Another major difference in ropes course approach that soon became obvious in the developmental stages of the program, involved the amount of time that the ropes facility was used with a group of students. As an OB instructor, I would plan to use the ropes course for one-half to a full day only as part of a full-day course. At PA the course is used throughout the year, depending upon the weather. When it became obvious that the ropes course was going to be used extensively as a training tool, I had doubts as to whether the students would maintain their interest over a year's time. No problem. The uniqueness of the program (new vocabulary, venue, emphasis on trying rather than performing, new games, ungraded system, no uniforms, etc.) captured the interest of an age group that was disinterested and bored with the alternative. Teaching the varied content of our expanding curriculum was a breeze. Compare teaching ancient history or calculus to teaching canoeing, rock climbing, or ropes course skills—see what I mean?

In 1972, as part of our grant proposal mission, we offered the Project Adventure model to neighboring schools. During that year we built ropes courses at Newburyport and Andover high schools and Houlton-Richmond Jr. High, all in Massachusetts. The following year, four more courses were built and the number has increased each year since then. PA is now building over 100 ropes courses each year.

The training model under our federal grant was to build a ropes course for a school system and then spend a semester teaching all the physical education classes at that school while the regular P.E. teachers assisted and observed. The participating PA staff began to feel more like a faculty member at the cooperating schools than at our parent organization. Spending that much time at an adopting school in order to implement a program was effective but obviously inefficient. We continued this implementation plan for a number of years, primarily because we didn't fully appreciate our developing role as a teacher training organization. Also, during those first 2 or 3 years I was the only one building ropes courses and conducting on-site training, so our effectiveness was necessarily limited by the small size of our staff.

Project Adventure was initiated at Hamilton-Wenham High as a full-year mandatory sophomore physical education requirement (and still operates at that level). The sophomore year was chosen because the federal grant that supported the Project was available for three years, and since most of us thought the program would come to a close after those initial years, it made sense that we begin at a student level that would allow us to evaluate the effectiveness of Project Adventure over that period of time; the sophomore, junior, and senior years.

Ropes course participation, mud walks, winter camping trips, fun runs, parachute sailing, hang gliding, cross-continent bicycle trips, unidentifiable games, boat-building, recycling, yurt construction, dory trips, salt marsh camping, Allagash canoe trips—Project Adventure became the vehicle for doing (not just conceptualizing) exciting curriculum events. And the Challenge By Choice philosophy continued to grow, although it had not yet been verbalized during these early years. However, we were well on our way toward developing a unique interpretation of what nationally was still a nebulous concept: adventure education.

The point at which we (PA) began to separate from our OB roots and develop roots of our own was the realization that, as dramatic a change in student self-concept could be achieved on campus as in a wilderness setting, and even more significantly, that students' choices of what, where, and how they wanted to challenge themselves were more important than how well they performed. What a relief (for both teacher and student) to know that you were not being tested on how well you did something, but rather how well you tried. Once a student recognized that the safety procedures were predictable and that participants did not have to perform on request or to someone else's expectation, the student's willingness to contemplate an "impossible" task increased. Much of this willingness to risk resulted from the group cooperation and communication that had been emphasized as part of each class session. It was a relief to the students to not be overly concerned with how they looked (during an attempt) or how they would be received by the group if they did not complete their goal. Being in tune with a group does not happen as the result of playing a couple of games and successfully completing an initiative problem or two. Experiencing many things together, sharing the experiences in a discussion format, and having the benefit of an adept facilitator working with the group (add some people-brewing-time), can result in extraordinary group dynamics—changes in attitudes and reactions that are measurable and remarkable.

If you tell a reluctant student to do something (because if the student doesn't, the student will get an F, because it's "good for them," or because that's the way it has always been done) that might make them "look bad" in front of their peers, there's a good chance that some type of negative behavior will result. If the request is couched in terms that allow the student to initially watch others make the attempt and it's obvious that performance level has negligible effect on their evaluation, that student is more apt to *try*.

There are three basic types of ropes course participation models: low and high ropes course events, and permanently installed initiative problems. At the beginning of a

Project Adventure semester session, it is important to spend 2 to 3 weeks away from the ropes course setting attempting to build those initially fragile feelings of trust within the group by working with the students in an open field or gymnasium situation. During this time various off-beat games, physical stunts, and trust activities are presented and attempted. It's not necessary for the teacher to do everything that the students do, or even to perform well, but the teacher should be ready to personalize each activity with their person. The teacher who is not willing to "fail" occasionally, cannot expect the students to give much of themselves either. Ropes course facilitation does not lend itself to take-a-lap teaching.

As the result of this valuable "field time," students will develop an appreciation for unpredictable activities and even look forward to a zany next class period. Having developed this type of positive anticipation, asking the students to perform the various unique and sometimes bizarre tasks on the ropes course will result in a level of acceptance that would not be achievable otherwise. You are also building the psyche value of the ropes course by doing things together that are ostensibly to build their fitness and flexibility level to a point that participation on the course will be facilitated. To what level this is true is relatively unimportant; eager anticipation is key.

Much of the field time is also spent building emotional and physical trust in one another. An individual will be much more apt to try an intimidating event knowing that the group will support the attempt. The fear to perform is often not of physical harm, but rather of ridicule.

Participating in low-level trust activities also teaches the students how to physically care for one another by emphasizing the skill of spotting. Knowing that someone will step forward to prevent a fast trip to the turf is a comforting bit of knowledge that provides incentive to try a risky event that otherwise might be avoided.

What follows is an example of a low element on the ropes course—The Triangular Tension Traverse:

> Three lengths of high tensile galvanized cable are tautly strung about 24-inches above the ground between three well-spaced trees (about 30 feet apart). In addition, two lengths of rope are attached to one of the support trees at a height of about 20feet. An individual attempts to walk each cable length (i.e., around the triangle) using one of the suspended ropes for suppport. Two to four spotters attend each participant, following their every move and being alert to the possibility of a slip from the cable, which happens frequently.

This is a particularly good low event because it challenges the individual and provides a responsible role for the spotters. By this time in the program the person walking the cable knows that his or her spotters have been trained and has faith in their ability to spot effectively. The cable walker also knows that if he or she falls after a disappointingly brief attempt, no one will deride the effort or the performance level, particularly knowing that their turn will soon be at hand. Aside from all that pedagogic rationale, challenging oneself to walk around the cabled triangle is good fun. It's also easy to become infectiously competitive with oneself—"I know I can do better than that next time." And, of course, there is a next time and another next time until the instructor perceives fading enthusiasm or a negative level of frustration. The Tension Traverse is an event that emphasizes trust, challenge, and enjoyment as an attractive preliminary to more demanding events.

Next is an example of an Initiative Problem on the Ropes Course—The Mohawk Walk:

> An initiative problem is a task that the instructor presents to the group with no solution offered. It is the instructor's role to be supportive, define the parameters of the problem, but not offer suggestions or physically help the group with their solution.

> Many of the popular initiative problems require no props and can be presented almost anywhere (Knots, Blindfold Line Up, Warp Speed, etc.); however, the use of a permanently set-up problem situation increases the visual challenge, resulting in greater student interest and participation. The Mohawk Walk consists of a series of taut cables connected to support trees in a zig zag fashion. The cables are suspended no more than 18-inches off the ground. The object (problem) is to move the entire group across these cables from beginning to end without touching the ground.

Cable lengths vary from 10-foot to about 30-foot. It's not overly difficult to scoot across a 10-foot cable, but not many people have the balance to navigate a 30-ft. length of the same cable. As with most good initiative problems, the crux becomes what an individual can accomplish as compared to what a group can achieve by working together.

It doesn't take much thinking or trial and error (mostly error) participation to figure out that to get the entire group from start to finish through the series of connected cables, each member of the group must help the others by providing balance support for one another. Five minutes into the problem everyone is fiercely (and unselfconsciously) holding someone's hand in order to balance themselves on the cable. The problem is obviously fabricated. The group's enthusiastic participation is real.

If a person inadvertently touches the ground while attempting passage, a penalty is recorded, and the wire walker regains his or her pre-fall position on the cable. When all participants have completed traversing the cable series, all penalties are recorded and added together to achieve a group score. The group then sits down together, debriefs the attempt and decides how best to improve their team effort on the next try.

There is genuine carryover from these adventure/play fabrications to real- life scenarios, but parents often ask, "Why does my son and/or daughter have to climb over this 12-foot one-dimensional wall, when the obvious and prudent and easy solution is to take a few steps around its edge?" An answer: In today's push-button world there are not as many unequivocal challenges for young people as there were 50 years ago. There are many obvious social, moral, and intellectual challenges for individuals youth, but few of the type that result in working together on a demanding physical task that involves reasonable risk but which is also visually stimulating and enjoyable. It is the high-risk/high-reward challenge situation (ropes course, canoeing) as contrasted to the high-risk/low-reward scenario (drugs, illicit sex). If a group is presented with a task that seems initially impossible, but as the result of a sustained group effort (cognitive and psychomotor) overcomes the challenge, the next "impossible" barrier won't appear so fearsome. Getting over a "fake" wall might not look impressive on a college application, but the personal rewards of having achieved a difficult goal result in carryover confidence that far exceeds the simplicity of the event itself.

The Pamper Pole is an example of a high ropes course event:

> This dramatic event consists of climbing to the top of a 30-foot to 70-foot vertical pole, standing on top of that pole, and diving for a suspended trapeze that hangs a tempting 6 feet to 7 feet from the precariously balanced climber.

Before you question the sanity of the participant, the institution, or Project Adventure for having developed this event, re-read the above section on the rationale of challenge. Climbing the pole and standing on top of the ridiculously small platform is obviously challenging, but the real challenge is overcoming the sometimes paralyzing fear associated with what is being attempted. A frequently heard comment from participants is, "The climb wasn't too bad, but diving for that trapeze was the hardest thing I have ever done." This astoundingly honest evaluation of commitment and emotion points out the largely mental aspect of this element in particular, but also of most of the ropes course events in general.

Looking at this separation of the physical from the mental challenge also provides an insight into the planning and rationale that must be considered before construction of these various elements can begin. A builder not only has to take into consideration performance potential and frustration levels for each individual or group challenge (including age and maturity capabilities), but also tries to arrange the elements in an aesthetic series of contiguous events. A hammer, saw, drill, and enthusiasm do not a ropes course make.

INDOOR ROPES COURSES

Indoor ropes courses and climbing walls have proliferated in areas where the weather is unpredictable (usually bad) or where ropes course security is a problem (unauthorized use and vandalism). Project Adventure has pioneered the construction and installation of both low and high elements inside gymnasiums, so that the events can either be hauled out of the way or entirely removed by using turnbuckles as the cable connecting devices. Almost all of the elements that make up an outdoor ropes course can be adapted to an indoor facility. Much of this adaptation, of course, depends upon the gym's construction—drop ceilings, I-beam construction, wainscotting, and so on.

The first indoor climbing wall built by the Project was "just up the road" at a local high school in the early 1970s. Our most recent "concrete" facility was installed at a school in Hong Kong a few weeks ago. The geography changes, but the challenges remain the same.

Climbing walls are essentially manmade facilities designed to duplicate as closely as possible the vertical difficulties inherent in rock climbing. Hi-tech and expensive climbing walls have received considerable publicity in the media lately, as world classclimbers choose these synthetic vertical venues to display their considerable skills. There's more to come on this high-profile aspect of the sport as the money versus ethics controversy has yet to be decided. But one thing I know for sure, having constructed over 100 of these ersatz walls, basic climbers and neophyte school participants are not nearly so concerned at a height of 30 feet with what the installed hold looks like, but rather with how large, grippable, and solidly installed it is.

EVOLUTION OF ROPES CHALLENGE FACILITIES

Earlier I had mentioned that the original ropes course built at Hamilton-Wenham was state-of-the-art. The state-of-the-art constantly changes within any viable growing organization, as the evolution of ropes course technology at Project Adventure has demonstrated over the years.

The first ropes course was just that, a series of challenge elements built of rope. Today most ropes courses are constructed almost entirely of galvanized aircraft-quality cable because the cable is considerably stronger than rope, more resistant to vandalism, and lasts longer. Rope is still used for swings (hands-on applications) and occasionally for crossing line, but function and use for the future point to the continued use of cable.

Another indication of growth in the area of ropes challenge courses is the development of belay hardware for use on the high elements. In the past, rock climbing and industrial hardware was borrowed or purchased and installed as belay devices because no one had developed specific safety gear for ropes course use. When it was found that carabiners were wearing out (developing deep grooves in the metal) as they were being tensioned over sections of belay cable, heavy industrial pulleys were substituted. These massively over-engineered pulleys proved superior to the use of single carabiner belay anchors, but it was obvious that something more site-specific was needed. In time, lightweight and sufficiently strong pulleys were designed to replace the ill-fitted and cumbersome substitutes. It was satisfying to see a product that had been designed to fill a need, eventually being used by people all over the world. These R.O.S.A. (Really Outstanding Safety Attachments) pulleys led to the development of a line of safety products that are specific to ropes course use.

Belay techniques were also borrowed from the sport of rock climbing, and even these well-accepted methods were changed and adapted as seemed most appropriate and necessary to a ropes course setting. Gravity's pull was still unrelentingly down, but the climber on a ropes course was invariably above the belayer, so the belay ropes positioning was different. And rather than anticipating a sliding fall on rock, the cable walker's mid-air positioning allowed comfortable slips into or onto nothing. With the faller free from contact with any solid object, the rope handler was able to apply a more comfortable dynamic belay, resulting in a happier climber (faller) and less wear on the rope. A dynamic belay (less abrupt than a static belay as the result of being able to let some rope play out during the braking process) in conjunction with a stretchy rope, give of the trees at the cable contact point, and movement of the belayer, produces a cushioned and safe stop in comparison to what would happen if all the factors above were static (no give).

Another example of the evolution in ropes course equipment is the improved braking system on the zip wire, also known as the Flying Fox. My first exposure to the zip wire event was at the Hurricane Island Outward Bound School in 1967. The "zip," located at the quarry rock climbing area, consisted of two parallel hawser-lay lengths of goldline stretched between two anchor points—perhaps 150 feet. The take-off was higher than the finish, and the area in between was typically a lot of nothing. The student was clipped, via carabiners on swiss seat and chest harness, onto both zip ropes, and was also attached to a "tag" line that measured the full zip length. The tag line acted as the braking device and was controlled by a belayer who was anchored to the rock near the zip start. All-in-all, this was not a bad way to slow a rapid zipper down, but unless the tag line was handled well, the rider would either go too fast or too slow and sometimes not at all. The temptation of a jaded belayer was to see how close you could let the rider come to the end without applying the brake; the result of slowing too many students in a row—an avoidable drawback.

The next step in the slow-down evolution of the Flying Fox was a bit of primitive hands-on braking attempted at the Outward Bound School in North Carolina. Six paired designated brakers stood near the bottom (end) of the zip ride. A blanket was held between each pair so that the held blanket was perpendicular to the cable. As the rider neared the end of the ride (disconcertingly near the support tree) he/she made mid-torso contact with the compassionately positioned and tautly supported blankets. By the time the rider had hit a couple successive blankets, momentum was slowed to the extent that the last blanket was seldom needed, except for the occasional impact of large (well-covered) riders. This slam-bam technique (although somewhat primitive) was effective, required considerable trust, involved lots of people, and was a kinetic spectacle not soon to be forgotten. The negative factor was that the first set of brakers were, as the result of their own task commitment and concern, pulled off their feet and propelled forcibly into one another by the impact of the speeding rider. The bowling pin analogy isn't far from what actually happened. As it turned out, hesitation to participate on this particular zip related more to volunteering for the braking job than committing to the ride.

The next chapter in this fast-moving and slow-stopping saga occurred at Project Adventure in New England. The stopping system of choice for a number of years was the predictable gravity brake. The zipper picked up speed quickly while riding down the initial steep section of cable, reached the bottom (belly of the cable), and began the slowing process by using up the momentum on the far incline. The rider stopped well before reaching the end of the cable (support tree anchor), then glided back down to the bottom of the "belly" to disengage. This gravity brake is still used by many ropes course builders around the country, because it's predictable and safe. After some time consuming trial and error tension adjustments have been made.

But we were looking for a braking system that would incorporate trust (more people involvement) and less "adjustment" (trial and error) time during construction; something predictable and exciting. The bunji brake block system meets those criteria, plus it's comfortable and safe.

The final chapter: A routed wooden block with a rubber end stopper is affixed to the zip cable via attachment bolts. A measured length of 1/2 inch bunji (shock) cord is attached to an eye bolt on the block. Two people then hold the far end of the bunji cord at an angle away from the zip cable. As the rider descends, the pulley eventually hits the rubber end of the brake block, causes the 30 to 80 foot length of bunji to stretch, and slowly brings the rider to a stop. Use of the block and cord allows the builder to set up the zip cable with much greater angle leeway and less concern about rider speed and ultimate stopping point. If the cable angle is considered too severe, two bunji cords (and more people) can be attached to the brake block.

The purpose of the paragraphs above were not to turn you on to zip wires or act as a construction guide (*don't* try to build a Flying Fox without experienced help—no matter what braking system you decide to use), but simply to demonstrate that ropes course construction and use have changed considerably over the last 20 years. I'm sure this inevitable curriculum and construction evolution will continue in the direction of increased safety, more efficient construction and innovative design.

Safety and liability matters have always been a concern to administrators, parents, teachers and all those individuals prudent enough to look beyond the fun and games aspect of adventure education. As a result, certain outdoor education pursuits are viewed as risky, including, among others, any water sports, horseback riding, rock climbing and rappelling, and ropes courses. True, there is an element of risk in these activities, but the sensation of risk is what makes participation valuable and attractive to the individual. It's important to understand that this type of programmed risk is largely perceived rather than real. (The definition of programmed adventure includes that the outcome of the chosen adventure be controllable and predictable.) Rappelling with a belay is an example of programmed adventure: predictable outcome, safe, controllable, exciting, and perceived risky by the participant.

Ropes courses have been a liability target in recent years for insurance companies and risk analysts because of this perceived risk. The incidence of accidents in school sports and regular physical education programs is considerably greater than participation on a ropes course, as reported by the Project Adventure 15-year safety survey. (Detailed results of this survey are available through Project Adventure, Inc.)

Ropes courses are being used today by a wide range of organizations and for a variety of purposes. Looking through Project Adventure's workshop brochure offers some indication of this variety of users, for example: teachers, administrators, outdoor educators, camp staff, social service workers, counselors, hospital and treatment center clinicians, business executives, management development professionals, interested parents, and others.

The use of a ropes course provides strong evidence to an individual that he/she can do more than they thought they were previously capable of accomplishing *and* have fun while doing it. Although the feeling 20 years ago was that ropes course participation was primarily for young individuals who needed a rites-of-passage symbolic challenge, today's challenge courses offer a dramatic educational medium for use by anyone who is interested in stretching their capabilities, working intensely with other people, and rediscovering the joy of playful participation.

Considering the number of ropes courses that Project Adventure is now building each year in this country and more recently around the world, there's no doubt in my mind that this unique challenge vehicle is on the way to becoming a universally recognized and effective curriculum tool.

Section Nine

THE CLIENTS OF ADVENTURE EDUCATION

Application of a Generic Model

The historical overview earlier in this volume revealed that the first clients of adventure education programming were well-to-do young men in an English public school. A quarter century after Hahn, the clientele of Outward Bound in the United States was still projected to be young men. One of the primary characteristics of the adventure education movement in the past quarter century has been a steady extension of adventure-based learning models to diverse clientele.

The nine contributors to this section reveal how ethnic minorities, women, school children, university students, business executives and senior citizens have been served by adventure educators. The clientele has become diverse, and will continue to do so. Practitioners of adventure education are only beginning to think about and implement some of these extensions. Women have become extensively, though perhaps not adequately, served. People with disabilities have benefited from great programming ingenuity, but there is much work to be done on that front. Experience has shown that adventure education approaches can be one ingredient in the much-needed overall improvement of American education, but only a beginning has been made in that work. Perhaps the greatest challenge of the future is serving the growing population of senior citizens.

The extension of adventure education to diverse clients reflects, perhaps more than any other development in the field, changes in the social environment. The 20th century has witnessed a progressive, if halting, movement toward equality and justice in America and elsewhere in the world. While adventure education is but a small piece of the social fabric, it has demonstrated its ability to play a significant role in this social evolution. The word "empowerment" has been so much used as to be rendered a cliché, but no word better describes the consequences for people participating in adventure education programs.

People gain strength from their adventure experiences, and can go further to meet other challenges. Some groups face greater challenges than others. By providing resources to these groups, educators of whatever ilk aid in the essential work of social progress. Adventure educators can count themselves among these contributors to progress, as the writings in this section attest.

Ethnic Minorities' Involvement with Outdoor Experiential Education

Frank B. Ashley
Texas A & M University

It is a known fact that minorities make up a very small percentage of the total individuals involved in experiential education. This includes not only leaders in the field but also participants involved in various programs and activities. Activities such as rock climbing, rafting, backpacking, and scuba diving do not seem to attract many minority participants. The question arises as to why minorities do not become more involved in these programs. In this manuscript I will not try to answer this question, but I will attempt to provide some insight as to why this situation may exist.

AN OVERVIEW

Unfortunately, there is not an abundance of information concerning minorities and their involvement in experiential education programs. Most of the information provided in this overview was obtained in cooperation with Richard Hall, whose thesis, *Linking Resources, Learning and Experience in a Multicultural World* (1987), provided an abundance of information pertinent to the subject.

Hall used an interview survey to determine the access of ethnic minorities to experiential education. The interviews were conducted with individuals in ethnic minority communities who had previous contact with experiential approaches such as adventure education or new games. These individuals ranged from a Chicano Mental Health worker and outdoor adventure instructor to a black Outward Bound instructor from New York. Interviews were also conducted with individuals in adventure and other experience-based programs who, according to Hall, "expressed a willingness to discuss the question of Minority Access."

Included in this study by Hall were interviews of: Mark Luna, a Chicano who had participated in the Minority Staff Training Program at the Colorado Outward Bound School; Ricky Tam, who works with ethnic Chinese in the San Francisco Bay Area; Arthur Conquest of the Outdoor Education area of the Thompson Island Environmental Education

Center in Boston; and Kathryn Nelson of the Danforth Foundation in St. Louis.

Each individual seemed to relate a need for more minority leaders in experiential education and also a need for providing experiential education experiences for minority youths. Inability of non-minority leaders to communicate with the minorities was another factor that caused low minority participation in experiential activities. The fact that some minorities may not be able to relate to an experiential education experience, and that such an experience is simply not a priority, are two other rationales for low minority participation given by Nelson and Conquest, who are involved mainly with black and disadvantaged youths.

Being from an ethnic minority myself, I have had friends and relatives constantly question my sanity because of my love for scuba, rock climbing, white-water rafting, and other adventure activities. My participation in these activities is done for recreation but also as a challenge, "to prove something to myself" —though sometimes I feel as though I am trying to prove something to others: "Yes I'm black, but I can do anything you can do!"

Being a black scuba instructor in a predominantly white profession can at times be a challenge. At a diving show two years ago, I had to restrain myself to not return an obnoxious comment to an individual who stated "What, a black scuba instructor? I thought that blacks couldn't even swim." It is because of preconceived stereotypes such as this that many minorities do not become involved in activities which they are not "supposed" to be interested in. To eliminate this problem, a need arises for minority leaders in experiential education programs. Minority youth need individuals that go against the typical stereotypes, individuals that can serve as models and can also allow youth an opportunity to explore the adventure and benefits that experiential programs can offer.

INTERVIEW SUMMARY

Hall (1987), in summarizing the discussions obtained from ethnic communities and experiential programs, recognized several key issues. Those issues and a discussion follow:

ISSUE	ETHNIC COMMUNITIES	EXPERIENTIAL PROGRAMS
awareness	lack of awareness of experiential education programs and resources in communities	unaware of potential interest and points of contact within ethnic minority
experience	outdoor adventure not within experience of most individuals, peers, family	experience with people from different cultural backgrounds is often limited.
role models	few available role models for adventure or environmental education	few ethnic minority role models on program staffs
economics	beyond scholarships: concerns about jobs, travel expenses, equipment, clothes, family support	underfunded without "venture" funds for program development; low staff salaries
time	time away from family and friends magnified by close ties and peer pressure resources	overburdened staff reluctant to increase demands on time, program

ISSUE	ETHNIC COMMUNITIES	EXPERIENTIAL PROGRAMS
skills	lack of basic skills, fitness levels (e.g., swimming or camping)—too threatening	staff often lacks skills (e.g., language, ability to relate to student's environment)
risk/failure	Who needs to fail or risk being seen unskilled, ill-equipped or inexperienced?	Why chance rejection by a "reluctant" population or risk not meeting needs?
environment	perceived hostile physical environment and an alien, white, Anglo-cultural environment	city or reservation seen as hostile, and cultural environment as inaccessible
utility	What use is this for my home community? Lack of perceived utility limits value of and motivation for experience	What's in it for us? A legitimate question for both programs and communities. How does this relate to program objectives?
legitimacy	Is this a legitimate way to make it? Will I gain or lose credibility with peers? Will I be able to make it economically, professionally?	Is the issue of minority involvement legitimate or is it guild-laden, do-gooder exploitation? Can we develop credibility and is this a viable enterprise?
priority	basic education and economic survival seen as competing priorities	institutional survival, maintenance seen as competing with ethnic minority outreach
power/initiative	Who articulates needs? Who teaches and who learns? Who controls programs?	Who has responsibility to initiate efforts to collaborate? Who sets program policy?
values	conflict with basic cultural values (e.g., "pushing your limits" having been taught to accept one's own limitations)	Are programs willing to re-examine their premises and include a wider range of beliefs and values?
feelings	fear of the unknown, of co-optation; anger at continued institutional racism	disappointment, guilt, frustration at failures of previous efforts to involve minorities
diversity	Ethnic communities are diverse within themselves with varying experiences, values, needs, and aspirations. It is even more in error to lump them all together as the "minorities."	Experiential programs are also diverse, going beyond Outward Bound, Foxfire, or Environmental Education, and include people with varying values, lifestyles, and commitments.
commitment	Will individuals and communities make mutual commitments with programs? Access?	Will program commit resources and make changes required for minority?
communication	Sharing information and experience is needed both with communities and with others.	Looking for common problems and concern could lead to collaborative responses.

REASONS ENCOURAGING NON-PARTICIPATION

So what is the major reason for the lack of participation in experiential education programs by minorities? Training more outdoor leaders and developing better lines of communication between ethnic minorities and experiential education programs may increase minority participation, but there will still be a need to understand and evaluate four key concepts:

No Interest or Desire to Participate

As I began working on this manuscript, a fellow minority faculty member walked into my office and inquired as to what I was working on. After giving him an explanation, he retorted, "Are you crazy? Why would someone raised in Brooklyn, New York, want to go out in the woods with mosquitoes, no bathroom, and no air conditioning? There's no logical reason to. Why sleep on the ground outside or risk breaking your neck climbing on the side of a mountain?" After explaining the concept of adventure to him he then asked, "Why do you need adventure? Growing up black in Brooklyn was all the adventure you needed for the rest of your life!" This reaction is not uncommon for many minorities. Some individuals feel that they do not need these kinds of experiences as challenges. To many of them, being a minority and trying to survive the challenges of everyday life is an adventure in itself.

Lack of Funds

Many minorities look at most experiential programs as "something that the rich people do." It can be expensive to buy equipment or clothing for these activities, and one also needs money to travel to wherever the activity is being held. Outward Bound and other schools that specialize in experiential activities are also very costly. Expense alone may be enough to discourage the person who may be trying to make it from pay period to pay period, as is the case with many minorities.

Lack of Knowledge or Understanding

Many individuals, minority or not, simply do not have the knowledge and understanding of what experiential education is or what it involves. They also may have no understanding of what is involved with participation in certain activities. For example, the term "survival" does not have to always imply learning how to survive in the desert or woods for weeks at a time, nor does "canoeing" always imply going down Class 5-rated rivers.

Strong Feelings of Distrust for Others

Some minorities, especially youth, have developed a distrust of individuals outside their race or economic class. This distrust may be caused by past experiences, something heard or said, or just an inbred feeling of distrust toward some individuals. This distrust is shown by some of my friends through comments such as, "I can't believe you're going down a river or out in the woods with a group of white guys? They may leave you out there." This distrust or concern for my safety was also shown by my family when they discovered that I was interested in scuba diving. I was told, "Make sure to watch out for yourself, because you can't depend on those others to watch out for you." The involvement of more minority leaders in experiential education programs may help reduce this problem. Also, if more minorities could be convinced to participate in experiential programs, many of the activities in these programs could help promote feelings of trust not only in oneself, but also in others.

WHAT NEEDS TO BE DONE

As stated in the introduction of this manuscript, I cannot provide answers, but only offer insight as to why there are so few ethnic minorities participating in experiential education programs. There does exist a need to increase the participation of minorities in such programs, if for no other reason than to give minorities the opportunity to experience all of the benefits that may be obtained through participation in them.

The training of more minority leaders in the field is needed in order to make programs more attractive to minorities. Outdoor schools should try to recruit minorities who have an interest in becoming outdoor leaders. Once the number of minority leaders increases, these leaders can return to their communities and recruit minority youth to become involved in experiential educational programs.

Secondly, there is a need for more research to be completed in order to develop a clearer understanding of the problem of ethnic minorities' access to and participation in experiential educational programs. Hall (1987) also states this need for research in his study, and he gives a list of possible steps that can be taken. Two of these include:

1. A need for an investigation of the frequency of minority involvement in selected experiential programs at participant, staff, and leadership levels, and the factors influencing such participation.

2. Documentation and dissemination of programs with strong multicultural involvement that address the needs of ethnic minority communities and include models derived from their own experiences and cultures.

Finally, there needs to be a way to make programs more economically accessible to individuals with low incomes. This may be done by community involvement or involvement through private corporate sponsorship. Experiential educators should meet with community leaders and explain to them the need for such programs and the contributions that it can make to the youth of the community.

REFERENCE

Hall, R. (1987). *Linking resources, learning and experience in a multicultural world.* Unpublished master's thesis, Mankato State University.

Adventure Activities for School Children

Gary Moore
The Ohio State University

Outdoor adventure programs have grown tremendously in the past decade. Initially envisioned strictly as a part of junior high and high school programs, adventure activities are slowly becoming evident in elementary physical education programs. Siedentop (1984) suggests several possible explanations for the popularity of these activities so early in the educational process.

1. Active participation regardless of skill level.
2. Success in challenging activities.

One additional explanation that may prove to be the most rewarding is an activity that provides a balance with competitive athletics; where games are designed so that cooperation among team members is necessary to achieve the objectives of the game. Adding a cooperative atmosphere to routines provides opportunities for children to practice some basic gymnastic skills, while adventure activities offer children the chance to develop cooperation, trust, and problem-solving skills. These skills, in turn, may enhance teamwork in organized sports.

It is interesting to note a few similarities between youth sports and adventure units within school programs. First of all, both offer situations where young athletes feel successful, and feeling good about oneself is often more important than actual performance.

I wish I could lay out this neat little package of a curriculum unit in an elementary school. This way I could follow the traditional method of fitting this nice unit into the overall yearly curriculum. Most of us let programs determine our goals. Those of you who decided to offer these activities to your students did so with the thought, "Hey, what a neat idea, let's try this with our students." We didn't think much about why we were doing them. Deep down you knew that it was different and that the students would welcome the change. But I'll bet the majority of you did not spend much time on how this fits into the graded course of study in physical education. I have to confess, I started the same way.

As the years go by, more and more I see the value of having adventure programming as part of the school curriculum. It becomes so easy for me to cut across curriculum lines and deal with the many issues that face the youth of today. Often we are confronted with conflict on the playground. From making friends to choosing teams to finding things to do when all the basketball courts are in use, and even incorporating what's going on in language arts into cooperative games and sport.

Growing up I had a chance to do all those neat outdoor activities; building rafts, tree houses, hiding from my brothers in the woods. I would try almost anything physical; heights or danger didn't seem to faze me. What did scare the heck out of me was having to stand up in front of the classroom full of my peers and give some sort of oral presentation. For days I would think about this dreaded event... I would even think about failing the subject, if I just didn't have to stand up there. I can still remember what those butterflies felt like. I'm sure today's youth have those same butterflies, but one dramatically different turn of events has made adventure programming even more important in today's society. A few years ago, I could probably ask a group of adolescents about some of the wild and crazy things they had done, and the answers might have dealt with cutting class, pulling off some prank, or some event that made them stand out in the crowd.

Today's youth still want to stand out, to be special, to feel good about themselves. Yet we find the environment becoming one in which drugs and alcohol play a major role. Today's risk-taker is the student with poor self-esteem being made special by others who have found a false sense of confidence through substance abuse.

Okay, now what has all this got to do with adventure programming in physical education?

Fact: Today's youth need a chance to take risks—to feel those butterflies in a supportive and productive environment. They need to walk out of an educational situation being excited, relieved, and willing to brag about what they did in school today. A chance to be the big cheese—not because they scored the winning goal, but because they did something they thought they had no chance of accomplishing, whether it be in a group or individual situation.

Fact: Today's youth need to be a part of a team. It is important at this point to explain my definition of a team. A team is a positive peer group with similar interest or focus in which each individual has an opportunity to contribute to the personal growth of each member. That team can come together in many different forms—the family, a youth sports team, a community service organization (Boy Scouts, Girl Scouts), a support group in school counseling, a close group of friends with similar beliefs and positive role models, or a school elementary physical education curriculum that focuses on "cooperative—be your best curriculum."

Fact: Today's youth need a balance with competitive sport. The value of cooperative play is often overshadowed in the youth sport movement. Winning has become the major goal of some sport programs.

The following is a description of how adventure programming has been integrated into the elementary school physical education curriculum. The situation in which this program takes place is a suburban elementary school of over 500 students, with one specialist in physical education, in which the children receive physical education one 50-minute period per week.

This somewhat nontraditional approach is being accomplished throughout the school year in four different ways.

First, adventure activities are woven into the basic instructional program. Three concentrated weeks of instruction are offered during the school year, and some other activities are taught year round.

The adventure activities fall into two categories:

1. Cooperative game and sport: During each sport unit, a strong emphasis is placed on the "team" value of the sport as it ultimately relates to the overall success of the team. My most enjoyable unit is volleyball—a sport in which there is a large amount of activity time for a small group with plenty of action. Although the students learn the basic skills, many of the skills are developed to provide for a "cooperative atmosphere." The activity of blanket beachball volley ball, four-way volleyball, involves skill testing with a large focus on group challenges (e.g., the number of successful sets within your group). Although some of these may seem rather traditional, what makes them special is the large amount of teacher feedback which is directed toward cooperative play.

2. Self-challenging activities: Traditionally, physical education specialists have long provided self-testing activities for their students. The President's Physical Fitness Program is one such traditional activity that challenged children to compete against the scores of others throughout the country. A mistake many physical education teachers make is to always associate sport with winning or losing—with the goal to be number one. Self-challenging in an adventure model means children competing against themselves to improve their performance or the performance of the group. Siedentop et al., have developed an elementary track-and-field program that rewards children for improving their performance while downplaying the importance of simply beating the other child. Anytime a sport or activity can be modified to instill a sense of "being your best" will enable a physical educator to meet course objectives in an innovative way.

One of these three "adventure" weeks is highlighted in particular. During this unit, students in grades 4 through 6 have the opportunity to scale one of three indoor climbing walls. The horizontal traverse wall, which progresses 60 feet along the gymnasium, introduces students to some basic climbing and spotting techniques. This teaching station requires a minimum amount of floor space and utilizes an often-neglected segment of the physical education classroom—the walls. Blocks of different sizes and configurations are bolted to the wall at a height of a few inches to five feet. The children traverse along the wall using a variety of hand and foot holds; they are never farther from the floor than the height of a balance beam. This one activity has tremendous value, for it offers an activity that can be made more or less challenging by using special color-coded blocks. Thanks to some clever painting by the school's art teacher, students scramble along the simulated mountain ridge in the company of rock climbers, mountain goats, and snakes. Near the end of the traverse wall are wall charts where children can indicate their level of success by signing their names. This simple traverse wall can be constructed for less than $100, provided a local lumber yard is willing to donate 50 to 60 mahogany blocks. The paint is brought in by the students urged on by statements such as: "Anyone who brings in a gallon of latex house paint is the first one to climb the wall." A talented and creative art teacher can mix the necessary colors to form a very attractive scene. At the same time, what has been created is an extremely effective public relations tool.

From the traverse wall, the students progress to one of two vertical climbing walls that reach 20 feet to the top of the gymnasium. Once on top, the students can sign their names to the snow-covered peak (or honk the horn, or touch the golden egg at the top of the "Bean Stalk" climb). An "I can" feeling soon prevails—it comes about when a student reaches the top or improves a previous best. These vertical climbing walls are somewhat more difficult to construct than the traverse wall, since this activity must depend upon "bomb proof" overhead belay anchors and specialized safety equipment. However, the vertical wall is still within reach of school programs. One must, however, get expert advice before sending students to the top. Otherwise they may come down considerably faster than one would like.

The second aspect of the school curriculum that contains some element of adventure is the intramural program. As with all skills, children need an opportunity to practice to improve; these activities are included to provide an alternative to total competitive events.

The third aspect of the curriculum that exposes youngsters to adventure experiences is the resident camp program. Sixth grade children have the opportunity to test these newly acquired adventure skills during a three-day camp session. Approximately 50 percent of the camp curriculum is devoted to extending the adventure program into a natural, outdoor environment.

The final portion allows for a series of one-day field trips to the Adventure Education Center. This local experientially based center offers a variety of adventure activities for area youth. Using a model developed by Ohio State University faculty, area teachers and recreation professionals are trained as instructors and facilitators. This model has had a tremendous impact on area school curriculums. Teachers are receiving graduate level credit for developing adventure alternatives within a variety of disciplines, and students are becoming "turned on" to school through some very innovative approaches. Teachers from around the state have used this experiential center with programs such as:

1. Gifted and Talented
2. Quest
3. Tribes
4. Physical Education
5. Art Education
6. Language Arts
7. Substance Abuse Prevention Programs
8. Leadership Programs
9. Student Council

A recent outgrowth of this model finds teachers wanting a longer experience with their students. Through a pooling of resources, students, equipment, ideas, and enthusiasm, these teachers have developed a five-day resident "Adventure Camp." It is interesting to note that these teachers come from a variety of school districts and have shared their common interest only by becoming a part of this adventure network. Students spend five days participating in camps that have central themes such as "Knights, Castles, and Dragons," and "Pirates, Rafts, and Treasure."

These theme camps have extended learning into the summer months both for teachers and students. A highlight of Knights, Castles, and Dragons involves building a real castle complete with drawbridge, walls, cardboard armor, shields, water balloon catapults, medieval feasts, and tournaments.

The excitement in Pirates, Rafts, and Treasure includes building a homemade raft of 100 milk jugs and PVC pipe and floating out of camp on the last day. The three-mile trip home involves protecting a recently discovered buried treasure from the infamous river pirate, "Morgan."

The Use of Adventure in Reducing and Preventing Socially Deviant Youth Behavior

Mike Laurence

&

Tim Stuart
Brock University

Each year a growing number of youth become involved in some form of socially deviant behavior. In an historically typical response, society pursues categorization of these young people in order to more clearly distinguish their behavior from societal norms. The usual resulting population labels have included, though are not limited to, what might be referred to as 3-D: disadvantaged, disturbed, or delinquent.

Juvenile training centers, detention centers, probation, parole, and community-based corrections have been the more traditional approaches to dealing with the problems of socially deviant behavior of 3-D youth populations. These five modalities have evolved since the mid-19th century state training schools of New York and Massachusetts.

A number of modern-day detention centers supplement detention with diagnostic procedures, educational programs, and therapeutic interventions. Regardless, statistical indicators (e.g., recidivism rates) suggest that traditional methods of juvenile rehabilitation are not very effective deterrents to continued deviant behavior. Furthermore, little research has been conducted regarding the potential for education, community organization, competency promotion, and natural caregiving as effective components of interventions aimed at minimizing deviant youth behavior.

In the late 1960s, a classic exploration into the effects of outdoor adventure on socially deviant youth took place with the cooperation of the Massachusetts Division of Youth Service and Outward Bound (Ewert, 1982). Pioneer researchers Kelly and Baer assigned 120 adjudicated juvenile delinquents, with a mean age of 16 years, to each of three different Outward Bound schools in the United States. Based on follow-up measures, significantly lower rates of recidivism led the authors to conclude that an Outward Bound-type of experience is a more effective rehabilitation tool than the traditional institutional management approaches. Perhaps the most significant information to be gleaned from this and several further studies (Kelly & Baer, 1969 &

1971, & Baer, 1975, as cited in Ewert, 1982) was the suggestion that youth with different background factors influencing their delinquent behavior might respond to different program formats. For example, close association with nondelinquent peers in a physically challenging program led to improved self-concept and social attitudes in some of the subjects.

The purpose of this chapter is to explore several outdoor adventure interventions designed to either *prescribe treatment for*, *reduce*, or *prevent* the socially deviant behavior of youth who are labeled as juvenile delinquents. As a prelude to the introduction of these model North American programs, a brief diversion is necessary to introduce aspects of the various theories of socially deviant youth behavior. Following these theoretical illustrations, several adventure-based program methodologies will be presented along with their conceptual foundations and philosophies.

Several theories have been put forth in explanation of antisocial youth behavior. However, an extensive review of the sociology, psychology, and human biology research into the socially deviant behavior of youth reveals several factors that are purported to influence the antisocial behaviors labeled as juvenile delinquency. The following variables are reported to be amenable to some forms of therapeutic intervention:

1. lack of moral judgment
2. academic failure in school*
3. lowered self-esteem*
4. structurally generated alienation ("powerlessness")*
5. lack of attachment to family
6. inadequate socialization in the family, other family deficits
7. lack of prestige and status
8. unconditional vs. qualified acceptance by parents ("satellization")
9. marginal malnutrition (insufficient vitamins and minerals in diet)
10. hypoglycemia, food intolerance, and neurotransmitters
11. low intelligence, minimal brain dysfunction, and learning disabilities

* often collectively referred to as "school affect"

Adventure-based interventions for youth at risk for delinquent or other socially deviant behavior often target one or more of the above variables for change. This author has selected the following contemporary programs for review based upon the unique nature of their approaches to the problems associated with socially deviant youth behavior.

THE SPRITE PROGRAM MADISON, WISCONSIN

Most state and provincial correctional services contract their adventure-based young offender rehabilitation programs to outside agencies. However, professionals of the Wisconsin State Division of Corrections have developed a unique model program designed to increase the maturation and responsibility levels of incarcerated clients through an adventure-based curriculum. The SPRITE Program (Support, Pride, Readiness, Involvement, Teamwork, and Education) is predicated on the supposition that delinquency results from prolonged exclusion from full societal participation. This exclusion occurs during a significantly long period of adolescence. Related or contributing factors such as poverty, institutional indifference, learning disabilities, parental neglect, and racial prejudice are likely to increase the probability that delinquent behavior will be manifested.

In the SPRITE Program, a typical intake results when an offender review committee (JORP) identifies a youth as "bottomed out" (one who likely acknowledges being in trouble), as having difficulty in coping with interpersonal relationship demands, perhaps in need of reconsidering personal values, or seeking different ways of communicating. The SPRITE Program is seen as both a testing ground for subsequent client release approval and as a therapeutic process. A major aspect of the intervention is client goal setting. Examples of actual goals that clients have formulated and sought to accomplish while at SPRITE include:

1. To develop empathy for my victims;
2. To learn a positive means of dealing with my anger and frustration;
3. To be able to resist negative peer pressure;
4. To learn to accept authority and rules.

It is not unusual to encounter JORP referrals which suggest that a client has had difficulty with the more cognitive therapeutic approaches to that individual's problems and that the more experiential approach of SPRITE would likely test and help solidify gains made so far during custody. Ropes courses, rock climbing, canoe tripping, backpacking, and winter camping are some of the adventure modalities employed in this program.

Another unique aspect of the SPRITE program is found in the partnerships undertaken with other state, federal, or corporate agencies. Young offenders gain an opportunity to learn some basic job skills before their release as they engage in service learning. Projects that the SPRITE clients have completed include trout stream and campsite improvements, ski trail development, and tree planting—work often done side by side with agency personnel (e.g., Forest Rangers) who serve as positive role models.

PROJECT CHALLENGE ATLANTA, GEORGIA

An effective alternative program model for adjudicated youth is community-based Project Challenge in Covington, Georgia. Conducted as an ancillary program of Project Adventure and the Georgia Division of Youth Services, this six-week intervention combines academics, adventure, and counseling (Lisa Galm, personal communication, 1989). Funding for Project Challenge is derived from individual and corporate donations, federal, and state grants. Clients are primarily referrals from court service workers, school personnel, or parents, and must undergo an extensive review process that includes an interview with Project Challenge staff. Four times per year, 14 students between the ages of 12 and 17 are selected to participate in the program.

The majority of students live at a contract home (similar to a foster home) during the six weeks spent in Covington. Staffing consists of two full counselors with the students all day, everyday, with a special education teacher meeting with the group at certain times. During expeditions or trips a third leader joins the group. A typical program starts with one week of academics (focus on reading, writing and math), followed by a week of camping and the Challenge Ropes Course. Weeks 3 and 4 are again classroom oriented, followed by a one-week backpacking expedition in a wilderness area. The final week of classroom activities culminates with a graduation banquet (see Kalisch, 1979, pp. 92-93 for further description of group closure).

A major program goal of this innovative curriculum is to help students change inappropriate antisocial behaviors so that they may successfully reintegrate back into the community. The staff communicate the high expectations they have for the students and work diligently to make students realize that all of their behaviors have consequences for which they must accept responsibility. The philosophical basis for Challenge suggests that students who accept this responsibility become more effective participants in the program which leads to improved self-concept and a decrease in their inappropriate behaviors. Several additional important program goals that foster student growth and development are as follows:

1. To accept personal weaknesses as areas to be strengthened rather than excuses for failure.

2. To appropriately communicate personal needs and feelings to others.

3. To accept obstacles and setbacks as real events in our lives that are to be over come as opposed to being excuses for quitting.

4. To delay gratification, to focus increasingly on the consequences of behaviors and on longer-range goals (Project Adventure, 1988).

The methodology utilized in Project Challenge is called Adventure-Based Counseling. This group change model utilizes a sequential progression of success-oriented activities designed to enhance participant trust, confidence, and coping skills. Within this model "group members are both the means of change and the persons to be changed ... like traditional groups, they can define new realities, offer acceptance, provide contracts for social comparisons, and be a potent context for affecting values and attitudes" (Project Adventure, 1984). For a more in-depth treatise of the Adventure-Based Counseling model, the reader is referred to Prouty, Radcliffe & Schoel (1988).

ROPES (JOHN HOWARD SOCIETY) ST. CATHARINES, ONTARIO

A unique community-based adventure program is operated by the John Howard Society in Ontario, Canada's Niagara Region. The parent organization is a national social service agency that assists convicted imprisoned individuals who are about to transition back to the community with employment, counseling, and other support services. ROPES is a primary prevention strategy that has been developed in an attempt to identify youth who are at risk to enter the criminal justice system and intervene in an effort to prevent delinquency and other antisocial behavior. Initially adventure-based, this multiphasic intervention employs several techniques, similar to those discussed by Gullota and Adams (1982), in a comprehensive approach to delinquency prevention. *Education*, *community organization*, *competency promotion*, and *peer counseling* are the four most significant techniques employed in this program.

Education

Through the use of open houses and media, ROPES conveys a message to young people and the community that is focused on their potential to succeed and on the accomplishments of others already in the program. This becomes, in fact, a form of advocacy for changing the community's expectations for its youth. In addition to these progressive public education strategies, the ROPES program has utilized more traditional educational settings by developing "partnerships" with a number of schools from four regional boards of education. A ROPES instructor, normally a university graduate with a degree in a human services area and adventure programming competencies, is placed in the school and conducts an adventure-based counseling program with students screened and selected by school faculty. Some of these programs have been designed for grades K through 8 in the elementary schools. Secondary school programs are presently under development. Cooperative games, initiative tasks, and ropes courses are the modalities utilized by these instructors.

Competency Promotion

The development of the personal life management skills necessary to cope with the demands of their community, school, and family lives is a major objective for clients in the ROPES program. Three strategies are utilized to empower these pre-delinquent youth to gain control over their own lives:

1. Youth work to reduce negative peer groupings followed by social integration with other young people who act as positive role models. A progressive high school cooperative education program and the field work require ments of a local university serve to facilitate the success of this strategy.

2. Stress reduction in the school setting by provision of program activities that more closely approximate the youth's needs and interests. Adventure-based counseling sessions are normally scheduled on a withdrawal basis rather than after school.

3. The promotion of self-esteem, internalization of acceptance of responsibility, and enhancement of positive attitude are all factors in developing resistance to those forces that lead to delinquent behavior. The small group challenge education is particularly well-suited to the success of these strategies. Additionally, backpacking and rockclimbing expeditions, and encouragement and support for participation in community recreation, are additional vehicles toward this end (adapted from Gullotta & Adams, 1982).

Peer Counseling

The basic premise of the adventure-based counseling model utilized by ROPES is the importance of the peer group as a counseling and socializing agent. Group facilitators give considerable attention to the development of a supportive group atmosphere in which peers can provide assistance (e.g., emotional support) toward the achievement of each individual's personal goals. It is believed that such peer support and opportunities to play the role of helpers can reduce tendencies toward delinquent behavior.

Several adventure-based program models have been presented in order to illustrate the range of options avaliable to treat, reduce, or prevent delinquent behavior. These programs are representative of the several hundred North American agencies that utilize challenge and adventure interventions in school-based, residential or wilderness settings.

REFERENCES

Ewert (1982). *Outdoor adventure and self-concept: A research analysis.* Eugene, OR: University of Oregon Center of Leisure Studies.

Gullota, T., & Adams, G. (1982). Minimizing juvenile delinquency: Implications for prevention programs. *Journal of Early Adolescence,* 2 (2), 105-117.

Kalisch, K. (1979). *The role of the instructor in the Outward Bound educational process.* Wheaton College, Three Lakes, WI: Author.

Project Adventure (1988). *Project challenge.* (program document). Covington, GA: Author.

Project Adventure (1984). *Adventure-based counseling.* Unpublished manuscript. Hamilton, MA: Author.

Schoel, J., Prouty, D., & Radcliffe, P. (1988). *Islands of healing. A guide to adventure-based counseling.* Hamilton, MA: Project Adventure.

Adventure Programs in Higher Education

Michael Gass
University of New Hampshire

INTRODUCTION

As adventure activities began to be adapted to meet the specific needs of certain populations, one of the first applications was for programs in higher education. In fact, in a meeting that led to the development of the Association of Experiential Education in 1974, a large number of conference participants were professionals from colleges and universities (Miner & Boldt, 1981). The intent and perspective of adventure programs in higher education are often extremely varied. From preparing sophomore high school students for the rigors of college to offering programs for students graduating from undergraduate programs, a number of efforts have been made to implement adventure experiences into programs in higher education.

While the existence of such programs is not a recent development in the field of adventure education, the growth and utilization of such efforts has been comparatively small. Most existing programs have not developed through a general need perceived by higher education professionals, but usually by the self-designed efforts of one or two individuals at a particular institution. These individuals, usually after participating in or learning of the values of adventure experiences, devised adventure programs to meet the specific needs of their program or institution. While this type of "internal" development has led to a variety of applications, adventure programs in higher education have just begun to receive external professional acceptance. Another factor that has limited the expansion of adventure programs in higher education is that programs tend to operate independently of one another. This independent growth has enabled creativity in development, but has also limited the potential expansion of such efforts.

The greatest development and application of adventure programs in higher education has been with incoming student orientation, continuing student development, and residential life training programs. Other applications have been utilized (e.g., potential college applicants, student teacher programs, physical education activity classes/curricula, the use of adventure experiences to enhance curricula) and will briefly be discussed at the end of this chapter, but these programs have not received the same level of professional acceptance.

INCOMING STUDENT ORIENTATION PROGRAMS

To ease the transition of incoming students into the educational and social experiences of university life, institutions of higher learning have implemented a variety of assistance programs, often falling under the label of "orientation programs." Since the inception of programs at Dartmouth College in 1935 and Prescott College in 1968, a number of schools have developed incoming orientation programs that incorporate adventure experiences. In a study done to examine the purposes of such programs, Gass (1984) identified 41 colleges and universities that utilize adventure experiences for incoming student orientation programs.

Most of these adventure programs focus on the same purposes as traditional orientation programs; to reduce the attrition of the undergraduate student and/or to ensure a more positive transition to college life. Other adventure programs exist that focus on other goals (e.g., providing a means of introduction to the school's outing club), but these instances occur less frequently.

Unfortunately, many early efforts in adventure programming for incoming students neglected to focus program goals on specific areas of student development. Failure to tailor these programs to the particular needs of these students inhibited many programs from reaching their full potential. Recognizing this problem, several individuals have advised program directors to focus the selection and utilization of adventure experiences to meet needs of the incoming college student. In a paper addressing this concern, Parchem (1975) provided the following thoughts for professionals:

> In a program run at Denison University during the summer of 1974, we had incorporated a four-day and three-night solo experience. Within the traditional Outward Bound framework the solo experience is considered to be an opportunity to reflect upon the recent challenging experience (such as a major climb), to test one's self-discipline by fasting (this differs from instructor to instructor), and to prepare oneself for the final expedition. These goals are well and good—for Outward Bound. But they did not adequately reflect what we believed college students should be getting out of a program run by an institution of higher education. In other words, we recognized that the use of the solo experience by us had different goals than such an experience has for Outward Bound. Consequently, we designed and conducted a series of value clarification exercises prior to putting people on solo. In addition, we told them in advance that part of their post-solo interview would be spent negotiating an informal contract as to what they were going to attempt to accomplish in the remainder of the course and what they wished to accomplish academically during the school year. (pp. 3-4)

Many existing programs have taken the direction of Parchem and others (e.g., Stogner, 1978; Hansen, 1982; Gass, Kerr & Garvey, 1986) and have focused program activities on developing certain areas pertinent to student adjustment. These developmental areas are crucial for all incoming student orientation programs, whether they utilize adventure experiences or more "traditional" methods. Achievement in these critical areas generally leads to positive integration of students into the college environment. Failure to reach these areas often results in adjustment problems for students, which can lead to individuals dropping out or leaving school. These areas crucial to the development of incoming students include:

1. Attachment to/isolation from peers;
2. Faculty-student interaction/isolation;
3. Focus on career development and major course of study;
4. Academic interest/boredom;

5. Inadequate preparation for college academics;
6. Dissonance/compatibility with college environment and student expectations.

Why Adventure Education for Incoming Students?

Given the positive effects of incoming student orientation programs using adventure experiences that focus on these six areas, what are the reasons for their success? How can placing incoming students into environments quite different than that of a university classroom (e.g., unfamiliar wilderness settings) have such a strong influence on a student's ability to adjust to school? Questions like these are often asked by administrators, parents, and incoming students. Clear and well-supported answers to such questions often mean the difference between maintaining an integrated, well-respected program or struggling with an isolated and often fragmented effort.

Several areas of explanation exist that substantiate the use of adventure experiences for incoming orientation programs. Most of these areas relate to the effectiveness of using an adventurous environment to reach the developmental areas described previously (see Figure 1). These areas, and examples of how adventure experiences are often utilized to reach these objectives, include:

Development of Meaningful Peer Relationships

One goal critical to student adjustment is the development of meaningful and positive peer relationships. Attachment to a positive peer group is seen as an extremely valuable step for students making the transition to university life. This has been particularly true in areas of academic success and persistence (Tinto & Cullen, 1973; Astin, 1975), positive academic and social integration skills (Astin, 1975), and greater levels of trust, independence, and individuality (Winston, Prince & Miller; 1983). Others (e.g., Tinto & Cullen, 1973; Astin, 1975; Faugh, 1982) have found isolation from peers highly related to academic failure and attrition from school.

Adventure activities, especially those that are conducted in small groups, are extremely well-suited to nurture the formation of positive peer group development with incoming students. The bonds and interdependence developed to overcome the difficulties of the wilderness are used to overcome similar difficulties experienced by students in their first year of school. These meaningful peer relationships continue to be reinforced as students utilize the behaviors learned and implemented from their adventure experience in their established peer reference groups as they enter college. Participants turn for help and to help fellow students at school, just as they gave and received assistance in the adventure experiences.

Faculty-Student Interaction

Interaction with faculty members has also proven to be extremely helpful in the transition of students to college life. Several researchers (e.g., Terenzini & Pascarella, 1980; Ramist, 1981; Faugh, 1982) have found it to be positively related to both student academic as well as interpersonal growth. Terenzini and Pascarella (1980) also reported that the lack of nonclassroom interaction with faculty, especially concerning intellectual or subject-related matters, is connected to student withdrawal.

Interaction with group members in adventure experiences requires support and reciprocity (Walsh & Golins, 1976; Kerr & Gass, 1987). Being placed in these types of situations with faculty members provides incoming students with a sense of personal validity and a feeling that the university is concerned about the student as an individual. It is also felt that by using adventure experiences as a base to begin such relationships, students and faculty will attain more accurate perceptions of one another. Students also develop a more comfortable feeling about approaching faculty

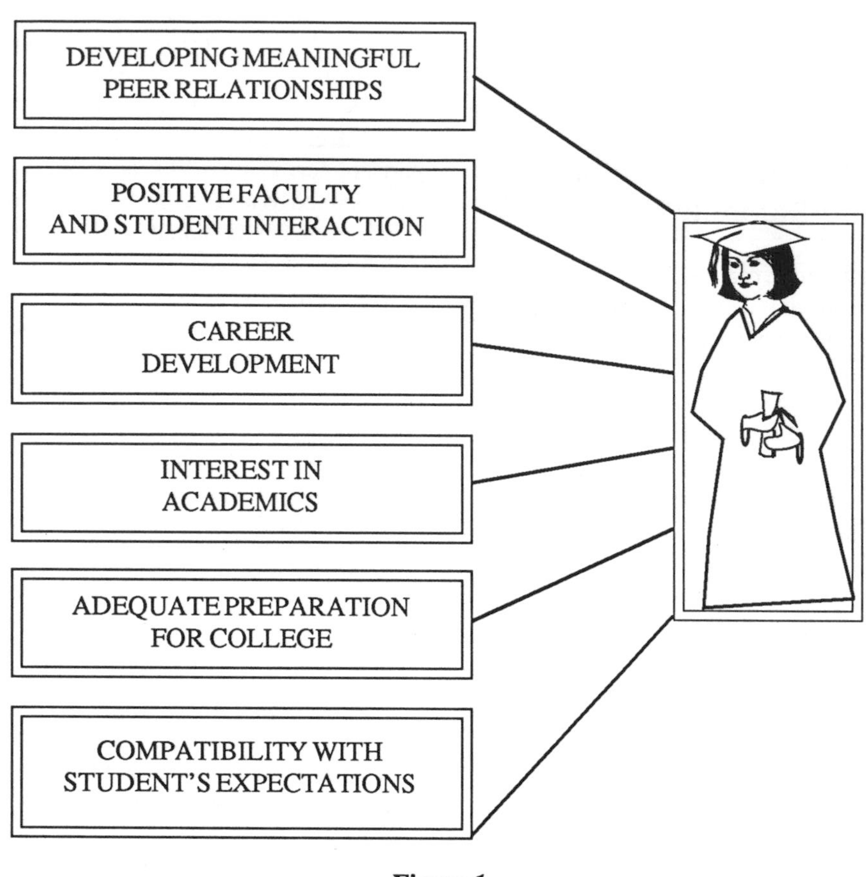

Figure 1
Areas that lead to Student Development

and positive relationships are fostered through involvement in adventure experiences. Such contacts are extended into the school year and act as a base for students to achieve positive integration into the university community. It is often felt that this type of medium is much more appropriate to use as a student's first interaction with faculty, rather than in a room with 300 other incoming freshmen during the first day of classes!

Focus on Career Development and Major Course of Study

A number of individuals (e.g., Tinto & Cullen, 1973; Ramist, 1981) have illustrated the negative effects of students lacking direction toward career goals or major areas of study. In the same study, Ramist (1981) found that even if students are unclear about a choice of a career or major, direction toward even tentative study plans led to greater motivation to do coursework.

Much of the time spent by faculty advising incoming students during adventure experiences focused on answering questions about being a student in a college setting and providing accurate information to plan appropriate goals for school and career. Faculty, staff, and upperclass students are often utilized as instructors or facilitators in adventure experiences for incoming freshmen.

When in this role, it is their intent to utilize adventure experiences as a means to generate discussions concerning career development and provide feedback to incoming students about the academic decisions they are contemplating.

One example of utilizing an adventure experience for career development can be seen in the planning of a hiking experience by the orientation group. Here the beneficial elements of planning the hiking experience are linked to the elements of planning a positive educational experience. In both situations, similar elements of providing appropriate resources, selecting appropriate goals based on personal and supporting resources, choosing a path that is challenging and enriching, and persisting to accomplish a long and difficult goal are required to complete both tasks. These tasks are metaphorically linked together so that learning the proper planning of the hiking experience facilitates the development of the student's decision-making process in preparing and planning for study areas and career considerations. This form of metaphoric transfer (Bacon, 1983) is critical in the utilization of adventure experiences for a variety of populations (see Chapters 4 and 5 for further information).

Academic Interest/Boredom

The amount of academic interest, and conversely, the lack of academic stimulation, have been found to play an important role in student transition and persistence in school. Several individuals (e.g., Tinto & Cullen, 1973; Astin, 1975; Ramist, 1981) have found that low academic stimulation and the inability of students to reach their potential in academic areas often leads to student withdrawal.

Metaphoric transfer from adventure experiences can also be used to provide incoming students with other perspectives of the academic world of higher education. The outdoors, like the world of academia, possesses a great deal of stimulating opportunities. There are other times, however, that an individual encounters activities in both environments that are not as exciting as others, yet necessary to achieve desired goals. Whether it be a student studying for a final examination, or the same person struggling over a mountain pass, each person must learn to search for personal relevance in one's efforts and determine the means to motivate oneself. The ability to provide personal motivation in one situation (e.g., tedious hiking to achieve a desired goal) is metaphorically linked to the other.

Inadequate Preparation for College Academics

Given the reduction of many schools' academic standards for admission, the number of students leaving due to inadequate preparation for school has increased (Green, 1985). While many of the factors in this lack of preparation include inadequate cognitive abilities (e.g., intellectual skills [Ramist, 1981]), other related factors also play an equally important role. These factors include an inadequate concept of the meaning of work and a lack of self-discipline (DeBoer, 1983), a lack of motivation (Robertson, 1978), and an inability to assume responsibility (Astin, 1975). In an interesting discussion of all of these factors, DeBoer (1983) found that students with this problem often overestimate their abilities, are too quick to discount the effects of greater effort, and are too eager to blame external factors for poor performance. He also found effort in academics to be equally as important as student ability.

While the ability of any incoming student orientation program to compensate for poor cognitive abilities is limited, there are several factors related to inadequate college preparation that adventure programs can positively influence. As stated previously, many of the difficulties students encounter in higher education can be resolved through more accurate self-perception, greater persistence and effort, and self-responsibility. When focused to address these issues, adventure experiences are well-suited to positively influence and motivate incoming students in these areas. This is particularly true when one considers the motivational characteristics inherent in such activities and that these activities are accomplished with the assistance of positive peer and faculty support.

An example of this can be seen through the use of an activity such as rock climbing. Here, students are presented with a novel learning situation that appears to be extremely demanding and one that will be difficult, if not impossible, to complete. Through taking personal responsibility for themselves and others, utilizing high levels of persistence, and receiving encouragement and support from peers and faculty, students succeed in accomplishing this difficult task. Students are encouraged to reflect on the processes they utilized to accomplish this task and acknowledge the factors that led to their success. The focus of this entire process is to integrate these factors (e.g., persistence, responsibility, not discounting the value of hard work) into the novel environment the student will be entering as an incoming first-year student.

Dissonance Compatibility with College Environment and Student Expectations

Noel (1977) identified that one of the strongest indicators of student adjustment was the relationship between what the incoming student expected college to be like and what it actually was. He also found that the larger the gap between these two factors, the more difficult the transition for students and the greater their chance of dropping out.

As incoming students approach their undergraduate education, they often rely on a number of sources of information to ascertain what "college life" is truly like. Many of these sources often provide these students with an unrealistic viewpoint of what higher education can provide for each individual. The gap between the students' expectations of college life and what it actually is can create an unpleasant dissonance as students search for perspective in their first year of school. Placing incoming students in an adventurous environment that mirrors such incongruence (i.e., one that in reality is quite different than what the person initially expected) can provide a positive environment for incoming students to reduce this dissonance. This is particularly true when one considers that these activities are done with students and faculty that are knowledgeable of the resources and realities of the school.

While it is not possible in some programs to focus on all six of these goals, adventure programs focusing activities based on these needs have demonstrated a large degree of success. This success has been found to translate into greater levels of student retention (Gass, 1987), higher first-year grade point averages (Stogner, 1978; Gass, 1987), greater levels of student development (Hansen, 1982; Gass, 1987), and increased levels of self-esteem (Wetzel, 1978; Jernstedt, 1986).

CONTINUING STUDENT ORIENTATION PROGRAMS

As efforts to enhance the orientation process in higher education have developed, there has been an expanding sensitivity to view the orientation of students to school as a continuing process, not just one that exists for individuals during their first year of school. A variety of models have been utilized in targeting the needs of these individuals (e.g., Chickering, 1969), with a predominate focus on the development of students' intellectual, moral, identity, and interpersonal abilities.

The focuses in these areas of development have also created the establishment of programs that utilize adventure experiences to help reach the goals of the upperclass student. While not as numerous as efforts with incoming orientation students, a number of programs exist that utilize adventure experiences to assist in the continuing orientation process of upperclass students (Smith, 1984; Gass, Kerr & Garvey, 1986.)

As with incoming student programs that use adventure experiences to enhance the orientation process, continuing programs have focused on using such activities to meet the needs and goals of students as they continue to grow in their university experience. Gass, Kerr, and Garvey (1986) describe one such model where the intellectual, identity, and interpersonal needs of upperclass students are met through a continuing orientation program that uses adventure experiences. These needs are achieved through the following six goals (see Figure 2).

Provide a forum for students, faculty, and staff members to participate as co-learners in a vigorous learning environment

By bringing students together with faculty and staff members as co-learners, students gain the opportunity to be involved in the "process" of problem-solving. In most traditional teacher/student relationships, students are often denied the opportunity to witness how a faculty member arrived at an answer. Adventure activities place faculty and students in a novel environment where the entire group works together as partners making decisions, analyzing various options, and following a plan to its conclusion.

Encourage the development of responsible behavior while working as a group member

Adventure activities are designed so that participants are required to exercise self-control, consideration of others, and good judgment related to understanding one's own strength and limitations. The success of the experience is often the result of the cooperative posture of group members. The focus of these activities is to transfer these qualities into the students' lives where responsible behavior is required, thereby contributing positively to the life and vitality of the campus.

Offer a variety of "vigorous learning environments" to the university community

Too often learning at universities becomes extremely theoretical and students experience very little mastery of the subject material. One of the goals of adventure experiences used in continuing orientation programs is to permit students to experience a wide range of learning environments that require the utilization and completion of tasks. The completion of such tasks broadens students' perspectives of how they learn and provides motivation to attempt new areas of learning and discovery.

Use the wilderness as a natural setting for the study of female/male roles

The wilderness provides an excellent setting for participants to gain an understanding of the limits inherent in traditional sex role stereotyping. Activities are structured so that participants are encouraged to transcend these limitations and explore new perspectives relative to the roles of men and women in other settings.

Provide non-alcoholic programs on weekends for students

Many institutions in higher learning are continually addressing the issue of alcohol and other drugs in campus life. By conducting non-alcoholic weekend experiences for students, programs ask students to focus on the role of alcohol in their lives (e.g., the requiring of alcohol to have a good time, the reasons why students use alcohol, the role of alcohol in relating to peers).

Provide learning experiences in leadership positions for students

Much of the learning in colleges precludes students from accepting responsibility and being placed in positions of leadership. The role of many continuing orientation programs

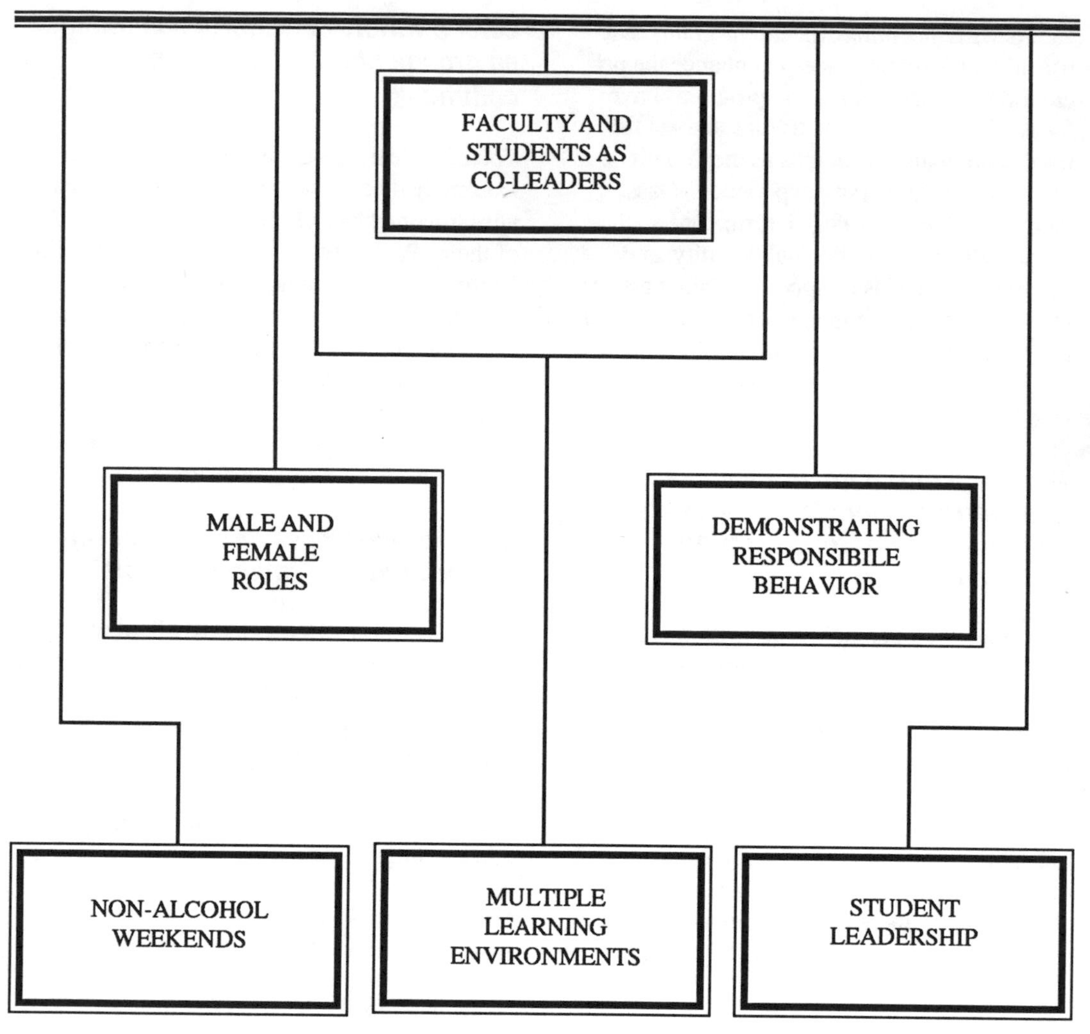

Figure 2
Development of Student Intellectual, Moral, Self-Identity, and Interpersonal Abilities

that use adventure activities is to place students in positions of leadership and responsibility that require problem-solving skills, intellectual growth, and practical application. Active forms of learning replace passive ones as students attain responsible leadership experience with the guidance and support of faculty and other students.

Other models also exist that provide a basis for continuing orientation programs utilizing adventure experiences. One common model is based on the work of Chickering (1969) and Winston, Miller, and Prince (1982). Here, the needs of the continuing student are identified through seven major "development vectors." These vectors include:

1. Achieving competence
2. Managing emotions
3. Becoming autonomous
4. Establishing identity
5. Freeing interpersonal relationships
6. Clarifying purposes
7. Developing integrity

These vectors represent areas critical to the growth and development of the undergraduate. In both of the models presented here, adventure activities are selected based on their ability to reach the goals of the particular model. It is important to remember that such activities are not being utilized as recreational outlets for the college student, but to provide a viable means of meeting needs critical to the development of the undergraduate.

ADVENTURE PROGRAMS FOR RESIDENT ASSISTANTS

Another common application of adventure programming in higher education has been the use of adventure experiences to train resident assistants. The job of a resident assistant (RA) is extremely critical to university life, yet one that is demanding and difficult. In these positions, undergraduate students are asked to work in direct contact with peers in a supervisory role, balancing both personal needs with the needs of the institution. As stated by Cook (1980):

> RAs have responsibilities to individual students, to student groups, to other RAs within the hall they are located, to their supervisory staff, and to the University. A special kind of person is needed who can successfully handle the variety of responsibilities, while still maintaining a personally successful and rewarding university program of study. (p. 4)

Because of the complexity of the position and the vital role that RAs play in higher-education systems, colleges and universities often implement training programs to enhance the skills necessary for RAs to be successful. While these models vary in application, most focus on one or all of the following four areas critical to the development of RAs:

1. Student development—learning about students' personal and academic development and the residential context where this occurs.
2. Self-awareness—learning about one's ability to interact with others.
3. Interpersonal skill development—actual skills needed when working with and relating to others.
4. Leadership development—ability to accomplish tasks in leadership situations.

One popular model that integrates all four of these factors into an RA training program is one created by Upcraft (1982) (see Figure 3). In this training model, the skills needed for RAs are broken down into four critical areas of development, and training activities are implemented based on their ability to enhance this development.

Independent from understanding the implications and direction of such a model, adventure programs have proven to be effective in assisting in the development of some of these areas. Schroeder (1976) found that adventure activities increased the ability of new RAs to understand group modeling skills. Cook (1980) found that the RA adventure training program at Penn State University developed group cohesion between RAs. In a program for Stetson University, Smith (1984) created an adventure program to develop leadership skills in RAs and increase their interpersonal skills and effectiveness. While the results of these programs illustrate some of the strengths that adventure programs hold for training RAs in requisite skills, they still fall short of the potential that these programs can reach.

Since these efforts, adventure programs have found that in order to reach their true potential in enhancing the training of RAs, they must directly address the specific needs of RAs while still utilizing the strength of adventure activities. Peterman, Pilato, and Upcraft (1979) have demonstrated the ability of experience-based training programs to positively influence RAs personally and on their ability to meet the responsibilities of their job. Based on the steps in the model illustrated in Figure 3, the following illustrations are offered as examples of how adventure activities can develop to have a stronger effect on the training of RAs:

Student Development in the Residential Context

One concept vital to the development of RAs is learning how to accept individual differences and promote growth in people with different levels of cognitive, affective, and physical development. The primary step in acquiring these skills is each RA understanding how they perceive and stereotype others and how this affects their interaction with people. Many of these perceptions are often observed in sex-role stereotypes and projections from past interactions with other individuals that "appear to be similar." Using the novelty of adventure environments as a microcosm of the resident halls or campus, training programs lead individuals to look at each person's true competencies and transcend sex-role, racial, and other types of inappropriate stereotyping.

Examples of this can be seen in a variety of contexts of adventure experiences—a female being an assertive leader for her male peers in a particularly demanding exercise, a male showing compassion to another individual as they struggle to complete a task, or an individual performing a skill in a manner that isn't expected based on the group's first impression of that individual. Each of these scenarios is complemented and enhanced by the straightforward and stimulating medium present in adventure activities. This learning is generalized from the RA adventure experience to use in interactions with others in the resident halls on campus.

Self-Awareness/Providing Appropriate Feedback

Two related concepts that are critical to the training of RAs are the development of an awareness of how one is perceived by others and the ability to provide appropriate feedback. Anytime people interact with other individuals, they are at some level of personal risk. This type of risk can have negative consequences (e.g., rejection, humiliation, loss of respect) or positive ones (e.g., greater trust, insight, better relations with others). Taking such self-exposing risks and learning under what conditions such risks are appropriate and which will provide positive, and not negative, outcomes is extremely important for each person. Using the risks presented in adventure experiences as a basis for directly and realistically focusing on these issues can provide RAs with valuable information for their residential setting on campus.

Also related to these principles is the ability of the RA to give and receive feedback from others. Upcraft (1982) defines feedback "...as the exchange of verbal and non-verbal responses among groups members based on commonly observed behavior" (p. 80). Appropriate feedback, based on this definition, has the following seven characteristics (Upcraft, 1982, pp. 81-83):

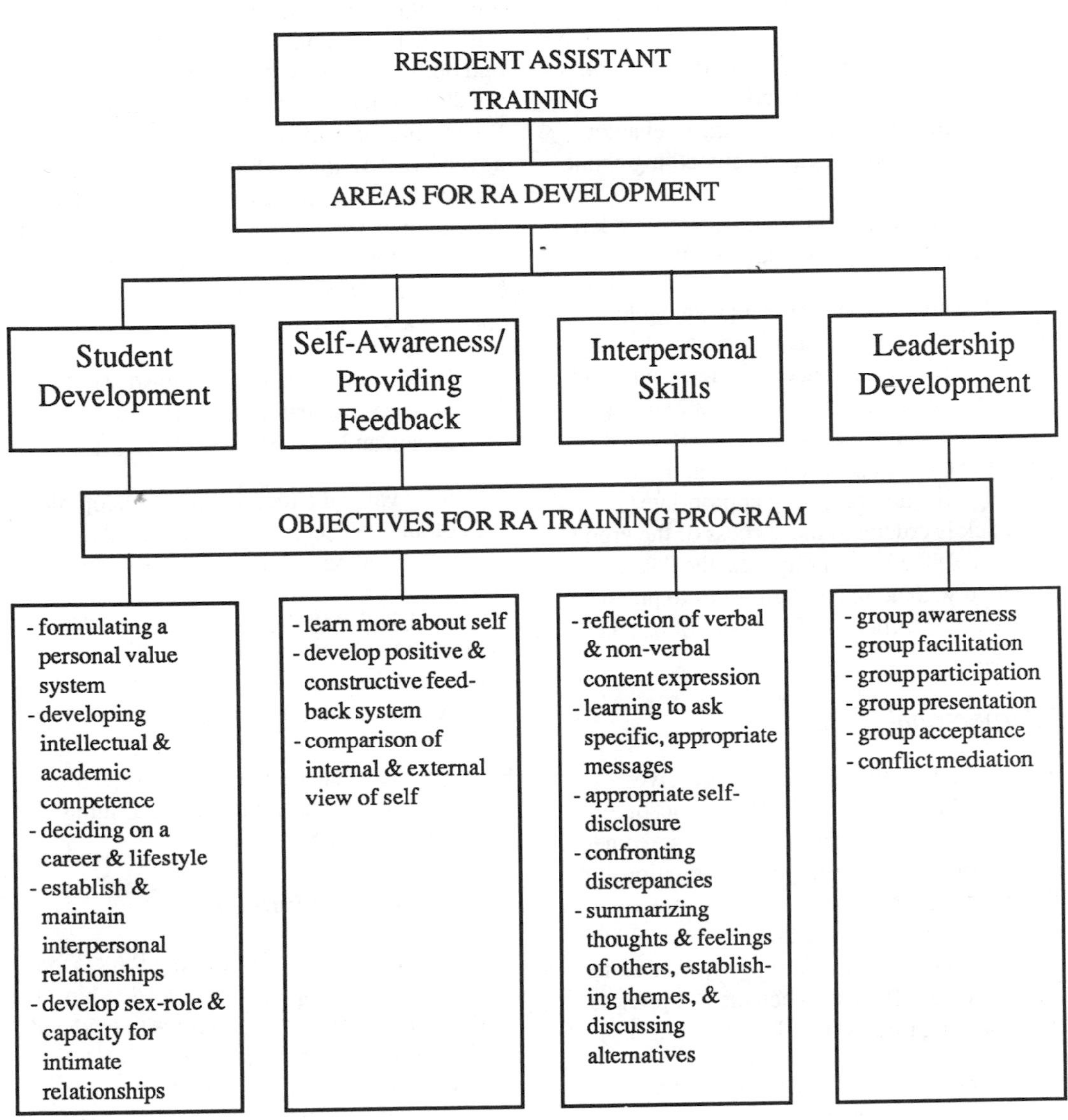
RESIDENT ASSISTANT TRAINING
AREAS FOR RA DEVELOPMENT
Student Development
Self-Awareness/ Providing Feedback
Interpersonal Skills
Leadership Development
OBJECTIVES FOR RA TRAINING PROGRAM
- formulating a personal value system
- developing intellectual & academic competence
- deciding on a career & lifestyle
- establish & maintain interpersonal relationships
- develop sex-role & capacity for intimate relationships
- learn more about self
- develop positive & constructive feed-back system
- comparison of internal & external view of self
- reflection of verbal & non-verbal content expression
- learning to ask specific, appropriate messages
- appropriate self-disclosure
- confronting discrepancies
- summarizing thoughts & feelings of others, establish-ing themes, & discussing alternatives
- group awareness
- group facilitation
- group participation
- group presentation
- group acceptance
- conflict mediation

Figure 3
Resident Assistant Training Program Model

1. It must be descriptive rather than evaluative.
2. It must be specific rather that general.
3. It must be well-intended.
4. It must be directed toward a behavior that the person can do something about.
5. It must be well-timed.
6. It must be checked out with the sender.
7. It must be checked out with the group.

Adventure activities create a valuable, safe, and non-threatening environment for RAs to experience these concepts as recipients and providers of feedback. While in a training session using adventure activities, RAs are placed in realistic, consequential activities where giving and receiving appropriate feedback is crucial to the success of the group. From these feedback processes, the RAs are provided with actual opportunities to practice appropriate methods of feedback for use on campus.

Interpersonal Skills

Related to how an individual is perceived by others is the person's ability to interact and work with others in periods of both agreement and conflict. These interpersonal relationship skills serve as the basis for RAs to effectively perform the functions of their position. In the model shown in Figure 3, interpersonal skills are viewed as effective when the RA possesses the following three skills (Upcraft, 1982):

1. Responding—a respectful and non-evaluative understanding of what a person is thinking and feeling, achieved through appropriate listening skills.
2. Self-disclosing—the ability to share one's thoughts and feelings openly and honestly.
3. Initiating skills—confronting or summarizing ideas from interpersonal interaction to bring about change.

Adventure activities can provide an effective medium to develop and achieve strong areas of competence with these three areas of interpersonal skills. Adventure experiences are conducted in small groups where success is highly dependent upon sharing the thoughts and opinions of each group member and resolving interpersonal conflict when it arises. Processing techniques also accompany adventure activities to further enhance the future utilization of these interpersonal skills. An example of one such technique is the "full value" or "no-discount" contract (Gass, 1985; Schoel, Prouty, and Radcliffe, 1988). This contract asks each individual to:

- fully value their own feelings/thoughts/opinions as they participate in the group, and

- fully value the feelings/thoughts/opinions of all other individuals that are also participating in the adventure experience.

Using such a policy requires each person to openly and honestly confront and address personal and group issues and work toward resolving such issues. Developing the interpersonal skills to accomplish a positive resolution to the problems encountered in the adventure experience provides an invaluable training medium for the RA.

Leadership Development

A final area necessary for training RAs is the development and application of leadership skills. Without strong capabilities to lead and work with groups, the ability of the RA to carry out the function of their job is severely diminished. Upcraft (1982) identifies these necessary capabilities as including:

1. A strong awareness of group dynamics.
2. The ability to facilitate groups in accomplishing tasks.
3. Active and effective participation by the leader in group activities.
4. The ability to present material to group members so it can be used/implemented.
5. Participation by the leader that is accepted and respected by group members.

Adventure activities provide a real and consequential medium to learn, enhance, and/or practice these qualities. Group dynamics become actual leadership issues, as individual as well as group decisions must be made in order to accomplish difficult tasks. As leaders of such tasks, RAs find they must take an active role to ensure that ALL OF THE members contribute and have their needs met. Leaders also find it necessary to take on different roles to accommodate the needs of different group members and mediate conflict as the group finds itself in stressful situations. A healthy respect for the meaning of leadership and its uses and abuses is also obtained with a personal and group knowledge of leadership strengths and weaknesses.

OTHER ADVENTURE PROGRAMS IN HIGHER EDUCATION

While the three models presented in this chapter represent the most common areas of use in applying adventure programs in higher education, they are by no means the limit to efforts that are presently occurring. As the adaptation, integration, and strength of adventure programs/models in higher education continue to develop, more applications will be created. The applications that will be discussed briefly here include pre-college preparation programs, student-teacher preparation programs, developments in college and university physical education departments, and curriculum enhancement programs.

Pre-College Preparation Programs

One such application in higher education that is receiving attention is the use of adventure activities with high school students preparing for college. Some of the programs involved in preparing these students have found adventure components to be extremely valuable in reaching certain specific objectives of their programs. One example of a successful application has been with Upward Bound programs. Upward Bound is a federally funded program designed to assist high-ability disadvantaged youth to enter and complete programs in higher education. One of the goals of this program is "to develop the motivation, self-confidence, attitude, and self-concepts necessary for high school graduation and matriculation in postsecondary education programs" (Steel, & Shubert, 1983). Upward Bound programs have applied the strengths of adventure education programs to assist them in successfully reaching this goal for their students. In a study done at Johnson State College, the Upward Bound program found that their outdoor experience program developed more positive attitudes, higher levels of self-concept, and greater levels of motivation in school work (Anderson, 1984).

Teacher Preparation Programs

Another use of adventure activities has been with teacher training programs. Here, adventure programs have been used as means to provide student teachers with insights into how students learn, what school is like for children that have difficulty learning, and how placing students in stressful situations affects their learning. Such programs have also focused on having student teachers assume responsibility for learning so they become more self-reliant and cooperative as teachers and highlighting the need for teachers to individualize learning for students based on their emotional as well as intellectual abilities. As stated by Eder (1976):

> What do the (adventure) experiences say about teaching? For the group, the rock face has become a metaphor for learning; the ropes have come to represent the different ways to learn. The meaning behind the symbols also became sharper. Since human diversity is a fact of school life, then they—as teachers—must be able to provide students with learning alternatives and an encouraging environment, just as the climbing instructors were doing for each of them. (p. 5)

Adventure programs have also been used with several applications for veteran teachers. Goals with these programs have included providing a means for enhancing current teaching effectiveness by providing teachers with safe yet novel environments to experiment with different curricula, instructional strategies, and staffing patterns (Eder, 1976).

Physical Education Programs

As illustrated in earlier chapters, physical education activity programs have commonly been a vehicle for adventure activity in higher education. In a recent study, Uhlendorf (1988) identified 200 colleges and university physical education departments that possess some type of activity class in outdoor leisure/adventure pursuits. The focus of such programs are often educational and/or recreational in purpose and usually serve the general university population as well as P.E. majors.

Two major concerns are presently being confronted by physical education departments in higher education pertaining to the offering of adventure activity classes. The first is the training and certification of physical education majors to become teachers. In the most recent publishing of the National Council for Accreditation of Teacher Education (NCATE) Guidelines (1987) for physical education preparation programs, it is required that all potential physical education teachers must demonstrate skill and knowledge regarding outdoor leisure pursuits "so they can plan, implement, and evaluate" (p. 53) such offerings in physical education programs. In her study analyzing such practices, Uhlendorf (1988) found that even though half of the P.E. programs in the United States have some form of outdoor leisure pursuit classes, most physical education teacher preparation programs are deficient in their ability to train students in these activities.

The other concern is the ongoing philosophical debate of physical educators on whether the use of physical activity primarily for affective development, and not psychomotor development, should be part of physical education curricula. Both of these concerns are important for physical education programs in higher education to address, and the urgency of answering both will be strong professional focuses in the next few years.

Adventure Education to Enhance Higher Education Curricula

Physical education departments are not the only academic programs that have incorporated adventure activities into higher education. While suffering from the same problems as other efforts in higher education addressed earlier (e.g., isolation of programs, programs revolving around one individual), there have been several successful efforts to utilize adventure education to enhance curricula in higher education.

Much of the success of these programs is due to the fact that the learning in adventure education is experience-based and incorporates both action and reflection to attain educational objectives. As stated by Medrick (1973):

> The student is placed in a situation where he (she) learns through direct experience and where what he (she) learns is immediately tested and, if workable, reinforced through his (her) achievements and successes. (p. 1)

The success of most curricula have been their abilities to integrate the learning from the adventure experiences into the particular academic needs of the college coursework, whether it be philosophy, areas of science, languages, education, literature, and so on. Illustrated in a series of articles, Beidler (1980, 1985, 1987) has demonstrated the ability to use adventure experiences to enhance the learning of college students. These activities place the students in novel situations where direct experience, personal and group interaction, individualized learning, and the benefits of problem-solving work to empower the learning processes.

CONCLUSION

As stated throughout the chapter, the applications of adventure experiences in higher education are extremely varied. Whether it is due to this variation, the novelty of this type of learning, and/or the isolation of existing programs, such experiences are far from reaching the potential influence they can have on institutions of higher learning. To reach this zenith, interested professionals must work to validate as well as demonstrate the true abilities of their programs and focus on the transfer of learning from adventure experiences to colleges and universities. Past accomplishments have provided an incomplete outline of what can be attained with such programs. The much more difficult tasks of improving and integrating adventure learning in higher education hold the merits of what can truly be achieved in the future.

REFERENCES

Anderson, J. (1984). *Results from the outdoor education component of the Johnson State Upward Bound program.* Johnson, VT: Johnson State College, Upward Bound Project.

Astin, A. W. (1975). *Preventing students from dropping out.* San Francisco, CA: Jossey-Bass.

Bacon, S. (1983). *The conscious use of metaphor in the Outward Bound experience.* Denver, CO: Colorado Outward Bound School.

Beidler, P. G. (1980). A turn down the harbor. *Journal of Experiential Education, 3*(2), 24-32.

Beidler, P. G. (1985). English in the tree tops. *Journal of Experiential Education, 8* (3), 34-41.

Beidler, P. G. (1987). Bee weekend. *Journal of Experiential Education, 10* (3), 23-27.

Chickering, A. W. (1969). *Education and identity.* San Francisco, CA: Jossey-Bass.

Cook, K. V. (1980). *The effectiveness of an outdoor adventure program as a training method for resident assistants.* Unpublished master's thesis, The Pennsylvania State University. (ERIC Document Reproduction Service No. 210 142.)

DeBoer, G. E. (1983). The importance of freshmen students' perception of the factors responsible for first-term academic performance. *Journal of College Student Personnel. 24* (4), 22-29. (ERIC Document Reproduction Service No. 287 893.)

Eder, S. (1976). Learning on the rocks. *American Education, 12*,(1), 24-29.

Faugh, S., et al. (1982). *Significant others: A new look at attrition.* Paper presented at the Annual Meeting of the American Counseling and Personnel Association, Detroit, MI. (ERIC Document Reproduction Service No. 225 446.)

Gass, M. A. (1984). *The value of wilderness orientation programs at colleges and universities in the United States.* Durham, NH: University of New Hampshire, Outdoor Education Program. (ERIC Document Reproduction Service No. 242471.)

Gass, M. A. (1985). Programming the transfer of learning in adventure education. *Journal of Experiential Education, 8* (3), 18-24.

Gass, M. A., Kerr, P. J., & Garvey, D. (1986). Student orientation in wilderness settings. Kraft, R. J. & Sakofs, M. (Eds.). *Experiential education in the schools* (pp. 320-330). Boulder, CO: Association for Experiential Education.

Gass, M. A. (1987). The effects of a wilderness orientation program on college students. *Journal of Experiential Education, 10* (2), pp. 30-33.

Hansen, R. N. (1982). QUEST: Career exploration in the wilderness. *Journal of College Student Personnel, 23* (4), pp.344-345.

Jernstadt, G. C. (1986). *Procedures, materials, notes for the Outward Bound impact study*. Hanover, NH: Dartmouth College.

Kerr, P. J., & Gass, M. A. (1987). Group development in adventure education. *Journal of Experiential Education, 10* (3), 39-46.

Medrick, F. W. (1973). *Outward Bound and higher education: A rationale and outline for college development.* Denver, CO: Colorado Outward Bound School.

Oppenheimer, B. T. (1984). Short-term small group intervention for college freshmen. *Journal of Counseling Psychology, 31* (1), 45-53.

Parchem, A. (1975). *Notes on the evaluation of outdoor experience programs.* Paper presented at the Annual Conference on Outdoor and Experiential Education, Mankato, MN.

Peterson, D., Pilato, G., & Upcraft, M. (1979). A description and evaluation of an academic course to increase interpersonal effectiveness of resident assistants. *Journal of College Student Personnel, 20,* 348-352.

Ramist, L. (1981). *College student attrition and retention college board report No. 81-1.* New York, NY: College Entrance Examination Board. (ERIC Document Reproduction Service No. 229 075.)

Robertson, T. (1978). *Title III proposal: Linfield out-of-doors.* An unpublished paper. Linfield College: McMinnville, OR.

Schoel, J., Prouty, D., & Radcliffe, P. (1988). *Islands of healing: A guide to adventure-based counseling.* Project Adventure: Hamilton, MA.

Schroeder, C. G. (1976). Adventure training for resident assistants. *Journal of College Student Personnel. 17* (1).

Smith, K. D. (1984). *Beyond wilderness skills: Education for the individual and group development.* Paper presented at the American College Personnel Association Conference, Baltimore, MD. (ERIC Document Reproduction Service No. 252 368.)

Steel, L., & Shubert, J. G. (1983, April). *The effectiveness of Upward Bound in preparing disadvantaged youth for postsecondary education.* Paper presented at the annual meeting of the American Educational Research Association, Montreal, Canada. (ERIC Document Reproduction Service No. 235 262.)

Stogner, J. D. (1978). *The effects of a wilderness experience on self-concept and academic performance.* Dissertation Abstracts International.

Terenzini, P. T., & Pascarella, E. T. (1980). Student/faculty relationships and freshmen year educational outcomes: A further investigation. *Journal of College Student Personnel, 21* (6), 521-528. (ERIC Document Reproduction Service No. 238188.)

Tinto, V., & Cullen, J. (1973). *Dropout in higher education: A review and theoretical synthesis of recent literature*. Washington, DC: Office of State Planning, Budget, and Evaluation, U.S. Dept. of Education, June 30, 1973. (ERIC Document Reproduction Service No. 078 802.)

Uhlendorf, K. (in press). *An investigation of outdoor adventure leadership and programming preparation in physical education baccalaureate degree programs.* Unpublished doctoral dissertation, University of North Carolina at Greensboro). Dissertation Abstracts International.

Upcraft, M. L. (1982). *Learning to be a resident assistant*. San Francisco, CA: Jossey-Bass.

Walsh, L., & Golins, G. (1976). *The exploration of the Outward Bound process.* Denver, CO: Colorado Outward Bound School.

Winston, R. B., Miller, T. K., & Prince, J. S. (1982). *Assessing student development.* Athens, GA: Student Development Associates.

Programming Adventure Education for Older Adults

Deborah Sugarman
Unity College

Several factors have produced an increasingly large number of older adults who have the time, health, and finances to pursue leisure activities and interests. People are living longer and are increasingly active at an older age. The life expectancy of an infant born in 1978 is 73.3 years compared to the 47 years of an infant born at the beginning of the 20th century. After retirement at age 65, a person has approximately 20 percent more years of life remaining before death occurs (Leviton, 1980). Secondly, the development of medical technology and the widespread application of medical care, public health, and consumer protection has made it possible for individuals to avoid many illnesses and diseases and to live a relatively healthy life (Peterson, 1983). Finally, the work force is increasingly white collar with workers in fields such as law, administration, and finance rather than in manufacturing or service industries (Ewert, 1983). According to the 1980 U.S. Bureau of Labor Statistics, about 60 percent of all elderly couples have incomes in the middle class range or above. Although about 90 percent of all elderly Americans receive income in the form of a Social Security pension, the reason that many retired people do reasonably well is because of private pension systems and personal investments (Schaie and Willis, 1986). Concurrently, a growing national interest in outdoor adventure programs has opened doors to older adults. According to the President's Commission on Americans Outdoors, the demand for outdoor activities has grown faster than the available resources in the past 25 years, with 90 percent of Americans seeking enjoyment from mountains, seashores, lakes, pathways and playgrounds. The Commission also found that the average age of outdoor enthusiasts is steadily climbing (Alexander et al., 1987).

With the increase in the number of people over 65, program administrators need to understand the concepts of aging and retirement as they relate to adventure education. The biological, sociological, and psychological aspects of aging have an impact on the individual and how he or she relates to others. With the knowledge of how these aspects impact leisure, administrators will be able to provide meaningful and satisfying programs for older adults.

BIOLOGICAL ASPECTS OF AGING

Biological aging refers to the physical changes that occur in an individual as he or she grows older. The changes caused by aging are a natural process and they vary greatly from person to person. The number of people with specific impairments begins to increase around the age of 40 and shows a sharp increase after 60. In general, the changes include a slowing down of biological functions, a breakdown in the functioning of body systems, a reduction in physiological reserves, and the altered structure of cells, tissues, and organs (Kraus, 1983). Older persons require a longer adjustment period after activity to resume normal respiration, pulse rate, and oxygen consumption. A decline is seen in speed, strength, endurance, coordination, and flexibility. Aging decreases the efficiency of body systems, and brings about progressive disabilities of the circulatory and nervous system. Decreases occur in the senses and cause changes in visual acuity, depth perception, and the ability to hear high frequency sounds. Changes are also seen in the amount and quality of sleep, and the tolerance for temperature extremes. There is also a decrease in the body's capacity for cell growth and tissue repair. Reduction of muscle mass occurs, as does a decrease in tissue elasticity and in the water absorbing capability of tendons. In terms of biological effects on the body, the program planner needs to consider the following:

1. Make sure there is plenty of light, avoid activities that need to be done close to the eyes, and give people time to adjust to changing light conditions.
2. When speaking, make sure everyone can see you, try to eliminate background noise that may mask what is being said, and do not speak rapidly.
3. Gradually build up physical capacity.
4. Schedule shorter sessions with breaks in between.
5. Allow time to warm up before doing activities to increase range of motion and flexibility.
6. Allow for longer rest times after strenuous activity.
7. Be aware of the diminished response to temperature changes.

SOCIOLOGICAL ASPECTS OF AGING

Sociological aging refers to the roles in which society places people when they reach a certain chronological age (Kraus, 1983). As individuals age, they are deprived of the major roles that occupied their adult lives, such as worker, parent, or spouse. Havighurst (1972) described the sociocultural tasks of later life as the following:

1. Adjustment to retirement. This significant change provides the opportunity for increased leisure time, while it reduces economic resources.
2. Adjustment to the death of a spouse. This task is faced by more women than men and involves social, personal, and economic adjustments.
3. Establishing an explicit affiliation with one's age group. This is important in order for older people to develop social networks.
4. Meeting social and civic obligations. Older adults have more time to become involved in creating social responsibilities to future generations and to society at large.

Adventure education can help the older adult to successfully deal with these tasks and begin to develop new roles with which they feel comfortable. Group-centered activities increase mutual support and trust in participants and begin to develop social networks that can be continued after the course is finished. Through successful completion of activities, participants can be recognized by the group as a person of worth and can recognize in themselves new roles with which they may feel comfortable.

PSYCHOLOGICAL ASPECTS OF AGING

Psychological aging refers to the emotional well-being of a person as he or she ages. Because of the increase in life expectancy, people are becoming more interested in the concept of "successful aging" which, according to Palmore (1979), has been equated with life satisfaction. The foremost predictors of life satisfaction are socio-economic status, personality, perceived health, activity and intimate friendships above and beyond one's family (Leviton, 1980). Researchers developed several theories to explain how older adults respond to aging. The "activity theory" of aging is concerned with the relationship between activity and life satisfaction in old age. Activity is seen as providing opportunities to gain the elements that predict life satisfaction. Through activity, adults can enhance personality, become healthier, and develop friendships, which are predictors of successful aging. The "disengagement theory" states that people experience some reduction in activities and in encounters with other people after retirement. They do not replace their lost roles, but become increasingly preoccupied with the self and decreasingly invested in persons or objects in the environment.

The development of these theories has stimulated much research into the relationship between activity and life satisfaction in old age. Most studies (Havighurst, Neugarten & Tobin, 1968; Hockschild, 1975; Lemon, Bengtson & Peterson, 1972; Longino & Kart, 1982) show a sizable correlation between activity and satisfaction. The strongest correlation is seen in informal activities such as those done with friends, neighbors, or relatives as opposed to formal activities involving participation in voluntary groups that have established agendas, such as attending meetings. Based on this research, it appears that intimate activity does provide strong role support and self-affirmation. The important implication of these studies is that not all activities are equal in helping older people adjust to aging or in helping them to reach the goal of successful aging. It is not the frequency of the activity that is important, but the quality of the activity (Schaie & Willis, 1986).

Although adventure challenge programs have little to do with socio-economic status, they do have a direct influence on the remaining predictors of life satisfaction: personality, perceived health, activity, and intimate friendships above and beyond one's family. The goals of adventure challenge programs relate directly to life satisfaction. As a result of the successful completion of challenging activities, the development of personality is seen through an increase in self-confidence and self-esteem, self-discovery, leadership development, creativity, and decision-making. People become aware of the importance of good physical and mental health. Many new skills are learned and developed on adventure courses, skills that participants can continue to use in their personal lives after the course is finished. Close bonds develop between group members as a result of intimate friendships, which continue long after the course is over (Miles, 1980).

PLANNING ADVENTURE PROGRAMS

Planning adventure programs for older adults, like planning programs for any specific population, involves a series of steps. The first step is to define the goals of the program.

What do you want to accomplish? What are the needs of the group? How can you mesh the group's needs with your goals? The administrator, in this first step, should be familiar with the three aspects of aging: biological, sociological, and psychological. With knowledge of the aging process and the importance of activity to life satisfaction, the planner can design goals that will fit the needs of older people. The goals should evolve from a holistic view of adventure education and include the social, emotional, and physical realms.

The next step involves designing the specific schedule of activities. When planning the schedule it is important to consider specific information concerning physical aspects (i.e., longer adjustment period after activity, decline in strength, endurance, and coordination, decrease in efficiency of senses, etc.), sociological aspects (i.e., importance of role development) and psychological aspects of aging (i.e., predictors of life satisfaction). Criteria for selecting the activities should include such considerations as the appropriateness of the activities to the clientele, suitability for the intended group, effectiveness of the activities in reaching the goals and objectives, and the pacing and variety of activities (Szczypkowski, 1980). In researching the meaning of the camping experience for older adults, Chenery (1987) found the following:

1. The importance of having a range of levels and kinds of activities;
2. The importance of having success-oriented activities;
3. The importance of having opportunities for varying levels of physical demands, social interaction, and newness of familiarity;
4. The importance of having the ability to choose among activities;
5. The importance of socialization.

Older people are process-oriented rather than product-oriented. That is not to say that they cannot push themselves physically and psychologically—they can and do! But there is much reflection and introspection in the process. When planning the schedule, the concepts of choice and process must be considered.

The next planning step involves resources. What will you need in order to run the program in terms of equipment, staff, environment, information, etc.? What adaptation of the resources will be necessary to fit the physical and emotional needs of the participants? Staffing and medical information are extremely important when working with an older adult population. Hiring and training a good staff is the key to an effective program. Staff should be mature and personable, be knowledgeable in the content areas of adventure education, have skill in teaching, and be able to facilitate the participants' abilities to pursue their own goals. The staff should be able to encourage continued growth and independence in older persons.

Instructors must be able to gain insight into the students' historical experiences, their beliefs and values, and their present situations. They need to be able to develop a warm, caring climate with mutual respect between themselves and the participants. They should foster the belief that both leaders and participants have roles in the teaching/learning process and that both can respect the knowledge and experience of the other. Staff should be trained in the specifics of working with older adults. They should understand health issues, the concept of successful aging, developmental aspects, how to provide an intense yet enjoyable experience, techniques for helping participants overcome stereotypes of themselves, and techniques for confronting behavior characteristic of this age group.

Medical information is specifically important in planning adventure education programs for older adults. The administrator needs to develop a medical form to be given to participants that will give complete medical information pertinent to the program. Specific questions pertaining to aging need to be included in the form, such as questions about age-related diseases, heart problems, lung problems, joint problems, sight/hearing loss, gastrointestinal or urinary problems, high blood pressure, medications a participant is currently taking, and current level of physical activities, among other key information. The form may include a physical examination, copies of a recent EKG, and/or a signed statement from the participant's physician. This specific information can help the administrator plan the program to more closely fit the physical abilities of the participants, and can help the instructors know what kinds of problems they may run into in the field.

The next planning step is to develop an information packet to be sent to participants before the course begins to avoid false expectations or misconceptions. Just like anyone else, older adults may feel inadequate when thinking about participating in an adventure experience. "Will I be able to do it? Am I too old? Will I hold the group back?" The administrator needs to be aware of these concerns and take steps to relieve people's worries. The participants should be given enough information concerning the goals of the course, the schedule, and the medical aspects before the course so that they can make a decision whether or not to participate. Expectations should be thoroughly explained so that participants know specifically what will be happening in the program and what they will be expected to do.

The last step in the planning process is to design evaluation procedures. How will the course be evaluated along the way and when it is completed? Evaluation can be done cooperatively between participants and instructors. Ideally the instructors have provided regular opportunities throughout the course for feedback from the group so that participants' perceptions, reactions, and evaluations can modify the program to more closely fit their needs and wants. Participants can provide useful feedback for future programs.

RUNNING THE PROGRAM

The development and learning techniques of older adults are different from any other age group. Adults are increasingly self-directed and are problem-centered in their learning. They have a rich background of experience that can play a vital role in their learning new skills. They learn new knowledge by relating it to what is previously known. Adults are more motivated by internal incentives than by extrinsic rewards. The instructor needs to tailor his or her teaching and leading styles to fit the unique characteristics of this particular group.

At the beginning of the course it is important for the instructors to learn participants' expectations of themselves and the leaders. The instructor, knowing the needs and desires of the group, will be able to direct the course to meet them. This will result in greater motivation and learning for participants. By providing an atmosphere of support and group cooperation, the instructor can help participants verbalize their fears and can continually strive to make those fears more manageable.

Participants should be involved in planning the content of the course. This will help make them feel more at ease, reduce anxiety, and result in more commitment to the course. Participants should be encouraged throughout the course to share their knowledge, ideas, and skills. They have a wealth of information, and sharing helps develop new roles within the group that can be carried into their lives at home.

Instructors should continually encourage the development of group cohesiveness and strive for a supportive, interactive group. They need to be aware of changes in the energy or enthusiasm of individuals in the group that could be caused by physical or emotional problems.

Instructors should consider the following when leading activities:

1. Concentrate on one task at a time and make sure that one item is satisfactorily learned before the next is undertaken.
2. Reduce the potential for distraction whenever possible.
3. Allow time for integration of new experiences.
4. Organize material into categories or sequences.
5. Keep learning concrete and deal with the present reality.
6. Design tasks to reduce the fear of failure, the chance of being made to look foolish, and the need to compete for rewards.
7. Design tasks so they need not be completed under pressure of time.
8. Keep sessions fairly short and space them out throughout the day, giving people opportunities for socialization and introspection.
9. Give constant, supportive, helpful feedback on performance.
10. Make sure that participants understand the meaning behind the activities.

At the end of the course it is important for instructors to process the total experience with the participants, and to talk about how to link the adventure experiences with everyday life. These links can provide more meaning to the experience. Participants must be able to bring closure to the experience and to process what it has meant to them. They must be helped and encouraged to develop ways to keep the social networks continuing after the course is over. Instructors and participants should discuss the concept that the course is a means, not an end.

CONCLUSION

Older adults are a growing segment of our population whose leisure needs must be met. They are a challenging population, and rewarding to work with. Several authors (Hupp, 1987; Kennison, 1985; Rillo, 1980; Rogers, 1982) feel that this population has been seriously neglected, and that there is a need to develop programs for them that revive former skills and interests and teach new ones.

Adventure education programs can challenge, revitalize, and provide new leisure directions for older persons. It is important for everyone who desires an adventure experience, no matter what their age or ability level, to be able to share the joys and satisfactions of living with a group in the wilderness.

One participant on an adventure education course said it best: "Thank you for letting me do this course. So many people think that old people can't do these things, and won't even let us try. I appreciate your giving us this opportunity."

REFERENCES

Alexander, L., et al. (1987). *President's Commission on Americans Outdoors.* Washington, DC: U.S. Government Printing Office.

Chenery, M. F. Research in action: Camping and senior adults. *Camping Magazine, 59*(5), 50-51.

Ewert, A. (1983). Adventure programming for the older adult. *Journal of Physical Education, Recreation, and Dance, 54*(3), 64-66.

Havighurst, R. J. (1972). *Developmental tasks and education.* New York: David McKay.

Havighurst, R. J., Neugarten, B. L., & Tobin, S. S. (1968). Disengagement and patterns of aging. B.L. Neugarten (Ed.), *Middle age and aging*. Chicago, IL: University of Chicago Press.

Hockschild, A. R. (1975). *The unexpected community,* Englewood Cliffs, NJ: Prentice-Hall.

Hupp, S. (1987). Camping in the third age. *Camping Magazine, 59*(3), 20-22.

Kennison, J. A. (1985). Outdoor education and recreation must not neglect the sixty-plus crowd. *Nature Study, 38*(2/3), 5-6.

Kraus, Richard, (1983). *Therapeutic recreation service: Principles and practices.* Philadelphia, PA: Saunders College Publishing.

Lemon, B. W., Bengtson, V. L., & Peterson, J. A. (1972). An exploration of the activity theory of aging: Activity types and life satisfactions among in-movers to a retirement community. *Journal of Gerontology, 27,* 511-523.

Leviton, D., & Santoro Campanelli, L. (Eds.). (1980). *Health, physical education, recreation, and dance for the older adult: A modular approach.* Virginia: American Alliance for Health, Physical Education, Recreation and Dance.

Longino, C. F., & Kart, C. S. (1982). Explicating activity theory: Formal replication. *Journal of Gerontology, 37,* 713-722.

Miles, J. C. (1980). The value of high adventure activities. Meier, J., Morash, T., & Welton, G. (Eds.), *High adventure outdoor pursuits organization and leadership.* Salt Lake City, UT: Brighton Publishing Col.

Peterson, D. A. (1983). *Facilitating education for older adults.* San Francisco, CA: Jossey-Bass.

Palmore, E. (1979). Predictors of successful aging. *The Gerontologist, 19*(5), 427-431.

Rillo, T. J. (1980). Outdoor education—The past is a prologue to the future. ERIC #212 392.

Rogers, E. S. (1982). Current status and future prospects of school camping, outdoor education, environmental education. ERIC #232 819.

Schaie, K., & Willis, S. (1986). *Adult development and learning.* Boston, MA: Little, Brown and Company.

Szczypkowkski, R. (1980). Objectives and activities. A. B. Knox and Associates, *Developing, administering and evaluating adult education.* San Francisco, CA: Jossey-Bass.

Women's Outdoor Adventures

Karen Warren
Hampshire College

Women-only outdoor programming has emerged in the past two decades as a significant development in adventure education. By creating courses for women, adventure organizations took great preliminary strides in validating women's outdoor experiences. Adventure leaders must recognize that a woman's experience in the wilderness is unique and that programming should correspond to this different perspective. To simply sign up a group of women for a standardized course and enlist the services of available women instructors ignores the specific needs of this special population.

In looking at adventure programming from a feminist perspective, relevant questions emerge. Is outdoor experiential education an effective methodology for women's growth? How can existing wilderness course models be adapted to respond to women's needs? How is the outdoor experience of this clientele unique and what implications does that have for programming? To answer these questions it is useful to explore several myths that underlie our conceptions of women's adventure experience. These myths, which cause adventure programs to be unresponsive to women through ignorance rather than intention, also serve as stoppers for women at various stages in their pursuit of meaningful outdoor challenges. After defusing the myths by recognizing their existence and reconciling their impact, adventure programs can respond to the special needs of women in the wilderness.

THE MYTH OF ACCESSIBILITY

The myth of accessibility is based on the misconception that outdoor experiences are widely available to women. As more women participate through organized coed programs as well as emerging women's tripping businesses, the appearance of equal access is fostered. However, women's reality doesn't support this notion as social and economic factors serve to limit women's participation. Women's economic inequity, well-documented in their statistically lower earning power, is the first deterrent to involvement in adventure programs. A woman struggling with the grocery bills may not be able to consider a backpacking trip. Furthermore, while a man has a sense of the value of adventure experiences based on previous exposure, a woman with no prior background may not be willing to assume the financial risk for an unknown commodity. She is unsure if adventure-based education makes economic sense.

Women's adventure organizations have consistently given attention to equitable accessibility. Woodswomen, Inc. and Women Outdoors, Inc. are among the women's programs offering scholarships. OceanWomen Kayaking uses a sliding scale course fee structure based on participant income. Other programs such as the Hurricane Outward Bound School have offered price discounts for women's courses.

The primary factor that advances the myth of accessibility is a woman's social conditioning. When deciding between the needs of her loved ones and her own desire for adventure, an outdoor trip seems frivolous and trivial compared to a child who might need her. Making the choice to take for herself when she is trained to always give to others creates an internal conflict. Guilt at pursuing her own needs is a powerful deterrent to seeking adventure opportunities.

In addition, social conditioning inundates a woman with the insistent message that the woods is no place for her. Not only must she reconcile her own doubts on a personal level (i.e., guilt at leaving the family alone, economic stress, etc.), a woman faces substantial societal risks in pursuing adventure experiences. Historically a masculine domain, the wilderness trip is painted by the message bearers of the media and tradition as a scary, uncomfortable, and intimidating event. The moment she steps into the woods her femininity is in question. Faced with these odds, it is a great social risk for women to be involved in outdoor programs. By not being a part of the male network that validates outdoor challenges, a woman misses the external prompting and support to seek the offerings of adventure programs.

Outdoor programs with a mandate for equal access will work along avenues women trust to minimize factors that prevent women's full participation in wilderness activities. Forming networks of women who have found value in the outdoors, promoting adventure options through women's educational and social organizations, and offering short courses that allow women to sample the wilderness without making a huge time or financial commitment are all possibilities for adventure institutions to pursue to avert inaccessibility.

THE MYTH OF EGALITARIANISM

This myth is predicated on the notion that the wilderness is an ideal place to revise prevailing social conditioning. As outdoor experiential educators, we are imbued with the power of the mountains to enact changes in people's lives. We therefore believe a viable corollary to the wilderness as social healer axiom is that the outdoors is the perfect place to eradicate any inequalities based on gender. We can encourage women to light stoves while the men do the cooking and in the process redefine acquired sex roles. The fallacy of this aspiration lies in the fact that the wilderness is not a natural place to break stereotypes. When it's pouring rain, the group has been hiking all day, and it's growing dark, the most expedient way to set up camp is for people to do tasks that are comfortable and familiar. In spite of our noble intentions of egalitarianism, when efficiency is important in a trying situation, women often do end up cooking. The coed wilderness trip also serves as a constant, insidious reminder to women that their intrinsic worth on the course is in doubt. Weight distribution on a backpacking course illustrates this point. Since women typically have lower weight-carrying capabilities than men, when it comes time to divide up group responsibilities, the message that subtly prevails is that the woman is not carrying her weight. Someone else is doing it for her. What the women makes up for in load transporting by her nurturing, endurance, and facilitation is often not given comparable acclaim because her contribution to the trip is more intangible.

It is important for adventure course leaders to understand how wilderness experiences that subtly emphasize physical prowess perpetuate the myth of egalitarianism and undermine a woman's experience outdoors. Since research has demonstrated that women have proportionately less absolute strength than men, wilderness course components that favor strength discriminate against women. Yet this discrimination is rarely blatant; therein lies its tyranny. My favorite example to show this elusive dynamic is about learning to single-carry a canoe while I was portaging in the Boundary Waters of northern Minnesota. As I repeatedly struggled unsuccessfully to raise a 77-pound Grumman to my shoulders, my male counterparts who also had not yet mastered the technique could still succeed by muscling the canoe up. My friends constantly reminded me that upper body strength was unimportant if I had perfect technique. These encouraging exhortations made it no less obvious that I was a failure because my technique was unrefined while my equally inexperienced male friends were shuffling down the portage trail with the canoe on their backs. This example shows that while both male and female participants may be similarly skilled in a particular course component, if the task is better suited to the male body type, the woman faces initial failure and feelings of inadequacy. Instead of changing the emphasis of the task, women are expected to be perfect and therefore may be discouraged from seeking additional adventure situations.

The myth of egalitarianism offers an excellent rationale for women-only programs. Since all the available roles on women's courses, including the traditionally male-held roles, must be filled by women, equality is promoted. Women have the opportunity to try out outdoor activities in a supportive atmosphere without immediate comparison to men's adventure experiences.

Adventure programs sensitive to the issues of egalitarianism have altered course components that unconsciously discriminate against women. Obviously it is not suggested that adventure programs simply make courses easier for women; that idea has been put to rest by those who realize that merely advocating an easier version of a standard course is condescending to women and not a useful methodology for their growth. What emerges is a different approach for women engaged in adventure education. For example, egalitarianism at the climb site means concentrating on climbs that emphasize less upper body strength and more grace. It means selecting ropes course events that will extend realistic challenges based on women's skills and abilities in endurance, flexibility, and balance and avert the predetermined failure intrinsic to elements that invalidate women's strengths. It also means elevating perceived risk while de-emphasizing intensive physical strength in challenging situations. By extending the feminist philosophy of comparable worth to the outdoor adventure field, the myth of egalitarianism could be unequivocally dispelled.

THE MYTH OF SQUARE ONE

The myth of square one is apparent at the start of most beginning-level wilderness education courses. Outdoor instructors often assume that beginners arrive with the same lack of skills and similar disadvantages; in other words, that all participants start at square one. This unfortunate assumption can be detrimental to women, especially if it affects the type of instruction they receive because of it. Lacking the same precursory experiences that men have acquired through their conditioning, women embark upon a wilderness adventure at a disadvantage. I have identified three major precursory experiences that directly influence the quality of women's outdoor undertakings. Because women lack technical conditioning, role models, and an internalized assumption of success, they are thwarted in maximizing wilderness learning situations.

The first precursory experience denied, technical conditioning, affects a woman's aptitude to easily and enjoyably learn wilderness skills. Mechanical unfamiliarity may hinder her ability to grasp stove use and repair, while math anxiety prevents her from learning map and compass skills as quickly as her male counterparts. Rock climbing, an activity that usually creates some anxiety in participants regardless of gender, becomes more problematic for a woman because she has not had the same opportunity to handle ropes and tie knots as her Boy Scout-trained cohorts. Therefore, it is paramount that enlightened adventure programs take women's shortage of technical training into account when planning instruction. When instructors do not recognize that they must first peel back the layers of technical apprehensiveness that trouble most women, they promulgate the myth of square one.

The invisibility of acceptable role models also prevents women outdoors from starting at square one. I remember very distinctly my first day instructing at the Outward Bound School in Minnesota when I found out the student patrol groups were named MacKenzie, Pond, Radisson, and Hennepin after the explorers and traders of the north woods. Where were the women? It's not that no role models exist; women have been active in the outdoors throughout history, yet their story is hidden, unspoken, trivialized, or ignored. It's time to reclaim the Isabella Birds, the Fanny Workmans, and the Mina Hubbards from their historical burial grounds and restore them as role models to young and old adventurous women. It's time to put aside our campfire tales by London and Service and share the women's outdoor stories in such books as Rivers Running Free, by Niemi and Wieser, or Daughters of Copper Woman by Cameron.

The final precursor deficient in a women's outdoor experience is an internalized assumption of success. A woman who constantly encounters surprise that "she got as far as she did in the wilderness" will soon internalize the message that she is expected to flounder. So not only is the woman's presence in the wilderness questioned, her ability to cope once there has been traditionally discredited. Realizing this social prejudice, it is understandable that when a women is faced with a challenging situation in the outdoors, the little voice of anticipated failure comes back to color her response. She is no longer simply figuring out how to fix a broken tent pole or taking a compass bearing, the woman is first forced to wrestle with her fear of defeat; her fear frequently becoming a selffulfilling prophecy.

The uniqueness of how women learn intervenes as well. While men have been urged to learn experientially, women are often left to learn by observation. Wilderness skills, which are usually task-oriented, allow a man to step forward buoyed up by the supposition that he will succeed. So inspired, he masters the task. On the other hand, the woman who watches the demonstration of an outdoor skill has the weight of a double doubt bearing down on her. Her confidence is undermined by both the absence of an internalized expectation of accomplishment as well as her inexperience in learning by doing. Adventure educators must be prepared to advocate for different styles of learning and to critically examine how their own attitudes may unconsciously contribute to women's inner predictions of failure.

THE MYTH OF THE SUPERWOMAN

While the effects of this myth eventually filter down to all outdoorswomen, the myth of the superwoman most acutely maligns women outdoor leaders. In order to achieve an advanced rank in the outdoor field, women leaders acquire exemplary competence in all outdoor skills. In this common scenario, the woman can carry the heaviest pack with a smile on her face. She demonstrates complete command of her campstove, compass and canoe. She is comfortable in the mountains and woods, confident in her unequaled proficiency. Yet the Catch 22 is exactly that competence that women leaders have worked years to gain and refine. For with superior abilities she becomes the superwoman, a woman unlike the rest of the population. Her students no longer have to view her competence for what it is: the ongoing struggle to gain parity in a male-dominated profession.

The effect of the superwoman on wilderness course participants is unintentionally detrimental. Participants, both men and women, struggle with the dissonance created by the conflict between their indoctrination that implies a woman doesn't belong in the wilderness and the reality of the woman outdoor leader guiding them. The existence of the superwoman gives them a way out of this nagging conflict. Due to her exemplary outdoor achievements the superwoman is the exception to other women. She's extraordinary, unique, not normal. As an anomaly the superwoman instructor can be cast aside and made invisible in the minds of her students. When she is perceived as being unrepresentative of ordinary women, participants are no longer forced to deal with their sexist conditioning; they need not reappraise their world view of women. They merely write off this one superwoman as incongruous and leave the course with the same cultural baggage they had when they arrived.

The implications for women participants are notably profound. While the woman instructor might serve as a wonderful role model to other women, her superwoman status disallows this. Women, especially beginners in the outdoor field, may feel great admiration for the superwoman but are intimidated by this woman who, in addition to her superlative technical skills, may display no apparent fears or doubts. The "I can never be like her" statement that rings in the minds of her female students robs the competent outdoor leader of her opportunity to be a role model.

Adventure program leaders and administrators can counter the myth of the superwoman by being conscientious of the style of leadership they value. Sharing leadership by consensus decision-making, demystifying competency, and revealing vulnerabilities may be one method of confronting the myth. With attention to the tenets of a feminist vision of outdoor leadership, the superwoman has no impetus to be born.

THE MYTH OF THE HEROIC QUEST

The final myth to be explored centers on women's spiritual identity in a wilderness adventure situation. A metaphor employed by adventure programs is a model of the heroic quest prevalent in classical and contemporary literature. The participant undergoes a real life experience in the wilderness that parallels the mythical quest of the hero. The student hears a call to adventure, leaves home, encounters dragons on the way and slays them, reflects on the conquest, and returns home as a hero with a clearer understanding of self.

Upon closer examination, the heroic quest is a metaphor that has little meaning to women. Each stage of a woman's journey in the wilderness is a direct contradiction of the popular quest model. A woman rarely hears a call to adventure; in fact, she is more often dissuaded by the factors discussed in the myth of accessibility from leaving home to engage in adventurous pursuits. The dragons looming in a woman's path on a wilderness course are equally ambiguous. Are these metaphoric limitations a personal block or are they societally imposed? It's impossible for her to sort out. Which dragons should she slay? Needing a point of reference to discern the difference, a woman finds confusion at this stage of the model. Furthermore, a woman's experience often is not compatible with viewing challenges in the wilderness in a militaristic framework; she is more likely to ally with the metaphoric dragons than to conquer them. Returning home is also problematic for women if the myth of the heroic quest is given credence. While a man's mythical journey in the wilderness parallels his everyday situation, a woman's does not. Encouraged to be bold and assertive in the woods, this style transfers readily for a man upon return. The woman who has learned to be strong, assertive and independent on a wilderness course encounters intense cognitive dissonance back home because these traits are not presently valued for her in society. Transfer of her newly acquired understanding of her strengths to her real world life is jeopardized. Finally, as argued in the section on the superwoman, the generic model of heroism, because it necessitates the emergence of a hero or superperson, incites a tradition that is a disservice to women.

The answer, therefore, is not to engage women in the heroic quest cycle, but to inspire a new heroic for adventure programming. A heroic based on bonding with the natural world rather than conquering it may be the foundation of a new metaphor for men and women alike. Adopting women's emphasis on merging with nature and the attention to spiritual completeness and process valued by many women outdoors, wilderness programs may increase the transfer potential and eventually the social significance of their course offerings.

IMPLICATIONS AND RECENT TRENDS

Outdoor adventure programs and businesses running all-women trips have made significant strides in developing a cogent philosophy of working with women in the outdoors. The development of a feminist model for outdoor adventure education has been the result of this work. It is important to remember that outdoor adventure education has traditionally been a white male-dominated field with programs evolving from and emulating these roots. Therefore, in order to be sensitive to the needs of women, programming needs to be articulated and implemented supporting a distinction from established adventure education philosophy. Leadership, decision-making, co-leading, diversity, and teaching styles are some areas of divergence from conventional wilderness education theory.

Leadership in a feminist model of adventure education is based on the premise that a group needs leadership rather than omniscient leaders. The role of the guide, then, is to facilitate rather than to control, to distribute leadership functions rather than to seek to fill them all, and to utilize the resources of the group rather than relying primarily on self. The result is that participants themselves have opportunities to experiment with different leadership styles. It also prevents the dynamic of the leader as superwoman.

Decision-making in traditional courses tends to be reserved to the judgment of the leader or, at best, democratic. In women-only programming there has been a trend toward consensus decision-making where the needs of each group member are heard and considered in the cooperative development of a decision. This avoids the up to 49 percent dissatisfaction possible in majority-rule decision-making. It also frees the leader from interpreting and determining the needs of the individuals in a group, as each member has the responsibility of voicing their own needs.

All-women's programs typically have eschewed a hierarchical style of leadership where there is a head instructor supported by assistant leaders. Co-leading, true shared leadership, is based on the supposition that all leaders bring valuable skills and experiences to a trip. While there are always power differentials based on experience, specific technical or communication skill proficiency, age, or gender, the goal of true co-leading is to recognize and minimize these differences. The work co-leaders do to downplay power inequalities reflects in the group as the message portrayed is that differences are appreciated and beneficial.

Women's programs have been on the cutting edge of advocating diversity. Making outdoor trips accessible to women of different backgrounds has been important enough to such organizations as Women Outdoors, Inc. that its brochure now includes a diversity statement. In addition, Women in the Wilderness and Outdoor Vacations for Women Over 40 are among women's businesses offering trips geared specifically for older women. New Routes, Inc. designs outdoor programs for survivors of domestic violence and incest. There has been a genuine emphasis in women's programs to encourage all types of women to participate.

Teaching styles used in all-women courses often shun dichotomous thinking, emphasizing that there are not right and wrong ways of performing skills. Teaching tends to acknowledge different learning styles and accentuate connections with other participants and the Earth. It is built on relationship rather than rules.

CONCLUSION

The goal of this discussion has been to point out that women bring to adventure experiences not only distinct needs that programs must acknowledge, but also a unique perspective that would be beneficial if incorporated in all facets of outdoor experiential education. By labeling myths that impede our realization of gender differences, we take the first step in ensuring that outdoor adventure will be a positive, holistic experience for women. The demise of the myths frees adventure leaders to conceive and restructure programs that will be on the cutting edge of growth for men and women alike.

REFERENCES

Andrews, R. (1984). No spare rib. *Mountain*, *97*, 22-29.

Bacon, S. (1983). *The conscious use of metaphor in Outward Bound.* Denver, CO: Outward Bound School.

Cameron, A. (1981). *Daughters of copper woman.* Vancouver, BC: Press Gang.

Christ, C. P. (1980). *Diving deep and surfacing.* Boston, MA: Beacon Press.

Del Rey, P. (1978). Apologetics and androgyny: The past and future. *Frontiers, 3*, 8-10.

Dewey, J. (1938). *Experience and education.* New York: Collier Books.

Fielder, E. (1979). Women and leadership. *Women in the Wilderness Quarterly*, 4-15.

Galland, C. (1980). *Women in the wilderness.* New York: Harper & Row.

Hardin, J. A. (1979). *Outdoor/wilderness approaches to psychological education for women: A descriptive study.* Unpublished doctoral dissertation, University of Massachusetts.

Kokopeli, B., & Lakey, G. *Leadership for change: Toward a feminist model.* Philadelphia, PA: New Society Publishers.

Maughan, J. J. *The outdoor woman's guide to sports, fitness and nutrition.* Harrisburg, PA: Stackpole Books, 1983.

Niemi, J., & Wieser, B., Eds. (1987). *Rivers running free.* Minneapolis, MN: Bergamont.

Warren, K., & Tippett, S. (1988). Teaching consensus decision making. *Journal of Experiential Education, 11* (3).

Professional Development Courses (PDP): A Case for Prescription Programming

Alan Ewert
USDA Forest Service

One of the more recent permutations in outdoor adventure programming is the development of courses specifically designed for managers and people involved in business. The underlying theory for this development is that many of the components inherent in an outdoor adventure course such as teamwork, confidence-building, and decision-making are important in the business world. A number of terms have been used to describe these types of courses, including Executive Development Programs (EDP), Executive Challenge, Management Development Programs (MDP), and Executive Training Programs (ETP). Within the context of this paper, these courses will be referred to as Professional Development Programs (PDP).

Currently, there exists a limited number of organizations offering PDP types of programs. Examples of these organizations include The Stroud Experience, Executive Challenge, Executive Venture, and Project Adventure. One of the earliest promoters of these programs has been Outward Bound. Outward Bound is generally recognized as the largest and leading organization in the field of adventure-based education with Professional Development Programs now constituting a substantial and growing portion of the total number of participants served.

From a financial standpoint, PDP provides a good example of a program using *specifically designed* adventure activities. In a sense, PDP programs represent a growing array of programs that are prescriptive rather than generic. Courses designed to enhance teamwork are often different than those designed to create feelings of confidence or risk-taking.

It is the author's contention that adventure-based programs should increasingly turn to prescriptive programming as a means to provide quality experiences to a clientele that is becoming more sophisticated and discriminating. The days of students with absolutely no adventure experiences or clients that are relatively unaware of other avenues in which to spend their money or time are quickly disappearing. To offer the same program to different participants is a recipe for ultimate failure. Without periodic redesign, no program has a curriculum that will continue to serve all the needs and characteristics of the participants. With respect to adventure-based programs, participants can vary along a number of factors including, but not limited to:

- Demographics: gender, age, socioeconomic status, group membership
- Objectives of the courses: benefits, expectations
- Professional occupations and positions
- Physical and emotional abilities
- Expectations of the course or adventure experience

To facilitate the development of PDP courses, the remainder of this paper is devoted to the designing of such experiences. While Outward Bound was the framework of the course design information, most, if not all, of the information can be applied to a variety of PDP courses from different organizations. The thrust of this exposition is necessarily practical and applied rather than theoretical. Correspondingly, the information is meant to be used in actual course design.

THE PDP MISSION, GOALS AND OBJECTIVES

The Professional Development Program should be designed to provide safe and environmentally sound adventure-based experiences that are relevant to the professional and work-related portions of an individual's life. Given this mission, a number of goals are recognized as important to the PDP course objectives.

With a PDP overall objective of enhancing an individual's ability to function within the workplace environment, such programs address the development of:

- Leadership/management skills
- Organization and team-building
- Commitment-building
- Self-confidence
- Action-oriented, problem-solving skills
- Willingness to take appropriate risks
- Career and life-renewal

A PDP course should be a highly focused and sophisticated experience. An underlying assumption is that adventure-based programs have something to say to the business and professional community, particularly in the areas of team-building, responsible behaviors, commitment to a set of goals, and effective but humanistic leadership. As society and its institutions such as businesses and corporations undergo transformation, often under adverse conditions, PDP experiences can be an empowering agent of change. While PDP courses often will concentrate on the groups, the unit of effect continues to be the individual.

COURSE DESIGN

With a Professional Development Program, instructors are expected to design courses that focus on providing for relevant learning experiences in addition to the standard offering of outdoor activities. In essence, what is needed is a course rich in metaphor and analogy supported by activities that are *congruent* and *relevant* to the individual participant or group. From an instructor's point of view, what this does *not* mean is that PDP courses can be generic outdoor experience, only with clients from a business or company. Indeed, this thinking is in line with the emerging view in outdoor experiential education that programs and courses need to become more sophisticated and relevant to the client.

Accordingly, this curriculum guide has divided an adventure-based PDP program into four phases. These phases should not be considered orthogonal but rather somewhat overlapping. Of even greater importance is the flow of the course design moving from Phase to Objectives, PDP Applications, and Activities. From a course design perspective, this is an unidirectional flow with the planning emanating from the objectives and applications for the course rather than just using the activities of the course. Thus, in any course design for PDP, the instructors need to consider the objectives of the course followed by what PDP applications can or should be made by the participants. After these issues have been addressed, the specific activities can be selected that generate these outcomes and are congruent with the demands of environment and program.

Curriculum plans and guides are not intended to replace the intuition and experience of the field instructor. It is the field instructor who actually produces a PDP experience for the clients. However, given this era of increasing competition and participant demands, offering a more specific and prescriptive experience makes for good business and philosophical sense. Putting the dollars aside, it is reasonable to believe that the better the product (i.e., courses and experiences), the more positive and powerful will be the outcomes for the participants and ultimately, adventure-based programs will have moved closer to achieving their potential as a positive force in our society.

THE PDP PARTICIPANT

Participants in an adventure-based PDP program often have several characteristics that distinguish them from more traditional students in outdoor programs. Instructors need to be cognizant of these differences in order to better design the adventure experience around the needs and goals of the student and organization. These differences include the following:

1. Clients are generally older and in poorer physical condition.
2. Many of the participants would not have voluntarily enrolled in the course unless a superior in the organization had not "suggested" that they attend.
3. Often because of the higher cost and fact that the participant comes from a business environment, the participant often brings to the course a heightened awareness of cost/benefits and a concern for getting his or her money's worth.
4. If the experience involves a contract course (the groups are made up of members from the same company), participants are often very cognizant of the rank or hierarchial ordering within their groups. In other words, they keep in mind who the boss of the company is and always act accordingly.
5. Stereotyping, particularly related to gender, is a commonly seen attribute of PDP groups.
6. While there is wide variance, activities common to many adventure-based programs such as camping and eating simple, basic foods are even more alien to PDP clients than to the general population. Another manifestation in a similar vein, is that many PDP clients tend to be rather materialistic and overly concerned with making money. Consequently, activities that do not directly relate to increasing productivity or increasing profits are often difficult for them to justify, both in terms of financial costs and time commitment.

PHASES OF A PDP PROGRAM

The phases of a PDP course are similar to those of many adventure-based programs. The difference is in an emphasis on the creation of opportunities for application and transference to the workplace, and in the type of participants.

The orientation phase of a PDP course focuses on beginning the course with expectations and goals that are understood by both the students and staff and are congruent with the objectives of the program. It is extremely important at this stage to address any concerns about self-efficacy and physical abilities that many of the participants are experiencing. This is particularly true since the participants are typically older and lead a relative sedentary lifestyle.

Related to these questions of personal ability are concerns about the safety of the course and the roles of each person on the course. More specifically, an early discussion about how the course will be conducted in a safe manner, with examples on how this will be done, is most appropriate.

Identifying new roles or assessing old ones is more difficult for both the staff and students. Staff should be aware that this is often a difficult and uncomfortable time for students, and act accordingly. A classic example of this might be the new role of the CEO (chief executive officer) or president of the client corporation. Should the corporate chiefs be regular students or should they still assume leadership roles within the group? Such questions are often not adequately addressed, resulting in unused insight on behalf of the executive, or a feeling that they were less than professionally treated.

As is usually the case in such situations, solutions to the problem are not to come from a manual but rest with the intuition and experience of the instructor. Instructors must be sensitive to these and similar potential problems and allow time for the group to sort out the situation. It is appropriate for the instructors to periodically "check-in" with selected people on the course such as the CEO or president to see if the course is meeting the needs of the group or selected individuals, and/ or should be redesigned.

The immersion phase of a PDP course extends the orientation phase by further providing opportunities for skills development, problem-solving, decision-making, group identity situations, and communication issues. During this period the participants are typically establishing some efficacy statements about themselves and forming relational linkages and opinions about the other members of the patrol and instructional staff. Because of the questions about personal abilities and environmental demands, the instructors should set up an early success from which participants can build confidence.

Given the fact that participants are involved in redefining roles, discovering levels of abilities, and establishing communication patterns, instructional staff need to provide adequate time to create discussional and reflective opportunities. *Caution to staff: Do not allow the course to become just a series of activities; discussional and reflective times are of growing importance throughout the remainder of the course.*

The application phase of a PDP course actually occurs throughout the entire experience. During this phase, the instructional staff attempt to provide a pathway from the outdoor activity to the workplace. This connecting of adventure activities with future work activities is often accomplished through the use of metaphors and other transfer techniques. These transfer techniques can involve direct, nonspecific, or metaphoric mechanisms. Direct transfers involve using the exact skills or attitudes learned in one situation and applying them to another. In PDP, one example would be having an intact work group develop a consensual decision-making process and then using that same process back at the workplace. Nonspecific transfers utilize general principles or attitudes learned in the adventure-based experience and apply them to another situation. Obviously, the process works in reverse as well. An example of this in the PDP setting would be the bonding that occurs when a group has a shared common experience and then carries those feelings of comradeship and shared purpose back to the workplace. Metaphoric transfers use specific examples or experiences gained from an outdoor experience to convey a feeling or point while in a different environment. A classic example of metaphoric transfer is paddle rafting, in which the term "shooting the rapids" moves from a river orientation to a situation requiring risk-taking, planning, and effective teamwork.

The application phase is the time when the group begins to assume its own identity and hopefully gels into an effective, self-functioning unit. It is critically important that staff facilitate this direction. *Caution: Instructional staff need to ensure that the course remains a process-oriented experience rather than allowing the participants to focus on simply completing the tasks.*

Similar to all the phases in a PDP course, the translation and integration phase is not limited to a specific time on the course. Rather, the intent here is to develop a framework in which the process of decision-making, group communication and working as a team continue to remain critical components. Components in this phase include providing opportunities and expertise in allowing the participants to translate and internalize the *meanings* of the activities rather than just the activities themselves. Moreover, it is at this stage where instructors would do well to emphasize the importance of building networks. This is especially true for open-enrollment courses where the usual case is that the participants will never see one another again unless they make a special effort to do so.

Relational configurations refer to providing opportunities and expertise in helping participants draw linkages about attitudes, behaviors, and outcomes. For example, PDP clients often have the attitude and belief that accomplishing the task is of paramount importance. PDP staff should consider that *how* the task is accomplished is often of equal importance. This attitude of task achievement at any cost can often lead to "ready-fire-aim" types of behaviors with corresponding outcomes of lack of investment in the decisions by some and covert or overt reluctance by others.

In sum, each phase should be considered a continuous, ongoing process that takes into account the participant, current situation, and course objectives. No one phase is inherently more important than any other although, in the eyes of the participant, the application and integration phases are more visible.

From an instructional staff perspective, it is important that the program emphasizes objectives and process and not activities or tasks. Many different activities can be used to produce a set of given course objectives. In a similar fashion, any number of tasks can be accomplished once an effective procedure for processing feelings and situations is in place.

ACTIVITIES

One of the unique aspects of a PDP experience in an adventure-based setting are the varied and interesting activities that can be accomplished. Keeping in mind that program objectives and process are the primary products, activities provide the real-life drama and examples through which the instructor(s) can weave the tapestry of a successful experience. The activities appropriate for a PDP experience go beyond the more traditional rock climbing, white-water rafting, or hiking. PDP instructors must keep in mind the program goals such as team-building, consensual decision-making, or project planning, when planning activities. Consider the following activities as examples of possible program components for a contemporary PDP course.

PROFESSIONAL DEVELOPMENT PROGRAM PHASES

PHASE	OBJECTIVES	PDP APPLICATIONS	ACTIVITIES
	Pick-up Expectations Goals	Communication Criteria for success Assessment	Name games Occupational stereotyping
ORIENTATION	Roles Tone Safety	Forming Personal responsibility	Initiatives Pick-up Skills
IMMERSION	Role identity Group identity Facilitation of communications	Teaming Resource/needs Leadership Managership	Camp-setup Dyads/group discussions Watches Cooking/rations
APPLICATION	Skill employment Performance-based assessment Positive stress Cohesiveness Interaction Feedback Focus	Planning Assessment Risk-taking Dealing with adversity Conflict management Clarification Redefinition Team-building Leadership	Rock climbing Rappelling River-rafting Hiking Route-planning Search/rescue Survival games I need/we need Expeditions Explore
TRANSFERENCE/ TRANSLATION	Synthesis Refinement and internalization Facilitation of the experience Relational configuration Transderivation searches Re-entry Bridging to the workplaces	Useful lessons Building commitment Action-planning Metaphors Resourcing Observations/ insights Networking	Journal writing Solo Closing activities Expanding map Leading vs. managing Kaleidoscoping Solo framing Support systems Checkpointing Pins/diplomas

1. Doctor, Lawyer, Indian Chief

Purpose: a. Introduce members of group to one another.

b. Introduce concept of occupational and personal stereotyping.

Materials: One 3x5 card per person.

Procedure: a. Have people print occupation on card.

b. Collect, mix up, and pass cards back out to participants (make sure individuals do not get their original cards).

c. Have everyone write one or two words on each card describing a person in that occupation.

d. Pass cards back to proper owner.

e. Have people introduce themselves using cards—Are descriptions true or false? What is reality?

f. Have participants keep cards as part of their personal literature.

Comments: Good activity as an introduction, particularly for open enrollment courses.
Can use with intact work groups by changing stereotypes of occupations to stereotypes of positions within a company.

Phases = Orientation, Immersion

2. Creating a Team-Building Agenda

Purpose: a. Generate a working agenda and focus for discussion.

b. Allow for course redesign.

Materials: a. Two 3x5 cards.

Procedure: a. Each participant is asked to think about the challenges facing that person and compare those challenges with the participant's perceived abilities.

b. Silently identify one change that would enhance personal effectiveness. List that change on a card entitled "I Need!"

c. Considering the challenges facing the group, on a card entitled "We Need!" Have each participant identify one change in the characteristics of the patrol that would increase the effectiveness of the patrol.

Comments: Ask the group how they will address these issues.
Work units (groups) often fail to address the private needs of the individual. Eventually these hidden needs can interfere with the functioning of the group.

Phases = Orientation, Immersion, Application

3. Spiders (Corporate) Web/Group Decision-Making Activity

Purpose: To provide an experiential decision-making and group communication situation.

Materials: a. Monofilament line for construction of web.

b. Recording material.

Procedure: a. Construct web without knowledge of group.

b. Have group "come upon" web.

c. Establish rules for going through web (e.g., spotting, not touching web, closing off openings).

d. Observe group and record observations.

e. Use a sociogram if possible.

f. Use time as a stressor.

Questions:

a. How did your group make decisions?

- Discount/no-discount
- Pairing
- Railroading
- Voting
- Trading
- Self-appointed decision
- Delegating
- Consensus

b. Is this an acceptable and appropriate method for this group? If not, how should it be different?

c. Were these decision-making and communication patterns similar to those at the workplace?

d. What difficulties are anticipated in changing how decisions are made personally or professionally?

e. Who can help?

Phases = Orientation, Transfer

4. Seven Steps to Peak Performance

Purpose: To provide tools through which the instructors can motivate participants for better performance.

Procedures: Whenever appropriate

a. Progressive Relaxation

- systematic tensioning of muscles
- centering (breathing and flow)
- practice

b. Stress Management

- self-assessment
- body reactions
- recognizing stress

c. Positive Thought Control

- think about situations that make you angry, frightened, etc.
- source of negative thoughts
- ways to control and identify barriers to performance

d. Self-Regulation

- identifying a winning past situation
- self assessment

e. Visual-Motor Behavioral Rehearsal (VMBR)

- use of imagery
- centering
- visualizing what it would look like to be successful
- developing "trigger phrases"

f. Concentration

- look at something broadly
- focus on various objects
- bring focus to something close
- bring focus to self
- beware of "attention narrowing"

g. Energy Control

- use centering to relax
- sense energy level and act when high
- capture the feeling of high energy

Phase = Implementation

5. Expanding the Horizons/Map

Purpose: To focus on planning for the future: career, personal, professional developments.

Materials:

a. One topo map per person (up to three people per map).

b. One sheet of flipchart or other type of paper.

c. One pencil or felt-tip marker per person.

d. Masking or first aid tape.

Procedures: a. Lay out maps.

b. Attach large sheet at side of exit.

c. Draw route as it extends off the map.

d. Have participants draw futures map with planned routes for personal, career, and professional developments.

e. Have participants establish a personal network:
- with whom
- communication
- checkpointing

f. Use wide-scanning and lifeline concepts if possible.

Phases = Implementation, Translation

6. Building a Support System/Lifeline

Purpose: a. To identify personal support systems.

b. To develop a more effective support system.

Procedures: People vary in their ability to be self-sufficient. This self-sufficiency can stem from any number of variables, including personal abilities and fortunate circumstances of internal motivation. Despite these differences, everyone needs and uses a personal support system or lifeline. Have participants address the following questions.

Questions: a. Who are people I need or like around me?

b. What can I count on from this person?

c. How is contact made with this individual?

d. How often is contact made and who initiates it?

e. Should I and how can I expand this system?

Example: Type of Need/Support

Current State of My System Expansion (?)

- loneliness
- belonging
- affirmation of competence
- crisis
- intimacy
- challenge
- stimulation
- other

Phase = Application

7. Resource Bank

Purpose: a. To identify the strengths of the individual.

b. To identify the weaknesses and strengths of the group.

Materials: a. One or two 3x5 cards per participant.

Procedures: a. On one card, have participants write down what internal resources they have and can contribute to the group.

b. These listings are then available for the entire group. The group can then determine what its areas of strengths and weaknesses are.

Phases = Orientation, Implementation

ADDITIONAL TEACHING OPPORTUNITIES FOR PDP

Navigation : Like other groups, PDP clients are usually not highly skilled at map reading or land navigation. Inevitably, the instructors are asked for locations, etc. If questions are overwhelming, consider having the patrol "buy the map." The patrol starts with $10 and every time the instructor is used, the group forfeits $2.

Cooking/Rations : Because of the typically short course length, PDP instructors are encouraged to take an active role in the packing, rationing, and food preparation for the course. This is especially true in the beginning of the course.

Travel : Setting up travel procedures throughout the course can often be likened to a business plan in that the patrol can be given the following tasks to solve: goals, individual responsibilities, chain of command, criteria of success, checkpoints, and evaluation.

Communicating with the Participants : PDP participants will often be more demanding and willing to express needs than students of typical adventure-based programs. Given this fact, the PDP instructors should strive for open, clear communication with an absence of gamesmanship and reverse questioning. Despite their often high level of education and management training, instructors should expect counterproductive communication patterns, sex role stereotyping, and poor listening skills. Creating awareness of the "cost" of these unproductive techniques is often the only improvement instructors can realistically expect. Effective debriefings, modeling good listening skills, and creating powerful learning experiences are tools at the disposal of the adventure-based instructor.

PDP clients will often come to a course with a significant questions concerning levels of ability and the amount of stress to be expected on a course. An effective PDP course should strike a fine balance between useful and dysfunctional levels of stress. *The instructors must keep in mind that this is a management training experience, first, and and outdoor adventure course, second.* As previously mentioned, the PDP client is often in poor physical condition and is typically older than traditional adventure-based program students. Moreover, given the choice, many would not come to an adventure-based PDP experience. These realities necessitate that instructors be constantly cognizant of "where the participants are at" and what activities are appropriate or inappropriate for them.

Solo : As with other groups, the solo can be a powerful component of the PDP experience. It does, however, need to be facilitated with an eye on stimulating participants into thinking what the course means with respect to their workplace and personal environment. Questions that can facilitate the solo experience include the following:

1. What are the expectations currently placed on you by your work environment and family?
2. How important is it to you that there is a balance between the commitments to your work and family? What is that balance right now?
3. Without immediately judging any of the possibilities, what would be some things you could do to improve that balance?
4. For each item in Question 3, what are some of the potential obstacles for each potential action?
5. What support from your family or work team would you need?

Risk-Taking : PDP clients are often used to taking financial risks but have little experience in physical or social risk-taking situations. While risk-taking is a natural component of Outward Bound, it needs to be congruent with the abilities of the participants and objectives of the course. Furthermore, risk-taking is not a natural situation for many PDP participants and as such needs to be processed and discussed more than is usually the case in many adventure-based programs. The following *questions* can be used to facilitate a discussion on risk-taking.

1. What thing(s) are you finding to involve the greatest risk?
2. On a scale of 1 to 10, what degree of risk do you feel? What makes these activities or events risky?
3. What motivates you to take risks while on your course? At the workplace?
4. What did you stand to gain or lose by taking these risks?
5. How did you feel after successfully completing the event/activity?
6. What support did you need from your team or team members?
7. How did you seek it?
8. How did the team or team members respond?
9. How did you respond when someone asked you for help?

Reasons for *not* taking a risk:

Fear of failure
- what people will think
- losing what you have
- uncertainty of outcome
- loss of control

Questions about
- competence
- image
- future working relationships

PARTICIPANT OBSERVATION AND FEEDBACK

One of the most powerful and important services that adventure-based program instructors can provide for their students is the giving of neutral and objective feedback based on observation. To be most effective, this observation and the resulting feedback need to be built around a systematic and accurate method of watching people. The following is a structure that can be used to guide the observational style of the field instructor.

Participant Observation Form

1. How is the group accomplishing its task(s)? (What procedures and processes are the group members doing?)
2. What kinds of information are being used and sought by the group? (task vs. process, technical vs. affective)
3. How are individual ideas received and sought out by the group?
4. What criteria are being used to evaluate the ideas?
5. How is the group making decisions? (voting, consensus, etc.)
6. What is your personal evaluation of:
   - The final product
   - The process the group used to achieve it
   - Your feelings about the experience

Within the professional development context, communication between group members is often of critical importance. Given this fact, it becomes extremely important that the instructor provide feedback to the group concerning the quantity and quality of its communication that is both factual and systematically grounded. Key words and phrases are often important teaching components in the sense that they often represent situations that are metaphoric and/or carry certain learning events.

FACILITATION AND TRANSFER OF LEARNING IN A PDP EXPERIENCE

Facilitating or processing the experience is a critical part of any adventure education experience. Within the framework of the Professional Development course, facilitation of the experiences will usually necessitate assisting the participants in linking the outdoor experience with the workplace or personal environment. The following questions can be useful in promoting discussion and thought, and ultimately facilitate the transfer of learning.

Communication:

1. Considering this past experience, what were the ways in which ideas were communicated?
2. Of those ways, which ones were effective and which were ineffective?
3. Did you learn something about communication that will be helpful later?
4. What things got in the way of communicating in the group?

Listening:

5. Who made suggestions for achieving the group goal(s)?
6. Were all these suggestions heard?
7. How did the group receive your suggestions?
8. How did you receive the suggestions of others?
9. Why were some suggestions acted upon and others not?
10. What interfered with your ability to listen to others?

Leadership:

11. Who assumed leadership roles during the activity?
12. Why did some people lead and other people follow?
13. What are the traits of a good leader?
14. Is it difficult to assume leadership in this group? Why or why not?
15. What type of leader would you aspire to be?

Group Decisions:

16. How were group decisions made in the group?
17. Were you satisfied with the way decisions were made in the group? How could they be made better?
18. What is the best way for this group to make decisions?
19. How would you like to see decisions made back at the workplace?

Trust:

20. What examples can you give of when you trusted someone in this group?
21. On a scale of 0 to 10, what level of trust do you have for this group?
22. What have you done to deserve trust from the others within this group?
23. What is the state of trust back at your workplace? How do you think it can be improved?

CONCLUSION

Like other adventure-based programs, PDP can provide an effective and exciting arena for learning and experiencing in the outdoors. Indeed, PDP can often provide the only avenues for the corporate executive to experience outdoor adventure and experiential learning. This paper has provided information and described activities that can be used to help transform an adventure-based course into a relevant and meaningful management training experience.

Increasingly, structured adventure program activities should be processed to provide the maximum amount of transference of meaning to the workplace and everyday life. Transference can be most effectively accomplished by thorough planning, careful execution, and honest evaluation as to the efficacy of the results of the program.

PDP participants can be exacting clients who expect to get their money's worth from any program. By demanding more than just a climbing or white-water experience, however, PDP participants force the course instructors to design a focused and well-conceived sequence and mix of activities. Mastering this type of demanding course necessitates the development of a highly skilled and motivated staff. The staff member who can consistently design and implement the PDP course will be well prepared for adventure-based education in the 1990s.

Adventure Tourism

Dale R. Christiansen
California Polytechnic Institute

Cross-country ski 600 miles over a two-month period to the South Pole, eat freeze-dried food, and sleep in tents in an environment that offers temperatures of 40 degrees below zero. For the adventure-minded tourist, this package, at a modest $69,500, is available from Mountain Travel, Inc., of Albany, California (Dolan, 1988). This and other exotic experiences are being offered tourists in an increasing array of travel packages that use various forms of adventure recreation as the core of the package.

Thrill seekers are pushing the limits of today's travel industry to meet modern-day travelers' needs by including everything from riding elephants to dehorning cows. "Vacationers who once settled for a couple of nice weeks at the beach are pushing for more challenging excursions, creating what travel agents call 'soft adventure.' This might include such cream-puff outings as hiking in the Alps or riding elephants in Thailand." (Dolan,1988). True thrill seekers, according to Dolan, have pushed experiential requirements a bit further.

Mountain Travel, Inc., as the prime contract tour packager for the nearly two-million-member cooperative Recreation Equipment Incorporated (REI), offers the traveler the opportunity to visit various areas in the Nepal Himalayas including Annapurna and Mt. Everest; trek the High Atlas in Morocco in North Africa; trek the Inca trail, including a stop at Machu Picchu; or take an extended kayak tour of Glacier Bay, Alaska, as well as other activities in areas throughout the world (REI, 1987).

The ultimate diving experience, according to Sterba (1988), involves eight days of chumming the seas off Port Lincoln, Australia, with tuna heads and oil, pet food, and horse blood, to bring great white sharks and tourists that have paid $2000 for airfare and $1000 per day, within camera distance and even touching distance of each other in a flimsy underwater cage. These experiences are examples, albeit the extremes, of today's buffet of offerings to travelers with the intent of fulfilling individual needs through adventure recreation.

Why are individuals willing to spend large sums of money for what appears to be and often is dangerous? According to Dolan (1988), Dr. Yale Kroll, a New York dentist, says: "It's stress replacement therapy. I enjoy it more than vegging out on the beach." Dr. Kroll went on to suggest that he returned to work more refreshed after experiencing 4 or 5 days of cross country skiing and winter camping or rock climbing than after the more sedentary vacation of mulling over work-related problems on a beach.

The adventure travel business is growing and shows patterns that can excite the entrepreneurial proclivity of students interested in pursuing a career in the outdoor recreation or adventure recreation profession. Dolan indicated that Mountain Travel, Inc. had experienced a 30 percent increase in business over the past five years. These and other indicators, such as the impending movement of that large segment of the population known as the "Baby Boomers" from an employed to a retired status, may make adventure recreation tourism a most interesting subject of study and discussion.

Therefore, contrary to the bulk of previous writings on the subject of adventure recreation, high-adventure outdoor pursuits, or risk recreation—where the activity is presented as individual or group activity without the influence of commercialization—the objective of this article is to briefly review adventure recreation as a growing segment in the tourism industry. It will provide suggestions on the definition and risk levels of adventure tourism, and considerations that can contribute to the successful provision of the adventure recreation experience through the services of the tourism industry. In the concluding portion, it will suggest some areas where trends may provide opportunity for the student seeking a career through adventure education either as part of a larger organization or as an aspiring entrepreneur.

TOURISM, TOURIST, AND TOUR PACKAGING

What do we mean by the terms tourism, tourist, and tour packaging? The term *tourist* has in fact defied a clear definition. Definitions of a tourist vary with the motivation of the body politic interested in qualitative and quantitative analysis of the movement and benefits derived from the segment of the population that are traveling between countries and within a given country. Tourism and tour packaging are easier to define, though some writers want to use the terms *tourist* and *tourism* interchangeably.

For our purposes, we will define the tourist as one who travels for pleasure to engage in some form of adventure recreation and travels at least 25 miles beyond the boundary of his/her community. This definition is similar to that used by the Canadian Government, except that the Canadian definition includes all travel activities apart from commuting to work and is consistent with the definition used by the U.S. Bureau of Labor to track certain food and lodging expenditures (McIntosh & Goeldner, 1984).

Tourism is defined as people taking trips away from home for recreation and embraces the whole range of transportation, lodging, food service, and other activities relating to and serving the traveler (McIntosh & Goeldner, 1984). Consequently, a tourist is someone who travels away from home. McIntosh and Goeldner go on to suggest that the terms "travel" and "tourism" are synonymous.

A 1986 study funded by the United States Senate has defined travel and tourism as: "An inter-related amalgamation of those businesses and agencies which totally or in part provide the means of transport, goods, services, accommodations and other facilities for travel out of the home community for any purpose not related to day-to-day activity." Using this definition, tourism becomes the largest business in the world, representing $2 trillion in expenditures. It is estimated that tourism expenditures in the United States in 1986 were $482 billion, or 47 percent more than the budget for military defense.

Tour packaging is an important component of the tourism industry and occurs when an individual or firm (tour operators or tour wholesalers, who organize but do not operate tours) arranges, organizes, and provides a package that may include all of the elements necessary for an individual to engage in a travel experience. In recent years, tour packaging may consist of saving the traveling consumer valuable time and money by agreeing to provide certain services in conjunction with a planned pleasure travel experience for a fixed price. The types of services the customer can expect may include arrangements for transportation, lodging, meals, guided tours, car rentals, and other selected elements appropriate for the tour.

An example would be a white-water river experience such as floating Idaho's Middle Fork of the Salmon River. The tour package may include obtaining the requisite permits from the U.S. Forest Service; the provision of guides, shelter, rafts, food, and beverages for the river trip, plus, depending on the time of year, arrangements for bush pilots to shuttle the tourist party into the point of departure on the river and for buses or vans to pick the party up at the take-out point downriver. This prepaid package is all-inclusive from where the outfitter, guide, or tour leader assumes responsibility to where the responsibility is relinquished, normally the same place. In the case of the river trip described, friends or family may pick the clients up at the take-out point on the Main Salmon River instead of waiting to pick the client up at the point where the client became the responsibility of those providing the tour, either McCall or Salmon, Idaho. Where tours transcend the boundaries of the United States, tour leaders may assume and relinquish their responsibility at an international airport, such as New York, Los Angeles, San Francisco, or Miami.

A HISTORICAL OVERVIEW

The concept of tour packaging is not new. Thomas Cook is credited with introducing the package tour in England in 1841. In Cook's time, transportation was primarily by train, although on occasion steamer travel was involved. Cook's tours included transportation and access to a planned event, but contrary to today's standards, did not include accommodations. In Cook's case, the traveler was issued a warrant that was honored at over 10,000 hotels or inns and guest houses throughout Europe. Accommodation managers of the time readily accepted the warrants issued by Cook because of a reputation for rapidly honoring the warrants for the amount involved. Cook's company ultimately provided guided tours to all parts of the world, including the United States. Cook's company is still one of the world's largest travel organizations (McIntosh & Goeldner, 1984).

The extent that tour packaging applies to adventure recreation in the 19th century is difficult to discern since little has specifically been written on the subject. The extent that the early climbers in the Alps, Caucuses, Dolomites, and other climbing regions in Europe were served by the entrepreneurial efforts of an emerging group of professional guides is also unclear. According to Bunting (1973), De Saussure's third ascent of Mont Blanc in 1787 included 18 villagers, who later became Alpine guides. Much of what we call adventure (or risk) recreation today that occurred during the 18th and the early part of the 19th centuries was organized by the participant or employees of the participant. A classic example of this type of travel was beautifully illustrated by the Italian photographer/illustrator, Vittorio Sella, when H.R.H. Prince Luigi Amedeo di Savoia, Duke of Abruzzi, made the first ascent of Mount St. Elias, Alaska, in 1897 (Fillippi, 1900).

Today's adventure recreation tour packaging is marketed in various forms and provides a wide range of perceived and real risks. Risk, or the perception of risk, is an important attribute of adventure recreation. Risk perception, as a component of the travel package, can take on various forms; these will be discussed later in this paper.

Where the normal tour package represents an opportunity for the customer/participant to engage in a pleasure travel activity that provides the benefits sought by the participant, such as socialization, cross-cultural experiences, escape, and ego enhancement, adventure recreation tends more toward excitement, optimal arousal (Ellis, 1973), or the "flow experience" (Csikszentmihalyi, 1975). Motivational factors contributing to an individual's participation in a particular activity are discussed elsewhere and will not be addressed in this article.

SOME FUTURE TRENDS

Godbey (1985) has introduced the concept of "time deepening" within recreation literature. Two of the components of time deepening are "undertaking an activity more quickly or satisfying some need through an activity more quickly," and "the use of time more precisely." These are both contributors to the growth that is occurring in the adventure travel industry today. With the growth in numbers of two-income families and the intensity of life's pace in an age of accelerating technological change, we are seeing an increase in discretionary income and a corresponding reduction in the amount of time available to pursue quality experiences.

Tour Packages
Risk/Adventure Levels

Risk	Soft Adventure	Adventure	High Adventure
High			- South Pole ski touring - Shark baiting - Sea kayaking - Storm skiing
		- Salmon River - Raft trip - Himilaya trek - Mexico volcano climb	
Low	- Grand Canyon float trip - Mule trip to Grand Canyon bottom		

Adventure Level

Table 1
Levels of Risk

Through the services provided by a wholesale tour packager and tour operators, the legal or medical professional, administrator, or other individual with ample funds and a shortage of discretionary time can maintain physical fitness through a strenuous program at a health club or on sophisticated equipment at home and then fly to locations throughout the world for a few days of intensive adventure recreation. This can range from climbing major volcanos like Popocatepetl, Orizaba, and Ixtaccihautl in Mexico, or Kilimanjaro and Mt. Kenya in Africa, to trekking in South America or the Himalayas, to running a river by kayak or raft in Idaho or Alaska.

For this experience, the client is paying for the knowledge and skill the tour operator has in understanding the needs and abilities of the client, trip organizational abilities, knowledge of local cultural mores, and the communicative skills necessary to negotiate with local vendors, guides, and political bodies that may have a material effect on the success of travel to and within a foreign nation or the more remote areas of the United States.

Time is saved by the client, for a price, that would otherwise be needed to research; communicate with individuals, organizations or governmental officials; organize; make reservations; negotiate prices and conditions of employment of equipment suppliers, guides, horse wranglers, bush pilots; and the list goes on and on. Without the services of the tour packager and the tour operator, who may be one and the same, the individual seeking the benefits of adventure recreation experiences would find it difficult if not impossible to accomplish the task of meeting those needs within the time available.

One of the prime considerations of those involved in marketing products or services is understanding the factors utilized by the client/consumer in making purchase decisions. Such is the case of those providing the adventure experience as a fee service. Ellis (1973), Priest and Martin (1985), Mitchell, Mortlock (1984), and Csikszentmihalyi (1974) have all conceptualized and put forth constructs to explain the motivating factors for individuals to seek a set of conditions that bring stimulation, or in Csikszentmihalyi's case, a state of "flow." These constructs can help identify what motivates the tourist seeking a satisfactory experience through adventure recreation. What separates the normal conception of a group of associates getting together to engage in a climb or rafting trip, and the commercial provider of such experiences is that the commercial provider is exchanging the desired experience and assuming many of the financial risks for a fee.

Adventure recreation can be perceived as being on a continuum that ranges from "soft adventure" to "high-risk adventure." While not clearly defined, one might arbitrarily break this continuum into three segments that would include levels of "soft adventure," "adventure," and "high-risk adventure." Each of these would provide the basis for targeting market segments seeking to break the boredom of their everyday environment and replace that boredom with elements of pleasure, excitement, a sense of freedom and risk. These levels of risk are shown in Table 1.

Soft adventure is directed toward those seeking a perception of risk and excitement with little actual risk. Examples of soft adventure in the extreme would be the rides found in a theme park such as Disneyland, where the general public can pay a fee for an experience that might include riding a "log" down a flume. Examples of soft adventure tourism would include rafting trips on the Grand Canyon of the Colorado River that use huge rafts, a mule ride into that same canyon and the mail jet boat trip from Gold Beach to Agnes on the Rogue River in Oregon. Each of these trips provides satisfying adventure experiences for those who are restricted by age, physical condition, and low perceived competence, or some other factor such as experiencing the initial stages of an adventure continuum that will ultimately take them to the extremes of adventure tourism.

It is suggested that if the extremes of the adventure continuum are soft adventure and high-risk adventure, then the middle point should be what might be construed as normal adventure recreation activities. Such activities would include those that provide a higher level of risk than the soft adventure activities but less risk than high-risk adventures. This category of adventure recreation would constitute the main body of activities provided by the larger providers of adventure recreation, such as the Sierra Club and Mountain Travel, Inc. Examples would include treks in the Himalayas and South American Andes, standard float trips in the Western United States utilizing 2-to-6 person rafts, and mountain climbing packages not involving high levels of individual technical skill and overall competence and providing moderate personal physical risk.

High-risk adventure includes those activities which have a high level of actual risk and often can involve restrictions as to the physical conditioning and specialized competencies of the individual. In the case of an extended cross-country ski trip or mountain climbing expedition, where individuals must live under stress in close proximity to each other, compatibility of individual personalities could be a major factor in the decision as to which individuals will be allowed to make the trip.

Private and commercial providers in the adventure recreation business are faced with the problem of providing the client with a perception of risk taking while at the same time doing it within an acceptable probability of safety. In risk-activity there is a possibility of injury or death. That is part of the attraction and is accepted by the client. In this day of over-legalization and high court awards where individuals are sued for negligence in legal cases involving injury or death while involved in recreation pursuits, the provider is faced with the decision how best to stay in business under these circumstances. Consequently, what constitutes acceptable risk from a legal and financial perspective is best answered by the individual or firm affected. Some of the best methods for reducing the sensitivity toward risk of this nature are the development of an excellent accident-free history, strong planning skills and adherence to the highest standards of leadership training, skills, and experience for adventure recreation leaders.

Providers of adventure recreation are finding insurance one of the major concerns of the tourism business. The Travel Industry World Yearbook (1987) indicates that if insurance can be obtained, the premiums are double or triple the premiums of 1985. Insurance industry representatives claim the increase in settlement size has been the cause of premium increases, but tourism and recreation officials say they have not been hit with large damage awards. In some states, park and recreation departments have canceled rafting and backpacking programs, and in 1986 the Sierra Club canceled 40 outings for members, including most of the boat trips. The American Professional Mountain Guides Association reported in 1987 that many national parks require that guides have $1 million or $2 million in insurance, while the maximum insurance the guides could obtain was $300,000. The result of high insurance premiums is that many operators providing adventure recreation activities are either going out of business or going without insurance. Tour operators call such gambling in the operation of their business without insurance "going dry."

SOME STEPS TOWARD SUCCESSFUL TOUR PACKAGING

Planning is not only necessary to ensure a successful adventure recreation business venture, but it is also one of the mechanisms that can reduce the level of liability and legal risk. Elements of such a plan might include a situation analysis that looks at the consumer base that is being targeted or has been served in the past, the competitors that are seeking to serve the same market segment with similar services or at least compete for the same dollars, and the legal/political, cultural, economic and environmental factors that can influence your offerings.

A critical element in risk management for adventure recreation is ensuring that the leadership used to serve the paying consumer has the skills, knowledge, and experience that will provide for a high level of good judgment under all circumstances. This is largely the focus of adventure education and strengthens the need for such programs. Adventure education should not be construed, however, to serve as a replacement for judgment skills that are developed through experience. Risk management plans should not be expected to replace recognition for key items such as equipment and sound leadership, nor should they become either dust-covered dinosaurs on a shelf, or fodder for the regulation-makers that lack an understanding of the activity or the individuals involved. A key responsibility of the leader is to know when and to what degree the participant must accept responsibility as control over the environment is lost (Ewert, 1987).

Networking, for our purposes, is the process of developing a working relationship with individuals and firms that are needed for the successful attainment of one's objectives. In the case of the adventure recreation tourism provider, the network could include individuals in the travel industry, hospitality industry, various levels of transportation (in foreign countries, this could include everything from helicopter pilots to locals providing human labor or animals for packing purposes), government officials, and local persons of influence. The network could also include representatives of the manufacturers of specialized equipment used in adventure recreation, such as boots, clothing, tents, rafts, food products, and communication devices. Sound networking requires an unobstructed two-way flow of information, especially where the information is directed toward the equipment used in serving the participants. Much of the modification of these items is the direct result of input from a population of specialized users.

The contingency or risk management plan is a must in the successful provision of adventure recreation experiences in the tourism industry. While hopefully never needed, a contingency plan must provide a precise strategy in the event some misfortune strikes a trip either while it is in progress or prior to the trip. As pointed out earlier, this plan must not be used to replace the necessary ingredients that include mature leadership with sound judgment and proper equipment.

Pre-trip contingencies would anticipate some catastrophic condition that would cause the trip to be canceled. Examples of this type of problem would include political or social unrest in the region to be visited, weather-related problems or some disruption of the transportation links to the region such as airline strikes, loss of landing rights, war, or even the possibility of the transportation company ceasing to be in business. It is an unfortunate reality that the provision of adventure experiences as well as other major tourism pursuits are the product of planning and organizational efforts over a long period of time. These efforts can be negated by any of the above, plus such problems as loss of the trip's key leaders due to illness or death, or not having a sufficient numbers of travelers contracted for the trip.

The other type of problem requiring contingency planning is of a more serious nature. These are the problems that arise in the event that a client is injured, becomes ill, or dies while involved in a trip. This is of particular importance should the problem develop in an isolated area and especially if it occurs in a foreign land. Questions should be answered such as:

- How do we communicate our needs to the appropriate individuals or authorities both technologically and culturally?
- What can be done to obtain appropriate medical attention?
- How do we move the individual or individuals to a suitable location for medical care?

Not only must a worst-case scenario be developed, but value judgment must be exercised as to what extent specific arrangements must be made. To reduce the impact of these kinds of problems, the provider must have a contingency plan that will reduce the possibility of not being able to meet the specific needs of the client or of a trip cancellation that causes the client anguish resulting from not being able to achieve the desired experience.

As in any planning process, the process of evaluation is cyclical and continuing, and periodic evaluation is a necessary element to continually strengthen the product offering to the traveling public. In short, a formalized plan for evaluation is mandated.

The adventure recreation segment of tourism offers an exciting but limited opportunity for individuals to have a sound adventure education. The tourism industry tends to be dominated by a few successful large providers, while the small operator has a difficult time experiencing financial success. This stems largely from the efficiencies of scale that are experienced by the larger organization. This is not to say that opportunity does not exist for the entrepreneur adventure recreation specialist that has developed, through experience and education, the skills necessary to attract a market segment large enough to support a financially successful business. One particular segment that would warrant special attention are the growing numbers of older consumers.

Trends would suggest an increasing focus on the aging baby boomers or "Grampies" as described by van der Merwe (1987). Grampies are identified by van der Merwe as follows:

- Growing numbers of people living to 60 or over
- Retired—more people are retiring earlier
- Active in lifestyle and consumption
- Monied
- People who are emotionally and physically
- In an
- Excellent
- State of health

One in 11 consumers will be over 60 by the end of this decade, and by the year 2000 one-tenth of the world's population will have reached this age group (van der Merwe, 1987). A number of personal acquaintances of the author in the over-60 age group have already shown the ability to participate successfully in adventure recreation activities provided by the tourism industry. Serving these groups can provide future opportunities for those educated in adventure.

Adventure education can play an important role in providing opportunities for individuals interested in entering the private/commercial tourism business—a business that provides various levels of adventure experiences for developing segments within the total population. Skills provided through adventure education can provide the basis for strengthening that portion of the tourism business that caters to those interested in heightened levels of perceived risk. Once again, it must be emphasized that education alone cannot ensure good judgment, which requires the added dimension of experience.

Trends in today's lifestyles make opportunities for serving individuals' experiential needs challenging and provide the potential for gratifying and rewarding entrepreneurial or service careers in the private/commercial business of tourism. For those interested in more academic pursuits, profound research opportunities exist that require the attention of the bright minds now focusing on adventure education and its role in enhancing the future of the human experience.

REFERENCES

Csikszentmihalyi, M. (1975). *Beyond boredom and anxiety.* San Francisco, CA: Jossey-Bass.

Dolan, C. (1988, March 18). Hard traveling: from riding elephants to dehorning cows, Americans flock to adventure trips. *The Wall Street Journal*, p. 5D.

Ellis, M. J. (1973). *Why people play.* Englewood Cliffs, NJ: Prentice-Hall.

Fillippi, F. de (1900). *The ascent of Mount St. Elias.* New York: Fredrick A. Stokes.

Godbey, G. (1985). *Leisure in your life, an exploration*, 2nd ed. State College, PA: Venture.

McIntosh, R. W., & Goeldner, C. R. (1984). *Tourism: principles, practices, philosophies*, 4th ed., p. 6. New York: John Wiley & Sons.

Meier, J. F., Morash, T. W., & Welton, G. E. (1987). *High-Adventure Outdoor Pursuits*, 2nd ed. Columbus, OH: Publishing Horizons.

Mortlock, C. (1984). *The adventure alternative.* Cumbria, UK: Cicerone.

Priest, S., & Martin, P. (1985). Understanding the adventure experience. *Journal of Adventure Education, 3*(1), 13-15.

Spacht, R. J. (1987). Precautions against liability. *Employee Services Management*, May/June, p. 15.

Staff, (1987). *REI adventures: Travel for outdoor enthusiasts.* Recreation Equipment Incorporated Cooperative.

Sterba, J. P. (1988, March 18). Blue water, white death, ten grand. *The Wall Street Journal*, p. 7D.

van der Merwe, S. (1987). GRAMPIES: A new breed of consumers comes of age. *Business Horizons*, November-December, p. 14.

Waters, S. R. (1987). *Travel industry world yearbook* . Vol 31. Organization for Economic Cooperation and Development.

Section Ten

A GLOBAL PERSPECTIVE ON ADVENTURE EDCUATION

Environmental Trends and Issues

What will be the future of adventure education? The prospect seems to be for a broadening and even a redefinition of "adventure" in the context of education. The picture that emerges from the essays in this book is of growing application of adventure education approaches to diverse clientele. The field, still young, reaches for foundations, organization and identity. Slowly, all three are being achieved. Hard work and hard thought, coupled with vision, imagination, cooperation, and political acumen, promise a bright future for adventure education.

Everything exists in an environment, including adventure education. It is surrounded by a social environment where people strive to satisfy their needs, yearn and work for safety, security and fulfillment. This social environment is a maelstrom of converging and diverging values. American society is an open arena in which interests compete constantly and sometimes viciously with each other. Decision-making is fraught with difficulties. Aspirations far exceed the resources necessary to achieve them. Wealth flows here and there, often gathering in the pockets of a few. The society leads the world in affluence, though even this is changing. Adventure education may have an increasingly important role to play in this charged social environment, as Dan Cohen points out. It may help people sort out their values, clarify what is truly meaningful in their lives. It may help people discover that fulfillment does not lie in the gathering of wealth and material things, that the winners are not those who die with the most toys. It may help people discover that the winners are those who care the most, who serve their world the best, who assure a liveable future for their descendants.

Everything exists also in a physical environment. The 1990s promise to be the "decade of the environment." Human population is growing rapidly, threatening to overwhelm the natural systems upon which all people depend. These human masses demand ever more food, fuel and services. Soil is lost in the rush for more food, and deserts advance. Oil is spilled, and forests are stripped for fuel wood. Carbon is released in combustion of fuel in homes, industries, and especially in automobiles, to rise as greenhouse gas into the atmosphere with well-known consequences. Ozone is depleted in the stratosphere, and the very fabric of nature is ripped. The human future, let alone the future of an enterprise like adventure education, is uncertain at this time. Many writers and thinkers today meditate on the "death of nature." Such a figurative and even literal death seems possible today.

Adventure education can even help to address the greatest of today's challenges—to learn what humans must do to sustain their natural environment, and to motivate them to action on its behalf. McLaren and Bunting suggest a role for adventure education in this large task. People can be helped to touch and understand nature. Adventure programs often immerse people in natural settings, and when they do, the potential is there to understand the nature of nature, a reality that insulated life in human-built and dominated places often obscures. The process of adventure education can also, as has been so often said in this volume, empower people. One daunting quality of the global environmental situation is that it is so vast. How can I do anything about such a huge problem, many ask. General confidence in self can move people to the position of saying, "Perhaps I can't solve the whole problem, but I can do some small good. I can, as the cliché has it, act locally while considering the global predicament." Thus can adventure education help in this global work, albeit indirectly.

Miles attempts to tie things together in the closing essay of this collection. He ends on a positive note. There is much work to be done, and adventure educators can help do it. The resource most essential for successful effort to solve the great problems today are educated people—caring, confident, dedicated, thoughtful, self-sacrificing and ethical people. The great circle of experiential educators at the Port Townsend Conference of the Association for Experiential Education that Miles describes suggests where such people may be found.

Planet Saving: The Ultimate Adventure

Milton McClaren
Simon Fraser University

We stand now in the place and limit of time
Where hardest knowledge is turning into dream,
And nightmares still confined in sleeping dark
Seem on the point of bringing into day
The sweating panic that starts the sleeper up.
One or another nightmare may come true,
And what to do then? What in the world to do?

(Nemerov, H., "Magnitudes" *TIME*, 1989)

Each year, at the outset of the new year, *TIME* magazine prints a special issue dealing with the person or issue that describes the most important topics of the year just completed. At the close of 1988 this issue was dedicated to the endangered Earth (*TIME*, 1989), our planet.

In all countries there is an increasing awareness that the environment that has so successfully nurtured our species may be having serious difficulty coping with the impact of ever-growing numbers of humans combined with our insatiable demand for resources and the rising tide of garbage, pollution, and effluent.

In Canada, *Maclean's* (1989) magazine in a special year-end poll conducted by the Decima corporation found that 55 percent of the respondents thought that tap water would not be drinkable by the year 2001 and that 61 percent would be prepared to add between $10 to $20 to their weekly expenses in order to purchase products less harmful to the environment. The Canadian Youth Foundation in a survey of 15 to 24-year-olds (Posterski & Bibby, 1988) found that they ranked "pollution" third in importance, nationally, among twelve social problems. The scientific community has been issuing increasing warnings about the significance of global climatic change, habitat destruction, loss of genetic diversity, and atmospheric pollution. However, in the midst of growing awareness there is a general uncertainty about what an individual can do to make any difference to these immense problems.

Adventure education has often been associated with wilderness experiences and the graduates and operators of adventure programs have often been in the vanguard of environmental campaigns. What has been less clearly developed, however, is an examination of the educational value of adventure education in the overall domain of environmental education. While there are a number of definitions of adventure, and descriptions of adventure education, the usual concept of adventure is that of an undertaking of uncertain outcome, entailing some risk or hazard. To the extent that adventure education prepares people to address uncertainty and to operate effectively in challenging situations, it can be seen as having important implications for the educational development of human beings in terms of their capacity to face, address, and eventually overcome the environmental problems now affecting the planet.

Low (1987) has developed the concept that human competence resides in the interaction among two sets of skills. He defines these as field skills and character skills. Field Skills are those things that we learn concerning the "how to" elements of action: information, skills, and concepts that are related to an area of performance. Character skills are more affective or involve concepts of purpose, value, wisdom, and characters such as courage, persistence, self-discipline, and patience. Thus, a person wishing to learn to play the piano would learn the field skills required, including the ability to read musical notation, finger exercises, hand movements, the ability to recognize various notes, chords, and tempos, and the ability to combine these in various pieces of music. Some of these field skills are also transferable to other musical instruments. However, in order to become a competent performer one will also need the character skills of patience, persistence, and self-discipline in order to hone the field skills to the level required for enjoyment and in-depth appreciation and interpretation of music. Many students in any field of endeavor fail not from a lack of ability in terms of the basic physical or intellectual prerequisites, but from a lack of the character skills.

Modern educationists have tended to regard character development as at best a side issue in schooling or curriculum development. They assume that people develop both field skills and the characters required for good citizenship by taking courses such as civics or social studies which attend directly to field skills. This assumption is questionable in the light of many modern social problems that relate to the role of citizens in modern democracy. Most primal societies, on the other hand, have developed curricula that address both field skills and character skills. This balance is often demonstrated in the preparations for entry to adult status in the tribe or band. Adventure education is a field in which there is an opportunity for a modern synthesis of field skills and character skills through conscious, considered curricular plans and operations. But why should this be important to the domain of environmental education and action?

In the year-end issue of *TIME* cited above, Senator Albert Gore described five major attitudinal barriers to environmental action. Briefly, they were as follows:

1. Faced with uncertainty as to the complete nature or severity of the problems, people tend to focus on the uncertainty or missing information and to magnify this as a justification for no action at all. We don't fully understand acid rain, hence, until we do have complete understanding, we should do nothing.

2. Current environmental problems are outside the bounds of human historical experience. The earth has never had a population of more than five billion before. Thus, people assign a certain unreality to modern problems. How can they be happening now; they have never happened before.

3. Some people accept that severe changes are occurring but have decided that human beings will adapt to these changes, whether biologically, through organic evolution, or culturally, or by the application of science and technology. They assume that adaptation will be easier than attempting to slow, correct, or reverse the changes. They neglect to consider, however, that the rate of change is accelerating and that this may make adaptation, if possible at all, too slow.

4. Lack of awareness of the severity of the problems by national leaders and by the general public leads to indifference or inaction. In some cases this lack of awareness is the result of deliberate lack of attention: What I can't see won't hurt me, so I won't look.

5. Many of the solutions to modern environmental problems are very difficult and will require immense effort at all levels. The solutions will require time to implement and take effect. These facts lead some people to decide simply not to try in the first place. Of course, a decision not to act is a decision, nevertheless.

It is evident that these five syndromes of inaction are also common problems addressed by instructors in adventure education programs. By its very nature, adventure involves uncertainty, often in all the dimensions of outcome, risks, methods, and self-knowledge or preparedness. Many people in the modern world, especially young people, feel rich in information about problems but poor in strategies to address them. This fact can lead to inaction and to the appearance of passivity or indifference. In fact, many young people are optimistic about their own futures, but far less so about the collective future of humankind or of the environment. However, lacking strategies for action and experience with action-oriented educational programs, they choose not to act. This is not the same as indifference.

Many modern curricula, especially in public education, are very restricted in the opportunity for students to carry their plans and intentions, their proposals and ideas into action. It is assumed, again, that knowledge *about* can be automatically translated into knowledge *how*. Moreover, there has been a general failure to recognize that there is a certain kind of information that can be gained in no other way than in the course of action. For example, imagine a person who plans and designs a house. As elegant as the designs may be, until the design is actually converted into a building, there is an entire class of information that can inform learning and develop experience that is simply available in no other way. Experiential educators have long realized this, but the understanding has had little impact on general curriculum design. We cannot, however, condemn the students of our schools or the graduates as being uncommitted or apathetic if in fact we have severely restricted their experience of action.

THE ELEMENTS OF ENVIRONMENTAL LITERACY

Table 1 on the following page summarizes Canada's official position concerning world environmental issues as expressed on two separate dates. The first column lists the items included in Canada's action proposals to the World Conference on the Environment in Stockholm, Sweden (Environment Canada, 1974). The second column lists items in an action plan described by the Hon. Tom Macmillan, Minister of the Environment in the previous federal government, in a recent speech (T. Macmillan, personal communication, 1988).

There are themes, if not specific items, common to both statements. Considering these lists as well as other similar major political or environmentalist statements about global problems and their possible solutions, I have attempted to define the concept of environmental literacy. If an educated person has an understanding of environmental problems and the capacity to address them, both personally and through political actions, what knowledge, skills, and attitudes must they possess? As I define it, environmental literacy comprises the following elements.

The Ability to Think About Systems

This might be described as the ability to think *eco-systematically*. The central message of modern ecology is that everything is in fact connected ultimately to everything else. It may be convenient, and even necessary to

Table 1 Two Canadian Environmental Goal Statements

Canada at the Stockholm Conference in 1974	Canadian Environmental Priorities
Goal 1. The Development of National Air Quality Standards	Goal 1. Canada Must Develop a Population Policy
Goal 2. The Development of National Water Quality Standards	Goal 2. Environmental Quality and Human Health Must be Linked
Goal 3. The Control, Reduction, and Elimination for Detergent Phosphates	Goal 3. Recycling is Essential
Goal 4. The Elimination of Mercury from the Environment	Goal 4. We Must Develop General, Usable Product Protocols Dealing with the Biodegradability, Energy Costs, and Pollution Potential of Common Products
Goal 5. The Reduction and Elimination of DDT and PCBs	Goal 5. We Need to Attend to the Impact of Agriculture
Goal 6. The Development of Motor Vehicle Emission Standards	Goal 6. We Need Widespread, Effective Energy Resource Management
Goal 7. The Control of Radioactive Cesium	Goal 7. We Need Special Attention to the Arctic Environment
Goal 8. Development of International Agreements Concerning Migratory Birds	Goal 8. We Must Protect Endangered Species
Goal 9. There Must be Planning for Environmental Emergencies	
Goal 10. There Must be Widespread Programs of Environmental Education	
Goal 11. We Need to Move the Management of Renewable Resources Toward Sustained Yield	
Goal 12. We Need Policies and Regulations in the Area of Marine Resources	

separate a system into components in order to analyze and understand it, but it is also required that we put things together again. Approximately one-third of all paper produced in North America is used in packaging. We take this for granted, but in the meantime the forests of the planet are vanishing at a rapid rate in order to produce things that have an actual use measured in minutes. Technology makes our lives easy, but it insulates us from the consequences of many of our actions. We don't know where our electrical power is produced, or where our wastes go when they disappear down the drain. It has been noted, with some measure of truth, that for many of today's urban children, meat is produced in the supermarket and milk comes from vats in the grocery basement. So, the first challenge to developing environmental literacy is to reconnect ourselves to the planet, to understand where things come from, where they go, and how much energy and material is used along the way.

The Ability to Think in Time: To Forecast, Think Ahead, and Plan

Along with systems thinking, we also need to introduce the concept of time. We need to work at extending people's capacities to think beyond the here and now. What seems to be a quick and convenient "fix" today has often turned out to be the genesis of serious environmental problems in years to come. Many human beings in the modern world seem to have genuine difficulty thinking beyond the term of their own lifespan. In fact, many seem to have difficulty thinking beyond this year. Most environmental problems will not be solved quickly. They will require extended effort over many years. Children living in an age of instant electronic miracles are impatient with the idea that something might produce results only after many years, if in their lifetimes. We need new modern fables and creative curricular activities to foster the capacity to think beyond the here and now.

The Ability to Think Critically About Value Issues

Almost all modern problems, environmental or otherwise, have an important component based in human value systems. Contemporary society is pluralistic and multicultural. We do not have a common, culturally agreed-upon set of values. Many environmental educators are people who value the outdoors in natural settings, if not real wilderness. Yet it has been estimated that the average North American now spends about 4 percent of his or her total life actually out of doors. For many children today, the shopping mall offers more attractions than the forest or seashore. What we value is reflected in our actions. If we really value a healthy environment, then we may have to sacrifice some of our conveniences. We will have to learn to ask hard questions even when besieged by the inducements offered through the mass media. We will have to learn to think about issues of quality.

The Ability to Separate Number, Quantity, Quality, and Value

Many people in the modern world are confused about the differences between these elements. People assume that bigger or faster or more expensive is better. We confuse the possession of many material possessions or money with higher moral authority. We have difficulty distinguishing between the medium and its messages. We assume that if a lot of people do something or believe something, that it must be right or true. We assign numbers to things that can really only be assigned qualities, and assume that because we have enumerated them we have also addressed their value. Why do we need more trees? Why should we try to have high-quality, clean water? Isn't the number of our possessions an indicator of our success and of the quality of our lives? Such problems are at the core of many environmental decisions. In the structure of modern life it is often apparently less expensive to pollute or to waste than it is to conserve. Only the capacity to think through number, quality, quantity, and value issues can enable us to challenge these assumptions.

The Ability to Distinguish Between the Map and the Territory

We are surrounded by high-quality representations of the world. We have photos in full color, video, stereo, models, and simulations. They can be very useful in helping us to understand components of the environment. But we often become so fond of our maps that we forget that they may not be entirely faithful representations of how things actually are.

Many of our notions about the environment are in fact elaborate stereotypes. We have learned ideas about animals from the cartoon creatures of our childhood. As enjoyable as these were, they are less than reliable representations of how animals actually behave. We also have stereotypes about the "wilderness" and about the beauties of nature. Not all natural environments are obviously beautiful in the "calendar art" sense of the term. Few North Americans have ever seen the equatorial rain forest and few are likely to. Most would find this incredibly important ecosystem uncomfortable and forbidding, if not frightening, at least at first. But this would hardly be an argument against its conservation. Natural environments seldom measure up to the manicured pleasure gardens we have been taught to expect.

The Capacity to Move From Awareness to Knowledge, to Action

The need to have people take personal actions that contribute to the solution of environmental problems has been widely recognized by writers about environmental education. A popular slogan has been: Think Globally, Act Locally. In actual fact, however, the link between awareness, knowledge, and action is poorly understood by many educators and curriculum designers. It is important to understand that knowledge, and certainly information, carries no automatic set of instructions converting it into appropriate actions. Many a young scientist learns the hard way that no matter how much data you gather, the data itself makes no decisions. Furthermore, there are things to be learned that can be learned only through action itself. Thus, a class may learn about water pollution and about how to test for various aspects of water quality. They may become aware of problems in a local creek. But, if they actually decide to act upon the problem then they move into new territory, territory where they will confront the need for tools, the requirement to act politically, to be able to interact with various community groups. From these experiences they will gain powerful new learning, most of it not available other than through action. By continually disconnecting the cycle of learning from action, we have removed some of the most important resources for educational development from schooling.

A Basic Set of Concepts and Facts Plus the Ability to Learn New Ones and to Unlearn the Old

There are concepts to be learned and useful facts to be recalled in the course of developing environmental literacy. Ecological principles and concepts are important organizers for experiences in the environment and provide insights to be applied to critical thinking about environmental issues. Students need to understand biological and geological cycles, bioenergetics, food and energy relationships, and concepts such as adaptation and diversity. But, equally as important, there is a need for students to become expert in learning how to access information and how to evaluate its quality. Environmental citizenship often requires the ability to use up-to-date, accurate information. Learning how to find this information is an important aspect of environmental literacy. At the same time, students must also learn to expect that many of the things they learn today, especially specific facts and figures, may prove to be wrong tomorrow. This is to be expected given the rate of growth of new knowledge and the deployment of new technologies. Lifelong learning is as essential to environmental education as to any other field.

The Ability to Work Cooperatively With Other People

There is scarcely any modern environmental problem that we can expect to be solved by a single person. It has been noted that many environmental issues are complex. They will require international cooperation as well as cooperation among neighbors in local communities. Effective skills in group processes and communication will be very important. Many specialists will have to work in interdisciplinary teams. These teams will have to learn to solicit and employ citizen participation.

Experts alone cannot solve environmental problems. Thus, cooperative learning becomes as critically important here as it is in many other fields of endeavor today.

The Capacity to Use Skills in Eight Processes: Knowing, Inquiring, Acting, Judging, Opening, Imagining, Connecting, and Valuing

This set represents an "ecosystem" of processes that are essential to effective intelligence. They are generic not only to environmental education, but to all forms of education. In order to develop them fully, curricula need to be designed to attend to them all at some time or another during the student's development in the course of schooling. Not all need to receive equal emphasis at all times, but all need emphasis during some phases of learning. All are equally important. They need not be seen as being in any universally appropriate logical sequence in all contexts. In some situations, students may begin with their awareness of a problem or opportunity (Opening). In others, taking stock of what is known and developing strategies for finding out more is of central importance (Knowing and Inquiring). In still other situations, starting with value positions may be most useful. However, by encountering a variety of educational problems and by learning in a variety of contexts, through a number of teaching models, students can develop proficiency in these process elements.

CONCLUSION

If this set of elements of environmental literacy is examined through the lens of field skills and character skills, it can be seen that information, concepts, specific skills, and personal characteristic will be required to attain it. It is worth emphasizing that in the field of adventure education the synthesis of the cognitive, affective, and psychomotor domains has always been a major goal. Adventure programs provide opportunities for students to develop their abilities to plan and effect action in situations that are novel, filled with uncertainty, and which often contain risk. The actions taken may lead to failure, from which the students will often have to learn, recover, regroup, and then act again. Effective group action has long been a major objective in many adventure or challenge programs. Thus, it is my contention that there are major elements of contact between adventure education and environmental education in the development of general environmental literacy. There are also obstacles in the path of such a fruitful synthesis.

First, both environmental education and adventure education have been marginalized in most public school curricula. Both fields entail many challenges to the conventional wisdom of curriculum design and operation. They recognize the importance of a wide range of action as a requirement for effective educational development. Second, both environmental education and adventure education recognize that as useful as schools are as foci of learning and teaching, they present a very limited amount of the total range of experiences that might have educational power. Thus, enhancing or widening the spectrum of instructional settings are characteristics of both. Unfortunately, the bureaucratic nature of many large modern school systems combined with a limited understanding of the requirements for the full development of human powers and capacities acts to severely restrict the implementation and operation of both adventure and environmental education.

It is to be hoped that as we recognize the gravity of the environmental problems we now face, and their social and economic concomitants, we will seek instructional strategies and educational programs that have potential value in the development of human competence to address them. If modern schooling was in part a response to, as well as a product of the Industrial Era, then it is likely that the characteristics of environmental education and adventure education may be employed in the development of a new description of post-industrial schooling.

REFERENCES

Low, K. (1987). *Character in a new light.* Briefing Paper. Calgary, AB: Action Studies Institute.

Posterski, D., & Bibby, R. (1988). *Canada's youth ready for today.* A comprehensive survey of 15-24 Year olds. Ottawa, ON: The Canadian Youth Foundation.

Environment Canada. (1974). *Canada at the Stockholm conference on the human environment.* Ottawa, ON: Author.

Planet of the year. Endangered earth. (1989, January). *TIME.* pp. 18-68.

A spotlight on Canadians. (1989, January). *Maclean's.* pp. 8-38. Interdependency: A key in environmental and adventure education.

Interdependency: A Key in Environmental and Adventure Education

Camille J. Bunting
Texas A&M University

Educational and adventure education both focus on the study of interrelationships. The term that has been coined for the study of our environmental home or the interrelationships of the biosphere, is *ecology* (Ford & Blanchard, 1985). The ecology movement of the late 1960s and 1970s gradually lost some of its intensity, but recently has been regaining a foothold in the educational world. Today, one of the most often used phrases for ecology is "environmental education."

A word worthy of expressing the interrelationships of the components of adventure education may be *gumnopedia.* Gumnopedia is taken from the Greek words *gumnao,* meaning the practice of strenuous activity in a natural outdoor environment, and *paideia,* meaning the process of learning. Adventure education is the process of learning through strenuous activity in a natural outdoor environment. Whenever there is physical activity that is dependent upon some type of interaction with the natural environment, challenge is a major ingredient of the activity. The exhilaration of challenge, with uncertain outcomes having actual consequences, is a strong motivator for many individuals. Couple such challenge with the natural setting of the outdoors, and you have outdoor adventure. Outdoor adventure has been defined as activities which involve humans grappling with problems that are naturally present in a particular environment, such as a white-water river, a rock face or mountain, or a gracefully curling wave (Miles, 1978). The adventure lies not in "overcoming" the natural challenge, but in "communicating" with it. Such "communication" requires appropriate skills, respect, and adequate knowledge of the particular environment. Outdoor adventures can be described as environmental communications because, as in interpersonal communication, there is an interdependency between the individuals involved. There is interdependency between participants as well as between the environment and the participants.

Interdependency is a key term for understanding environmental concepts and interrelationships. The food chain, adaptation, habitat, energy, and so on, are all ecological concepts relating to the interdependent nature of our natural environment. In the life/Earth science area, this is one of the dominant themes. Although there is a general understanding and acceptance of the concept of interdependency in nature, there has been little, if any, discussion of the relevance of that concept for adventure pursuits.

With this in mind, the following two premises will be discussed:

1. Seven major ecological concepts, as set forth in Steve Van Matre's *Sunship Earth,* are also major concepts for adventure education; and
2. Although interdependency is a term relevant within both environmental and adventure education, these two branches of outdoor education are also interdependent upon one another.

The idea of having basic concepts to teach in environmental education is not at all abstract or foreign to that field of study. However, the field of adventure education is still in its formative stage as far as the development of its basic concepts and principles. As the field of adventure education has been evolving, observation, research, and evaluation have provided information pertinent to the value of adventure and the learning it can provide (Gass, 1985; Bunting, 1982; Teaff & Kablach, 1985; Toft, 1987). Most of this information can be directly related to concepts that are generally accepted as basic to the field of ecology.

It must be kept in mind that environmental education is education about our natural environment and how it functions, while adventure education is a vehicle for learning about ourselves and about interrelationships. Despite this difference of content versus method or experience, the desired outcomes are quite similar. In Table 1 on the following page, seven ecological concepts are listed with a brief explanation of each as it relates to both environmental and adventure education.

In any field of study, there is a need for establishing some basic concepts to act as building blocks. By their very nature, ecology and outdoor adventure are closely related and it is therefore fitting that some of the ecological concepts are also applicable to adventure education. Since one of the primary objectives of adventure education is to provide a means of understanding oneself and interpersonal relationships, the concepts are appropriately expressed in these terms.

Outdoor adventure is synonymous with challenge, and it is this challenge, stress, exhilaration, or creative tension that provides the *energy.* This flow of energy is transferred from a situation to the participants, as well as from participant to participant. Due to the interaction of group members in adventure activities, this "tension" may not always be euphoric in nature, but can prove to be challenging and energizing if dealt with properly.

One of the common denominators of adventure education is that it is experiential in nature. When experiential learning is most effective, it is *cyclical.* One means of expressing such a cycle is with a model developed to illustrate appropriate sequencing of initiative activities (see Figure 1). As learning takes place, further experiences are needed that are more complex and have increased consequence.

The concepts of *diversity, community, and interrelationships* are very closely intertwined in the realms of both ecology and gumnopedology. In the realm of gumnopedology they are directed toward complexities of interpersonal relationships rather than environmental relationships. M. Scott Peck, in his book *The Different Drum,* has much to say about the understanding and appreciation of individual differences and their importance in interrelationships and community.

Table 1
Ecological Concepts

ENVIRONMENTAL EDUCATION	*CONCEPTS*	*ADVENTURE EDUCATION*
Sunlight energy is transferred from plants to animals to food decomposers	ENERGY FLOW	Challenge and creative tension is transferred to and from situations and individuals
Nutrient cycles in the earth's reservoirs of air, soil, and water allow life to continue	CYCLES	Experiential learning goes in a cycle from: experience to observation, to processing to learning, and on to another experience
Different nutrient and sunlight requirements permit diverse plants and animals to share the Earth	DIVERSITY	Individual diversities increase the potential for learning and growth
Plants and animals co-exist where essential nutrients best meet their individual needs	COMMUNITY	Mutual support is developed in situations that require individual needs to be met by other group members
Constant interaction with each other and surroundings as plants and animals meet one anothers' needs	INTERRELATIONSHIPS	Constant interaction with each other and surroundings as individuals meet one anothers' needs, as well as meeting needs of the environment, and the environment meeting their needs
Resulting from all of the above, all plants and animals are in the process of becoming something else	CHANGE	The sum of our experiences —if learning is the result—allows us to remain "becomers"
Some plants and animals improve as a result of the ever-changing conditions of where they live	ADAPTATION	The result of energy, cycles, diversity, community, interrelationships, and change for those desiring growth

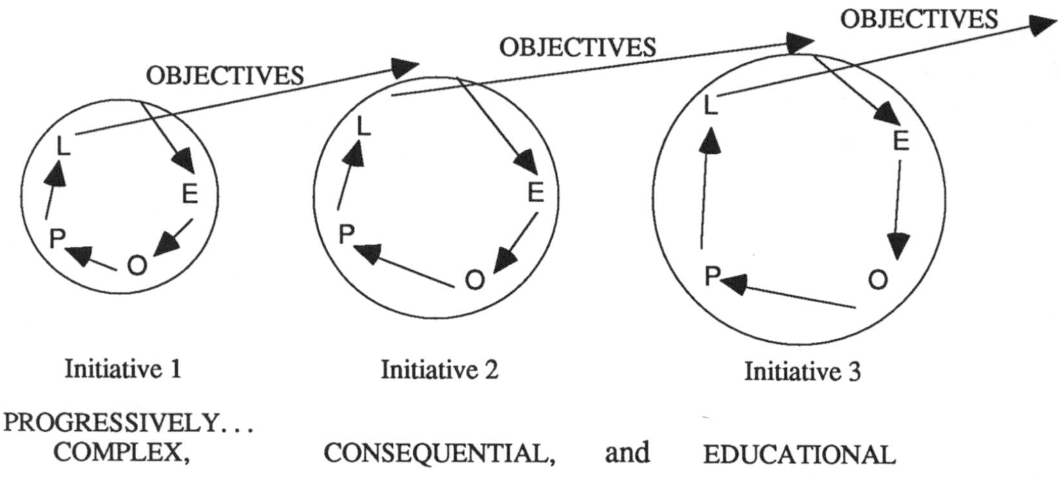

Figure 1
Initiative Task Sequencing Model

> The very genetic code is such that (except for the rare aberration of identical twins) each of us is not only subtly different biologically from any other human being who ever existed but is substantially dissimilar from the moment of conception. And if that were not enough, all of us are born into different environments and develop differently according to a unique pattern throughout our own individual lives. (Peck, p. 53)

Our individual differences offers us unlimited growth potential as we learn how to work and play together. Without this diversity, much of the challenge would be missing, thereby reducing the energy flow. However, as the energy does flow and interrelationships are developed through the mutual meeting of needs, a "connectedness" is formed that can often be identified as community. "The experience of true community is a unique way of communicating, of sharing our deepest thoughts and feelings without fear or guilt" (Peck, 1987). This is a worthy objective for adventure education.

As the concepts of diversity, community, and interrelationships are intertwined, so are the concepts of *change* and *adaptation.* Through the process of experiential learning, our experiences should continue to change and challenges increase as we grow and change. If, in fact, learning has occurred in keeping with the building blocks of adventure education, then adaptation will be the result; adaptation to ourselves, others, and our environments. This is not to say that adventure education is the only means for such personal adaptation to occur, but that it can be one method.

The sum of these concepts for environmental education and adventure education is *interdependency.* According to the second premise of this paper, not only are the concepts interdependent within each branch of outdoor education, but the two branches are also interdependent upon one another. Several years ago, learning about the environment meant memorizing names of trees, flowers, insects, species, and so on, a method quite dissimilar from experiential learning. However, in the early 1970s, Steve Van Matre spawned the "acclimatization" idea for environmental education. The objective of acclimatization is experiential learning, and that is to become "one" with your environment through sensory awareness activities. As a result of such "adventures," an individual becomes naturally inquisitive about the environment and motivation for learning is greatly increased. About the same time that Van Matre came out with *Acclimatization*, there were many projects that developed outdoor activities for teaching environmental concepts. All of these attempted to capitalize on the motivational impact of adventure or experiential learning. There were projects, such as, Outdoor Biology Instruction Strategies, The Green Box, Project Wild, Project Learning Tree, and other environmental activity books. Environmental education was becoming dependent upon the adventure or discovery method of learning.

The other side of this interdependency is adventure education's dependency upon environmental education. This is an area most frequently neglected. Although outdoor adventurers are dependent upon the natural environment to provide appropriate settings for their experiences, the importance of being good stewards of the environment is often overlooked or ignored. Such a negligent attitude can be attributed to a lack of understanding in regard to the interdependency concepts and/or a very one-sided introduction to the world of outdoor adventure. It is in this matter of introduction and education that adventure educators have a major responsibility for instilling an appreciation for the interdependent values and concepts of environmental and adventure education. It is beyond belief that adventurers would fail to be diligent with the resources so necessary for their activities, yet such is often the case. It could be that those individuals were introduced to their activities by someone who did not understand the basic concepts, and therefore was able only to pass on what they knew—technical skills. This type of cycle needs to be broken. Without a commitment to environmental education on the part of adventure educators, the method of adventure education may not be an option for future generations due to the deterioration of our adventure environments.

Interdependency is key. It is the concept that is totally relevant within and between environmental and adventure education. In fact, it is significant to the point that we in the fields of experiential, environmental, and adventure education are dependent upon one another to teach the concepts of the "connectedness" of our interdependency.

REFERENCES

Bunting, C. J. (1982). Managing stress through challenge activities. *The Journal of Physical Education, Recreation and Dance—Leisure Today, 53*, 48-49.

Bunting, C. J. (1985). *Venture dynamics*. College Station: Texas A&M University Outdoor Education Institute.

Ford, P., & Blanchard, J. (1985). *Leadership and administration of outdoor pursuits*. State College, PA: Venture Publishing.

Gass, M. A. (1985). Programming the transfer of learning in adventure education. *The Journal of Experiential Education, 8*, (3).

Miles, J. C. (1978). The value of high adventure activities. *The Journal of Physical Education, Recreation and Dance—Leisure Today*, 3-4.

Peck, M. S. (1987). *The different drum*, New York: Simon and Schuster, Inc.

Teaff, J., & Kablach, J. (1987). Psychological benefits of outdoor adventure activities. *Journal of Experiential Education, 10,* (2), 43-46.

Toft, M. (1987). Finding high-level wellness through outdoor pursuits. *High Adventure Outdoor Pursuits,* Meier, Morash, & Welton (Eds.) 16-22.

Environmental-Values Education

Daniel Cohen

This section will address the topic of environmental-values education and its integration within adventure education programs. Initially, a connection between environmental-values and adventure education must be drawn. Then, the meaning of the term "value" will be discussed. Once this fundamental definition has been assessed, the subject of environmental values and valuing will be examined. It will then be shown that adventure educators can and should include environmental-values education in their programs. Various aspects and approaches to values education will be delineated. Finally, a sample of appropriate environmental-values education activities will be given.

THE BASIC PREMISE

The significance of this section of the book is generated from one premise: that adventure educators should include environmental-values education as an integral part of their programs. There are three sound reasons for the adventure-environmental values education connection. First, adventure educators' field classrooms provide a superior opportunity for such endeavors. The potential for meaningful environmental learning is naturally increased when the learning experiences occur in natural settings.

Second, environmental-values education can introduce students to various aspects of the natural world and students can also explore the meaning and value of the environment. This introduction and exploration should lead students to an understanding of themselves and how they might view their personal responsibility toward the environment.

Finally, the adventure educator must recognize that his or her program is dependent on available wilderness settings. Most adventure education programs utilize pristine environments to achieve the goals of the programs. This being the case, it would only seem logical that adventure educators should lead others to understanding the necessity of preserving and caring for natural wilderness areas.

Lengthy volumes have been written on the subject of values. The purpose of this section is not to delve fully into the meaning of "value." Rather, a brief description of the term is in order. An efficient method of addressing the meaning of "value" will expose the definition of the term in two distinct ways by answering the following two questions:

1. What is the *value* of X?
2. What are person (or society) X's *values*?

An entity, living or not, obtains value in two distinct ways. The value of entity X can be measured *instrumentally* or *intrinsically.* To have instrumental value is to be valuable in terms of serving a purpose. Things with instrumental value are seen as means to an end. A typewriter is valuable because it enables one to communicate with others. A fallen tree is valuable because it serves as a niche for an ant colony or because it can be made into some kind of wood product. Living trees are valuable because they supply the atmosphere with oxygen or because they provide a perfect setting for adventure education programs.

Intrinsic, or inherent, value is a complex subject. An entity is said to be intrinsically valuable when it obtains value by virtue of its mere existence. Simply put, X is valuable in and of itself. It is difficult, particularly in Western philosophy, to attribute intrinsic value to any of the entities in the preceding examples. The mere existence of a typewriter or a tree does not warrant any value in our society. While there is a move by environmentalists to view trees and other natural objects an entities worthy of intrinsic value, this is certainly not a commonly held view. The only entity that holds intrinsic value in our society is the human being. This is manifested in certain laws and beliefs known as human rights.

It should be noted that certain nonentities seem to hold instrumental and intrinsic value. Honesty, love, truth, and happiness are such nonentities.

An individual has certain values that lead in determining what is good, what is right, what is moral and what is desirable. Values additionally play a major role in societal beliefs and behavior. Knapp (1983, p. 22) defines "value" as follows: "The term 'value' is defined as a standard that guides and determines personal behavior." This definition can be expanded to include the whole system of value that guides the social group and thus the individual members of that group.

Consider the following theoretical definitions of the term "value." According to Kluckhohn, (1951, p. 35)

> A value is a conception, explicit or implicit, distinctive of an individual or characteristic of a group which influences the selection from available modes, means and ends of action." This behavioristic approach is also emphasized by Sikula in defining values as preferences for action. "Values represent 'wants' or preferences . . . A person's values describe the things or ideas that matter most to him, things which he will strive and sacrifice for in order to obtain.... (1:35)

So it is recognized that individuals and groups hold certain values that prescribe their beliefs and behaviors. As Kluckhohn mentions, these values may be explicit or implicit, which means some people may not be aware of their own values. (Becoming aware of one's values is an integral part of values education.)

In summary, the term "value" has been briefly defined in two ways: the *value* of an entity (instrumental and intrinsic) and the *values* held by an individual or a society (as guidelines for behavior).

Environmental Values

The task of defining the term "environmental values" demands that two familiar questions be answered:

1. What is the *value* of the environment?
2. Of what importance is the environment in our *values* system?

A complete answer to these questions is attainable only if we understand the "environment" in three integral, yet distinct, ways. The first two views of the environment are called ecosystemic and ekistic relationships. (7.2) (Priest, 1859)

Ecosystemic relationships are the connections between members of an ecosystem that create what is called interdependence. This is the view that all inhabitants of an ecosystem depend on each other for survival. *Ekistic* relationships deal specifically with the relationship between humans and nature. This view examines the influence of human behaviors on the natural world. The view also examines the effect the natural world has on human beings.

A third view that is an integral part of environmental values is the understanding that parts of the environment are also individuals. While the environment consists of systems and influences, it is also inhabited by individual parts: animals, plants, lakes, rocks, and so on. This third view understands that the individual parts of the environment are worthy of consideration as individuals as well as parts of systems.

Identifying environmental values, based on the three views of the environment as described above, will determine the instrumental and intrinsic value of the natural world. It will also determine the importance of the environment with regard to our values system. Several questions will help with this identification, or clarification. What purpose does the environment serve? To what ends do plants and animals serve as means? Does the environment, or an ecosystem, or a tree, or a river hold intrinsic worth? How do I value the environment compared to, say, my personal comfort and lifestyle? These are the types of questions that lead to discussions of environmental values. Such discussions enable individuals to answer the ultimate question: what is desirable conduct and behavior affecting the environment?

Environmental Valuing and Adventure Education

What is the act of valuing and does environmental valuing belong in adventure education programs? "Valuing is the link between thinking and action. It transcends pure reason by including the non-rational (as opposed to irrational) with the rational. Thinking may help us to see alternatives which are relevant, and valuing helps us in the process of choosing from among alternatives." (Cummings, 1974, p. 18)

The act of valuing is the act of making behavioral choices from relevant alternatives and identifying the values that led to those choices. Therefore, environmental valuing would be the act of choosing specific behaviors that have some sort of impact on the environment and identifying the environmental values that may have led to these behaviors.

At first glance, it may be difficult to see a connection between environmental-values education and adventure education. Since the thrust of adventure education is to bring out the best in the people participating in the programs, the primary goal of adventure education is an anthropocentric goal. Using perceived risks to build self-confidence and esteem and to direct group cohesiveness, adventure education seems to be centered on achieving a quality human experience. This motivation exhibits the value of human enrichment. Wilderness helps with the enrichment, thus serving an instrumental value, but any serious environmental valuing does not appear to take place during a purely human-centered program. Consider this summation by Priest (7:1):

> Adventure educators have a primary responsibility to assist their students in learning about interpersonal relationships (how people interact in groups—leadership, trust, cooperation, communication, problem solving, etc.) AND intrapersonal relationships (how people regard themselves—self-concept, independence, confidence, skill, experience, etc.). These are the main goals of adventure education.

I would like to introduce a third primary responsibility of adventure educators. I believe this responsibility to be a facet that is covertly inherent in most adventure education programs and an implicit part of most adventure educators' styles. The "new" primary responsibility is to assist students in finding their place as living beings in the natural world—physically, emotionally, and philosophically. There is no better way to accomplish this goal than to utilize various forms of environmental values education.

As stated before, adventure education programs tend to utilize wilderness areas for trips and/or ropes courses. These settings are usually beautiful and stimulating environments. The field classroom is ideal for learning biological, ecological, and geological concepts. Wilderness classrooms are also superb settings for environmental valuing exercises. Therefore, environmental values education activities would help any wilderness living and learning experience reach its full potential.

There is an ethical aspect to connecting adventure education and environmental values. By asserting that environmental valuing is an integral part of adventure education, one seems to be initiating the idea that people, because they are part of, immersed in, and have an influence on nature, have some obligation to understand and care for the environment. I believe most adventure educators adhere to this ethic.

Of course, the obvious justification for the use of values education strategies by adventure educators is the fact that their programs depend on available wilderness areas. Adventure educators believe a wise use of the environment is to utilize pristine places for their programs. One must therefore value the choice of preserving wilderness for adventure programs. Environmental-values education would be the likely method for identifying and teaching these values.

How Environmental-Values Education Works

The objectives of environmental-values education are based on the belief that humans make critical decisions regarding behaviors that influence the quality of the natural world. "Men and institutions are faced with the necessity to make decisions that affect the quality of the environment, and these decisions are, to an extent, influenced by the prevailing valuative norms present in the individual or the institution." (Miles, 1966, p. 6) If it is true that decisions regarding behaviors are directed by value sets, then changes in behavior may occur when value sets have been clarified and analyzed. "Studies generally confirmed that changes in environmental attitudes and behavior are most effectively brought about by [environmental-values education] strategies that increase the learner's level of knowledge of emotional involvement, and experience in the area being addressed." (Caduto, 1983, p. 14)

The primary goal of environmental-values education is to direct individuals in the development of their values system as it pertains to human behaviors that influence the quality, integrity, and diversity of the environment. Achieving this goal will depend mostly on the abilities of the educators who employ strategies in environmental-values education. Consider this proposal by Caduto (1983, p. 17) as he maps a strategy:

> ...the adaptation of environmental [adventure] educators of the role of catalysts who enhance learner self-awareness ... This would consist of helping people to understand clearly what their own and other people's values are. It is of critical importance to foster a strong awareness of how each of our values and behaviors affects other people and the environment, and how these compare to those that are most beneficial to social and environmental welfare.

There are several approaches, or methods, to values education. Some of these approaches are widely used, others are still in development stages. It seems that of the five specific methods, three are appropriate for the field classroom. They include *inculcation, values clarification*, and *action learning*. Two other methods, values analysis and cognitive moral development, will be mentioned briefly.

Inculcation

The fundamental belief with inculcation is that specific values should be taught. Inculcation involves the direction of students to the understanding that certain values are more desirable than others. Some desirable values might include honesty, friendliness, unselfishness, happiness, and the gift of love. Some undesirable values might include stealing, cheating, lying, and vandalism.

One implicit way of inculcating is to role model. Educators who feel strongly about certain values will no doubt exhibit these values through their behaviors and appearances. Students, who look up to instructors, can be influenced by the image portrayed by their instructors.

Implicit inculcation occurs in several other instances. For example, if students are requested not to litter, or to pack out whatever they pack in on a wilderness trip, the value of a clean environment or the value of leaving no trace of human impact is implied. Even without mentioning the word "value," students will "osmotically" be introduced to the value of a clean environment. "The purpose of inculcating values is to instill in learners certain chosen values or to shift learner values toward those desired ends" (Caduto, 1983, p. 15).

Values Clarification

As the most commonly used approach to any type of values education, values clarification seems to be the safest method for a democratic society. Students are encouraged to explore and identify their personal values, the values of others, and to decide for themselves which values they will act on. Miles (1976, p. 10) shows that values clarification is a process that:

1. Poses a problem of valuing in an open and free environment;
2. Urges students to identify their positions on the problem;
3. Provides an opportunity to view a range of alternative value positions;
4. Allows affirmation and action upon the value position taken;
5. Involves no normative judgment of right and wrong or good and bad;
6. Gives practice in the process of perceiving and evaluating alternatives.

Action Learning

Action learning utilizes the approach of experiential education. It is a method that goes beyond thinking, feeling, and discussing to include action. Action learning encourages students to explore the realm of real-life experiences in their learning experiences. Activities for this approach include volunteer work, internships, and community service programs.

The foundation for action learning is based on the belief that the best way to learn concepts or values is to experience them. A student can learn much about recycling from lectures, readings, and video programs. The student can learn about the process involved in recycling, the physical and chemical changes that occur, and the economic and environmental value of recycling. But, participating in a recycling campaign, working at a recycling plant, or driving a recycling pick-up route will enrichen the student's experience. A student will feel a sense of involvement, purpose, and value in things he/she experiences first-hand.

The final two approaches to values education, values analysis and cognitive moral development, are currently too academic and too theoretical in nature to be of much use in the field classroom. Nevertheless, they will be briefly mentioned.

Values Analysis

Taking values clarification one step further, values analysis focuses on the motivating force in the act of making a decision. Where values clarification seeks to identify the values that lead to decisions and behaviors, values analysis scrutinizes the consequences of each of the alternatives to be decided on. The goal here is to lead students to identifying the consequences of their behaviors.

Cognitive/Moral Development

The last of the approaches to values education, cognitive moral development, is perhaps the most complex. This approach serves as a guideline for educators when they begin to incorporate values education into their curriculum. The guideline is based on the belief that students go through a progression of stages of moral development where the student's abilities to deal with value-laden issues depend on which level of moral reasoning has been achieved by the student. These stages predicate the approach an educator should utilize when choosing values education activities for their students.

Three viable approaches to values education have been described. One point must be made clear: no approach stands alone. Most educators will agree that the various approaches complement each other, that an efficient and worthwhile endeavor into environmental-values education will incorporate, at one time or another, the use of all appropriate approaches. Ryan (1981, p. 31) refers to this as a "Synthesis Approach." He points out that each approach has strengths that lead to certain ends and that people living in a free society are too complex to be served by one approach. If the goal of values education is to have students know their values, to analyze the values and their consequences in a decision- making process, and to act on the values, then educators must be willing and able to employ each of the appropriate approaches.

One theory that seems to unite the various approaches is Priest's Ladder of Environmental Learning (1988, p. 6). On this metaphorical ladder exist what might be termed "rungs of achievement," each leading up the ladder to the eventual goal of environmental values education. The advancement from rung to rung requires the use of several values education approaches.

Environmental...Values Education Activities

Inculcation

1. The primary mode of inculcating is, as mentioned before, to role model the values an adventure educator feels the students should embrace. The standard "practice what you preach" certainly holds true here.
2. While waiting between normal program events, or as an integral part of an adventure program, have students imagine a world where the dominant species valued the environment purely as something to be used, rich in resources for human consumption. Have the students draw mental or physical pictures of how such a world might look. Discuss the virtues (if any) of this type of world and have students decide if this is how they would like their world to be.
3. As mentioned before, simply expressing the value of a wilderness setting for the practice of adventure education programs will instill a feeling for this type of environmental value. Those students that have a memorable experience in an adventure education program will come to realize the connection between pristine environments and the ability to maintain a future in adventure education.
4. If part of an adventure education program requires students to obey minimum-impact camping (not littering,

staying on trails, using fire rings), students will be introduced to the value of choosing to create as little impact on the environment as possible.

Values Clarification

1. Pose the following situation and follow it up with the activity given.

SITUATION: The natural setting the group is using for their adventure education program is being considered for development as a resort site. There are no other wilderness areas near this setting, so there is no other location in the area suitable for a resort development.

ACTIVITY: Students will make two lists. First, they should list five benefits derived from the resort development. (The lists may include income for developers, local employment, human relaxation and recreation, etc.) Second, students should list five benefits from leaving the area in its natural state. (These lists might include the continuation of adventure education programs, the welfare of nature, etc.)

Break up into small groups, of three or four people, and discuss the lists.

Return to the lists and rank each benefit in terms of importance.

Finally, bring the students together and identify the values that influenced the ranking of the benefits. After some values have been clarified, have the students attempt to identify some of their personal behaviors that might reflect these values.

2. Using the same situation as above, have the students divide into three groups: the resort developers, the local town people, and an environmental activist group. The group that each student is in will determine the character each is to role-play. Students must try to envision themselves as developers, local people, and environmentalists in order to accurately portray the role. Tell the students that there will be a judicial meeting in 30 minutes to determine the fate of the setting in question. Each represented group will have a chance to plead their case as to what should become of the potential resort and the wilderness area. (This type of activity is an attempt to have students clarify and understand the values held by persons other than themselves. Usually the instructor plays the role of judge or moderator.)

3. Have students list their five favorite modern conveniences. Then tell the students that they are moving to a place where they may have only three of their conveniences. Have the students choose which three of the original five they will take. Then ask the students to determine what environmental effect these conveniences have.

4. Have students discuss the various values (if any) they hold for the environment or any value the environment itself possesses independent of the students. Then have the students identify any five personal behaviors that they feel have some impact (positive or negative) on the environment.

A note on initiating exercises in values clarification: Before beginning the activity, the instructor should put forth some ground rules for the discussions. First, each person who wishes to speak will be given the opportunity. All persons must respect the speaker and devote full attention to that speaker. It will be understood that no one viewpoint is the correct viewpoint and that all persons will agree to these guidelines. A gentle, relaxed and peaceful tone will create an open and free environment.

Action Learning

As part of the adventure education program, have students participate in the following events:

- Ecological restoration of the program setting
- Trail maintenance
- Litter clean-up
- Ropes course repair
- Leading their peers in values exercises
- Land use planning

SUMMARY

The term "value" has been defined in two ways: as an entity having either instrumental and/or intrinsic value; and as pertaining to an individual's or group's set of values. Environmental values have been shown to define values in terms of ecosystemic, ekistic, and individual relationships. It has been exhibited that the act of valuing should be an integral part of adventure education and that environmental values education has a definite place in adventure education programs. Three approaches to values education have been delineated, with a call for a synthesis approach included. A sample of environmental values activities has also been included.

The duty does henceforth fall on adventure educators to familiarize themselves with the philosophy of values and the various approaches to environmental values education. Devotion to this duty will result in worthwhile endeavors into environmental valuing and a population of sound environmental thinkers.

REFERENCES

Baker, M. R., Doran, R. L., & Sarnowski, A. A., An analysis of environmental values & their relation to general values. *Journal of Environmental Education*, (vol. no. unknown), 35-40.

Caduto, M. (1983a). A review of environmental values education. *Journal of Environmental Education, 14*(3), 13-21.

Caduto, M. (1983b). Toward a comprehensive strategy for environmental values education. *Journal of Environmental Education, 14*(4), 12-18.

Cummings, S. I. (1974). A methodology for environmental education. *Journal of Environmental Education*, 6(2), 16-20.

Knapp, C. E. (1983). A curriculum model for environmental values education. *Journal of Environmental Education, 14*(3), 22-26.

Kluck, C. (1951). Values and values orientations in the theory of action. Parsons, T. and Shils, E. A. (Ed.), Toward a General Theory of Action. Campridge, MA: Harvard University Press,

Miles, J. C. (1976). The study of values in environmental values education. *Journal of Environmental Education, 8*(3), 5-17.

Priest, S. (1988). The ladder of environmental learning. *Journal of Adventure Education and Outdoor Leadership, 5*(2), 23-25.

Ryan, K. (1981). *Questions and answers on moral education.* Bloomington, IN: Phi Delta Kappa Educational Foundation.

The Future of Adventure Education

John C. Miles
Western Washington University

This collection of writings about adventure education presents the thoughts of leading practitioners in the late 1980s on this relatively new approach to teaching and learning. Adventure education in the United States has been developing for a mere 25 years. It has emerged from changes in society and education. The emergence of modern technology and the relative affluence of the United States has removed much risk from daily life and separated people from the natural world. The so-called "information age" has led to domination of information assimilation approaches to learning, with students more and more manipulating symbols of the world in carefully controlled and contained classrooms. The direct, risky and often adventurous experience of the world and life in it that had so long been a central process of human development has receded in importance. Now adventure education and other approaches to experiential learning have come along to inject this experience back into education.

Conventional schooling has recently come under attack from all directions. Critics assail the perceived inadequacy of American education, blaming it for an array of societal difficulties ranging from the trade deficit and a reduced rate of technological innovation, to the breakdown of conventional values and the drug abuse problem. Suggested cures for the crises in education are many and include more time in school, more training and greater professional rewards for teachers, more accountability and standardized tests, and more basic education, among others. At the moment, in 1989, many agree that there are serious problems, but few agree on solutions.

Adventure education is not the solution to education's ills, but it may be part of the solution. Experiential education, of which adventure education is one powerful form, can inject important ingredients into education. Among these ingredients are powerful intrinsic motivation, personal relevance, excitement, lessons about risk and responsibility, and service. Education has many missions. While adventure education may not contribute directly to the acquisition of skills necessary to be better mathematicians, engineers, computer programmers, and businesspersons, it can certainly do so indirectly. People can learn about dedication, commitment, cooperation, trust, empathy, compassion, tolerance, success, failure, patience, and fulfillment, among other things. All of this knowledge, highly personal in nature, can help people decide why to work and toward what ends. We have, as many people have observed, a plethora of means and a paucity of ends. What good are greater skills if we know not why we have them and for what purpose we should use them? Experiential and adventure education can help with these fundamental valuative dimensions of education, which is where, in my view, American education needs the most help.

Does adventure education have a future? If so, what will it be? Will it continue to grow in importance? Will it fade in the face of a reactionary "back to basics" emphasis in education? Will it be a luxury enjoyed only by a rich few in America and other parts of the world? There is one certainty. The world will change and adventure education will change with it. The next version of this collection of writings on adventure education, if there is one, will inevitably document changes in this field.

What might some of these changes be? They will reflect changes in the societal context, so we should reflect on some of the trends in the world today that might have implications for the future of adventure education. We can identify several global trends of interest:

1. The global population is increasing. The world is becoming more crowded.
2. The environment is increasingly stressed and deteriorating badly in some places.
3. The dominant global culture is increasingly empirical, rational, utilitarian and manipulative.
4. Information is growing very rapidly as are the technological systems for storing and delivering this information.
5. The world is shrinking as communication and transportation technologies develop.
6. There is increasing global integration of markets—for goods, services, technology, and ideas.

There are trends in America that may have implications for adventure education. Some of these are:

1. More two-earner families appear as people strive to maintain a high level of consumption.

2. There are increasing numbers of "latch-key children" as both parents are away at work.

3. The economy is shifting from an industrial to a service economy, with lower worker pay.

4. Status and roles for women are changing.

5. The age structure of the population is changing; the "graying of America" is underway.

6. Increasing numbers of people change careers during their working lives.

7. Public morality is deteriorating, as indicated by stock market scandal, sale of political influence, and other abuses of the public trust.

8. Social values trend toward consumption, domination, and manipulation rather than conservation and compassion.

9. Mortgaging of the future to sustain the affluence of the present is an increasingly acceptable public policy.

10. There is a growing intellectual, cultural and ethical anomie among American young people that results in more drug abuse, crime, and teenage suicide.

11. American society becomes ever more litigious.

We have seen some trends in adventure education reflected in the essays in this collection. These include:

1. Expansion and diversification of the field.
2. Slow incorporation of concepts and methods of adventure education into conventional schooling.
3. A growing effort to bring the program to the learner, rather than the learner to the program, as in growing efforts to develop urban programs.
4. An increasingly complex managerial environment for adventure programs.
5. A shrinking outdoor adventure setting for adventure programming with consequent exploration of alternatives such as artificial environments.
6. A slow maturation of adventure education as a field through formulation of self-examining questions, development of a body of knowledge, professional guidelines and standards for practitioners and a strong association of people working in the field.

All of these trends suggest that what we have here defined as adventure education will continue to thrive, grow, and exert considerable influence on the future of American education. It can help society cope with some of the problems associated with these trends. Adventure can infuse excitement and challenge into otherwise dull lives. It can offer unique perspectives through reflection on life's normal values and routines. It can infuse challenge and excitement in healthy forms into young lives tempted to find these in crime and drugs. People beaten down and depressed by overwhelming prospects of nuclear holocaust and environmental collapse can find hope, personal power, and self-confidence in adventure, which then transfers back home. Lessons about trust, cooperation, honesty, and openness, antidotes to domination and manipulation, can be learned. So, too, can lessons about responsibility—to self and others, even others in remote lands and of future generations. Adventure, occurring as it often does in natural settings, can help people renew appreciation for nature, rekindle awe and wonder, and even contribute to understanding of and respect for life, including other persons and even other life forms. Adventure education can and will be, it seems likely, an important element in American education in the future.

All of this is cause for optimism about the future of adventure education, but there is cause for concern as well. There seem to be ever-expanding demands on limited financial resources, at least in the public arena. Adventure education is today a "fringe" element in the array of educational enterprises. Faced with too many demands on too little money, educational decision-makers are likely to opt to allocate their scarce resources to "mainstream" activities. Adventure educators face a large challenge in demonstrating to those with the dollars that they can assist more conventional school people in addressing the fundamental goals of the teaching and learning enterprise.

A part of this demonstration will involve empirical evidence of the value of work that adventure educators do. Many, perhaps most, adventure educators know instinctively that they are doing good and helpful work. This knowing is enough for them, but not for the larger society that demands more concrete evidence of achievement. This means that adventure educators must more thoroughly document the effects of their work than they have done so far. Research in this field is difficult to do. It can be a nuisance, even interrupt the smooth flow of a program, but it must be done. Unless it is, the potential of its contribution to the growth of people may not be realized.

Another challenge is to take the programs to the people. The cost of transporting urban youth from Chicago to the Colorado wilderness is prohibitive. There will only be enough money to take a very few there. Yet, as Steve Proudman so well reveals in his paper, the need for adventure education in Chicago is very great. Will instructors skilled in meeting the challenges of wild and remote outdoor environments go to Chicago to offer their leadership and skill? They undoubtedly will, but the challenge to leaders of this field will be to train instructors to be as effective in urban environments as they have been in their more familiar wilderness haunts. Since the opportunity to spend at least part of their lives "in the mountains" is a powerful inducement to many who work as adventure educators, ways will have to be found to allow instructors to go back and forth from the wilds to the city.

Will instructors go to work in the less attractive urban environments for the same extremely low pay they have earned in their wilderness work? They are willing to live simply on a limited income in order to enjoy the rewards of the outdoor life. Furthermore, their cost of living while working in the outdoors is relatively low. If programs are to attract leaders to the cities, they will have to provide more financial rewards. This will, of course, increase the cost of doing the adventure education business and that, in the face of shrinking financial resources available to programs, is itself a monumental challenge.

Yet another challenge facing adventure educators involves the outdoor environments that they have long used. Wilderness and natural areas are scarce today, and will become more so in the future, as I pointed out in my earlier essay in this collection. As the population grows, demands for resources will increase. Many of those resources are in areas currently natural and therefore available for adventures. The search for commodities will erode these resources in the future. The challenge of maintaining the quality of what wild and natural areas are left will be very great. Undoubtedly the restrictions on users of such areas will increase. Perhaps the costs to the users will increase as well. Certainly it will be a challenge for adventure educators to work with land managers to solve problems. If adventure educators realize early in the game that their self interest will be served by cooperating with agencies in managing scarce natural resources (and the beginnings of such realization are visible today), then long-term use of the natural environment for adventure education will be assured.

The diverse group of people who practice adventure education can and will assure the continued evolution of their field. Their resources were revealed to me on a November morning in 1987. The occasion was the closing ceremony of the 15th annual conference of the Association of Experiential Education. About 400 people were still around after three intense days of workshops and many other programs. We sat on the floor of the "theater" that had been the principal large-group meeting place throughout the conference. After a slideshow depicting what we had been doing, various people "testified" to their commitment and dedication to their work. They spoke from the heart. Tears flowed from speakers and listeners alike. We had all enjoyed a powerful shared experience and we would carry that power away to our various homes. We would, we declared, work for a better world, for more effective education.

The group linked hands and snaked, single file, out of the building to a large field. Energy seemed to pass through the chain. Once before, at an AEE conference at Santa Fe, New Mexico, I had felt this energy. Here, nearly 10 years later, it was stronger than ever.

We formed a huge circle around the field, and as we did so, the sun burst from the late-November sky. One person ran to the middle of the circle and led us in thanks to the Earth for its blessings. We embraced Earth, and then we embraced each other. I have never felt so much shared joy and energy. Knots of people stood around in the sun for a while, talking, not wishing to let go of this experience.

Why bring this up in an essay on the future of adventure education? Because it seems to testify to the strength, cooperation, spirit, love, and energy of the people who must assure a future for this approach to education. Adventure education is people work. Love, will, dedication, compassion, and deep resources of energy are necessary to do this work. The Port Townsend group was richly endowed with these qualities and they will carry on the work of building an important future for adventure education.

OTHER BOOKS FROM VENTURE PUBLISHING

Acquiring Parks and Recreation Facilities through Mandatory Dedication: A Comprehensive Guide, by Ronald A. Kaiser and James D. Mertes

Amenity Resource Valuation: Integrating Economics with Other Disciplines, edited by George L. Peterson, B.L. Driver and Robin Gregory

Behavior Modification in Therapeutic Recreation: An Introductory Learning Manual, by John Dattilo and William D. Murphy

Beyond the Bake Sale - A Fund Raising Handbook for Public Agencies, by Bill Moskin

The Community Tourism Industry Imperative - The Necessity, The Opportunities, Its Potential, by Uel Blank

Doing More With Less in the Delivery of Recreation and Park Services: A Book of Case Studies, by John Crompton

Evaluation of Therapeutic Recreation Through Quality Assurance, edited by Bob Riley

The Evolution of Leisure: Historical and Philosophical Perspectives, by Thomas Goodale and Geoffrey Godbey

The Future of Leisure Services: Thriving on Change, by Geoffrey Godbey

Gifts to Share - A Gifts Catalogue How-To Manual for Public Agencies, by Lori Harder and Bill Moskin

International Directory of Academic Institutions in Leisure, Recreation and Related Fields, edited by Max D'Amours

Leadership and Administration of Outdoor Pursuits, by Phyllis Ford and James Blanchard

The Leisure Diagnostic Battery: Users Manual and Sample Forms, by Peter Witt and Gary Ellis

Leisure Diagnostic Battery Computer Software, by Gary Ellis and Peter Witt

Leisure Education: A Manual of Activities and Resources, by Norma J. Stumbo and Steven R. Thompson

Leisure Education: Program Materials for Persons with Developmental Disabilities, by Kenneth F. Joswiak

Leisure in Your Life: An Exploration, 3rd Edition, by Geoffrey Godbey

A Leisure of One's Own: A Feminist Perspective on Women's Leisure, by Karla Henderson, M. Deborah Bialeschki, Susan M. Shaw and Valeria J. Freysinger

Outdoor Recreation Management: Theory and Application, Revised and Enlarged, by Alan Jubenville, Ben Twight and Robert H. Becker

Planning Parks for People, by John Hultsman, Richard L. Cottrell and Wendy Zales Hultsman

Playing, Living, Learning: A Worldwide Perspective on Children's Opportunities to Play, by Cor Westland and Jane Knight

Private and Commercial Recreation, edited by Arlin Epperson

The Process of Recreation Programming Theory and Technique, 3rd Edition, by Patricia Farrell and Herberta M. Lundegren

Recreation and Leisure: An Introductory Handbook, edited by Alan Graefe and Stan Parker

Recreation and Leisure: Issues in an Era of Change, 3rd Edition, edited by Thomas Goodale and Peter A.Witt

Recreation Economic Decisions: Comparing Benefits and Costs, by Richard G. Walsh

Risk Management in Therapeutic Recreation: A Component of Quality Assurance, by Judy Voelkl

Schole: A Journal of Leisure Studies and Recreation Education

A Social History of Leisure Since 1600, by Gary Cross

Sports and Recreation for the Disabled - A Resource Manual, by Michael J. Paciorek and Jeffery A. Jones

A Study Guide for National Certification in Therapeutic Recreation, by Gerald O'Morrow and Ron Reynolds

Therapeutic Recreation Protocols for Treatment of Substance Addictions, by Rozanne W. Faulkner

Understanding Leisure and Recreation: Mapping the Past, Charting the Future, edited by Edgar L. Jackson and Thomas L. Burton

Wilderness in America: Personal Perspectives, edited by Daniel L. Dustin

Venture Publishing, Inc
1999 Cato Avenue
State College, PA 16801
814-234-4561